Scots
Commercial
Law

Scots Commercial Law

General Editor

Iain G MacNeil LLB, PhD

Alexander Stone Professor of Commercial Law
at the University of Glasgow

Avizandum Publishing Ltd
Edinburgh
2014

Published by
Avizandum Publishing Ltd
25 Candlemaker Row
Edinburgh EH1 2QG

First published 2014
Reprinted 2015

ISBN 978-1-904968-56-6

British Library Cataloguing in Publication Data
A catalogue entry for this book is available from the British Library

Typeset by AFS Image Setters Ltd, Glasgow
Printed and bound by Bell & Bain Ltd, Glasgow

Authorship of this volume

Chapter 1: Introduction to Juristic Persons
Ross G Anderson, Advocate

Chapter 2: General Principles of Contract Law
Dot Reid

Chapter 3: General Principles of Property Law
John MacLeod

Chapter 4: Agency
John MacLeod

Chapter 5: Partnerships, LPs and LLPs
Ross G Anderson, Advocate

Chapter 6: Sale of Goods
Andreas Rahmatian

Chapter 7: Insurance
Iain G MacNeil

Chapter 8: Money and Debt
Ross G Anderson, Advocate

Chapter 9: Payment Obligations
Matteo Solinas

Chapter 10: Conventional Security: Cautionary Obligations
Paul McClelland

Chapter 11: Non-Judicial Real Security
John MacLeod

Chapter 12: Judicial Security: Diligence
Frankie McCarthy

Chapter 13: Insolvency: Bankruptcy
Frankie McCarthy

Chapter 14: Corporate Insolvency and Dissolution
Ross G Anderson, Advocate

Chapter 15: Alternative Dispute Resolution
Lindy Patterson QC

Preface

It can sometimes be difficult to match the scope and depth of university courses in Scots commercial law with texts that provide appropriate coverage but do not at the same time lose track of some of the basic principles that form the bedrock of the law. Our aim in producing this book has been primarily to provide students with a text that gives a prominent place to general principles alongside a concise treatment of the relevant special rules in the field. Thus, the first part the book provides an introduction to the law of persons, contract and property before focusing on specialist topics in the second part. In addition to students, we hope that practitioners will find some merit in the book as an initial point of reference on commercial law.

While the book is framed so as to cover all the topics normally covered in the LLB curriculum for commercial law, we have also included aspects of commercial law in its broader sense which may be placed elsewhere in the curriculum. The most obvious examples are the chapters on money and debt and diligence. These chapters deal with issues which may arise in connection with any of the transactions or forms of business organisation that are dealt with in the other chapters. We have also included a chapter on corporate insolvency. Although that is a matter in principle reserved to the Westminster Parliament, there is a distinct Scottish dimension to the law resulting from its historic links with the law of sequestration. Taken together with the influence of the EU Insolvency Regulation, the result is that the law is often difficult to access and to understand. Thus, Ross Anderson's consolidated outline of the law in Chapter 14 is a particularly welcome development.

The book is the outcome of collaboration between staff at the University of Glasgow School of Law, our former colleague Ross Anderson, Advocate, and Lindy Patterson QC of CMS Cameron McKenna. Each chapter has been written by an author with specialist expertise and with a view to incorporating elements of practice that are important for understanding the law. The expertise and co-operation of the contributors has meant that my own role as general editor has been very much of a light touch nature. While I am grateful to all the contributors, special mention must go to those contributing more than a single chapter: Ross Anderson (four chapters); John MacLeod (three chapters); and Frankie McCarthy (two chapters).

The law is stated as at 28 February 2014 although every attempt has been made to include later developments where possible. The Land Registration etc (Scotland) Act 2012 has been treated as though it was in force but we have been unable to include references to the important changes contained in the Small Business, Enterprise and Employment Bill 2014.

Finally, we would like to thank Margaret Cherry at Avizandum Publishing for her encouragement to undertake this project and for her patience in seeing it through to completion.

Iain MacNeil
5 September 2014

Contents

Authors

Ross G Anderson, Advocate practises at the Scottish bar mainly in the fields of corporate and financial law, trusts law, and property law, as well as general commercial litigation. A graduate of the University of Edinburgh (LLB (Hons), PhD, DipLP), he lectured full-time in corporate and financial law in the University of Glasgow between 2008 and 2012, where he is now an Honorary Research Fellow. He has been the Visiting Professor of Immovable Property Law at the Institute of Law in Jersey since 2010. His publications include a monograph on *Assignation* (2008), 'Security over Bank Accounts in Scots law' (2010) 4 *Law & Financial Markets Review* 593–604; and 'Words and Concepts: Trust and Patrimony' in *Judge and Jurist: Essays in Memory of Lord Rodger of Earlsferry* (2013).

Frankie McCarthy is a senior lecturer in private law at the University of Glasgow. Her teaching and research interests focus on property and family law, and the human rights aspects of both. She has published in the *Edinburgh Law Review, Child and Family Law Quarterly* and the *European Human Rights Law Review*, and written textbooks on *Succession Law* (2013) and (with Anne Griffiths and John Fotheringham) *Family Law* (3rd edn, 2013).

Paul McClelland graduated from the University of Glasgow with a first class honours degree in law before qualifying as a solicitor with Shepherd and Wedderburn LLP in 2010. He is currently a part-time PhD candidate in the fields of private law and legal history, studying the pre-history of the Scots doctrine of innocent misrepresentation. His other research interests include commercial law and property law. Paul is also a lecturer in law at the University of Glasgow, teaching undergraduate courses in business law, property law and obligations.

John MacLeod graduated with an LLB from the University of Edinburgh, and then worked as a legal assistant at the Scottish Law Commission. During his PhD studies he spent a year at the Max Planck Institute for Foreign and International Private Law in Hamburg. He graduated with a PhD on 'Fraud and Voidable Transfer: Scots Law in European Context' in 2014, also from the University of Edinburgh. He has been a lecturer in commercial law at the University of Glasgow since 2010.

Iain MacNeil has been the Alexander Stone Professor of Commercial Law at the University of Glasgow since 2005. He is a graduate of the

Universities of Glasgow (LLB) and Edinburgh (PhD). Before taking his PhD and entering the academic world he worked for eight years as an investment analyst in the City of London. His teaching and research interests are primarily in the fields of company law, financial markets and related aspects of contract law. Iain is a member of the editorial board of the *Capital Markets Law Journal*, a former general editor of the *Law and Financial Markets Review* and a member of the International Law Association's Committee on International Securities Regulation. He is the author of *An Introduction to the Law on Financial Investment* (Hart, 2nd edn, 2012) and has published widely on corporate governance and financial regulation. He has recently acted as special adviser to the House of Lords European Committee on financial regulation and is a member of the UK Research Evaluation Framework (REF) 2014 Law Panel.

Lindy Patterson QC is a partner in CMS Cameron McKenna and a specialist in arbitration, adjudication and commercial litigation. She is qualified in both English and Scots law and was appointed a Queen's Counsel in Scotland in August 2010. Lindy is a Fellow of the Chartered Institute of Arbitrators and a Fellow of the Chartered Institution of Civil Engineering Surveyors. She is also the only woman on the international FIDIC President's List of Adjudicators, having been appointed in 2012. She is on the Arbitral Appointments Committee of the newly constituted Arbitration Centre in Scotland. She is an honorary member of the RICS. She regularly acts as arbitrator and dispute board chair both within and outside the UK.

Andreas Rahmatian is a senior lecturer at the University of Glasgow where he teaches intellectual property law and commercial law. After having completed an LLM at the University of London with an emphasis on comparative and intellectual property law, he worked as an associate attorney at law in a law firm in Vienna where he specialised in intellectual property law, before returning to the United Kingdom for qualification as a solicitor. His research interests include intellectual property law, property law and theory, commercial law, private law, comparative law, and intellectual history and the law. His most recent book, *Copyright and Creativity: The Making of Property Rights in Creative Works* (Edward Elgar, 2011), was shortlisted for the Peter Birks Prize for outstanding legal scholarship in 2012 by the Society of Legal Scholars.

Dot Reid is a lecturer in private law at the University of Glasgow School at Law, having previously taught at Strathclyde University. Her research and teaching focus is in the law of obligations and property, with an interest in theoretical aspects of private law and the history of ideas. She also writes and researches on succession law, providing a perspective that takes account of the impact of social policy on modern Scots law. She holds degrees from the Universities of Glasgow (MA (Hons) in French and Spanish), Strathclyde (LLB) and Edinburgh (PhD) and is currently the assistant editor of the *Edinburgh Law Review*.

Matteo Solinas is a lecturer in corporate and financial law at the University of Glasgow. He holds degrees from the London School of Economics (PhD), Universita' Cattolica (LLB), Bocconi (MSc), and the University of Warwick (LLM). In 2008 in worked as legal researcher at the Financial Markets Law Committee c/o Bank of England. Prior to undertaking an academic career, Matteo practised criminal law and corporate law in Milan. He is a qualified solicitor in England and Wales and a member of Lincoln's Inn.

Table of Statutes

Table of Orders, Rules and Regulations

Table of Cases

Chapter 1

Introduction to Juristic Persons

INTRODUCTION

Law of persons

1.01 'All our law is about persons, things and actions.'[1] In other words, *who* has rights, *what* rights they have, and *how* they are enforced.[2] But what is the law of persons? It is not much taught at any Scottish university. There are no UK books on the subject,[3] and yet the law of persons is one of the great pillars of private law. It is not possible in the short space available here to sketch the entire law of persons and to explain, for example, how the University of Glasgow was originally incorporated by Papal Bull; how the Aberdeen Harbour Board is considered to be the UK's oldest commercial corporation;[4] or why unincorporated associations do not, in Scots law, generally enjoy legal personality.[5] For present purposes, suffice it to say that, in commercial law – as well as many other areas of legal practice – the law of persons is of fundamental importance, not least because, more often than not, the parties to commercial transactions are juristic rather than natural persons. It is thus necessary to identify certain fundamental principles of legal personality before turning to consider the particular rules that apply to the juristic persons considered in this book: partnerships, limited partnerships and limited liability partnerships.

---

1 Gaius, *Institutes* I, 8.
2 G L Gretton and A J M Steven, *Property, Trusts and Succession* (2nd edn, 2013) para 1.14.
3 P J Fitzgerald (ed) *Salmond's Jurisprudence* (12th edn, 1966) pp 298–328 remains the best treatment available.
4 J Micklethwait and A Woodridge, *The Company: A Short History of a Revolutionary Idea* (2003; pbk 2005) p 23 confer on the Aberdeen Harbour Board, which can trace its origins to at least 1136, the accolade of the oldest UK corporation.
5 Cf. C Hemström, 'Associations' in *International Encyclopaedia of Comparative Law* (2006) vol III/2, ch 8.

GENERAL PRINCIPLES OF LEGAL PERSONALITY

Legal personality

1.02 The concept of legal personality is central to any legal system.[6] Only a legal person can enter into legal transactions or hold patrimonial rights. Natural persons – human beings – acquire, on being born alive, legal personality. Historically, one of the most extreme sanctions a legal system could impose on a natural person was to declare that person an 'outlaw' or a rebel, resulting in a loss of civil legal personality.[7] So fundamental is legal personality to vindicating legal claims, that the very right to be recognised as a person is enshrined in the UN's Universal Declaration of Human Rights[8] and, for similar reasons, some national constitutions tightly regulate the related issue of the withdrawal of citizenship.[9] One practical effect of a loss of legal personality is patrimonial: what happens to that person's assets? Personality ceases with death; yet, between death and confirmation of executors, there is a legal limbo (the *haereditas jacens*): a patrimony but no person to represent it.[10]

1.03 Natural persons have the right to form associations; and, in the EU, there is a fundamental economic freedom to establish undertakings.[11] An undertaking established as a juristic person in one EU member state may do business in any other member state.[12] But not all associations of natural persons create juristic persons. Unincorporated associations, such as sports and social clubs, do not have legal personality and cannot, therefore, hold patrimonial rights or be a party to juridical acts.[13] In contrast, commercial undertakings formed as partnerships, limited partnerships, limited liability partnerships or companies are all juristic persons and may enter into juridical acts and hold patrimonial rights. Death by

---

6 D N MacCormick, *Institutions of Law: An Essay in Legal Theory* (2007) ch 5; MacCormick, 'General Legal Concepts' in *Stair Memorial Encyclopaedia* (Reissue) (2008).

7 The Scottish procedure, now abolished, was that of 'denunciation as a rebel', following a process of 'horning': Stair, *Institutions* III.3.1; G Watson (ed) *Bell's Dictionary and Digest of the Law of Scotland* (7th edn, 1890) s.v. 'Denunciation'; and *Lord Advocate v Marquis of Zetland* 1920 SC (HL) 1 at 27 per Lord Shaw of Dunfermline.

8 Universal Declaration of Human Rights, Art 6: 'Everyone has the right to recognition everywhere as a person before the law.'

9 As in the German *Grundgesetz* Art 16.

10 For all this, see L Smith, 'Scottish trusts in the common law' (2013) 17 Edin LR 283.

11 Treaty on the Functioning of the European Union, Art 49.

12 Case C-212/97 *Centros Ltd v Erhvervs-og Selskabsstyrelsen* [2000] Ch 44, ECJ; Case C-208/00 *Überseering BV v Nordic Construction Co Baumanagement GmbH (NCC)* [2005] 1 WLR 315, ECJ.

13 Cf. an 'Owners Association', created in conjunction with a scheme for a housing development, which is a body corporate created at the time specified in the registered deed: Title Conditions (Scotland) Act 2003, s 71 and Title Conditions (Scotland) Act 2003 (Development Management Scheme) Order 2009 (SI 2009/729), Art 4(2).

liquidation and dissolution of juristic persons presents special problems. A paradigm situation involves the dissolution of a company which still holds assets. The effect of dissolution is that the assets pass to the Crown.[14] These issues are dealt with below.

Capacity

1.04 Recognition as a legal person does not in itself define that person's legal capacity. Capacity determines whether, and to what extent, a legal person can enter into juridical acts, hold patrimonial rights and incur liabilities. The legal capacity of a child, an adult, a company and a partnership may each be different. The differences can be clarified by examining legal capacity in its active and in its passive sense.

Active and passive capacity

1.05 Active capacity focuses on two characteristics of a legal person. The first aspect is the ability to enter into juridical acts, the paradigm example of which is a contract. This ability to enter into juridical acts is sometimes known as 'transactional capacity'. Transactional capacity may vary. The capacity of a child to enter a contract is limited compared to that of an adult.[15] A person suffering from mental illness or infirmity may also lose transactional capacity. There are detailed provisions in private law for dealing with natural persons lacking transactional capacity.[16] The second aspect relates to the ability of a person to commit legal wrongs, such as delicts.

1.06 A person may have no active legal capacity, but may nonetheless have passive legal capacity. Passive legal capacity is the ability to benefit from unilateral juridical acts[17] or to benefit from the protection of the law of delict. At the simplest level, this form of capacity identifies the capability of an entity to fall within the protection of the law. A related and controversial question is whether juristic persons (as opposed to natural persons) fall within the protection of human rights legislation.[18]

---

14 Companies Act 2006, s 1013 ff. See, further, Chapter 14: Corporate Insolvency.

15 Age of Legal Capacity (Scotland) Act 1991, s 1(1)(a) and s 2 (transactional capacity); Children (Scotland) Act 1995, s 9 and s 10 (property).

16 Adults with Incapacity (Scotland) Act 2000, for which see generally A D Ward, *Adult Incapacity* (2003).

17 Bilateral juridical acts, by definition, require the consent of both parties. A person with no active legal capacity, by definition, cannot give consent.

18 Juristic persons, as a general principle, benefit from the European Convention on Human Rights: R G Anderson, 'Fundamental rights of juristic persons' in E Reid and D Visser (eds), *Private Law and Human Rights in Scotland and South Africa* (2013).

Attribution of acts to a juristic person

1.07 Juristic persons, being creations of the law, can act only through human agency.[19] In relation to commercial transactions, the law of agency allows juristic persons to enter into juridical acts. Suppose Alpha Limited wishes to enter into a contract with Bravo Limited. Alan, a director of Alpha Ltd, acts for and on behalf of Alpha Ltd; Brian, a director of Bravo Ltd, acts for and on behalf of Bravo Ltd. On conclusion of the agreement, the parties to the contract are the principals, namely Alpha Ltd and Bravo Ltd.

Juristic persons in commerce

Overview

1.08 Company law is a specialist area on which there are many excellent introductory texts.[20] Company lawyers tend to focus, understandably, on a paradigm vehicle in order to illustrate the general principles. That paradigm is normally the private company limited by shares. But that is only one of a number of different possible vehicles available under the Companies Acts and related legislation. In summary, the following are possible:

- An unlimited company[21]
- A company limited by guarantee (Ltd)[22]
- A private company limited by shares (Ltd)
- A public company (plc)
- Community Interest Companies (CIC)[23]
- Societas Europaea (SE)[24]

1.09 Only a public company can apply to be listed on a regulated exchange. It is worth emphasising, however, that not all public com-

---

19 Companies Act 2006, s 155 requires a company to have at least one director who is a natural person.

20 P Davies, *An Introduction to Company Law* (2nd edn, 2002); P Davies and S Worthington, *Gower and Davies Principles of Modern Company Law* (9th edn, 2012); R Kraakman et al, *An Anatomy of Corporate Law: A Comparative and Functional Approach* (2nd edn, 2010).

21 Companies Act 2006, s 3 and s 102. An unlimited company can re-register as a limited company, although it may do so only once: s 102(3) and s 105(2). The name of a company with unlimited liability does not contain a suffix indicating its status. Unlimited companies are more common than might be imagined not least because they are not subject to rules on capital maintenance. Take, for example, *Re Lehman Brothers International (Europe) (in administration)* [2012] UKSC 6. Lehman Brothers International (Europe) (registered number 02538254) was an unlimited company.

22 Not all companies limited by guarantee need to include 'Limited' or 'Ltd' in their name: Companies Act 2006, s 60 (which also contains a small number of exceptions for companies limited by shares).

23 See part II of the Companies (Audit, Investigations and Community Enterprise) Act 2004.

24 Council Regulation (EC) No 2157/2001 on the Statute for a European company: see P Davies and S Worthington, *Gower and Davies Principles of Modern Company Law* (9th edn, 2012) para 1-33 ff.

panies are listed. Otherwise, of the entities listed above, only the private company limited by shares (Ltd) and the public limited company (plc) are commonly encountered in commercial life. In addition to companies, three other juristic persons, which are covered in this book, are common:

- A limited liability partnership (LLP)
- A limited partnership (LP)
- A partnership

1.10 With this limited knowledge of the law of juristic persons, it should – in principle if not in practice – be possible instantly to verify the vehicle adopted by a business to pursue its commercial activities: companies, like LPs and LLPs, have to publicise their status on all their business documents, including emails and websites. The designation plc, Ltd, LLP or LP is a mandatory part of the registered name for these respective vehicles – it is not an optional suffix. A solicitor who is a notary public sometimes uses the suffix 'NP', after his or her name: its use is optional. But the plc, Ltd, LLP or LP designation is as much a part of the company name as a natural person's surname. At this juncture, it is worth recording an obvious observation about the use of the word 'limited'. That term is a misnomer. Companies, LLPs and LPs do not have limited liability: their liability is unlimited. The limitation being advertised by the suffix of Ltd, plc, LLP or LP is rather the liability of certain persons behind the vehicle – the shareholders, members or limited partners – who have no direct liability to the creditors of these entities. Scottish partnerships, as we will see, are unusual: although a partnership is a juristic person and primarily liable for its own debts, the partners are expressly held by statute to be secondarily liable – essentially guarantors – for the firm's debts.[25]

PERSONALITY AND PATRIMONY

Concept

1.11 Every person has a patrimony. A patrimony contains the totality of that person's assets.[26] Assets are a person's patrimonial rights: real rights, personal rights and intellectual property rights. The general principle of personal liability (whether of a natural or a juristic person) is that a creditor may look to all the debtor's assets to satisfy the creditor's claim, by way of diligence or, ultimately, through bankruptcy. It is for this reason that a personal obligation granted by a juristic person with plentiful assets (relative to its liabilities) may often be more valuable

---

25 A point made in *J H Rayner (Mincing Lane) Ltd v Department of Trade and Industry* [1990] 2 AC 418 at 479H–480A per Lord Templeman and at 508D–E per Lord Oliver of Aylmerton.

26 G L Gretton and A J M Steven, *Property, Trusts and Succession* (2nd edn, 2013) paras 1.9–1.12. Sometimes the word 'estate' is used as a synonym for patrimony, as in 'trust estate', 'bankrupt estate', 'deceased's estate'.

than a real right in security in a thing that is of fluctuating value or for which there is no ready market. A bank guarantee (a personal obligation) is commercially preferable to a standard security (a real security) over an owner-occupied residential property.

1.12 Although all assets in the debtor's patrimony are available, it is *only* the debtor's patrimony that is available: assets held in a separate patrimony are not available to the debtor's personal creditors. The classic example for explaining this distinction is the trust. A trustee is bound to segregate trust assets from his personal assets. The trust assets are thus considered to be held in a patrimony that is separate from the trustee's personal patrimony. The significance of the distinction is that trust assets are not available to the personal creditors of the trustee; nor are the trustee's personal assets available to creditors who have contracted with the trustee on the basis that only the trust assets shall be available to satisfy the creditor's claim.[27]

Asset partitioning: juristic persons

1.13 Every person, natural or legal, has a patrimony, but, generally, only one patrimony. The creation of a juristic person as a vehicle for a business involves the creation of a new person and thus a new patrimony. Assets acquired by the business vehicle, let us suppose it is a company, are held in the company's patrimony, not the patrimony of individual shareholders. Two aspects of asset partitioning between the company and its shareholders are worth highlighting.[28] The first, sometimes known as *entity shielding*, exists for the benefit of the company. The personal insolvency of a shareholder does not – at least directly[29] – affect the company's assets. The second aspect (asset partitioning) arises by virtue of the company's separate legal personality and the idea of limited liability: individual shareholders are not liable to the company's creditors on the company's insolvency, although the shareholders may be affected in other ways: if a company cannot pay its creditors, then shareholders will not receive back the money they originally invested in the company.

1.14 Sometimes, however, asset partitioning for particular purposes is more specifically intended. A special purpose vehicle ('SPV') or special purpose entity ('SPE') is, normally, a juristic person whose only purpose is to hold particular assets. An SPV is often incorporated to hold assets rather than to trade. The assets are partitioned in theory because they

---

27 *Gordon v Campbell* (1840) 2 D 639, affd (1842) 1 Bell's App 428. Where a trustee commits a breach of trust, the beneficiaries may seek to satisfy their claim from the trustee's personal assets.

28 The ideas are well explained in R Kraakman et al, *The Anatomy of Corporate Law* para 7-11.

29 It may do so indirectly because the shareholder's insolvency administrator may be able to take control of the shares and thus the company. Once in control of the company the insolvency administrator could, in principle, wind up the company.

are held by a separate juristic person; but that partition is reinforced in practice because the basic premise of the SPV is that it holds rather than trades. An SPV is an entity that does not incur debt; and, because the entity has no debts, it has no creditors who can enforce court judgments against the vehicle's assets.

Asset partitioning: trusts

1.15 Another possibility for asset partitioning is the trust.[30] A trust is *not* a legal person, but gives rise to the creation of a separate patrimony.[31] A trust must have trustees. The trustees must be natural or juristic persons, for only persons enjoying legal capacity can enter into juridical acts. A trustee is in an exceptional position because the trustee has more than one patrimony. One patrimony is that in which her personal assets are held. The additional patrimony is that in which the trust assets are held. In principle, a trustee, a single person, can contract on such terms as to choose which patrimony is benefited and burdened by the contract. What, then, if the trustee becomes insolvent? The general principle is that assets held by a trustee in her capacity as trustee may not be attached by the trustee's personal creditors.[32]

Trust companies

1.16 A 'unit trust' may be a trust; but more usually it is a juristic person subject to some sort of trust deed. A REIT (a real estate investment trust), despite its name, cannot be a trust and must be a public limited company whose shares are traded on a recognised stock exchange.[33] A 'trust company' is normally a company acting as a trustee.

Limited liability

1.17 All persons, natural or juristic, are liable for their debts without limitation. In this sense, the liability of everyone is *unlimited*. What, then, is the concept of 'limited liability'? In historical terms, it is a relatively recent private law development. In Roman law every juristic person (*universitas*) had limited liability in the sense that only the *universitas* was liable for debts. But the Roman law business organisation, the partnership (*societas*), was never a *universitas*: juristic persons existed only in public law. The revolution in the modern world was to fuse *societas* (business but not person) with *universitas* (person but not business) thus creat-

---

30 See Gretton and Steven, *Property, Trusts and Succession*, ch 22.
31 G L Gretton, 'Trusts without equity' (2000) 49 International and Comparative Law Quarterly 599; K G C Reid, 'Patrimony not equity: the trust in Scotland' (2000) European Review of Private Law 427, cited with approval in *Ted Jacob Engineering Group Inc v Robert Matthew, Johnson-Marshall & Partners* [2014] CSIH 18, para [90] per Lord Drummond Young.
32 Bankruptcy (Scotland) Act 1985, s 33(1).
33 Corporation Tax Act 2010, s 528.

ing the modern company (both business and person), with explosive consequences.[34] Today, 'limited liability' means that the liability of a *member* of a company or an LLP, and a limited partner in a limited partnership, for the debts of the company, LLP or LP as the case may be, is limited by reference to the capital that is contributed by the member.[35] The limitation of the liability of the member or limited partner carries no implications for the liability of the juristic person. The juristic person's liability for its debts, like the liability of a natural person for his or her own debts, is unlimited.

PUBLICITY

Juristic persons

1.18 In the case of companies, LLPs and LPs, registration with the Registrar of Companies[36] is essential to the creation of these entities as juristic persons.[37] Registration serves the purpose of providing a central public record of information relating to the entity for the benefit of creditors, members and others who may have dealings with the entity. In the case of companies and LLPs they must have a registered number, a registered name and a registered office. The registered number does not change even if the name of the company or LLP changes. In addition to the publicity required for incorporation, a company or LLP has continuing reporting requirements, the most important of which is the public filing of annual audited accounts.[38] A company must disclose to the Registrar of Companies its directors and its members; it must also keep registers of this information at its registered office, which registers are, essentially, open to public inspection.[39] LPs require to be registered; they have a registered number, but only a principal place of business, which, curiously, need not actually be in Scotland.

1.19 Ordinary partnerships are not subject to registration in any form. An ordinary partnership may be formed simply by the conduct of persons carrying on a business in common with a view of profit,[40] which

---

34 This insight is gratefully acknowledged to be that of the Lord President Reid Professor of Law in the University of Edinburgh, Professor G L Gretton.

35 Cf. *J H Rayner (Mincing Lane) Ltd v Department of Trade and Industry* [1990] 2 AC 418 at 479H–480A per Lord Templeman and at 508D–E per Lord Oliver of Aylmerton. In the case of companies limited by guarantee, members' liabilities are limited to the guarantee provided in the memorandum of association.

36 The Registrar of Companies for Scotland is based in Edinburgh. There are separate Registrars for England and Wales (in Cardiff) and Northern Ireland (in Belfast).

37 See Companies Act 2006, s 16; Limited Liability Partnerships Act 2000, s 3; Limited Partnership Act 1907, s 8C.

38 Companies Act 2006, s 394.

39 Companies Act 2006, s 116 now imposes a 'proper purposes' test on applicants wishing to consult the registers kept at the company's registered office. For discussion, see *Burry & Knight Ltd v Knight* [2014] EWCA Civ 604, [2014] BCC 393.

40 See Partnership Act 1890, s 1.

means that, in contrast to registered business structures, its very existence may not always be clear. There is no easy way for third parties to establish, from an independent source, whether a partnership has been constituted, who the partners are, and where it does business. Since a partnership is not subject to the same reporting requirements as a company or LLP it might be thought that there is an obvious loophole: to form a partnership where the only partners are themselves companies. But specific anti-avoidance provisions have closed this loophole.[41] There are no requirements of registration or publicity for trusts, with the result that there is often no way of telling whether particular assets are held in trust.[42]

1.20 Publicity means that, in theory if not in practice, any contractual creditor of a corporate entity should be able to inform itself of the nature of the entity with whom a prospective contract is to be concluded. Some creditors, however, are involuntary – delict victims, for instance, do not choose their wrongdoer. Nonetheless, the courts have consistently held that it is legitimate to use the corporate form to structure matters in a way that effectively limits the claims of involuntary creditors, such as employees who are victims of delicts, to claims against a particular corporate entity, a subsidiary company responsible for employing workers, but which has few assets.[43]

Trusts

1.21 Trusts may be latent. There may be no way of telling whether particular assets are held in trust. Although trusts may be used for all kinds of legitimate purposes, they may not be used for purposes which are contrary to public policy. A trust which has only one purpose – to ring-fence assets from the trustee's lawful creditors – is not a valid trust.[44] The point is important to emphasise because, in the corporate and financial world, where there are no statutory prohibitions on exclusion of trustee duties,[45] constant recourse is made to trusts which often

---

41 Partnership (Accounts) Regulations 2008 (SI 2008/569), reg 3. The Companies and Partnerships (Accounts and Audit) Regulations 2013 (SI 2013/2005) introduced anti-avoidance provisions aimed at the use of Scottish LPs where the partners are companies or LLPs but where there is a nominal natural person as a limited partner.

42 The law on whether trusts may continue to be created without publicity may change: see n 63 below.

43 *Adams v Cape Industries plc* [1990] Ch 433. In *Chandler v Cape plc* [2012] 1 WLR 3111, however, the Court of Appeal held that a parent company may owe a duty of care to employees of a subsidiary. The principles on which the courts may ignore formal corporate structures are set out in *Prest v Petrodel Resources Ltd* [2013] UKSC 34.

44 G L Gretton and K G C Reid, *Conveyancing 2004* (2005) p 81. A striking English example is *Midland Bank plc v Wyatt* [1997] 1 BCLC 242.

45 There are various statutory prohibitions on exclusion of duties by trustees of occupational pension schemes, of issues of debentures, of unit trusts, or of contractual structures: see I MacNeil, *An Introduction to the Law of Financial Investment* (2nd edn, 2012) p 178.

have few, if any, legitimate trust purposes and in which the normal duties of a trustee are largely excluded. There are some English decisions where the courts have allowed sophisticated parties to exclude almost all of the duties of a trustee without invalidating the trust.[46] But whatever may be the English position (and there is a conflict of authority on the point in England) it is highly doubtful that a purported trust, without legitimate trust purposes, and in which the putative trustees have limited fiduciary obligations, is valid.

JURISTIC PERSONS AND BODIES CORPORATE

1.22 All 'bodies corporate' are juristic persons, but not all juristic persons are bodies corporate. Of the three vehicles with which this book is concerned (partnerships, LPs and LLPs), all are juristic persons, but only one – the LLP – is a body corporate. Companies are also bodies corporate. Bodies corporate enjoy what is known as 'perpetual succession': that is to say, their legal personality continues without reference to their members. A change in membership of a body corporate has no effect on the body's legal personality. Neither partnerships nor LPs, in contrast, automatically enjoy this attribute.[47] All other things being equal, a change in the constituent partners of a partnership – whether by death, resignation, bankruptcy or assumption of new partners – may result in the dissolution of one, and the reconstitution of a new, juristic person.[48]

BUSINESS ORGANISATIONS: THE LEGAL FRAMEWORK

Sole trader

1.23 A sole trader is a natural person who trades in that capacity without using a juristic person as a business vehicle. The 'sole' descriptor emphasises the solitary nature of this form of business organisation: it is possible for a sole trader to have employees and agents but if there is more than one person engaged as a principal (contributing capital and entering contracts) it is likely to be considered as a partnership. The sole trader bears full liability for all debts incurred in the business and faces the risk of bankruptcy if those debts cannot be paid.[49]

46 Cf. *Spread Trustee Co Ltd v Hutcheson* [2012] 2 AC 194. The leading Scottish case is *Lutea Trustees Ltd v Orbis Trustees Guernsey Ltd* 1997 SC 255.

47 'Person', in terms of the Interpretation Act 1978, Sch 1 and the Interpretation and Legislative Reform (Scotland) Act 2010, Sch 1, includes bodies *unincorporate*. We read '*unincorporated* associations' and reason that they have no legal personality. But 'unincorporated' does not equal 'no legal personality'. Scottish partnerships and limited partnerships are perhaps the classic example of bodies with juristic personality but which are not bodies corporate.

48 See para **5.40**.

49 Cf. *Accountant in Bankruptcy v Butler* 2007 SLT (Sh Ct) 200.

Partnerships and limited partnerships

1.24 A partnership is 'the relation which subsists between persons carrying on a business in common with a view of profit'.[50] Partnership is primarily an owner-manager form of business entity in which the owners (partners) themselves manage the business. Before the introduction of the limited company in Scotland in 1856,[51] and for some time thereafter, partnership was the dominant form of business organisation. The limited partnership ('LP') differs from the LLP in that it is not a body corporate. The LP's main commercial application is as a vehicle for investment management in which limited partners (investors) contribute capital to be managed by a professional manager (the general partner).

1.25 All partnerships in Scotland are juristic persons. General partnerships are governed by the Partnership Act 1890.[52] The 1890 Act comprises both default provisions which are capable of modification by the partnership agreement (the relations of partners to one another) as well as mandatory provisions (relations between the firm and third parties). The Limited Partnerships Act 1907 made available the limited partnership, which combined aspects of the traditional partnership (legal personality, privacy) with limitation of liability (for limited partners). But except in so far as inconsistent with the terms of the 1907 Act, the 1890 Act applies also to limited partnerships.

Limited liability partnerships (LLPs)

1.26 The Limited Liability Partnerships Act 2000 was introduced largely in response to demand from professional firms for protection from the potential liability to which their partners were exposed under the general law of partnership. An LP under the 1907 Act was not satisfactory since it did not provide limited liability for partners involved in management (and partners in professional firms are involved in management); nor did it clearly provide for perpetual succession on the death or resignation of general partners. Since the 2000 Act, most professional firms have adopted the LLP model. And so too have many commercial firms who see it as an alternative to a company, especially with regard to the different approach to taxation applied to partnerships compared to companies.[53]

50 Partnership Act 1890, s 1.
51 Joint Stock Companies Act 1856. For further discussion, see Chapter 5: Partnerships, LPs and LLPs below.
52 See Partnership Act 1890, s 46, preserving the common law except so far as inconsistent with the Act.
53 Partnerships are generally taxed according to the 'look-through' principle whereby profits are treated as earned by the individual partners (which may be companies) whereas companies pay corporation tax as entities separate from their members.

Companies

1.27 Companies represent the dominant form of business organisation. While limited liability and corporate status is now also available in the form of the LLP, the company still has a number of attractions that are not available in other business structures. These include the separation of ownership (members) and control (the board of directors) which enables external investors to contribute capital to be managed by others. The availability of a detailed and well-tested legal regime offers certainty for investors. In the case of public companies there are also the attractions of access to public capital markets, enabling large projects to be financed, and a liquid market in shares enabling investors to sell their shareholding in a regulated market.

1.28 Companies are governed by the Companies Act 2006. Earlier Companies Acts have been largely repealed. But companies incorporated under previous Companies Acts remain subject to the model articles prescribed by the Act under which the company was formed.[54]

Trusts

1.29 A Scottish trust is *not* a legal person, but gives rise to the creation of a separate patrimony.[55] A trust must have trustees. The trustees must be natural or juristic persons, for only persons enjoying legal capacity can enter into juridical acts. A trustee is in an exceptional position because the trustee has more than one patrimony. One patrimony is that in which her personal assets are held. The additional patrimony is that in which the trust assets are held. In principle, a trustee, a single person, can contract on such terms as to choose which patrimony is benefited and burdened by the contract. An important patrimonial question arises on the trustee's insolvency. The general principle is that assets held by a trustee in her capacity as trustee may not be attached by the trustee's personal creditors.[56] It is possible for one patrimony held by a trustee to be insolvent while the trustee's private patrimony remains solvent. A trust patrimony can be sequestrated, or have a judicial factor appointed to administer it.

Contractual liability of trustees

1.30 As a general rule creditors who have contracted with the trustee on the basis that only the trust assets (the trust patrimony) are liable, cannot attach assets held in the trustee's personal patrimony. There are conflicting cases on this extremely important practical issue. In *Gordon v*

---

54 Companies Act 2006, s 20(2).
55 G L Gretton, 'Trusts without equity' (n 31); K G C Reid, 'Patrimony not equity: the trust in Scotland' (n 31).
56 Bankruptcy (Scotland) Act 1985, s 33(1).

Campbell,[57] signature of a bond by trustees '*qua* trustees only' was held by the House of Lords sufficient to limit the creditors' rights to the trust funds; the trustees had no additional personal liability. In two subsequent decisions of the House of Lords,[58] however, registration of trustees as shareholders 'as trustees' was held, in terms of the relevant companies legislation, to be insufficient to prevent an imposition of personal liability on the trustees (the shares in question being held in banks with unlimited liability). As a matter of civil procedure, a decree against a defender in a representative capacity ('as judicial factor') has been held sufficient to limit the holder of the decree to recourse against the trust patrimony.[59] As a general rule, therefore, a decree against a representative, as representative, imposes no personal liability; a decree, without qualification, imposes personal liability but accords to the representative a right of relief against the fund held; and a decree against a representative 'personally' imposes personal liability and excludes a right of relief.[60] There is no equivalent of the *ultra vires* rules for creditors contracting with Scottish trustees. Third parties acting in good faith are protected even where the trustee has acted in breach of trust.[61]

1.31 The trust did not evolve as a business structure and is not often employed in Scotland for that purpose. But it may be that a trust is created in association with a specific transaction or course of dealing. For example, trusts are commonly used in various forms of financing because they offer the following benefits: separation of title and benefit (e.g. a pool of financial assets held and managed by professionals for investors); privacy; and insolvency effect (the pool of assets is ring-fenced on the insolvency of the trustees). The formal requirements for creating a trust are minimal.[62] There are no compulsory public registration requirements (although, in Scotland, many trusts are in fact registered in the Books of Council and Session). In the case of shares in a Scottish company held in trust, the existence of the trust may be publicised on

---

57 *Gordon v Campbell* (1840) 2 D 639, affd (1842) 1 Bell's App 428, an approach followed by a court of seven judges in *Craig v Hogg* (n 59).

58 *Lumsden v Buchanan* (1864) 2 M 695 (Whole Court), revd (1865) 3 M (HL) 89, (1865) 4 Macq 950 and *Muir v City of Glasgow Bank* (1878) 6 R 392, affd (1879) 6 R (HL) 21, (1879) 4 App Cas 337. A modern case dealing with some of these issues is *Brown v Rysaffe Trustee Company (CI) Ltd* [2011] CSOH 26.

59 *Craig v Hogg* (1896) 24 R 6 at 21 per Lord M'Laren following the decision of the House of Lords in *Gordon v Campbell* (n 57). The opinion of Lord Young (at 13–19), writing for the majority, is instructive and not limited to questions of expenses.

60 *Kilmarnock Theatre Co v Buchanan* 1911 SC 607; *Dyer v Craiglaw Developments Ltd* 1999 SLT 1228.

61 Trusts (Scotland) Act 1961, s 2. The trustee's personal patrimony will, however, be available to satisfy any losses brought about by his breach of trust.

62 Only so-called 'truster-as-trustee' trusts (where the truster declares a trust over his own assets in which he also acts as trustee) require to be in writing: Requirements of Writing (Scotland) Act 1995, s 1(2)(a)(iii).

the company's register of members, whereas in the case of English trusts, there is a prohibition against trusts appearing on the register.[63]

Charities

1.32 A charity is not a business organisation in the normal sense because it is established for public rather than private benefit. Nor is a charity necessarily a juristic person. Most juristic persons may apply to become a charity,[64] but not all charities are juristic persons: non-persons, such as trusts or unincorporated associations, may be registered as charities with the Office of the Scottish Charity Regulator ('OSCR').[65] Of the entities encountered above, companies limited by guarantee are commonly used for 'not-for-profit' activities. Similarly, a registered charity may or may not have charitable status for tax purposes. Only one juristic person *must* be a charity: the Scottish Charitable Incorporated Organisation ('SCIO').[66]

JURISTIC PERSONS AND CONTRACTS

Overview

1.33 Transactional capacity is a necessary pre-requisite for a natural or juristic person to enter into juridical acts. A juristic person, in addition, can act only through human agents. In those cases, it is necessary for the agent to have the requisite authority to bind the juristic person. Two separate issues thus arise for contracts to be concluded by juristic person: (a) does the juristic person as principal have capacity to enter the contract; and (b) does the juristic person's agent have authority to bind it to the contract?

Capacity

1.34 Historically, the contractual capacity of a company was linked to the objects clause (found in the memorandum of a company formed

---

63 See Companies Act 2006, s 126 for the prohibition. But the government has proposed that both the existence of a trust of shares and the identity of the beneficiaries in respect of more than 25% of the shares, should be publicly registered: Small Business and Employment Bill 2014, sch 3, which will introduce a new Part 21A into the Companies Act 2006.

64 But not all. A community interest company (CIC), for instance, cannot be entered on the OSCR register: Companies (Audit, Investigations and Community Enterprise) Act 2004, s 26(3)(b).

65 www.oscr.org.uk.

66 Charities and Trustee Investment (Scotland) Act 2005, s 49 ff and Scottish Charitable Incorporated Organisations Regulations 2011 (SSI 2011/44). This entity is perhaps the nearest equivalent in Scots law to the *foundation* found in other European systems: cf. K Hopt et al (eds) *The European Foundation: A New Legal Approach* (2006).

prior to the entry into force of the Companies Act 2006). The objects clause defined the permissible business activity of the company. Acts outside those objects, such as purported contracts, were held to be *ultra vires* and void.[67] The underlying rationale of this approach was that members and creditors could better estimate the risk to which they were exposed if there was a clear limit to the activities of the company.

1.35 The problem with the *ultra vires* doctrine was that it created uncertainty for creditors, especially as companies began to adopt broader objects clauses so as to permit a wide range of activities. As a result of the EC company law harmonisation programme, measures were adopted in the UK to provide greater protection to third parties dealing with a company. The Companies Act 2006 now provides that the validity of an act done by a company shall not be called into question on the ground of lack of capacity by reason of anything in the company's constitution.[68] Any objects clause in the company's constitution does not limit the company's capacity so far as third parties are concerned, but it will operate internally: any contract concluded for and on behalf of the company by a director who has exceeded his powers may leave the director liable to the company for any losses the company incurs.

Authority and agency

1.36 The common law of agency enables an agent to bind the principal to a third party.[69] Third parties, however, can normally never know the agent's *actual* authority. Third parties are concerned with what is described as the agent's apparent or ostensible authority. The extent of an agent's ostensible authority is determined by the representations made by the principal regarding the agent's authority. Providing an agent acts within his ostensible authority, the principal is bound, even if that act was not actually authorised.[70] But it is an important general principle of the law of agency that an agent can have no greater powers than his principal. Historically, therefore, a company agent's powers were subject to the *ultra vires* rule. That rule exposed third parties to the risk that directors (or other agents) acting on behalf of a company might lack the requisite authority.[71] The result would be that the third party could not enforce the contract against the principal (although there might be a claim against the agent for breach of warranty of authority).[72]

1.37 As a result of the EC company law harmonisation programme, third party creditors now have similar protection to that of a creditor

67 *Ashbury Railway Carriage and Iron Co Ltd v Riche* (1875) LR 7 (HL) 653, applied in *Piggins & Rix Ltd v Montrose Port Authority* 1995 SLT 418.
68 Companies Act 2006, s 39.
69 See generally L J Macgregor, *The Law of Agency in Scotland* (2013).
70 *Freeman & Lockyer v Buckhurst Park Properties (Mangal) Ltd* [1964] 2 QB 480.
71 The decision in *Royal British Bank v Turquand* (1856) 6 El & Bl 327, 119 ER 886 limited the full rigour of this rule.
72 For breach of warranty, see e.g. *Cheshire Mortgage Corporation Ltd v Grandison* 2013 SC 160.

dealing with a Scottish trustee: a contract concluded for and on behalf of a company by an officer such as a director, binds the company by virtue of the director's ostensible authority. But where a director, in so acting, has exceeded his actual authority, the company will, in principle, have a right of relief against the director. The same principles that apply to companies apply also to LLPs.[73]

1.38 In the case of partnerships, partners' ostensible authority covers 'acts for the carrying on in the usual way business of the kind carried on by the firm of which he is a member'.[74] Questions regarding the authority of partners to bind the firm to contracts generally focus on the issue of whether the particular contract entered into by a partner is within the scope of the business of the firm.

PRACTICALITIES: SUBSCRIPTION AND SIGNING

General requirements for writing[75]

1.39 As a general rule contracts may be formed in Scots law without formality. There are three major practical exceptions to that rule. Writing is required for the creation, transfer, variation or extinction of a real right in land; for the creation of a gratuitous unilateral obligation undertaken other than in the course of business; for the creation of a truster-as-trustee trust;[76] and for wills.[77] Where writing is required, the document must be subscribed by the granter of it, or, if there is more than one granter, by each of the granters.[78] Subscription means signing at the end of the last page of the document, excluding any annexations.

Execution by juristic persons

Formal validity

1.40 Juristic persons can act only through human agency. The Requirements of Writing (Scotland) Act 1995 (the '1995 Act') sets out who can properly execute written documents for and on behalf of a juristic person. Many, perhaps most, commercial contracts do not *require* to be in writing. But they are normally reduced to writing for the sake of certainty.

1.41 Given the prevalence, in commercial practice, of written documents whose draftsperson may have been familiar only with English law,

---

73 Limited Liability Partnerships Act 2000, s 6.
74 Partnership Act 1890, s 5.
75 See generally Gretton and Steven, *Property, Trusts and Succession*, ch 30; Gretton and Reid, *Conveyancing* (4th edn, 2011) ch 17.
76 Requirements of Writing (Scotland) Act 1995, s 1(2)(a).
77 1995 Act, s 1(2)(b) and (c).
78 1995 Act, ss 1(7) and 2(1) respectively. In the case of contracts constituted by separate offer and acceptance documents, each must be subscribed (s 2(2)).

it is worth making three general observations about execution of commercial documents under Scots law. In the first place, the 1995 Act applies to 'written documents'. 'Deed' is not a term of art in Scots law.[79] Valid execution under the 1995 Act requires the parties to the contract to 'subscribe': that means signature by the granter 'at the end of the last page'.[80] Secondly, it is standard practice, for documents drafted with execution under English law in mind, to have free-standing signature pages – i.e. pages which do not otherwise make reference to the document to which they belong. Such pages do not, however, comply with Scots law, since subscription must be on 'the last page' of the document. In practical terms, therefore, in order to ensure a contract complies with the 1995 Act, the page on which the first signatures appear should also contain the last clause of the agreement.[81] Thirdly, in the modern commercial world, the parties to a commercial contract governed by Scots law may be spread out around the world. Careful thought needs to be given to how the documents can be executed remotely.[82] In principle, however, it is possible for each party to print off a copy, subscribe it before a witness and deliver the document (electronically) to the other parties or to an agent appointed for that purpose. Some legal uncertainty surrounds this practice, but that uncertainty will be removed when the draft Legal Writings (Counterparts and Delivery) (Scotland) Bill 2014[83] is brought into force.

Validity and probativity

1.42 Companies subscribe by either a director or the secretary or an authorised person for and on behalf of the company. In the case of an LLP, subscription is by a member for and on behalf of the LLP. In the case of a partnership, subscription is by a partner, or other authorised signatory, for and on behalf of the Firm. In addition to ensuring that the document is formally valid, it is standard practice to have the documents executed in such a way as to confer probative status. Probativity refers to the evidential presumption that the document was executed by the granter and, if the document included a date and a place of execution, that the document was indeed executed on that date and at that place.[84] Probativity is about form rather than substance: the presumption allows

---

79 Cf. *Walker v Whitwell* 1916 SC (HL) 75 at 79 per Lord Dunedin and *Low & Bonar plc and Low & Bonar Pension Trs Ltd v Mercer Ltd* [2010] CSOH 47 at para [21] per Lord Drummond Young.
80 1995 Act, s 7(1).
81 For an example, see Scottish Law Commission, *Report on Execution in Counterpart* (No 231, 2013) para 3.7.
82 See Scottish Law Commission, *Discussion Paper on Execution in Counterpart* (DP No 154, 2012) and n 81 above; as well as R G Anderson, 'Subscription and settlement by fax and email' 2010 SLT (News) 67 and 'Fax and email in corporate completions' 2010 SLT (News) 73.
83 Cf. the Appendix to the SLC Report (n 81).
84 1995 Act, s 3(1) and (8).

reliance to be placed on a document without recourse to extrinsic evidence. But a probative document may nonetheless be invalid: a party who bears to have signed as an authorised signatory of the granter company, for instance, may not, in fact, have been authorised to sign.[85] The general rule for achieving probative status is that the subscription of someone authorised to sign on behalf of the company must be witnessed;[86] and the witness must be designed by name and address. This means, in the case of companies, that signature by a director and a witness is sufficient. There is, however, an alternative method, which is that the document may be signed by a second signatory. There are three permitted combinations:

(1) two directors;
(2) a director and the company secretary; or
(3) two authorised signatories.[87]

1.43 LLPs execute documents by a member signing for and on behalf of the LLP in the presence of a witness; or by two members signing for and on behalf of the LLP.[88] Partnerships execute documents by a partner, or other authorised signatory, signing for and on behalf of the firm in the presence of a witness.[89] Uniquely among juristic persons, a partnership can validly subscribe a document by the partner or authorised signatory signing the name of the partnership rather than his or her own name.[90]

Other bodies corporate

1.44 There may be many other types of juristic person, not least foreign entities, which enter into commercial transactions governed by Scots law. In general terms, such entities execute documents in terms of the residual provisions of the 1995 Act on 'other bodies corporate'.[91]

Digital documents and signatures

1.45 The Land Registration etc (Scotland) Act 2012 allows for the generation and authentication of digital documents in such a way as to

---

85 1995 Act, s 3(1C), as substituted by Sch 2, para 3(5)(a).
86 1995 Act, s 3(1)(b), as substituted by Sch 2, para 3(5)(a).
87 1995 Act, s 3(1A), as substituted by Sch 2, para 3(5)(a).
88 1995 Act, Sch 2, para 3A(1) and (4) and (5). Curiously, no reference is made, in the case of LLPs, to signing by an authorised signatory. But the ordinary principles apply and there is nothing to prevent an LLP specifically authorising a non-member, such as an employee, to sign on its behalf. Such a document would be validly executed.
89 1995 Act, Sch 2, para 2(1). In legal practice, incorporated law firms often sign the LLP or company name on formal missive letters purporting to contain substantive contractual provisions. Such signatures are not, however, valid.
90 1995 Act, Sch 2, para 2(2).
91 1995 Act, Sch 2, para 5. These provisions, in practice, are applied also to foreign juristic persons which have legal personality but are not bodies corporate.

obtain the equivalent evidential status of a probative paper deed. But the digital signatures used for the purposes of authentication of a digital document will have to comply with the regulations that are to be made under the 2012 Act. In addition, and importantly for corporate lawyers, the Legal Writings (Counterparts and Delivery) (Scotland) Bill 2014 will permit execution of contracts in counterpart.

JURISTIC PERSONS AND DELICT

Introduction

1.46 A juristic person may have rights to claim damages in delict or it may be liable to pay damages for delicts. For a juristic person to be liable in delict, it is normally necessary to attribute the acts of a natural person to the juristic person for the purposes of establishing liability. A related issue concerns the losses incurred by a juristic person for which damages may be due.

Vicarious liability

1.47 As a general rule, a person is liable only for his own acts and omissions and not for the acts and omissions of others.[92] The rule reflects the principle that liability is based on the wrongdoer's fault (*culpa*). Vicarious liability is an exception to the general rule since it has the effect that liability attaches to another person. Vicarious liability differs from the primary or direct liability of the wrongdoer in that it can arise only when liability attaches to the wrongdoer and cannot arise in the absence of such liability. Vicarious liability is additional to the primary liability of the wrongdoer. The wrongdoer and the party vicariously liable are, as far as the party with the right to claim damages is concerned, jointly and severally liable to the injured party.

1.48 Vicarious liability applies in many situations. An employer is vicariously liable for the delicts of an employee committed in the course of employment. A distinction is drawn between employees who are employed under a contract of employment (and for whose acts or omissions the employer is normally vicariously liable);[93] and independent contractors who are employed under a contract for the provision of services (and for whose acts or omissions the employer is not normally vicariously liable). But the parameters of an employee's scope of employment and control are often difficult to draw.[94] Vicarious liability may also arise in the case of principal and agent. Employment and agency

---

92 The principle is reflected in the maxim *culpa tenet suos auctores*: 'fault binds its authors'.
93 *Wilsons & Clyde Coal Co Ltd v English* 1937 SC (HL) 46.
94 See discussion in *Vaickuviene v J Sainsbury plc* [2013] CSIH 67; *Catholic Child Welfare Society v Various Claimants* [2013] UKSC 56, [2013] 2 AC 1; *Lister v Hesley Hall Ltd* [2002] 1 AC 215.

may well overlap in circumstances where scope of employment is linked to the authority granted by an employer to an employee.

1.49 Other than in the case of partnerships, the instances of vicarious liability mentioned above are not defined by reference to the legal person who bears the liability. Thus, for example, a sole trader who has employees faces the same risk of vicarious liability as a partnership or a company. A similar view can be taken of the potential vicarious liability of a principal for an agent. A company or LLP may incur delictual liability either in its capacity as an employer or as a principal. There are, however, two additional issues which arise in the context of companies and LLPs. The first is that the *ultra vires* doctrine, such as it is, does not limit the delictual liability of a company.[95] So where a company elects[96] to have an objects clause restricting its activity, its capacity to commit a delict is not restricted. The second is that, in the case of the delicts of misrepresentation or negligent provision of advice, it must be shown that the wrongdoer voluntarily assumed responsibility for the advice or information provided to the third party who has suffered loss.[97] Where an agent (such as a director) assumes responsibility for advice or information given by a company to a third party in the course of the company's business, only the company is liable to the third party.[98] However, in the case of other delicts, where assumption of responsibility is not a necessary requirement for liability, an agent may be personally liable, and the company vicariously liable, to the third party.[99]

Claims against third parties

1.50 A juristic person may pursue remedies for injury or loss suffered as a result of delicts committed by third parties, so companies may recover for damage caused to the company's property,[100] reputation[101] or creditworthiness.[102] A clear distinction should be drawn between (a) loss suffered by the company as a juristic person and (b) loss suffered by other persons related to a company. Members, directors or employees have no rights to sue for damage to the company's assets. One exception to this principle arises in the case of derivative actions.[103]

1.51 The board of directors of a public or private company has respon-

---

95 *Houldsworth v City of Glasgow Bank* (1880) 7 R (HL) 53.
96 Companies Act 2006, s 31.
97 *Bank of Scotland v Fuller Peiser* 2002 SLT 574, following *Henderson v Merrett Syndicates Ltd* [1995] 2 AC 145.
98 In *Williams v Natural Life Health Foods* [1998] 1 WLR 830, a (one-man) company had been dissolved and the plaintiffs attempted, unsuccessfully, to have the managing director and principal shareholder held personally liable for misrepresentation.
99 *Standard Chartered Bank v Pakistan Shipping Corporation (No 2)* [2003] 1 AC 959.
100 *Macaura v Northern Assurance Co Ltd* [1925] AC 619.
101 *Jameel v Wall Street Journal Europe Sprl (No 3)* [2007] 1 AC 359.
102 *Downtex plc v Flatley* [2003] EWCA Civ 1282.
103 These are briefly discussed in para **5.65** below.

sibility for the management of a company's business and the board may exercise all powers of the company. This responsibility, subject to the company's articles, extends to the control of litigation by the company.[104] Any action the board elects to pursue is pursued in the company's name. In the case of a general or limited partnership, the default rule is that the decision to bring or defend an action is taken by the majority of (general) partners.[105]

Termination of legal personality

1.52 Dissolution of companies and LLPs is dealt with in Chapter 14: Corporate Insolvency. The dissolution of partnerships and limited partnerships is also dealt with in that chapter.

JURISTIC PERSONS AND CRIMINAL LIABILITY

Introduction

1.53 A juristic person is capable both of committing a criminal offence and being the victim of a criminal offence.[106] The criminal liability of juristic persons, however, poses particular problems of attribution. Not only must conduct (*actus reus*) be attributed to the juristic person, but also criminal intent (*mens rea*). Criminal intent may not, however, form part of the *corpus delicti* of many statutory offences which essentially impose strict liability. In contrast with the law of delict, vicarious liability has not been employed in order to attribute criminal liability to a juristic person. The following section deals with the attribution mechanisms employed by the criminal law.

Attribution

1.54 The 'identification doctrine' has been developed in the context of companies but, in principle, applies also to other juristic persons.[107] That doctrine identifies those individuals (in principle an open category) who stand above the company's employees and agents and who may be considered the embodiment of the company.[108] Such individuals are

---

104 Companies (Model Articles) Regulations 2008 (SI 2008/3229), Model Articles for private companies limited by shares, Art 2, Model Articles for public companies, Art 4.
105 Partnership Act 1890, s 24(8).
106 Scottish Law Commission, *Discussion Paper on Criminal Liability of Partnerships* (DP No 150, 2011), para 3.1. However, there are some criminal offences which can be committed only by an individual because it is not possible to attribute the act and intent to a juristic person: they include murder (but not culpable homicide) and rape. Similarly, a juristic person cannot be a victim of crimes against the person (e.g. murder, assault, rape).
107 Scottish Law Commission, *Discussion Paper on Criminal Liability of Partnerships* (DP No 150, 2011) ch 3.
108 *Tesco Supermarkets Ltd v Nattrass* [1972] AC 153 at 170 per Lord Reid, applied in *Transco plc v HM Advocate* 2004 JC 29.

sometimes referred to as the 'directing mind and will' of the company. The actions and intentions of such individuals are therefore considered to be attributable to the company. The individuals likely to be considered a company's embodiment must, of their nature, be senior management. The identification doctrine is narrower in scope than the principle of vicarious liability; but as in the case of vicarious liability, the manager's personal culpability must be established in order to attribute it to the company he or she manages.

1.55 Alternative models of attribution have been adopted in the case of various statutory offences. For example, the criminal liability of an employer under section 3 of the Health and Safety at Work etc Act 1974 – failure to maintain a safe place of work – is a form of personal liability: in the case of a juristic person, section 3 liability can be established without the need first to establish the personal liability of an employee or agent.[109] In the case of corporate homicide, the statutory model of attribution has been described as 'holistic' because it is based on management failure within the organisation and not on the action/intent of a single individual.[110] Similarly, the attribution model adopted by the Bribery Act 2012 is broader than the common law approach because it holds a juristic person liable for failing to take action to prevent bribes being paid by its employees (as well as attaching liability to employees who arrange bribes).

1.56 Beyond senior managers, other individuals within a corporate structure may incur criminal liability in two ways. In the first place, individuals may be found to have acted 'art and part' in the commission of an offence committed by others within the company, or by the company itself, or both. Secondly, individuals may commit the secondary offence of assistance in respect of the commission of a primary offence.[111] In such a case, conviction for the secondary offence does not require that there has already been a successful prosecution for the primary offence.

Effect of dissolution

1.57 Termination of legal personality poses similar problems for criminal law as in the law of delict since there is no longer a legal person that can be prosecuted. In *Balmer v HM Advocate*[112] a prosecution under the Health and Safety at Work etc Act 1974 was brought against a partnership for breach of duties which had caused the deaths of fourteen people in a fire. Prior to the indictment being served, however, the partnership had been dissolved. As a result, it was held that the indictment was incompetent.[113] The Scottish Law Commission subsequently investigated

---

109 *R v British Steel plc* [1995] 1 WLR 1356.
110 E.g. Corporate Manslaughter and Corporate Homicide Act 2007, s 1.
111 E.g. Health and Safety at Work etc Act 1974, s 36.
112 2008 SLT 799.
113 There was no charge brought against the partners 'art and part' or under the accessory liability provisions of s 36 of the Health and Safety at Work etc Act 1974. For the prosecution of trustees, see *Aitkenhead v Fraser* 2006 JC 231.

the matter and its report has led to a change in the law whereby a partnership can be prosecuted for a criminal offence committed within five years of its dissolution.[114]

Criminal sanctions

1.58   The most serious sanction for conviction of a criminal offence is imprisonment. Juristic persons, however, cannot be imprisoned. The common sanction, therefore, is to apply financial penalties to juristic persons. In the case of a partnership, a fine is a debt owed by the partnership and may be recovered from the personal assets of the partners if the firm's assets are inadequate.[115] Companies cannot indemnify directors for liability arising from a fine (and indeed civil liability for negligence, default, breach of duty or breach of trust) imposed on directors personally.[116] The rationale for that approach is that an indemnity would effectively shift the cost of mismanagement on to members.

114 Partnerships (Prosecution) (Scotland) Act 2013, s 1.
115 Scottish Law Commission, *Report on Criminal Liability of Partnerships* (No 224, 2011) para 3.1. The principle of limited liability prevents a fine levied on a juristic person being recovered from the personal assets of company shareholders, LP limited partners or LLP members.
116 Companies Act 2006, s 232. Under s 233, however, a company may obtain insurance for its directors against such liabilities. But it is a general principle of the law of insurance that it is not normally possible to insure against fraud or other criminal conduct.

Chapter 2

General Principles of Contract Law

2.01 Contracts are quintessentially about relationships. In the usual case, two (or more) parties enter into an agreement in which they commit themselves to certain obligations to each other. The relationship between the parties is of relatively little importance in over-the-counter sales or even in the high-value world of financial trading, where transactions are concluded instantaneously. However, commercial parties often enter into contracts which last for many years and the provisions of the contract are the backdrop against which they do business with each other. At the beginning of the life of a contract both parties optimistically hope that the courts need never be involved and, in most cases, the content of the contract remains a private matter which regulates their business relationship without contention. It perhaps seems strange that the law should intervene at all in private commercial agreements and, in the Common Law world, there has traditionally been reluctance for either governments or courts to interfere with the operation of commerce. That reluctance stems from the belief that individual and commercial freedom creates the best environment for business to flourish and for the economy to grow. However, when things go wrong it is important for business confidence and commercial certainty that the agreement the parties have made with each other is enforceable and that the remedies it provides can be relied on. Commercial contracts, therefore, have two principal functions: to provide certainty by setting out clearly and concisely in advance the parties' respective rights and obligations; and to provide a solution when things go wrong through application of the default rules of contract law.

2.02 Much of what we refer to as commercial law is founded on the application of the law of contract in a corporate and business context. Whilst particular types of contract have their own specific rules, for instance insurance law or employment law, there are general principles that apply to all contracts. The objective of this chapter is to provide a selective overview of the general principles of Scots contract law which are most relevant in a commercial context.[1] Attention is also given to the

---

1 The assumption is made that the parties to a commercial contract are businesses, unless otherwise stated. No attempt will be made to outline the growing number of rules which apply to consumer contracts. The law of promise is also excluded from this chapter.

content of commercial contracts and some of the most commonly used terms. A more comprehensive treatment can be found in specialist textbooks.[2]

FUNDAMENTAL CONCEPTS IN CONTRACT LAW

Freedom of contract

2.03   The most important theoretical principle in contract law is *freedom of contract*. The development of contract law coincided with a period when Scotland's economy changed from being largely agrarian to one that was industrial and commercial. By the end of the nineteenth century contract cases dealt less often with transactions concerning horses and cows and more frequently with obligations incurred by banks, shareholders and company directors. In this period of transformation entrepreneurs and investors were needed to oil the wheels of commerce and the role of law was not to impede progress by placing obstacles in their way. Hence, within certain limits, business people were free to decide both whom they wanted to conduct business with and the terms on which they entered into contractual relationships. Unless the contract had been entered into using deceit, force or under a fundamental error,[3] or it dealt with illegal or immoral activities,[4] the rules of contract law would not interfere with what the parties agreed. The purpose of contract law was to facilitate commerce and the growth of wealth for the benefit of society as a whole, as encapsulated in Jessell MR's well-known statement:[5]

> [I]f there is one thing which more than another public policy requires it is that men of full age and competent understanding shall have the utmost liberty of contracting, and that their contracts when entered into freely and voluntarily shall be held sacred and shall be enforced by courts of justice.

Legal certainty

2.04   What then was the role of the courts if not to interfere with commercial bargains? The second part of the quotation tells us that it was to ensure that contracts were enforced. This is the related principle of *sanctity of contract* which contains the idea that the law will respect commercial bargains, holding them as 'sacred', and will ensure that the parties perform the obligations they have freely entered into. Contracts are entered into against the backdrop of legal enforcement and legal sanctions which in turn give both parties the legal certainty required in the commercial world. If you cannot be sure that the agreements you

2 W W McBryde, *The Law of Contract in Scotland* (3rd edn, 2007); H L MacQueen and J Thomson, *Contract Law in Scotland* (3rd edn, 2012).

3 See paras **2.57–2.71**.

4 See paras **2.78–2.83**.

5 *Printing and Numerical Registering Co v Sampson* (1875) LR 19 Eq 462 at 465 per Jessell MR.

make have the support of the law, you cannot plan with certainty the future of your business. And if businesspeople enter into high-value contracts they need reassurance that if the other party fails to deliver they have recourse to the courts to protect their assets and investment. Freedom and certainty go hand in hand to create the best commercial environment for economic growth in that once the parties have exercised their freedom they are legally bound by the obligations they have undertaken. It is therefore good for the state and for society as a whole as a matter of legal policy. Certainty is particularly important since the commercial world is inextricably linked to the operation of credit. Loans and other credit transactions are the day-to-day business of banks, financial institutions and many businesses, but they are possible only because the law of contract stands behind them as both a carrot and a stick.

Limitations on freedom of contract

2.05 Freedom of contract was the legal equivalent of economic liberalism, or *laissez-faire*, which had its heyday in the nineteenth century.[6] However, freedom has its limits and in some circumstances may be illusory, particularly where the parties are not on an equal footing. Even in a commercial context a small business may find itself subject to harsh contract terms when dealing with a much larger business: for instance, a local newsagent dealing with a multinational company for the supply of goods may be bound by that company's standard terms and conditions with no opportunity to negotiate a deal. In those circumstances it cannot be said in reality that the newsagent has had true freedom of contract to decide the terms on which any purchase is made. Freedom of contract is most meaningful where the parties enter into contracts on relatively equal terms, where both parties can negotiate about the terms and can tailor the contract to their specific needs. Over the course of the last fifty years judges and legislators have intervened to place limits on the parties' freedom where there was an imbalance of power and particularly if one of the parties was a consumer dealing with a business.[7] The Law Commission and the Scottish Law Commission have recently acknowledged that a similar regime is needed to protect small businesses.[8]

Good faith and fair dealing in a commercial context

2.06 Another underlying, although not uncontested, concept in contract law is good faith. The modern debate on the subject began after Lord Clyde referred in *Smith v Bank of Scotland* to 'the broad principle in the field of contract law of fair dealing in good faith'[9] which sparked a flurry of academic writing reflecting a broad range of views as to

---

6 For a fuller discussion see P S Atiyah, *The Rise and Fall of Freedom of Contract* (Oxford, 1979).

7 For instance, the Unfair Contract Terms Act 1977, see paras **2.116–2.123**.

8 See *Joint Report on Unfair Contract Terms* (Law Com No 292, Scot Law Com No 199, 2005) part 5.

9 *Smith v Bank of Scotland* 1997 SC (HL) 111 at 121.

whether or not such a principle existed.[10] Some argued that good faith was indeed an underlying principle and appeared throughout the law of contract in various guises; others were sceptical about the development of a concept which was ill-defined and could lead to uncertainty. Since then it has been affirmed at the highest judicial level that 'good faith in Scottish contract law . . . is generally an underlying principle of an explanatory or legitimating rather than an active or creative nature',[11] and yet the Scottish judiciary remains resistant as a recent statement from the Outer House demonstrates:[12]

> It is, of course, no part of Scots law that, in the absence of agreement, parties to a contract should act in good faith in carrying out their obligations to each other.

2.07 English law is similarly resistant to a general principle of good faith[13] but the courts have been willing to uphold a duty to act in good faith (either express or implied) in particular commercial contracts.[14] Commercial parties often expressly embody the principle of good faith in their agreements.[15] If further proof were needed of its value two of the world's most successful market economies, the United States and Germany, do not appear to have suffered for doing business under a legal regime which places good faith at its core.[16]

PRE-REQUISITES TO FORMATION OF CONTRACT

Agreement: *consensus in idem*

2.08 Contracts are voluntary obligations entered into by the parties of their own free will. The core idea behind contractual agreement is that of consent or *consensus in idem*, a meeting of the minds. The parties' intentions must coincide about the mutual rights and obligations they are about to undertake towards each other. Establishing whether or not agreement has been reached is often analysed by reference to the offer

---

10 See contributions in A D M Forte (ed), *Good Faith in Contract and Property* (1999).

11 *R v Immigration Officer at Prague Airport, ex parte European Roma Rights Centre* [2004] UKHL 55, [2005] WLR 1 at para 60 per Lord Hope.

12 *EDI Central Ltd v National Car Parks Ltd* [2010] CSOH 141 at para [23] per Lord Glennie.

13 *Mid Essex Hospital Services NHS Trust v Compass Group UK and Ireland Ltd (t/a Medirest)* [2013] EWCA Civ 200 at para 265 per Jackson LJ.

14 *Berkeley Community Villages Ltd v Pullen* [2007] EWHC 1330 (Ch); *CPC Group Ltd v Qatari Diar Real Estate Investment Co* [2010] EWHC 1535 (Ch); *Yam Seng Pte Ltd v International Trade Corporation* [2013] EWHC 111; *Bristol Groundschool Ltd v Intelligent Data Capture Ltd* [2014] EWHC 2145.

15 One of the world's most important standard contractual documents – the English law-governed International Swaps and Derivatives Association (ISDA) Master Agreement – contains various clauses which expressly impose duties of good faith on the counterparties. For further discussion of good faith and best endeavours clauses see below at paras **2.107–2.108**.

16 Bürgerliches Gesetzbuch [BGB] (German Civil Code) § 242; American Uniform Commercial Code art 2.

and acceptance framework.[17] Besides the central notion of agreement there are certain other pre-requisites which must be satisfied before a contract comes into existence: the parties must have legal capacity to transact; they must intend to enter into a legal relationship; and the essential terms of their agreement must be ascertainable. It should be noted that a bare agreement is sufficient to conclude a contract in Scots law and, unlike English law, there is no requirement for consideration. The term consideration is sometimes found in Scottish case law but not as a term of art and it is not a pre-requisite for formation of contract. However, in English law a contract is binding only if supported by consideration. This means, broadly speaking, that there must be reciprocity or *quid pro quo* and that each party must receive something in return for giving something.[18] By contrast, Scots law recognises the enforceability of unilateral or gratuitous promises.[19]

Legal capacity

2.09 In every legal transaction there is a requirement that the party or parties concerned must have the legal capacity to transact, i.e. they must be legally capable of entering into obligations. Where individuals are concerned they may be deemed to lack capacity because they are too young[20] or because they lack sufficient understanding or mental capacity to enter into legal obligations. The consequence of entering into a contract with a party lacking capacity is that the contract will be treated as void, as if it never existed, and no rights or obligations can arise for the parties in such circumstances.

2.10 In a commercial context, artificial legal entities such as companies and partnerships also require legal capacity,[21] which arises when they are constituted as legal persons under the relevant legal framework. If such a body acts outwith the powers conferred on it, it will be acting *ultra vires*, i.e. it will lack legal capacity and any contract entered into will be void. The Companies Act 2006 has significantly altered this position in order to prevent such situations arising and to protect all parties to a contract involving a company.[22] The rule also applies to other bodies who act under statutory authority, for instance local authorities or trades unions. A recent example of this can be seen in *Morgan Guaranty Trust Co of New York v Lothian Regional Council*[23] in which the local authority acted beyond the powers prescribed in the Local Government

17 See para **2.21** ff below.
18 For further detail and an account of developments in the definition of consideration see E McKendrick, *Goode on Commercial Law* (4th edn, 2010) p72 ff; also J Adams and R Brownsword, 'Contract, consideration and the critical path' (1990) 53 MLR 536.
19 *Regus (Maxim) Ltd v Bank of Scotland plc* [2013] CSIH 12, 2013 SC 331.
20 Age of Legal Capacity (Scotland) Act 1991.
21 See Chapter 1: Introduction to Juristic Persons.
22 See paras **1.35–1.36**.
23 1995 SC 151.

(Scotland) Act 1973 with the result that the contract it had entered into was void. If money or other assets have changed hands there is no remedy in contract law (because there is no contract in existence) but there may be in the law of unjustified enrichment.

Intention to create legal relations

2.11 A second pre-requisite for entering into a contract is that the parties must seriously intend the transaction to be a legally enforceable obligation, sometimes known as the doctrine of 'intention to create legal relations'. Here context is important and there is a distinction between agreements made in a social context and those in a commercial context.

Social and domestic agreements

2.12 There is a general presumption that obligations undertaken in a social or domestic context are not intended to create legal obligations, especially between family members. However, this is only a presumption and there are likely to be many exceptions, for instance separation agreements between couples or loans between family members. In *Robertson v Anderson*[24] an agreement between two friends to share their bingo winnings was held to be a legally enforceable obligation, illustrating that the Scottish courts will easily look beyond the presumptions to the facts and circumstances of an individual contract. Lord Reed explained that the presumptions do not amount to 'watertight compartments', rather 'it is . . . essential to look at the particular facts to discover whether those facts reveal an intention to conclude a contract'.[25]

Commercial agreements

2.13 Conversely, the presumption in a commercial context is that the parties intend their agreements to be legally binding. Again the presumption can be rebutted but the words used must be very clear that any agreement reached is not intended to have legal force. Phrases such as 'ex gratia' or 'subject to contract' would tend to suggest that the parties are still at the negotiating stage prior to reaching a final agreement and have been so held in England. In *Wick Harbour Trs v The Admiralty*[26] an agreement was held to be binding despite the use of the words 'ex gratia', Lord Sands taking the view that '[i]f he has agreed to a payment it does not matter what he calls it'.[27] However, there is no hard and fast rule and the Scottish courts will consider individual facts and circumstances in reaching a view about whether or not the parties intended their agreement to be binding.

2.14 Particularly problematic are cases where the parties have osten-

24 2003 SLT 235.
25 At para 13.
26 1921 2 SLT 109.
27 At 112.

sibly reached agreement but the final step of embodying that agreement in writing has not yet been taken. The question that arises is whether or not there is an enforceable contract without that final stage. There is no doubt that freedom of contract demands that the parties can stipulate when the contract comes into force and prior to that they retain the right to withdraw (*locus poenitentiae*), but the words used must be clear and unambiguous.[28] In *W S Karoulias SA v The Drambuie Liqueur Co Ltd*[29] the two companies had a long-standing business relationship and a number of previous contracts. When their agreement came to be renewed the negotiations between them were concluded in an email attaching the 'final draft' of the agreement with confirmation that two copies would be sent for signature if everything was in order (which Karoulias agreed it was). However, it transpired that Drambuie was in negotiations with another distributor and did not intend to sign the final contract. The court held that there was no binding agreement as both parties had intended to be bound only when the agreement was signed. Similarly in *Royal Bank of Scotland plc v Carlyle*[30] a telephone conversation in which a bank informed its customer that a loan of several million pounds had been approved was not held to be a legally enforceable agreement without being in writing, in part because their prior dealings had always been in writing and because the details of the obligations which the parties would be entering into were not specified.

Agreement on essential terms

2.15 The exercise of drafting a contract is an attempt to look into the future, to cover all eventualities and to provide for the possibility that things may go wrong. However, even if all the details are not settled, the parties must agree on the *essential* terms before a contract can come into existence and those vary depending on the type of contract:[31]

> As a matter of the general law of contract all the essentials have to be settled. What are the essentials may vary according to the particular contract under consideration.

2.16 In a contract of sale the subject matter and the price, or method of fixing a price, must be agreed. For a lease to be enforceable the essential terms are the parties, the rent, the subjects to let and the duration or *ish*. Agreeing on 'a reasonable and fair market rent' without stipulating how such a figure would be arrived at has been held to be too vague and an indication that there was no consensus on this essential term.[32]

2.17 However, there have been exceptions to this general rule and

---

28 Such a right was recognised in *H T Van Laun & Co v Neilson, Reid & Co* (1904) 6 F 644 and *Stobo Ltd v Morrisons (Gowns) Ltd* 1949 SC 184.
29 [2005] CSOH 112, 2005 SLT 813.
30 [2013] CSIH 75, 2014 SC 188.
31 *May & Butcher Ltd v The King* [1934] 2 KB 17 at 21 per Viscount Dunedin.
32 *Gray v University of Edinburgh* 1962 SC 157.

situations have arisen where essential elements of a contract have not been agreed at the start. In *R & J Dempster Ltd v Motherwell Bridge & Engineering Co Ltd*[33] the parties were contracting against the backdrop of a steel shortage in which businesses had to operate on a quota system. Such was the demand for the product that the industry was operating an 'open order' system whereby work was carried out on the basis that the price would be worked out later. The court concluded that price was a secondary issue to supply: 'in the market conditions operating when this contract was made, all the essentials were settled'.[34] As well as the unusual market conditions, it was relevant that the parties were already performing the contract as well as the fact that not agreeing a price was standard trade practice within the industry. In line with the principle of freedom of contract the courts are reluctant to hold commercial agreements invalid and will allow the parties considerable latitude.

2.18   Another important exception can be found in *Avintair Ltd v Ryder Airline Services Ltd*[35] where one party was already providing services to the other without having agreed a rate of commission. Despite the apparent lack of an essential term the court did not find the contract invalid.[36] The fact that performance had already taken place was highly significant in the court's decision to substitute the missing term and to imply that a reasonable sum should be paid for work done. Some commentators have been critical of the court's decision, arguing that a term should only be implied where it is clear the parties intended the matter to be settled at a later date, but not where it was the very issue on which they could not agree.[37]

Uncertainty of expression

2.19   Despite believing they have reached agreement, there may in fact be no contract between the parties if the words used are too vague or if there are contradictory terms which would undermine consensus. The contract may be 'void from uncertainty' if that is the case. For instance a description of a share in a partnership as being 'a substantial interest' was too vague to be enforceable;[38] likewise a description of property as 'the ground at present being quarried by our clients and the surroundings' with no identification of the boundaries.[39] The key is whether or not the contract can be enforced as it stands, in which case some uncertainty can simply be ignored. Alternatively, if the uncertainty arises from an error in drafting, the offending term can be rectified under section 8 of the Law Reform (Miscellaneous Provisions)(Scotland) Act 1985.

33 1964 SC 308.
34 At 329 per Lord President Clyde.
35 1994 SC 270.
36 See also more recently *RTS Flexible Systems Ltd v Molkerei Alois Müller GmbH & Co KG* [2010] UKSC 14.
37 MacQueen and Thomson, *Contract Law*, para 2.8.
38 *McArthur v Lawson* (1877) 4 R 1134.
39 *Grant v Peter G Gauld & Co* 1985 SC 251.

FORMATION OF CONTRACT

2.20 The idea of predicating the formation of a contract on the agreement of the parties derives from a will theory of contract, so-called
because the parties are deemed to have intended and chosen the obligations they enter into. However, there is a philosophical as well as a
legal difficulty with this theory in that it leads logically to an enquiry
into the state of mind of the parties at the time of contracting. This is, of
course, an entirely subjective matter and one which would be unworkable in practice. However, while maintaining agreement as the central
concept in the formation of a contract, the law will ascertain the existence and the terms of that agreement *objectively*. Instead of conducting
an investigation into the subjective intentions of the parties the question
for the court is not whether the parties actually consented but whether
they *appeared* to consent. This is assessed according to what they say and
what they do rather than what they think, according to the standards
of a reasonable person:[40]

> Commercial contracts cannot be arranged by what people think in their
> inmost minds. Commercial contracts are made according to what people
> say.

The offer and acceptance framework

2.21 The principal technique used by the courts to determine whether
or not agreement exists is the offer and acceptance framework. The conduct or words of the parties is analysed objectively as an offer or an
acceptance until the point of agreement is reached. A contract is formed
when the terms of the offer are met with an unqualified acceptance. For
instance, after a successful job interview you would normally receive a
formal letter offering employment on certain terms and conditions,
including the salary. You are invited to respond to that offer, sometimes
within a certain time, by accepting the job on the terms specified. A contract comes into existence at the moment the offer is accepted: 'an offer
accepted is a contract, because it is the deed of two, the offerer and the
accepter'.[41]

Limitations of the offer and acceptance analysis

2.22 It is perhaps worth noting that the offer and acceptance framework does not adapt well to every contractual situation and is not the
only way in which a contract can be formed. Where formation of contract and its performance are instantaneous, for instance over-the-counter sales, it is somewhat artificial to say that a newsagent 'offers' a
newspaper for sale and that I accept by handing over payment. Simi-

---

40 *Muirhead & Turnbull v Dickson* (1905) 7 F 686 at 694 per Lord President
    Dunedin.
41 Stair, *Institutions* I.10.3.

larly, at the other end of the spectrum, where there are long and complex negotiations with multiple drafts of documentation it can be difficult to ascertain which version is an offer and which an acceptance. Many, perhaps most, commercial contracts involve such a process and the parties are free to stipulate that the contract will come into existence only when negotiations are concluded and they have signed the final draft of their agreement.[42]

Coincidence of offer and acceptance

2.23   In order for there to be *consensus in idem* the terms of the offer and the terms of the acceptance must coincide. In *Mathieson Gee (Ayrshire) Ltd v Quigley*[43] Dr Quigley was a GP in Renfrewshire who wanted the mould removed from a pond on his property, so he contacted MG about the work. MG wrote offering 'to supply the necessary mechanical plant for the excavation and removal . . . of the mould' to which Dr Quigley replied 'confirming my verbal acceptance of your offer to remove the silt and deposit from the pond'. In retrospect it is clear that the parties were at cross purposes, one offering to supply machinery, the other believing he had a contract to carry out the work of removing the mould from his pond, and the House of Lords held that this was a case of *dissensus* and that no contract existed. However, the case was litigated through the Scottish courts without such a conclusion and with differing interpretations of what the contractual obligations of the parties were, thus demonstrating that applying the offer and acceptance analysis is not always straightforward.

The offer

2.24   One of the difficulties in contract formation is classifying whether a communication from one of the parties amounts to an offer.

Pre-contractual statements not amounting to an offer

2.25   Often people will, by their words or their actions, indicate that they are willing to do business but without intending to begin the process of contract formation. These types of pre-contractual statements or actions are sometimes referred to as 'invitations to treat' and must be distinguished from offers. Indeed, the response to an invitation to treat is usually an offer, thus beginning the contractual process. A key distinction is that a willingness to do business does not involve an intention to enter into a legal obligation: it merely invites offers. Case law suggests that making that distinction is not always straightforward, but as a general rule the following are considered invitations to treat:

---

42 See discussion in Scottish Law Commission, *Discussion Paper on Formation of Contract* (Scot Law Com DP 154, 2012) para 2.1ff (henceforth 'SLC DP 154').
43 1952 SC (HL) 38.

- Advertisements are generally regarded as 'trade puffs' whose purpose is to generate business, even if they use the wording 'special offer'.[44]
- Mail order catalogues are not offers even if they invite customers to place orders.[45] This also accords with business sense for if every order placed amounted to a concluded contract the supplier could easily find himself in breach of contract if stock was in short supply.
- Window and shop displays are equivalent to advertising and are not offers.[46] It may be that a similar analysis would apply to websites offering goods for sale although there is little authority to date.
- Inviting tenders to be submitted amounts to an invitation to treat, the response to which is to make an offer by submitting a bid.[47]

Characteristics of an offer

2.26 An offer is a proposal to enter into an agreement which invites acceptance. It is therefore implicit that if the party to whom the offer is made accepts, then a binding contract is formed. The terms of the offer must be sufficiently definite to create legal obligations and the offeror must intend to be legally bound. Offers (and acceptances) are usually in words, either written or spoken, but an offer can also be inferred from conduct, for instance when you take products from a supermarket shelf to the checkout.[48] For an offer to be effective it must be communicated to the offeree and, logically therefore, acceptance cannot take place or be inferred prior to the offer being communicated.

2.27 An offer is usually made to a specific offeree, particularly in a commercial context. However, it is possible for an offer to be open to the general public. In an exception to the general presumption that an advertisement does not constitute an offer, one placed in a newspaper advertising a reward of a specific sum of money to anyone who complied with its terms[49] was held to constitute an offer 'open to the world' which was sufficiently specific in its terms to show an intention to be legally bound upon acceptance. Likewise automatic ticket and vending machines have been held to amount to 'standing offers' open for acceptance by anyone.[50]

---

44 *Fenwick v Macdonald, Fraser & Co Ltd* (1904) 6 F 850; *Philp & Co v Knoblauch* 1907 SC 994.
45 *Grainger & Son v Gough* [1896] AC 325 at 334 per Lord Herschell.
46 *Fisher v Bell* [1961]1 QB 394.
47 *Harvela Investments Ltd v Royal Trust Co of Canada (CI) Ltd* [1986] AC 207.
48 *Pharmaceutical Society of Great Britain v Boots Cash Chemists (Southern) Ltd* [1953] 1 QB 401.
49 *Carlill v Carbolic Smoke Ball Co* [1893] 1 QB 256.
50 *Thornton v Shoe Lane Parking Ltd* [1971] 2 QB 163.

Revocation of offers

2.28 An offer can be withdrawn at any time prior to acceptance. The offeror can change his mind and has the right to withdraw the offer (*locus poenitentiae*) unless the offer contains within it a promise to keep it open for a specific period (a 'firm offer'). Withdrawal or revocation of an offer must be communicated before it is effective.[51] In exceptional circumstances the offeree may be deemed to have been notified that the offer has been withdrawn because communication is assessed objectively. In *Burnley v Alford*[52] the fact that the solicitor was on a shooting trip and not in his office to receive a telegram withdrawing an offer did not prevent the withdrawal being deemed to have been communicated. Communication depends on the operation of normal business hours and practices and had they been followed in this case the withdrawal would have been received. A modern equivalent may be a business which does not take care to check emails on a regular basis or fails to deal with an inbox that is full.

Lapse of offers

2.29 Where a time limit has been set in the offer it must be accepted within that time period or it lapses. The precise wording of the offer will determine whether or not the offer can be withdrawn before the time period ends. An offer stating that it will be open for acceptance for three days has been held to contain a promise to keep it open and it cannot be withdrawn;[53] however, an offer stating that it must be accepted within three days has a different semantic meaning and can be revoked during those three days.[54] If no time limit has been specified an offer will lapse within a reasonable time. What is considered reasonable may be influenced by factors such as trade practice; market fluctuations; the mode of communication adopted by the parties; and a material change of circumstances which renders the offer redundant.[55]

2.30 If an offer is rejected by the offeree it will lapse. Rejection is implied if the offeree makes a counter-offer in response to the offer.[56] Finally, the death or insanity of the offeror will bring the offer to an end, but his insolvency will have no effect.[57]

The acceptance

2.31 Once an offer is met with an unqualified acceptance indicating consent to its terms a contract is formed. Offers and acceptances are

---

51 *Thomson v James* (1855) 18 D 1.
52 1919 2 SLT 123.
53 *Littlejohn v Hadwen* (1882) 20 SLR 5.
54 *Heys v Kimball and Morton* (1890) 17 R 381.
55 See McBryde, *Contract*, paras 6-49–6-50.
56 See paras **2.32–2.33** below.
57 There is little authority on the effect of insolvency on the process of contract formation but see the discussion in SLC DP 154 (n 42) paras 3.39–3.42.

generally made verbally, either orally or in writing, and if the offer prescribes a certain mode of acceptance, for instance that it must be in writing, the acceptance must be in the prescribed form. The law is fairly relaxed on this question and if no mode of communication is mentioned then the acceptance can take any form although normally the acceptance will follow the form in which the offer is made. An offer can also be accepted by conduct if actions imply consent to the offer.[58] Where a landlord allowed his tenant to remain in possession of a farm after the lease had come to an end, continued to accept payment of rent and allowed the tenant to carry out improvements, the landlord's actions were deemed to amount to consent and the constitution of an agreement of lease.[59] Another example involves accepting payment by cashing the offeror's cheque.[60] However, silence does not amount to acceptance because there must be some positive indication by words or conduct of consent to the offer.

Qualified acceptances

2.32 If an acceptance attempts to alter material terms of the offer it amounts to a qualified acceptance, with two dramatic results:

  (a) it rejects the original offer which then lapses and is no longer open for acceptance; and
  (b) the qualified acceptance in itself becomes a counter-offer which is open for acceptance.

2.33 This analysis can lead to confusing results for the parties involved and highlights one of the limitations of the offer and acceptance framework. The parties may believe they are negotiating to the point of agreement, but imposing a legal analysis which categorises their communications as either offers or acceptances can lead to unintended results. For instance in *Wolf and Wolf v Forfar Potato Company*[61] an offer to supply potatoes was made by telex from one company (FPC) to the other (WW) and it included terms relating to delivery, carriage, inspection and payment. The responding telex from WW 'accepted' the offer but made alterations in relation to some of the terms (hence it was a counter-offer). A phone call then took place between the parties subsequent to which WW sent another telex accepting the original offer. However, the court held that the original offer had been struck down by the counter-offer and was no longer available for acceptance, contrary to the expectations of the parties. Where two cross-offers are made without knowledge of or reference to each other, both have been held to amount to offers open for acceptance.[62]

58 *Carlill v Carbolic Smoke Ball Co* [1893] 1 QB 256; *University of Edinburgh v Onifade* 2005 SLT (Sh Ct) 63.
59 *Morrison-Low v Paterson* 1985 SC (HL) 49 at 78 per Lord Keith of Kinkel.
60 See McBryde, *Contract*, para 6-83.
61 1984 SLT 100.
62 *Findlater v Maan* 1990 SC 150.

Standard form contracts and the 'battle of the forms'

2.34 The rule relating to counter-offers is particularly problematic in a commercial context where parties often use standard form contracts, i.e. pre-printed forms containing detailed terms of the contract which are standard for the business in question and are not individually negotiated. Indeed both parties to a commercial contract may have their own standard terms and conditions and the question in those circumstances is which set is to regulate the contract?

2.35 On a strict application of the counter-offer rule the party who sends their standard terms last will prevail. This is known as *the battle of the forms* and the rule boils down to the fact that whoever fires the last shot wins. For instance, Company A makes an offer subject to its standard terms. Company B accepts subject to Company B's standard terms, which would amount to a counter-offer and A's offer would lapse. If Company A then performs the contract, B's counter-offer is impliedly accepted and B's terms will prevail. This application of the offer and acceptance framework is problematic and can work against the fundamental principle of freedom of contract.

2.36 Lord Denning suggested in the late 1970s that a different approach might be adopted:[63]

> In many of these cases our traditional analysis of offer, counter-offer, rejection, acceptance and so forth is out of date. . . .. The better way is to look at all the documents passing between the parties – and glean from them, or from the conduct of the parties, whether they have reached agreement on all material points – even though there may be differences between the forms and conditions printed on the back of them.

This suggestion has not been adopted in the last thirty-five years, but the problem continues to attract the attention of law reformers and academics.[64] The Scottish Law Commission recommends an approach similar to that proposed in international instruments such as the Draft Common Frame of Reference:[65] the principal question is whether or not there is sufficient agreement and intention to establish the existence of a contract between the parties so long as they are agreed on the matters essential to that contract, for instance supply of goods or services and price. Where there are conflicting standard terms those in common will form part of the contract and those which conflict will not. Any gaps would then be filled by the general law of contract, with implied terms playing a particularly important role. These seem sensible suggestions, although they do transfer much of the work of establishing the terms of a contract onto the courts rather than the contracting parties.

63 *Butler Machine Tool Co Ltd v Ex-Cell-O Corporation (England) Ltd* [1979] 1 WLR 401 at 404.
64 SLC DP 154 (n 42) ch 5.
65 SLC DP 154 (n 42) para 5.20.

Communication of the acceptance

2.37   For an acceptance to be effective it has to be communicated to the offeror. The general rule, as for offers, is that an acceptance is valid once it has been brought to the attention of the offeror, hence the offeror must be aware of the acceptance. However, the *form* in which the acceptance is given is highly significant because there are different rules for acceptances depending on whether the mode of the acceptance is considered to be an instantaneous or a non-instantaneous communication.

The postal acceptance rule

2.38   An important exception to the general rule that offers and acceptances must actually be communicated to the other party is the postal acceptance rule which provides that where an acceptance is sent by post a contract is concluded at the point of sending rather than the point of receiving the letter. The rationale behind the rule is that the acceptor has done everything he could to accept and that he has no control over the postal service and any delays which may occur.[66]

2.39   This leads to difficulty when there is a competition between different forms of postal communication, depending on how they are classified. In the important case of *Thomson v James*[67] one of the negotiating parties posted an acceptance on 1 December and on the very same day the other party posted a withdrawal of the offer – both letters arrived on the same day. The court had to decide what the priority was between one party's wish to accept and the other's wish to withdraw from the contract. It was held that a contract had been concluded at the point of posting the acceptance, applying the postal acceptance rule, and that an offeree was entitled to assume that an offer was open until he heard otherwise.

2.40   The rule will apply even if there is a long delay in the letter arriving,[68] although it must ultimately reach its destination for a contract to be formed.[69] It should also be noted that although it is a default rule it is open to the parties to disapply it and to agree that all communications between them must be received before they are effective to conclude a contract.

Classification of modes of communication

2.41   Most communications between the parties are likely to be instantaneous, therefore they must be received and understood by the other

---

66   *Dunlop, Wilson & Co v Higgins & Son* (1848) 6 Bell 195.
67   (1885) 18 D 1.
68   *Jacobsen Sons & Co v Underwood & Son Ltd* (1894) 21 R 654.
69   *Mason v Benhar Coal Co Ltd* (1882) 9 R 883 at 890 per Lord Shand.

party. Hence telephone conversations and, by analogy, other communications like telex and fax which make use of telephone lines are considered instantaneous. There is a duty on the party communicating an offer, a withdrawal or an acceptance to take reasonable steps to ensure the other party has received and understood the communication. For instance in a conversation by mobile phone should signal be lost it would be reasonable for the other party to call back and check that communication had been properly understood.[70] There is little authority on modern forms of communication such as text message or email, but most commentators take the view that they would also be treated as instantaneous forms of communication even though they are not always so,[71] and given the problematic nature of the postal acceptance rule it seems unlikely that the courts will extend its reach to other forms of communication.

2.42 The rationale behind the postal acceptance rule is that the offeree has done all he can to accept by putting his acceptance in the hands of a trusted agent, the Post Office or now the Royal Mail, to deliver it to the offeror. By analogy it has been extended beyond communications that are posted to telegrams which are delivered into the hands of that same trusted agent. It may be that courier firms would fall into the same category.

Proposed reforms of the postal acceptance rule

2.43 The rule has been criticised as being artificial and contrary to the expectations of most contracting parties. Its original purpose was to protect an offeree against withdrawal of the offer, but arguably the balance has swung too far in favour of the acceptor and there is a need for the law to balance the interests of both parties to a contract. Under the current law if an acceptance is posted the acceptor has full knowledge of the risks whereas the offeror will usually be unaware that a contract has come into existence until the acceptance arrives. The acceptor could carry out certain activities in performance of the contract, but the offeror has no such advantage.

2.44 The Scottish Law Commission has recommended abolition of the postal acceptance rule since 1977 and continues to do so,[72] but recommends retaining it in one instance in order to provide more protection for the offeree. The proposal is that an offer should not be able to be withdrawn once an acceptance has been posted.[73] The result in *Thomson v James* would, therefore, be no different.

---

70 *Entores v Miles Far East Corporation* [1955] 2 QB 327.
71 MacQueen and Thomson, *Contract Law*, para 2.35; McBryde, *Contract*, para 6-118. For a contrary view see A D Murray 'Entering into contracts electronically: the real w.w.w' in L Edwards and C Waelde (eds), *Law and the Internet* (2nd edn, 2000).
72 SLC DP 154 (n 42) para 4.13.
73 At para 4.14.

Contracts and writing

2.45 It is a general principle that most contracts do not need to be in writing in order to be valid.[74] Commercial contracts are often detailed written documents, running to hundreds of pages, so that the terms of the agreement are clear and can subsequently be referred to in case of doubt. The written document also marks a clear transition between the negotiation stage and the contract proper and the parties can therefore rely on the terms of the written document rather than what was said in the negotiation process. However, this is a choice made by the parties or their lawyers and there is no legal requirement to do so.

The Requirements of Writing (Scotland) Act 1995

2.46 The rules on writing and formal validity of contracts are set out in the Requirements of Writing (Scotland) Act 1995 ('the 1995 Act') which begins by stating that general principle.[75] The main exception to the general rule is that writing is required for contracts relating to real rights in land.[76] This includes missives for the sale of heritable property, standard securities and leases of more than one year,[77] as well as other contracts which create, transfer, vary or extinguish any of the fixed list of real rights.[78] Such contracts must be 'subscribed', or signed at the bottom of the document, by each granter in order to be valid and they can be traditional paper documents, subscribed in pen and ink,[79] or electronic documents authenticated by an electronic signature.[80] The Scottish Law Commission has pointed out that in modern life many if not most traditional documents start out in electronic form but are later printed and signed in the usual way. It appears that the character of a document, whether traditional or electronic, will be determined at the point of execution according to the type of signature used.[81] Contracts relating to a real right in land do not, therefore, exist unless they are in the form prescribed in the 1995 Act and the parties are free to withdraw from negotiations.

2.47 However, in certain circumstances the parties are personally barred from denying that a contract exists even if it is not in writing when it ought to be. Four conditions must be satisfied:[82]

- There must be a *prima facie* contract, i.e. the parties must have

---

74 Certain specific contracts regulated by statute do require writing, for instance the Consumer Credit Act 1974 and the Employment Rights Act 1996: see MacQueen and Thomson, *Contract Law*, para 2.44.
75 1995 Act, s 1(1).
76 1995 Act, s 1(1)(2)(a)(i).
77 1995 Act, s 1(7).
78 See para **3.22**.
79 1995 Act, s 2(1).
80 1995 Act, s 9B(1).
81 SLC DP 154 (n 42) para 7.9.
82 1995 Act, s 1(3)–(4).

reached agreement on all the essentials and intend to be legally bound.

- One party ('the first person') must have acted in reliance on the putative contract.
- Those actions must be carried out by the first person with the *knowledge and acquiescence* of the other party ('the second person').
- The first person (who has acted in reliance) must be affected to a material extent by his actions, for instance by having incurred expenditure, and must also be adversely affected to a material extent if the second person were to withdraw from the agreement.

If all of these conditions are satisfied, the second person cannot withdraw from the obligation even although it has failed the test for formal validity. The contract will survive.

2.48   An example will illustrate the operation of these provisions. Alan and Bob orally agree that Alan will buy Bob's land as the site of his new development. Before the paperwork is complete Alan begins digging the foundations, keen to make a start. On his way to work Bob notices that Alan has brought in his mechanical digger and that work has begun but he does nothing to prevent it. A week later Bob receives a much higher offer for the land and has his solicitor draw up missives to sell it to Charles. Alan and Bob certainly have an agreement but it is not formally valid in terms of the 1995 Act. However, Alan has acted in reliance on it and Bob knows this but does nothing to stop the work. The only remaining condition is that Alan must be affected to a material extent by his actions, for instance if he hired the digger or paid workmen; and he must also be materially affected if the sale does not go ahead, for instance if he had taken out a fixed-term loan for the purchase and was committed to paying interest on it. A contract would exist despite it not being in writing.

Execution in counterpart and remote transactions

2.49   In a global economy commercial contracts are often entered into by multiple parties who may be spread across Scotland, the UK or the world. As mentioned previously, it is possible for contracts to come into existence other than by reference to offer and acceptance, particularly in a commercial context where it is common for the parties to agree that the contract will only come into existence once they have signed a final written document incorporating all of their negotiations. If their agreement is to be embodied in a single written document, or set of documents, until now this would mean a single 'signing ceremony' in which all of the parties are gathered together in one location at significant cost once travel and billing hours are taken into account for all concerned. At the time of writing a new Bill is before the Scottish Parliament to allow the parties to an agreement to sign and execute identical agreements (counterparts) remotely, in their own geographical location, and for those documents to be regarded as a single agreement between the parties.[83]

2.50 The Legal Writings (Counterparts and Delivery) (Scotland) Bill[84] was introduced into the Scottish Parliament in May 2014 and it provides a legal basis for parties to conclude a contract by signing their own counterpart of the agreement and then delivering it to the other party or parties. In terms of contract formation, it is only once each counterpart has been signed and delivered to the other parties that a contract is formed unless the parties have agreed an alternative. The Bill allows for a single nominee to take delivery of all counterparts to avoid the complexity of sending multiple copies to a range of parties. It also provides for digital signatures and electronic delivery of documents but envisages that in most cases the documents will be signed by hand in the traditional way, but will subsequently be transmitted to the other parties or to the nominee electronically as an email attachment or a fax. A further innovation is to allow only part of the counterpart to be delivered so long as that part is clearly part of the counterpart which has been signed. As a minimum the signature page must be delivered. The electronically scanned or faxed version of the counterpart does not have probative value and if the parties wish to register the contract in the Books of Council and Session the original signatures, duly witnessed, will need to be gathered together into a single document for registration.

Third party rights: *jus quaesitum tertio* ('JQT')

2.51 The parties to a contract may agree that a third party should be given rights or benefits under their contract. In Scots law this is referred to by the Latin phrase *jus quaesitum tertio*, the right of third parties. The most obvious example is a life assurance policy which is a contract between the insured and the insurance company but which will usually stipulate that in the event of the insured's death the proceeds of the policy go to a family member. That person (known as the 'tertius') will have a legally enforceable right in the contract although not a party to it.

For a valid JQT to exist the following conditions must be satisfied:

- There must be a contract in the first place – a JQT can only arise from a contract and not from another legal transaction such as a trust.
- There must be *intention* on the part of the contracting parties to benefit the tertius and this must be clearly expressed in order to be legally enforceable.[85]
- The third party must be clearly identified even if not specifically named or in existence.[86]

83 For greater detail see SLC DP 154 (n 42) part 3.
84 SP Bill 50, 2014.
85 *Finnie v Glasgow & South-Western Railway Co* (1857) 3 Macq 75.
86 *Morton's Trs v Aged Christian Friend Society of Scotland* (1899) 2 F 82.

- The right must be made irrevocable.

Irrevocability

2.52   It is an essential feature of a JQT as the law currently stands that it must be rendered irrevocable, i.e. it must be put beyond the power of the contracting parties to change their minds. This may be done by intimation or delivery to the tertius but it may be enough for the third party to know about the right.[87] In the leading case[88] a life assurance policy had not been delivered but the tertius knew it existed and this was enough to constitute a JQT. Lord Dunedin commented that irrevocability can be shown in various ways either expressly or by inference and much will depend on the circumstances of the individual case.

INVALID AND UNENFORCEABLE CONTRACTS

2.53   This section will consider situations in which contracts are either invalid or unenforceable and are, therefore, ineffective. The first part examines ways in which a contract can be nullified because there is deemed to be no consent or flawed (vitiated) consent and as a result the contract is essentially invalid. Three classic vitiating factors are examined: fraud, error, and force and fear. The second part examines situations in which a contract may become unenforceable, i.e. the contract remains valid but it cannot be enforced usually because of external events outwith the control of the parties or on grounds of public policy. These two categories clearly have different conceptual underpinnings but they are treated together since both have the effect of bringing performance of the contract to an end.

Void and voidable contracts

2.54   A void contract, sometimes referred to as being null or *null ab initio*, is one that has no legal effect and contractual remedies are thus not available to the parties. Usually a contract will be void because there is a flaw in the consent of one or both parties that is so severe that the law deems there to have been no contract from the outset. By contrast a voidable (or annullable) contract is one that has come into existence but is retrospectively set aside because a vitiating factor, such as misrepresentation, has later come to light with the result that consent turns out to have been flawed. A voidable contract exists up to the point when it is rescinded at which point the parties are obliged to restore each other to their original starting positions (*restitutio in integrum*) by undoing any effects of the contract, for instance by returning money or property that has already changed hands.

---

87 See MacQueen and Thomson, *Contract Law*, paras 2.76–2.78 for discussion of other ways in which a JQT might arise.
88 *Carmichael v Carmichael's Executrix* 1920 SC (HL) 195.

Implications for third parties

2.55   Usually it will be of little consequence to the contracting parties whether a contract is deemed to be void or voidable. However, it is a crucially important distinction where third parties are involved. The distinction is illustrated in the well-known cases of *Morrisson v Robertson*[89] and *MacLeod v Kerr.*[90] In both a plausible rogue pretending to be someone else tricked the owner of goods into selling them to him: in the first case, on the credit of the party for whom the rogue was pretending to act; in the second, by paying with a cheque from a stolen chequebook which was subsequently dishonoured. In both cases the rogue sold the goods on to a good faith third party (and in both the rogue was later convicted of the crime of theft). In both cases there was a competition for the goods between the original owner/seller and the third party who had bought in good faith. In *Morrisson* it was held that an essential error as to the identity of the buyer rendered the contract void, that the rogue had therefore never acquired title to the goods and so neither did the good faith third party. The owner regained his cows. In *MacLeod*, by contrast, the owner was held to be the victim of fraud, the contract was voidable and, therefore, the good faith third party was entitled to keep the car in question.

2.56   In such a scenario the law has to make a policy choice. There are two innocent parties: the seller and the innocent third party buyer who has no knowledge of the deception. Who should be protected? Normally the law favours the third party and this is indeed the rule where a contract is voidable, on condition that the third party has given value and is in good faith (i.e. has no actual or constructive knowledge of the flaw). However, if a contract is void the third party is not protected and cannot acquire rights under a void contract. This will be a relatively rare occurrence and only if the flaw in consent is so serious that no contract has come into existence in the first place. A contract can be void where there is *dissensus*, incapacity, force and fear and, in some cases, error. In all other cases it will be voidable.

Fraud

2.57   Historically fraud had a wide meaning in Scots law and could encompass a spectrum of behaviour ranging from deliberate deceit to simply taking advantage of someone in an unscrupulous way.[91] Under the influence of the important English case of *Derry v Peek*[92] the meaning of fraud narrowed so that in modern Scots law fraud amounts to inten-

---

89 1908 SC 332.
90 1965 SC 253. For comment see D Reid and H L MacQueen, 'Fraud or error: a thought experiment?' (2013) 17 Edin LR 343.
91 See D Reid, 'The doctrine of presumptive fraud in Scots law' (2013) 34 Journal of Legal History 307.
92 (1889) LR 14 App Cas 337.

tional or reckless deceit or 'a machination or contriv
Within this narrow definition it has been said that
fraud are never closed'[94] and any behaviour whi
designed to deceive will amount to fraud. Fraud wil
voidable and, as it also amounts to an intentional del
claimed. The principal manifestation of fraud in the 1
law of misrepresentation.[95]

Misrepresentation

2.58 A misrepresentation is any inaccurate statement of fact which would have resulted in any reasonable person refraining from entering into the contract had that statement not been made. Advertisements are not generally presumed to be statements of fact unless they claim to have a factual basis, for instance in scientific research; nor are statements of opinion or statements of future intent. Although misrepresentations generally are to be found in written or oral statements, they can also take the form of positive misleading conduct. Deliberately placing reproduction furniture which had been distressed to make it look old among genuine antiques amounted to a misrepresentation because of the seller's positive misleading conduct.[96] In a recent case involving a fake antique table (described as being 'designed to deceive') which was offered at auction the court held that in order for it to amount to a misrepresentation there must be intention to deceive, i.e. fraud.[97]

2.59 A misrepresentation cannot generally be constituted by silence unless there exists a duty of disclosure;[98] for instance where there is a fiduciary or quasi-fiduciary relationship between the parties, or in the special category of contracts which are considered of the utmost good faith (*uberrimae fidei*) such as insurance contracts or partnership agreements.

2.60 Four conditions must be satisfied for a misrepresentation to be operative:[99]

   (a) the misrepresentation must be made by the other contracting party – or their agent – and not a third party to the contract;

   (b) it must be made prior to formation of the contract, generally in the course of negotiations between the parties;

---

93 Erskine, *Institute* III.1.16.

94 McBryde, *Contract*, para 14-03.

95 It should be noted that many commentators regard misrepresentation as an aspect of the law of error, MacQueen and Thomson, *Contract Law*, para 4.27; for discussion see Reid and MacQueen (n 90).

96 *Patterson v H Landsberg & Son* (1905) 7 F 675.

97 *Lyon and Turnbull v Sabine* [2012] CSOH 178. See M Hogg, 'A Regency drama: misrepresentation by appearance, reduction and *restitutio in integrum*' (2013) 17 Edin LR 256.

98 *Broatch v Jenkins* (1866) 4 M 1030.

99 *Ritchie v Glass* 1936 SLT 591.

misrepresentation must cause the other party to be under a
material error; and

there must be a causal link between the error and the reason for
entering into the contract.

Consequences of a misrepresentation

2.61   An operative misrepresentation will render a contract voidable
and it can be rescinded if *restitutio in integrum* is possible. In *Boyd & Forrest
v Glasgow & South-Western Railway Co*[100] the contract could not be
annulled even although an innocent misrepresentation was established
because construction work had already been carried out: 'unless the
railway is obliterated, restitutio in integrum is impossible'.[101] Despite the
fact that the House of Lords has advocated a more flexible approach[102]
the Scottish courts continue to apply this condition strictly.

2.62   Misrepresentations can be made fraudulently, negligently or
'innocently' (i.e. without intention or negligence) and the distinction is
important in relation to remedies. A fraudulent misrepresentation
involves making an inaccurate statement intentionally or recklessly without regard to its truth. As well as rendering the contract voidable damages
can be claimed in delict, since fraud is an intentional delict. A misrepresentation may also be made negligently, most notably by professional or expert advisers whose opinions are likely to be relied on.[103]
For such negligence damages can be claimed in addition to any contractual remedy.[104] However, if a misrepresentation is made innocently, i.e.
where a person honestly believes in the statement they are making but
it is false nevertheless, the only remedy is contractual (rescission) and no
damages can be claimed.[105]

Error

2.63   'Error arises when there is a discrepancy between reality and a
party's belief.'[106]
   One of the most complex areas which contract law must deal with is
the situation when people make mistakes. If I have entered into a contract under some kind of error, how should the law deal with that error?
Subjectively, if I have made a mistake it would appear to be unfair to
insist on performance of the contract. On the other hand, setting aside
the contract on the grounds of my error may be equally unfair to the
other party, not to mention the difficulties of proof, and contracting

---

100 1915 SC (HL) 20.
101 At 36 per Lord Shaw.
102 *Spence v Crawford* 1939 SC (HL) 52 at 70 per Lord Thankerton.
103 This is an exception to the rule that statements of opinion do not constitute a
      misrepresentation: *Esso Petroleum Co Ltd v Mardon* [1976] QB 801.
104 Law Reform (Miscellaneous Provisions)(Scotland) Act 1985, s 10.
105 *Boyd & Forrest v Glasgow & SW Railway Co* 1915 SC (HL) 20.
106 McBryde, *Contract*, para 15-36.

parties need to be able to rely on obligations that have been entered into. Much of the confusion which can be found in decisions involving error comes back to the familiar tension between the subjective and the objective approach. The application of objective criteria to an essentially subjective problem is the heart of the error dilemma.

2.64 There are three basic types of error in contracts.[107] First, there may be an error in expression where the terms of a written contract do not match the agreement of the parties.[108] Such errors can be rectified.[109] Secondly, there may be an error in performance, for instance if money is paid in error or goods delivered to the wrong person. The remedy in these cases usually lies in unjustified enrichment if it was not caused by the fault of either party.[110] Thirdly, there may be an error in the consent of one or both parties, consensual error.

2.65 Scots law has always offered a remedy for a consensual error. The traditional approach was that for the contract to be reduced the error must be in 'the substantials' of the contract, sometimes referred to as essential error. Error in the substantials must fall within one of five pre-defined categories:[111] the subject of the contract, the identity of the debtor in the obligation, the price, the quality of the thing bargained for, or the nature of the contract. Such an error in theory prevents formation of a contract with the result that any putative contract will be void.[112]

2.66 Three types of consensual error are recognised: common error, mutual error and unilateral error. A common error occurs where the parties are mistaken as to the same thing,[113] for instance the extent of boundaries in the sale of property. A mutual error occurs where the parties are both mistaken but are at cross purposes.[114] Both types of error will prevent formation of a contract and can be considered examples of *dissensus*. Both will also be rare.

2.67 The most problematic case is where only one of the parties is labouring under an error, i.e. a unilateral error. A key question to ask is whether the error was induced or not by the other contracting party. If it was induced, this amounts to a misrepresentation and the contract will be voidable.[115]

---

107 McBryde, *Contract*, para 15-01.
108 *Anderson v Lambie* 1953 SC 94.
109 Law Reform (Miscellaneous Provisions)(Scotland) Act 1985, ss 8, 9.
110 *Morgan Guaranty Trust Co of New York v Lothian Regional* Council 1995 SC 151.
111 Bell, *Principles* § 11; *Stewart v Kennedy* (1890) 17 R (HL) 25.
112 *Morrisson v Robertson* 1908 SC 332.
113 *Hamilton v Western Bank of Scotland* (1861) 23 D 1033.
114 *Mathieson Gee (Ayrshire) v Quigley* 1952 SC (HL) 38.
115 See paras **2.58–2.62** above. There is some discussion to the effect that an induced error (i.e. a misrepresentation) which falls within one of the five categories of error in the substantials ought to lead to a void contract, as in fact was the case in *Morrisson v Robertson*. There is little authority on this issue, but see the English case of *Shogun Finance Ltd v Hudson* [2003] UKHL 62, [2004] 1 AC 919.

2.68 An uninduced error will not be sufficient to annul a contract.[116] However, if such an error is combined with an additional factor it may be operative:[117]

(a) if the contract is gratuitous;[118] or
(b) if the other party is aware of the error and takes advantage of that error.

The second suggestion has both older and more recent authority in Scots law and amounts to punishment of bad faith and sharp practice. In *Steuart's Trs v Hart*[119] a contract was reduced on grounds of an uninduced unilateral error because the seller knew about the purchaser's error and took advantage of it, Lord Deas holding that 'the purchaser is not fairly entitled to take advantage of such an error'.[120] More recently in *Angus v Bryden*[121] and *Parvaiz v Thresher Wines Acquisitions Ltd*[122] that principle has been affirmed.

Force and fear

2.69 Force and fear or extortion was one of the earliest grounds of challenge to a contract in Scots law. The terminology is misleading in that it suggests that to be a valid ground of challenge two elements are required, namely force and fear. It would be more accurate to call this ground of challenge force or fear since either may be sufficient depending on the circumstances, and most of the cases focus on fear:[123]

> although we couple together force and fear as one ground of reduction, the act of force is truly only one means of inducing fear, the true ground of reduction being extortion, through the influence of fear induced in [the] various ways.

2.70 In English law the equivalent terminology is duress. Force and fear will be a relevant ground of challenge where some form of coercion or pressure is applied to secure consent. The essence of the challenge is that a deed was granted or a contract entered into without consent because it was induced by fear and often threats. Force and fear is historically regarded as being such a serious matter that consent is excluded completely and any contract will be void.[124]

---

116 *Steel v Bradley Homes (Scotland) Ltd* 1972 SC 48; *Royal Bank of Scotland plc v Purvis* 1990 SLT 262; *Spook Erection (Northern) Ltd v Kaye* 1990 SLT 676.
117 This borrows from McBryde's 'error plus' analysis, i.e. a unilateral error requires an additional factor before it will be operative, see McBryde, *Contract*, para 15-23.
118 *Hunter v Bradford Property Trust Ltd* 1970 SLT 173.
119 (1875) 3 R 192.
120 At 200.
121 1992 SLT 884.
122 2009 SC 151.
123 *Priestnell v Hutcheson* (1857) 19 D 495 at 499 per Lord Deas.
124 Stair, *Institutions* I.9.8. For discussion see J E du Plessis, *Compulsion and Restitution* (2004) para 6.2.2.

2.71 The force or threat must be sufficient to annul consent; therefore futile or empty threats will not be sufficient. In addition, the threat itself must be illegitimate,[125] for instance threatening assault or harassment of a family member but not a threat to report illegal behaviour to the police, which would not be unlawful. In a commercial context English law has developed the concept of economic duress. However, legitimate commercial pressure, no matter how unpleasant it may be to undercut a competitor's prices or create other financial difficulties for him, will not be sufficient as the law currently stands in Scotland unless it is unlawful behaviour. Generally the law of contract will accept that in a capitalist system economic pressures are a legitimate part of the operation of the free market.

Unenforceable contracts

2.72 Contracts may become unenforceable because of events outwith the control of the contracting parties which they have not foreseen, or on grounds of public policy. It is important to note that, unlike contracts which are void or voidable, the contract is not nullified retrospectively. The contractual relationship between the parties still exists and transactions which have already taken place, such as payment, are not invalidated. However, if the contract cannot be enforced it simply stops and any future performance is suspended. Frustration of contract and illegality both render contracts unenforceable.

Frustration of contract

2.73 Frustration of contract arises where some external event 'supervenes' between the time when the contract is formed and the time when performance is due which renders performance illegal or impossible or radically different in nature from what the parties had contemplated when they entered into the contract. Frustration is a relatively rare occurrence and most commercial contracts will contain *force majeure* clauses which accept the risk that unforeseen events will happen but provide that the contract will continue nonetheless. They may even stipulate how the risk is to be allocated, in which case the parties have made their own agreement about the consequences and they have contracted out of the frustration regime.[126] Since frustration does not bring the contract to an end any relevant terms of the contract remain enforceable (e.g. an arbitration clause). It is only performance which is suspended. For a contract to be frustrated neither party must have caused the supervening event – the idea that neither of the parties is at fault is an important one.[127]

---

125 *Earl of Orkney v Vinfra* (1606) Mor 16481.
126 MacQueen and Thomson, *Contract Law*, para 4.86.
127 *Maritime National Fish Ltd v Ocean Trawlers Ltd* [1935] AC 524.

Supervening illegality

2.74 Supervening illegality arises where there has been a change in the law between the time a contract is formed and the time when performance is due. Many of the cases on frustration deal with the outbreak of war.[128] A modern equivalent could perhaps be found in the consequences facing companies that were trading with Iraq when sanctions were imposed. Often supervening illegality is caused by emergency legislation: for instance a wartime ban on importing pine wood rendered a contract for the supply of wood illegal;[129] and a Scottish company found itself trading with an enemy alien (an Austrian company) after the outbreak of the First World War, thus rendering any future supply of marine engines illegal.[130] Had there been a state of war between the UK and Austria when they entered into the contract the rules on illegal contracts would have applied from the start.[131]

Supervening impossibility

2.75 Supervening impossibility arises where performance of the contract has become impossible, not simply more difficult or more expensive, because of a supervening event. For instance, the subject matter of the contract may have been destroyed (*rei interitus*)[132] or it may be held *constructively* to have been destroyed if it has become impossible to use it for its original purpose, such as a property that became impossible for a tenant to live in because it had been requisitioned by the military.[133] The same principle would apply where the qualities of a person are essential to the contract (*delectus personae*), for instance a concert pianist or a particular artist with unique and irreplaceable skills. The change of circumstances must be outwith what the parties had contemplated when they entered into the contract. Some changes may make performance impossible, for instance a strike by workers, but a frustrating event must be outwith the normal range of risks that the parties impliedly undertook when they entered into the contract.

Supervening radical change of circumstances

2.76 A third category of events may frustrate a contract if they amount to a radical change of circumstances. In this case the supervening event does not render performance impossible or illegal but instead it destroys the basis of the agreement between the parties, i.e. performance would be radically different from what the parties had envisaged. It is not

---

128 See W W McBryde and I Scobbie,'The Iraq and Kuwait conflict: the impact on contracts' 1991 SLT (News) 39.
129 *James B Fraser & Co v Denny, Mott & Dickson* 1944 SC (HL) 35.
130 *Cantiere San Rocco SA v Clyde Shipbuilding and Engineering Co Ltd* 1923 SC (HL) 105.
131 See para **2.78** ff.
132 In *Taylor v Caldwell* (1863) 3 B & S 826, a building was destroyed by fire.
133 *Mackeson v Boyd* 1942 SC 56.

enough for performance to be more difficult or less profitable[134] but it must destroy the common assumptions of the parties at the point when they entered into the contract.

The consequences of frustration

2.77 Frustration renders a contract unenforceable (not void or voidable) with the result that future performance is suspended and the parties are free from their obligations after the supervening event has occurred. Frustration only has *future* effect, so that any contractual effects which have occurred before the supervening event took place will survive and are not struck down. If one of the parties has already incurred costs, for instance by having paid for a service that becomes impossible to render, in principle the losses lie where they fall and no damages are payable. Where the effects of frustration are inequitable the courts have been willing to grant a remedy in unjustified enrichment.[135] More recently the Supreme Court has acknowledged that there may be scope in future for an alternative approach based on 'equitable adjustment' of the contract where it has been frustrated.[136]

Illegal contracts

2.78 In all areas of private law court decisions are sometimes made not on the grounds of a specific rule of law but on the grounds of public policy and this is clearly illustrated in the area of illegal contracts, sometimes referred to as *pacta illicita*.[137] As in the case of frustrated contracts, if a contract is set aside on grounds of illegality it is neither void nor voidable, but it becomes unenforceable and any future performance simply stops.

2.79 Some contracts are illegal from the outset because they are in explicit contravention of either a rule of common law or a statutory provision, for instance entering into a contract with someone to commit a theft or an act of deception. Others may be impliedly illegal in that they do not directly contravene a rule of law but the illegality is to be found in the way in which the contract is performed. For instance, in *Jamieson v Watts Tr*[138] under wartime regulations it was necessary to obtain a licence to carry out construction work. Mr Jamieson, a joiner, did have

---

134 *Tsakiroglou & Co Ltd v Noblee Thurl GmbH* [1962] AC 93 where the cost of shipping increased because of the closure of the Suez Canal but although the contract was less profitable it was not held to be frustrated; see also *Davis Contractors Ltd v Fareham Urban District Council* [1956] AC 696.
135 *Cantiere San Rocco SA v Clyde Shipbuilding and Engineering Co Ltd* 1923 SC (HL) 105.
136 *Lloyds TSB Foundation for Scotland v Lloyds Banking Group plc* [2013] UKSC 3 at para [46] per Lord Hope; for further comment on equitable adjustment following the Outer House decision in *Lloyds* see L Macgregor, 'Long-term contracts, the rules of interpretation and "equitable adjustment"' (2012) 16 Edin LR 104.
137 Only a brief overview of principles is set out below. For a more extensive treatment of this complex area see McBryde, *Contract*, ch 19. Immoral contracts would also come into this category but are not dealt with in this chapter.
138 1950 SC 265.

the necessary licence to carry out work up to the value of £40 but he exceeded the permitted value. His contract with his customer was not in itself illegal but the way in which he had performed it was and as a result the court would not 'lend its aid in any way to one who has to found on what he has illegally done or on his own turpitude'.[139]

Illegality and fault

2.80 As a general principle illegal contracts are not enforceable. However, the consequences vary depending on the degree the parties are to blame for the illegality either through their behaviour or their state of knowledge. Where the parties are equally to blame (*in pari delicto*), i.e. where both parties intend to commit or have knowledge of an illegal act, the courts will refuse to implement the contract or to allow damages for its breach. Any losses will lie where they fall.[140] On the other hand where the parties are not equally blameworthy, in principle an innocent party can sue under the contract to recover losses. In *Dowling & Rutter v Abacus Frozen Foods Ltd*[141] illegal workers were supplied by Dowling to work in Abacus' fish processing factory. However, since the company had no knowledge that the workers were illegal the court considered it would be inequitable to deny them payment under their contract with Abacus. Even where the parties are *in pari delicto* a remedy in unjustified enrichment may be allowed if there is 'no moral turpitude' and the court considers it equitable to do so.[142]

Illegality and restraint of trade

2.81 A restrictive covenant or a covenant in restraint of trade is perhaps the most common type of illegal contract and an early example of the operation of competition law. Any contract, or clause within it, which unreasonably restricts a person's freedom to trade is potentially illegal and therefore unenforceable. Attempts by employers to restrict the future employability of employees will be carefully scrutinised. Commonly employees may be asked to agree not to reveal the employer's trade secrets or not to work for a competitor. As a general rule if a contract or term of a contract restricts a person's economic freedom to an unjustified extent, in light of what is reasonable in a market economy, that term will be illegal and unenforceable.

2.82 In deciding if the contract or clause is reasonable there are some general principles that provide guidance:

- It must be reasonable between the parties at the time the contract is formed and in the public interest.[143]

---

139 At 279 per Lord Jamieson.
140 *Cuthbertson v Lowes* (1870) 8 M 1073.
141 2002 SLT 491.
142 MacQueen and Thomson, *Contract Law*, para 7.20.
143 *Nordenfelt v Maxim Nordenfelt Guns and Ammunition Co Ltd* [1894] AC 535.

- It must be necessary to protect a legitimate interest and the question to be asked is whether a lesser restriction would reasonably have protected that interest. Factors such as the duration of the restriction, its geographical extent, the range of people it applies to, the nature of the business and the status of the employee within that business are relevant.

2.83 If a restraint of trade clause is shown to be unreasonable it will be unenforceable. However, where possible, unreasonable elements may be severed from reasonable ones or from the rest of the contract (the 'blue pencil' rule).[144]

CONTRACT TERMS: THE CONTENT OF A CONTRACT

2.84 Previously we have considered how contracts are created and ways in which they may turn out to be flawed resulting in annulment or non-performance of the obligations undertaken by the parties. This section considers the content of the contract and what the parties have agreed to, i.e. the terms of the contract which will determine the respective rights and duties of the contracting parties. First, we will consider the *express terms* of the contract, namely those which have been expressly agreed by the parties. Questions may arise as to the precise scope of those terms, the relationship between the terms of the agreement and the prior negotiations of the parties and whether additional terms may have been incorporated into the agreement (incorporation of terms). Secondly, no matter how careful the drafting, inevitably contracts cannot cover every eventuality and where there are gaps in the express terms the courts may be required to *imply terms*. Many contracts consist of a mixture of express terms, including terms incorporated by reference, and implied terms. This section will also examine briefly the approach of the Scottish courts to interpreting contracts where there is ambiguity as to their meaning. Finally, more detailed consideration is given to good faith and best endeavours clauses, suspensive and resolutive conditions and exclusion clauses.

Express terms of the contract

2.85 The terms of a contract can derive from a number of different sources and, since contracts generally do not need to be in writing, some terms of the contract may have been orally agreed. For instance, if I bargain with a salesman about the price of a new car and we reach agreement on a suitable price that will be an express oral term of our contract which will normally be incorporated into a written document for signature. Even when the contract is in writing the express terms may be found in several different documents. For instance, when negotiating a property sale, offers and counter-offers are likely to go back and

---

144 *Hinton & Higgs (UK) Ltd v Murphy* 1988 SC 353.

forth between the parties as they negotiate about the terms and conditions of the sale. The express terms will be in writing between the parties but may be found in several different documents. There are three principal sources where the express terms of a contract may be found: in a written document, in the negotiations between the parties or in an external written source.

Terminology

2.86   It is worth noting that Scots law generally refers to the provisions of a contract as *contract terms* without distinction. This can be contrasted with English law which classifies terms as *conditions* (material terms which go to the root of the contract) and *warranties* (less fundamental terms), a distinction which is important when identifying remedies for breach of contract. In Scots law conditions and warranties are particular types of contract term, as discussed below.[145]

Express terms in a written document

2.87   If there is a written agreement that will be the starting point for determining the rights and obligations of the parties, but it may not be the end point. The safest way to be sure of the content of an agreement is to reduce the terms to writing and the presumption will be that the express terms of the contract are to be found only in the written document or documents:[146]

> Where a document appears (or two or more documents appear) to comprise all the express terms of a contract or unilateral voluntary obligation, it shall be presumed, unless the contrary is proved, that the document does (or the documents do) comprise all the express terms of the contract or unilateral voluntary obligation.

This presumption can be rebutted if it can be proved that the parties agreed additional terms not found in the written agreement, for instance if they had come to an agreement orally on specific details.[147]

2.88   If, however, the contract contains an 'entire agreement' or 'entire contract' clause no evidence can be led of other express terms.[148] However, this does not generally prevent the introduction of implied terms, which are treated as an intrinsic part of the agreement.[149] An entire agreement clause is designed to prevent the other party from relying on any-

---

145   For warranties see paras **2.90**–**2.91**; for conditions see paras **2.109**–**2.112**.
146   Contract (Scotland) Act 1997, s 1(1); see also *Macdonald Estates plc v Regensis (2005) Dunfermline Ltd* [2007] CSOH 123, 2007 SLT 791 at para [126] per Lord Reed.
147   Contract (Scotland) Act 1997, s 1(2).
148   Contract (Scotland) Act 1997, s 1(3).
149   *MacDonald Estates plc v Regenesis (2005) Dunfermline Ltd* at para [131] per Lord Reed. A recent English decision leaves open the possibility that a contract could include 'an express specific exclusion of such implied terms', see *Axa Sun Life Services plc v Campbell Martin Ltd* [2011] EWCA Civ 133 at para 41.

thing outwith the written document, for instance prior statements made, the conduct of the parties or any other communication between them. However, such a clause cannot exclude liability for fraud[150] nor is it thought that it would be effective to exclude liability for pre-contractual misrepresentations.[151] An entire agreement clause which operates in effect as an exclusion clause must be reasonable in terms of the Unfair Contact Terms Act 1977.[152]

Negotiations and express contract terms

2.89 When discussing formation of contract the general rule is that there is no agreement between the parties until an offer has been met with an unqualified acceptance. In principle, while the parties are at the stage of negotiating their agreement they are entitled to withdraw and are not generally under any legal obligation to enter into the contract (although there may be a moral one if they have incurred costs and spent time in the negotiating process). However, the negotiations are not completely irrelevant to establishing contract terms. Indeed, as previously discussed, in a commercial context there may be many meetings, telephone calls, emails and letters which pass between the parties discussing particular contractual issues before anything is put in writing and some of the details of those communications may not make it into the final written agreement. The question may then arise as to which of the issues discussed in negotiations can be regarded as terms of the contract. Some statements made in the course of negotiations have no legal effect; others may amount to representations; some will amount to terms of the contract (sometimes called warranties).

2.90 Statements which only amount to an invitation to treat, advertising puffs or techniques used by salesmen, bargaining positions adopted by the parties and expressions of opinion or future intention – none of the above are deemed to have legal effect unless it is proved they were intended to be part of the contract. Statements made which may have induced or influenced the other party to enter into the contract are known as representations. These may have legal effect in a negative sense in that there may be a right of action if they amount to an inaccurate statement of fact, i.e. the law of misrepresentation. If so the contract may be reduced if *restitutio in integrum* is possible and there will be a remedy in damages if the representation has been made fraudulently or

---

150 *Boyd & Forrest v Glasgow & South-Western Railway Co* (1915) SC (HL) 20 at 35 per Lord Shaw.

151 *Inntrepreneur Pub Co (GL) v East Crown Ltd* [2000] 2 Lloyd's Rep 611; *Axa Sun Life Services plc v Campbell Martin Ltd* makes the distinction between what the parties have agreed and 'representations' which induced one party to enter into the agreement and which are, logically, outwith the scope of an entire agreement clause (at para 81 per Rix LJ). See also I MacNeil, 'Excluding liability for misrepresentation' (1998) 3 Scottish Law and Practice Quarterly 226.

152 *Thomas Witter Ltd v TBP Industries* [1996] 2 All ER 573; see paras **2.116–2.123** below.

negligently. Statements of fact made in negotiations which become part of the contract are express terms or warranties. If a warranty is false the remedy will lie in breach of contract.[153]

2.91 There is considerable difficulty in distinguishing between representations and warranties with little judicial guidance in Scotland other than a general principle of looking objectively at the absence or presence of contractual intention. The timing of the statement will be relevant and the nearer it is to the point of formation of the contract the more likely it is to be a warranty.[154]

Terms outwith the negotiations

2.92 Another possible source of express terms are those which have not been discussed by the parties at all in negotiations. Parties may attempt to introduce new terms at the point of formation of the contract, for instance standard pre-printed forms containing details of the contract which have not previously been discussed in any detail. This is referred to as incorporation of terms and can take place in three ways: by signature; by reference; or by a prior course of dealing between the parties.

Incorporation by signature

2.93 Contracts do not need to be in writing, nor do they need to be signed in order to be valid. However, if the parties have put their signature to a document they are bound by its terms and the express written terms are deemed to have been incorporated by the signature of the parties. A signature is taken to be 'conclusive'[155] and to indicate agreement regardless of whether the parties have taken the time to read the document carefully (unless the signature has been obtained by fraud or duress).

Incorporation by reference

2.94 There are occasions on which a contract may refer to a separate external document which contains additional terms in an attempt to incorporate those terms by reference. Many of these cases concern tickets in various forms. For instance, the purchaser of a train ticket in Scotland will find on the reverse of the ticket that it is 'issued subject to National Rail Conditions of Carriage' which are available either on the National Rail website or 'available from staffed stations'. Few of us are likely to make any effort to find those conditions, far less read them, and yet our contract of carriage with the rail company is subject to those terms. A Glasgow Underground ticket is similarly 'subject to published con-

---

153 For discussion see MacQueen and Thomson, *Contract Law*, paras 3.14-3.19.
154 *Malcolm v Cross* (1898) 25 R 1089.
155 *McCutcheon v David MacBrayne Ltd* 1964 SC (HL) 28 at 40 per Lord Devlin.

ditions' without any indication of where said conditions may be found. The question is whether or not such terms have been effectively incorporated and the courts apply a three-stage test to determine whether or not they have become express terms of the contract.

(a) *Is the document itself contractual in nature?* Tickets are generally deemed to have contractual effect, particularly travel tickets and tickets of deposit, but in some situations they merely function as a receipt showing that the customer has paid.[156] The function of the document will be relevant; hence invoices, receipts and delivery notes do not generally have contractual effect.

(b) *Are the terms and conditions known to the parties prior to formation of the contract?* Consistent with the principle that consent is required, the terms of the contract must be known to the parties prior to formation of the contract. Notices or documents containing contract terms must therefore be displayed in such a way that they can be read and understood when the contract is entered into. For instance, a notice in a car park excluding liability for any damage caused must be displayed prior to taking a ticket from the machine and entering the car park.[157] Similarly, online transactions usually require an act of consent to indicate acceptance of the seller's terms and conditions prior to payment.

(c) *Has sufficient notice been given?* Where contract terms are particularly unusual or onerous, they must be drawn to the other party's attention:[158]

> The question really is whether a particular condition is of such an unusual nature that it should specifically be drawn to the attention of the other party rather than being left simply as part of a large collection of other terms and conditions which are of a fairly standard nature

Clauses excluding liability or imposing a personal cautionary obligation are sufficiently onerous to warrant attention being drawn to them in a specific way.[159] If, for example, a notice excluding liability for loss or damage in a nightclub cloakroom is not displayed prominently and drawn to a customer's attention questions may arise as to the validity of such an exclusion clause.[160]

Incorporation by a prior course of dealings

2.95 One final means of incorporation is where the parties have had a prior course of dealings. This may be true even if the term was not specifically brought to the other party's attention prior to formation of the

---

156 *Taylor v Glasgow Corporation* 1952 SC 400.
157 *Thornton v Shoe Lane Parking Ltd* [1971] 2 QB 163.
158 *Montgomery Litho Ltd v Maxwell* 2000 SC 56 at 59 per Lord Sutherland.
159 *Hood* v *Anchor Line (Henderson Bros) Ltd* 1918 SC (HL) 143.
160 Exclusion clauses are also regulated by the Unfair Contract Terms Act 1977, see para **2.116** ff.

contract. In order for a term to be successfully incorporated there must be a regular and consistent course of dealings between the parties which is sufficient to demonstrate that they knew about and consented to the term or terms in question.[161] Contract terms which are known to operate within a particular commercial sector may also be relevant.[162]

Implied terms

2.96 Implied terms may be needed where there are gaps in the agreement between the parties and issues arise which the express terms of the contract do not provide for. In certain circumstances the courts can find that terms have been implied into the contract. This may be regarded as controversial and an unwarranted intrusion upon the freedom of the parties because, it could be argued, the courts are writing terms for the parties and are taking control of the contractual process. In the commercial world parties do not want to rely on implied terms since they can introduce uncertainty and the aim is for the express terms of the contract to cover as much as possible.

2.97 There are two broad categories of implied terms: terms implied in law, which apply to all contracts of a particular type, and terms implied in fact which apply to the particular facts of the individual case before the courts and which are needed to fill any gaps left by the express terms. In both cases the common intention of the parties is a priority: terms implied in law are included *unless* the intention of the parties is otherwise indicated in the contract; terms implied in fact will only be implied if the intention of the parties can be deduced from the facts and circumstances.

Terms implied in law

2.98 Terms can be implied into certain nominate contracts by statute. The most common example is the Sale of Goods Act 1979 which contains a number of implied terms, for instance that goods sold are to be of satisfactory quality.[163] Terms can also be implied by the common law, for instance in contracts of hire, loan, insurance or employment. Historically terms could also be implied from custom and trade practice within a particular commercial sector,[164] but this will be relatively rare in modern times.

Terms implied in fact

2.99 Terms will only be implied in fact if the court deems it would have been the intention of the parties to agree to those terms had they

---

161 *McCutcheon v MacBrayne* 1964 SC (HL) 28.
162 *United Central Bakeries Ltd v Spooner Industries Ltd* [2013] CSOH 150.
163 Sale of Goods Act 1979, s 14(2) and see Chapter 6: Sale of Goods.
164 *William Morton & Co v Muir Bros & Co* 1907 SC 1211.

considered it. Any implied term must, therefore, be *reasonable* for both parties in the circumstances:[165]

> If the condition is such that any reasonable man on the one part would desire for his own protection to stipulate for the condition, and that no reasonable man on the other part would refuse to accede to it then it is not unnatural that the condition should be taken for granted . . . without the necessity of giving it formal expression.

This suggests an approach which attempts to discern what two reasonable contracting parties would have agreed to had they considered the issue and any implied term should not, therefore, be heavily weighted in favour of one party.[166]

2.100 The implied term must also be *necessary* to give effect to the contract. This is sometimes referred to as a test of what business efficacy requires,[167] the underlying idea being that the contract would not work as the parties had intended it to without implication of the term:[168]

> [W]hat the law desires to effect by the implication of terms is to give such efficacy to the transaction as must have been intended at all events by both parties who are business men; not to impose on one side all the perils of the transaction, or to emancipate one side from all chances of failure.

The courts will not go further than is necessary for the working of the contract.

Interpretation of contracts

2.101 Interpretation of contracts is a complex topic and only a brief overview of the general principles is possible in this chapter. The Scottish Law Commission has recently reviewed this area and extensive detail can be found in its Discussion Paper on Interpretation of Contract.[169]

2.102 As well as being able to imply terms where reasonable and necessary, another method of judicial control of contracts is through interpretation of the express terms of the contract where the parties are in disagreement. Law is a linguistic discipline and words are inherently uncertain and ambiguous and their meaning can change depending on the context. The aim of interpretation is once again to give effect to the common intention of the parties and the judicial approach is objective. The starting point is the written word, what the parties have expressed in the contract itself, not what they did or said in the context of negotiation or after the bargain was concluded.

---

165 *William Morton v Muir Bros* at 1224 per Lord McLaren.
166 *J & H Ritchie Ltd v Lloyd Ltd* 2007 SC (HL) 89.
167 *Ritchie v Lloyd* at para 37 per Lord Rodger.
168 *The Moorcock* (1889) 14 PD 64 per Bowen LJ.
169 Scottish Law Commission, *Discussion Paper on Interpretation of Contract* (Scot Law Com DP 157, 2012), henceforth 'SLC DP 157'.

The English approach

2.103 English law altered its course after the landmark decision in *Investors Compensation Scheme v West Bromwich Building Society*[170] in which Lord Hoffmann adopted a purposive approach to interpretation. This involves having regard to the context in which words are used, including surrounding circumstances and the 'factual matrix' of the contract – i.e. anything which would have affected the way in which words would have been understood by a reasonable person in possession of all the relevant background knowledge at the time of contracting. However, English law has not gone so far as to include prior negotiations between the parties.[171]

The Scottish approach

2.104 Lord Hoffmann's approach has certainly been acknowledged by the Scottish courts, but not enthusiastically embraced thus far, perhaps displaying greater reluctance to interfere with the freedom of the contracting parties.[172] The current position of Scots law can be summarised by the following seven principles borrowed from the Scottish Law Commission's analysis of recent Scottish case law:[173]

1. The words used by the parties must generally be given their ordinary meaning.
2. A contractual provision must be construed in the context of the contractual document or documents as a whole.
3. Where a contract has been professionally drafted the words may be expected to have been chosen with care and to be intended to convey the meaning which the words chosen would convey to a reasonable person.
4. The process of construction is objective, according to the standards of a reasonable third party aware of the commercial context.
5. Regard is to be had to the circumstances in which the contract came to be concluded to discover the facts to which the contract refers and its commercial purposes objectively considered, although this is

---

170 [1998] 1 All ER 98.
171 *Chartbrook Ltd v Persimmon Homes Ltd* [2009] 1 AC 1101.
172 See most notably *Bank of Scotland v Dunedin Property Investment Co Ltd* 1998 SC 657; also *Multi-Link Leisure Developments Ltd v North Lanarkshire Council* [2009] CSIH 96, 2010 SC 302.
173 SLC DP 157 (n 169), para 5.13. These principles have been distilled from analysis of the following recent Scottish cases: *City Wall Properties (Scotland) Ltd v Pearl Assurance plc* [2003] CSOH 21, 2004 SC 214; *Middlebank Ltd v University of* Dundee [2006] CSOH 202; *Macdonald Estates plc v Regenesis (2005) Dunfermline Ltd* [2007] CSOH 123, 2007 SLT 791; *Autolink Concessionaires (M6) plc v Amey Construction Ltd* [2009] CSIH 14; *MRS Distribution Ltd v DS Smith (UK) Ltd* 2004 SLT 631; *Emcor Drake & Scull Ltd v Edinburgh Royal Joint Venture* [2005] CSOH 139, 2005 SLT 1233; *Forbo-Nairn Ltd v Murrayfield Properties Ltd* [2009] CSIH 94; *Credential Bath Street Ltd v Venture Investment Placement Ltd* [2007] CSOH 208.

limited to matters known or reasonably expected to be known by both parties.

6. Where more than one construction is possible, the commercially sensible construction is taken to be what the parties intended.

7. The court must not substitute a different bargain from that made by the parties.

2.105 These principles of interpretation demonstrate that the Scottish courts could be said to adopt a modified purposive approach, 'seeking to give effect to the actual words used in the light of the circumstances surrounding the parties at the time they entered their contract',[174] but careful to preserve the intention of the parties and reluctant to rewrite their contracts. How this approach will be applied in future cases is not yet entirely clear. The recent decision of the Supreme Court in *Lloyds TSB Foundation for Scotland v Lloyds Banking Group plc*[175] is in line with the modified Scottish approach outlined above,[176] if the surrounding circumstances are taken to include the state of knowledge of the parties at the time of formation of the contract. However, the application of that same approach led the Inner House and the Supreme Court to reach opposite conclusions based on what they thought it reasonable for the parties to have known at the time.[177] It remains the case, both in Scotland and in England, that pre-contractual negotiations are not generally permitted as an interpretative tool in relation to the intentions of the parties (sometimes referred to as the 'exclusionary rule'),[178] but they may be used in a limited way to shed light on the surrounding background circumstances.[179]

Particular contract terms

2.106 Three particular types of contract terms are considered in more detail below, namely good faith and best endeavours clauses, suspensive and resolutive conditions, and exclusion clauses.

Good faith and best endeavours clauses

2.107 Since the decision in *Smith v Bank of Scotland*[180] lawyers in Scotland have become increasingly familiar with the idea of good faith and

---

174 SLC DP 157 (n 169), para 5.1.
175 [2013] UKSC 3.
176 I.e. that the 'words must be read in the light of what a reasonable person would have taken them to mean, having regard to what was known in 1997 [the time of formation of the contract]' at para 46 per Lord Hope.
177 Compare the Supreme Court decision, [2013] UKSC 3 at para 34 per Lord Hope, with that of the Inner House, [2011] CSIH 87, 2012 SC 259 at para 12 per Lord President Hamilton.
178 *Bank of Scotland v Dunedin Property Investment Co Ltd* 1998 SC 657; *Luminar Lava Ignite Ltd v Mama Group plc and Mean Fiddler Holdings Ltd* [2010] CSIH 01, 2010 SC 310; *Chartbrook Ltd v Persimmon Homes Ltd* [2009] UKHL 38.
179 SLC DP 157 (n 169), paras 5.17–5.20.
180 1997 SC (HL) 111 at 121.

its role in domestic legislation[181] as well as in international instruments.[182] And in a commercial contract it is not uncommon for the parties to agree to act in good faith or equivalent terms. This goes back to the fact that they are often in a long-term business relationship and in practice, as well as in law, commercial parties want to act towards each other in a way that is fair and transparent in order to preserve that relationship.

2.108   A number of recent cases have considered the content and effect of clauses which require the parties to use 'all reasonable endeavours' or 'best endeavours', which the courts consider closely analogous to a good faith principle. It is instructive to consider how the Scottish courts have interpreted the content of such an obligation. In *Mactaggart & Mickel Homes Ltd v Hunter*[183] the contract provided that one of the parties should 'use reasonable endeavours' to obtain planning permission for a development. Lord Hodge suggested that there was a hierarchy in the standard of behaviour expected: the obligations imposed by a requirement to use 'reasonable endeavours' is less onerous than those requiring 'all reasonable endeavours' (which raises the question whether there were any reasonable steps that could have been taken but were not), which in turn is less onerous than the even higher standard of 'best endeavours', which 'requires a party to take all the reasonable courses he can.'[184] However, such obligations do not mean that a party must act completely altruistically or disregard its own commercial interests in the process.[185] Further guidance is given by Lord Glennie who had to consider a clause to 'use all reasonable endeavours', linked to an obligation to act in good faith. In his view the distinction between using 'all reasonable' and 'best' endeavours was 'likely to be metaphysical rather than practical',[186] but it would involve being 'prudent'. This suggests that the party under such an obligation must consider his own financial and commercial interests; is not required to continue making such endeavours when it becomes clear they are unlikely to be successful; and if difficulties are encountered he should inform the other party.[187] A contractual obligation to act in good faith involves observing 'reasonable commercial standards of fair dealing'.[188] The Inner House has confirmed this

---

181 Most of which emanates from European Union Directives, for instance Unfair Terms in Consumer Contracts Regulations 1999 (SI 1999/2083); Commercial Agents (Council Directive) Regulations 1993 (SI 1993/3053); and Consumer Protection from Unfair Trading Regulations 2008 (SI 2008/1277).

182 Draft Common Frame of Reference III.–1:103; Convention on the International Sale of Goods, art 7.

183 [2010] CSOH 130.

184 At para 63, quoting with approval *Rhodia International Holdings Ltd v Huntsman International LLC* [2007] EWHC 292 (Comm), 2 Lloyd's Rep 325 at para 33.

185 *Mactaggart v Hunter* at para 63.

186 *EDI Central Ltd v National Car Parks Ltd* [2010] CSOH 141 at para 20.

187 At paras 20–21.

188 At para 23, adopting the words of Morgan J in *Berkeley Community Villages Ltd v Pullen* [2007] 3 EGLR 101 at para 97.

approach and, in addition, has stated that it would be a defence to an action for breach of contract to show that taking particular steps would not have been successful in achieving the desired result.[189]

Suspensive and resolutive conditions

2.109 Obligations may be contingent – i.e. they are conditional on some future event happening or not happening. It is possible for a condition to delay the contract coming into existence, for instance a stipulation that the parties' agreement must be embodied in a written document and signed by both.[190] This should be distinguished from the situation where the contract exists but *performance* of the parties' obligations is conditional on some other event. In Scots law there are two principal types of condition: suspensive and resolutive, the former suspends performance of an obligation, the latter resolves (or dissolves) it.[191]

2.110 A suspensive condition (sometimes called a condition precedent) is the most common type of condition where the parties agree to delay performance until a future event has happened or not happened. For instance, A and B are respectively the buyer and seller of property which A plans to develop into a block of flats. A and B may have agreed all of the essential terms of the missives but they may also agree that the sale will only go ahead if planning permission for the block of flats is granted by the local authority. The contract between A and B exists but the respective obligations to transfer title to the property and to pay the price will not be triggered unless the condition is fulfilled or 'purified'. If planning permission is not granted the contract will effectively come to an end because performance is unenforceable. If no date is specified, performance cannot be suspended indefinitely and the condition must be fulfilled within a reasonable time.

2.111 By contrast, a resolutive condition is one which, when fulfilled, brings the contract to an end. The condition is often a time period or date. This is a relatively uncommon term of a contract but, for instance, A and B entered into a sub-letting agreement which was conditional on obtaining the head landlord's consent by a certain date otherwise either could resile from the contract. However, the letter of consent was not obtained until eight days after the date stipulated. Lord Sutherland held that this was a resolutive condition and failure to obtain consent by that date brought the contract to an end.[192]

---

189 *EDI Central Ltd v National Car Parks Ltd* [2012] CSIH 6 at para 28 per Lord Mackay.

190 Such a term may be contained in a preliminary agreement, such as 'Heads of Terms', used to record the outcome of negotiations for the sale of a business.

191 For a fuller discussion see J Thomson, 'Suspensive and resolutive conditions in the Scots law of contract' in A J Gamble (ed), *Obligations in Context: Essays in honour of Professor D M Walker* (1990).

192 *Ford Sellar Morris Properties plc v E W Hutchison Ltd (No 4)* 1990 SC 34 at 37.

2.112 There is another sub-division in that suspensive and resolutive conditions can be either potestative or casual conditions: a potestative condition is one which is within the power of one or both parties to fulfil; by contrast, a casual condition is not within the power of the parties, but fulfilment depends on a third party or on chance. If one party has it within his power to fulfil the condition he must not do anything to prevent it being fulfilled; otherwise, on grounds of fairness, the condition will be held to be fulfilled.[193] Much will depend on the construction of the contract but it makes good business sense as well as good legal sense for the parties to act reasonably in fulfilling conditions that are within their power to fulfil unless they are clearly optional.

Exclusion clauses

2.113 Finally, in considering the terms of a contract, consideration must be given to the way in which the law exercises control over exclusion clauses, i.e. clauses where parties attempt to avoid (an exclusion clause proper) or limit (a limitation clause) their liability. Such clauses are common in commercial contracts as a way of allocating risk between the parties and if the parties are broadly of equal bargaining power it may be a commercially sensible approach. However, the law is somewhat hostile to such clauses, particularly where they have not been individually negotiated, and a range of judicial controls developed to subject them to further scrutiny. First, the rules of incorporation of terms can be applied to determine whether or not an exclusion clause contained in a notice or in a set of standard terms and conditions has been effectively incorporated into the contract.[194] Secondly, the courts will interpret such clauses narrowly. Thirdly, the Unfair Contract Terms Act 1977 ('UCTA') places statutory controls on exclusion clauses.

Interpretation of exclusion clauses

2.114 It is not uncommon in written contracts for the parties to draft exclusion clauses widely to minimise any risk to themselves, even to the point of excluding liability for loss or damage caused by their own fault or negligence. Where an exclusion clause attempts to exclude liability for negligence it must be carefully drafted in order to be effective. Unless the word 'negligence' is used unequivocally (in which case the clause will stand) the clause will be interpreted narrowly and the *contra proferentem* rule of interpretation will apply to any ambiguity, meaning that the court will prefer the interpretation which least favours the party attempting to rely on the clause. The rationale for such a rule is a pre-

---

193 Bell, *Principles* § 50; *Smith v Stuart* 2010 SCLR 131, affd 2010 SC 490.
194 See paras **2.94–2.95**.

sumption that one party is unlikely to release the other from liability for his own negligence.[195]

2.115 Limitation clauses (whereby there is no attempt to exclude liability, merely to limit its value) 'are not regarded by the courts with the same hostility as other clauses of exclusion; this is because they must be related to other contractual terms.'[196] The rules developed in relation to exclusion clauses proper do not apply to limitation clauses, which should be interpreted according to general principles.

The Unfair Contract Terms Act 1977

2.116 The intervention of Parliament to control contract terms runs contrary to the principle of freedom of contract, and it does so for policy reasons. The Unfair Contract Terms Act 1977 is a UK-wide statute, Part II of which, along with Schedule 2, applies to Scotland. As the title indicates, despite the judicial controls available, there was governmental concern at the potential for abuse of contract terms, particularly where there is a risk of unfairness in the terms of contracts and where contracts are drawn up in advance on the basis of standard terms. However, in another sense the title is misleading in that UCTA does not regulate all unfair contract terms, only those attempting to avoid liability, i.e. exclusion clauses.[197]

The scope of UCTA

2.117 UCTA applies to clauses inserted by businesses (widely defined to include companies, firms, professions, sole traders, government departments, local and public authorities) into contracts either with a consumer or with another business. Its scope is wide in that most types of contract (and non-contractual notices) are included[198] except for insurance contracts, contracts relating to the creation or transfer of a real right in land, and contracts setting up or dissolving corporate entities such as companies and partnerships.

---

195 *W & S Pollock & Co v Macrae* 1922 SC (HL) 192; Lord Wilberforce regarded it as 'inherently improbable that one party should agree to discharge the liability of the other party for acts for which he is responsible' (*Smith v UMB Chrysler (Scotland) Ltd* 1978 SC (HL) 1 at 7).
196 *Ailsa Craig Fishing Co v Malvern Fishing Co Ltd* 1982 SC (HL) 14 at 57 per Lord Wilberforce.
197 Detailed consideration is only given to provisions which deal with contract terms between commercial parties, although UCTA provides additional protection for consumers. Unfair contract terms are also controlled by the Consumer Contract Regulations 1999 (SI 1999/2083) but these apply only to consumer contracts and are not discussed in this chapter.
198 UCTA, s 15.

Statutory controls

2.118   Two different control mechanisms are used in the Act depending on what type of liability the business is attempting to exclude: the first declares the clause to be void, the second subjects it to a fair and reasonable test. The broadest provision of UCTA concerns attempts to exclude liability for any breach of duty (which would include a duty arising from contract or from delict, including liability for negligence) 'arising in the course of a business' or 'from the occupation of business premises'.[199] Section 16 applies whether or not the clause was negotiated between the parties. Section 16(1)(a) states that clauses which attempt to exclude or limit liability for personal injury or death will always be void. Section 16(1)(b) states that attempts to exclude or restrict liability for any other loss or damage will be effective only if the court judges them to be fair and reasonable. The party who is attempting to rely on the clause bears the onus of proving that the clause is fair and reasonable.[200]

Standard form contracts

2.119   Section 17 provides that attempts to exclude liability for breach of contract (either non-performance or performance that was substantially different from what could reasonably have been expected) where the contract is concluded on one of the party's standard terms, even in a commercial context, are also subject to the fair and reasonable test. To come within the scope of section 17 the standard terms must be in a pro forma document and the same terms must invariably be imposed on customers.[201]

2.120   Some guidance is given on what is to be regarded as 'fair and reasonable' both in UCTA and in subsequent case law. The following factors are relevant:[202]

(a)   the state of knowledge of the parties at the time the contract was entered into;

(b)   equality of bargaining power, i.e. the extent to which the parties are on an equal footing;

(c)   availability of goods and services elsewhere, the extent to which there is freedom of contract in the particular market;

(d)   the difficulty of the tasks to be performed;

(e)   the practical consequences of not allowing the exclusion; and

(f)   insurance implications – could the business insure itself and does the other party know that the business has insurance cover?

---

199   UCTA, s 16(1).

200   UCTA, s 24(4).

201   *Border Harvesters Ltd v Edwards Engineering (Perth) Ltd* 1985 SLT 128.

202   UCTA, s 24 and *Smith v Eric S Bush* [1990] 1 AC 831. For detailed discussion of the fair and reasonable test see D Cabrelli, *Commercial Agreements in Scotland: Law and Practice* (2006) paras 22.16–22.17.

Limitation clauses

2.121 UCTA provides additional factors to be taken into account when assessing whether a limitation clause is fair and reasonable:[203]

   (a) the resources available to the party seeking to rely on the limitation clause; and

   (b) how far it was open to that party to cover himself by insurance.

Breach of implied terms

2.122 Special provision is made in sections 20 and 21 for any exclusion of liability for breach of implied terms in contracts of sale or hire purchase. Any attempt to exclude the obligation to pass good title will be void. Attempts to exclude other implied terms are subject to a fair and reasonable test. The range of factors to be considered in this context is set out in Schedule 2:

   (a) strength of bargaining power;

   (b) whether there was true freedom of contract and whether the customer had a choice of contracting with another party;[204]

   (c) knowledge of the term; and

   (d) whether the goods were specially made or adapted for the customer.

2.123 Although the legislation provides different factors for assessing what is fair and reasonable in different contexts the courts have indicated that any of the factors can be referred to by a court.[205] Since the test is flexible in the first place, the court is not limited in what it can consider.

BREACH OF CONTRACT

2.124 The concept of breach of contract is fundamental to contract law and is the most common reason why contract cases end up in court. The law of breach of contract provides a default set of rules setting out what constitutes a breach and which remedies are available when things go wrong. However, before examining the rules of breach it should be pointed out that the vast majority of contracts are either performed to the satisfaction of the parties or, if things do go wrong, they are likely to attempt to find resolution through negotiation or other dispute resolution processes such as arbitration or mediation. Remedies for breach are a last resort, particularly if the parties are in a long-term commercial relationship, because it is highly likely that litigation will mark the end of that relationship, not to mention the considerable time and cost involved for both sides.

---

203 UCTA, s 24(3).
204 Considered in *Denholm Fishselling Ltd v Anderson* 1991 SLT (Sh Ct) 24.
205 *Singer Co (UK) Ltd v Tees and Hartlepool Port Authority* [1988] 2 Lloyd's Rep 164.

2.125   There are various ways in which the parties may fail to perform their obligations under a contract. Company A enters into a contract with Company B to install a new computer system having agreed the cost and the date for installation to begin. If B fails to appear on the agreed date it will be a breach of contract. If B gives advance notice that some of the components have not arrived and this would result in a delay, it is an anticipatory breach of contract. If B completes the installation but no-one in the company can access the company's server it amounts to defective performance. If only half of the staff can access the server it amounts to a partial failure to perform. All of these scenarios constitute a breach of contract and in Scots law the type of breach is generally irrelevant as regards the remedies available, although there is an important distinction between breaches that are *material* and those that are not.

2.126   Scots law, like English law, also distinguishes between what are known as self-help remedies, which allow the innocent party to take action to defend his position, and judicial remedies which require the intervention of the courts.

Self-help remedies for breach of contract

The mutuality principle

2.127   Underpinning the so-called self-help remedies is the idea that in most contracts there is an element of reciprocity in the obligations that the parties undertake towards each other. Those obligations are often interdependent in that the performance of one party is dependent on the performance of the other. This is referred to as the mutuality principle which has two effects in relation to a breach of contract: where obligations are interdependent if one party (the breaching party) does not perform his obligations he cannot enforce performance by the innocent party; and, as a logical counterpart, the innocent party can withhold his performance and cannot be compelled to perform with the result that the breaching party may not be entitled to a remedy. This principle underpins the remedies of retention and rescission.

Retention

2.128   Retention allows the innocent party to withhold his reciprocal performance in the event of a breach and is the most obvious application of the mutuality principle. Before retention can be applied it must be shown that the obligations undertaken are genuinely counterparts, which will be presumed unless there is evidence to the contrary.[206] An obvious example is withholding payment if work has not been carried

---

206 *Inveresk plc v Tullis Russell Papermakers Ltd* [2010] UKSC 19, 2010 SC 106 at para 42 per Lord Hope. This may not be the case in relation to employment contracts: see D Cabrelli, 'The mutuality of obligations doctrine and termination of the employment contract: *McNeill v Aberdeen City Council (No 2)*' (2014) 18 Edin LR 259.

out as agreed in order to persuade the workman to rectify the problem. However, payment can only be retained for the work it relates to, i.e. the obligations must be direct counterparts. So, where payments under a contract are made in instalments, an instalment can be withheld only for the breach to which it corresponds but not for obligations performed before or after the breach.[207] In an employment context the manager of Celtic football club was unable to suspend his obligation to be resident in Glasgow when he argued that it was in response to his employer's breach of the obligation of 'mutual trust and confidence' because it was not a direct counterpart.[208]

2.129 Retention of performance by the innocent party does not bring the contract to an end; rather it is designed to rescue the contract by persuading the other party to perform his side of the bargain. Where retention is permissible the innocent party is not treated as being in breach of contract despite his failure to perform.

Rescission

2.130 Rescission is where the innocent party brings the contract to an end or rescinds. Rescission is only available in response to a material breach or a repudiation by the wrongdoer (indicating that he no longer wishes to be bound by the contract). In principle there must also be a material breach before retention is available, but the degree of materiality required may be less than for rescission although the issue has been little explored.[209]

Material breach

2.131 There is no definitive statement of what constitutes a material breach of contract but it is sometimes described as going to the root or being of the essence of the contract. It is open to the parties to agree that certain terms are fundamental to the contract and any breach thereof will be treated as a material breach entitling the innocent party to rescind. There is, however, a danger for the innocent party. If he rescinds in response to what he believes to be a material breach and it turns out not to be, his actions will in themselves amount to a breach of contract. In the classic Scottish case *Wade v Waldon*[210] the popular comedian George Robey was hired to appear in Glasgow. Shortly before he was due to appear Robey discovered that the show had been cancelled. The manager had relied on clause 6 of the contract with Robey which provided:

> All artistes engaged . . . must give fourteen days notice prior to such engagements, such notice to be accompanied by bill matter.

207 *Bank of East Asia v Scottish Enterprise* 1997 SLT 1213.
208 *Macari v Celtic Football & Athletic Club* 1999 SC 628.
209 See MacQueen and Thomson, *Contract Law*, paras 5.11–5.12.
210 1909 SC 571.

Since Robey had neither notified nor sent publicity materials the manager took this to be a material breach and cancelled the shows. However, the court found that Robey's failure to perform was indeed a breach but it did not go to the root of the contract and therefore did not constitute a material breach. The manager was not entitled to rescind the contract and, in addition, cancellation of the shows was in itself a material breach entitling Robey to damages.

2.132 Whether or not late performance or defective performance amounts to a material breach is a question of facts and circumstances, unless the parties have so stipulated.[211] The question is whether the consequences of such a breach are so severe that the contract has to come to an end. In most cases of late or defective performance it will be more practical to allow the party in breach an opportunity to cure the problem rather than bring the contract to an end. In relation to payment the party in breach must be given a reasonable time to pay before it can be treated as a material breach justifying rescission.[212]

Repudiation

2.133 A second scenario in which a party is entitled to rescind is in response to a repudiation. This is sometimes referred to as an anticipatory breach and it arises where the other contracting party has indicated his refusal to perform his obligations under the contract. Technically repudiation is not in itself a breach and only becomes one when it is 'accepted' by the other party. Acceptance turns the repudiation into a breach and entitles the acceptor to rescind. Returning to the computer installation example above, if Company B telephones in advance to indicate that it is unable to perform the contract on the stipulated date because some of the components are not in stock, this does not necessarily amount to a repudiation. Company B may be able to procure the components elsewhere and may begin the work a few days later than planned, which may be acceptable to Company A. However, if time is of the essence, Company A may 'accept' the failure to perform, rescind the contract, thus bringing it to an end, and hire an alternative provider.

2.134 The question of whether there is in fact a refusal to perform is judged objectively, and must be more than a mere threat or anticipation of non-performance that may never be fulfilled.[213] However, once refusal has been indicated it is open to the innocent party to rescind immediately for anticipatory breach, which may be of practical value and allows time to find an alternative contractor, or to wait until the date of performance and rescind for actual breach of contract.

2.135 It is also open to the innocent party to insist on performance of the contract rather than accept repudiation. In *White and Carter (Councils)*

---

211 For further detail see MacQueen and Thomson, *Contract Law*, paras 5.35–5.39.
212 *Rodger (Builders) Ltd v Fawdry* 1950 SC 483.
213 *Blyth v Scottish Liberal Club* 1982 SC 140.

Ltd v McGregor[214] a contract for advertising on litter bins contained an accelerated payment clause under which, if there was failure to pay for one month's advertising, the whole amount due under a three-year contract would become payable. McGregor attempted to repudiate, indicating he wished to cancel the contract, but the company did not accept the repudiation, choosing instead to affirm the contract and implement the accelerated payment clause. The company was entitled to payment because it had a 'legitimate interest'[215] in performance of the contract and it may also have been relevant that it was able to perform its obligations under the contract without the co-operation of the breaching party. The Scottish Law Commission has voiced criticism of the decision recognising that it could lead to wasteful or unreasonable conduct and has proposed modifications of the rule.[216]

Consequences of rescission

2.136 It is not entirely accurate to say the contract is at an end when it is rescinded for material breach. Its effect is to free the innocent party from future obligations but not from obligations, for instance payment, corresponding to satisfactory performance prior to the breach.[217] In limited circumstances the law of unjustified enrichment may provide a remedy after a breach of contract where partial performance of a contract has taken place[218] although the courts tread warily so as not to undermine the rules of contract law.[219]

Judicial remedies for breach of contract

2.137 Remedies for breach of contract are *cumulative* and the use of self-help remedies does not prevent the innocent party from applying to the courts for a judicial remedy, nor does one judicial remedy exclude others. The available remedies can broadly be classified as those which are designed to compel performance and those which compensate the innocent party for failure to perform.

Specific implement

2.138 Specific implement has been described as a 'primary remedy' in Scots contract law[220] in that it is always apposite for the innocent party to seek to compel performance following a breach of contract.[221]

---

214 1962 SC (HL) 1.
215 At 14 per Lord Reid.
216 Scottish Law Commission, *Discussion Paper on Remedies for Breach of Contract* (Scot Law Com DP no 109, 1999) paras 5.12–5.17, henceforth 'SLC DP 109'.
217 *Graham v United Turkey Red Co* 1922 SC 533.
218 H L MacQueen 'Unjustified enrichment and breach of contract' 1994 JR 137.
219 *Connelly v Simpson* 1993 SC 391.
220 SLC DP 109 (n 217), para 6.1.
221 Although some doubt has been cast on its primacy given how rarely it is sought or granted (see MacQueen and Thomson, *Contract Law*, para 6.6).

The underlying principle is that the parties should get what they contracted for and the courts will enforce performance. Non-compliance can lead to imprisonment of the party in breach.[222] However, like all judicial remedies, it is discretionary and may be refused in the following circumstances:[223]

(a) Where the decree sought is not sufficiently precise. In *Retail Parks Investments Ltd v Royal Bank of Scotland plc (No 2)*[224] the bank was under an obligation to keep the premises open for 'retail purposes' but had proposed leaving only cash withdrawal machines which was held to breach the terms of the lease. However, in relation to specific implement it was held that the court could specify the goal (retention of premises for retail banking) but need not specify the precise means by which performance was to be achieved.

(b) Where performance is impossible.

(c) Where performance would cause exceptional hardship or injustice.

(d) Where performance would be of a highly personal nature, for instance in contracts which depend on relationships such as employment contracts.

(e) Where replacement performance is readily available, for instance if the goods or services are readily available elsewhere.

Action for payment

2.139 An action for payment is the most common judicial remedy since the most common method of breaching a contract is failure to pay. It is procedurally distinct in that enforcement is by way of diligence to recover any sums due.[225]

Interdict

2.140 The judicial remedy of interdict can be viewed as the reverse of specific implement in that it prevents rather than compels actions. It can be sought to prevent conduct likely to lead to a breach of contract and is therefore anticipatory in nature. It is possible to obtain an interim interdict which acts as a temporary remedy pending a full investigation of the facts and circumstances. Before granting interim interdict the court must consider whether on the balance of convenience an order should be granted. The innocent party must first present a *prima facie* case.

2.141 An interdict cannot be granted in order to require somebody to do something. However, the distinction between positive and negative obligations may be a fine one. In *Church Commissioners for England v Abbey*

---

222 Law Reform (Miscellaneous Provisions)(Scotland) Act 1940, s 1(1).

223 This summary borrows from SLC DP 109 (n 217), paras 6.2–6.7.

224 1996 SC 227; see also *Highland and Universal Properties Ltd v Safeway Properties Ltd* 2000 SC 297.

225 See Chapter 12: Judicial Security: Diligence.

National plc[226] Abbey National were in breach of a 'keep open' clause in a lease requiring them to occupy premises in a shopping centre. The landlord sought to interdict the defenders from failing to occupy the premises and was ineffective because it amounted to compelling the tenants to do something and to fulfil their obligations under the lease. Lord President Hope noted that the *function* of an interdict is 'a negative one . . . namely to prevent taking of action in breach of the obligation, not to compel performance of it directly by order of the court'.[227]

Damages

2.142 The final remedy to be considered is different in nature from the other judicial remedies considered above in that it seeks financial compensation as a substitute for performance. In effect, the breaching party is permitted to pay rather than perform. However, damages must directly relate to any loss suffered by the innocent party as a result of the breach and Scots law does not allow punitive damages.[228] The aim is to put the innocent party in the position they would have been in had the contract been performed. Damages can be claimed for actual loss caused; for consequential losses, i.e. losses which flow directly from the actual loss caused; and it may be possible in some circumstances to claim a 'nominal' award of damages if the innocent party has suffered 'trouble and inconvenience' as a result of the breach.[229] For instance, if Company B installs a computer system defectively with the result that none of the employees of Company A can access a computer for a period of three days, Company A will be entitled to compensation for the cost of rectifying the problem by calling in other experts (the loss caused). However, if a three-day shut-down of all computers has also led to a loss of revenue those losses can also be claimed as consequential losses. Claims for damages must not be unreasonable.[230]

Causation

2.143 A further limitation on claims for damages is the rule of causation that the loss must be caused by the breach of contract. This is sometimes expressed as asking whether 'but for' the breach the loss would have occurred. The breach may not be the only operative cause of the loss but it must be a material cause.[231]

Other limitations on claims for damages

2.144 Not all losses can be compensated and the law has developed a

---

226 1994 SC 651.
227 At 660.
228 Nor has Scots law thus far provided 'gain-based' damages as English law did in *Attorney-General v Blake* [2001] 1 AC 268.
229 *Wilkie v Brown* 2003 SC 573 at para 21 per Lord Justice-Clerk Gill.
230 *Ruxley Electronics and Construction Ltd v Forsyth* [1996] AC 344.
231 *Monarch Steamship Co v A/B Karlshamns Oljefabriker* 1949 SC (HL) 1.

number of limiting devices to prevent excessive claims. The test of remoteness[232] requires that the loss must arise directly in the ordinary course of events (without special knowledge on the part of the contracting parties)[233] and must be of such a type as the parties might reasonably have contemplated.[234] In addition the parties are under a duty to mitigate their losses and avoid incurring losses where possible. This could again be seen as amounting to a requirement that the parties act reasonably.

232 *Hadley v Baxendale* (1854) 9 Exch 341.
233 *Balfour Beatty Construction (Scotland) Ltd v Scottish Power plc* 1994 SC (HL) 20.
234 See H L MacQueen, 'Remoteness and breach of contract' 1996 JR 295.

Chapter 3

General Principles of Property Law

WHY DOES PROPERTY LAW MATTER
FOR COMMERCIAL LAW?

3.01 Commercial law is to a large extent the law of trade. Trading assets involves buying and selling them. This is often financed by loans which are secured against other assets. Buyers will not be content merely to have a contract obliging the seller to make them owners of goods, they want that contract to be fulfilled. A lender may only be willing to lend if the borrower gives a right in security which allows the lender to sell some of his or her property if the debt is not paid.

3.02 Trade also involves risk. Things may not work out as parties hope. If commercial transactions do not work out as parties hope, they may find that their assets are not sufficient to meet their obligations. That means that the debtor will not be able to pay every creditor in full. This situation is known as insolvency and it is handled through processes such as sequestration and liquidation, which are discussed later in this book. Crudely put, they involve selling off the debtor's assets and sharing the proceeds between the creditors. No-one gets all that they are entitled to because there is not enough to go round.

3.03 In this situation, property rights in the debtor's assets are much more valuable than contractual rights against the debtor. They give direct access to the assets without the need to share with other creditors. Imagine that Susan has four tonnes of wheat and no other assets. She gets a bit confused and makes contracts for the sale of a tonne of wheat with six different people. She does not have enough wheat to fulfil all of the contracts. Insolvency processes are about sharing the four tonnes of wheat between the six buyers. None of the buyers will get a whole tonne (or its value) from the insolvency official.

3.04 If, however, Susan has transferred a tonne of wheat to Brenda (one of the buyers) before the insolvency process starts, then Brenda will not have to share her wheat with the other buyers. The insolvency process is about sharing Susan's assets between her creditors. Brenda's tonne is no longer one of Susan's assets. It belongs to Brenda and she does not owe any obligations to Susan's creditors. Of course, this means that the others now have to share three tonnes between five buyers. Brenda received full performance but that makes things worse for everyone else.

3.05 Cases like this show that a sound grasp of the basic principles of property law is essential for the commercial lawyer. This chapter is intended to give a brief outline of these principles. For reasons of brevity, citation of authority will be kept to a minimum. For a more detailed account, texts devoted to property law should be consulted.[1]

KINDS OF RIGHTS

Real and personal; absolute and relative

3.06 The key distinction in property law is between personal and real rights.[2] Personal rights are the 'correlative' or mirror image of obligations. If David has borrowed £100 from Colin, then he owes Colin £100 (and perhaps some interest as well). That, in turn, means that Colin has a personal right against David for payment of the £100 (and the interest). Colin's personal right against David and David's obligation to Colin are two sides of the same coin. Put another way, a personal right is a right that somebody does or refrains from doing some action. The person against whom the right is held is obliged to act or refrain from acting in that way.

3.07 Personal rights are so called because they are enforceable against a certain person or group of persons (whoever owes the relevant obligation) and only them. Colin can sue David for enforcement of the right to the £100 but he cannot sue anyone else because only David owes the obligation. Contracts are the most important source of personal rights in commercial law, but personal rights can also arise from delict, unjustified enrichment, *negotiorum gestio* (benevolent intervention in another's affairs) and trusts. Personal rights are sometimes said to be relative because they express the specific relationship between particular persons. Whatever the origin of a personal right, it behaves in much the same way once it has been created.

3.08 Real rights are different from personal rights. Where a personal right is a right against a person or group of persons for the fulfilment of a particular obligation, a real right is a right 'in' a thing. The term 'real right' is derived from the Latin word for thing: *res*. Because the object of the real right is a thing rather than conduct by a particular person, it is valid against the whole world. Most importantly, it can usually be enforced against whoever is in possession of the thing. Because they can be enforced against the whole world, real rights are said to be absolute rather than relative.

---

1 G L Gretton and A J M Steven *Property, Trusts and Sucession* (2nd edn, 2013); K G C Reid *The Law of Property in Scotland* (1996).
2 See the judgment of Lord Hope in *Sharp v Thomson* 1995 SC 455, especially at 461–75.

3.09 Thus, if Olivia owns a car and it is stolen, she can recover it from the person in whose possession it is found, irrespective of how that person got hold of the car. This can be contrasted with the position of someone with a contractual right to the car. Imagine that Olivia contracts to sell the car to Brian. Before ownership is transferred to Brian, the car is stolen. The thief 'sells' the car to Peter. Peter had no idea it was stolen. Olivia can sue Peter to recover the car because she owns it. Brian, on the other hand, has a personal right to the car arising from the contract of sale but he has no real right. His personal right means that he can sue Olivia for breach of contract seeking damages (or, if she has recovered the car, delivery of the car itself). Peter, however, is not a party to the contract of sale so it cannot be enforced against him.

3.10 Some rights, particularly intellectual property rights such as copyright, patents and trademarks are enforceable against the whole world without there being an obvious 'thing' for the right to be in. In relation to these, it might be suggested that they are absolute rights (i.e. rights which are good against the whole world) but not real rights because there is no *res* (thing). Although copyright can protect an artistic work such as a picture, it does not concern the physical picture itself. Rather it relates to the expression of ideas found in the picture.

3.11 However, it is also possible to see the intellectual products which are covered by the intellectual property right (whether that be a picture, song or work of literature protected by copyright, an invention covered by a patent or an image, phrase or sound protected as a trademark) as incorporeal things and the relevant intellectual property rights as real rights in these things. Some care must be taken with this approach. If a song is a thing which can be the subject of real rights, we might expect that it is possible to own the song. That, however, is not the case. The greatest right which the law admits in the song is copyright, which is not the same as ownership.

3.12 Intellectual property rights work by conferring a monopoly on the rightholder: the holder of a patent over an invention is the only one who is allowed to manufacture the relevant product. Thus they can be said to be exclusive privileges. Historically, there were other types of exclusive privilege, such as the monopoly rights of royal burghs in respect of trade. In the modern era, however, intellectual property rights are the only important rights of exclusive privilege as a result of the general hostility to monopolies.

Ownership and the subordinate real rights

3.13 Scots lawyers explain a person's relationship with his or her corporeal property in terms of ownership: the principal real right. The concept appears to be a simple and familiar one. If a car belongs to Oliver, he is said to own that car. The aspiration to own a home is a regular topic in news reports.

3.14 Various attempts have been made to define ownership: it is some-times said to be the exclusive and absolute right of use and enjoyment of the thing.[3] Others feel that this does not capture everything which an owner can do and simply say that it is 'the most complete right a person can have in a thing'[4] or 'the main real right'.[5] Some present it as the 'residual' right in a thing;[6] still others are sceptical about the possibility of or need to offer a definition of ownership.[7] To some extent, the scepti-cism about a definition and the idea of ownership as a residual right spring from a common root: the grant of subordinate real rights.

3.15 The owner of a thing can grant subordinate real rights in it. For instance, if Lionel owns some land, he might grant a lease to Teresa and a standard security to Calum. Once he has granted these rights, the free-dom which Lionel has to deal with his property is limited. Teresa, rather than Lionel, is entitled to possess the property, and Lionel can only transfer it subject to Calum's standard security. The rights which Teresa and Calum enjoy can be enforced against someone to whom Lionel transferred the property because they are real rights.

3.16 In some sense, Lionel's rights in respect of the property are dimin-ished. For this reason subordinate real rights can be described as encum-brances on Lionel's right of ownership. On one view, Lionel has carved out a bit of his ownership and transferred it to someone else. This has led some scholars, particularly in the French legal tradition, to describe sub-ordinate real rights as dismemberments of ownership.

3.17 We might think of ownership as being a bit like a box of chocolates: as the owner grants subordinate real rights he gives away chocolates. Even after all the chocolates have been given away, the owner is still holding the box and is therefore still the owner.[8] Even if Lionel has burdened his property with so many subordinate real rights that he has no meaningful freedom to decide what happens to it, he is still the owner just as much as he was before he granted the rights. For this reason, it is difficult to define ownership in terms of what the owner can do since that can vary quite a lot from case to case. Thus some con-sider ownership to be a residual right.

3.18 We should be conscious that ownership is not as simple as first appears but it is important not to overstate the difficulties. The concept of ownership in Civilian systems such as Scots law has been worked out

---

3 Erskine, *Institute* II.i.1; Bell, *Principles* § 1284. This is sometimes expressed with the Latin expression *ius utendi fruendi abutendi*.

4 E.g. Draft Common Frame of Reference VIII–1:202.

5 Stair, *Institutions* II.i.28.

6 S J Grossman and O D Hart, 'The costs and benefits of ownership: a theory of vertical and lateral integration' (1986) 94 Journal of Political Economy 691.

7 S R Simpson, 'Towards a definition of "absolute ownership": II' (1961) 5 Journal of African Law 145.

8 The analogy is not completely accurate since, in theory, it is always possible to grant further subordinate real rights so the box of chocolates is never empty.

over thousands of years and it helps us to analyse many of the most important property law problems. We can be relatively confident in saying that ownership establishes a default rule: in the absence of any rule or right to the contrary, the owner gets to decide what happens to his or her property. It is up to someone who wants to object to the owner's conduct in respect of the property to point to the rule of law or right which restricts his or her freedom.

3.19 Ownership is the right which a person has in his or her own things. Subordinate real rights are the rights which a person can have in other people's things.

3.20 Scots law recognises a fixed list of types of subordinate real rights. This is known as the principle of *numerus clausus*. Attempts to create real rights outside this list will be ineffective. This principle is one of the major features which distinguishes the law of property from the law of contract. The reason for the principle is the third party effect of real rights. Since contracts do not impose obligations on third parties, third parties have little or no interest in being able to discover the content of the contract. Therefore, the contracting parties are generally entitled to craft their contracts as they wish, creating bespoke regimes which fit their needs. The position is somewhat different for real rights.

3.21 As explained above real rights affect everyone. They are particularly important to singular successors: those who acquire the property from a former owner. Therefore, third parties (particularly those who are considering acquiring the property) have a strong interest in discovering which real rights affect an asset. This process is made much easier if there is a limited number of potential real rights to consider and if the creation of these rights is attended by some publicity.

3.22 The subordinate real rights are:

- rights in security: which allow the security holder to realise the value of an asset in order to satisfy a debt due to him or her and/or to retain possession until payment;
- proper liferent: which allows the liferenter to possess property for his or her lifetime;
- lease of land:[9] which allows possession for a specified period of time on condition of payment of rent;
- servitudes: which allow the rightholder to make some use of the property burdened by the servitude, typically for the benefit of neighbouring property. The classic example is a right of way; and
- the right to enforce a negative real burden: which allows the rightholder to veto certain uses or modifications of property by the owner.

9 The position of leases is slightly more complex than that of other subordinate real rights. In many Civilian systems, a lease is considered as a contract which transfers to successors with or without their consent, rather than as a subordinate real right.

Some would also suggest that being in possession confers a real right not to be forcibly dispossessed, which is a distinct real right.[10] This view might be contested on the basis that a bare possessor could not be maintained in possession in the face of a judicial challenge by the owner, while the other real rights would remain. It has also been suggested that rights held by the public, such as public rights of way, are real rights because they are generally enforceable.[11]

3.23   As noted above, some would see intellectual property rights and other rights of exclusive privilege as real rights because they are enforceable against the whole world. Others would suggest that they are absolute but not real because there is no *res*.

Common ownership

3.24   The potential for the grant of subordinate real rights shows that more than one person can have a real right in a thing. Can more than one person own a thing? They can. Indeed they can do so in two different ways: common ownership and joint ownership. The most important instance of the latter is the trust and joint ownership is discussed along with the rest of the rules on trusts below.

3.25   In common ownership the right of ownership is shared, reflecting each person's share of the property. Each common owner is entitled to make normal use of the property, transfer his or her share and grant rights in security over it. Acts which would affect other owners, such as leasing the property or granting servitudes, can only be done with their consent.[12] Each common owner is entitled to raise an action for division and sale under which the property will be sold and each common owner will receive his or her share of the proceeds.[13] If property is transferred to more than one person, the assumption is that they will have equal shares but it is possible to vary this so that one party has 75 per cent and another 25 per cent or one 60 per cent and another 40 per cent.

Competing rights

3.26   One of the most important differences between real and personal rights is the way in which they compete with other rights. There are three basic principles: personal rights rank *pari passu*; real rights trump personal rights; and competing real rights rank by date of creation.

Personal rights rank pari passu

3.27   An earlier personal right does not normally enjoy priority over a later one. Each creditor is entitled to seek satisfaction without worrying too much about other creditors. If the debtor does not have enough

---

10 K G C Reid, *The Law of Property in Scotland* (1996) para 5.
11 Reid, *Law of Property*, para 5.
12 Bell, *Principles* § 1072–5.
13 Bell, *Principles* § 1079.

assets to satisfy all creditors, insolvency law will usually compel each one of them to take a proportionate cut.

3.28 Imagine that Gary has a gambling problem. He borrows £3,500 from Frances on Monday and loses it on the horses. On Tuesday, he borrows £4,500 from Serena which he loses in the casino. Chastened by his losses, he goes home to stay with his mum who gives him free board and lodgings. After some time, he is sequestrated. After gathering in Gary's assets, the insolvency official finds that Gary has £5,000 of assets but £8,000 worth of debts. The *pari passu* principle means that Frances cannot claim full payment on the basis that her debt was constituted first. Instead each of them will be entitled to five-eighths of their debt: so Frances would get £2,187.50 and Serena would get £2,812.50.

Real rights trump personal rights

3.29 Since a real right is good against the world, it is good against the holders of any personal rights with which it is in conflict. Peggy concludes a contract with Harriet under which Harriet has the right to use Peggy's car every Tuesday. Peggy then pledges the car to Cathy in security for a debt which she owes her. When property is pledged, the pledgee (Cathy) is entitled to possession until the debt is paid.[14] Harriet's right and Cathy's right appear to be in conflict: when Tuesday comes, Harriet's contract says she is entitled to take the car but Cathy's pledge says she is entitled to hold onto it. In such a situation, Cathy wins. Her right of pledge is a real right, which is enforceable against Peggy, Harriet and anyone else. Harriet's personal right, on the other hand is only enforceable against Peggy and so is no use in a dispute with Cathy. Harriet would, however, be able to sue Peggy for breach of contract.

3.30 The most common cause of a conflict of rights is insolvency and it is here that rights in security come into their own. Consider the following case. Widget Co Ltd has four creditors, each of whom is owed £100,000. It owns a factory worth £200,000 and other assets worth £100,000. Total assets are therefore £300,000 and total liabilities are £400,000. If expenses are ignored, each unsecured creditor would get around £75,000. If, however, two of the creditors (Al and Betty) had secured their debts by way of standard securities over the factory, the picture would be different. Al and Betty would be entitled to sell the factory and share the proceeds between themselves, taking £100,000 each. The two unsecured creditors would be left to share the remaining £100,000 worth of assets, leaving them with £50,000 each.

3.31 This story is a little bit like that of Susan, Brenda and the wheat which was discussed at paras **3.03–3.04**. But the secured creditors' preferential treatment cannot be explained on the basis that the factory belongs to them and not to Widget Co Ltd. Although the company has granted standard securities, it remains the owner. Rather, the result is

14 See para **11.27**.

explicable on the basis that a standard security is a real right and may therefore be invoked in disputes with the other creditors just as much as it can be used against the company.

3.32 The rule that personal rights are trumped by real rights means that holders of personal rights are very vulnerable in insolvency situations: they have to share the assets equally and the assets start being shared out only after those with real rights have taken their entitlement.

Real rights rank by date of creation

3.33 The rule that real rights rank ahead of personal rights in respect of the item of property which they affect governs the interaction of real rights and personal rights. Since it is possible for more than one real right to exist in an asset, a rule is also needed to regulate the relationship of these rights to one another.

3.34 Al and Betty both had a standard security which burdened the factory. Since the value was enough to satisfy both of them, their respective priority did not matter. If, however, the factory was only worth £150,000, then its sale would not be enough to satisfy both Al and Betty. Unlike personal rightholders, Al and Betty will not rank *pari passu*. They will rank according to the date of creation (sometimes expressed in the Latin phrase *prior tempore potior jure*).[15] Therefore, if Al's standard security was created first, Betty would not receive any of the proceeds of the sale of the factory until Al had been paid in full.[16] It is possible for Al and Betty to make an agreement between themselves which alters this, so that both rank together (and thus take a proportionate cut in the case of the assets being of insufficient value). Alternatively, Al may agree to give up his prior rank so that Betty ranks ahead of Al.

TRUSTS

3.35 Under normal circumstances the owner of property uses it for his or her own benefit. There is one important exception to this however: the trust. The basic idea behind the trust is that property is owned by a trustee or trustees but not used for their benefit. Rather they administer it for the benefit of other parties, known as beneficiaries, in accordance with a set of aims known as trust purposes. The situation is set up by a truster who transfers the property to the trustee and imposes the duty to administer it for the benefit of beneficiaries.[17] In the typical case, there are at least three parties: a truster, a trustee and a beneficiary. Tracey might transfer a number of buy-to-let properties to Trudy in trust for Bertie. Trudy owns the properties but profits arising from rental income should go to Bertie (although his precise entitlement would depend on

---

15 Which means 'first in time, stronger in right'.
16 Conveyancing and Feudal Reform (Scotland) Act 1970, s 27(1).
17 Bell, *Principles* § 1991.

the terms of the trust). Bertie and Tracey have personal rights against Trudy which they can use to compel her to act in accordance with the trust.

3.36 It is also possible for one person to perform two roles. So Tracey might transfer the properties to Trudy to be held for Tracey's benefit. In that case, she would be both truster and beneficiary and Trudy would be the trustee. Alternatively, Tracey might declare that, from now on, she would hold the properties for Bertie. This needs to be done in writing and intimated to Bertie[18] but once these steps have been fulfilled, Tracey is the trustee in respect of those assets and Bertie is the beneficiary. The only combination which is not possible (because it would be pointless) is being a trustee and beneficiary. In that situation, the trustee would be obliged to administer the property for his or her own benefit, but that is what a normal owner does anyway.

3.37 Where there is more than one trustee, the trustees are said to have joint ownership. In contrast to common ownership, individual trustees have no share of the property which they can deal with individually and, where a trustee ceases to perform that role, he or she ceases to be owner of the trust property automatically. Where a new trustee is assumed, he or she acquires joint ownership automatically.

3.38 Trusts have one characteristic which has given rise to extensive use of the trust in commercial contexts: trust assets are protected from the trustee's personal creditors.[19] This means that the beneficiaries under the trust enjoy exclusive access to these assets held in trust for satisfaction of their rights. This has led some to question whether the beneficiaries' rights can be said to be truly personal and others to doubt whether it is possible to properly rationalise the trust in Scots law.

3.39 The trust can be explained without abandoning the principle that the beneficiaries' rights are personal by the idea of separation of patrimonies. As discussed in Chapter 1, a patrimony is the totality of a person's assets.

3.40 A patrimony can be thought of as a suitcase, into which all your property is put. Your creditors are entitled to seize and sell items from the suitcase in order to satisfy your debts to them. A trustee has two suitcases: a personal patrimony containing his own assets which is liable for his personal debts, and a trust patrimony which is liable for the trust's debts (most importantly the personal rights of beneficiaries). The beneficiaries do not have to share these assets with the personal creditors of the trustee but that is because the assets are in a different patrimony, not because the beneficiaries' rights are stronger than any other personal rights. They do not have access to the second suitcase.

---

18 Requirements of Writing (Scotland) Act 1995, s 1(2)(a)(iii); *Allan's Trs v Lord Advocate* 1971 SC (HL) 45.
19 *Heritable Reversionary Co Ltd v Millar* (1892) 19 R (HL) 43; Bankruptcy (Scotland) Act 1985, s 33(1)(b).

3.41 By comparing the position of creditors of the trust we can see that separation of patrimonies, rather than some special quality of the beneficiaries' rights, explains the trust's insolvency effect. Trust creditors are entitled to payment in priority to the beneficiaries.[20] An example might be a plumber who does work on the buy-to-let properties which Trudy holds in trust for Bertie. Bertie is not entitled to payment until it is clear that there are sufficient assets to pay the plumber.

3.42 The fact that a trust can be sequestrated independently of sequestration of any of the trustees also points to the trust being a separate patrimony.[21] As discussed in Chapter 13, in personal insolvency, sequestration is the mechanism by which the assets of a person whose liabilities outweigh the contents of his or her patrimony are gathered in, sold off and distributed to the creditors. In the same way, the creditors of the trust can petition for the sequestration of the trust. If the trust merely consisted of a special right held by the beneficiary, it is difficult to see how such an insolvency treatment could make sense.

3.43 The idea of the trust as a separate patrimony also helps to explain the operation of the trustees' joint ownership. The asset is in the trust patrimony, which is a single patrimony controlled by multiple trustees. Since it is a trust patrimony, power over the patrimony is vested in the trustees because they are trustees. If someone resigns as a trustee, he or she necessarily gives up authority over the trust patrimony.[22] This contrasts with common ownership where each common owner has his or her own right of ownership in his or her personal patrimony. The contrast between joint and common ownership can thus be illustrated in these diagrams.

Common ownership:

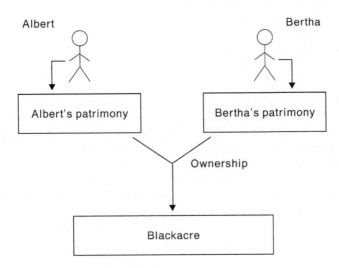

20 *Lamond's Trs v Croom* (1871) 9 M 662.
21 Bankruptcy (Scotland) Act 1985, s 6(1).
22 Trusts (Scotland) Act 1921, s 20.

Trustees' joint ownership:

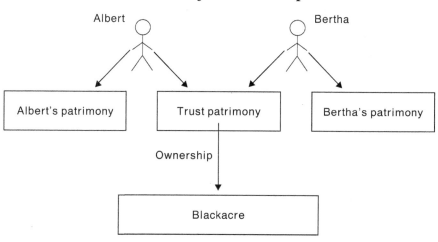

KINDS OF PROPERTY

Rights as rights and rights as things

3.44 Real rights and personal rights do have one very important thing in common however. They are ways in which the law conceptualises relationships between persons and the 'real world'. Personal rights express the relationship between persons. Saying Christine has a right to payment against Debbie expresses something about the relationship between Christine and Debbie which is relevant to the law: Debbie is obliged to pay a sum of money to Christine and the courts will give Christine aid in her efforts to secure that payment. Real rights express something about a person's relationship with a thing. Saying that Brian has a servitude of access over a piece of land expresses something about Brian's relationship with that piece of land and (by virtue of that fact) his relationship with everyone else: namely Brian is entitled to take access to his property (e.g. his house) across that piece of land and everyone else must refrain from obstructing Brian's efforts to do this. Rights express the relationship between persons and the real world but the law must also find a way of expressing the relationship between a person and his or her rights.[23]

3.45 This is important because rights themselves are important assets which can be traded. In fact, many of a business's more important assets will be rights: real rights such as leases or standard securities, personal rights against debtors, intellectual property rights such as copyright,

23 Strictly speaking, where this chapter says 'his or her', it should say 'his, her or its' since juristic persons such as partnerships, companies and limited liability partnerships can have personal and real rights in just the same way as natural persons.

patents and trademarks. These rights can be transferred in more or less the same way as physical things. Transfer of a right has a special name. It is known as assignation.

3.46 The traditional approach to conceptualising the relationship between a person and his or her rights in Scotland, as in the rest of Europe, is based on a scheme presented by the Roman jurist Gaius in his *Institutes* ('the Gaian scheme'). He proposed a general class of things, which he subdivided into corporeal and incorporeal things:

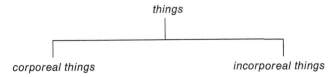

3.47 Corporeal things are items with a real, physical existence such as plots of land, cars, lorries, sacks of coal and so on. Incorporeal things, on the other hand, are assets which cannot be touched. The main items in this class are rights. Since all things can be owned, the real right of ownership expresses the relationship between a person and his or her assets. Christine owns her personal right against Debbie or a lease over another plot in much the same way as she owns a plot of land. On this model, a person's patrimony comprises things which he or she owns. Christine's affairs may be illustrated in the following way:

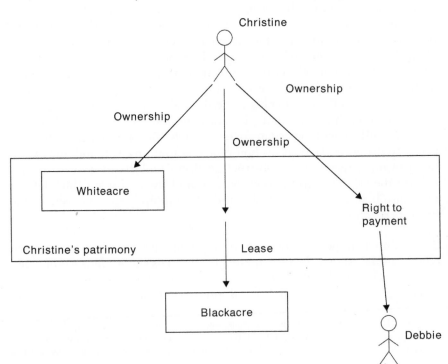

3.48 This approach makes it easy to explain why rights are transferable and to apply principles developed in the context of corporeal property to incorporeal assets. Just as the owner of a plot of land can transfer it, so can the owner of a right to payment. In every case, what is transferred is ownership of the relevant thing. In one case the thing is the plot of land; in the other it is the right to payment. Further, if subordinate real rights (such as rights in security) are conceptualised as burdens on or dismemberments of ownership, then it is easy to understand which subordinate rights might be granted in incorporeal things.

3.49 Such an approach does, however, face one major challenge: ownership is generally recognised as a real right. Indeed, it is the principal real right. If real rights are things, and ownership is a real right, then it appears that it should be possible to own ownership. That, however, sets up a problem of perpetual regression, since the same thing could be said regarding the ownership of the right of ownership, so the ownership of the ownership of the ownership would be owned, and so on.

3.50 There are various possible responses to this problem. One is to suggest that ownership is a special kind of real right which cannot be owned.[24] Another is to suggest that ownership is not a real right.[25] Both of these approaches can be seen as efforts to retain the Gaian scheme or a modification of it. A further option is outright rejection of the Gaian scheme. This rejection is most closely associated with German scholars, in particular with the Pandectist school, but it is also adopted by some modern scholars in Scotland.[26]

3.51 Key to the Pandectist approach is the idea that a patrimony rather than ownership is the mechanism which explains the relationship between a person and his or her rights. On this view, the patrimony contains a person's rights but nothing else. Rights reach out from the patrimony to things in the real world.

3.52 This approach avoids the problem of perpetual regression in the ownership of ownership. It is possible to apply principles of transfer developed in relation to land or corporeal moveables to dealings with rights to payment or leases because each case involves moving a right from one patrimony to another. If Christine assigns her right against Debbie, it moves from her patrimony to that of the assignee. If she transfers Whiteacre, the real right of ownership over Whiteacre moves from

---

24 Reid, *Law of Property*, para 16.
25 The most famous statement of this view is S Ginossar, *Droit réel, propriété et créance: Élaboration d'un système rationnel des droits patrimoniaux* (1960). In addition to being in French, this work is very difficult to locate. A good summary of Ginossar's views and those of his later interpreters can be found in G Gretton 'Ownership and its objects' (2007) 71 Rabels Z 802 at 810–815.
26 Most notably Gretton 'Ownership and its Objects' (n 25 above) and R G Anderson, *Assignation* (2008), para 1-09.

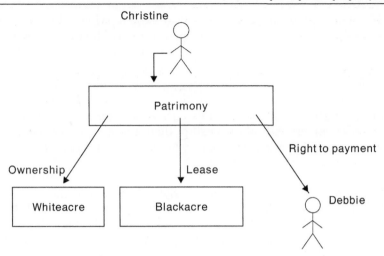

her patrimony to that of the transferee. On the Pandectist view, nothing more need be said.

3.53 The Pandectist approach faces greater challenges with subordinate rights in rights. If Christine wants to grant a right in security over the lease of Blackacre, it is relatively easy for the Gaian scheme to explain it: the lease is a thing and can therefore be the object of a real right in security. The fact that Christine owns the lease explains why she should be able to burden it. Should Christine become insolvent, the security holder's real right explains the priority over unsecured creditors.

3.54 The Pandectist can say that she should be able to deal with the lease because it is part of her patrimony, but there is more difficulty in explaining the nature of the subordinate right which she grants. Similarly, the status of the right in security as a real right is more difficult to invoke to explain any insolvency protection. Explanations of how this may be are possible but they are rather complex and, in the view of the writer of this chapter, a little awkward.[27] The other, more pragmatic problem with the Pandectist approach is that most lawyers in the western tradition have been using Gaian language for a very long time and it would take a significant intellectual effort to displace that tendency.

3.55 Both views of the relationship between persons and their rights are respectable. Each helps to explain one part of the law and struggles with another. They have implications for the language used in discussions of assignation and rights in security but few, if any, implications for the substance of the rules used. Once the basics of both systems are properly grasped, it becomes possible to translate from one view to the other without too much difficulty. The rest of this chapter and the chapters on rights in security are written from a Gaian perspective, although the

---

27 See further Gretton 'Ownership and its objects' (n 25 above) at 840–844.

alert reader will have noticed the Pandectist approach in the diagrams at paragraph **3.43**.

Kinds of property: heritable and moveable; corporeal and incorporeal

3.56 As well as recognising different kinds of rights, Scots law recognises different kinds of property. The distinction between corporeal and incorporeal things has already been discussed. There is a further distinction between heritable and moveable property.

3.57 The heritable–moveable distinction is basically a distinction between land and rights in land on the one hand, and everything else on the other. In many systems, the equivalent of heritable property is called immoveable property because land cannot really be moved. Of course, it would be possible to dig up a lot of the soil from a plot of land, put it in a lorry and drive it away but the digging up of the soil would separate it from the land. This separation of the soil from the earth would mean it was no longer part of the land and therefore no longer heritable. As well as land itself, rights in land are heritable: so servitudes or rights in security over land are examples of incorporeal heritable property.

3.58 The term heritable derives from the old Scots law of succession, under which the land passed to the heir, while the moveable property passed to an executor who administered it according to either the deceased's will or the law of intestate succession. There are some examples of heritable property not connected to land,[28] but they are not important for the purposes of this book.

3.59 Combining the two divisions of types of property gives four possible categories:

Corporeal heritable	Incorporeal heritable
Corporeal moveable	Incorporeal moveable

While the basic principles remain the same, the details of the rules about how property is dealt with vary depending on which of the four categories a right falls into.

ACQUIRING AND DEALING WITH PROPERTY

Publicity principle

3.60 Since property rights affect third parties it is important that they are discoverable by third parties, particularly potential purchasers. For

28 Erskine, *Institute*, III.ii.6.

that reason, a public act is usually required for the constitution or transfer of real rights. Until that act is completed, the grantee will not acquire the real right.

3.61 Publicity benefits third parties but it imposes costs on the parties to the transaction because it means doing something extra for the sake of notifying others. There is a balance to be struck between the effectiveness of the notice and the burden it puts on the transacting parties. Where this balance lies varies depending on the type of property and the nature of the transaction (as will be discussed below). The principal means of publicity are registration and change of possession.

Specificity principle

3.62 The other general principle which plays an important role in the rules on acquiring and dealing with property is the principle of specificity. Since real rights are rights in particular things, it is important to know which thing is being burdened or transferred. For this reason, a disposition[29] of 'some of my land' could not effectively transfer anything. The Keeper of the Register would not know which plot was being transferred. This principle explains why section 16 of the Sale of Goods Act 1979 requires goods to be ascertained before ownership can pass. Like the publicity principle, the specificity principle is not always strictly adhered to. The main exception is found in section 20A of the Sale of Goods Act 1979 and it is discussed in Chapter 6: Sale of Goods below.

Original acquisition

3.63 Most property which is relevant to commercial life is already owned by someone and is acquired by a grant from that person. However, it is possible to acquire property without the involvement of any prior owner, indeed, without there being any prior owner at all. This is known as original acquisition of property. It is so called because the owner acquires a fresh right to the property rather than having someone else's right transferred to him.

3.64 There are a number of different mechanisms for original acquisition. The key common factor is that, in every case, the legal effect results from some physical act done to the property, which explains the irrelevance of any prior owner. The terms for the various mechanisms by which this occur may look rather puzzling. They are derived from Latin and this area of property law draws very heavily on Roman law.

Occupation

3.65 The simplest method of original acquisition is occupation. If property is ownerless, anyone may acquire it by taking possession of it with

---

29 The special term for the voluntary transfer of land. The deed by which land is disponed is known as a disposition.

the intention of becoming owner. This principle derives from Roman law and is expressed in the maxim *quod nullius est fit occupantis*. However, it is of very limited relevance.

3.66 It has no application to land because land in Scotland cannot be ownerless. Where no other owner can be identified, land is deemed to be in the ownership of the Crown. This is a remnant of the now abolished feudal system of land tenure. Secondly, occupation cannot apply to property which has been owned. If property has been owned and is then lost or abandoned, another maxim applies to it: *quod nullius est fit domini regis* – what is owned by no-one belongs to the Crown. That means that even when property is lost or abandoned, it does not become ownerless.

3.67 Taking these two factors together, only moveable property which has never been owned is liable to occupation. Wild animals form a slight exception to this. It is impossible to tell whether a wild animal has never been captured or has been captured and escaped. Therefore, wild animals are treated as capable of occupation even if they have been owned and then escape.

Specification

3.68 Where items are taken and used to make a new thing (a *nova species*: thus the name) specification occurs. Of course, if the items belong to the person who makes them, there is no issue. If Spencer bakes bread using flour, yeast and water which belong to him then the ingredients are his and so is the loaf. The law of specification addresses what happens when a new thing is made from someone else's property, as where Spencer uses Olivia's flour and yeast to make his loaf. The rationale for the rule is that the raw materials have ceased to exist and that the person who made the new thing is entitled to it, although the owner of the raw material is entitled to compensation from the acquirer.[30]

3.69 Where the process is irreversible and the manufacturer is not aware that the property belongs to another, the manufacturer becomes the owner of the new thing.[31] Where, however, the process can be reversed, ownership remains with the owner of the raw materials. So Spencer owns the loaf, even if he uses Olivia's ingredients. If, however, he had made a salad by adding some cherry tomatoes to some mixed leaves which belonged to Olivia, she would remain owner of the leaves because it would be easy enough to pick out the tomatoes and thus return things to their former state.

Accession

3.70 A similar logic is apparent in accession. This applies where one thing becomes attached to another in such a way as to be subsumed into

---

30 *International Banking Corporation v Ferguson, Shaw & Sons* 1910 SC 182.
31 Bell, *Principles* § 1298; *McDonald v Provan (of Scotland Street) Ltd* 1960 SLT 231.

it. The thing which is subsumed (the accessory) becomes part of the other thing (the principal). The result is that the accessory ceases to have an existence independent of the principal. This in turn means that, if the accessory belongs to one person and the principal to another, the owner of the accessory will lose his or her right of ownership because the object of the right will disappear. As a matter of law, nothing new is acquired by the owner of the principal: the whole point of the doctrine is that the identity of the principal remains the same. Thus where paint is used to paint a wall, the paint becomes part of the wall. However, the operation of accession may significantly increase the value of the principal.

3.71 There are three elements to accession: attachment, functional subordination and permanence.[32] All must be present in some degree for accession to take place. The need for attachment is obvious: without it there would still be two separate objects. Functional subordination is important because it provides guidance as to which of two objects is the principal and which is the accessory. In some cases this is obvious: moveables accede to land rather than the other way around. Where there are two moveables, however, working out which has acceded to the other is important because it is the former owner of the principal who becomes owner of the item. Functional subordination is not the same as value. A diamond may be worth very much more than the ring it sits in but it is nonetheless functionally subordinate to it.[33] The better view is that the parties' intentions are not relevant to the operation of accession. Unless the attachment has some degree of permanence, one object can hardly be said to become part of the other. If the three elements of attachment, functional subordination and permanence are present, the fact that the person who did the attaching did not intend that accession should operate is irrelevant.

3.72 Where an object is productive, the items produced by the object belong to its owner. So, if Bob owns a cow and it has a calf, the calf belongs to Bob. If he has an apple tree, the apples belong to him. This is sometimes said to be accession by fruits. This title is somewhat perplexing since these processes are the opposite of accession: one thing is coming out of another rather than being subsumed by it.[34] Nonetheless, the rule has commonsense appeal. It is difficult to see who else could reasonably be owner of the new thing.

Confusion and commixtion

3.71 In specification and accession, one right of ownership is lost because its object has disappeared. Commixtion and confusion cover the case where properties belonging to two different people are mixed together in such a way that it is impossible to separate what belongs to one owner from what belongs to another. In both cases, the result is that

32 Reid, *Law of Property*, para 571.
33 Stair, *Institutions*, II.i.39.
34 Stair, *Institutions*, II.i.34.

the 'contributing' owners become common owners of the result of the combination.[35]

3.74 Confusion applies to liquids: so if 600 litres of petrol belonging to Enid are mixed with 300 litres of petrol belonging to Freddy the resulting 900 litres are owned in common by Freddy and Enid. Enid has a two-thirds share and Freddy gets a one-third share. Commixtion applies to solids: so if five tonnes of wheat belonging to George are mixed with five tonnes which belong to Helen, the resulting ten tonnes of wheat are owned in common by George and Helen. Each has a half share.

Prescription

3.75 The methods of original acquisition discussed so far operate more or less instantaneously. They are the law's response to an action which fundamentally affects the physical state of the thing in question. There is, however, another method of original acquisition which only happens after a long period of time: positive prescription. Positive prescription only affects land and the requirements vary slightly depending on whether ownership or a subordinate real right is being acquired.

3.76 To acquire ownership of a piece of land, it is necessary to have a foundation writ and to possess it as of right, 'openly, peaceably and without judicial interruption' for ten years. A foundation writ is a registered deed (usually a disposition) which would have entitled the possessor to the land had it been effective.[36] From this it becomes evident that the effect of positive prescription here is to cure a void transfer. This process is, however, excluded in cases where the deed is forged and the grantee is aware of that fact.[37] Suppose that Bob forges Bill's signature on a disposition to Carol (who is unaware of the forgery). Carol registers the disposition and takes possession of the property. These acts will not make Carol the owner because the disposition was not granted to her by Bill, the owner of the property. If, however, she possesses the land for ten years after registering the disposition, she will become the owner of the plot instead of Bill.

3.77 The possession requirements are designed to ensure that the owner has opportunity to challenge the prescriptive acquirer's right. The possession needs to be as of right so that someone who only possesses the plot because the owner lets them do so will not acquire it by prescription. The possession needs to be open so that the owner is alerted to the need to challenge the possessor's right to the plot. Possession is peaceable and without juridical interruption if no-one challenges the possessor's right to possess. Taken together, the requirements mean that the possessor is behaving as owner and no-one with a relevant interest has ques-

---

35 Bell, *Principles* § 1298.
36 Prescription and Limitation (Scotland) Act 1973, s 1(1).
37 1973 Act, s 1(2)(b).

tioned this for ten years. That being the case, it makes sense to bring the legal situation into line with the facts on the ground.

3.78 In the majority of cases where it operates, positive prescription cures voidness of which the grantee is not aware. However, it also plays a role in bringing land whose owner cannot be traced back into circulation. This is done by registering an *a non domino* disposition (that is, a disposition by a non-owner) and waiting for the clock to run out. Of course, for this to operate, the Keeper must be willing to accept the *a non domino* disposition. The Keeper will only accept such a disposition if the land has been in possession of the *a non domino* disponer and/or the grantee for at least a year counting back from the application to register the deed. Further, the Keeper will only accept the registration if notification of the application to register has been given to the person who is currently entitled to the property or, if no such person can be traced, to the Crown.[38] If the Keeper decides to accept the deed for registration, she must notify the person entitled to the property or the Crown, if this is reasonably practicable.[39] These requirements are designed to ensure that the property is truly out of circulation before the *a non domino* disposition can be registered and that, even after this happens, the owner has every opportunity to step in and assert his or her right to the property.

3.79 It is also possible to acquire subordinate real rights by positive prescription.[40] Possession still requires to be open, peaceable and without judicial interruption, and as of right, but requires to be for twenty years rather than ten.[41] In practice, the most important subordinate real rights acquired by prescription are rights of way, which are a type of servitude which allow the holder to access his property by passing over the burdened property. In contrast to other subordinate real rights, it is possible to acquire a servitude by prescriptive possession without having registered a relevant deed.[42] For servitudes, the notion of possession is somewhat difficult: the servitude is not a thing which can be held. However, exercise of the right is taken to be equivalent to possession.

Voluntary grant of real rights

3.80 Since most property which is commercially significant is already owned by someone, the most important method for acquisition of property or of a subordinate real right is by a grant from someone else (usually the owner of the property). This is sometimes known as derivative acquisition because the acquirer's right derives from someone else's right. Thus where Olivia grants a disposition of a piece of land to Albert and he registers it, Albert's right is derived from Olivia. Similarly, if Albert

---

38 Land Registration etc (Scotland) Act 2012, s 43(3)–(4).
39 2012 Act, s 45(1)–(2).
40 1973 Act, ss 2–3.
41 1973 Act, ss 2(1)(a) and 3(1) and (2).
42 1973 Act, s 3(2).

then grants a standard security to Bank of Alba Ltd, the bank's right is derived from Albert's.

3.81 The basis for recognition of these grants is the owner's freedom to deal with property as he or she wishes. For the same reason, the holder of a subordinate real right is entitled to discharge the right and thus to disencumber the property.

3.82 The fact that the acquisition derives from the granter's act implies three requirements for an effective grant: the granter must intend to bring the transfer about; since real rights are being transferred or created, this intention must usually be expressed in some formal, external act to give third parties notice of the right; and the granter must have the power to make the relevant grant (usually because he owns the property which is transferred or encumbered).

Intention

3.83 From the requirement of intention, it follows that if Victoria is physically forced to sign a deed which purports to transfer property to William, that deed will be ineffective. Ineffective grants are typically said to be void. Even if William complies with the requisite formalities, he will not become owner because Victoria did not consent to the transfer. Similarly, if Ivor intends to transfer a cow to David but delivers it to Daniel, who knows of this, Daniel will not acquire the cow because there was no intention to make him the owner.[43]

3.84 In most cases, the property which is being dealt with has some value. For that reason, the main focus of discussion is on the granter's intention. However, there may be situations where someone tries to make a grant to someone who does not want it. For instance, the property in question might be very expensive to maintain. Therefore, the consent of the acquirer is also required for a valid transfer. Since both granter and acquirer must consent to a transfer, it is commonly said that a transfer or real agreement is necessary.

3.85 Often, however, the acquirer's intention is less formally expressed than that of the granter. Thus, where land is disponed, the transferor's intention to transfer must be expressed in formal writing. The acquirer's intention, on the other hand, is inferred from their accepting delivery of the deed and presenting it for registration. Similarly, an assignor must express his or her intention to transfer a personal right to the assignee but very little is required of the assignee in terms of indicating consent to the transfer. It is even open to the assignor to make the intimation which completes the transfer.

---

43 Illustrated by the facts and result but not the reasoning in *Morrisson v Robertson* 1908 SC 332.

Formalities: heritable property

3.86 The intention to grant a real right usually requires some formal expression. In the case of heritable property, the formalities are quite extensive: the grant must be made in formal writing[44] and the written grant must usually be registered in the Land Register.[45] This writing can be either traditional writing on paper, subscribed with pen and ink,[46] or an electronic document authenticated by an electronic signature.[47] This serves to preserve the terms of the grant in a durable medium and as an 'indication of seriousness' which helps to ensure that grants made are truly intended. Registration is in a public register and is thus a mechanism for giving notice to third parties. The requirement of registration is an application of the publicity principle.

3.87 Failure to register can have serious consequences if the seller resells the property or becomes insolvent. Until registration, the seller remains the owner and thus retains the power to transfer the property. As discussed at paras **3.100–3.101**, the fact that the seller is still the owner also means that the property is open to seizure by the seller's creditors.

Formalities: corporeal moveable property

3.88 There is no general register of corporeal moveable property.[48] The main reason for this is that corporeal moveables have tended to be of less value than land. For the same reason, there was less concern about preserving the terms of any grant or making sure that grants were seriously intended. At Scots common law, the only applicable formality was delivery. Both constitution of rights in security and transfers of ownership were effected by delivery accompanied by intention on the part of granter and grantee.[49] This remains the main rule for Scots law: where corporeal moveables are transferred as a gift or bartered, ownership will not pass before delivery. The rule is, however, subject to one very significant exception.

---

44 Requirements of Writing (Scotland) Act 1995, s 1(2)(b).
45 Registration of Leases (Scotland) Act 1857, s 20B; Conveyancing and Feudal Reform (Scotland) Act 1970, ss 11 and 14–17; Land Registration (Scotland) etc Act 2012, ss 50–51. There are some exceptions to the requirement for registration. Constitution of a lease of less than 20 years is completed by taking possession: Registration of Leases (Scotland) Act 1857, s 1. Where a servitude is granted, it may be completed by exercise of the servitude right rather than by registration: *Campbell's Trs v Corporation of Glasgow* (1902) 4 F 752 at 757 per Lord Kinnear.
46 Requirements of Writing (Scotland) Act 1995, s 2(1).
47 1995 Act, s 9B(1). An electronic signature is a mechanism similar to the chip and PIN devices used for payment by debit or credit card.
48 The register of keepers of vehicles kept by the Driver and Vehicle Licensing Authority does not have property law effect because it is a register of keepers rather than owners. There is a register of ships, and dealings with ships are effected by registration in that register: Merchant Shipping Act 1995, Sch 1, para 1. There is also a Register of Aircraft Mortgages in which security rights over aircraft may be registered: Mortgaging of Aircraft Order 1972 (SI 1972/1268).
49 Bell, *Commentaries*, II, 11.

3.89 Victorian legislative reforms which are now embodied in the Sale of Goods Act 1979 removed the requirement of delivery for transfers which are made in pursuance of contracts of sale. Section 17 of the 1979 Act provides that, where goods are sold, ownership will pass from seller to buyer at the moment when the parties intend as long as the goods are specific or ascertained (i.e. as long as the principle of specificity is satisfied). This means that ownership can pass before delivery or, if the parties prefer, at some point after delivery (usually when the price has been paid). An agreement to delay transfer until the price or other debts owed by the buyer to the seller have been paid is known as a retention of title clause.

3.90 Often, there will be no discernible intention regarding the moment of transfer. If that is the case, then section 18 supplies five rules which effectively create presumptions about when ownership is to pass. They are discussed in Chapter 6: Sale of Goods.

Formalities: incorporeal moveable property

3.91 Incorporeal moveable property cannot be delivered because there is no physical thing which can be handed over. Of course, intention to transfer still requires to be expressed and, in the case of intellectual property rights, this requires to be done in writing.[50]

3.92 In some special cases, there is a register on which transactions can be publicised.[51] It should be noted that the existence of such a register does not necessarily imply a straightforward transfer by registration regime, like the one which applies to land, but even in such cases, those who rely on the register will generally be protected from unregistered dealings.[52] One of the most important instances of the use of a register to publicise dealings with incorporeal property is company shares.

3.93 Company shares can be transferred only by changing the entry in the shareholders' register maintained by the company. A share certificate (in effect an extract from the register of shareholders) is sufficient evidence, unless the contrary is shown, of the shareholder's right to the relevant shares.[53] Since it is only prima facie evidence, a true owner (e.g. a person from whom a share certificate is stolen by a thief who succeeds in having his name inserted on the shareholders' register) is entitled to vindicate his rights against a person wrongly recorded as the

50 Registered Designs Act 1949, s 15B(3); Patents Act 1977, s 31(6); Copyright, Designs and Patents Act 1988, s 90(3); Trade Marks Act 1994, s 24(3).
51 Registered Designs Act 1949, s 17; Patents Act 1977, s 32; Trade Marks Act 1994, s 63; Companies Act 2006, ss 113 and 771. The fact that most shares are held and traded through intermediaries (effectively bodies which hold shares in trust for those who want to invest in the companies) limits the significance of the companies' register of members in those cases.
52 Registered Designs Act 1949, ss 15B(2) and 19; Patents Act 1977, s 33(1); Trade Marks Act 1994, s 26(3).
53 Companies Act 2006, s 768; s 127.

owner and to have the register corrected. However, a bona fide purchaser of shares is entitled to rely on a certificate issued by the company as evidence of the seller's right to the shares. If the seller is not in fact entitled to sell the shares, the buyer cannot be registered as a shareholder but is entitled to damages from the company at the market price of the shares.[54]

3.94   Where there is no register and no possibility of delivery, another mechanism for publication must be found. For the transfer of personal rights, that method is intimation to the debtor. So, if David owes Cecil £50 and Cecil wants to transfer his right to payment to Angela, two stages are necessary: a transfer agreement known as an assignation and intimation of the assignation to David.

3.95   As with corporeal property, failure to complete the second step exposes the grantee to the risk either of transfer by the assignor to a second assignee who intimates first, or of the assignor's insolvency. Further, intimation plays a role in protecting the debtor from prejudice. Until intimation is made, payment to the assignor will relieve the debtor of liability. Further, the debtor is entitled to set off against the assigned claim any debt owed by the assignor to the debtor which was constituted prior to intimation.

The 'nemo plus' rule: power to make the relevant grant

3.96   In addition to an intention to make the grant properly expressed, it is required that the granter has the power to make it. This is sometimes expressed by the maxim *nemo plus juris ad alium transferre potest quam ipse haberet*: no one can transfer to another a greater right than he himself has.[55] If Ferdinand purports to dispone a field which belongs to Geraldine, his action will be ineffective. Geraldine owns the field so she is the one with power to transfer it or burden it with subordinate real rights. The rule is not without exceptions, which are discussed below, but it remains a cornerstone of Scots property law.

3.97   In the majority of cases, the only person with the power to make the relevant grant is the owner of the asset affected by the grant. However, that is not always the case. Many rights in security empower the security holder to sell the relevant property if the debt is not paid. When the security holder does so, he or she is able to transfer the property from the current owner to the buyer. What is necessary, therefore, is the power to transfer or burden the thing. The owner has that power but it

---

54 *Re Bahia and San Francisco Railway Co Ltd* (1868) 3 QB 584 at 594. In English law, the company's liability is based on the principle of estoppel: it cannot deny the title of the seller because the certificate issued by the company causes the buyer to believe that the seller owned the shares. It is likely that the same rule would be applied in Scotland based on personal bar (which is the Scottish equivalent of this type of estoppel).

55 A briefer but broadly equivalent maxim is *nemo dat quod non habet*: no-one can give what he does not have.

can also be granted to others. When the right in security is granted, the owner grants a conditional power to transfer to the security holder. (It is conditional because the security holder will only have the power to sell if the debtor fails to pay the debt.)

3.98 The *nemo plus* rule means that it is important for potential purchasers to know that the person they are buying from owns the property (or has the power to sell it for some other reason). The general rule is that a non-owner cannot make anyone else the owner. Therefore, if you buy from a non-owner, the true owner will be able to come and demand what you bought back from you. It does not matter that you really believed that the seller owned the relevant asset. Of course, you will have a right to damages from the seller but he or she might have made off with the money by then.

3.99 It should also be borne in mind that a granter may have the power to make an effective transfer although he acts wrongfully in making the transfer. Making the grant was a breach of an obligation. However, since the obligation was not owed by the grantee, he or she may be able to rely on the grant despite its wrongful nature.

3.100 To take a simple example: Sophie concludes a contract with Florence to sell her flat for £150,000. The next day, Gary (who is unaware of the contract) offers to buy the flat for £200,000. Sophie decides that she could do with the extra money so she quickly concludes a second contract with Gary and dispones the flat to him. Gary registers the disposition, still unaware of the prior right. Sophie's conduct is wrongful: she has breached her contract with Florence. In that sense, she was not entitled to act as she did.

3.101 However, her grant to Gary is effective. Sophie was still the owner of the flat when she made the grant to Gary. She still had the ownership and so what she gave to Gary was no greater than what she had herself. Therefore, the *nemo plus* rule is not a problem for Gary. Sophie's breach of contract will of course make her liable to Florence in damages since the transfer does not set aside her contractual obligations.

The 'nemo plus' rule: scope of the right

3.102 The rule says that no one can transfer a *greater* right than he himself has. This has implications, not only for cases where a granter has no right at all but also for cases where the granter's right is limited. If Alf has a servitude over Blackacre, he can transfer the servitude to someone else. However, having the servitude does not entitle Alf to make anyone the owner of Blackacre. Similarly, if Tessa has a lease of a shop for 30 years, she may be entitled to transfer it to someone else but when she does so, she can only transfer an entitlement for so much of the lease as is still to run. In other words, no-one can expand the scope of a right by transferring it to another.

3.103 This aspect of the *nemo plus* rule is particularly important in the context of assignation where it is expressed in its own maxim *assignatus utitur jure auctoris*: the assignee uses the right of the author. The *assignatus utitur* rule (or rather, the *assignatus utitur* aspect of the *nemo plus* rule) has important implications for debtor protection.

3.104   Rights are assets which, in the absence of any special rule, the rightholder is entitled to transfer without the consent of the debtor. The justification for this is that the right belongs to the rightholder and persons are generally entitled to deal with their assets as they see fit. However, since the debtor does not have a say in whether the transfer takes place, he or she should not be prejudiced by its occurrence.

3.105   The *assignatus utitur* rule plays a key role in ensuring this protection. It means that any defences which the debtor had against the assignor may also be invoked against the assignee. If David owes Colin £100 under a contract for the supply of goods, David will typically be entitled to withhold payment until the goods are supplied. Colin can assign his right to Agnes before delivering the goods but, if he does so, Agnes will not be able to force David to pay unless Colin has supplied the goods.

Transfer by non-owners: currency and negotiable instruments

3.106   The normal rule is that a grant by someone who lacks the power to make the relevant grant is ineffective.[56] In some circumstances, the law will protect those who deal with certain granters who lack the power to make the relevant grant. The main reason for these protections is to facilitate commerce. Were such protection not afforded, expensive and time-consuming attempts to establish sellers' rights would need to be undertaken. This would be bad for the economy as a whole.

3.107   The commonest example of this kind of rule is so deeply embedded that most people do not even think about it: cash payment. If Anna sells something to Brian and he pays her in notes or coins, she will not ask him to demonstrate that he owns them. It is quite possible that Brian may have stolen them or found them on the street but in the absence of special circumstances such as notes which are stained with special ink, Anna would have no way of knowing this. For this reason, the presumption of ownership which generally arises from possession is much stronger in the case of money and the person from whom Brian stole the money would not be able to reclaim it from Anna.[57]

3.108   Similar protections are afforded to recipients of negotiable instruments.[58] These are documents which embody a right to payment. One of the purposes of this embodiment is to allow the right to be transferred by transferring the document. The ease with which negotiable

---

56 E.g. Sale of Goods Act 1979, s 21(1).

57 Stair, *Institutions*, II.i.34; Bell, *Principles* § 1333.

58 Negotiable instruments are discussed in more detail in Chapter 9: Payment Obligations.

instruments can be transferred is enhanced by the fact that anyone who receives a bill of exchange in good faith (i.e. without knowing that the transferor does not own it) and for value is treated as the owner of the instrument.[59]

3.109 The protection afforded to those who receive cash and negotiable instruments is very extensive. Protection for those who receive other types of property is more limited. The protections cover situations where the third party is particularly likely to be misled into thinking that the granter has the power to transfer the asset in question or to grant a subordinate real right in the asset.

Transfer by non-owners: Sale of Goods Act 1979

3.110 In the Sale of Goods Act 1979, there are three main cases where buyers are protected: where the owner is personally barred from denying the seller's authority to sell; where ownership has passed but the seller is still in possession; and where ownership has not passed but the buyer is already in possession.

3.111 The first case is addressed in section 21(1). It sets out the basic *nemo plus* rule but then makes an exception for cases 'where the owner of the goods is by his conduct precluded from denying the seller's authority to sell'. This covers the situation where the owner has given the impression that the seller had authority to sell and this has been relied on by the buyer. So if Olivia leads Bertie to believe that her dog is in fact owned by Sidney, section 21(1) would mean that Bertie would become owner if Sidney sold him the dog.

3.112 The other two situations, covered by sections 24 and 25, deal with the consequences of the abandonment of the delivery requirement. As noted at paragraph **3.89** above, the 1979 Act removed delivery as a requirement for transfer of ownership in sale situations. Delivery was a means of giving notice to third parties of the transfer. Once it was abandoned, it became more difficult for third parties to identify the owner of the goods. Sections 24 and 25 protect third parties who are misled. In both cases, the third-party acquirer needs to be in good faith (i.e. to believe that the person in possession is the owner) and to have taken delivery of the goods.[60]

3.113 Section 24 deals with the case where ownership has passed but there has been no delivery. In such a situation, the seller remains in pos-

---

59 Bills of Exchange Act 1882, s 38(2).
60 Both sections refer to 'delivery or transfer' to the third party, which seems to suggest that transfer is an alternative to delivery. However, in *Michael Gerson (Leasing) Ltd v Wilkinson* [2000] EWCA Civ 250, [2001] QB 514, the Court of Appeal suggested that transfer of possession was necessary in all cases, although constructive delivery (where the transferee acquires possession by virtue of the fact that the person who has physical control of the goods acknowledges that they are held on the transferee's behalf) was accepted as sufficient.

session but a third party dealing with the seller has no way of knowing that the seller no longer owns the goods in question. A third party who buys the goods from the seller in good faith and takes delivery of them is protected. Section 24 says that such a delivery 'has the same effect as if the person making the delivery or transfer were expressly authorised by the owner of the goods to make the same'. Thus, the seller is treated as the first buyer's agent and so a transfer is effected from the first to the second buyer.

3.114   For example, Olivia sells her dog to Sidney but Sidney asks her to keep it for the weekend when he will be away on holiday. During the weekend, she sells the dog a second time to Bertie who is in good faith and takes possession. The application of section 18, rule 1 means that Sidney became the owner of the dog as soon as the contract with Olivia was concluded. However, section 24 operates to protect Bertie so ownership passes from Sidney to Bertie.

3.115   Section 25 deals with the converse case: where there is a retention of title clause meaning that the goods are still owned by the seller but the seller has allowed the buyer to take possession of them. As with section 24, it would be difficult for a third party to know about this arrangement.

3.116   The wording of section 25 is a little complex but, broadly stated, it works in the same way as section 24: the buyer in possession is treated as the seller's agent and so ownership is transferred directly from the seller to the third party. So if Olivia sells the dog to Sidney but they agree that she will remain owner for a trial period of two weeks, so Sidney can see if she and the dog get along, Olivia will retain ownership although she delivers the dog to Sidney. If, however, Sidney sells the dog to Bertie after two days, Bertie will become owner provided that he is in good faith and takes delivery. Ownership would pass directly from Olivia to Bertie.

3.117   Subsection (2) of section 25 sets out an important exception to the protection in section 25. It does not apply where the buyer in possession had acquired the goods under a consumer credit agreement. 'Consumer credit agreement' is defined in section 8(1) of the Consumer Credit Act 1974. Confusingly, the definition does not require that the credit be given to a consumer. It simply defines a consumer credit agreement as an agreement under which an individual gets credit of any amount. Equally bizarrely, the Consumer Credit Act 1974 defines the term 'individual' as including partnerships of two or three partners, at least one of whom is not a body corporate, and unincorporated associations.[61]

3.118   Since the most common reason for retention of title is that the goods have been supplied on credit, this means that section 25 protection will usually be limited to third parties who buy from companies or

61 Consumer Credit Act 1974, s 189.

limited liability partnerships. The situation is further complicated by section 27 of the Hire Purchase Act 1964. That section provides equivalent protection to that found in section 25 of the 1979 Act for third parties who buy cars from hire purchasers or buyers in protection. Unlike section 25 of the 1979 Act, section 27 of the 1964 Act does not exclude consumer credit agreements but its protection is limited to third parties who are 'private purchasers'. That means that it does not extend to third parties whose business is the sale of motor vehicles or the financing of such sales.[62] None of this reflects well on the architects of the relevant legislation. It may be clarified somewhat by some examples.

3.119 Edward sells some computers to Cawdors and Associates, a firm of solicitors which operates as a partnership. The computers are supplied on credit and Edward and Cawdors agree that ownership will remain with Edward until he is paid. Cawdors sell the computers on to Peterson Thirlstane, another firm of solicitors. Cawdors go bust and Edward tries to get the computers back from Peterson Thirlstane. Can Peterson Thirlstane rely on section 25?

3.120 Cawdors were a buyer in possession and they delivered the goods to Peterson Thirlstane who were in good faith, so all the requirements of section 25(1) were fulfilled. However, Cawdor had received the goods on credit and, as a partnership, they are an individual in terms of the Consumer Credit Act 1974. Since they are an individual and they received the goods on credit, this is a consumer credit agreement within the terms of section 8 of the 1974 Act. That in turn means that the exception in section 25(2) applies, so Peterson Thirlstane are not protected.

3.121 If, however, Cawdors and Associates had been a limited liability partnership rather than a general partnership, Peterson Thirlstane would have been safe. A limited liability partnership is a body corporate[63] so it is not an individual in terms of the 1974 Act. That means that the supply to it of computers on credit would not be a consumer credit agreement in terms of section 8 of the 1974 Act. Therefore, the exception in section 25(2) of the Sale of Goods Act 1979 would not apply. Since Peterson Thirlstane fulfil the requirements of section 25(1), they would be protected.

3.122 Alternatively, if Edward had supplied cars rather than computers to Cawdors and these had been sold on, Peterson Thirlstane would be entitled to rely on section 27 of the Hire Purchase Act 1964 since Peterson Thirlstane's business does not involve dealing in motor vehicles or financing such dealing.

Transfer and grant by non-owners: Land Registration etc (Scotland) Act 2012

3.123 Most transactions which affect land must be registered so third

---

62 See the definition of 'trade or finance purchaser' and of 'private purchaser' in the Hire Purchase Act 1964, s 29.
63 Limited Liability Partnerships Act 2000, s 1(2).

parties have notice of what has happened. This might be thought to be all the protection potential purchasers would need against dealing with a non-owner who purports to sell them land or grant a subordinate real right over it. If every transaction is publicly registered, it should be possible to work out who owns each piece of land. However, mistakes occur even in the process of registration. It may be, for instance, that a fraudster has forged a disposition and managed to convince the Keeper of the Register to enter him or her as owner when in fact they are not. A third party consulting the register would then be misled.

3.124   The Land Registration etc (Scotland) Act 2012 ('the 2012 Act') contains rules which protect third parties who transact with those who appear from the register to be owners but in fact are not. This makes the register more reliable for those who are buying property and thus facilitates dealings with land. Of course, protecting the buyer who relies on an inaccurate entry on the register has a downside. If the buyer becomes owner, the former owner loses his or her right. This downside also exists in relation to currency and corporeal moveables but it has been taken more seriously in the context of land because land tends to be more valuable. The 2012 Act makes provision, not only for the protection of those who rely on the register but also for the compensation of those who lose out as a result of that protection.

3.125   There are two levels of protection for those who rely on the register: a money guarantee from the state and validation of void grants. For the sake of simplicity, the transfer of ownership will be used as an example but the 2012 Act also protects other grantees.

3.126   The money guarantee is known as the Keeper's warranty. When the Keeper accepts a putative transferee's application for registration, she warrants to the applicant that the register is correct in showing him or her as owner and that none of the subordinate real rights which should be shown on the register as affecting the property have been missed out.[64] The Keeper may exclude or restrict the warranty in circumstances where it is appropriate (usually because of doubts about some aspect of the rights claimed by the applicant).[65] If it turns out that the applicant did not become the owner, perhaps because the register was inaccurate in showing that the person who granted the disposition to the transferee was the owner, then the register will be rectified to reflect the true position[66] and the transferee who made the application will be entitled to compensation from the Keeper.[67]

3.127   Bob sees a nice house in an area he would like to move into. He checks the Land Register and finds that the owner is Frank, who was registered as owner and moved in one month ago. Frank agrees to sell

---

64 Land Registration etc (Scotland) Act 2012, s 73.
65 2012 Act, s 75.
66 2012 Act, s 80.
67 2012 Act, s 77(1).

the house to him. Bob pays the price, moves in and registers his disposition. Two months later, Olivia appears. She says that she is the true owner of the property and that Frank appeared on the register because he had forged her signature on a disposition. If she can prove that this is the case, the register will be rectified and Bob will get a pay-out under the Keeper's warranty. Of course, since Olivia owns the house, Bob will have to move out unless he comes to some arrangement with Olivia.

3.128 The Keeper's liability is excluded in a number of circumstances, set out in section 78 of the 2012 Act. The most important exceptions are set out in paragraphs (b) and (c). An applicant who knows that the register will not be accurate when his or her entitlement is entered is not entitled to compensation. Neither is an applicant who caused the Keeper to make an inaccurate entry by a failure to take reasonable care in making the application. So, if Bob knew that Frank was not the owner at the time when he registered his disposition, his right to compensation under the Keeper's warranty would be excluded.

3.129 Assuming that none of the section 78 grounds applies, Bob may well be grateful for the money since Frank is likely to be long gone and the chances of recovering damages from him may be minimal. However, what Bob wanted was the house not the money. There are circumstances in which Bob would get the property rather than mere monetary compensation: that is the second level of protection. Of course, giving that protection to Bob involves taking the property away from Olivia, so more stringent conditions are applied.

3.130 The conditions are set out in section 86(3) of the 2012 Act. As with the Keeper's warranty, Bob requires to be in good faith and the disposition needs to be accepted by the Keeper without excluding warranty. The extra requirement is that property had either been possessed for one year by the disponer; or, alternatively, the disponer and the applicant had possessed the property for a year between them without the inaccuracy being drawn to the Keeper's attention.

3.131 So, if Frank had acquired the house eighteen months before selling it to Bob, then on registration, Bob would become the owner of the house.[68] Alternatively, if Frank had taken possession one month before the sale but more than eleven months expired before Olivia returned to challenge Bob's right, he would be safe. In that case, Bob would become owner eleven months after moving in because that would be the point when the combined possession of Bob and Frank reached one year.[69] In either case, the result is that ownership passes directly from Olivia to Bob. Frank never was and never becomes the owner. If that happens, Olivia is entitled to compensation from the Keeper.[70]

---

68 2012 Act, s 86(4)(a).
69 2012 Act, s 86(4)(b).
70 2012 Act, s 94.

3.132   There are equivalent rules which protect assignees of registered leases[71] and grantees of servitudes.[72] Grantees of standard securities are only protected by the Keeper's warranty. The reason for this is that, unlike the other rights just mentioned, money from the Keeper can give the grantee of security complete satisfaction. All that the standard security entitled its holder to do was to sell the property for the satisfaction of a debt. It should be a matter of indifference whether the money is generated by the sale of the property or comes from the Keeper's funds; therefore, there is no good reason for curing the standard security and thus burdening the real owner's title.

Voidable grants

3.133   The problems discussed so far are problems which would mean that the grantee did not acquire the right at all: if there is no intention to make the grant, if the proper formalities are not complied with or if the granter did not have the power to make the relevant grant, the result is that the grant is void. That means that it is totally ineffective and no right is conferred on the grantee.

3.134   However, there is another class of cases where there is a problem with the grant but it has less drastic consequences. Some grants are said to be not void but voidable. This means that the grant is initially effective but that someone has a personal right against the grantee which entitles him or her to have the grant reversed. Usually, the reason for this is that the grant involved a wrong against the person who is entitled to have it reversed.

3.135   The simplest example is a fraudulently induced transfer. In that case, the transferor truly intends to transfer the property but that consent has been wrongfully obtained. For instance, Freddy might lie to Vanessa, telling her that he is her long-lost grandson. She might gift some land to him because she believes this. She really intended to transfer the land to him but that intention was induced by Freddy's fraud. Therefore the transfer is voidable at Vanessa's instance.

3.136   In many cases the granter is the person who is entitled to avoid the transaction but this is not necessarily the case. Some of the most important grounds of voidability involve cases where a third party is entitled to set the transaction aside.

3.137   If a creditor of the granter has used the diligence of inhibition against the granter, then any grant of a real right affecting heritable property will be voidable at that creditor's instance.[73] Similarly, grants made by an insolvent debtor which operate to the prejudice of his or her

---

71   2012 Act, s 88.
72   2012 Act, s 90.
73   See paras **9.35**–**9.42**.

creditors may be voidable at the instance of those creditors or of the insolvency official acting on their behalf.[74]

3.138 Further, although a contract of sale will not prevent the seller from transferring the subjects of sale to a third party or from burdening them if the buyer has not yet become owner, the grant to the third party may be voidable at the buyer's instance under the so-called 'offside goals rule'.[75] It allows the holder of a personal right to a real right (e.g. someone with a contractual right to have property transferred or to have a subordinate real right granted) to set aside a grant made by the party obliged under that right on two conditions. The first is that the grant which is challenged must prejudice the prior personal right in some way. This is fairly obvious in the case of a double sale: if the seller has transferred the object of the sale to someone else he will no longer be in a position to transfer it to the buyer. The second condition is that the subsequent grantee must either know about the prior personal right or have received the grant gratuitously.

3.139 Sidney contracts with Bertie to sell his house and then makes a second contract with Glenda for the sale of the house. Glenda registers her disposition first so she becomes the owner. However, Bertie will be able to set aside the transfer from Sidney to Glenda if he can show that Glenda knew of Bertie's contract with Sidney when she concluded *her* contract with Sidney. If the transfer to Glenda was not a sale but a gift, Bertie would be able to set it aside without the need to show that she was in bad faith.

3.140 The justification for the offside goals rule is connected to the rules allowing challenge to acts by an insolvent debtor. In each case, the actions of the granter would, if allowed to stand, defeat the interests of a prior personal right holder. Where the recipient of the second grant is in bad faith or gratuitous, this is not thought to be fair.

3.141 As far as the grantee is concerned, it makes little difference whether the grant is void or voidable: in either case challenge will lead to loss of enjoyment of the right or the property. However, the difference between a void grant, where the grantee receives no right and a voidable grant, which is effective albeit liable to be set aside, is very important for successors.

3.142 If the initial grant is void, then the *nemo plus* rule means that any attempt by the grantee to pass on what was granted will be ineffective and the owner will be able to recover the property even if it has been transferred on to a third party. If, however, the grant is merely voidable, then the grantee has the relevant right unless and until the grant is set aside. That means that he is able to transfer the right or burden the relevant property. The recipient of this further grant is not bound by the

---

74 See paras **10.25–10.54**.
75 *Rodger (Builders) Ltd v Fawdry* 1950 SC 483.

personal right which enables the first grant to be set aside. Therefore, the recipient of the further grant is safe.

3.143 So, if Glenda was in bad faith regarding the contract between Sidney and Bertie, the transfer to her would be voidable. Her right is precarious because Bertie could come along and have it set aside in court. If, however, she sells the house on to Tracy (who is unaware of any of this), Tracy will become the owner and will not be subject to any challenge from Bertie. Glenda was the owner and so she had the power to make Tracy the owner, and Bertie's personal right against Glenda is none of Tracy's business.

3.144 The recipient of the further grant will find him or herself vulnerable, however, if that grant was gratuitous or if the recipient was in bad faith (i.e. knew or should have known that his or her author's right was voidable). This rule is set out for sale of goods in section 23 of the 1979 Act but it also applies as a matter of common law to transfers of other kinds of property and to rights burdening them. So, if Tracy knew about the circumstances in which Glenda acquired the house, Bertie could set aside the transfer from Glenda to Tracy and the transfer from Sidney to Glenda. That would enable him to enforce his contract against Sidney and thus become owner of the house. Since the further grant defeats the personal right to reverse the transaction, Tracy's vulnerability, as being of bad faith and a gratuitous recipient, in this situation can be seen as an application of the offside goals rule.

Judicial acquisition

3.145 In certain circumstances, the court will intervene to transfer property from one person to another or to grant subordinate real rights. This is done in order to secure the fulfilment of the former owner's obligations. Although judicial acquisition occurs without the consent of, and usually against the will of, the former owner it is nonetheless a form of derivative acquisition. For that reason the *nemo plus* rule applies to judicial acquisition: the court can confer no better right on the acquirer than it takes from the former owner.

Adjudication in implement and execution by the sheriff clerk

3.146 The simplest form of judicial acquisition is adjudication in implement. It is a long-recognised but rarely used remedy by which effect can be given to an obligation to convey heritable property. It is done by raising an action in the Court of Session, the end result of which is that the relevant heritable property is declared by the court to belong to the pursuer,[76] which is then completed by registration.[77]

3.147 Adjudication in implement is a Court of Session remedy, which

---

76 J Graham Stewart, *A Treatise on the Law of Diligence* (Edinburgh, 1898) pp 667–69.
77 Titles to Land Consolidation (Scotland) Act 1868, s 62.

means that it is quite expensive for the parties involved. However, an equivalent is supplied by section 5A of the Sheriff Courts (Scotland) Act 1907, which provides that the sheriff may direct the sheriff clerk to execute the deed which should have been granted by the defender and that a deed so executed is effective as if it had been granted by the defender.

Reduction

3.148 Where a grant which affects heritable property is voidable, the personal right to reversal of the transaction is given effect by reduction. Like adjudication in implement, reduction of a transfer operates as a judicial conveyance. Reduction only takes effect against good faith third parties on registration of the decree in the public register.[78]

Insolvency officials

3.149 The appointment of a trustee in sequestration operates to vest everything in the debtor's patrimony (other than exempt assets) in the trustee in sequestration.[79] However, with regard to heritable property, this vesting requires to be completed by registration and the trustee must leave 28 days from the date of publication of the sequestration proceedings before registering.[80] The purpose of this window is to allow those to whom the bankrupt has granted real rights to register their grants. If they do not do so prior to the trustee's registration, they will not get the right which they were granted and will rank as unsecured creditors in the sequestration.

3.150 Where the insolvent debtor is a company rather than a natural person, the relevant mechanism for selling off the assets for creditors' benefit is liquidation rather than sequestration. In most cases, this does not involve transfer of assets to the insolvency official: the liquidator simply takes control of the company and uses that authority to dispose of the assets. However, the liquidator may apply to the court for an order which vests the company's property in him or her.[81]

Diligence

3.151 As well as acquiring ownership as a result of judicial action, it is also possible to acquire rights in security in the debtor's assets. The general Scots law term for this mechanism is diligence.[82] However, the term diligence has a slightly broader scope than judicial rights in security. It covers both freeze diligences, which restrict the debtor's capacity to make grants affecting his or her property, and seize diligences, which give the creditor a right in security in the asset against which diligence is done.

---

78 Conveyancing (Scotland) Act 1924, s 46.
79 Bankruptcy (Scotland) Act 1985, s 31. See paras **10.26–10.31**.
80 1985 Act, ss 31(1A)–(1B).
81 Insolvency Act 1986, s 145.
82 See generally Chapter 12: Judicial Security: Diligence.

Chapter 4

Agency

INTRODUCTION

What is agency?

4.01 The idea that one person can transact on behalf of another is essential to modern business practice. The person on whose behalf an action is done is known as the principal, the person doing the act is known as the agent. In this chapter, for the sake of ease of expression, the principal will be referred to with the feminine pronoun, the agent with the masculine, and the third party with the neuter pronoun ('it'). So, in the typical case, a male agent will be transacting on behalf of a female principal with a third party which is a juristic person.

4.02 The core idea is that the agent acts but this act is attributed to the principal; it is treated as if the principal had done it herself. If Peter is Alice's agent and he makes an offer to buy some whisky from Teldi Ltd on Alice's behalf then the contract which would result from Teldi's acceptance is one between Alice and Teldi. Peter made the offer but it is treated as if it was made by Alice.

4.03 Many of the materials which discuss agency do so in terms which suggest that all agents do is conclude contracts on behalf of their principals. However, it is clear that agents can also perform other juridical acts[1] on their principals' behalf: they can transfer property,[2] appeal decisions of courts or tribunals,[3] and make or accept payments.[4]

4.04 Many European systems have a broader notion of agency. They recognise that agents may carry out acts in the principal's name which are attributed to the latter. They call this direct agency. However, they also recognise a second category: indirect agency. In indirect agency, the agent acts in his own name but does so for the principal's benefit. Crudely put, the result is that acts done are attributed to the agent but agency rules regulate the relationship between principal and agent.

---

1 In this chapter, the term 'juridical act' is used in a very broad sense to mean any voluntary conduct intended to affect someone's legal position.
2 E.g. Factors Act 1889, s 2(1), applied to Scotland by Factors (Scotland) Act 1890, s 1(1).
3 *Goodall v Bilsland* 1909 SC 1152.
4 *International Sponge Importers Ltd v Andrew Watt & Sons* 1911 SC (HL) 57.

4.05 This means that, as far as the rest of the world is concerned, the principal has no part in the transaction. However, the agent will have a duty to communicate the benefit of the transaction to the principal and the principal will have a duty to indemnify the agent for any expenses associated with it. To return to the earlier example, if Peter was an indirect agent he would make the offer to buy the whisky in his own name. That would make him a party to the contract of sale so he would be liable to Teldi for the price and Teldi would be obliged to supply the whisky to him rather than to Alice. However, Peter would be obliged to pass the whisky on to Alice (or to deal with it in accordance with her instructions) and Alice would be obliged to pay Peter the price which he paid Teldi. Lawyers in the UK have tended not to classify this kind of arrangement as agency, although agency on behalf of an undisclosed principal (discussed at paras **4.56–4.66** below) might be regarded as half way between direct and indirect agency.

Why might an agent be used?

4.06 There are many reasons why a principal may prefer to transact through an agent rather than acting personally. The simplest and one of the commonest is lack of time. If Stella owns and runs a shop and wants to keep it open when she is at the wholesaler buying more stock, she might employ Alf to look after things while she is away. Since Stella is a sole trader, a customer who buys something from the shop when she is there makes a contract of sale with her. Is it any different if Alf is manning the till when the purchase is made? No, Alf is Stella's agent, selling on her behalf. This remains so even if Alf is an employee as employees often act as agents.

4.07 Another common reason is that the agent has special knowledge or expertise which the principal lacks. This is why most people who are buying or selling a house do so through a solicitor (sometimes called a law agent). The solicitor knows what needs to be done and what problems to look out for. Similarly, a company looking to expand into a new country may employ an agent who understands the local business conditions to run its affairs there.

4.08 A company has another important reason for transacting through an agent. A company is a juristic person, with no physical body. As such, it lacks the physical presence necessary to express consent. Since expressions of consent or intention are essential to most juridical acts, this is a problem. It is addressed to some degree by the Requirements of Writing (Scotland) Act 1995, which has procedures for subscription by various kinds of juristic person.[5] They are, however, relatively cumbersome and are of no relevance where writing is not used. If the shop was owned by a company rather than by Stella, Alf's position as an agent would be

---

5 Requirements of Writing (Scotland) Act 1995, Sch 2. See Chapter 1: Introduction to Juristic Persons, paras **1.40–1.43**.

even more important. Unlike Stella, the company could not man the tills and sell directly to customers. Its only practical means of selling is through agents.

4.09 In agency, there are three parties whose interrelationships need to be considered: the principal, the agent and the third party. If everything works properly, there should be a relationship between the principal and the third party by virtue of the agent's act on the principal's behalf. There will also be legal relations between the agent and the principal by virtue of the rules which regulate the agent's duties to the principal and vice versa. There should be no legal relations between the agent and the third party because the agent is merely the conduit through whom the principal acts. If things go wrong, however, the agent may find himself liable to the third party. Each of the three relationships will be considered in turn.

PRINCIPAL–THIRD PARTY RELATIONS

4.10 Under normal circumstances each person transacts on his or her own behalf but not on behalf of anyone else. This is important because juridical acts involve the exercise of private autonomy: they are part of the way in which the law enables us to live our lives as we choose. Autonomy does not make much sense if someone else is making the decisions. If giving effect to the contracts which Alice makes is part of the law's recognition of her private autonomy, it is difficult to see how this end is served if the contract comes into existence because of Peter's actions rather than Alice's.

4.11 Further, persons are usually entitled to choose with whom they deal. In a sense this is also part of private autonomy. When Bill decides to enter into a contract of sale he may wish to buy from Sally but not from Sophie and the law respects that choice.

4.12 The law of agency seems to challenge both of these basic values: the agent does the act but it is the principal who is bound, and the third party deals with the agent but ends up transacting with the principal. These apparent anomalies are dealt with by two concepts which are central to the relationship between principals and third parties: authority and disclosure.

Authority

4.13 Agency involves an agent acting on behalf of the principal but that is not the first step. Peter cannot just wake up one morning and decide that he will conclude a contract on Alice's behalf with Teldi Ltd or that he will make a gift of her car to Trudy. If Peter had no authority to conclude the contract with Teldi, then Teldi will not be able to enforce the contract against Alice. If Peter had no authority to give the car to Trudy then Alice will be entitled to get it back from her.

4.14 If Peter is to be Alice's agent, Alice must do something which gives him the authority to bind her. Without authority to bind Alice, no juridical act which Peter does in Alice's name will be attributed to her. In this way, Alice's autonomy is recognised. Peter can do things which bind Alice but his power to do so derives from Alice's actions. Alice exercises her autonomy in conferring the power on Peter. All of this means that, when trying to work out if an act of a purported agent binds the alleged principal in a question with a third party, the first question to ask is whether the agent had authority to do the relevant act.

Scope of authority

4.15 It is rare for a principal to want to confer universal authority on the agent. The agent will usually be authorised to do some acts but not others. When Stella leaves Alf in charge of the shop, she wants him to be able to sell goods to customers but not to sell the premises to a property developer. Therefore, it is necessary to ask not just whether the person who acted was the principal's agent but also whether the act in question was within the scope of his authority. The scope of authority can vary widely: an agent may be commissioned to undertake a specific sale or purchase or to manage all of the principal's business affairs. Agents whose authority is limited to particular tasks are sometimes referred to as special agents and those with wider authority as general agents.[6] However, in every case the key question is whether the agent had authority to do the particular act in question.

Kinds of authority

4.16 There are three broad types of authority: actual, retrospective and apparent. Actual authority is authority which has been granted by the principal prior to the transaction at issue. Retrospective authority, which is usually called ratification, is granted after the fact by the principal. Apparent authority covers situations where the principal has not granted authority either before or after the agent's act but is nonetheless bound because she is responsible for the third party's belief that the agent was authorised.

Actual authority

4.17 An agent has actual authority when the principal has granted power to do the relevant act beforehand. This grant is a juridical act by the principal and it is usually done in the context of a contract between the principal and agent in which the latter takes on obligations to the principal.[7]

4.18 It is often suggested that an agent need not have active capacity

---

6 E.g. Bell, *Principles* § 219.
7 E.g. *Freeman and Lockyer v Buckhurst Park Properties (Mangal) Ltd* [1964] 2 QB 480 at 502 per Diplock LJ.

since he is a mere conduit for the principal's act.[8] If this is the case, it implies that the conferral of authority may be a unilateral act by the principal since requiring the agent's consent would imply his participation in the constitution of the agency relationship. Someone without active capacity would not be able to so participate and thus could not become an agent in the first place.[9] In England, it is accepted that agency may arise from a unilateral conferral of authority by the principal.[10] Of course, explaining the basis of the agent's duties to the principal becomes more difficult if agency can come into existence without the agent having to consent.

4.19   Like most other juridical acts, the conferral of authority need not be in writing and need not take any particular form. It may be done expressly or impliedly. In the latter case, the principal does not state explicitly that he or she authorises the agent. Rather, the authority is implied from the circumstances of the case.

4.20   Thus, where an agent is given a task, authority is given to do everything necessary to complete the task,[11] so a solicitor who is asked to purchase land on someone's behalf is authorised to have searches made of the land register to make sure that there are no problems with the seller's title. Further, appointment to some roles implies authority to enter into certain kinds of transaction: a partner in a general partnership has authority to bind the firm in its usual business relations[12] and the managing director of a company has wide-ranging authority to bind the company.[13] This authority will often depend on what is usual in the given field of activity.[14]

4.21   Implied authority is based on the presumption that this is what the principal intends but that principle can be rebutted. So it would be open to someone instructing a solicitor to require the solicitor to get specific authority before ordering a search of the land register and section 5 of the Partnership Act 1890 envisages that the partners may agree to limit the authority of some or all of the partners.

Ad hoc *agency*

4.22   A recent line of decisions in the Outer House has suggested a further category of agency which, if it is accepted, is best considered as a

8 E.g. J J Gow, *Mercantile and Industrial Law of Scotland* (1964) p 516; A D M Forte and J P Van Niekerk, 'Agency' in R Zimmermann, D Visser and K Reid (eds), *Mixed Legal Systems in Comparative Perspective*, p 240 at 245. As to the meaning of active capacity see Chapter 1: Introduction to Juristic Persons, para **1.05**.

9 E.g. Age of Legal Capacity (Scotland) Act 1991, ss 1(1)(a) and 9(b).

10 P Watts and F M B Reynolds, *Bowstead and Reynolds on Agency* (19th edn, 2010) para 1-006.

11 *Black v Cornelius* (1879) 6 R 581.

12 Partnership Act 1890, s 5.

13 *Freeman and Lockyer v Buckhurst Park Properties* (n 7).

14 *Black v Cornelius.*

type of implied authority.[15] It is known as *ad hoc* agency. The concept is the creation of Lord Drummond Young and its precise contours are not yet clear. The basic idea is that, in cases where there is a mismatch between the parties to a contract and those who are performing the obligations and enforcing the rights, the person who is acting as a *de facto* party to the contract can be considered to be the agent of the true contracting party in order to get round the mismatch.

4.23 The usual reason for the mismatch is either that the contract has been concluded by one member of a group of companies but is then performed by another member of the group, or that a business is restructured. A sole trader may transfer her business to a limited company of which she is the shareholder and director but neglect to assign contractual rights to the company or secure the consent of the other parties to the delegation of the obligations to the company.

4.24 Thus, in *Laurence McIntosh Ltd v Balfour Beatty*, a contract was entered into by a partnership called Laurence McIntosh & Sons. The partners of that firm later created Laurence McIntosh Ltd and were in the process of transferring the business from one to the other. Lord Drummond Young deployed the concept of *ad hoc* agency to cover the gap between the practical moment when the company took over the business and the legal transfer of rights and responsibilities. During that gap, the company was considered to be the agent of the partnership.[16]

4.25 The basis for *ad hoc* agency appears to be that, in a given situation, the best method of making sense of what the parties are doing, in a way that keeps all the contracts running, is to assume that one person acts on behalf of another. It should be borne in mind, however, that Lord Drummond Young did not consider the inference appropriate in 'formal' situations like litigation.[17]

4.26 The idea has been subject to academic criticism[18] and has not been endorsed at appellate level so it is not clear whether it will become an established part of the Scots law of agency. The basis for the implication of authority certainly differs from classic implied authority since, in cases of the type envisaged by Lord Drummond Young, it is likely that the 'agent' would consider itself to be acting for its own benefit and thus on its own behalf rather than that of the nominal principal.

Retrospective authority (ratification)

4.27 Agents do not always remain within the bounds of the authority

---

15 *Whitbread Group plc v Goldapple Ltd (No 2)* 2005 SLT 281; *Laurence McIntosh Ltd v Balfour Beatty Group Ltd* [2006] CSOH 197; *Stirling v Westminster Properties Scotland Ltd* [2007] CSOH 117.

16 [2006] CSOH 197 at paras 15–19.

17 *Stirling v Westminster Properties Ltd* at para 20.

18 L Macgregor and N Whitty, 'Payment of another's debt, unjustified enrichment and *ad hoc* agency' (2011) 15 Edin LR 57.

granted to them by their principals. The reasons why this may happen are diverse but one obvious one is a misunderstanding of the scope of the authority on the part of the agent. In more extreme cases, someone with no authority at all may purport to act as agent for another. In some cases, however, the person in whose name the act was done may be happy with the transaction which the purported agent has undertaken. In those circumstances, it is open to the 'principal' to ratify the actions. This effectively amounts to granting authority after the fact. The effect of ratification is that the act is treated as always having been authorised.[19]

4.28   The justification for allowing ratification is that everyone is getting what they want: the principal clearly wants to approve the transaction (otherwise she would not be ratifying it) and the third party thought that the agent was acting on the principal's behalf anyway. Therefore, the ratification just brings the legal situation into line with what the third party thought it was. The requirements for an effective ratification are fourfold.

1. The ratifier must make a decision

4.29   Ratification depends on the will of the ratifying party. Therefore, ratification can only occur where there is evidence that she has decided to approve the relevant transaction. This approval may be express but it is more common for it to be implied by the principal's actions. There is English authority which suggests that it may even be implied by the principal's inaction for a reasonable period of time in circumstances where the principal can be expected to take steps to disown the transaction,[20] and that this evidence need not have been communicated to the third party in order to take effect.[21]

4.30   The fact that the principal requires to make a decision means that the principal cannot be held to have ratified an agent's act merely on the basis of actions for which she had another good reason, such as recovering her property. Further, nothing done by the principal before she becomes aware of what the agent has done can imply a ratification of the agent's actions.[22]

2. The principal must have had legal capacity at the time of the act which was ratified[23]

4.31   This follows from the fact that ratification is retrospective in effect. As noted above, when an agent acts within the scope of his or her

19   *Bolton Partners v Lambert* (1889) 41 Ch D 295.
20   *Bank Melli Iran v Barclays Bank (Dominion, Colonial and Overseas)* [1951] 2 Lloyd's Rep 367.
21   *Harrisons & Crossfield Ltd v London and North-Western Railway Co* [1917] 2 KB 755; *SEB Trygg Liv Holding AB v Manches* [2006] 1 WLR 2276.
22   *Forman & Co Pty Ltd v The Liddesdale* [1900] AC 190.
23   *Boston Deep Sea Fishing and Ice Co Ltd v Farnham* [1957] 1 WLR 1051.

authority, the act is attributed to the principal. Since ratification means that the agent is treated as having had authority at the time of the act, it would mean the contract or other transaction being attributed to the principal at a time when she was incapable of so acting. This would make no sense.

4.32 The requirement that the principal have legal capacity at the time of the agent's act implies a requirement that the principal existed at the time of the relevant act since there can be no capacity without existence. The most common application for this rule relates to the formation of companies. Those behind a company may want to line business up for it before it is formed by incorporation and to have the contracts ratified once the company has been created. The retrospective effect of ratification makes this impossible. Instead, section 51 of the Companies Act 2006 provides that those who purport to contract on behalf of the company in those cases are personally liable.

3. The agent must have held himself out as acting as an agent

4.33 If part of the rationale for accepting ratification as binding on third parties is that it gives them what they thought they were bargaining for in the first place, it should be obvious that ratification can only be allowed where the third party is aware that the agent is not acting on his own behalf. Were that not the case, the third party might expect to contract with the agent and end up contracting with the principal.

4. There must have been no material change in circumstances between the agent's act and the ratification

4.34 This is sometimes expressed as the requirement that the ratification must be reasonable in all the circumstances. Ratification gives the principal the power to make a retrospective change. This has the potential for significant abuse. For instance, if the agent placed a bet on a football match in the principal's name, it would not be appropriate to let the principal decide to ratify the gambling contract after the match was over. However, the courts have been willing to recognise ratification of a contract of insurance after the peril against which the insurance was taken out has occurred.[24]

4.35 Thus, where an act requires to be done within a certain time (perhaps an offer made subject to a time limit), both the agent's act and the ratification must occur within the time limit.[25] Otherwise the time limit would be deprived of all effect. Similarly, if someone else has acquired a real right in the principal's property, this cannot be prejudiced by a subsequent ratification.[26] Thus, if Alf purports to pledge Phillipa's car to Terence and, in the meantime, Phillipa sells the car to Trudy, Trudy

---

24 *Williams v North China Insurance Co* (1876) 1 CPD 757.
25 *Goodall v Bilsland* 1909 SC 1152.
26 *Bird v Brown* (1850) 4 Exch 786.

will not be affected by the pledge to Terence, even if Phillipa ratifies it. However, an attempt by the third party to withdraw an offer on learning that the agent has acted without authority can be defeated by a ratification.[27]

Apparent authority

4.36 The existence and extent of the agent's authority are the result of private dealings between the agent and the principal. As such, it is difficult for third parties to determine whether or not someone who purports to be an agent actually has the necessary authority for the transaction in question. For this reason, rules are required to protect third parties who are misled into dealing with someone whom they believe to have authority.

4.37 This protection takes two forms: the agent's warranty of authority and the validation of juridical acts performed by a person with apparent authority to do them. The former protection renders the purported agent liable to the third party and so it is considered below in the section on agent–third party relations.

4.38 Apparent authority (sometimes referred to as ostensible authority), however, concerns the relationship between the principal and the third party. If the principal has done something which justifies the third party in believing that someone has authority to do a particular act on her behalf and the third party relies on that impression by transacting with the agent, the principal will be bound.

4.39 Often apparent authority results from cases where an agent is deprived of his authority but those whom the agent has dealt with in the past are not informed of the loss of authority. It can also arise where someone is appointed to a post which usually carries a certain degree of implied authority but the principal and agent agree that the latter's authority shall not extend to the usual range.

4.40 So, if Alice appoints Peter to manage her affairs and then dismisses him for misconduct, she will need to inform those with whom Peter has been dealing on her behalf. If she does not do so, they will be justified in continuing to deal with Peter on the basis that he can bind Alice. The initial appointment gave the impression of continuing authority, so the onus rests on Alice to tell people that the situation has changed. Peter will not have actual authority but he will have apparent authority and that will be enough to enable those who contract with Peter before Alice informs them of the change to enforce their contracts against Alice.

4.41 Similarly, if Stella leaves Alf in charge of her shop but tells him not to sell certain products, Alf will not have actual authority to sell these products. He will, however, have apparent authority to do so

---

27 *Bolton Partners v Lambert* (1889) 41 Ch D 295.

because someone who works behind the till in a shop usually has authority to sell all of the products in the shop. If Stella does not want to be bound by such sales by Alf, she would need to do something to warn potential customers such as putting up a sign in the shop.

Requirements for apparent authority

Impression given by the principal

4.42   The third party's belief must result from the principal's conduct. The justification for binding the principal to acts done by agents with apparent authority is that the principal is responsible for the misunderstanding. This can only be the case where the principal has done something which justifies the third party's belief.

4.43   Despite that, apparent authority has been held to exist on the basis of minimal action by the principal. This is illustrated by *International Sponge Importers Ltd v Andrew Watt & Sons*.[28] In that case, an agent sold sponges on behalf of the pursuer. The pursuer's terms and conditions required payment to be made by a cheque to the principal, although such cheques could be delivered to the agent. The agent induced a number of customers to pay by cheques in his name or in cash. He had no authority to do so. The agent absconded with some of the money paid to him and the principal attempted to claim the price from customers who had paid the agent in unauthorised ways. The agent was held to have apparent authority to receive payment in this way. The basis for the decision was that the agent had greater actual authority than was usual in being able to take delivery of cheques and that the pursuers had been aware of at least one of the instances of irregular payment but did not communicate any objection to the defenders.

4.44   Among other things, the requirement that the principal give an impression of authority means that a claim to have authority made by a purported agent will not usually give rise to apparent authority.[29] However, it should be borne in mind that a statement made by an agent with authority to communicate on behalf of the principal will be attributed to her.

4.45   The idea is well illustrated by the facts of *First Energy (UK) v Hungarian International Bank*:[30] there a company was negotiating a loan with a bank employee who acknowledged that he did not have authority to grant it. However, he then purported to contact his superiors to get authorisation (i.e. specific authority) for the relevant transaction. He told the company's representatives that he had done so, although this was not in fact the case, and the loan was agreed. The Court of Appeal held that the bank was bound by the loan agreement. While the employee did not have authority to grant the loan, he did have authority to

---

28 1911 SC (HL) 57.
29 *Armagas Ltd v Mundogas SA (The Ocean Frost)* [1986] AC 717.
30 [1993] 2 Lloyd's Rep 194.

make representations on behalf of the bank. That meant that his (incorrect) representation that the loan was approved by his superiors was attributed to the bank, i.e., it was treated as if the bank had made it. Since it gave rise to the legitimate belief that he was authorised to agree the loan, the employee had apparent authority to make the loan agreement.

4.46 The decision has been subject to criticism on the basis that it opens the door to agents creating their own apparent authority but the logic of the decision is difficult to argue with. The Court of Appeal returned to the idea that a representation by an agent with actual authority could be attributed to the principal and thus create apparent authority for a further act in *SEB Trygg Liv Holding AB v Manches*.[31] The comment was merely an *obiter dictum* but the *First Energy* analysis seems to be on the way to being established.

Giving rise to a reasonable belief that the agent has authority

4.47 The purpose of the rule is to protect third parties who are misled into believing the agent to be authorised. Therefore, it cannot be invoked if the third party was aware of the agent's lack of authority. Furthermore, that belief must have been reasonable since the principal cannot bear the risk of unjustifiable inferences which the third party might draw.

Transaction on that basis

4.48 The third party cannot be said to rely on the representation unless a transaction has been concluded with the agent. So, a belief that the agent has authority which is not followed by a juridical act will not affect the principal. Similarly, there is no reliance on the inaccurate impression unless the agent acts in the principal's name rather than his own. If the agent acts in his own name then his lack of authority does not affect the third party.

Prejudice

4.49 There is some dispute about whether the third party also requires to demonstrate prejudice flowing from the principal's disavowal of the agent's transaction.[32] If such prejudice is required, however, it is thought to be satisfied in every case where the other requirements are satisfied because the loss of the benefit of the relevant transaction will be considered as prejudice.

Rationale

4.50 In England, apparent authority has often been said to be based

---

31 [2006] 1 WLR 2276 at para 32 per Buxton LJ.
32 *Gregor Homes Ltd v Emlick* 2012 SLT (Sh Ct) 5.

on estoppel[33] and some Scots lawyers have followed this by suggesting that it is based on personal bar.[34] However, the estoppels/personal bar analysis has been doubted in both jurisdictions.[35]

4.51 There are two main reasons for this. First, the conduct on the part of the principal which can give rise to the impression of authority is not as extensive or definitive as would usually be required for personal bar. Secondly, personal bar typically requires that the party invoking the bar (the third party who dealt with the apparent agent in this case) has acted in reliance on the false impression in a way which would mean he or she would be prejudiced if the barred party was allowed to back out. In apparent authority, the only reliance which the third party needs to show is the conclusion of the transaction with the apparent agent and the only prejudice is the loss of the benefit of that transaction. It is open to question whether this reliance and prejudice of this kind would suffice for personal bar in another context.

Disclosure

4.52 The requirement that the agent have authority for the relevant transaction protects the principal's autonomy. However, the third party also requires protection since it has an interest in being able to choose whom it deals with. This interest is protected by the rules surrounding disclosure of agency.

4.53 Discussion of disclosure of the principal's identity tends to be limited to contracts. In principle, other juridical acts may be performed on behalf of an undisclosed principal but the policy issues surrounding disclosure of the principal's identity are less sharp. A transferee or payee will usually be unconcerned about the identity of the transferor as long as the transfer is effective. A transferor has few grounds to object to an agent receiving a transfer on behalf of another when it would have been open to the agent to transfer the relevant asset on. Therefore, discussion in this section will focus on contracts concluded on behalf of an undisclosed principal.

4.54 There are three possible levels of disclosure: where the principal is disclosed and identified; where the principal is undisclosed and where the principal is disclosed but not identified.

---

33 *Freeman and Lockyer v Buckhurst Park Properties* [1964] 2 QB 480 at 503 per Diplock LJ.
34 *Bank of Scotland v Brunswick Developments (1987) Ltd (No 2)* 1997 SC 226 at 234 per Lord Rodger; E C Reid and J W G Blackie, *Personal Bar* (2006) para 13-01; H L MacQueen and Lord Eassie (eds), *Gloag and Henderson: The Law of Scotland* (13th edn, 2012) para 18.23.
35 *Gregor Homes Ltd v Emlick*; *Bowstead and Reynolds on Agency*, para 8-029.

Disclosed and identified principal

4.55 Where the agent discloses the identity of the principal to the third party and acts in her name, there can be no doubt that the third party intends to deal with the principal and that the contract is between the third party and the principal.

Undisclosed principal

4.56 Basic principles of private law suggest that where the agent purports to act on his own behalf the principal should be unaffected. The third party agreed to transact with the agent not with the principal. However, for pragmatic reasons, the law allows a principal who has not been disclosed to step in and enforce the contract made on her behalf by an agent despite the fact that the agent acted in his own name.[36] As might be expected, the principal can only do this where the agent has authority to act and intends to do so on behalf of the principal.

4.57 Where an agent has contracted on behalf of an undisclosed principal, the third party is entitled to choose whether to enforce its rights against the agent or the principal and can use any defence which could have been raised against the agent against the principal.

4.58 The rationale for allowing the undisclosed principal to enforce the contract is that, in most transactions, people do not mind to whom they make performance. This assumption also underlies the general rule which allows assignation without the debtor's consent. If that is the case, the third party is sufficiently protected by ensuring that it can insist on having rights against the agent rather than against the principal.

4.59 If Alf concludes a contract for the sale of sheep to Trudy with Stella as his undisclosed principal, Stella can enforce the contract by bringing an action against Trudy for the price. However, if Alf owed money to Trudy, she would be entitled to set that off against Stella's claim for the price. Once Stella reveals herself, Trudy has a decision to make. She can enforce against Alf or Stella. This choice is known as an election. Once she has chosen, she cannot then go back and try to enforce the contract against the other party. So, if she decides to choose Alf as her seller and he fails to deliver, she will not be entitled to sue Stella.[37]

4.60 The choice need not be made expressly. It is implied by conduct which suggests that one party or the other is liable, such as pursuing an action for enforcement of the contract to the point of judgment, or ranking in an insolvency procedure.[38] If the litigation is abandoned before final judgment, however, it will not be considered as an election.

---

36 The basic principles are set out in *Siu Yin Kwan v Eastern Insurance Co Ltd* [1994] 2 AC 199.

37 *David Logan and Son Ltd v Schuldt* (1903) 10 SLT 598.

38 *Meier & Co v Kuchenmeister* (1881) 8 R 642; *David Logan and Son Ltd v Schuldt*.

4.61   There are limits to the law's willingness to allow an undisclosed principal to step in. It is open to the third party to stipulate at the time that it is only willing to conclude the relevant transaction with the agent personally. Such a stipulation rebuts the argument that the identity of the person to whom performance must be made is a matter of indifference. Even if no such stipulation is made, if the contract is a 'personal' one, where the person to whom the performance is due is a central part of the obligation, no undisclosed principal can step in and enforce it. The standard example of such a contract is a contract to paint a picture.[39] This example is not without its difficulties.

4.62   The difficulty arises from the fact that the rules on undisclosed principals allow the separation of rights from obligations and not all of the obligations arising from the contract are personal. In cases where the undisclosed principal intervenes the third party can elect to treat the agent as liable and therefore demand performance from him rather than from the principal. The only effect which the intervention of the undisclosed principal has on the contract is to change the person to whom the performance is to be made. The contract to paint a picture is personal in the sense that the painter is likely to have been chosen for his or her particular characteristics. On the other hand, it is not obvious that the painter has particular concerns regarding the person who commissions the picture since the commissioner's obligation is to pay.

4.63   If the undisclosed principal commissions the painting, her identity is presumed to be a matter of indifference to the painter (the third party). If, on the other hand, the third party commissions an undisclosed agent to paint the picture, it can ensure that the agent paints the picture by electing to take the undisclosed agent as its debtor in the contract rather than the principal. Although it can demand that the agent paints the picture, the third party can be forced to pay the price to the undisclosed principal but it is unlikely that this will be against the third party's interests.

4.64   There are, however, other examples where the third party can be presumed to have taken account of the identity of the person to whom obligations are to be performed. For instance, the third party may have a contract to provide services which involve close personal contact (such as bathing or dressing the creditor) or living with her (for instance, as a nanny).

4.65   There is also authority which suggests that the principal's intervention is excluded if the agent has concealed her identity for the purpose of deceiving the third party. The particular facts of the case were peculiar. Someone who knew he was not welcome at a particular theatre obtained a ticket for an opening night by getting an agent to apply for the ticket for him. The court held that the theatre owners were

39 E.g. *Siu Yin Kwan* at 210.

entitled to refuse him entry because the agent had been used to deceive them.[40]

4.66 This restriction needs to be handled with care, however. Many circumstances where the principal is not disclosed will involve a principal with some interest in concealing her identity or involvement in the relevant transaction. Such concealment necessarily implies a degree of deception. Were the restriction applied to all such cases, there would be little point in sanctioning transactions made on behalf of an undisclosed principal. Therefore, the rule ought to be read narrowly and restricted to cases where the principal is aware that the third party would be unwilling to deal with her specifically.

Disclosed but unidentified principal

4.67 The agent may make full disclosure or no disclosure at all but it is also possible that the agent will disclose the fact that he is acting on another's behalf without identifying the principal. This might be regarded as something of a mid-point between the undisclosed and the fully disclosed principal.

4.68 There has been some conflict in the authorities on the proper analysis of this midpoint. The main Scottish authorities which discuss the disclosed but unnamed principal involve an attempt by the third party to enforce the contract against either the agent or principal. Therefore they do not address whether the contract is enforceable by the principal. Given that a principal who has been neither disclosed nor identified can usually enforce the contract, it seems likely that it is. The fact that the third party knew that there was some other party behind the agent would make it difficult to argue that the contract was personal in a sense which would prevent a principal stepping forward and taking up the rights.

4.69 One approach has been to treat the situation in the same way as an undisclosed principal would be treated: giving the third party an election as to whom it wishes to hold liable under the contract.[41] The other approach is to ask whose credit the third party relied on when making the contract and to treat that person, be it principal or agent, as the party liable on the contract.[42] The expression 'giving credit' is perhaps a little obscure but it simply means asking who the third party looked to for payment under the contract.

4.70 The Inner House returned to the issue in *Ruddy v Marco*,[43] where the court stressed the responsibility of the agent to make clear to the third party that the principal, and only the principal, is liable, if the agent wants to escape personal responsibility. The fact that the third

---

40 *Said v Butt* [1920] 3 KB 497.
41 *Ferrier v Dods* (1865) 3 M 561.
42 *Lamont, Nisbett & Co v Hamilton* 1907 SC 628.
43 2008 SC 667.

party is aware that there is a principal standing somewhere in the background is not necessarily enough to discharge this burden. If this burden is not discharged (as was the case in *Ruddy*), the general presumption that people who contract make themselves liable on the contract applies and the agent finds himself liable.

4.71 A similar analysis applies to the execution of documents by an agent. The mere fact that the person to whom the document is addressed knows that the signatory is an agent is not sufficient to release the agent from liability under the document. Rather, the signature should be qualified in such a way as to make clear that the document is subscribed on behalf of the principal rather than in any personal capacity.[44]

4.72 Drawing all this together, when an agent acts for a disclosed but unidentified principal, it is likely that the principal will be able to enforce the contract against the third party provided that this is not clearly excluded. Whether the agent will be liable to the third party depends on whether the agent has made clear to the third party that he accepts no personal liability on the contract.

AGENT–THIRD PARTY RELATIONS

4.73 Since the agent transacts with the third party on behalf of the principal rather than on his own behalf, the agent will not normally find himself liable to the third party. There are three major exceptions to this: where the principal is not disclosed (discussed at paras **4.56**–**4.66** above); where the parties agree otherwise or the agent makes a promise to the third party; and where the agent does not have authority to do the relevant act. The fact that the agent may take on obligations to the third party by agreement or promise is a simple application of basic principles of contract or promise. A little more needs to be said, however, about the agent's liability in cases where the authority is exceeded.

4.74 Agents acting without authority are sometimes thought to be personally bound by the relevant obligation, particularly where the purported principal does not exist. As noted at para **4.32** above, there is a special rule which makes those who contract on behalf of a company which is yet to be formed personally liable. However, the general rule is that where the agent acts outwith his authority the relevant act does not bind him personally. Instead, he is liable to the principal for breach of warranty of authority.[45] The rule was developed in England, where promise is not generally recognised as a basis for obligations, and so the warranty is described as a collateral contract between the agent and third party. In Scotland, it might have been possible to explain the rule

---

44 *Stewart v Shannessy* (1900) 2 F 1288.
45 *Irving v Burns* 1915 SC 260 at 269 per Lord Salvesen; *Halifax Life Ltd v DLA Piper Scotland LLP* [2009] CSOH 74.

as an implied promise by the agent but the English collateral contract analysis has in fact been followed.

4.75   Where the agent was not authorised to do the relevant act, he is thus liable to the third party for breach of contract. The contractual basis of the obligation means that the liability is strict so it does not matter that the agent honestly believed himself authorised to do the relevant act. The contractual basis also determines the extent of the damages which the agent must pay. Contract damages usually aim to put the injured party in the position it would be in if the breach had not occurred.

4.76   Therefore, the agent must pay the third party enough to secure the benefit of the transaction because that is what the third party would have had if the warranty had been true. So, if the third party had contracted to sell goods to the principal, the agent would usually be liable for the profit which the third party would have made on the sale.[46] However, if the principal was insolvent and not able to pay for the goods anyway, then the agent may not be liable at all since the third party would have made a loss on the sale.

4.77   From this it should be obvious that the agent only warrants that he is authorised by the principal. The agent does not warrant that the principal has any particular attributes or characteristics. In particular, the agent does not warrant that the principal owns any property over which rights are being granted or is otherwise able to perform any obligations which arise under the transaction.[47]

PRINCIPAL–AGENT RELATIONS

4.78   Principals and agents owe duties to one another. As with most personal rights and obligations, they may usually be varied by agreement between principal and agent.[48] The agent is entitled to payment for the work he does on the principal's behalf. The method of calculating how and when the agent is to be paid will usually be agreed between the parties. It is common for the agent to be employed on commission. An agent who is on commission receives a percentage of the price or the profit in transactions which he performs or negotiates on the principal's behalf, provided that the agent has made a substantial contribution to the transaction. As well as payment, the agent is entitled to relief from any liabilities and to reimbursement of any expenses which have been incurred in the course of the proper performance of his duties as agent.[49]

---

46 *Irving v Burns.*

47 *Cheshire Mortgage Corporation Ltd v Grandison* [2012] CSIH 66, 2013 SC 160.

48 An important exception to this in the case of commercial agents is discussed at para **4.94** ff below.

49 *Stevenson v Duncan* (1842) 5 D 167; *Tomlinson v Scottish Amalgamated Silks' Liquidator* 1935 SC (HL) 1.

4.79 In some cases, the agent will agree to act for the principal without any payment. Such gratuitous agency is known as mandate. In mandate, the principal is known as the mandant and the agent as the mandatary. In such cases, the mandant is still entitled to relief and reimbursement.[50]

4.80 The duties imposed on the agent ensure that he carries out the task or tasks with which he has been entrusted properly. For this reason, the agent is obliged to follow the principal's instructions and to exercise reasonable skill and care when acting as agent. The agent is obliged to compensate the principal for losses occasioned by breaches of these duties.

4.81 One of the most important applications of the duty to follow instructions is the duty not to exceed his authority. Of course, in many cases, an act which exceeds authority will not prejudice the principal because the act will not bind her. However, the principal may find herself bound if the act was with the agent's apparent authority. In such cases, the agent would be liable for any loss suffered by the principal in the relevant transaction.[51]

4.82 The situation with ratification is a little more complex. The agent has strayed outwith his authority but the principal is only bound because she has decided to ratify the act. It might be argued that the principal cannot have it both ways: ratifying the transaction on the one hand and claiming against the agent for the loss occasioned by an act outwith authority on the other. In most circumstances, ratification will imply a waiver on the part of the principal of any right of recovery against the agent for exceeding his authority.

4.83 However, the courts recognise that the principal may have good reasons, such as preservation of her commercial reputation, for ratifying a transaction although she would not have sanctioned it beforehand. In such cases, the principal is simply making the best of a bad situation and this should not bar recovery from the agent. Therefore, it is possible to ratify the agent's act without waiving the right to compensation for excess of authority.[52] If the principal wishes to retain her right against the agent, she must make this clear at the time of the ratification.[53]

4.84 Agents are also sometimes said to have an obligation not to delegate the task entrusted to them on the basis of the maxim *delegatus non potest delegare* (one to whom something has been delegated cannot delegate it). However, this is only a general presumption and may be rebutted by evidence of the custom in particular cases.[54] Of course,

---

50 Bell, *Principles* § 218.
51 *Milne v Ritchie* (1882) 10 R 365.
52 *Suncorp Insurance and Finance* v *Milano Assicurazioni SPA* [1993] 2 Lloyd's Rep 225; *Wyatt v Crate* [2012] CSOH 197, 2013 SCLR 323.
53 *Wyatt v Crate* at para 30 per Lord Boyd.
54 Bell, *Commentaries* I, 516–17.

where the agent has an obligation not to delegate, he also lacks the authority to create contractual relations between the principal and the delegate.

Fiduciary duties

4.85 The duties to use reasonable skill and care and to follow instructions amount to simple duties incumbent on the agent to carry out the task or work which he has agreed to undertake. As such, they are of a type to be found in most contracts. However, agents are also subject to another class of duties which address the fact that the principal necessarily puts a lot of trust in the agent by conferring upon him the power to alter her legal position. Duties in this class are known as fiduciary duties. The law supplies default fiduciary duties but they can be varied by contract to meet individual circumstances.[55]

4.86 Fiduciary duties are duties of loyalty to the principal. The general principle which underlies them is that, within the scope of his sphere of responsibility as an agent, the agent must put the principal's interests ahead of his own. This general duty of loyalty may be broken down into two broad categories.

Duty to avoid conflicts of interest

4.87 In order to ensure that the agent puts the principal's interests first, he is obliged to avoid situations where his interests conflict with those of the principal. The most extreme version of this situation is self-dealing: where the agent deals on behalf of the principal with himself. If Alex sells goods to Paula, his principal, there is a clear conflict of interest.[56] His duty to Paula means that he should try to get the goods as cheaply as possible for her but his personal interest lies in getting as high a price as possible.

4.88 A slight variant on this case would involve Alex acting for two principals who are both involved in the same transaction: buying on behalf of Paula and selling on behalf of Terence. Again there is a clear conflict of interest: Alex's duty to Paula is to negotiate as low a price as possible; his duty to Terence is to negotiate as high a price as possible.[57] He cannot do both.

4.89 An agent may have a conflict of interest if he is representing multiple principals whose products are in competition. The agent cannot give his full energies to promoting one principal's products because he also has a duty to promote those of the other. For this reason, the terms of the agent's contract will often bar him from representing competing principals.[58] However, there are many common business situations

---

55 See *Kelly v Cooper* [1993] AC 205.
56 *McPherson's Trs v Watt* (1877) 5 R (HL) 9.
57 *Aberdeen Railway Co v Blaikie Bros* (1853) 15 D (HL) 20.
58 *Graham & Co v United Turkey Red Co Ltd* 1922 SC 533.

where the same agent represents a number of principals, such as a solicitor or estate agent acting in the sale of a number of homes in the same street. In many cases, this is to the advantage of all of the principals because potential customers or buyers may be more likely to visit or listen to an agent who has a wide range of potential deals to offer them. Therefore, there is no general principle that an agent may not act for competing principals.[59]

Duty to communicate benefits to the principal

4.90 Since the agent is engaged to act for the principal, the agent is obliged to pass on any benefits which he receives to the principal, unless these form part of the remuneration which was agreed between agent and principal. This in turn implies a duty to account (i.e. inform) the principal of all benefits received in the course of agency activities.[60] Together these rules are sometimes referred to as the rule against secret profits.

4.91 The most common sources of incidental benefit to the agent are use of property or information which the agent has because he is an agent;[61] mistakes in payments to or from the principal;[62] and payments or other benefits received from the third party with whom the agent deals on the principal's behalf.[63] The last example, sometimes referred to as a secret commission, overlaps with the conflict of interest rules because the agent may be tempted to enter into a transaction which is not beneficial to the principal as a result of his desire to secure the benefit from the third party. For this reason, the principal is entitled to set aside the transaction concluded by the agent and the third party wrongs the principal by making the payment.[64]

Consequences of breach of fiduciary duties

4.92 As with 'normal' duties, an agent who breaches a fiduciary duty must compensate the principal for any harm suffered as a result. That does not represent the limit of his potential liability. Rather, the agent is also obliged to pay over to the principal anything which he has received as a result of breach of his fiduciary obligations.[65] The agent also forfeits any right to payment or commission for the relevant transaction.[66] There is English authority suggesting that, where it is equitable to do so, the court may allow the agent to retain a proportion of the commission

---

59 *Lothian v Jenolite Ltd* 1969 SC 111. See also *Kelly v Cooper* [1993] AC 205.
60 *Trans Barwil Agencies (UK) Ltd v John S Braid & Co Ltd* 1988 SC 222.
61 *Boardman v Phipps* [1965] Ch 992.
62 *Trans Barwil Agencies.*
63 *Ronaldson v Drummond and Reid* (1881) 8 R 956; *Imageview Management Ltd v Jack* [2009] EWCA Civ 63, [2009] 2 All ER 666.
64 *Aberdeen Railway Co v Blaikie Bros* (n 57).
65 *Ronaldson v Drummond and Reid.*
66 *Ronaldson v Drummond and Reid; Imageview Management Ltd v Jack.*

despite a breach of fiduciary duty.[67] The allowance is made to reflect the value of the services which the agent rendered to the principal and is usually limited to cases where the breach of fiduciary duty was an honest mistake.

4.93 The fiduciary duties place particularly stringent demands on agents and there may be circumstances in which the principal may be content for the agent to receive an additional benefit or for the agent to supply goods which she is looking to buy. If the situation is disclosed to the principal and she consents, then there is no breach of duty.

Commercial agents

4.94 Both Scots and English law have tended to see the regulation of the relationship between principal and agent primarily in terms of protecting the principal from wrongful conduct on the part of the agent. However, the late twentieth century saw European legislation intended to establish protection for commercial agents. This legislation was implemented in the United Kingdom by the Commercial Agents (Council Directive) Regulations 1993.[68]

4.95 The regulations are primarily concerned with establishing the agent's rights to remuneration, notice prior to termination of the agency, and payment on conclusion of the agency relationship. Underlying these rules is a presumption that commercial agents play a role in building up goodwill for their principals for which they are entitled to appropriate reward.

Sphere of application

4.96 The protections in the regulations apply only to commercial agents, as defined in regulation 2(1). In order to qualify as such, the agent must be (a) self-employed; (b) have continuing authority to negotiate the sale or purchase of goods on behalf of the principal; and (c) not be excluded by the regulation.

4.97 The term continuing authority suggests that the agent must carry out more than a single transaction on behalf of the principal but it can cover a single contract where the agent has ongoing authority from the principal to negotiate extensions to that contract.[69]

4.98 The requirement that the agent negotiate might be taken to suggest that the agent has some say in the terms of the bargain between principal and third party. However, it has been read very broadly. Provided that the agent does some work to generate goodwill or drum up business, he will be considered as negotiating for the purposes of the

---

67 Summarised in *Imageview Management Ltd v Jack* at paras 54–61.
68 SI 1993/3053.
69 *Poseidon Chartering BV v Marianne Zeeschip Vof* (C-3/04) [2006] ECR I-2505.

regulations.[70] However, an agent to whom customers come without any
effort on the part of the agent, such as a licensee who operated a petrol
station on behalf of an oil company, did not fall within the ambit of the
regulations.[71]

4.99   There are two types of specific exclusion: those based on the office
held by the agent and those based on the nature of the agent's activity.
Both types of exclusions are designed to focus the application of the
regulations on those who were thought to require protection. The
office-based exclusions cover those in posts which already have a well-
established legal regime and where the protections in the regulations are
not needed. Company officers such as directors, partners in partnerships
and insolvency practitioners are excluded,[72] as are gratuitous agents,
commodity traders and Crown Agents.[73]

4.100   The activity exclusion prevents the application of the regulations
to persons whose activity as a commercial agent is secondary.[74] Guidance
on when this is the case is found in the schedule to the regulations. Paragraph 2 of the Schedule sets out when the commercial agent's activity
will be primary: where the principal's business is the sale or purchase of
a particular type of goods; where the contracts are individually negotiated; and where securing transactions is likely to build up goodwill and
thus the principal's chances of further success.

4.101   Paragraph 3 of the Schedule provides a number of indicators
that this is the case: where the principal manufactures, imports or distri-
butes goods; where the goods are particularly identified with the principal; where the agent's time is substantially taken up with representing
the principal; where the agent is the main means by which the principal's goods are available in the relevant market; and where the parties
describe the relationship as one of commercial agency. Conversely, paragraph 4 lists contra-indicators, which suggest that the agent's activity is
secondary: where promotional material is sent to potential customers
directly rather than through the agent; where the principal appoints
agents without consideration of whether the relevant market is already
covered by another agent; and where customers select goods themselves
and merely place their orders through the agent. Further, paragraph 5
contains absolute exclusions for mail order catalogue agents and consumer credit agents.

4.102   The nature of the criteria in the Schedule further emphasises the
legislative intent to protect agents' interests in the goodwill which they
build up for their principals. The greater the agent's input into building
up goodwill associated with the principal's product and the more impor-

70 *Nigel Fryer Joinery Services Ltd v Ian Firth Hardware Ltd* [2008] EWHC 767 (Ch).
71 *Parks v Esso Petroleum Co Ltd* [2000] ECC 45.
72 Reg 2(1).
73 Reg 2(2).
74 Reg 2(3)–(4).

tant that goodwill is to the principal's business, the more likely the agent's activities are to be considered as primary rather than secondary.

Conduct of commercial agency

4.103   In addition to the rules on remuneration, notice of termination and payment at the end of the agency relationship, the regulations contain some brief provisions relating to the behaviour of the agent and principal. These impose an obligation to act dutifully and in good faith on both parties.[75]

4.104   In the case of the agent, the content of this duty is further specified as making proper efforts to negotiate and conclude the transactions entrusted to him, communication of necessary information and complying with reasonable instructions.[76] In the case of the principal, it is further specified in terms of provision of necessary documentation to the agent and notification of anticipated changes to the volume of transactions and of whether she has accepted, refused or failed to comply with any transaction which the agent has procured.[77] These obligations may not be excluded by the parties[78] and the agent is entitled to a signed, written document setting out the terms of the contract,[79] but otherwise they add little to the obligations entailed by an agency relationship at common law.

Remuneration

4.105   The regulations provide a default rule, entitling the agent to such remuneration as is customary (where there is a relevant custom in his place of operation) and to reasonable remuneration where there is no relevant custom.[80] Where remuneration takes the form of commission there are further rules detailing which transactions are to be considered as giving rise to entitlement to commission,[81] when commission is due,[82] and the agent's rights to information in order to determine the commission due to him.[83]

Termination

4.106   The most significant provisions in the regulations relate to the agent's rights at the end of the agency relationship. First, the commission rules entitle an agent to commission on transactions concluded after termination if the order was placed prior to termination or if the trans-

75 Regs 3(1) and 4(1).
76 Reg 3(2).
77 Reg 4(2).
78 Reg 5(1).
79 Reg 13.
80 Reg 6(1).
81 Regs 7–9 and 11.
82 Reg 10.
83 Reg 12.

action is mainly attributable to the agent's efforts and is concluded within a reasonable time after the termination.[84]

4.107 If the agency is for an indefinite period, either party may terminate the contract by notice. The regulations provide minimum periods of notice which vary depending on how long the agent has been in place: one month in the first year, two months in the second year, and three months in the third year and thereafter.[85] However, these minimum periods do not prevent immediate termination for material breach of contract or in exceptional circumstances (e.g. frustration).[86]

4.108 Where the agency relationship comes to an end, the agent will usually be entitled to a payment from the principal.[87] The entitlement arises although the principal has not done anything wrong.[88] It even applies where the agency is terminated by the agent's death.[89]

4.109 However, the right to payment is excluded where the principal has terminated the contract for material breach, where the agent has transferred his rights and duties under the contract to a third party, or where the agent has terminated the contract.[90] The last exclusion does not apply where the termination is justified by the principal's conduct or where age or illness makes it unreasonable to expect the agent to continue to perform his duties. Broadly speaking, the right to payment is excluded where the termination of the agency contract is caused by the agent's fault or free choice.

4.110 The regulations give the agent and principal two options for the payment on termination: the agent may receive either indemnity (calculated as directed by regulation 17) or compensation (calculated as directed by regulation 18). If no choice is made by the parties, compensation applies.[91] No agreement to derogate from the rules on compensation and indemnity made prior to the termination of the agency contract will be effective if it operates to the agent's detriment.[92] So the parties cannot exclude the agent's right to a payment on termination in their contract or make provision varying the rules for calculating indemnity or compensation in a way which leaves the agent with less than he would otherwise have received. However, a variation on the calculation mechanism which increases the agent's entitlement or an agreement to discharge the right made after the agency contract had come to an end would be effective.

4.111 Both indemnity and compensation are designed to give the agent

84 Reg 8.
85 Reg 15.
86 Reg 16.
87 Reg 17(1).
88 *Cooper v Pure Fishing (UK) Ltd* [2004] 2 Lloyd's Rep 518.
89 Reg 18(8).
90 Reg 18.
91 Reg 17(2).
92 Reg 19.

some reward for his role in building up the principal's goodwill. The two methods are available because of the political process which led up to the passing of the directive: indemnity is modelled on pre-existing German rules; compensation on pre-existing French rules.[93]

4.112   Under the indemnity system, the extent of the payment depends on the extent to which the agent has brought new business to the principal from which the latter continues to derive benefit after the end of the agency relationship.[94] Regard is to be had to all the circumstances of the case, with particular reference to the commission the agent would have earned had the agency not been terminated.[95] The amount payable is capped by the agent's average remuneration over the last five years, unless the agent has been working for less than five years in which case the average is taken over the whole period of agency.[96]

4.113   Compensation is calculated by reference to the damage which the agent suffers as a result of the termination of the agency relationship, in particular the loss of the opportunity to earn commission and to cover costs incurred in the performance of the agency contract.[97] After some initial doubts, it is clear that damage is determined in the conventional manner: i.e. by comparing the true position with what the agent's position would have been had the contract not come to an end.[98]

93 *King v T Tunnock Ltd* 2000 SC 424 at para 11.
94 Reg 17(3)(a).
95 Reg 17(3)(b).
96 Reg 17(4).
97 Reg 17(6)–(7).
98 *Lonsdale v Howard & Hallam Ltd* [2007] UKHL 32, [2007] 1 WLR 2055.

Chapter 5

Partnerships, LPs and LLPs

INTRODUCTION

Overview

5.01 The juristic persons available for conducting commercial life in the UK are:

- A company (a 'Company') incorporated under the Companies Act 2006 (the '2006 Act')
- A partnership (a 'Firm') formed under the Partnership Act 1890 (the '1890 Act')
- A limited partnership ('LP') formed under the Limited Partnerships Act 1907 (the '1907 Act')
- A limited liability partnership ('LLP') incorporated under the Limited Liability Partnerships Act 2000 (the '2000 Act') and regulated by the Limited Liability Partnerships Regulations 2001 (SI 2001/1090) (the '2001 Regs')

5.02 This chapter is concerned with the general principles applicable to three of these four entities: partnerships, LLPs and LPs. Company law must to some extent be touched upon and not least because, under what will be referred to as the '2009 Regs', Parliament has applied many of the provisions of the 2006 Act, sometimes with modifications, sometimes without, to LLPs.[1]

5.03 At the outset, it is worth observing that these different Acts of Parliament are drafted in markedly different styles. The principles of construction that can be applied to the 2006 Act cannot be applied in the same way to the 1890 and 1907 Acts. The 1890 Act has, on occasion, been described as model legislation.[2] But even its supporters are forced to admit that it lacks coherence. Lord Penrose, for instance, compliment-ing the light-touch regulation of the time, conceded that attempts to develop an 'over rationalised analysis' of the terms of the 1890 Act, para-

---

1 Limited Liability Partnerships (Application of Companies Act 2006) Regulations 2009 (SI 2009/1804).
2 *Spicer v Mansell* [1970] 1 WLR 333 at 335 per Harman LJ.

doxically, increase the risk of error in solving partnership problems.[3] The individual provisions of the 1890 Act, never mind the interaction of different terms of the Act, are often extremely difficult to understand. The Law Commissions have thus recommended wholesale reform of both the 1890 and the 1907 Acts.[4] Only in Scotland, however, does there appear to be any appetite for implementing these sensible proposals.

HISTORY

Common law companies

5.04   Scots law, like a number of other European legal systems, has long treated juristic persons as forming a major part of that fundamental chapter of private law, the law of persons. As a result it has sought to apply, at common law, general principles which can be applied to different cases as and when they arise. Scots law has long recognised many common law corporations – the Faculty of Advocates, the Society of Writers to the Signet and the Royal Faculty of Procurators in Glasgow are just three examples from the legal profession of bodies whose status as juristic persons is recognised at common law – as well as more short-lived business associations, such as partnerships, as having legal personality.[5]

Arran Fishing Company

5.05   Perhaps the most famous case is that of the Arran Fishing Company: *Stevenson v Macnair*.[6] In that case the Court of Session appeared to hold that Scots law, following the law set down by a number of European writers on commercial law, recognised at common law a sort of limited partnership – akin to the *société en commandite* recognised in French law – whereby sleeping partners, who contributed only capital but who were otherwise not engaged in the day-to-day business of the firm, had no liability for the firm's debts beyond their capital contribution. According to first principles, indeed, where the law recognises a juristic person it is exceptional to hold others – the partners – liable for the juristic person's liabilities. For reasons that have never been entirely clear,[7]

---

3 *Maillie v Swanney* 2000 SLT 464 at 468.
4 Law Commission and Scottish Law Commission, *Report on Partnership Law* (Law Com No 283; Scot Law Com No 192, 2003).
5 Many of the authorities and principles are canvassed in the opinions of the consulted judges in *University of Glasgow v Faculty of Surgeons* (1837) 15 S 736, affd (1840) 1 Rob 397.
6 (1757) Mor 14560 and 14667, 5 Br Sup 340, Kames Sel Dec 191 discussed in J Robertson Christie, 'Joint stock enterprises in Scotland before the Companies Acts' (1909) 21 JR 128.
7 J A Lillie, 'Company' in Lord Dunedin et al (eds) *Encyclopaedia of the Laws of Scotland* vol 4 (1927) para 2: in the case of common law companies, 'the liability of the members is unlimited, notwithstanding the decision in *Stevenson v M'Nair*, which was never followed'. Curiously, Bell mentioned *Stevenson v Macnair* for the first time only in the fourth edition of his *Commentaries* published in 1821: II, pp 621–23.

the Arran Fishing Company case was not followed in the litigation that arose out of the collapse of the Ayr Bank,[8] and has never been followed since. In the result, the development of limited liability business vehicles has been almost entirely a matter for UK legislation.[9]

Incorporation by Act of Parliament

5.06 Prior to the advent of the modern form of registered company, there were three ways in which a company could be brought into existence: by Act of Parliament; by Royal Charter; or by private association. Prior to the Union, many of the earliest trading companies in Scotland were incorporated by Acts of the Parliament of Scotland: companies such as the Company of Scotland trading to Africa and the Indies (known to subsequent students of Scottish history as the Darien Company)[10] or the better known example of The Governor and Company of the Bank of Scotland.[11] The Royal Bank of Scotland was founded by Royal Charter of 1727, which was renewed in 1738.[12] In 1746, the British Linen Company was formed by Royal Charter as a Scottish chartered company, and its charter also conferred note-issuing powers.

Chartered companies

5.07 Following a detailed report to Parliament in 1837, the Chartered Companies Act 1837[13] was passed, empowering the Queen to grant, without incorporation,[14] certain privileges and immunities to 'joint-stock companies'. One such privilege, despite the apparent lack of legal personality that such a company, at least in England, would have, was limited liability on the members and officers.[15] In Scots law, it seems, such a joint stock company was a juristic person but not a body corporate. Letters patent issued under the 1837 Act did, however, allow for the privilege of transferable stock, all transfers to be registered with the Lord Clerk Register.[16]

Separation of companies from partnerships

5.08 When the modern company was first introduced, by statute, in

---

8 *Douglas Heron & Co v Hair* (1778) Mor 14605, 8 Fac Coll 57.
9 The law of business associations is a matter reserved to Westminster under the Scotland Act 1998.
10 RPS 1695/5/104 (www.rps.ac.uk/mss/1695/5/104).
11 RPS 1695/5/239. The Governor and Company of the Bank of Scotland came to be registered as a public limited company under the Companies Acts only in 2006 by virtue of a private Act of Parliament: HBOS Reorganisation Act 2006 (c i).
12 The Royal Bank of Scotland Group plc was incorporated under the Companies Acts in 1968.
13 7 Will 4 & 1 Vict c 73.
14 Chartered Companies Act 1837, s 3.
15 Chartered Companies Act 1837, s 4.
16 A short summary is found in Bell, *Principles* (4th edn, 1839; repr 2010) §§ 397–403.

England and Wales, it was on the terms that the members were guarantors of the company's debts.[17] Limited liability was first introduced, in England, under the Limited Liability Act 1855. Like the first Joint Stock Companies Act, however, the 1855 Act did not apply to Scotland.[18] Limited liability was first introduced in Scotland in 1856.[19] Banking companies were first allowed to incorporate in England in 1844[20] and in Scotland from 1846.[21] But incorporation conferred no limitation on the liability of shareholders.[22] Under this regime, therefore, even those who held transferable shares in huge 'companies', such as international banking businesses, had unlimited liability for the company's debts.

5.09   The potentially ruinous consequences for investors, often as far removed from management as creditors, were highlighted in the calamitous collapse of the City of Glasgow Bank in 1878.[23] The international restructuring of this bank – it had significant positions in American railroad concerns, and in Australian and New Zealand land – dominated the pages of the Scottish law reports into the twentieth century.[24] The consequences of the collapse, immediately and painfully felt in Scotland, were much wider: within a couple of years almost all UK banks incorporated themselves under the Companies Acts with limited liability – an option that had been available from 1856 for general commercial companies[25] and from 1858 for banks.[26] By then incorporation with limited liability also entailed an auditing regime introduced as a direct result of the City of Glasgow Bank collapse.[27]

---

17 Joint Stock Companies Act 1844, ss 13 and 25: see discussion in *J H Rayner (Mincing Lane) Ltd v Department of Trade and Industry* [1990] 2 AC 418 at 507D–F per Lord Oliver of Aylmerton. The 1844 Act did not, however, apply to Scotland: see s 2. In California, company shareholders remained guarantors of the company's debts until 1931: R Kraakman et al, *The Anatomy of Corporate Law* (2nd edn, 2010) p 9, n 25.

18 Limited Liability Act 1855, s 18.

19 Joint Stock Companies Act 1856.

20 Joint Stock Banks Act 1844.

21 Joint Stock Banks (Scotland and Ireland) Act 1846. The Joint Stock Banks (Scotland) Act 1856 extended the period for which Her Majesty was able to grant letters patent to a bank beyond twenty years.

22 Joint Stock Banks Act 1844, s 7; Joint Stock Banks (Scotland and Ireland) Act 1846, s 2.

23 For which, see K G C Reid, 'Embalmed in Rettie: the City of Glasgow Bank and the liability of trustees' in A Burrows, D Johnston and R Zimmermann (eds) *Judge and Jurist: Essays in Memory of Lord Rodger of Earlsferry* (2013) p 489.

24 In what may have been the first use of a 'good assets' SPV, 'The Assets Company Ltd' was incorporated under the Companies Acts and it acquired the remaining assets of the bank under a local Act of Parliament the City of Glasgow Bank (Liquidation) Act 1882 (45 & 46 Vict, c clii). The Assets Company Ltd was litigating to the House of Lords and Privy Council as late as 1905 and was finally wound up only in 1955.

25 Joint Stock Companies Act 1856, superseded by the Companies Act 1862, ss 6, 7, and 8.

26 Joint Stock Banks Act, s 1; Joint Stock Companies Act 1858, s 1.

27 Companies Act 1879, s 7(6).

FORMATION

Basics: constitution, name, place of business

5.10 The modern law for companies is now found in the Companies Act 2006. But its provisions are not limited to companies. Taking companies in the context of other business associations, there is one basic point to observe from the outset. It is possible to have a one-(wo)man company – that is to say, a company with only one member and one director.[28] But that is not possible in the case of partnerships, LPs and LLPs: as the 'partnership' part of the designation suggests, these are associations that can be formed only by two or more people.[29] If a partnership has only two partners, both of whom are natural persons, and one dies, the partnership comes to an end. LLPs are different: despite the death of its members, the LLP remains in existence. But if it remains in existence for more than six months with only one member, that member becomes jointly and severally liable with the LLP for the payment of LLP debts contracted[30] after the six-month period.[31]

Registration

5.11 It was once the case that all businesses, whether corporate or not, had to register their business name in the 'Register of Business Names'.[32] That register was abolished in 1981.[33] Since the abolition of the register, it is necessary only for companies, LLPs and LPs to be registered at Companies House. There are separate indices of companies, LLPs and LPs. Each has a registered number and a registered name. In the case of companies and LLPs there must also be a registered office. Companies and LLPs may be registered either in Scotland; in England and Wales; or in Northern Ireland. There is a separate registrar for each jurisdiction.[34] A company incorporated in Scotland must have its registered office in Scotland.

Registered numbers: juristic DNA

5.12 All registered entities have a unique number. A Scottish company number is prefixed by the letters 'SC'. A Scottish LLP is prefixed with the letters 'SO'. A Scottish LP's registered number is prefixed with 'SL'.

---

28 It is a requirement of EU law that member states provide a 'one man' corporate vehicle. In the UK, however, public companies require two directors: 2006 Act, s 154(2). All companies must have at least one director which is a natural person: 2006 Act, s 155. Where the number of members in a public company falls below two, it is competent to petition for the company's winding-up: Insolvency Act 1986, s 122(1)(e).
29 1890 Act, s 1(1); 1907 Act, 4(2); 2000 Act, s 2(1)(a).
30 It is not clear why the wording is limited to debts incurred by way of contract.
31 2000 Act, s 4A(2).
32 Registration of Business Names Act 1916.
33 Companies Act 1981.
34 2006 Act, s 1060.

The importance of the registered number for a corporate entity cannot be overemphasised. Corporate entities can change their name by special resolution and companies do this with surprising regularity.[35] More confusing still is the situation where companies or LLPs swap names.[36] So suppose John enters into a contract on day 1 with Alpha Ltd (SC00001). Alpha Ltd is part of a corporate group. Another company in the group is called Beta Ltd (SC00002). On day 20, Alpha Ltd (SC00001) resolves to change its name the same day to Beta Ltd and, simultaneously, Beta Ltd resolves the same day to change its name to Alpha Ltd. On day 30, John wants to sue the debtor under his contract. Which entity should he sue? The answer is the company with whom he has a contract, whatever its name may now be. The company with whom he had a contract is that with the number SC00001, which is now called Beta Ltd. It is therefore good practice always to include, in any document where a registered entity is being referred to, that entity's registered number so that it can be unambiguously identified. It is the registered number, not the registered name, which is the entity's unique identifier, its DNA. It is not possible to register a company with a name that is the same as a name already registered on the Registrar's index of companies.[37]

5.13 LPs too must be registered at Companies House and they have a registered number.[38] The control on the names of partnerships and LPs is found in a separate part of the Companies Act 2006 dealing with business names.[39] Partnerships and LPs must therefore comply with the detailed rules regulating the words and letters which may be used in the business's name,[40] which are applicable to all businesses, irrespective of the particular business vehicle employed. But there is no requirement for an LP to have a registered office, still less a registered office in Scotland. LPs require only a principal place of business but that principal place of business need not be in Scotland.[41] As a result, some Scottish LPs on the register have an address that is not in Scotland, but in places like St Peter's Port, Guernsey.

5.14 Ordinary partnerships have no registered number, no registered office, no publicity at all. Determining whether a partnership exists is an altogether more metaphysical test, which is considered below.

---

35 2006 Act, ss 77–81.
36 See e.g. *FJ Neale (Glasgow) Ltd v Vickery* 1973 SLT (Sh Ct) 88.
37 2006 Act, s 66.
38 1907 Act, ss 8, 8A, 8B.
39 2006 Act, Part 41.
40 Companies (Trading Disclosures) Regulations 2008 (SI 2008/495); Company, Limited Liability Partnership and Business Names (Sensitive Words and Expressions) Regulations 2009 (2009/2615); Company and Business Names (Miscellaneous Provisions) Regulations 2009 (SI 2009/1085).
41 1907 Act, s 8A(e).

Regulation of business names

5.15 Companies and LLPs must publicise the fact that their members are not liable for the debts of the company or LLP. Indeed, in terms of general principle, it is the position of partnerships and LPs that is exceptional. Companies and LLPs do not have limited liability; and the fact that their members are not liable for the debts of the company or LLP is entirely consistent with the basic principles of the general law. The exceptional vehicles are partnerships and LPs where the (general) partners are effectively guarantors of the vehicle's debts.

5.16 For the purposes of the law of business names, however, there is no prohibition on founding a partnership with an identical name to another partnership; and the Companies Act gives express authority for the use of the partners' surnames in the partnership name.[42] The only protection available to a partnership or limited partnership from another partnership trading under the same name is the common law of passing off or the law of registered trademarks. Where a firm uses a name that does not contain the surnames of all the partners, however, the firm is required to disclose in all business documents the name of each partner together with an address at which documents may be served on them.[43] Failure by companies, LLPs and partnerships to make these disclosures is a criminal offence, which attracts a daily fine for every day of default. Whether there are any civil consequences for breach of the trading disclosures regulations has not been decided but would be possible in egregious cases.[44]

5.17 There is one final point to mention about business names. Sometimes third parties make speculative registration of company names. So suppose Glaxo and Wellcome announce they are to merge. A third party, hearing this news, makes a speculative registration of Glaxo-Wellcome Limited.[45] All other things being equal, Glaxo and Wellcome cannot now use that name because it would be the same as one already on the register.[46] The third party who registered the name offers to change the name of his company in consideration of a large fee. The 2006 Act now allows the possibility of an application to the Company Names Adjudicator,[47] based at the Intellectual Property Office in Cardiff, to order a company to change its name.[48] These provisions deal, among other situations, with the problem of speculative company name registrations that are not made in good faith.[49] Indeed an application

---

42 2006 Act, s 1192.
43 2006 Act, s 1201.
44 Cf. *Nigel Lowe & Associates v John Mowlem Construction plc* 1999 SLT 1298.
45 The example is taken from *Glaxo plc v Glaxo-Wellcome Ltd* [1996] FSR 388, decided under the pre-2006 law.
46 2006 Act, s 66.
47 www.ipo.gov.uk/cna/cna-factsheet.htm. The adjudicator's decisions are available at www.ipo.gov.uk/cna/cna-decisions.htm.
48 2006 Act, s 73.
49 2006 Act, s 69.

may be made by any person (which would include a sole trader, Scottish partnership or limited partnership) on the ground that the company name is the same as a business name associated with the applicant, and in which the applicant has goodwill. Once an applicant establishes that the respondent business has the same name as one in which he enjoys goodwill, it is for the respondent company to justify why the application should not be granted.[50]

EXTERNAL RELATIONS

Liability

5.18 As legal persons, companies, partnerships, LPs and LLPs have unlimited liability. Each can contract liabilities which exceed its assets; and, if that leads to an inability to pay debts as they fall due, the entities can be dissolved, put into administration or liquidation (in the case of companies and LLPs), or sequestrated (in the case of LPs and partnerships). Of cardinal importance, however, is the liability of those who stand behind these vehicles: the shareholders, partners and members. As is well known, in the case of a company or LLP, the members have no liability beyond the amount they agreed to contribute by way of capital – the nominal value of the share (plus any premium) or the amount they have agreed to contribute under an LLP members' agreement. To that extent, therefore, there is an element of 'limited liability'. The position of partnerships and LPs is different and, indeed, exceptional. It is a general principle of private law that each person is liable only for his or her own debts. The position of partners in a partnership, or general partners in an LP, are two well-defined exceptions to this principle, for which express statutory wording was required.[51] So, in a Scottish partnership, partners are jointly and severally liable for the debts of the partnership.[52] For LPs, that means the general partners, if more than one,[53] are jointly and severally liable for the LP's debts; in practical terms, anyone involved in the day-to-day management of an LP is a general partner. It is this aspect of the law of partnership that can make partnerships unattractive to entrepreneurs; but sometimes the reasons for difficulties

---

50 2006 Act, s 69(4). For the procedure, see the Company Names Adjudicator Rules 2008 (SI 2008/1738).
51 *J H Rayner (Mincing Lane) Ltd v Department of Trade and Industry* [1990] 2 AC 418 at 508E per Lord Oliver of Aylmerton.
52 1890 Act, s 9. Partners in an English partnership are jointly, but not severally, liable for the partnership's debts. Confusingly, the words 'joint' and 'several' have exactly opposite meanings in Scots and English law: see W W McBryde, *The Law of Contract in Scotland* (3rd edn, 2007) para 11-01. See para **8.15**.
53 A limited partnership must have more than one partner, but it needs only one general partner.

arise less out of the incidents of a partnership but rather from a lack of attention to the wording used in documentation.[54]

Agency

5.19 Because, in Scots law, partnerships and LPs are juristic persons, each of the partners is an agent of the partnership or LP as the case may be. Curiously, however, the 1890 Act says that the partners are also agents for each other.[55] The provision is drafted with English law in mind, where a partnership has no legal personality. In Scots law, the better view is that the 'agent for each other' element of section 5 needs to be interpreted away.[56] By way of analogy, no one would suggest that directors of a company are agents for each other. To hold that partners of a Scottish firm are agents of each other may cause all sorts of problems. Suppose Alan and Beth form a partnership (AB Partners). Charlie and David form a partnership (CD Partners). Because both entities are juristic persons, it is possible for AB Partners and CD Partners to enter into a partnership or joint venture: ABCD Partners. This structure is not possible under English law. In English law the partners of ABCD Partners are Alan, Beth, Charlie and David. In Scots law, however, the partners of ABCD Partners are two separate partnerships. If section 5 were read literally, however, it would mean that, in the case of the Scottish partnership structure, David was an agent of AB Partners, a partnership of which he is not a partner.

5.20 The general partners, but not the limited partners, have authority to bind an LP;[57] and the members of an LLP have authority to bind an LLP.[58] But a partnership, LP or LLP may be bound also by an agent who has actual or ostensible authority to bind the firm, LP or LLP as the case may be.[59]

---

54 In *AIB Group (UK) Ltd v Martin* [2001] UKHL 63, [2002] 1 WLR 94, for example, a bank (X) advanced moneys to an English firm of two partners, A and B. A and B were jointly and severally liable not just for the loan, but for any other money advanced to either of them by X. X subsequently advanced additional funds only to A. The House of Lords found B jointly and severally liable to repay those funds, though B had never had any benefit of those funds.

55 1890 Act, s 5.

56 *Major v Brodie* [1998] STC 491, 70 TC 576 involved a Scottish partnership, of English QCs running a Scottish farm, subject to Scots law; the case was pursued in the English courts and expert evidence on Scots law was taken from Professor George Gretton and Professor John Murray QC: their opinions are reproduced in an appendix to the case. Professor Gretton's opinion represents the better view of Scots law, although Professor Murray's opinion was preferred as a matter of fact in the English court. See too P Stein, 'The mutual agency of partners in the civil law' (1959) 33 Tulane L Rev 595 at 604 ff.

57 1907 Act, s 6(2).

58 2000 Act, s 6.

59 For ostensible authority, see *Freeman and Lockyer v Buckhurst Park Properties (Mangal) Ltd* [1964] 2 QB 480, [1964] 1 All ER 630.

INTERNAL DECISION-MAKING

5.21   One of the advantages of the private company limited by shares is that, on incorporation, if the members do nothing else, the law provides a default set of terms on which the company is to conduct its affairs: the Model Articles. LLPs and LPs cannot be constituted otherwise than by registration and this additional formal act is usually sufficient to focus the minds of those wishing to employ such a vehicle on the terms on which those vehicles are to conduct business. It is thus normal practice for the affairs of an LLP or LP to be regulated by a written members' or partnership agreement. Matters may be different with a partnership. Since it is possible to get into a partnership without knowing it, partnerships are often encountered which have no written partnership agreement. More common still is the written agreement the provisions of which are either difficult to interpret or say nothing about the problem in question.

5.22   The 1890 Act, however, confers certain basic rights and imposes certain basic obligations on the partners – such as a right to inspect the firm's books[60] – which will be considered in more detail below.

SPECIALITIES: PARTNERSHIPS

Formation

General principles

5.23   No formalities are required to enter into a partnership. This is one of the attractions of a partnership: not only are there no formalities for formation, there is also no continuing publicity in respect of accounts. For this reason, Scottish partnerships may be desirable vehicles – they provide the benefits of legal personality without the commercial inconvenience of publicity. But because there are no formalities at all, it may be difficult, in a case of UK-wide businesses, to determine whether the partnership is Scottish or English or whether there are separate Scottish and English partnerships.[61] All that is required is a 'relation which subsists between persons carrying on a business in common with a view of profit'.[62] Some commercial purpose is thus required.[63] A partnership may arise because there is the carrying on of a business in common with a view of profit, though the business never advanced beyond the prepar-

---

60 1890 Act, s 24(9); 1907 Act, s 6(1) (for limited partners); Limited Liability Partnerships Regulations 2001 (SI 2001/1090) reg 7(8) (for members).
61 See the decision of the First Division in *Mortgage Express Ltd v Dunsmore Reid & Smith* 1996 GWD 40-2295. Cf. Civil Jurisdiction and Judgments Act 1982, s 42(4).
62 1890 Act, s 1(1).
63 *Religious Tract and Book Society v Inland Revenue* (1896) 23 R 390; *Inland Revenue Comrs v Falkirk Temperance Café Trust* 1927 SC 261.

ations for trading.[64] In contrast, where there is merely a prospectus setting out a proposal to enter into a partnership, but those proposals are never implemented, no partnership comes into existence:[65]

> Partnership is a legal status with legal implications. There are certain features which are usually to be found in a partnership. None are present here. There was no firm name, no partnership premises, no partnership employees and no partnership bank account. Nor is there any averment that steps were being taken to establish any of these. There were no partnership accounts or tax returns. None of these is fatal to the contention that there was a partnership, but the lack of any of such things points strongly against the likelihood of there being one.

5.24 A joint venture between two or more people for a particular purpose – such as the development of a plot of land – may amount to a partnership.[66] Partnerships may be formed for a fixed period of time;[67] or for an undetermined period of time – the so-called partnership at will.[68] Where a partnership for a fixed period of time continues beyond its intended period, the terms of the original agreement may nonetheless continue as terms of the partnership-at-will.[69]

5.25 Not all joint ventures of commercially-minded people, however, are partnerships. There may be another basis for the relationship such as a company, a limited partnership or LLP.[70] In the corporate world, 'joint ventures' often, though not always,[71] use a corporate vehicle. Or there may be no intention or any other basis for a partnership at all: English barristers' chambers – unofficial partnerships of freelances – are perhaps the best example.

Indicia of partnership

5.26 Although partnership is a contract, in cases where the parties have perhaps not clearly directed their minds to the nature of their relationship, an avowed lack of any intention to share in the firm's losses does not prevent a finding that the defender is a partner, especially

64 *Miah v Khan* [2000] UKHL 55, [2000] 1 WLR 2123 (fitting out of a restaurant amounted to a partnership though the restaurant never commenced trading).
65 *Pine Energy Consultants Ltd v Talisman Energy (UK) Ltd* [2008] CSOH 10 at para [28] per Lord Glennie.
66 *White v McIntyre* (1841) 3 D 334; *Mair v Wood* 1948 SC 83 at 86 per Lord President Cooper.
67 1890 Act, s 27, for which see *Wallace v Wallace's Trs* (1906) 8 F 558.
68 1890 Act, s 26(1), 'no fixed term'. In *Maillie v Swanney* 2000 SLT 464, Lord Penrose held that a partnership at will (with 'no fixed term') could be terminated without dissolving the partnership under s 32(c), which provides that a partnership for an 'undefined term' may be dissolved on notice. For the interaction between s 26 and s 32, see G Morse, *Partnership Law* (7th edn, 2010) paras 2.07–2.10.
69 *M'Gown v Henderson* 1914 SC 839.
70 1890 Act, s 1. *Chahal v Mahal* [2005] 2 BCLC 655 at para [37] per Neuberger LJ; *Ilott v Williams* [2013] EWCA Civ 645 at para [20] per Arden LJ.
71 See e.g. *Emcor Drake and Scull Ltd v Edinburgh Royal Joint Venture* 2005 SLT 1233.

where there is evidence of an intention to share in profits.[72] Establishing the existence of a partnership is classically a question of substance rather than form:[73]

> If a partnership in fact exists, a community of interest in the adventure being carried on in fact, no concealment of name, no verbal equivalent for the ordinary phrases of profit or loss, no indirect expedient for enforcing control over the adventure will prevent the substance and reality of the transaction being adjudged to be a partnership; and I think I should add, as applicable to this case, that the separation of different stipulations of one arrangement into different deeds will not alter the real arrangement, whatever in fact that arrangement is proved to be. And no 'phrasing of it' by dexterous draftsmen, to quote one of the letters, will avail to avert the legal consequences of the contract.

5.27 But identifying the moment a partnership has been formed, particularly in a case where there is no formal documentation, is a notoriously difficult task.[74] The 1890 Act provides some very general guidance, identifying various factors which may be indicative of a partnership. These factors are set out in s 2 of the 1890 Act:

(1) joint tenancy or common property does not of itself create a partnership, irrespective of what is done with profits;
(2) sharing of gross returns of itself does not create a partnership; and
(3) receipt of a share of profits of a business is prima facie evidence of a partnership, but that evidence may be neutralised where the receipt is: (a) by way of repayment of a debt; (b) remuneration for services;[75] (c) by way of an annuity paid to a widow, widower or civil partner; (d) by way of repayments made pursuant to a written contract of loan;[76] or (e) by way of annuity or otherwise a share of the profits in respect of the consideration payable by virtue of a sale of the goodwill.

5.28 Section 24 prescribes various default rights which, in the absence of an agreement to the contrary,[77] each partner in a firm is entitled to exercise, including: a right to an equal share in the profits; a right to indemnity for expenses; a right to interest on loans made to the partnership (not including capital contributions); a right to participate in management of the business; and a right to sight of the firm's accounts.

---

72 *Pooley v Driver* (1876) 5 Ch D 458 at 483 per Sir George Jessel MR followed in *Brown & Co's Tr v M'Cosh* (1898) 1 F 52 at 60 per Lord President Robertson, affd (1899) 1 F (HL) 86; *Stewart v Buchanan* (1903) 6 F 15.

73 *Adam v Newbigging* (1888) 13 App Cas 308 at 315 per Lord Halsbury LC.

74 Two examples where the parties' relations were bedevilled by informality are *Gillespie v Gillespie* [2011] CSOH 189 and *Maritsan Developments Ltd v HMRC* [2012] UKFTT 283 (a decision of J Gordon Reid QC sitting in Edinburgh).

75 So the drowned fisherman, remunerated by a share of the boat's gross returns, in *Clark v G R & W Jamieson* 1909 SC 132 was held to have been an employee, not a partner. Cf. *Sharpe v Carswell* 1910 SC 391.

76 *Stewart v Buchanan* (n 72).

77 For construction of an agreement held to oust the default rule in s 24, see the decision of the First Division in *Heaney v Downie*, 11 February 1997, unreported.

But these rights are often used by the courts for descriptive purposes too: in considering whether a business relationship amounts to a partnership, the exercise of any or all of the rights that would be conferred by s 24 on a partnership is often taken as indicative of the existence of a partnership. And where someone has effective control of a business, including sharing in profits, contributing capital and having an unfettered right to appoint someone as a partner in the business, such control is indicative of that person being a partner in the business.[78] Conversely, someone who has no share of profits may nonetheless be held to be a partner and liable for its debts where, in the case of a law firm, it was necessary for him to be held out as a partner for regulatory purposes.[79]

Trading

5.29 In terms of s 1(1) of the 1890 Act, 'Partnership is the relation which subsists between persons carrying on a business in common with a view of profit.' Section 45 defines a 'business' as 'carrying on a trade, business or profession'. What amounts to a 'trade, business or profession' is of some importance to Scottish partnerships and limited partnerships which are used as vehicles for the holding of assets or investments. It is sometimes said that investing in assets and drawing the profits from the investments is not a 'trade'.[80] But investing in moveable or immoveable assets and drawing the profits from rents or dividends or capital gains, would today be considered to fulfil the definition of 'carrying on a trade, business or profession'. Lord Justice-Clerk Macdonald has formulated the question, admittedly in the context of a tax case, as: 'Is the sum of gain that has been made a mere enhancement of value by realizing a security, or is it a gain made in an operation of business in carrying out a scheme for profit-making'?[81] The Law Commissions, having considered whether to legislate in this area, decided no clarification was necessary: 'it is difficult to conceive of a term wider than "business" to cover all commercial undertakings. The term seems clearly apt to include investment activities as a commercial venture'.[82] The House of

---

78 *Brown & Co's Tr v M'Cosh* (1898) 1 F 52 at 60 per Lord President Robertson, affd (1899) 1 F (HL) 86.

79 *M Young Legal Associates Ltd v Zahid (a firm)* [2006] EWCA Civ 613, [2006] 1 WLR 2562.

80 Cf. *Glasgow Heritable Trust v Inland Revenue* 1954 SC 266 at 284 per Lord President Cooper: 'Mere realisation of capital assets is not a trade'. But the business in that case was not one that was otherwise concerned with selling capital assets. Other tax cases of high authority have held that drawing rents may amount to a business: e.g. *American Leaf Blending Co Sdn Bhd v Director-General of Inland Revenue* [1979] AC 676, [1978] 3 All ER 1185 (PC).

81 *Californian Copper Syndicate Ltd v Harris* (1904) 6 F 894 at 898, a test approved by the Privy Council in *Commissioner of Taxes v Melbourne Trust* [1914] AC 1001 at 1010 and by the House of Lords in *Ducker v Rees Roturbo Development Syndicate Ltd* [1928] AC 132 at 139.

82 *Discussion Paper on Partnership Law* (Law Com No 159; Scot Law Com No 111, 2000) para 5.10. And see too the view of HMRC reproduced in Law Commission and Scottish Law Commission *Report on Partnership Law* (2003) para 16.25.

Lords has also held that a partnership can be formed with a view to profit though it never commences trading.[83]

Property

5.30 Purchasing property for the business may itself be evidence of subsisting partnership.[84] The technical rules, which historically prevented Scottish firms from owning heritable property, no longer exist.[85] But it remains uncommon for professionally advised partnerships to take title to ownership of land in the name of the partnership, one of the reasons being that a change of partners can give rise to terrifying difficulties regarding entitlements to the partnership assets.[86] Perhaps the only situation where a professionally advised partnership would take title to heritable property in the name of the partnership is where the partnership is being deliberately used as a tax transparent vehicle.

5.31 The near universal practice, therefore, is for the partners for the time being to take title to any heritable property in their own names as trustees for the firm. The rights of individual partners are personal rights against the firm.[87] There are thus three layers: trustees – firm (beneficiary) – partners.[88] Death, retirement or resignation of a partner under this structure does not give rise to property law problems. Trust title is the paradigm case of the elastic title found in joint ownership:[89] the departing partner's share accrues automatically to those who remain; but if the law is clear in principle, that clarity is not reflected in the decided cases. So in one case the lease was granted to the partners 'as trustees for the... firm and the survivors and survivor of them as trustees and trustee'. That title should have been unaffected by any change in the partners. Nonetheless it was held that the lease was terminated on a change of partners – in other words, a change in the personality of the beneficiaries of a trust to which the landlord was a stranger.[90]

5.32 In *Jardine-Paterson v Fraser*,[91] the Lord Ordinary held that a tenant under the lease was the 'business' or (trading) 'house' rather than a recognised juristic person. The difficulty with that proposition is that it

---

83 *Miah v Khan* [2000] UKHL 55, [2000] 1 WLR 2123.
84 *Christie Owen & Davies plc v Raobgle Trust Corporation* [2011] EWCA Civ 1151.
85 Abolition of Feudal Tenure etc (Scotland) Act 2000, s 70. See generally G L Gretton, 'Who owns partnership property?' 1986 JR 163.
86 In *Lujo Properties Ltd v Green* 1997 SLT 225 the lease was granted to '[the firm] and [..] the Partners of said firm as trustees for the said firm'. On one view, that clause must be void for uncertainty.
87 *McIrvine v McIrvine* [2012] CSOH 23 at para [21] per Lord Brodie.
88 *Duncan v The MFV Marigold PD145* [2006] CSOH 128, 2006 SLT 975 at para [16] per Lord Reed (dealing with registration of partners as owners of a fishing vessel under the Merchant Shipping (Registration of Ships) Regulations 1993 (SI 1993/3138)).
89 See K G C Reid, *The Law of Property in Scotland* (1996) para 20.
90 *Moray Estates Development Co v Butler* 1999 SLT 1338. The soundness of this decision may be doubted.
91 1974 SLT 93 at 97.

does not identify a tenant. The idea of a lease in favour of a (trading) 'house' may simply mean, in practical terms, a lease in favour of a particular person (natural or juristic) plus implied consent to assignation of the lease to associated entities of that tenant.[92] Alternatively, the idea of a trading 'house' may be no more than an ostensible holding out by the partners to the world that the business carried on by the original partnership is continuing. The wider world has no way of finding out from a public register what the basis of any 'new' partnership actually is. As a result, the partners cannot seek to rely on the provisions of s 33 to frustrate the claims of a third party creditor,[93] for whereas third parties can normally never know the actual authority of an agent, so too can third parties never know the actual terms of a private partnership agreement. A similar rationale underlies the rules imposing liability on a business (irrespective of its form) which acquires the assets of a partnership, including its name, and continues to allow the business to trade under that name.[94]

Relations of partners *inter se* and knowledge

5.33 Partners owe fiduciary duties to the firm.[95] In Scotland, because a firm is a juristic person it makes sense for the duties to be owed to the firm rather than by each and every partner to the other. But partners also owe each other duties of good faith,[96] and these duties may even arise before the partnership agreement is concluded, imposing, for instance, duties of disclosure in the context of formation of the partnership agreement.[97] There are specific statutory duties to account for private profits[98] and not to compete with the firm.[99] In addition, the Act provides that 'partners are bound to render true accounts and full information of all things affecting the partnership to any partner or his legal representatives'.[100] That duty is not one, it has been said, which is owed at all times; it arises rather in specific circumstances, as when one

---

92 Cf. *Renfrew District Council v AB Leisure (Renfrew) Ltd* 1988 SLT 635.
93 Bell, *Commentaries* (7th edn, 1870) II, p 528. Cf. *Inland Revenue Comrs v Graham's Trs* 1971 SC (HL) 1 at 20 per Lord Reid. See para **5.42**.
94 See para **5.72** below.
95 *Aberdeen Railway Co v Blaikie Brothers* (1853) 15 D (HL) 20, (1854) 1 Macq 461. For modern examples of breaches of duty in the context of solicitors' firms: see *Finlayson v Turnbull (No 1)* 1997 SLT 613 and *Ross Harper & Murphy v Banks* 2000 SC 500, 2000 SLT 699.
96 *Duncan v The MFV Marigold PD145* (n 88) at para [45] per Lord Reed; *O'Neill v Phillips* [1999] UKHL 24, [1999] 1 WLR 1092 at 1098–99 per Lord Hoffmann: 'company law has developed seamlessly from the law of partnership, which was treated by equity, like the Roman *societas*, as a contract of good faith'. See too *Helmore v Smith* (1880) 35 Ch D 436 at 444 per Bacon VC ('utmost good faith'), quoted with approval in *Sim v Howat* [2012] CSOH 171 at para [39] per Lord Hodge.
97 *Manners v Whitehead* (1898) 1 F 171.
98 1890 Act, s 29.
99 1890 Act, s 30.
100 1890 Act, s 28.

partner seeks information from a fellow partner in the context of negotiations between the partners.[101]

5.34 A partner of a firm (like a member of an LLP or a director of a company) is not an employee.[102] Conversely, an employee of the firm who is held out to the world as a partner (the so-called 'salaried partner') is likely to be held to owe similar duties of loyalty and good faith to the firm and to his or her fellow partners. Where partners owe duties, whether to the firm or to fellow partners, the standard of care is, today, an objective standard; looking at the matter objectively, a court will ask what an honest person would have done in the circumstances.[103] Duties of care and skill owed by the firm to third parties are considered in the following section. There is a detailed line of case law setting how and when a company director's knowledge may be attributed to a company.[104] For partnerships, however, the 1890 Act contains a specific provision that notice to a partner is deemed notice to the firm.[105]

Delicts

5.35 Section 10 of the 1890 Act provides that a firm is liable for the wrongful acts of a partner incurred in the ordinary course of the firm's business. The firm is liable for misappropriations of money made by a partner in the course of business.[106] The partners of the firm are jointly and severally liable for such delicts.[107] Wrongful acts include negligent acts or acts which amount, for example, to dishonest assistance.[108] There is, however, an exception with regard to property held by one of the partners in trust: a breach of trust by a partner does not impose on his

---

101 *Sim v Howat* (n 96) at para [40] per Lord Hodge. See too *Ferguson v Patrick & James WS* 1984 SC 115 and *Smith v Barclay* 1962 SC 1.

102 *Bates van Winkelhof v Clyde & Co LLP* [2014] UKSC 32, [2014] 1 WLR 2047: an LLP member was held not to be an employee, but was nonetheless a 'worker' for the purposes of whistleblowing legislation.

103 *Royal Brunei Airlines Sdn Bhd v Tan* [1995] 2 AC 378 at 389 (PC); *Twinsectra Ltd v Yardley* [2002] UKHL 12, [2002] 2 AC 164; *Barlow Clowes International Ltd (in liquidation) v Eurotrust International Ltd* [2005] UKPC 37, [2006] 1 WLR 1476 at para [15]. Similar formulations are adopted by Lord Hodge, in a different context, in *Frank Houlgate Investment Company Ltd v Biggart Baillie LLP* [2013] CSOH 80, 2013 SLT 993 at paras [40]–[45].

104 *Moore Stephens (a firm) v Stone & Rolls Ltd (in liquidation)* [2009] UKHL 39, [2009] 1 AC 1391; *Meridian Global Funds Management Asia Ltd v Securities Commission* [1995] 2 AC 500 (PC).

105 1890 Act, s 16. Despite what is said in *Zurich GSG Ltd v Gray & Kellas* [2007] CSOH 91, 2007 SLT 917, the rationale for s 16 may be in order, for the purposes of English law, to mirror the terms of s 5.

106 1890 Act, s 11, for which see *New Mining and Exploring Syndicate Ltd v Chalmers & Hunter* 1912 SC 126.

107 1890 Act, s 12.

108 *Dubai Aluminium Co Ltd v Salaam* [2002] UKHL 48, [2003] 2 AC 366. For Scots law, see the *obiter dicta* of the Lord Ordinary (Lord Reed) in *Commonwealth Oil & Gas Co Ltd v Baxter* [2007] CSOH 198 at para [197], affd [2009] CSIH 75, 2010 SC 156.

fellow partners personal liability for those breaches of trust.[109] In the late 1940s, the First Division held that a partner who suffered loss as a result of a negligent act of a fellow partner could not sue the partnership as being vicariously liable for the partner's wrongful acts.[110] That case has been followed in modern decisions. But while it may be a general principle that a principal is not *ipso jure* vicariously liable for the acts of his agent,[111] there seems no good reason in the modern law to deny a partner, injured by a negligent act of a fellow partner acting in the course of the firm's business, a claim against the firm.

Partner liability: holding out

5.36 Section 14(1) of the 1890 Act provides that

> Every one who by words spoken or written or by conduct represents himself, or who knowingly suffers himself to be represented, as a partner in a particular firm, is liable as a partner to any one who has on the faith of any such representation given credit to the firm, whether the representation has or has not been made or communicated to the person so giving credit by or with the knowledge of the apparent partner making the representation or suffering it to be made.

5.37 Ordinary principles of agency apply to individuals such as employees or consultants. So someone who is not a partner in the firm, but is held out to the world as such – as in the case of a 'salaried partner' – has ostensible authority on the ordinary principles of agency to bind the firm in the course of the firm's business.[112] Section 14(1), however, is directed not to authority but to personal liability. In the ordinary course of events, an agent acting within his authority has no personal liability on a contract concluded on behalf of a disclosed principal. Section 14(1) provides that, where an individual 'suffers himself to be represented' to a creditor as a partner, that individual becomes liable as a partner to a creditor who, on the strength of that representation, gives credit to the firm.

5.38 A useful example is *UCB Home Loans Corporation Ltd v Soni*.[113] An English solicitor, Mr Soni, had an unorthodox structure of separate businesses based at different offices, each trading under the same business

---

109 1890 Act, s 13.
110 *Mair v Wood* 1948 SC 83 at 86 and 90. But the decision in *Mair* was heavily influenced by the position of employees. A firm employee, at that time, did not have a delictual claim if injured by a fellow firm employee because of the doctrine of 'common employment'. The Division was reluctant to confer on a partner better rights than those enjoyed by an employee. The First Division advised its opinions on 19 December 1947. The doctrine of common employment was abolished six months later: Law Reform (Personal Injuries) Act 1948.
111 In *McE v Hendron* [2007] CSIH 27, 2007 SC 556 at para [131]; Lord Osborne, sitting in an Extra Division of the Inner House, reserved his opinion on the soundness of this view.
112 *Freeman and Lockyer v Buckhurst Park Properties (Mangal) Ltd* [1964] 2 QB 480.
113 [2013] EWCA Civ 62.

name, 'Soni & Co'. Mr Soni was a sole practitioner in respect of the London office. But there was an Essex office where he was in partnership with a Ms Khedrin. Mr Soni obtained mortgage finance from UCB. In these circumstances, since the borrower was a partner in a firm of solicitors acting for UCB, UCB required another partner to sign off the notice of title. Mr Soni forged Ms Khedrin's signature. UCB never received its 'charge by way of legal mortgage'.[114] UCB obtained a judgment against Mr Soni, but it proved worthless. The question was whether Ms Khedrin was also liable to UCB under s 14(1). She had appeared on Soni & Co's usual letterhead as operating from the Essex office and, it was argued, she had therefore 'suffered herself to be represented as a partner in a particular firm'. The judge and the Court of Appeal held that Ms Khedrin had indeed held herself out as being a partner in the firm of Soni & Co. Nonetheless, the Court of Appeal held that she was not liable under s 14(1). The firm of which she was a partner did not trade from the London address and it was clear from the letterhead she used that she operated only from the Essex office. Mr Soni, in order to keep his fraud secret from Ms Khedrin, did not disclose in his correspondence with UCB the existence of the Essex office. Ms Khedrin could not therefore be said to have suffered a representation to be made that she was a partner in the firm trading from the London office.

5.39   Some circumstances, however, will place a third-party creditor on enquiry: as where someone otherwise held out as a partner seeks to borrow money at uncommercial rates; or purports to grant a cautionary obligation on behalf of the firm in respect of the indebtedness of an individual who has no apparent firm connection. In such a case, the third party will not be able to rely on the partner's ostensible authority.[115]

Change of partners

5.40   One of the major difficulties with a partnership is that, without specific agreement on the point, it does not benefit from 'perpetual succession'; in other words, a change of partners gives rise to dissolution of one partnership and creation of another.[116] That may have important consequences for contracts which are said to include an element of *delectus personae*, since a change in the personality of the firm will give the creditor an option to terminate the contract.[117] Nonetheless, the 1890 Act provides, in words which do not fully recognise the ordinary effect of a change in the partnership,[118] that 'a person who is admitted as a partner into an existing firm does not thereby become liable to the creditors

---

114 The English equivalent of a standard security.

115 1890 Act, s 7 and *Paterson Brothers v Gladstone* (1891) 18 R 403; *Fortune v Young* 1918 SC 1; *Walker v Smith* (1906) 8 F 619.

116 *Inland Revenue Comrs v Graham's Trs* 1971 SC (HL) 1 at 4 per Lord Hunter (sitting in LVAC).

117 *Garden, Haig-Scott and Wallace v Prudential Approved Society for Women* 1927 SLT 393.

118 *Sim v Howat* [2011] CSOH 115 at para [13] per Lord Hodge.

of the firm for anything done before he became partner'.[119] But the law of prescription, as it applies to a series of transactions in which goods or services are sold or supplied despite a change of partners, presumes there to be an element of continuity.[120]

Termination and dissolution

5.41 The 1890 Act lacks clarity on (a) the respective relations of the partners inter se, and (b) between individual partners and the firm. As a result of this, perhaps, it is possible for a partner to terminate the agreement he had with the other partners without dissolving the firm.[121] But a partner who is himself in material breach of the partnership agreement may thus lose his right to dissolve the firm based on that agreement.[122] Moreover, a partner who has misused firm assets for private purposes may be liable to pay compound interest on the cost to the firm for his unauthorised use of those assets.[123]

Dissolution

General

5.42 Winding up of the firm's affairs can be carried out by the former partners, under s 38; or by the court, under s 39. In order to understand the consequences of partnership dissolution it is helpful to start with involuntary dissolution. The classic examples of involuntary dissolution provided by the 1890 Act are a partner's death or bankruptcy.[124] The provisions on dissolution in the 1890 Act, however, are expressed to be 'subject to any agreement between the partners'.[125] A partnership agreement may therefore provide that the partnership will continue notwithstanding the death or bankruptcy of one of the partners.[126] The 1890 Act is silent on the question of the effect of retirement or resignation of a partner or the assumption of a new partner. The general view, therefore, is that, without an express agreement to the contrary, retirement, resignation or assumption of a new partner may dissolve the existing partnership and lead to reconstitution of a new partnership. In large commercial partnerships which have traded for many years, such an approach would be unworkable. In such cases, the 'agreement' to oust s 33 may be easily implied in order to reflect the commercial realities of the situation.[127]

---

119 1890 Act, s 17(1).
120 Prescription and Limitation (Scotland) Act 1973, Sch 2, para 1(3).
121 *Maillie v Swanney* 2000 SLT 464.
122 *Hunter v Wylie* 1993 SLT 1091.
123 *Roxburgh Dinardo & Partners' Judicial Factor v Dinardo* 1992 SC 188.
124 1890 Act, s 33(1).
125 1890 Act, ss 32, 33(1), 43 and 44.
126 *Warner v Cunninghame* (1798) Mor 14603 approved in *Hill v Wylie* (1865) 3 M 541 at 543 per Lord Justice-Clerk Inglis.
127 *Inland Revenue Comrs v Graham's Trs* (n 116) at 19–20 per Lord Reid; *Lujo Properties Ltd v Green* 1997 SLT 225 at 235 per Lord Penrose.

Nature of dissolution

5.43 Whereas, with companies, the Insolvency Act 1986 envisages a winding-up of the affairs of the company before the company's final liquidation and removal from the register, the Partnership Act 1890 envisages that dissolution of the partnership may occur prior to the affairs of the partnership being wound up, at least in the case of death or bankruptcy of a partner.[128] The rule is inconvenient, although it is not unique, for this is essentially the position with natural persons: personality ceases with death, yet between death and confirmation of executors there is limbo, a patrimony but no person to represent it. In the case of a dissolved partnership being wound up, however, Lord Reed has suggested *obiter* that the partners are not to be described as trustees.[129] Nonetheless, on dissolution following a partner's death, it has been said to be not only the surviving partners' *right* to realise the firm's assets for the purpose of winding up the firm's affairs, but to be their *duty* to do so.[130]

Winding up by the partners

5.44 Section 38 presumes that the firm has been dissolved and no longer exists. And, if it no longer exists, then, all other things being equal, any purported acts of the partners on the dissolved firm's behalf must bind the partners only personally.[131] But since, in the eyes of the law all persons have a patrimony, the cessation of legal personality does not lead to the extinction of the former person's patrimony. Section 38 recognises the right of the former partners in the firm to intromit with the firm's assets, including existing patrimonial relationships such as contracts which, *ex hypothesi*, must have been terminated on the dissolution of the firm,[132] for although such contracts with the firm must, on the firm's dissolution, come to an end, the partners' secondary liabilities for the firm's debts under those contracts, as a result of s 38, do not.

---

128 *Chahal v Mahal* [2005] 2 BCLC 655 at para [27] per Neuberger LJ.
129 *Duncan v The MFV Marigold PD145* 2006 SLT 975 at paras [52], [65] and [67] per Lord Reed, preferring Lord Westbury's speech in *Knox v Gye* (1871–72) LR 5 HL 656 at 675 (no trust) to Lord Dunedin's speech in *Hugh Stevenson & Sons Ltd v Aktiengesellschaft für Cantonnagen-Industrie* [1918] AC 239 at 248 (remaining partners trustees). The point merits further consideration.
130 *Re Bourne* [1906] 2 Ch 427 at 431–32 per Romer LJ.
131 *Tinnevelly Sugar Refining Co Ltd v Mirrlees Watson and Yaryan Co Ltd* (1894) 21 R 1009.
132 *Inland Revenue Comrs v Graham's Trs* (n 116) at 4 (IH sitting as LVAC) per Lord Hunter: 'Possibly a more accurate statement may be that the surviving partners of the dissolved firm have, in such circumstances, the rights and powers necessary to enable them to wind up the affairs of the dissolved firm and distribute its assets: *Collins v Young* (1853) 15 D (HL) 35 at 36 per Lord Cranworth LC; Bell's *Principles* (10th edn) § 379. Such rights and powers may, in appropriate cases, include the completion of depending contracts. In my opinion, the foregoing view of the law accords with the terms of section 38 of the Partnership Act 1890, and avoids the logical difficulty of asserting that the partnership continues in existence after it has been dissolved by the death of a partner.'

Section 38 thus provides a legal basis for the surviving partners to take such steps as may be necessary to wind up the firm; to attribute those steps to the firm's patrimony; and to ensure that the individual partners (including the estate of any deceased partner) is each bound by the acts of a former fellow partner.[133] It has been held, however, that whatever the juridical nature of the rights and duties imposed on surviving partners, s 38 'does not make the surviving partners parties to the firm's contracts and so keep those contracts alive'.[134]

5.45 What, then, does s 38 authorise? Winding up the firm, as Lord Reed said in *Duncan v The MFV Marigold PD145*,[135] may take different forms: the business may be disposed of as a going concern to a third party; or disposed of to a new firm formed by the surviving partners. In other cases, individual assets may simply be sold to different buyers. The House of Lords has held that a surviving partner has no authority 'to undertake new transactions on behalf of the firm';[136] and that 'the surviving partners have no right to bind the assets of the dissolved firm by making new bargains or contracts'.[137] But these statements cannot be read literally; if assets are to be liquidated and sold – winding-up *par excellence* – the surviving partners will have to enter into contracts of sale – new contracts – with prospective buyers. The dicta from the cases must therefore be read in the context of the commercial realities of the situation. And there may even be cases which warrant the continuation of the business for a limited period. For, as Lord Reed has observed,[138]

> [T]here may be practical advantages in enabling the business of a dissolved partnership to be carried on during the twilight period of winding up: a business may be realised to best advantage as a going concern, and the continuation of trading may be necessary to maintain the value of goodwill.

5.46 The doubts expressed about the former partners' authority to enter into 'new' contracts must therefore be limited to new 'trading' contracts.[139] Contracts concluded for the purposes of winding up the dissolved firm's affairs are expressly authorised by the section.

5.47 The s 38 power may include the power to assign a lease granted in favour of the old partnership in favour of the partners of the old partnership, even if the lease permitted assignation only with the landlord's express written consent.[140]

---

133 It could be that, in this situation, s 5, in so far as it seeks to render the partners agents of each other, has a meaningful application in Scots law.

134 *Inland Revenue Comrs v Graham's Trs* (n 116) at 21 per Lord Reid.

135 2006 SLT 975 at para [22].

136 *Dickson v National Bank of Scotland Ltd* 1917 SC (HL) 50 at 52 per Lord Findlay LC.

137 *Inland Revenue Comrs v Graham's Trs* (n 116) at 21 per Lord Reid.

138 *Duncan v The MFV Marigold PD145* at para [43] per Lord Reed.

139 *Duncan* at para [44] per Lord Reed.

140 *Renfrew District Council v AB Leisure (Renfrew) Ltd* 1988 SLT 635.

Voluntary departures of partners

5.48 It is in the interests of both the firm and any departing partner to agree expressly the effect of his or her departure, either in the original partnership agreement or in an express severance agreement.[141] But any express agreement between the partners is not of itself sufficient to bind third parties. In order to publicise that the partner no longer has ostensible authority to bind the firm, and that the partner is no longer jointly and severally liable for the firm's debts, notice of the partner's departure ought to be placed in the Edinburgh Gazette.[142] The departing partner's right to a share of profits made since his departure and attributable to his share of the partnership assets is a reference to net assets.[143] In the absence of agreement the preferable remedy for a departing partner is to bring an action for count, reckoning and payment against the firm (if it continues) and the other partners.[144]

Dissolution by the court: s 39

5.49 There are also provisions for dissolution to occur under the supervision of the court, on grounds of mental incapacity, prejudicial conduct, persistent breaches of the partnership agreement, business able to be carried on only at a loss, or on the basis that it would be 'just and equitable' to dissolve the partnership.[145] In practical terms, dissolution by the court under s 39 takes place by way of a petition to appoint a judicial factor to wind down the partnership's affairs.[146] But the office of judicial factor is wider and more flexible than appointment under s 39. A judicial factor may be appointed to any 'estate' or patrimony in cases of deadlock, incapacity or alleged illegality.[147] Because of the expense involved in appointment of a judicial factor, however, it must be 'necessary or expedient' to appoint, as where there is a 'danger of loss',[148] for it is a remedy of 'last resort'.[149] The dissolution of LLPs is dealt with in Chapter 14: Corporate Insolvency.

---

141 For the prescriptive periods that apply to obligations prestable on or after termination of the partnership agreement, see Prescription and Limitation (Scotland) Act 1973, Sch 2, para 3; and *Harper v John C Harper & Co (No 1)* 2003 SLT (Sh Ct) 102.

142 1890 Act, s 36(2).

143 1890 Act, s 42(1) discussed in *Sandhu v Gill* [2005] EWCA Civ 1297, [2006] Ch 456.

144 *Green v Moran* 2002 SC 575.

145 1890 Act, s 35(f).

146 *Carabine v Carabine* 1949 SC 521; *McCulloch v McCulloch* 1953 SC 189; *Mahmood, Petr* 2010 GWD 37-753.

147 *Thurso Building Society's Judicial Factor v Robertson* 2000 SC 547. A judicial factor may complete title to heritable property: Titles to Land Consolidation (Scotland) Act 1868, s 24. Where a judicial factor is appointed and the title is in the GRS, the appointment itself vests 'title to the land or real right in land' in the factor: Conveyancing (Scotland) Act 1874, s 44.

148 *Gow v Schulze* (1877) 4 R 928 at 934 per Lord Shand.

149 *Rosserlane Consultants Ltd, Petr* [2008] CSOH 120 at para [20] per Lord Hodge.

Dissolution: other issues

5.50 In the event that the remaining partners fail to deal with all of the firm's assets, the default position is that the Crown, represented by the Queen's and Lord Treasurer's Remembrancer, succeeds to them as *bona vacantia*.[150]

5.51 In principle, Scottish partnerships may commit criminal offences.[151] But in the same way that only the living can be prosecuted, so too can juristic persons be prosecuted only if they exist. It is unusual to have a company restored to the register in order to bring criminal proceedings against it, not least because dissolution of a company is irrelevant to most corporate criminal cases: it is often the management rather than the company who are served with indictments. Sometimes, however, as in the case of health and safety legislation, the criminal offence is committed by the juristic person, not the board members, shareholders, partners or members. In such a case, therefore, ritual suicide has a greater appeal for the juristic rather than the natural person. So in *Balmer v HM Advocate*,[152] a partnership accused of culpable homicide, rendered the indictment incompetent by the simple expedient of dissolving the partnership: a dissolved juristic person could no more be indicted than a corpse. As a result of the decision in *Balmer*, however, the Scottish Parliament has acted to permit partners from dissolved partnerships to be prosecuted for the criminal offences of a firm that has since been dissolved.[153]

Closing accounts

5.52 Section 43 provides that amounts due by surviving partners to a deceased or retiring partner are 'a debt accruing at the date of dissolution or death'. The date on which the debt becomes due is important for the purposes of the prescriptive period. But the valuation of that debt can often occur only after the firm's affairs have been wound up: the assets realised and the debts paid.[154] Section 44 provides the basis on which the partnership's closing accounts should be drawn up. Losses are paid first out of profits, then out of capital and, in the event of a shortfall of capital, by the partners individually 'in the proportion in which they were entitled to share the profits'. In other words, the partner who would have benefitted the most from the firm's success will bear the brunt of the losses as between the partners inter se. All assets, including work in progress, are brought into account.[155] Importantly, there is a

---

150 It may be possible to obtain a retransfer from the QLTR: *Slattadale Ltd v Tilbury Homes (Scotland) Ltd* 1997 SLT 153.
151 See e.g. Corporate Manslaughter and Homicide Act 2007.
152 2008 SLT 799.
153 1890 Act, s 38 and Partnerships (Prosecution) (Scotland) Act 2013, s 1.
154 In *Duncan v The MFV Marigold PD145* 2006 SLT 975 at para [51], Lord Reed described the debt as being '*debitum in praesenti, solvendum in futuro*'. See too *Purewall v Purewall* [2008] CSOH 147, affd 2010 SLT 120.
155 *Bennett v Wallace* 1998 SC 457.

statutory rate of interest of 5 per cent on sums outstanding to partners in the closing accounts.[156]

5.53 Following the approach of the House of Lords in *Cruickshank v Sutherland*,[157] the Court of Session has consistently held that, unless there is a clear agreement to the contrary,[158] the valuation of the firm's assets on dissolution should be done on the basis of current market value rather than historic book value.[159] In England, in contrast, the Court of Appeal has held that there is no such presumption.[160]

5.54 It is important to emphasise, however, that s 44 applies only between the partners *inter se*. Creditors may treat any partners of the firm as being jointly and severally liable for the firm's debts – even if that partner has a counterclaim against his fellow partners for breach of contract; the relations of the partners between themselves are not a matter with which creditors need trouble themselves.[161]

Insolvency

5.55 In England, though partnerships are not juristic persons, there are bespoke provisions for the insolvency of partnerships.[162] In Scotland, ironically, where partnerships do have juristic personality, they are nonetheless subject to the law of personal bankruptcy.[163]

SPECIALITIES: LIMITED PARTNERSHIPS

General principle

5.56 The general principle of law regulating limited partnerships is that, unless otherwise specified, partnership law applies to them.[164]

Uses

5.57 Limited partnerships have varied practical uses. One important traditional use was to hold agricultural leases; indeed, by the end of the

---

156 1890 Act, s 42(1) applied in *Dyce v Fairgrieve and Morisons Solicitors* [2013] CSOH 155.
157 (1923) 92 LJ Ch 136.
158 One example is *Thom's Exrx v Russel & Aitken* 1983 SLT 335.
159 *Noble v Noble* 1965 SLT 415; *Shaw v Shaw* 1968 SLT (Notes) 94; *Clark v Watson* 1982 SLT 450; *Wilson v Dunbar* 1988 SLT 93.
160 *Re White* [2001] Ch 393; *Drake v Harvey* [2011] EWCA Civ 838, [2012] 1 BCLC 724.
161 *Hurst v Bryk* [2002] 1 AC 185.
162 Partnership Insolvency Order 1994 (SI 1994/2421).
163 Bankruptcy (Scotland) Act 1985, s 6(1)(b) and (d). See too *Smith, Petr* 1999 SLT (Sh Ct) 5. There are specific provisions in the Financial Services and Markets Act 2000 in terms of which it is possible for Scottish partnerships and limited partnerships engaged in regulated activity to be placed into corporate insolvency procedures.
164 1907 Act, s 7.

twentieth century, nearly all agricultural leases were granted to limited partnerships.[165] As a result of new legislative provisions in 2003,[166] however, the use of LPs in agricultural leases has become much less common. The other use of the LP is as an investment vehicle, particularly in private equity transactions.[167] Some examples of transactional structures can be gleaned from the case law.[168] The Scottish LP is particularly attractive because it has legal personality, yet offers limited liability, minimum publicity and sometimes tax transparency.

Formation

5.58 Formation of a limited partnership requires registration[169] at Companies House.[170] Each LP therefore has a unique registration number.[171] It is necessary in any limited partnership that at least one partner is designated the general partner. Unlike a partnership, an LP is not automatically dissolved on the death, bankruptcy or mental incapacity of a limited partner.[172] An LP therefore comes close to enjoying perpetual succession. But because there is no similar provision providing for continuation of the LP on the death, bankruptcy or incapacity of the general partner, it cannot be said that an LP enjoys full perpetual succession. As with partnerships, however, the default provisions of the 1890 and 1907 Acts may be modified by express agreement between the partners.

General partner

5.59 As has been seen, all LPs must have at least one partner with unlimited liability for the LP's debts. In practice, it is therefore common to employ a juristic person to act as the general partner.[173] These companies are often easy to spot: the general partner of Alpha Bravo LP might be called Alpha Bravo (General Partner) Ltd.

---

165 For the background to this ingenious use of the LP: see *MacFarlane v Falfield Investments Ltd* 1998 SC 14 at 29 ff per Lord President Rodger; and *Salvesen v Riddell* [2012] CSIH 26, 2012 SLT 633 at paras [8]–[12] per Lord Justice-Clerk Gill (revd on a different point [2013] UKSC 22).

166 Agricultural Holdings (Scotland) Act 2003, ss 72 and 73.

167 I MacNeil, *An Introduction to the Law of Financial Investment* (2nd edn, 2012) pp 151–52, 184–85. See e.g. *Inversiones Frieira SL v Colyzeo Investors II LP* [2011] EWHC 1762; [2012] EWHC 1450.

168 *Greck v Henderson Asia Pacific Equity Partners (FP) LP* [2008] CSOH 2. Another example involving a Scottish LP – interesting for the facts, rather than the law – is *Berghoff Trading Ltd, GEA Holdings Ltd, Caspian Energy Group LP v Swinbrook Developments Ltd* [2009] EWCA Civ 413.

169 1907 Act, s 5.

170 1907 Act, s 15(1).

171 1907 Act, s 8C(3)(b).

172 1907 Act, s 6(2).

173 The 1907 Act makes express provision only for corporate *limited* partners: 1907 Act, s 4(4), but the competence of the use of corporate general partners has never been doubted and their use is widespread.

Partners' relations inter se

5.60   The rights and obligations of a limited partner, as his designation would suggest, are limited: limited partners are not agents of the LP;[174] they have no right to dissolve the LP by notice;[175] and they have only limited voting rights. Management decisions, in the absence of any agreement to the contrary, are a matter for the majority of the general partners.[176] A limited partner does have the right to inspect the LP's books and, in the words of the 1907 Act, 'to examine into the state and prospects of the partnership business and advise the [general] partners thereon',[177] but that right is a limited right and, in some circumstances, the general partners may be able to refuse to provide information to a limited partner.[178] Crucially, a limited partner has no ostensible authority to bind the LP;[179] and he has no right to engage in management (and thus he has no right to vote on managerial decisions). The Act contains a strong disincentive against limited partners attempting to participate in management decisions: the limited partner who purports to do so becomes personally liable for the LP's debts as if he were a general partner,[180] without necessarily obtaining the rights of a general partner.[181]

5.61   Any LP agreement gives consideration to exit provisions, since the Act provides that, in the event that a limited partner, during the life of the LP, seeks to leave and have his capital contribution repaid, the investor attracts liability 'for the debts and obligations of the firm up to the amount so drawn out or received back'.[182] In practical terms, therefore, exit may often be by way of assignation of the limited partner's share, with the exiting partner obtaining his investment by way of payment from a third party as consideration for the assignation. In LPs, a limited partner can transfer his share in the LP, although, as in partnerships, the consent of the general partners (but not the limited partners) is required. In addition, assignation of a limited partner's share requires publication by notice in the Edinburgh Gazette and, until that notice is published, the assignation 'is deemed to be of no effect'.[183] It is probably

---

174   1907 Act, s 6(1).
175   1907 Act, s 6(5)(e).
176   1907 Act, s 6(5)(a).
177   1907 Act, s 6(1).
178   For limited partners' rights to see documents relating to the LP's investments, see *Inversiones Frieira SL v Colyzeo Investors II LP* (n 167).
179   1907 Act, s 6.
180   1907 Act, s 6(1).
181   So, in *Limited Partners in Henderson PFI Secondary Fund II LP (a firm) v Henderson PFI Secondary Fund II LP* [2012] EWHC 3259 (Comm), [2013] QB 934, where the limited partners in an LP were permitted to bring a common law derivative action, the judge held that the bringing of such an action would amount to management and the limited partners would thus become liable as general partners for the LP's debts.
182   1907 Act, s 4(3).
183   1907 Act, s 10(1).

the case, however, that, since a limited partner's share is arrestable,[184] such a share remains arrestable by the transferor's creditors until the date of publication of the notice in the Gazette.

SPECIALITIES: LLPs

General principles

5.62 An LLP is a body corporate.[185] Despite its name, an LLP therefore has more in common with a company than a partnership. As a result, large swathes of the Companies Act 2006 and associated delegated legislation apply to LLPs:[186] corporate names; accounting; company charges; dissolution: these are just four examples where the regime that applies to LLPs is the corporate regime.

External relations

5.63 Each member of an LLP has ostensible authority to bind the LLP. So too does anyone else held out as having equivalent authority, such as someone who is designated as a 'partner' (as is the case with most professional services firms). On the flip-side, a claim under a contract purportedly concluded on the LLP's behalf by an agent before incorporation does not bind the LLP.[187] But a representation made by a person, R, to an individual, I, who subsequently incorporates an LLP, which LLP, to R's knowledge, acts in reliance of the representation, may give rise to a duty of care owed by R to the LLP.[188]

Members inter se

5.64 Although there are many aspects of the LLP that are similar to companies, there remain aspects that are akin to partnerships. The default rights of members, for instance, are similar to those found in the 1890 Act: the right to share in profits; right to indemnification for expenses incurred in the course of the LLP business; right to participate in management; no right to remuneration; and no right to assign interest in the LLP without consent of the other members.[189] Each member has a right to call other members to account for their intromissions with the LLP's assets; that right to an accounting extends also to provision of 'full information'.[190] The default provision on decision-making is that of a bare majority of the members.[191] That provision appears to envisage a

184 This is implied from 1907 Act, s 6(5)(c).
185 2000 Act, s 1(2).
186 2009 Regs.
187 2006 Act, s 51 (applied to LLPs by 2009 Regs, reg 7); *Tinnevelly Sugar Refining Co Ltd v Mirrlees Watson and Yaryan Co Ltd* (1894) 21 R 1009; *Cumming v Quartzag Ltd* 1980 SC 276.
188 *Cramaso LLP v Viscount Reidhaven's Trs* [2014] UKSC 9, 2014 SLT 521.
189 Limited Liability Partnerships Regulations 2001 (SI 2001/1090) reg 7(1)–(5).
190 2001 Regs, reg 7(8).
191 2001 Regs, reg 7(6).

vote on the basis of one member, one vote rather than, as is the norm in bespoke members' agreements, voting tied to capital accounts. Only two matters require unanimity (although, again, it is quite competent for the members' agreement to modify these rules). These two matters are a decision to change the nature of the LLP's business;[192] or a decision to expel a member.[193] Members of an LLP owe their fiduciary duties to the LLP, not to each other – unless the members' agreement expressly so provides.[194]

Unfair prejudice and derivative actions

5.65 LLPs are subject to the provisions of the Companies Act 2006 on unfairly prejudicial conduct.[195] The right of petition for unfair prejudice is conferred on individual members. The court has a wide discretion in the orders it may make. Unlike rights arising on insolvent liquidation, a member's right to petition for unfair prejudice is an 'optional right'.[196] As a result, it is possible for members of an LLP by unanimous written agreement to exclude a member's right to petition the court for an order in respect of unfairly prejudicial conduct.[197] A similar result may be achieved where the membership agreement refers all disputes among the members to arbitration.[198] There are no provisions in the Regulations conferring on members of an LLP the right to bring a derivative action under s 265 of the Companies Act 2006. But it is likely that such a right exists at common law:[199] it has been held that it is possible, in principle, for the limited partners of an LP to bring a derivative action;[200] and it has been further held in England that a member of an LLP, which LLP was the sole shareholder in a company, could bring a derivative action on behalf of the company.[201] In Scotland it is likely that any such common law derivative action would now proceed as if it were being brought under the 2006 Act.[202]

---

192 2001 Regs, reg 7(6).
193 2001 Regs, reg 8.
194 *F & C Alternative Investments (Holdings) Ltd v Barthelemy* [2011] EWHC 1731, [2012] Ch 613.
195 2006 Act, s 994 as applied by 2009 Regs, reg 48.
196 *Fulham Football Club (1987) Ltd v Richards* [2011] EWCA Civ 855, [2012] Ch 333 at para [78] per Patten LJ.
197 2006 Act, s 994(3) as applied by 2009 Regs, reg 48 (sub-paragraph (3) does not appear in the version of s 994 in the 2006 Act as it applies to companies).
198 As a result of which, the court would be bound to sist the petition: Arbitration (Scotland) Act 2010, s 10.
199 For which, see *Anderson v Hogg* 2002 SC 190, 2002 SLT 354 and *Wilson v Inverness Retail & Business Park Ltd* 2003 SLT 301.
200 *Limited Partners in Henderson PFI Secondary Fund II LP (a firm)* (n 181).
201 *Universal Project Management Services Ltd v Fort Gilkicker Ltd* [2013] EWHC 348 (Ch), [2013] 3 WLR 164.
202 2006 Act, s 266, the procedure for which is elaborated in *Wishart v Castlecroft Securities Ltd* [2009] CSIH 65, 2010 SC 16.

Company charges and insolvency

5.66 The floating charge is not recognised at common law.[203] The floating charge is thus part of Scots law only as a result of the statutory provisions which permit incorporated companies and industrial and provident societies to create them.[204] LLP legislation applies various provisions on company charges to LLPs, namely the provisions on ranking and alteration of floating charges and one of the definition sections is applied to floating charges.[205]

5.67 An LLP, like a company, must register any charges at Companies House within twenty-one days of creation.[206] Partnerships and limited partnerships have no capacity to grant floating charges. One complication, however, arises where one of the partners is a company or LLP. In a limited partnership, the general partner is very often a company. In both partnerships and LPs, the normal practice is for the partners (the general partners in the case of an LP) to hold assets of the partnership or LP in trust for the partnership or LP. In that situation, where the partner or general partner holding the assets in question is itself a company or LLP, it is possible for a corporate general partner to create a floating charge over the assets it holds, in its capacity as trustee for the partnership or limited partnership as the case may be.

Incorporation of partnership as LLP

5.68 A partnership may agree to 'incorporate' as an LLP or limited company. There are a number of ways of doing so. But perhaps the most famous company law case of all time, *Salomon v A Salomon and Co Ltd*,[207] provides a useful case study for incorporating an existing business. The normal case, which the law presumes,[208] is that the business and assets of the partnership are purchased by the corporate entity, the consideration for the purchase being equity in the company, and the partnership is thereupon dissolved. Since a Scottish partnership is a juristic person, any sale of partnership property to a corporate entity, the seller to which the consideration (in equity) should be paid is the partnership not the individual partners. The presumption is that the partnership is dissolved

---

203 *Carse v Coppen* 1951 SC 233.
204 Companies Act 1985, s 462; Industrial and Provident Societies Act 1967, s 3. See further para **14.52**.
205 2001 Regs, Sch 2, part I, applying ss 464, 466 and 486 of the Companies Act 1985 to LLPs (but not, curiously, s 462). See too Limited Liability Partnerships (Amendment) Regulations 2009 (SI 2009/1833), reg 2(2).
206 2006 Act, s 859A(4) as applied to LLPs by 2009 Regs, reg 32 (added by Limited Liability Partnerships (Application of Companies Act 2006) (Amendment) Regulations 2013 (SI 2013/618).
207 [1897] AC 22. In *Salomon*, the consideration was partly paid in equity, and partly in debt; the debt was secured by a floating charge in favour of the seller over the property acquired by the company. The result was not only that Mr Salomon obtained limited liability for the future, but he became a secured creditor for the balance of the purchase price.
208 *Chahal v Mahal* [2005] 2 BCLC 655 at para [29] per Neuberger LJ.

on the incorporation of the business, but the presumption may be rebutted.[209]

Dissolution

5.69 LLPs are subject to the corporate winding-up regime. In the event that the liquidator fails to deal with LLP assets, the default position is that the Crown, represented by the Queen's and Lord Treasurer's Remembrancer, succeeds to them as *bona vacantia*.[210]

BUSINESS ACQUISITIONS

Assets or equity?

5.70 Generally speaking there are two basic structures for corporate acquisitions. The first can apply only to a target business which is a body corporate: an equity acquisition whereby the majority of the target company's share capital is acquired. The second possibility is to acquire individual assets of the target business.

5.71 There are important practical consequences as between the two approaches. As a general principle, acquisition of individual assets means the buyer acquires only the assets; the seller's liabilities remain with the seller. But the transfer of many individual assets of large businesses is a cumbersome exercise. A buyer that acquires the equity in a company, in contrast, takes the company warts and all: the buyer acquires the shares in the company, not any rights in individual assets held by the company. The change in the company's members has no effect on the company's personality and thus no effect on the company's liabilities. The value of the company to the buyer in those circumstances is only as good as the company's liabilities. It is for these reasons that, in corporate acquisitions, long and drawn-out 'due diligence' exercises are often undertaken.

Partnership acquisitions

5.72 Where a new firm acquires the assets of an old firm by sale and payment of a price, the general rule is that the new firm, as a separate juristic person, has no liabilities for the debts of the old firm.[211] But matters are often unclear, as where little thought is given to the effect on the firm's assets on a change of partners, where there is little in the way of formal documentation, no express transfers of any assets, and the

---

209 As indeed it was in *Chahal v Mahal*.
210 See 2006 Act, ss 1012–1013, 1020–1022, applied in amended form to LLPs by 2009 Regs, reg 54. Assets which have been inherited by the Crown by oversight may be reacquired, subject to agreement, by a conveyance from the QLTR: see e.g. *Slattadale Ltd v Tilbury Homes (Scotland) Ltd* 1997 SLT 153.
211 *Stephen's Tr v MacDougall & Co's Tr* (1889) 16 R 779; *Thomson & Balfour (a firm) v Boag & Son* 1936 SC 2.

business carries on as before. As has been seen, the effect of a change in partners is, in principle, to dissolve the firm and, if the business continues, to constitute a new firm. If the new firm pays for the assets of the old firm, then the old firm's creditors are protected: they can look to the purchase price.[212] But where there has been no consideration paid, the law, in order to protect the creditors of the old firm, holds the new firm liable for the old firm's debts.[213] The doctrinal basis for the new firm's liability for the debts of the old has been said to be an implied unilateral undertaking.[214]

5.73 It is sometimes said that a new firm becomes liable for the old firm's debts where a new partner is assumed, creating a new firm which carries on as before, but the new partner in the firm has not contributed any capital. As Lord Hodge has pointed out, however, a capital contribution to the new firm is of limited assistance to the creditors of the old firm.[215] A court will therefore look at the whole circumstances of the case, including the terms of any contractual provisions; but what is of particular importance is whether payment was made for any assets acquired by the new firm from the old. A contractual provision between the old firm and the new firm, or a provision in the new firm's partnership agreement that the new firm is not liable for the debts of the old firm, may be ignored by the court where there is no evidence of payment for the assets.[216]

5.74 The doctrine is not, however, generally applied to the situation where the business of a firm has been acquired by a company. One attempt to argue that the doctrine applied to the case where the transferee was a company was unsuccessful because the transferee company had paid a considerable consideration for the assets it acquired.[217]

COMPARATIVE CONSIDERATIONS

Corporate mobility: UK companies and the European Union

5.75 The general principle, we have seen, is of one-person, one-patrimony. That person may be a natural person (such as a sole trader) or a juristic person (such as a company). In both cases, however, all that person's assets are liable to satisfy the claims of creditors. In the UK, it is possible to form a private limited company with a share capital of £1 with very little formality. Such a company, registered in Scotland, can

---

212 *Henderson v Stubbs Ltd* (1894) 22 R 51 at 55 per Lord Adam.

213 *M'Keand v Laird* (1861) 23 D 846 (a decision of seven judges); *Heddle's Exrx v Marwick & Hourston's Tr* (1888) 15 R 698; *Miller v MacLeod* 1973 SC 172.

214 *Sim v Howat* [2011] CSOH 115 at para [33] per Lord Hodge.

215 *Sim v Howat* at para [31].

216 *M'Keand v Laird* at 851 per Lord Justice-Clerk Inglis.

217 *Ocra (Isle of Man) Ltd v Anite Scotland Ltd* 2003 SLT 1232. Cf. *National Bank of Greece and Athens SA v Metliss* [1958] AC 509 and *Britton v Maple & Co Ltd* 1986 SLT 70.

then be used to run a business in any EU country.[218] Other European countries, in contrast, often require a more significant minimum paid-up capital contribution before it is possible to incorporate a company:

Partnerships, LPs, LLPs

5.76 It should be mentioned that, in the UK, a full suite of partnership vehicles is not available. So, in English law, an LP with legal personality is not possible; in Scots law an LP without legal personality is not possible; and, in neither Scots nor English law is it possible to have an LP which is a body corporate.[219] Other jurisdictions, particularly offshore jurisdictions such as Jersey, offer a full suite of possibilities.[220]

Foreign companies in UK transactions

5.77 In corporate and financial transactions it is often the case that the parties to a transaction, governed by Scots law, are juristic persons formed or incorporated under the laws of foreign jurisdictions. In such cases it is common for a law firm in the jurisdiction where the foreign company is incorporated to be asked to provide a 'power and capacity' legal opinion confirming that the vehicle in question has the requisite power and capacity under its own law to enter into a transaction subject to Scots law. Similarly, Scots lawyers are often asked to provide power and capacity legal opinions for foreign lawyers that Scottish entities – companies, LLPs, LPs and partnerships – have the requisite power and capacity to enter into transactions governed by a foreign law.

---

218 Case C-212/97 *Centros Ltd v Erhversvs-og Selskabsstyrelsen* [1999] ECR I-1459; Case C-208/00, *Überseering BV v Nordic Construction Company Baumanagement GmbH* [2002] ECR I-9919. See generally P Davies and S Worthington, *Gower and Davies Principles of Modern Company Law* (9th edn, 2012) para 6–17 ff.
219 It was not always so: under the Companies Act 1867 (30 and 31 Vict, c 131), ss 4–8, it was possible to incorporate a company in terms of which the shareholders had limited, but the directors had unlimited, liability for the company's debts. Because such a company was a body corporate, however, it was different from the limited partnerships introduced by the 1907 Act (which are juristic persons, but not bodies corporate).
220 LP with no juristic personality; LP with juristic personality; LP with juristic personality and a body corporate.

Chapter 6

Sale of Goods

6.01 This chapter discusses Scots law in relation to the contract of sale of goods as governed by the Sale of Goods Act 1979. It concentrates on the structure and the essential aspects of this area of the law. Therefore it does not deal with contracts for hire and for hire purchase, and it does not discuss the Consumer Credit Act 1974, save for a few points which are considered very briefly. It does not examine the Unfair Contract Terms Act 1977 ('UCTA') and the Unfair Terms in Consumer Contracts Regulations 1999 either.[1] This chapter presupposes knowledge of the general principles of contract and property law which are set out elsewhere.[2]

6.02 The Sale of Goods Act 1979 is based on the Sale of Goods Act 1893, a piece of English legislation, which was, however, almost immediately adopted also in Scotland.[3] The original terminology was therefore according to English law, but, fairly recently, amendments to the Sale of Goods Act 1979 have inserted the proper terminology of Scots law in most instances.

THE CONTRACT OF SALE OF GOODS

Definition of sale, distinction from other contracts

6.03 The contract of sale is an agreement in relation to a subject matter and its price, paid in money, between the seller and the buyer for the purpose of transferring ownership in the subject matter to the buyer. Where the subject matter in question is 'goods', as defined by the law,

---

1 For these statutes one may consult more comprehensive works on contract law and the law of sale of goods, e.g. H L MacQueen and J M Thomson, *Contract Law in Scotland* (3rd edn, 2012) pp 299–318; J Adams and H L MacQueen, *Atiyah's Sale of Goods* (12th edn, 2010) pp 216, 244, 248. In this chapter the potential amendments by the Consumer Rights Bill which is currently going through Parliament could not be considered.

2 See Chapters 2 and 3.

3 The 1893 Act applied (formally) in Scotland since 1 January 1894: see R Brown, 'Sale of Goods Act' (1893) 1 SLT 536. See also 'Current topics: Sale of Goods Bill' (1889) 1 JR 310 at 311; A F Rodger, 'The codification of commercial law in Victorian Britain' (1992) 108 LQR 570 at 581–83.

we have a sale of goods contract. The definition of the sale of goods contract is in s 2(1) of the Sale of Goods Act 1979:[4]

> A contract of sale of goods is a contract by which the seller transfers or agrees to transfer the property in goods to the buyer for a money consideration, called the price.[5]

6.04 The contract of sale in general, or of sale of goods specifically, has to be distinguished from other contracts, such as *barter* (exchange of goods against goods, not against money[6]), *gift* (transfer without money in exchange), or the *contract of deposit* (delivery of goods to place them in the custody of another who must prevent the loss or damage of the goods and return them to the owner/depositor as agreed).[7]

6.05 An important exclusion can be found in the Sale of Goods Act 1979 itself: a contract of sale which is intended to operate by way of mortgage, pledge, charge, or other security contract is not a contract of sale of goods under the Sale of Goods Act (s 62(4)). Thus the Act does not apply to a contract to sell goods where the true intention is using the goods as a security for a loan of money. In such cases the debtor 'sells' goods to the creditor, with the intention that they will be transferred back when the debt is paid off. Since all the creditor wants is security for the debt, the creditor will usually allow the debtor/'seller' to retain possession. Section 62(4) means that the special rules in the Sale of Goods Act 1979 which allow ownership to pass without delivery do not apply and the creditor will not obtain the real right of ownership.[8] In these cases the courts seek evidence whether the transaction was genuinely intended to be a sale. If it was really a method to raise finance, then this is not a sale.[9]

The formation of the contract

6.06 The formation of a contract of sale of goods follows the general rules of the formation of contract as discussed in Chapter 2: General Principles of Contract.[10] Capacity to buy and sell is regulated by the

---

4 Section numbers in this chapter without further reference are to the Sale of Goods Act 1979 (c 54).

5 In more precise terminology according to Scots law this section would read: 'A contract of sale of goods is a contract by which the seller transfers or agrees to transfer *ownership* in goods to the buyer for *money*, called the price.'

6 Part exchanges, typically the sale of a new car against money *and* the buyer's old car, are regarded as sales, not barters, see *Sneddon v Durant* 1982 SLT (Sh Ct) 39.

7 This is discussed in Chapter 2: General Principles of Contract. See also Bell, *Principles* (4th edn) § 85 on the criteria of the contract of sale, and MacQueen and Thomson, *Contract Law in Scotland*, pp 4–5.

8 The Scots common law of property would apply in place of the Sale of Goods Act 1979, but that would require delivery of the goods for the passing of ownership (see K G C Reid, *The Law of Property in Scotland* (1996) para 609), and that does not happen.

9 *Ladbroke Leasing (South West) Ltd v Reekie Plant Ltd* 1983 SLT 155 at 159.

10 See para **2.20** ff.

general law concerning capacity to contract and to acquire and transfer property.[11] There must be a *consensus in idem* (typically by way of offer and matching acceptance) as to the essential terms of the contract – in the case of a contract of sale these are the subject matter or commodity and the price. Otherwise there is *dissensus* (e.g. seller wants to sell for 100, buyer wants to buy for 80). If there is seemingly consensus but the objective intention of one of the parties (or even both) is not reflected in the consensus ostensibly expressed (so there is objectively no *consensus in idem*), then there is *error* (and potentially misrepresentation) which vitiates the consensus and the formation of the contract. The contract is also defective if one party fraudulently induced the other to enter into the contract.[12]

6.07   The Sale of Goods Act 1979 distinguishes between *contracts of sale* (the property in the goods is transferred from the seller to the buyer), and *agreements to sell* (the transfer of property in the goods is to take place at a future time, or subject to some condition later to be fulfilled).[13] Sale of goods contracts may be absolute or conditional.[14] There is also a sale of goods contract where the seller initially acquires the goods depending on a contingency which may or may not happen.[15] A typical example would be the (contingent) sale of future crop.[16]

6.08   The actual formation of a contract of sale is not subject to any formality requirements for its validity. Contracts of sale can be made in writing (with or without seal), orally, or partly in writing and partly orally. A contract of sale may also be implied from the conduct of the parties (s 4(1)). Everyday purchases are often contracts of sale implied by conduct, for example putting the goods on the conveyer belt at the supermarket checkout, or pointing to the goods and the seller handing them over, without necessarily any exchange of words. The only situations when formality requirements apply is in the case of hire-purchase and credit-sale contracts governed by the Consumer Credit Act 1974.[17]

6.09   There is a distinction between *commercial contracts* of sale, when both parties are dealing in the course of business, and *consumer contracts* of sale, in which case a buyer not in the course of business (often, not

11 s 3(1).
12 See also e.g. MacQueen and Thomson, *Contract Law in Scotland*, pp 39–40, 45, 51, 162, 167–68, 180. On the general treatment of the formation of contract, see para **2.20** ff.
13 s 2(4) and (5). The *agreement to sell* becomes a *sale* when the time elapses or the conditions are fulfilled subject to which the property in the goods is to be transferred, see s 2(6).
14 s 2(3).
15 s 5(2).
16 If the crop does not come into existence, the sale can be considered as a contingent sale in which case the condition has not been fulfilled, so that the contract does not become operative in the first place. Or this scenario can also be interpreted as a case of s 7 (goods perishing after agreement to sell and before sale): see Adams and MacQueen, *Atiyah's Sale of Goods*, p 81.
17 See brief outline below in paras **6.16**, **6.17**.

always, a private individual) contracts with a seller who is dealing in the course of business.[18] Such a buyer is the 'consumer'. This distinction is particularly important in the context of buyer's remedies for a seller's breach of the contract of sale.[19] There are also purely *private contracts* of sale where neither party is dealing in the course of business. This distinction between commercial/consumer sales and private sales is important for the assessment whether in a contract of sale the implied terms as to the right quality of goods apply.[20]

Definition of 'goods' (s 5(1), s 61(1))

6.10 The Sale of Goods Act 1979 applies only to contracts of sale of *goods*.[21] 'Goods' are defined as 'all corporeal moveables except money' (s 61(1)).[22] This also includes an undivided share in goods.[23] Thus heritable property (land), and incorporeal moveable property, such as company shares and intellectual property, are excluded. Following the statutory definition of 'goods' timber which is felled by the buyer on the seller's land under a contract of sale with the seller falls under the definition of 'goods'.[24] According to (not entirely convincing) case law,[25] extracted minerals are, however, not 'goods', but subject to an agreement granting a title to land.

6.11 While incorporeal moveable property is excluded, software may be 'goods' for the purpose of the Act. Relevant here is not the software itself as a copyright-protected work, but the carrier, for example a computer disk. The decisions are inconsistent. In *Beta Computers v Adobe Computers*[26] it was held that a contract for the supply of computer software is a *sui generis* contract, with elements such as sale of goods and licence contracts. However, in *St Albans v International Computers*[27] the court said that computer disks are within the definition of 'goods' under s 61, although this statement was obiter.

6.12 The division between specific and unascertained goods is particularly relevant to the question of transfer of ownership and of risk.[28] *Specific goods* are goods 'identified and agreed on at the time a contract of

---

18 MacQueen and Thomson, *Contract Law in Scotland*, p 5.
19 ss 48A–48C. See paras **6.98–6.107** below.
20 See the different rules of applicability of s 13 and s 14, discussed below in paras **6.56** ff.
21 s 1(1).
22 This includes particularly 'emblements, industrial growing crops, and things attached to or forming part of the land which are agreed to be severed before sale or under the contract of sale': s 61(1).
23 s 61(1).
24 *Munro v Liquidator of Balnagown Estates Co Ltd* 1949 SC 49. This is an application of the definition of 'goods' in s 61(1).
25 *Morgan v Russell & Sons* [1909] 1 KB 357.
26 *Beta Computers (Europe) Ltd v Adobe Systems (Europe) Ltd* 1996 SLT 604.
27 *St Albans City and District Council v International Computers Ltd* [1996] 4 All ER 481.
28 See para **6.18** ff below.

sale is made' (s 61(1)). *Unascertained goods*[29] are (a) purely generic goods, such as 100 tonnes of rice; (b) goods to be manufactured or grown by the seller; or (c) an unidentified part of a specified whole, such as 200 tonnes out of a particular load of 500 tonnes of wheat.[30] Goods in class (b) are necessarily also *future goods* (see immediately below), while goods in classes (a) and (c) are either existing or future goods, depending on the circumstances.

6.13 The Act distinguishes further between *existing goods* and *future goods* (s 5(1)). Existing goods – whether specific or unascertained – are those goods which the seller owns or possesses when the contract is concluded. Future goods are goods to be manufactured or acquired by the seller after the formation of the contract of sale. This means the goods are either not yet in existence, or they are already in existence but not yet acquired by the seller. Where under a contract of sale the seller sells future goods,[31] this contract operates as an *agreement to sell* these goods.[32]

Ascertainment of price, valuation (ss 8–9)

6.14 The second essential element of a sale of goods contract is the price. The seller transfers the property in goods to the buyer for a *price*,[33] paid in money. This price is normally fixed by the contract, but it may also become fixed in a manner agreed by the contract, or it may be determined in the course of dealing by the parties (s 8(1)). If an agreement as to the price is absent, this is a 'fundamental lack of consensus' and no contract has been concluded.[34] Problems arise where the parties conclude a sales contract 'at a price to be agreed by the parties'. Some cases accept such a stipulation and regard this as a binding contract, since the parties had the intention to be bound.[35] Other decisions do not recognise an agreement in relation to a price 'to be agreed' as a contract.[36] Where there is a failure to stipulate a price (*not* where there is a *dissensus* about the price), the law can step in. Where the price is not determined as set out in s 8(1), the buyer must pay a reasonable price (s 8(2)); what constitutes a reasonable price is a question of fact depending on the circumstances of each particular case (s 8(3)).

6.15 It is also possible to have the price fixed by the valuation of a third party who then determines the price in the contract (s 9(1)). If the

---

29 Unascertained goods are not defined by the Sale of Goods Act 1979.
30 Detailed discussion e.g. in Adams and MacQueen, *Atiyah's Sale of Goods*, p 82.
31 See definition in s 5(1).
32 s 5(3).
33 s 2(1).
34 *May & Butcher v The King* [1934] 2 KB 17 (HL).
35 *Foley v Classique Coaches Ltd* [1934] 2 KB 1. In that case, however, the agreement contained an arbitration clause which enabled a reasonable price to be fixed if there was disagreement between the parties.
36 *Courtney & Fairbairn Ltd v Tolaini Bros (Hotels) Ltd* [1975] 1 WLR 297.

third party cannot or does not make the valuation, the contract is avoided:[37] this is a case of a contract without a determinable price which lacks one of the *essentialia negotii* (minimum content)[38] of a contract of sale.[39] Where, due to the fault of either the seller or the buyer, the third party is prevented from making the valuation, the party not at fault can claim damages from the party at fault.[40]

Formalities for consumer sales under the
Consumer Credit Act 1974

6.16   Our present economic system relies heavily on purchases of goods one does not necessarily need with money one does not necessarily have. Sales on credit are therefore of great importance. The Consumer Credit Act 1974 seeks to protect individual debtors in consumer credit agreements.[41] This complex piece of legislation cannot be discussed here;[42] only a few principal points relevant to sale of goods contracts can be highlighted. Credit agreements under the Consumer Credit Act arise in connection with sale of goods contracts when the buyer obtains a loan to enable him to buy the goods. The lender/creditor can be a third party unrelated to the seller, such as the buyer's credit card company or bank (this is called debtor-creditor agreement). Or the lender/creditor can be a third party having an arrangement with the seller/supplier, or the seller/supplier is also the lender/creditor (both are cases of a debtor-creditor-supplier agreement).[43]

6.17   Consumer credit agreements have to comply strictly with the formalities required by the Consumer Credit Act 1974 to be enforceable. An improperly executed regulated agreement is enforceable against the debtor on an order of the court only.[44] Section 60 and regulations passed under this section prescribe the form and content of any credit agreement. The prescribed content includes: a prominent heading on the first page stating that this agreement is regulated under the Consumer Credit Act 1974; names and addresses of all parties; the cash price where appropriate; the amount of any required deposit or advance payment; the

---

37 s 9(1).
38 This is a Civil law/Scots law expression. In English law this would probably be termed as 'fundamental lack of consensus', but the outcome (i.e. void contract) is the same.
39 Where, however, goods have already been delivered and accepted/appropriated by the buyer, the buyer must pay a reasonable price for them: see s 9(1).
40 s 9(2).
41 Consumer Credit Act 1974, s 8.
42 The Consumer Credit Act 1974 is an almost inaccessibly technical piece of legislation. See, e.g. for discussion of this Act with background information for illustration, I Ramsay, *Consumer Law and Policy* (2nd edn, 2007) pp 530 ff. The classic source for all matters concerning the Consumer Credit Act 1974 is the looseleaf work Goode, *Consumer Credit Law and Practice* (from 1977).
43 Consumer Credit Act 1974, ss 12, 13. On the issue of connected lender liability under s 75, see paras **6.110–6.113** below.
44 Consumer Credit Act 1974, s 65(1).

amount or limit of credit; the APR and how it is calculated; the total amount payable; details about the timing and amount of payments; the duration (or minimum duration) of the agreement; the details of default charges,; and details about any security provided by the debtor. The debtor has a cancellation right of the credit agreement under certain circumstances.[45]

The performance of the contract of sale of goods in outline

6.18   Every contract for the sale of goods has a *personal component* and a *proprietary component*,[46] reflecting the distinction in private law between (a) personal (relative) rights, here arising out of contract, and (b) real (absolute) rights.[47] The personal component (a) ('contract') deals with an obligation or bundle of obligations: these are personal rights enforceable against the other contracting party, particularly the seller's duty to deliver the goods and the buyer's duty to accept and pay for them. The proprietary component (b) ('conveyance') deals with the transfer of the real right (property right) of ownership in the goods sold from the seller to the buyer.

The personal component

6.19   The parties' rights and duties under the contract concluded are determined by the terms of the contract, whether express or implied.

6.20   *Express terms* are terms expressly stated by the parties to the contract. In contrast, terms which have not been expressly stated by the parties are *implied terms*. Contracts do not usually contain terms which address every situation which might arise during contractual performance, so that, to cover these gaps, the courts imply terms which a reasonable person would have accepted or wished to have included. These terms are said to be terms *implied in fact*, because their implication depends on the particular facts of the case in question. In contrast, implied terms can also be *terms implied in law*. The law may imply these terms by way of case law, but the most important source of such terms is legislation. In this context the particularly important ones are ss 12–15 of the Sale of Goods Act 1979, but the Act contains further special provisions on implied terms which govern the contractual obligations of the seller and the buyer. This central area of sale of goods law is discussed in separate sections below.[48] If either the seller or the buyer is in breach of contract because the express or implied terms of the contract are not complied with, the rules about remedies apply.[49]

---

45 Consumer Credit Act 1974, ss 67, 68.
46 See Bell, *Principles* (4th edn) § 86: 'contract' (*'titulus transferendi dominii'*) and 'transference'.
47 See in more detail Chapter 3: General Principles of Property Law.
48 For implied terms concerning the seller's duties, see paras **6.57** ff and for implied terms concerning the buyer's duties, see paras **6.67** ff.
49 For seller's remedies, see paras **6.84** ff and for buyer's remedies, see paras **6.94** ff.

6.21 English law distinguishes between different types of terms: conditions (important terms where even a minor breach entitles to rescission/termination of the contract); warranties (less important terms where their breach entitles to damages only); and innominate terms (breach may discharge the other party only if the nature and consequences of the breach are sufficiently serious to justify discharge[50]). *Scots law does not make this distinction*: these are all 'terms' and there is no substantive difference.[51] Hence in Scots law the aggrieved party may terminate the contract if there is a *material breach* of a *term*, whether express or implied, by the other party.[52] Since 1994[53] the Sale of Goods Act has taken account of this different legal concept in Scots law with an appropriately amended terminology.

6.22 The contract must be performed according to the express and implied contractual terms. However, sometimes the performance of the contract becomes impossible because the subject matter of the contract has been destroyed: this is a case of frustration due to supervening impossibility. Or it is a case of initial impossibility if the subject matter of the contract has been destroyed at the time of the formation of the contract. In such situations the general principles of contract law apply, but the Sale of Goods Act 1979 has a few provisions concerning the impossibility/frustration of performance in special cases. Where there is a contract for the *sale* of *specific* goods, and the goods without the seller's knowledge have perished at the time when the contract is made, the contract is void (s 6). Similarly, where there is an *agreement to sell* for *specific* goods, and subsequently the goods, without any fault on the part of the seller or the buyer, perish before the risk passes to the buyer,[54] the agreement is avoided (s 7).

The proprietary component

(a) Matters of terminology

6.23 According to the implied term in s 12, the seller has an obligation to transfer the property or title to the goods to the buyer. This requires that the seller has the right to sell the goods (without necessarily being the owner of the goods himself).[55] The usual terminology in this context is fairly imprecise. What is typically referred to as 'property' or 'title' here (also by Scots lawyers) is really 'ownership', the most comprehensive property right or real right. 'Title' is an expression appropriate in

---

50 *Hong Kong Fir Shipping Co Ltd v Kawasaki Kisen Kaisha* [1962] 2 QB 26.
51 See e.g. MacQueen and Thomson, *Contract Law in Scotland*, p 130. Scots lawyers often refer to terms, especially undertakings as to certain factual conditions (e.g. of goods), as 'warranties', but that is an untechnical use of this word. See also Adams and MacQueen, *Atiyah's Sale of Goods*, p 95.
52 See s 15B(1).
53 Amendment by the Sale and Supply of Goods Act 1994.
54 On the rules discussing the passing of risk, see paras **6.43–6.47** below.
55 For discussion of the implied term of s 12, see paras **6.49–6.52** below.

the property conception of English law, but misleading in the Civilian '*dominium*' conception of ownership in Scots property law. The Sale of Goods Act 1979 complicates matters further in that in s 61(1) it refers to the unencumbered property right or unrestricted real right (that is: ownership) as 'general property' and calls 'special property'[56] what would be subordinate real rights in Scots law.[57] So in the understanding of Scots property law, s 12 contains an implied term according to which the seller, entitled to transfer ownership by virtue of being owner himself or authorised by the owner, has a duty to confer ownership in the goods on the buyer. This ownership conferred must not be subject to a restricted real right by a third party,[58] unless known or disclosed to the buyer before the contract is made.[59] This is what is commonly referred to in England and in Scotland as 'the seller's duty to pass a good title to the goods'.

(b) Transfer of ownership/passing of property in general (ss 17, 18)

6.24   We now have to examine how ownership is transferred from the seller to the buyer. For that we have to consider the definitions of specific and ascertained goods. *Specific goods*, as has already been said, are 'identified and agreed on at the time a contract of sale is made'.[60] *Ascertained goods* are initially unascertained goods (generic goods etc[61]) but are individualised or made specific by way of having been identified, earmarked, segregated, set aside and the like. Thus specific goods are already identified as at the time of the contract ('this watch'), while ascertained goods are goods that have been identified at a later stage ('these 400kg of rye'). In a contract for the sale of specific or ascertained goods the property (ownership) in them is transferred to the buyer at such time as the parties to the contract intend it to be transferred. This is the general rule on the passing of property in s 17: ownership passes when the parties intend it to pass, thus not necessarily at the time of the delivery of the goods (delivery is defined as 'voluntary transfer of *possession* [not ownership] from one person to another': s 61(1)). The rule in s 17 is a departure from Scots common law which requires delivery (together with the parties' intention to transfer ownership) for the passing of ownership.[62]

6.25   The parties will often agree that the purification of a condition should be a prerequisite for the passing of ownership, that is, the seller may reserve the right of disposal of the goods until certain conditions are

---

56 On this term see e.g. M Bridge, *Personal Property Law* (3rd edn, 2002) p 30 for English law.
57 On the terminology in Scots property law, see e.g. Reid, *Law of Property in Scotland* (1996) paras 4–6, and Chapter 3: General Principles of Property Law.
58 On the floating charge in Scots law see briefly Reid, *Law of Property in Scotland*, para 8.
59 See s 12(2)(a).
60 According to the definition in s 61(1).
61 See para **6.12** above.
62 Reid, *Law of Property in Scotland*, paras 609–610, 613.

fulfilled (s 19(1)). A widely used application of this rule is the retention of title clause, being essentially a suspensive condition: ownership only passes when the price of the goods is fully paid by the buyer and so the suspensive condition is fulfilled.[63]

6.26 Generally, the parties' intention to pass ownership is to be ascertained by looking at the terms of the contract, the conduct of the parties and the circumstances of the case (s 17(2)). The law, however, contains some presumptions in s 18 for ascertaining the parties' intention when ownership is to pass if the actual intention of the parties is not apparent. If the intention of the parties is clear, s 18 does not come into play.[64]

6.27 Under s 18, rule 1, where there is an unconditional contract for the sale of specific goods in a deliverable state the property (ownership) in the goods passes to the buyer when the contract is made. It is immaterial whether the time of payment or the time of delivery, or both, is postponed. In many cases, however, one will be able to discern an intention of the parties that ownership of specific goods is to pass only on delivery or payment,[65] so the practical applicability of this rule should not be overestimated.

6.28 Under s 18, rule 2, if the seller is required to do something to put the goods into a deliverable state, ownership does not pass until the thing is done and the buyer has notice of that. In *Cockburn's Tr v Bowe & Sons*[66] the seller was required to sell his potato crop and to lift, pit and drive the potatoes to the station or harbour. The seller went bankrupt and the buyers claimed that they had acquired ownership before the date of the seller's sequestration, because in their view ownership supposedly passed when the contract was made (s 18, rule 1). The court took the view that, at the time of the contract, the potatoes were not in a deliverable state; they were put in a deliverable state after pitting and carting them to the station or harbour, so ownership passed according to s 18, rule 2.

6.29 Under s 18, rule 3, where the seller is required to weigh, measure, test the goods or do some other act to ascertain the price, ownership does not pass until the act or thing is done and the buyer has notice of that.

6.30 According to s 18, rule 4, where goods are delivered to the buyer on approval, or on sale or return, ownership passes to the buyer in two separate scenarios: (a) ownership passes when the buyer signifies the approval or acceptance to the seller or does any other act adopting the transaction; or (b) ownership passes if the buyer does not indicate his approval but retains the goods without notice of rejection beyond an agreed time limit for the return of the goods, or, if no time limit has been agreed, when a reasonable time has expired. In *Weiner v Gill*[67] the terms

---

63 See also discussion of seller's possessory remedies in paras **6.87** ff.
64 *Woodburn v Andrew Motherwell Ltd* 1917 SC 533 at 538.
65 *R V Ward Ltd v Bignall* [1967] 1 QB 534 at 545 per Lord Diplock.
66 (1910) 2 SLT 17.
67 [1906] 2 KB 574.

of the contract stated that goods that were on approbation or on sale or return remain the property of the seller, until paid in cash or returned by the buyer. It was held that such goods were not delivered within the meaning of s 18, rule 4, and the seller retained ownership until payment in cash.

6.31   The main consequences of the passing of ownership to the buyer are: the buyer will be able to maintain his ownership right in case of the seller's insolvency,[68] especially if the seller is still in possession of the goods; the buyer as owner obtains the right to sue a third party for damages for loss and damage to the goods sold; the risk passes prima facie with the transfer of ownership of the goods.[69]

6.32   The general rule of passing of ownership in s 17 principally applies to *specific* or *ascertained* goods only.[70] Also, s 18, rules 1–4 apply only to specific goods. Where there is a contract for the sale of unascertained goods, ownership passes to the buyer only if and when the goods are ascertained (s 16). But there are exceptions which will be discussed now.

(c) Transfer of ownership/passing of property in unascertained goods (s 17, s 18, rule 5), and in undivided shares (ss 20A, 20B)

6.33   *Passing of ownership in unascertained goods (s 18, rule 5)*: While according to s 17 ownership normally passes only in relation to specific or ascertained goods, s 18, rule 5 provides for the passing of ownership in unascertained goods. As already said, *unascertained goods* are (i) purely generic goods, (ii) goods to be manufactured or grown by the seller, or (iii) an unidentified part of a specified whole. Relevant here are also *future goods*: these are goods to be manufactured or acquired by the seller after the formation of the contract of sale (s 5(1)). In a contract for the sale of *unascertained* or *future* goods by description,[71] ownership passes if goods of that description and in a deliverable state are unconditionally appropriated to the contract by the seller or the buyer, with the express or implied assent of the other party, respectively (s 18, rule 5(1)). 'Unconditional appropriation' means that some ascertained and identified goods must be irrevocably attached or earmarked for the particular contract in question.[72] For example, the seller puts the goods in a different room in his warehouse and notifies the buyer of that. There is an element of common intention to unconditional appropriation, and the appropriating act is usually the last act in the seller's performance of the

---

68 Compare the example of *Cockburn's Tr v Bowe & Sons* (n 66).
69 On the passing of risk, see paras **6.43–6.47** below.
70 The definition of specific goods is goods 'identified and agreed on at the time a contract of sale is made' (s 61(1)).
71 On implied term that goods must correspond with the description, see paras **6.57–6.61** below.
72 Adams and MacQueen, *Atiyah's Sale of Goods*, p 323.

contract; if the seller only selects the goods in question but can still change his mind later unilaterally, this is not sufficient.[73]

6.34 Another case of an unconditional appropriation is s 18, rule 5(2): the seller delivers the goods to the buyer or to a carrier to transport them to the buyer and does not reserve the right of disposal (i.e. the right to retain control over the goods);[74] the seller is regarded as having unconditionally appropriated the goods to the contract.

6.35 Under s 18, rule 5(3), if goods are part of a bulk and the bulk is reduced in such a way that all that is remaining is due to one buyer, this is considered as appropriation (appropriation or ascertainment by exhaustion). So if B buys 5 tonnes of wheat flour from a bulk, but only 5 tonnes are left in the bulk, there is appropriation by exhaustion and ownership passes to B. This rule leads to the question of the sale of undivided shares in goods.

6.36 *Passing of ownership in undivided shares in goods forming part of an identified bulk (ss 20A, 20B).* When a seller S has 100 tonnes of wheat flour and the buyer B has bought 40 tonnes, these 40 tonnes cannot be ascertained, as one cannot determine which 40 tonnes out of the 100 tonnes are B's. Ownership cannot pass to the buyer (s 16). However, where the buyer has paid *in advance* for a *specified quantity* of goods which are part of a bulk that has been *identified* by the parties, he acquires an undivided share in the bulk and becomes an owner in common with the seller and/or other buyers, according to s 20A(1) and (2). So if the conditions of s 20A(1) are met (goods of a specified quantity being part of an identified bulk, advance payment by the buyer), in the example above the buyer B will be an owner in common with the seller S, following s 20A(2)(a) and (b). If there is also another buyer B1 for 50 tonnes, B (40 tonnes) will be owner in common together with S (10 tonnes) and B1 (50 tonnes).[75] If B1 has bought and paid for 60 tonnes, B will be owner in common with B1 only.

6.37 It needs to be stressed again that s 20A presupposes (i) the sale of a specified quantity, (ii) the supply of the goods from an identified bulk, and (iii) payment by the buyer for some or all of the goods. An identified bulk can be a cargo of wheat in a named ship; a mass of barley in an identified silo; the oil in an identified storage tank; cases of wine of the same kind in an identified cellar; bags of fertiliser (all of the same kind) in an identified storehouse and so on.[76] The rule of s 20A applies only in the absence of an express agreement by the parties.[77] Under s 20B,

---

73 *Carlos Federspiel & Co SA v Charles Twigg & Co Ltd* [1957] 1 Lloyd's Rep 240 at 255 per Pearson J.
74 See s 19(1) for the exercise of the seller's right to retain control.
75 For the presumed amount of the shares, see s 20A(3). Part payment of the price is treated as payment for a corresponding part of the goods: see s 20A(6).
76 Examples from the Law Commissions' joint report, *Sale of Goods Forming Part of a Bulk* (Law Com No 215, Scot Law Com No 145, 1993) para 4.3.
77 See in s 20A(2).

anyone who has become an owner in common of a bulk according to s 20A is deemed to have consented to any delivery of goods out of the bulk to any other owner in common of the bulk due to that other owner under his contract. So the general common law rule that all common owners must agree to any dealing with the property does not apply here. Otherwise, if the consent of each owner in common would have to be obtained specifically, dealings with the goods out of the bulk could become hampered.

(d) Transfer by a non-owner (ss 21–25)

6.38 The principal rule governing transfers by non-owners is *nemo dat quod non habet* (from Roman law: *nemo plus iuris ad alium transferre potest quam ipse habet*[78]): nobody can transfer more rights to another than he has himself. This also applies to the ownership right. Where the goods are sold by a person who is not their owner, the buyer acquires no better title to the goods than the seller had (s 21). But there are several exceptions to this rule. The most common one is that the seller is not owner but he sells the goods under the authority (e.g. as agent[79]) or with the consent of the owner: in that case the buyer acquires ownership.[80] A connected exception is that the seller does not really have authority from the owner to sell, but the conduct of the owner precludes him from denying the seller's authority, an example of a personal bar which operates against the owner: again, the buyer acquires ownership.[81]

6.39 There are two more exceptions which are based on the principle that the possession of goods prompts a presumption of ownership in them.[82] They are also the result of the fact that the delivery of goods is not required for the passing of ownership according to the Sale of Goods Act 1979. These two exceptions are regulated in s 24 and s 25. They are dealt with in more detail elsewhere,[83] so a few brief comments suffice.

6.40 Section 24 concerns a second sale by a seller who has remained in possession of the goods after the first sale of these goods. A third party, who buys the goods from the seller in possession (that possession gives rise to the presumption of the seller's ownership in the goods) and is in good faith and without notice of the previous sale, acquires ownership. According to s 24 the seller is deemed to be the first buyer's agent. The courts have interpreted the meanings of 'possession' and 'delivery' widely.[84]

---

78 Digest 50, 17, 54.
79 See the special rule regarding the sale by a mercantile agent in the Factors Act 1889, s 2(1).
80 See s 21(1).
81 Set out in s 21(1).
82 Generally for corporeal moveables, see Stair *Institutions* IV, 45, 17.
83 Chapter 3: General Principles of Property Law.
84 *Michael Gerson (Leasing) Ltd v Wilkinson* [2000] EWCA Civ 250, [2001] QB 514, [2000] 3 WLR 1645.

6.41   Section 25 deals with the converse scenario: the seller has allowed the buyer to take possession of the goods although the seller has retained ownership under a retention of title clause. If the buyer in possession of the goods that are still owned by the seller sells these goods to a second buyer, and that second buyer is in good faith and without notice of any right of the original seller in the goods, the second buyer acquires ownership.[85] The rule in s 25 therefore usually renders retention of title clauses ineffectual against a third party in good faith.

6.42   If the seller sells goods with a voidable title to them (so the title is valid until avoided), the seller can transfer ownership to the buyer, provided the buyer buys in good faith and without notice of the seller's defect of title (s 23). If the title is avoided after the sale and delivery to the buyer B but before a subsequent sale to a second buyer B1, the buyer B in possession of the goods may be able to pass title to B1 under the rules of s 25.[86] It is, however, unclear what applies if the contract is void *ab initio*, that is, the law deems the contract never having been valid in the first place, so that, for the operation of s 25, the necessary consent of the seller to the buyer's obtaining possession is deemed not to have happened. In such a case, the buyer B1 can presumably not benefit from s 25.[87]

The passing of risk

6.43   According to s 20, the passing of ownership typically entails the passing of the risk. The party who bears the risk must perform the contract when the goods accidentally perish or deteriorate. If the goods are at the seller's risk, the seller normally remains liable to the buyer for non-delivery if the goods are accidentally destroyed or damaged;[88] if the goods are at the buyer's risk, the buyer must pay the purchase price if the goods are accidentally destroyed or damaged.

6.44   The goods remain at the seller's risk until ownership ('the property') in them is transferred to the buyer. Once ownership is transferred to the buyer the goods are at the buyer's risk, irrespective of whether the goods have also been delivered to him or not, that is, irrespective of whether the goods are in the buyer's actual possession. The parties can depart from the principal rule – risk passes with the property – by agreement (s 20(1)).

---

85 s 25(1). This rule does not apply where the buyer in possession has acquired the goods under a consumer credit agreement as regulated by the Consumer Credit Act 1974 (s 25(2)).

86 *Newtons of Wembley v Williams* [1965] 1 QB 560.

87 *Shogun Finance Ltd v Hudson* [2003] UKHL 62, paras 50–52, which was decided under s 27 of the Hire-Purchase Act 1964, being the substantially equivalent rule to s 25.

88 Note the special rule of s 7 for specific goods: if, in an agreement to sell for specific goods, the goods perish before the risk passes to the buyer without the fault of either party, the agreement is avoided.

6.45   The general rule in s 20(1) is qualified by two exceptions. First, where delivery has been delayed by the fault of either party, the goods are at the risk of the party at fault. Any loss which might not have occurred but for that party's fault has to be borne by the party at fault (s 20(2)). So, for example, if the buyer has delayed in providing instructions about the delivery of apple juice which subsequently deteriorates, the buyer has to bear the risk of deterioration although the ownership in the apple juice is still with the seller.[89] The second exception is set out in s 20(3): despite the passing of risk rules, the duties of either party as custodier of the goods of the other party remain. Thus the party in possession is liable to the other party as custodier for any loss as a result of his negligence.

6.46   There is a principal exception to the passing of risk rules under s 20. If the contract in question is a consumer contract in which the buyer is a consumer, then the rules concerning the passing of risk under s 20(1)–(3) do not apply, and the goods remain at the seller's risk until they are delivered to the consumer (s 20(4)).

6.47   The problem of risk should not be confused with the problem of frustration.[90] If a contract to be performed is frustrated, that is, performance becomes impossible, then neither party is under any liability to the other. If, however, the goods are at the risk of one party, then that party is liable to the other party for non-delivery or the price, as the case may be. The Sale of Goods Act 1979 has a few provisions in ss 6 and 7 concerning the frustration of performance in relation to sales of, or agreements to sell, specific goods, which have already been discussed.[91]

CONTENT OF THE CONTRACT I: SELLER'S DUTIES

6.48   The contract of the sale of goods, once concluded, contains duties of the seller and of the buyer. We will consider the seller's duties first. The essence of a contract of sale is that the buyer obtains ownership (and usually possession) of goods which are of the quality and quantity agreed by the parties. The seller's duties, as specified in the contract, are directed to this end.

Duty to deliver and to pass good title

6.49   The seller has to deliver the goods (and the buyer must accept and pay for them).[92] 'Delivery' does not mean physical handing over only; it is any kind of 'voluntary transfer of possession from one person to one another.'[93] So there is no requirement to send the goods to the

---

89 *Demby Hamilton & Co Ltd v Barden* [1949] 1 All ER 435.
90 See Bridge, *The Sale of Goods*, pp 178–80.
91 See para **6.22** above.
92 s 27. On the buyer's duty, see para **6.84** ff below.
93 According to the definition in s 61(1).

buyer; whether the buyer has to take possession or whether the seller has to dispatch the goods to the buyer, depends on the terms of the contract, either express or implied.[94] In any case, the seller has to put the goods into a deliverable state and has to bear the incidental costs to effect that.[95] The place of delivery is the seller's place of business if he has one, otherwise it is his residence.[96] If the goods to be delivered are with a third person, then there is only delivery if and when the third person acknowledges to the buyer that he holds the goods on the buyer's behalf.[97] This rule may be slightly narrower than Scots common law on this matter.[98]

6.50 Under s 12(1), the seller has a duty to pass good title. This duty is independent from *when* title is supposed to pass – during delivery or before or after, as stipulated: title need not pass together with delivery.[99] 'Passing of title (or: property)' here means transfer of ownership, as has already been explained:[100] the buyer must become the new owner of the goods sold. The law implies a term on the part of the seller that he has (a) the right to sell the goods, (b) that the goods are, as at the time of the passing of title, free from any charge or encumbrance undisclosed or unknown to the buyer before the contract is made, and (c) that the buyer will enjoy quiet possession of the goods.[101] There is no requirement that the seller must be the owner. The seller must have a right to pass ownership. So there are cases in which a seller is not the owner but can confer a good title on the buyer because the owner has authorised him to do so, and there are situations in which an owner has no power to transfer ownership.

6.51 In *Niblett v Confectioners' Materials Co Ltd*[102] an American company sold condensed milk in tins to the plaintiffs, but when the goods arrived in the UK they were seized by the customs authorities because the goods were labelled with brands which infringed the registered trademark of another manufacturer. The defendants breached the implied term under s 12(1): although they had the power to confer good title (here they were owners), they did not have the right to sell the goods because the trademark holder could bring an injunction to prevent the sale of the goods. In *Butterworth v Kingsway Motors Ltd*[103] A took a car on hire purchase and mistakenly thought she had the right to sell it if she continued her repay-

---

94 s 29(1).
95 s 29(6).
96 s 29(2). If the contract is for the sale of specific goods, which to the knowledge of the parties at the time of the contract are in some other place, then that place is the place of delivery.
97 s 29(4).
98 Reid, *Law of Property in Scotland*, para 620.
99 This is discussed above in para **6.23** ff.
100 See para **6.23** ff above, also in relation to the accurate terminology in Scots property law.
101 s 12(1)–(2).
102 [1921] 3 KB 387.
103 [1954] 2 All ER 694.

ment in instalments. A sold the car to B, and the car was sold several times, ultimately by the defendant D to the plaintiff P. Meanwhile A kept paying the instalments. Nearly a year later the hire-purchase company notified P of its ownership (which it obviously retained). P reduced the contract with D because of breach of s 12(1) and obtained the return of the full purchase price. However, immediately after P's reduction of the contract A paid off the balance of the hire-purchase price to the hire-purchase company. The court found that with the payment of the last instalment title to the car vested in A and perfected title of all subsequent sales. The court did not decide whether there would have been a breach of s 12(1) if the last instalment had been paid before P's reduction of the contract. It arguably would have been a breach because the first seller A did not have the right to pass ownership at the time of the first sale.

6.52 The situations in which a buyer may obtain good title although the seller is not owner and has no right to confer title have been discussed above.[104]

Delivery at the right time

6.53 According to s 10(2), whether time of *delivery* is to be of the essence of the contract or not is determined by the contractual stipulations. If time of delivery is of the essence, the buyer can treat the contract as terminated if the seller's delivery is delayed. (Time of *payment* is prima facie not of the essence of a contract of sale, unless the contractual terms reveal an intention to the contrary.[105]) However, the courts are of the view that 'in ordinary commercial contracts for the sale of goods the rule clearly is that time is prima facie of the essence with respect to delivery'.[106] Agreements stipulating shipping or other delivery within a fixed time period or before a fixed date indicate that time is of the essence.[107] Any departure from the stipulations of the contract allows the other party to treat the contract as terminated.

6.54 Where the contract of sale requires the seller to send the goods to the buyer, but no time to do so has been fixed, the seller is bound to send them within a reasonable time.[108] What is reasonable depends on the circumstances at the time of delivery.[109] If time of delivery was stipulated to be of the essence, and delivery did not happen in breach of this term, but the buyer still insists on delivery, he has lost the right to reduction of the contract: the buyer's conduct then indicates that time of delivery is no longer of the essence. If nothing further was agreed specifically, that would be an agreement requiring the seller to deliver within

---

104 On ss 24 and 25, see para **6.23** ff.
105 s 10(1).
106 *Hartley v Hymans* [1920] 3 KB 475 at 484.
107 *Bowes v Shand* (1877) 2 App Cas 455.
108 s 29(3).
109 Adams and MacQueen, *Atiyah's Sale of Goods*, p 127.

a reasonable time,[110] as an alteration of the original contract. If the buyer waives the right to terminate the contract for non-delivery by continuing to press for delivery, it is open to the buyer to stipulate a new delivery date. In that case he can treat the contract as at an end if there is no delivery on the new due date, provided he has given reasonable notice that delivery must be made by a certain date.[111]

Delivery in the right quantity

6.55 Section 30 provides that the seller has the duty to deliver the right quantity of goods. The buyer is entitled to reject the goods if the seller delivers to the buyer a quantity of goods less than he contracted to sell. The buyer need not accept delivery in instalments (e.g. delivery of a part one day and the rest later), unless agreed otherwise.[112] If the buyer nevertheless accepts the goods as delivered he must pay for them at the contract rate. If the seller delivers a greater quantity than contracted, then the buyer has a choice: he may accept the goods as contracted and reject the rest, or he may reject the whole delivery.[113] The court decisions are not entirely consistent as to whether a very small shortfall or excess may entitle the buyer to reject (*de minimis* principle).[114]

Delivery in the right quality

6.56 · The Sale of Goods Act implies certain terms that impose obligations regarding the characteristics of the goods. These *implied terms* are found in ss 13–15: sale by description (s 13); implied terms about quality and fitness (s 14); and sale by sample (s 15). In addition to these, the parties are free to include *express terms* making further provision about the goods which the seller is obliged to supply. These are particularly common in commercial transactions.

Implied term that goods must correspond with the description (s 13)

6.57 Where there is a contract for the sale of goods by description, there is an implied term that the goods will correspond with the description (s 13(1)). It is important to note that s 13 also applies to private sales, not only (as is the case with s 14) to sales in the course of a business.[115]

6.58 In *Ashington Piggeries*[116] the court said that 'description' in s 13 does not comprise all descriptive words. 'Description' is confined to those words in the contract which were intended by the parties to identify the

---

110 s 29(3).
111 *Charles Rickards Ltd v Oppenheim* [1950] 1 KB 616.
112 s 31(1).
113 s 30(1) and (2).
114 More extended discussion in Adams and MacQueen, *Atiyah's Sale of Goods*, p 135.
115 *Varley v Whipp* [1900] 1 QB 513; *Beale v Taylor* [1967] 1 WLR 1193.
116 *Ashington Piggeries v Christopher Hill Ltd* [1972] AC 441.

kind of goods to be sold, and it is up to the parties whether they choose a broader or narrower description.[117] In that case herring meal was sold to mink breeders, but this foodstuff was poisonous to mink and resulted in the death of thousands of mink; the court held that for the purpose of s 13 the description 'Norwegian Herring Meal, fair, average quality' was accurate (it was indeed that foodstuff) despite the presence of the toxic agent, so there was no breach of s 13. (There was, however, a breach of s 14(2),[118] which shows that terms under s 13 and s 14 can apply concurrently in principle.) A similar case was *Border Harvesters Ltd.*[119] A grain dryer was sold but did not achieve the stated capacity. The description in the contract was held to be 'grain dryer' and did not extend to statements about its capacity. What the dryer was capable of doing was not part of the description, so s 13 was not breached.[120] In such cases it depends very much on the exact statement of the description.

6.59   A description need not be in words (only), but can also be in figures, images and so on. In *Beale v Taylor*[121] ·a car was advertised for sale as 'Herald, convertible, white, 1961'. The plaintiff bought it after having examined the metallic disc on the back of the car which read '1200' and led the plaintiff to believe that the car was a first model of the '1200' series. In fact, the car was made of parts of two different models welded together, only one having been from a 1961 model. The court held that the words '1961 Herald' were part of a contractual description, here in the form of a year and model number of the car in an advert affixed to the car.

6.60   A description does not specifically have to be relied on to qualify as a sale by description. However, for a sale by description the description has to have an influence on the sale, and the court must be able to attribute to the parties a common intention that the description would become a term of the contract. In *Harlingdon & Leinster Enterprises Ltd*[122] two paintings were sold as paintings of a 'Gabriele Münter'. The buyers enquired, but the sellers knew nothing about this artist.[123] The paintings turned out to be forgeries, and the buyers brought an action for recovery of the purchase price, founded on breach of s 13. The court found that there was no sale by description. This description, the name of the painter, did not have a sufficient influence in the sale to become a term of the contract. The buyer's reliance would be a strong indication for such an influence, but here the buyer did not rely on the identity of the artist. This case shows that not all descriptive words are automatically regarded as descriptions within the meaning of s 13.

---

117 *Ashington Piggeries* at 503–504.
118 See para **6.62** ff below.
119 *Border Harvesters Ltd v Edwards Engineering (Perth) Ltd* 1985 SLT 128.
120 *Border Harvesters Ltd* at 131.
121 [1967] 1 WLR 1193.
122 *Harlingdon & Leinster Enterprises Ltd v Christopher Hull Fine Art Ltd* [1991] 1 QB 564.
123 Gabriele Münter (1877–1962) was a German expressionist painter, associated with the group of 'Der Blaue Reiter' and especially with Kandinsky.

6.61 Clearly, s 13 applies to cases where the buyer has not seen the goods, but is relying on the description alone. Furthermore, sales of future or unascertained goods are necessarily sales by description under s 13.[124] However, s 13 can also apply where the buyer has seen the goods, and may even have selected them, as in ordinary sale in a shop. Section 13(3) underlines that.[125] In *Grant v Australian Knitting Mills Ltd*[126] Lord Wright said that 'there is a sale by description even though the buyer is buying something displayed before him on the counter: a thing is sold by description, though it is specific, so long as it is sold not merely as the specific thing, but as a thing corresponding to a description.'[127]

Implied term that goods must be of satisfactory quality or fitness (s 14 (2))

6.62 Under s 14(2), where the seller sells goods in the course of a business, there is an implied term that the goods supplied under the contract are of satisfactory quality. There are several aspects of this rule: (a) s 14(2) is conclusive; the law does not recognise implied terms beyond those stated in this section;[128] (b) s 14(2) (and also s 14(3)) only applies to sales in the course of a business; (c) s 14(2A) and (2B) define further, but not exhaustively, the term 'satisfactory quality'; and (d) s 14(2C) contains a proviso which limits the applicability of the implied terms in s 14(2A) and (2B) in certain circumstances. Each will be discussed in turn.

(a) Implied terms under s 14(2) are an exhaustive list

6.63 The implied terms under s 14(2) are an exhaustive list. It is, however, possible that the buyer stipulates or makes known to the seller that the goods sold must be fit for a particular purpose, in which case a corresponding term will be implied. This will be discussed under s 14(3) below.

(b) Section 14(2) only applies to sales in the course of a business

6.64 Section 14(2) applies only to sales by a seller in the course of a business. In practice that means that private sales (for example sales of second-hand goods) will not be covered, but only sales by manufacturers, wholesalers and retailers. In contrast, s 13 also applies to private sales. The expression 'in the course of a business' has a wide meaning.

---

124 *Joseph Travers & Sons Ltd v Longel Ltd* (1947) 64 TLR 150 at 153.
125 s 13(3): 'A sale of goods is not prevented from being a sale by description by reason only that, being exposed for sale or hire, they are selected by the buyer.'
126 [1936] AC 85.
127 At 100.
128 s 14(1).

In *Stevenson v Rogers*[129] a fisherman sold his first fishing vessel, the main asset of his fishing business. The defendant claimed that this was only a one-off sale – there was no regularity of dealing. The court held that (after an amendment) the Sale of Goods Act no longer required habitual dealing in the type of goods sold: a 'one-off' sale in the course of a business is sufficient and s 14(2) applies.[130] In *Buchanan-Jardine v Hamilink*[131] the seller sold the entire stock of the business (sale of a farm and its livestock and deadstock). The pursuer-seller claimed that he could not have been selling in the course of a business where in fact he sold the business itself to the defender. The court disagreed: the law required a sale in the course of *a* business, not in the course of business, so a displenishing sale is a sale in the course of a business, even if it may well have been the last act in the business.

6.65 Section 14(5) makes clear that the provisions of s 14(2) apply to a sale by a person who in the course of a business is acting as agent for another as they apply to a sale by a principal in the course of a business. This addresses the problem of a private seller who sells through an agent. The private seller cannot defend himself by saying that it was a private sale, if the sale was made through an agent in the agent's course of a business: s 14(2) still applies to the principal (whether disclosed or undisclosed) as private seller,[132] unless the principal is not selling in the course of a business and either the buyer knows that fact or reasonable steps have been taken to bring it to the buyer's notice before formation of the contract.[133]

(c) The definition of 'satisfactory quality'

6.66 A number of court decisions had to deal with the meaning of the implied term 'satisfactory quality'. To clarify the case law, amendments have been made to s 14 as s 14(2A) and (2B). According to s 14(2A), the quality of goods is satisfactory if the goods meet the standard that a reasonable person would regard as satisfactory, taking account of the description and price of the goods and any other relevant circumstances. Section 14(2B) defines quality further: 'quality' includes the state and condition of the goods. Furthermore, aspects of the quality of goods contain (s 14(2B)(a)–(e)):[134]

(a) fitness for all the purposes for which goods of the kind in question are commonly supplied;
(b) appearance and finish;
(c) freedom from minor defects;

---

129 [1999] QB 1028, [1999] 1 All ER 613.
130 *Macdonald v Pollock* [2013] CSIH 12, 2013 SC 22 followed the reasoning in *Stevenson v Rogers*, see para [24].
131 1983 SLT 149.
132 *Boyter v Thomson* 1995 SC (HL) 15, 1995 SLT 875.
133 s 14(5), final passage.
134 The list is not exhaustive.

(d) safety;
(e) durability.

6.67 The original term was 'merchantable quality' and a great deal of case law grew around this old term until it was replaced by the present one of 'satisfactory quality' in 1994. However, where the new law does not conflict with the old court decisions, these are still relevant.[135] Satisfactory quality is considered from the position of a (hypothetical) reasonable person, expertise is not required.[136] Thus the test of satisfactory quality is an objective test: the court puts itself in the position of the objective reasonable buyer with knowledge of all the relevant facts.[137] The implied term of s 14(2) also applies if the buyer does not rely on the seller's skill and judgment.[138] The expression 'satisfactory quality' does not denote a high standard – it rather means 'average', perhaps even 'mediocre'. A conclusive definition is impossible. As Rougier J said in *Bernstein v Pamson Motors* (in the context of whether a car is considered as being of merchantable quality): 'Any attempt to forge some exhaustive, positive and specific definition of such a term, applicable in all cases, would soon be put to mockery by some new undreamt of set of circumstances.'[139] In *Shine v General Guarantee Corporation*[140] the court said that the term 'merchantable quality' not only required the condition of the goods to be considered, but also the purchaser's reasonable expectations about the goods at the time of the sale. In that case the buyer bought a second-hand enthusiast's car without knowing that the car had been written off by the insurance company because it had been submerged in water for 24 hours. There had been a breach of the implied term because nobody, having been aware of this history, would have bought this car at other than a substantially reduced price. Whether this ruling also applies to the modern term of 'satisfactory quality' is, however, not clear.

6.68 *Fitness for all common purposes.* The law before 1994 was potentially narrower because then goods had to be fit 'for all the purposes for which goods of that kind are commonly bought' as it was reasonable to expect in the circumstances, while now 'fitness for all the purposes for which goods of the kind in question are commonly supplied' is required. This has to be taken into account when analysing older case law.[141] In *Kendall v Lillico*[142] the plaintiffs bought animal feeding stuff for their pheasants. One of the ingredients, a substance contained in Brazilian ground nut

---

135 Adams and MacQueen, *Atiyah's Sale of Goods*, p 159.
136 *Clegg v Andersson (t/a Nordic-Marine)* [2003] EWCA Civ 320.
137 *United Central Bakeries Ltd v Spooner Industries Ltd* [2013] CSOH 150 at para [73].
138 This is different from s 14(3), where the buyer's reliance is required. On s 14(3), see paras **6.75–6.78** below.
139 *Bernstein v Pamson Motors (Golders Green) Ltd* [1987] 2 All ER 220 at 222.
140 [1988] 1 All ER 911.
141 E.g., the decision of *Aswan Engineering Establishment Co v Lupdine Ltd* [1987] 1 WLR 1.
142 *Henry Kendall & Sons v William Lillico & Sons Ltd* [1969] 2 AC 31.

extraction, contaminated the animal feeding stuff which made it unsuitable for making feeding stuff for pheasants. But it was entirely satisfactory for animal feeding stuff for cattle and other animals. According to the House of Lords it would be unreasonable to regard the goods as not merchantable because they were unsuitable for only one of several main purposes for which these goods were commonly bought. If a buyer wanted goods to be suitable for a particular use, he would need to conclude his contract of sale under s 14(3) and comply with the specific requirements of that rule.[143]

6.69 *Appearance and finish.* In *Rogers v Parish*,[144] Mustill LJ said that 'deficiencies which might be acceptable in a second-hand vehicle were not to be expected in one purchased as new'. And not merely the buyer's purpose of driving a car is relevant, but also doing so 'with the appropriate degree of comfort, ease of handling and reliability, and ... of pride in the vehicle's outward and interior appearance.' In *Bernstein v Pamson Motors*, again involving the sale of a car, Rougier J indicated a test depending on the nature of the goods: 'in appropriate cases cosmetic factors will also apply depending on the description and price applied to an individual car'.[145] So the buyer of a Rolls Royce would not need to tolerate the slightest blemish on the exterior paintwork, while a buyer of a much cheaper car 'might be less fastidious'.

6.70 *Freedom from minor defects.* Often this criterion is related to 'appearance and finish'. Before the insertion of this requirement in s 14(2), the courts' attitude was quite robust. In *Millars of Falkirk v Turpie*[146] a buyer of a car complained about oil leaking from the steering box. The seller attempted to repair this fault, but the leakage had not been eliminated. The buyer refused another repair attempt and rejected the car, but the seller did not accept the rejection and sued for the price. The court regarded the leakage as a minor defect which could easily be dealt with at a small cost, the sellers were also willing to repair it, and many new cars have on delivery some small defects. Hence the car was of merchantable quality. In *Bernstein v Pamson Motors*, the court was of the opinion that 'no system of mass production can ever be perfect: mistakes and troubles ..., generally minor, are bound to occur from time to time, being often referred to as teething troubles. Nowadays ... even the buyer of a new car, must put up with a certain amount of teething troubles and have them rectified.'[147] However, the Inner House in *Lamarra v Capital Bank plc*[148] adopted a more consumer-friendly position. In that case, a

---

143 See discussion below in paras **6.75–6.78**.
144 *Rogers v Parish (Scarborough) Ltd* [1987] QB 933 at 944 per Mustill LJ.
145 At 228 per Rougier J.
146 1976 SLT (Notes) 66.
147 At 228–29 per Rougier J.
148 [2006] CSIH 49, 2007 SC 95, 2006 SLT 1053, and at para 50.

car was sold (in fact it was a hire purchase[149]) with several defects.
When driven, it pulled to the left. The pedals were positioned incorrectly, so the buyer's foot became trapped underneath the brake pedal.
There was a loud noise from the engine or the transmission system, and
other faults. The sheriff rejected the buyer's argument that the car was
not of satisfactory quality, apparently assuming that a manufacturer's
guarantee can be relied upon. The Inner House reversed the decision,
and held that the sheriff misdirected herself in law by omitting to take
into account the implied term of freedom from minor defects. 'The court
is required to put itself in the position of a reasonable person and ask
itself whether, in the state in which it was shown to be when it was delivered, this Range Rover was of satisfactory quality for such a vehicle.'
In this case the court found it was not.

6.71 *Safety and durability.* Goods may be safe in themselves but be
rendered unsafe by inappropriate instructions. In *Wormell v RHM Agricultural (East) Ltd*[150] a farmer bought a weedkiller from sellers of agricultural chemicals and herbicides which could be used for a longer period
than normal. The instructions stated that the herbicide would be effective for a long time during the growth of crop. In reality the herbicide
became ineffective at an earlier stage of crop growth. The sellers claimed
that the fact that the instructions caused the herbicide to be applied
when it had become ineffective did not make the herbicide unmerchan-
table or unfit for purpose. The court held, however, that 'goods' also
includes any instructions supplied with these, and wrong and misleading
instructions would render goods unsafe or unfit for purpose.

6.72 Where a foreign object has been supplied with the goods sold, that
may also render the goods unsafe. In *Wilson v Rickett, Cockerell & Co
Ltd*[151] coal merchants supplied the buyer with Coalite, a manufactured
fuel. However, one piece of coal contained an explosive which was delivered with the Coalite. When the buyer used the Coalite, an explosion
occurred in the fireplace. The defendant argued that the explosive was
not supplied under the contract; it was not part of the goods sold. The
court decided that the consignment of Coalite was delivered as a whole
and must be considered as a whole. Hence the detonator rendered the
whole consignment unfit for burning and unsafe. An earlier Scottish case
ruled exactly the opposite on substantially the same facts,[152] but one
should arguably follow the more convincing later English decision as
persuasive authority. As regards durability, goods are taken to last for a
certain period of time after purchase. In the case of second-hand cars,
this can be interpreted quite narrowly. In *Thain v Anniesland Trade*

---

149 By virtue of s 10 of the Supply of Goods (Implied Terms) Act 1973, the implied
     terms under the Sale of Goods Act (here s 14(2)) also apply to hire-purchase
     agreements.
150 [1986] 1 All ER 769.
151 [1954] 1 QB 598.
152 *Duke v Jackson* 1921 SC 362.

Centre[153] a five-year-old car with 80,000 miles developed an intermittent droning noise two weeks after having been sold. The fault was in the gearbox but it was uneconomic to replace, so the car was a write-off. The court regarded the car as reasonably fit for its purpose during the initial period of use after its acquisition if there was a justifiable basis to conclude that the defect was not present at the time of the sale. Since the defect could have emerged at any time, given the age and mileage of the car, durability was not a quality that a reasonable person would have demanded of a car of that kind. The price is also relevant in deciding what quality the buyer can expect.

6.73   Under s 14(2A), to assess whether the quality of goods is satisfactory one needs to take into account the description and price of the goods and any other relevant circumstances. Section 14(2D) provides that such relevant circumstances under s 14(2A) include any public statements on the specific characteristics of the goods made about them by the seller or producer (or his representative), particularly in advertising or labelling.[154] Section 14(2D) applies only if the contract of sale is a consumer contract.[155]

(d) Restriction of liability under s 14(2A) and (2B) by s 14(2C)

6.74   Section 14(2C) restricts the applicability of s 14(2A) and (2B) in certain circumstances. There is no liability for breach of the implied term of satisfactory quality in relation to any matter which is specifically drawn to the buyer's attention before conclusion of the contract. The same applies where the buyer examines the goods before the contract is made, and that examination ought to reveal the unsatisfactory quality of the goods.[156] The present law seems to be more generous to the buyer than the previous law. Older case law suggests that a superficial examination by the buyer may take him out of the protection of s 14(2), because a proper examination ought to have revealed that the goods were not of merchantable quality.[157] The statute was, however, amended in 1973. While in the past the statute read 'where the buyer examines the goods ... which *such* examination ought to reveal', it has now been changed to 'where the buyer examines the goods ... which *that*

---

153   1997 SLT (Sh Ct) 102.
154   This provision does not apply in the cases set out in s 14(2E): the buyer is not aware of the statement at the time of the contract, or the statement was withdrawn or publicly corrected before the contract was made, or the decision to buy the goods could not have been influenced by the statement.
155   See s 14(2D): 'in Scotland, if a contract of sale is a consumer contract ...'.
156   Furthermore, s 14(2C) provides that goods sold by sample are not covered by s 14(2A) and (2B) if the sample would have made apparent the unsatisfactory quality on a reasonable examination of the sample. On the sale by sample according to s 15, see para **6.79** below.
157   *Thornett & Fehr v Beers & Son* [1919] 1 KB 486. In that case the buyers did not inspect whether glue in barrels was of merchantable quality but only looked at the barrels from the outside.

examination ought to reveal'. So relevant is the examination actually
carried out by the buyer, even if cursory. Older decisions therefore have
uncertain authority on this point.

Implied term that goods are fit for a particular purpose (s 14(3))

6.75 Section 14(2) concerns the implied term for fitness for all common
purposes. However, the buyer can stipulate that the goods must be fit for
a particular purpose. According to s 14(3), where the buyer, expressly
or by implication, makes known to the seller any particular purpose for
which the goods are being bought, there is an implied term that the
goods supplied under the contract are reasonably fit for that purpose.[158]
To establish a liability for the seller under s 14(3), the buyer must sufficiently communicate his purpose.[159] It is not relevant whether the stipulated purpose is a purpose for which such goods are commonly
supplied.[160] The seller can become liable under s 14(3) only if he sells
goods in the course of a business.[161]

6.76 Furthermore, s 14(3) does not apply if the buyer does not rely
on the skill or judgment of the seller, or if it is unreasonable for the buyer
to rely on the seller's skill or judgment.[162] In *Jewson v Boyhan*[163] the
buyer, a property developer, who purchased boilers from a hardware
store for installation in converted flats in one of his developments, did
not rely on the seller's skill or judgment, nor was it reasonable for him to
have done so. What the buyer could rely on was that the boilers were fit
for their purpose as boilers. But since the buyer did not give the seller
any information which enabled the seller to form a view as to the effect
which the boilers would have on the flats' energy ratings, the buyer
could not reasonably have thought that the seller realised that the buyer
was relying on the seller's skill and judgment regarding the effect of the
installation of these boilers in the flats. Thus he failed under s 14(3)
when he sued for breach of contract because of the disappointingly low
energy ratings of the flats. In *Grant v Australian Knitting Mills Ltd*[164] Lord
Wright said that 'the reliance will seldom be express: it will usually arise
by implication from the circumstances'. In a situation like the present
case – purchase from a retailer – one will infer the reliance from the fact
that 'a buyer goes to the shop in the confidence that the tradesman has

---

158 According to s 14(4), trade usage may annex an implied term about quality or
     fitness for a particular purpose.
159 *United Central Bakeries Ltd v Spooner Industries Ltd* [2013] CSOH 150 at para [76].
160 Under s 14(3)(b), the same rule applies where the purchase price or part of it is
     payable by instalments and the goods were previously sold by a credit-broker to
     the seller; in this case the buyer must make known to the credit-broker the
     particular purpose.
161 This is the same as liability under s 14(2).
162 This is different from liability under s 14(2).
163 [2003] EWCA Civ 1030.
164 [1936] AC 85 at 99.

selected his stock with skill and judgment'. Lord Wright also made clear that the buyer has no duty to make known an obvious purpose: 'there is no need to specify in terms the particular purpose for which the buyer requires the goods, which is none the less the particular purpose within the meaning of the section, because it is the only purpose for which any one would ordinarily want the goods.' In this case, the buyer contracted dermatitis as the result of wearing a woollen garment which contained excess sulphites. The buyer did not need to state the obvious purpose: the garments were naturally intended to be worn next to the skin.

6.77   In *Flynn v Scott*[165] the issue was the rejection of a van by the buyer because it was not suitable for the carriage of furniture and livestock. The court found that the buyer had not made known to the seller this particular purpose, and so the seller had not warranted the fitness for such a purpose, and s 14(3) did not apply. Section 14(2) did not apply either in this case because the van was fit for all common general purposes.[166]

6.78   Liability under s 13 and under s 14 can overlap, and both sections may be breached if the criteria of both sections are met: for example, in *Beale v Taylor*[167] there was a private sale, so s 13 could apply, while s 14 could not; but had the sale been in the course of a business, s 14(2) would most likely have been breached. In *Ashington Piggeries*,[168] s 13 was not breached, but s 14(2) was. However, had the description been worded differently, both sections could have applied.

Sale by sample (s 15)

6.79   A contract for sale by sample is a contract where there is an express or implied term stipulating a sale by sample (s 15(1)). This means that merely a sample made available for the buyer's inspection does not make the contract a sale by sample. There has to be an intention that the sale is to be a sale by sample. The sample shall 'present to the eye the real meaning and intention of the parties with regard to the subject matter of the contract which, owing to the imperfections of language, it may be difficult or impossible to express in words. The sample speaks for itself.'[169] If there is a contract for sale by sample, then according to s 15(2) there is an implied term that (a) the bulk will correspond with the sample in quality, and (b) that the goods will be

---

165 1949 SC 442 (OH).

166 Similarly *B S Brown & Son v Craiks Ltd* 1970 SC (HL) 51: use of cloth not for industrial purposes, as the seller believed, but in fact for making dresses. The buyer has to make known to the seller such unusual uses to benefit from s 14(3). But s 14(2) will probably not apply either because this is not a common general purpose.

167 [1967] 1 WLR 1193.

168 *Ashington Piggeries v Christopher Hill Ltd* [1972] AC 441.

169 *Drummond v Van Ingen* (1887) 12 App Cas 284 at 297 per Lord Macnaghten.

free from any defect, making their quality unsatisfactory, which would not be apparent on reasonable examination of the sample.[170]

CONTENT OF THE CONTRACT II: BUYER'S DUTIES

6.80 Most duties of the buyer are the mirror image of the seller's duty to deliver, so this chapter should be read in conjunction with the respective sections on seller's duties.[171]

Duty to take delivery (s 37)

6.81 The seller must be ready and willing to give possession of the goods to the buyer.[172] The buyer, in turn, must be ready and willing to take delivery of the goods.[173] Section 37(1) provides that, if the buyer does not take delivery within a reasonable time after a request by the seller to do so, the buyer is liable to the seller for any loss the seller suffers as a result of the buyer's neglect or refusal to take delivery. The buyer is also liable for a reasonable charge for care and custody of the goods. In the courts' interpretation the seller's duty of delivery time is prima facie of the essence.[174] Time is presumed not to be of the essence for the buyer's duty of *payment*.[175] The same normally applies to the buyer's duty to take delivery: time is not of the essence.[176] However, if the contract is for the sale of goods of a perishable nature, time is of the essence with regard to taking delivery. If the buyer fails to take delivery, the seller has the right to rescind (reduce) the contract and to resell the goods,[177] in the same way as an unpaid seller of perishable goods under s 48(3).[178]

Duty to pay the price (s 28)

6.82 The buyer has to accept[179] and pay for the goods (and the seller has the duty to deliver them) in accordance with the contractual terms.[180] Section 28 provides that delivery of the goods and payment of the price are concurrent conditions (unless otherwise agreed): 'the seller must be ready and willing to give possession of the goods to the buyer in exchange for the price and the buyer must be ready and willing to

---

170 On the general implied term that goods must be of satisfactory quality, see discussion on s 14(2) in para **6.62** above.
171 Paragraphs **6.49–6.53** above.
172 s 28.
173 s 37(1).
174 *Hartley v Hymans* [1920] 3 KB 475 at 484.
175 s 10(1).
176 *Kidston v Monceau Iron Works Co Ltd* (1902) 7 Com Cas 82 (buyers were late in furnishing specifications for a quantity of iron to be manufactured by the sellers).
177 *Sharp v Christmas* (1892) 8 TLR 687.
178 See paras **6.91–6.92** below.
179 On non-acceptance by the buyer, see para **6.86** below.
180 s 27.

pay the price in exchange for possession of the goods'. If no time is fixed when payment is to be made, the seller can claim payment on conclusion of the contract, provided he is ready and willing to deliver the goods.

6.83 Unless stipulated otherwise, only payment in cash constitutes payment. If the seller accepts a bill of exchange or cheque or other negotiable instrument, this is normally[181] considered as a conditional payment,[182] and the seller may retain the goods until the bill is met (cheque is cleared). If the bill of exchange or cheque is dishonoured, the seller may sue on the instrument itself (which constitutes a separate obligation) or on the underlying contract for the price of the goods.[183]

6.84 According to s 10, time of payment is not of the essence of the contract of sale, unless a different intention appears from the terms of the contract. (The rule on time of *delivery* does not contain such a presumption.[184]) There seems to be a tension between this provision and s 28, whereby delivery of the goods and payment of the price are concurrent conditions. In fact, however, s 10 only makes clear that a buyer who does not make payment by the time stipulated is in breach of contract which entitles the seller to damages but not reduction of the contract.[185] If time of payment is supposed to be of the essence (so a breach allows the seller to reduce the contract), this must be agreed specifically. Even the buyer's repeated failure to pay in time (in case of an instalment contract) may not allow reduction by the seller if there is no serious risk that the buyer will not pay at all.[186]

BREACH OF CONTRACT I: SELLER'S REMEDIES

Seller's personal remedies

Action for price (s 49)

6.85 If the buyer is in breach of contract, the seller has certain personal remedies against the buyer: he can bring an action for the price (s 49), and he can bring an action for damages (s 50). From a pecuniary point of view there is usually a remarkable difference between the price of the goods and the damages the seller has suffered for non-acceptance. In addition, the action for price under s 49 applies when property (ownership) in the goods has passed to the buyer, while damages under s 50 are

---

181 It is possible to stipulate that payment by cheque or other instrument constitutes absolute, unconditional payment, but an intention to accept cheques as absolute payment must be strictly shown: see *Maillard v Argyle* (1843) 6 M & G 40.
182 *Leggat Bros v Gray* 1908 SC 67.
183 See Chapter 9: Payment Obligations.
184 s 10(2).
185 Adams and MacQueen, *Atiyah's Sale of Goods*, p 299.
186 *Decro-Wall International SA v Practitioners in Marketing Ltd* [1971] 1 WLR 361 at 380.

appropriate when property has not yet passed, or, in any case, the buyer has wrongfully neglected or refused to accept and pay for the goods.[187]

6.86   The seller has an action for the price according to s 49(1), where the property has passed to the buyer and he wrongfully neglects or refuses to pay for the goods according to the terms of the contract. The same action is available under s 49(2), even if property has not passed, where the price is payable on a day certain irrespective of delivery, and the buyer wrongfully neglects or refuses to pay for the goods. 'Day certain' is a fixed date, but a date determined by some future event (e.g. submission of an invoice) is not a day certain.[188]

Damages for non-acceptance (s 50)

6.87   Where the buyer wrongfully neglects or refuses to accept and pay for the goods, the seller may maintain an action against him for damages for non-acceptance (s 50(1)). This is the only personal remedy the seller has if property has not passed.[189] The damages are measured according to the estimated loss directly and naturally resulting in the ordinary course of events from the buyer's breach.[190] Where there is an available market for the goods, the damages will be ascertained by the difference between the contract price and the market price/current price at the time when the goods ought to have been accepted or have been refused.[191] Where the seller retained the goods after the breach and later resold them for more than the market price at the time of the breach, the seller can obtain the difference between the contract and market price and does not have to account for the greater price at which he had actually sold the goods.[192] In general, the seller who resells the goods cannot recover from the buyer the loss below the market price at the date of the breach if the market falls, and he does not have to account to the buyer for a profit if the market rises.[193]

Seller's possessory remedies

6.88   The seller also has certain remedies based on his possession of the goods beside the personal remedies, as the personal remedies may be unsatisfactory. According to s 39, the unpaid seller[194] ('unpaid' also includes cases of part payment only or where a negotiable instrument

---

187 The problem with this distinction is that in the case of s 50 (damages for non-acceptance) property may also have passed already, since property often passes before delivery: see para **6.18** ff.

188 *Henderson & Keay Ltd v A M Carmichael Ltd* 1956 SLT (Notes) 58.

189 If property has passed but the buyer neglects to take delivery, the seller can choose between the action for price and the action for damages.

190 s 50(2).

191 s 50(3).

192 *Campbell Mostyn (Provisions) Ltd v Barnett Trading Co* [1954] 1 Lloyd's Rep 65.

193 *Jamal v Moolla Dawood, Sons & Co* [1916] 1 AC 175 (PC) at 179 (this case involved the retention of shares by the seller after the breach).

194 This includes the agent of the seller: see s 38(2).

has been dishonoured[195]) has three real (proprietary) remedies, even though property in the goods has passed to the buyer: (a) a lien on the goods or right to retain them for the price while in possession of them; (b) after the seller has parted with possession, a right of stopping the goods in transit if the buyer becomes insolvent; and (c) a right of resale. The complicated proprietary dimension of these remedies, especially where property (ownership) has already passed to the buyer, cannot be discussed here.[196]

Unpaid seller's lien (ss 41–43)

6.89 The seller has a lien (right of retention), provided he is unpaid and in possession of the goods. This means that he is entitled to retain possession of the goods until payment, if, either (a) the contract of sale did not contain a stipulation as to credit, or (b) the sale did contain a stipulation as to credit, but the term of credit has expired, or (c) the buyer becomes insolvent.[197] Where the unpaid seller has made part delivery of the goods, he may exercise his lien on the remainder, unless one can infer from the circumstances of the part delivery an intention to waive the lien.[198] The seller loses his lien (i) when he delivers the goods to a carrier for further delivery to the buyer without reserving the right of disposal of the goods, (ii) when the buyer (or his agent) lawfully obtains possession of the goods, or (iii) when the seller waives the lien.[199] Once the lien is lost, it cannot be resurrected. In *London Scottish Transport v Tyres (Scotland) Ltd*,[200] the seller delivered the goods and then took them back (with the buyer's consent) because he suspected imminent insolvency of the buyer, which subsequently really happened. The buyer's liquidator could recover the goods because the seller's lien, lost on delivery, cannot be revived.

Stoppage in transit (ss 44–46)

6.90 When the buyer of goods becomes insolvent the unpaid seller who has parted with the possession of the goods has the right of stopping them in transit, so he can resume possession of the goods as long as they are in course of transit, and retain them until payment.[201] Whether property has already passed to the buyer is irrelevant.[202] The goods are in transit once they are delivered to the carrier until the buyer (or his agent) takes delivery from the carrier.[203] If the buyer obtains delivery of

---

195 s 38(1)(a) and (b).
196 See e.g. Adams and MacQueen, *Atiyah's Sale of Goods*, pp 447–49 for further discussion.
197 s 41(1)(a)–(c).
198 s 42.
199 s 43.
200 1957 SLT (Sh Ct) 48.
201 s 44.
202 s 39(2).
203 s 45(1).

the goods before scheduled arrival, transit is at an end;[204] the same applies when the goods are delivered to a carrier who is an agent of the buyer.[205] However, if the buyer rejects the goods and the carrier continues in possession of them, the transit is deemed to continue.[206] The seller can exercise stoppage in transit either by taking actual possession of the goods or by giving notice of his claim to the carrier who is in possession of the goods.[207] Where a carrier obtains a notice in time to stop the goods in transit but the carrier delivers to the buyer regardless of the notice, the carrier is liable in damages to the seller.[208] When the goods are stopped in transit, they must be redelivered to the seller, or according to the seller's directions, and the seller must bear the cost of the redelivery.[209]

Effect of sub-sale by buyer on seller's lien/stoppage in transit (s 47)

6.91 If the buyer has sold goods which were subject to the unpaid seller's exercise of his lien or stoppage in transit, the seller's rights are not affected, unless the seller has assented to the sale,[210] so a third-party buyer is bound by the seller's lien/stoppage in transit. The seller's 'assent' which affects the seller's right of lien/stoppage, must show in the circumstances that the seller intends to renounce his rights against the goods. Only giving notice of the sub-sale to the seller, and the seller acknowledging receipt of the notice, is not sufficient.[211]

Right of resale (s 48)

6.92 Mere exercise of the seller's lien or of stoppage in transit does not rescind ('reduce')[212] the contract.[213] However, according to s 48(4), where the seller expressly reserves the right to resell in case of the buyer's default, and resells the goods on the buyer's default, the original contract is rescinded (set aside), but any claim for damages the seller may have remains. Under s 48(2) the seller can, after having exercised his lien or stoppage in transit, resell the goods, and then the new buyer acquires a

---

204 s 45(2).
205 That appears from s 45(5).
206 s 45(4). This applies even if the seller refuses to receive the goods back.
207 s 46(1).
208 *Mechan & Sons Ltd v North Eastern Railway Co* 1911 SC 1348. The case concerned a railway company which ignored a notice from the seller to stop the goods in transit after the seller had heard of the buyers' insolvency.
209 s 46(4).
210 s 47(1).
211 *Mordaunt Bros v British Oil & Cake Mills Ltd* [1910] 2 KB 502.
212 In s 48, the use of the term 'rescission' is arguably outdated. What is meant in s 48, is 'termination' of the contract (e.g. for breach) which is of prospective effect, unlike rescission, which, strictly speaking, means voiding a contract *ab initio* (e.g. for fraud, misrepresentation/error), that is, retrospectively. See *Johnson v Agnew* [1980] AC 367, and Adams and MacQueen, *Atiyah's Sale of Goods*, pp 465–66.
213 s 48(1).

good title to the goods as against the original buyer. This goes beyond the rule of s 24 (acquisition of good title by the second buyer after second sale by the seller who has continued to be in possession after the first sale):[214] here, even when the first buyer has already obtained title, the seller still has the power to resell the goods and thereby pass a good title to the new buyer, a third party.[215]

6.93 Under s 48(3), where the goods are perishable, or where the unpaid seller gives notice to the buyer of his intention to resell, and the buyer does not pay within a reasonable time, the seller may resell the goods and recover from the original buyer damages for the loss suffered by the buyer's breach of contract. Section 48(3) does not provide, in contrast to s 48(4), that in the case of such a resale the original contract is rescinded, but it seems that the courts do presume such a rescission for a resale under s 48(3) as well, with property revesting in the seller.[216]

Operation of reservation of title (ownership) clauses (ss 17, 19)

6.94 In commercial practice a most important protection measure of the seller against the buyer's non-payment and insolvency is the stipulation of reservation of ownership or retention of title clauses. The idea of such retention of title clauses is that even after delivery the seller can regard the goods delivered as a (real) security for the payment of the price. Effectively such clauses are part of contracts of sale with a suspensive condition: ownership does not pass, for example, on delivery, but it is stipulated that ownership passes when a suspensive condition is purified, that is, the price of the goods is fully paid by the buyer. Sections 17(1) and 19(1) recognise such clauses: property passes when the contracting parties intend it to pass; and the seller may contractually reserve the right of disposal of specific goods until certain conditions are fulfilled. The courts have identified reservation of title clauses as applications of these statutory provisions.[217]

BREACH OF CONTRACT II: BUYER'S REMEDIES

Acceptance of goods

6.95 The buyer's primary remedy for breach of contract by the seller is to reject the goods and potentially to rescind the contract. This presupposes a discussion when the buyer can or is deemed to accept the goods, and when there is a breach by the seller because the buyer cannot accept them.

---

214 See discussion in para **6.18** ff above.
215 If the seller still has the property in the goods (e.g. depending on the stipulation when passing of property is supposed to have been effected), or if the seller is still in possession of the goods after property has passed (a s 24 scenario), there is not a problem which needs to be covered by s 48(2).
216 *R V Ward Ltd v Bignall* [1967] 1 QB 534.
217 *Armour v Thyssen Edelstahlwerke AG* 1990 SLT 891, [1991] 2 AC 339 (HL).

6.96 If not agreed otherwise, the seller must give the buyer a reasonable opportunity to examine the goods for the purpose of ascertaining whether they conform to the contract.[218] The buyer is not deemed to have accepted the goods until he has had a reasonable opportunity of examining them to see whether they are in conformity with the contract.[219] According to s 35(1), the buyer is deemed to have accepted the goods when (a) he expressly intimates to the seller that he has accepted them, or (b) after delivery to him, he does any act in relation to the goods inconsistent with the seller's ownership. According to some older decisions (not in all details necessarily still valid), if the seller delivers to a third party at the behest of the buyer, this in itself is not an act inconsistent with the seller's ownership,[220] while if the seller delivers to a carrier for the purpose of selling on by the buyer to a third party (which was not a stipulation of the original contract), this was at one time seen as inconsistent with the seller's ownership and the buyer was deemed to have accepted the goods.[221] In *Clegg v Andersson*[222] it was held that if the buyer seeks further information from the seller which the seller has agreed to supply, so that the buyer can make an informed choice whether to accept or reject, this cannot be interpreted as an acceptance; the buyer has retained the right to reject.

6.97 If the buyer retains the goods and does not intimate to the seller that he has rejected the goods, then, after the lapse of a reasonable time, he is deemed to have accepted them.[223] A reasonable time in which rejection is to be intimated is the time actually taken to resell the goods together with an additional period in which they can be inspected and tried out by the sub-purchaser.[224]

6.98 Section 35(6) provides that the buyer is not deemed to have accepted the goods merely because he asks for, or agrees to, the repair by (or under an arrangement with) the seller, or because the goods are delivered to another under a sub-sale or other disposition. In *J & H Ritchie v Lloyd*,[225] the buyers bought a seed drill and power harrow combination for their farm, but the harrow operated inadequately with vibrations from its drive chain. The buyers returned the goods to the

---

218 s 34. In the case of a contract for sale by sample, the buyer must have the reasonable opportunity to compare the bulk with the sample.

219 s 35(2), echoing s 34. Again, in the case of a sale by sample, the buyer must have the reasonable opportunity to compare the bulk with the sample, otherwise he is not deemed to have accepted the goods (s 35(2)(b)).

220 *Hammer & Barrow v Coca-Cola* [1962] NZLR 723.

221 *E & S Ruben Ltd v Faire Bros & Co Ltd* [1949] 1 KB 254. This case is potentially in conflict with the present provision of s 35(6)(b) (buyer is not deemed to have accepted because the goods are delivered to another under a sub-sale or other disposition), depending on the circumstances of the case in question. This section is the result of an amendment well after the decision in *E & S Ruben*.

222 [2003] EWCA Civ 320, [2003] 2 Lloyd's Rep 32 at para 75.

223 s 35(4).

224 *Truk (UK) Ltd v Tokmakidis GmbH* [2000] 1 Lloyd's Rep 543 at 551.

225 [2007] UKHL 9, 2007 SLT 377.

sellers who repaired the harrow without asking the buyers for agreement. The buyers were informed of the repair, but the engineer's report was withheld. The buyers, concerned that the vibrations may have damaged other parts of the machine, rejected the machine; also because, in order to use and test it, they would have had to wait until the following spring. The House of Lords ruled that the buyers could reject, although the judges based their rulings on two different arguments. One view (by Lord Hope) was that there is an implied term that the buyer retains the right to reject until he has been provided with the information needed to make an informed choice, and the seller's refusal to give the buyers the report was a breach of this term. The other view (by Lord Rodger) was that the repair of the goods was covered by a different, gratuitous, contract which contained the implied term that as long as the sellers performed their obligations under it (information as to the nature of the defect, repair as to proper standard), the buyers could not rescind the contract of sale. This decision clarifies the law, because s 35(6) preserves the right to reject if the buyer agrees to the repair, but is silent as to what happens if the repair has already been attempted. According to *J & H Ritchie* the buyer can still reject after a repair attempt if he cannot conduct tests and has not been given the necessary information which would enable him to make an informed choice. In *Douglas v Glenvarigill*[226] the buyer bought a car with several latent defects which only became manifest about a year after delivery, including a defective engine management system which suddenly reduced the speed of the car considerably. The buyer returned the car which remained with the sellers for six months. During this time the buyer sought information about the nature of the defects, but the sellers gave no explanation. Finally the sellers told the buyer that they had repaired the car, but the car broke down when the buyer drove it home. The buyer attempted to reject the car, but the seller refused to take it back. The court decided that rejection had come too late; the buyer could only claim damages. The delay was indeed for some fifteen months, but the defect was latent for about twelve months (if manifest it would clearly have entitled the buyer to rejection). The court found that at some stage 'commercial closure' would be required.[227]

Rejection of goods

General remedies (s 15B(1)(b))

6.99   If the seller is in breach of any term of the contract of sale, and if that breach is *material*, the buyer is entitled to reject any goods delivered under the contract and treat the contract as repudiated (s 15B(1)(b)).

---

226 *Douglas v Glenvarigill Co Ltd* [2010] CSOH 14, [2010] SLT 634 (OH).
227 At para 34. See also note on this case by R G Anderson, 'UK sales: loss of the right to reject goods' (2011) Zeitschrift für Europäisches Privatrecht 655–68.

6.100   In particular, the buyer may reject if the seller delivers to the buyer a quantity of goods less than he contracted to sell (s 30(1)), but only if the shortfall is material (s 30(2D)). The same applies, *mutatis mutandis*, to delivery in excess of what the seller has contracted to sell: the buyer can reject the whole, but only if the excess is material; in addition the buyer can choose to keep the contractually agreed quantity and reject the rest.[228] When the buyer chooses to keep the excess quantity, he has to pay for it at the contract rate.[229] The buyer has no duty to return the rejected goods to the seller.[230]

6.101   The loss of the buyer's right to reject by way of acceptance under s 35 has already been discussed. Section 35A(1) provides that acceptance of part of the goods does not extinguish the right of partial rejection. If the buyer, entitled to reject goods because of the seller's breach (which affects either some of the goods or all of them), accepts some of the goods (including all goods unaffected by the breach), he does not lose his right to reject the rest by accepting some of the goods. Thus s 35A also covers cases in which the buyer rejects either all or only some of the goods which do not conform (and in the latter case accepts some non-conforming goods).

Additional remedies for consumers (s 15B(2), ss 48A–48C)

6.102   As said, under s 15B(1)(b), in the case of a material breach by the seller, the buyer is entitled to reject any goods delivered under the contract and treat it as repudiated. If, however, the contract is a consumer contract, then every breach is material. A material breach for this purpose is a breach of (a) any term in relation to the quality of the goods or their fitness for a purpose; (b) any term that, in a sale by description, the goods correspond with the description; or (c) any term that, in a sale by sample, the bulk corresponds with the sample in quality (s 15B(2)). Thus for breaches of implied terms under s 14(2) and (3), s 13 and s 15, the buyer in a consumer contract is always entitled to reject and repudiate the contract.

6.103   Buyers who are consumers under a consumer contract have *additional* remedies alongside those of s 15B(2) where the goods do not conform to the contract of sale at the time of delivery.[231] These are set out in ss 48A–48C. The rule of s 48A provides that the buyer has (a) the right to require the seller to repair or replace the goods, according to the rules in s 48B; or (b) the right to require the seller to reduce the purchase price of the goods by an appropriate amount or to rescind the contract of sale, if the conditions in s 48C are met.

---

228   s 30(2) and (2D).
229   s 30(3).
230   s 36.
231   Section 48F defines that goods do not conform to a contract of sale if there is, in relation to the goods, a breach of an express term or of an implied term of the contract according to ss 13, 14 or 15.

6.104 Under s 48B the buyer may require the seller to repair[232] the goods or to replace the goods. In that case, the seller must repair or replace the goods within a reasonable time but without causing significant inconvenience to the buyer, and must bear any necessary costs of repair or replacement (s 48B(2)(a) and (b)). If the buyer invokes this remedy, the seller must be given a reasonable time in which to repair or replace the goods. Otherwise the buyer cannot reject the goods and treat the contract as repudiated.[233] However, the buyer cannot require repair or replacement if that is impossible or disproportionate in comparison to other remedies, including the remedies of reduction of purchase price or rescission (s 48B(3)). In assessing whether the remedy of s 48B is disproportionate, one has to take into account the value of the goods, the significance of the lack of the conformity of the goods, or the availability of other remedies without significant inconvenience to the buyer, having regard to the nature and purpose of the goods.[234]

6.105 Under s 48C another remedy is available, but only *on condition that* (see s 48C(2)) either (a) the buyer may require neither repair nor replacement of the goods in accordance with s 48B(3) (impossibility, disproportionality of the remedy), or (b) the buyer has required the seller to repair or replace the goods, but the seller, breaching his obligation under s 48B(2)(a), has not done so within a reasonable time and without significant inconvenience to the buyer. If that condition under s 48C(2) is fulfilled, the buyer may (i) require the seller to reduce the purchase price by an appropriate amount, or (ii) rescind the contract (s 48C(1)). So s 48C is *not* an alternative remedy to s 48B, but is only available if the remedies in s 48B cannot be exercised.

6.106 These remedies specifically for the consumer which have been introduced in 2002 clarify the law, but do not change it significantly. One may recall, for example, *Rogers v Parish*,[235] concerning the sale of a car with a defective engine and gearbox. The seller attempted the repair of the defects, but failed: the buyer was allowed to reject. Today this would be dealt with in accordance with s 48C(2)(b), so the buyer can rescind under s 48C(1)(b). Alongside these specific consumers' remedies, the general remedies under s 15B remain available to the consumer.

Damages for non-delivery (s 15B(1)(a), s 51)

6.107 The buyer is entitled to claim damages for the seller's breach of any express or implied term of the contract. If the breach is not material, then this is the only remedy the buyer has (s 15B(1)(a)). If the breach is material, then the buyer can *also* reject the goods and repudiate the

---

232 Section 61(1) defines 'repair' as 'to bring the goods into conformity with the contract'.
233 s 48D(1) and (2)(b).
234 s 48B(4)–(5).
235 *Rogers v Parish (Scarborough) Ltd* [1987] QB 933.

contract, as already discussed (s 15B(1)(b)).[236] (Note: if the buyer is a consumer under a consumer contract, then a breach of the implied terms under ss 13, 14 and 15 is always deemed to be a material breach, so the buyer can always reject and repudiate.[237])

6.108 Where the seller wrongfully neglects or refuses to deliver the goods[238] to the buyer, the buyer may sue the seller for damages for non-delivery (s 51(1)). The measure of damages is the estimated loss directly and naturally resulting, in the ordinary course of events, from the seller's breach of contract (s 53A(1)).[239] Like the seller's remedy for non-acceptance,[240] the buyer's remedy for non-delivery has a market price rule: where there is a market for the goods in question, the damages are prima facie assessed by the difference between the contract price and the market price at the time of delivery (or refusal of delivery).[241] A (usually higher) resale price is irrelevant in this calculation because if the seller does not deliver, the buyer is assumed to buy at market price to fulfil his contract with a third party. In *Williams v Agius*,[242] the seller of coal sold for 16s 3d per ton, while the market price was 23s 6d, and the buyer contracted to resell for 19s: the buyer was awarded damages which were the difference between contract and market price. A buyer may be required to mitigate the loss by buying replacement goods at a favourable price.[243]

Damages for breach of term relating to quality (s 53A(2))

6.109 Where the seller's breach consists in the delivery of goods which do not conform to the quality required by the contract and the buyer retains the goods, the buyer is again entitled to damages which correspond to the estimated loss directly and naturally resulting from the seller's breach.[244] In the case of a loss because of defective goods, such damages are prima facie the difference between the value of the goods at the time of the delivery and the value they would have had if they had

---

236 The buyer may have lost the right to reject because of acceptance under s 35. See discussion in paras **6.94–6.97** above.

237 s 15B(2).

238 'Wrongfully' means that the seller has no justification, especially a breach of contract by the buyer, to refuse delivery of the goods ('neglecting' means not making the necessary efforts to put the goods into a deliverable state).

239 Section 53A(1) restates s 51(2). Since Scots law does not distinguish between conditions, warranties and innominate terms, as English law does, a special provision for Scots law, s 53A, had to be introduced instead of s 53 for English law.

240 s 50.

241 s 51(3).

242 *Williams Bros v Agius* [1914] AC 510.

243 *Kaines (UK) Ltd v Österreichische Warenhandelsgesellschaft Austrowaren GmbH* [1993] 2 Lloyd's Rep 1. In the highly volatile oil market, the buyer should have bought alternative goods once the seller indicated he would not deliver, and damages were calculated accordingly, not on the basis of the difference between contract and market price.

244 ss 51(2), 53A(1) and (2).

conformed to the contract (s 53A(2)). Damages for consequential loss are assessed in the same way as damages in the delict of negligence.[245] Damages should therefore reflect physical injury[246] or damage to property[247] which the buyer has suffered as a result of the defective nature of the goods.

Specific implement (s 52)

6.110 If a seller is in breach of a contract to deliver specific or ascertained goods, the buyer can apply to the court to direct the seller to perform the contract specifically, thus without giving the seller the option of retaining the goods and paying damages instead.[248] This specific performance rule of English law also applies to Scotland, but it only supplements the general rules of specific implement in Scots law; it does not repeal them.[249] In Scots law, unlike in English law, specific implement is a general right for breach of contract,[250] but in reality the application of the remedy of specific performance and the right of specific implement are hardly different in both jurisdictions.[251]

Connected lender liability under the Consumer Credit Act 1974, s 75

6.111 This is not a remedy for the seller's breach of contract as such, but often arises as an associated situation, so it is appropriate to discuss the connected lender liability in this context. A typical case is the debtor-creditor-supplier agreement under the Consumer Credit Act 1974: the buyer buys goods on credit, the purchase price being payable in instalments over a period of time after delivery. In that case either the seller/supplier is also the lender who makes available the credit (two-party transaction), or a third party, such as a bank or finance house, makes available the credit to the seller/supplier, and the buyer pays the price in instalments to the finance house, that is, the buyer repays the credit (three-party transaction).[252] In the second scenario, if the goods do not conform to the contract and the seller is in breach, the finance house could theoretically insist on the performance of the independent and separate loan agreement.

6.112 To avoid that outcome, the parties, seller/supplier, creditor and buyer/debtor, have been connected together by s 75 of the Consumer

---

245 Compare *Hadley v Baxendale* (1854) 9 Ex 341.
246 *Godley v Perry* [1960] 1 WLR 9.
247 *Wilson v Rickett Cockerell & Co Ltd* [1954] 1 QB 598.
248 s 52(1).
249 s 52(4).
250 MacQueen and Thomson, *Contract Law in Scotland*, pp 233–34.
251 See e.g. *Union Electric Co v Holman & Co* 1913 SC 954.
252 Consumer Credit Act 1974, s 12(a) and (b) in connection with s 11(1)(a) and (b).

Credit Act. If a debtor under a (restricted-use and unrestricted-use[253]) debtor-creditor-supplier agreement in the form of a three-party transaction, has, in relation to a transaction financed by the agreement, any claim against the supplier in respect of a misrepresentation or breach of contract, he shall have a like claim against the creditor. This connected lender liability means that the creditor and the supplier are jointly and severally liable to the debtor.[254] For example, the seller (supplier) S has sold goods on credit which do not conform to the contract. Credit is provided by the bank (creditor) B, to be repaid by the buyer. The buyer (debtor) has the same remedies for breach of contract against B as he has against S.

6.113   There are some exceptions to the rule in s 75. It does not apply to non-commercial agreements and to a claim relating to a single item to which the supplier has attached a cash price of up to £100 or more than £30,000.[255] That means, if a defective toaster priced at £50 causes a fire in the kitchen with damage of £3,000, the creditor is not liable.

6.114   In addition, the debtor can also pursue his breach of contract claim against the creditor for transactions of goods or services with a cash value of more than £30,000[256] under certain circumstances: if (a) the supplier cannot be traced; (b) the supplier has not responded after having been contacted by the debtor; (c) the supplier is insolvent; and (d) despite having pursued his claim reasonably against the supplier, the debtor has not obtained satisfaction for his claim.[257] There are several provisos to this rule which cannot be discussed in this context.[258]

---

253 See Consumer Credit Act 1974, ss 75(1), 12(b) and (c), and 11. A restricted-use credit agreement under the 1974 Act, s 11(1) involves use of credit to finance a specific transaction between debtor and supplier, while an unrestricted-use credit agreement under s 11(2) allows the debtor to use the credit as he wishes, e.g. an overdraft or a credit card. Section 75 applies to credit cards: see *Office of Fair Trading v Lloyds TSB Bank plc* [2007] QB 1.
254 Consumer Credit Act 1974, s 75(1).
255 Consumer Credit Act 1974, s 75(3)(a) and (b). There are further exceptions.
256 Consumer Credit Act 1974, s 75A(6)(a) in connection with s 75(3)(b). Legislation has decided to keep s 75 unchanged and to add a new s 75A that applies to agreements outside the scope of the current s 75.
257 Consumer Credit Act 1974, s 75A(1) and (2).
258 Especially Consumer Credit Act 1974, s 75A(6).

Chapter 7

Insurance

INSURANCE CONTRACTS

The purpose of insurance

7.01 Insurance is, in essence, a mechanism whereby risk can be transferred to an insurer. Some risks (e.g. the destruction of one's home by fire) carry such severe financial consequences that it is not possible for one person to make adequate provision for the possibility of the occurrence of the risk. Insurance offers a means for a large number of people to contribute to a fund which will meet the cost of specific forms of loss or damage. As only a fraction of all the contributors are likely to suffer loss in any one year, the cost can be borne more easily by a large number than by an individual. This spreading of risk across large numbers makes it possible for insurers to charge premiums which represent only a fraction of the sums which can be recovered by an insured who suffers a loss. In order for the mechanism to work fairly it is necessary that policyholders contribute to the common fund according to the degree of risk that they pose and withdraw from it according to the cover agreed in their policy. These objectives are reflected in the various principles of insurance law which are discussed in this chapter.[1]

Definition of an insurance contract

7.02 There is no statutory definition of an insurance contract. Organisations engaged in carrying on insurance business are regulated by the Financial Services and Markets Act 2000, but the definition of insurance business in the Act largely follows the common law definition adopted in *Scottish Amicable Heritable Securities Association Ltd v Northern Assurance Co.*[2] In that case, Lord Justice-Clerk Moncreiff defined insurance as a contract in which 'the insurer undertakes, in consideration of the payment of an estimated equivalent beforehand, to make up to the assured any loss he may sustain by the occurrence of an uncertain contingency.' It is essential that the insured stands to lose by the occurrence of the insured event and that the timing of the insured event is uncertain. The

---

1 For the history, see A Forte, 'Insurance' in K G C Reid and R Zimmermann, *A History of Private Law in Scotland* (2000) II, chapter 13.
2 (1883) 11 R 287 at 303.

insured event itself does not have to be uncertain: in the case of life assurance, for example, death is a certain event, but its timing is uncertain and therefore it is an insurable risk. Uncertainty is determined at the time when the contract is concluded.[3] Nor is it necessary that the insurer agree to pay a sum of money to the insured on the occurrence of an insured event. In *Department of Trade v St Christopher Motorists Association Ltd*,[4] it was held that the provision by the insurer of chauffeur services to motorists convicted of drink-driving offences was insurance even though payment was in a form other than money. This approach was clarified in the later case of *Medical Defence Union Ltd v Department of Trade*,[5] which held that insurance was a contract for 'the payment of money or for money's worth' but that the payment of some other form of benefit could not be considered to be insurance. Following that approach, 'breakdown' cover provided by motoring organisations is considered to be a form of insurance.

7.03 Insurance contracts should be distinguished from manufacturers' guarantees and cautionary obligations. The former, in particular, can appear similar to insurance contracts, in that they provide for the manufacturer to bear the cost of an uncertain event in the future, for example the breakdown of an appliance. The law has approached manufacturers' guarantees from the perspective of the related contract for sale of goods rather than from the perspective of risk transfer.[6] Nevertheless, where a retailer offers an extended warranty to a customer covering the risk of breakdown, this may amount to a contract of insurance if the elements outlined in the paragraph above are present.[7] Cautionary obligations, by contrast, are in their nature different from insurance contracts in that they are accessory and not direct obligations:[8] thus, an insurance contract can be enforced against the insurer immediately following an insured event, whereas a cautionary obligation can only be enforced following the default of the debtor in the primary obligation.

3 *Department of Trade and Industry v St Christopher Motorists Association Ltd* [1974] 1 All ER 395, [1974] 1 WLR 99.
4 [1974] 1 WLR 99.
5 [1980] Ch 82 at 93 per Megarry V-C, [1979] 2 All ER 421, [1979] 1 Lloyd's Rep 499. The issue in this case was whether the Medical Defence Union was an insurer. It could, at its discretion, undertake or defend legal proceedings on behalf of members and could provide an indemnity in relation to awards arising from such proceedings. It was held that the discretionary power of the MDU prevented it having a contract with each member.
6 For example, manufacturers' guarantees are governed by the Unfair Contract Terms Act 1977 whereas insurance contracts are not.
7 In *Re Digital Satellite Warranty Cover Ltd* [2013] UKSC 7 it was not disputed that an extended warranty was a contract of insurance at common law. An extended warranty is additional to the protection given to the customer by the terms implied into the contract of sale by the Sale of Goods Act 1979.
8 *Scottish Amicable Heritable Securities Association Ltd v Northern Assurance Co* (1883) 11 R 287 at 303 per Lord Justice-Clerk Moncreiff.

TYPES OF INSURANCE

Indemnity

7.04 The most fundamental distinction is between indemnity and non-indemnity insurance. Indemnity contracts are intended to compensate the insured to the extent of her financial loss resulting from the occurrence of an insured event. Common examples are motor and home insurance. Non-indemnity contracts provide for the insurer to pay a specified amount on the occurrence of the insured event. They are used where the financial loss resulting from the occurrence of an insured event is not readily ascertainable. The most common form of non-indemnity insurance is life assurance.[9] As the loss resulting from a person's death cannot be known in the same manner as, for example, the cost of replacing a car, the sum to be paid by the insurer under a life assurance contract is specified when the contract is agreed.

First party and third party

7.05 A distinction can also be drawn between first party and third party insurance. First party cover is intended to protect against the risk of loss of or harm to the insured. Common examples of such insurance are the cover against causing damage to one's own car or having the contents of one's home stolen. Third party cover protects against legal liability arising from damage caused to a third party. Motor policies, for example, provide cover for this risk both in relation to personal injury and property damage. Where third party cover is provided, the policy wording makes clear that the insurer will only be liable in situations in which there is a legal liability to a third party. The result is that the normal principles of delictual liability apply to determine if the insured is liable to a third party and it is only if that liability is triggered that the policy provides cover to the insured.

Voluntary and compulsory

7.06 In the case of most types of insurance, the decision to insure is made voluntarily by the insured. However, there are some instances in which insurance is required by law. Two examples of this are third party motor vehicle insurance and employers' liability insurance. Section 143 of the Road Traffic Act 1988 requires a vehicle to be insured in respect of death or bodily injury caused to any person or damage to property caused by the use of the vehicle on a road in Great Britain. Employers are required to insure against the risk of bodily injury or disease sus-

---

9 The use of the terms assurance and insurance leads to some confusion. 'Assurance' is associated primarily with life assurance, as the insured event (death) is an assured event. However, it is also common practice in marine insurance to refer to the insured as the assured, despite the fact that the contract is referred to as insurance. (See the definition of a marine insurance contract in the Marine Insurance Act 1906, s 1.)

tained by employees in the course of their employment by section 1(1) of the Employers' Liability (Compulsory Insurance) Act 1969.

Life assurance

7.07 In its simplest form, life assurance provides protection against the financial consequences of early death. Such policies can take two forms. A whole life policy provides for a sum to be paid on the death of the assured, whenever that occurs. A term policy provides for a sum to be paid if the assured dies during a certain period (e.g. ten years) and no sum is payable if the assured survives to the end of that period. The more complex forms of life assurance are those which combine protection against early death with an investment. The most common example is endowment assurance, where part of the premium is invested by the insurer to provide the assured with a capital sum at the end of the policy term. This type of policy may be used in conjunction with mortgages and fulfils two functions: first, if the assured dies before the mortgage is repaid, the sum assured under the policy will repay the mortgage; second, if the assured survives to the end of the mortgage term, he will have a capital sum to repay the mortgage.

SOURCES AND STRUCTURE OF INSURANCE LAW

7.08 Insurance has a long history as a means of sharing the risks faced by merchants in their trading activities. Early forms of insurance involved merchants themselves, rather than insurers, assuming the risks of ships sinking or cargoes being lost, but as trade expanded and risk assessment became more complex, it became common for insurance to be underwritten[10] by insurers. The law relating to insurance underwent its most rapid development in the latter part of the eighteenth century. The influence of Lord Mansfield, an expatriate Scot who became Lord Chief Justice of England, was particularly evident in this period. By the time of Lord Mansfield's retirement in 1788, the basic principles of the common law governing insurance contracts had been put in place. The development of the law in Scotland leant heavily on the law in England, which benefited from the emergence of London as an international centre for insurance and shipping.

7.09 Insurance continued to be governed primarily[11] by the common law until the passing of the Marine Insurance Act 1906 ('the 1906 Act'). The Act codified the law relating to marine insurance. It specifically preserved the common law governing marine insurance in so far as it was not altered by the Act.[12]

---

10 The term 'underwrite' originates from the practice of subscribing the names of the persons bearing the risk ('underwriters') on the insurance contract.
11 As outlined below, legislation was introduced to control the abuse of insurance for the purpose of speculation.
12 1906 Act, s 91(2).

7.10 Other types of insurance are not covered by the Act.[13] However, there has always been a tendency on the part of the courts to extend the general principles of marine insurance to other types of insurance. This resulted from marine being the major class of business in the early days of insurance. As other types of insurance, such as fire and motor, were introduced, it was natural to look to the principles which had already been established for marine insurance. In *Thomson v Weems*[14] Lord Blackburn said: 'I think that on the balance of authority the general principles of insurance law apply to all insurances, whether marine, fire or life.' It follows that, to the extent that it states general principles of insurance law, the 1906 Act corresponds to the common law governing non-marine contracts.

7.11 Insurance contracts do not fall within the scope of the Unfair Contract Terms Act 1977.[15] Their treatment under the Unfair Terms in Consumer Contracts Regulations 1999[16] is more complex. In principle insurance contracts can fall within the definition of a consumer contract under the Regulations.[17] However, there is a substantial 'carve-out' of insurance contracts from the Regulations. The recitals provide that, 'The terms which clearly define or circumscribe the insured risk and the insurer's liability shall not be subject to such assessment [unfairness] since these restrictions are taken into account in calculating the premium paid by the consumer.' The effect is to remove many of the main terms of an insurance contract from the scope of the Regulations but subsidiary terms such as those requiring notice of loss or co-operation in the claims process[18] may nevertheless fall within the scope of the Regulations.

REGULATION OF INSURANCE BUSINESS

7.12 A range of activities associated with insurance is regulated by the Financial Services and Markets Act 2000 ('FSMA 2000'). The objectives of the Act are: to maintain confidence in the financial system; to promote financial stability; the protection of consumers; and the reduction of financial crime.[19] An authorisation, issued by the Financial Conduct Authority ('the FCA'), is required by any person engaging in insurance business in the United Kingdom, including those persons who advise on

---

13 1906 Act, s 2(2).
14 (1884) 9 AC 671 at 684.
15 Sch 1(1)(a) disapplies ss 2–4 for the purposes of English law and s 15(3)(a)(i) disapplies ss 16–18 for the purposes of Scots law.
16 SI 1999/2083.
17 Although it should be noted that the definition of a consumer contract is not the same as that adopted under the Consumer Insurance (Disclosure and Representations) Act 2012: see para **7.39**.
18 See further para **7.70**.
19 See FSMA 2000, ss 3–6.

insurance contracts (such as insurance brokers).[20] Before granting an authorisation, the FCA must be satisfied that the organisation will be soundly and prudently managed and that the individuals managing the organisation are fit and proper persons. An authorisation brings a person within the 'regulatory perimeter' of FSMA 2000 and results in that person being bound by the regulatory rules made by the FCA under statutory authority as well as the process of supervision and enforcement associated with those rules. The FCA's regulation and supervision can be divided into two categories: prudential supervision which focuses on solvency and financial stability; and conduct of business regulation which focuses on the relationship between authorised persons and their customers.

Prudential supervision

7.13 Prudential supervision focuses on controlling the solvency and liquidity of participants in financial markets. There are two objectives. The first, which may be termed 'micro-prudential regulation', focuses on the solvency of individual financial enterprises and attempts to ensure that customers are not threatened by the risks to which financial institutions are exposed in the normal course of their business. In the case of insurers, the main risk faced by policyholders is that the pool of premiums held by the insurer may not be adequate to cover claims. That may be the result of unexpectedly high levels of claims or a fall in the value of investments in which premiums are held by insurers. The second, which may be termed 'macro-prudential regulation', focuses on the stability of the financial system as a whole and the risks posed to it by the collapse of a financial firm and the instability that may spread across the entire financial system in those circumstances. Regulators attempt to protect customers from these risks by requiring insurers to have minimum levels of shareholders' capital (sometimes referred to as regulatory capital) and to hold a certain proportion of their assets in a liquid (readily-realisable) form. This has the effect that, if the firm were to face financial difficulties, losses would be borne by shareholders before customers (policyholders) became affected. In this sense, prudential supervision uses regulatory capital to protect customers. Shareholders in financial institutions, on the other hand, receive no special protection from the system of prudential regulation. They are assumed to face the normal risks arising from investment in any business, which includes insolvency.

Conduct of business regulation

7.14 Conduct of business regulation focuses on the relationship between

---

20 FSMA 2000, s 19 and s 22(1). It is also possible to engage in insurance business in the UK through a branch or by way of freedom of services on the basis of an authorisation granted by another member state of the EEA (so-called 'passporting').

a financial firm and its customers and operates through rules that control the manner in which individual financial transactions are conducted. They impose different types of obligations in different circumstances. Many are in effect disclosure (or related) obligations, such as the rules that require disclosure of information to a customer before a transaction is agreed. Others go beyond disclosure and limit the freedom of action of authorised persons or have important implications for the structure of the market.[21] Insurance has a specific set of conduct of business rules ('ICOB') as well as falling under the more general rules ('COBS') which apply to all authorised persons.[22] While these conduct of business rules are essentially public law rules that do not form part of the contract between an insurer and a policyholder, they can have important implications for the contractual relationship. For example, so-called 'mis-selling' claims made by policyholders with regard to payment protection insurance ('PPI') are based on the failure on the part of insurers to observe conduct of business rules and have resulted in the insurance industry paying many billions of pounds in compensation to policy-holders.[23]

INSURABLE INTEREST

The rationale for insurable interest

7.15 The principle of insurable interest is that only those who have a financial interest in the occurrence of the insured event should be permitted to enter into and claim under an insurance policy. The origins of insurable interest as a legal principle lie in the abuse of early forms of insurance as a form of gambling. This typically involved a person taking out a life insurance policy on a person in whose life they had no financial interest. Although gambling contracts were void under the common law in Scotland,[24] they could be enforced under the common law in England.[25] Parliament intervened to deter this abuse of insurance contracts by passing various Acts requiring insurable interest. As detailed at paras **7.16–7.24** below, the scope of these Acts does not make it entirely clear that insurable interest is a statutory requirement for all types of insurance. However, as the requirement of insurable interest is also recognised by the common law in Scotland, the problem of the scope of the statu-

---

21 See further I MacNeil *An Introduction to the Law on Financial Investment* (2nd edn, 2010, Hart Publishing) chapter 6.

22 See the FSA Handbook at www.fsa.gov.uk.

23 For a discussion of the legal and regulatory background to PPI claims see *R (ex parte British Bankers Association) v Financial Services Authority* [2011] EWHC 999.

24 The decision in *Bruce v Ross* (1787) Mor 9523 marked a change in the law as gambling contracts had previously been enforceable. The common law prohibition did not, however, prevent enforcement of contracts for the sharing of the proceeds of a gaming contract: see *Robertson v Anderson* 2003 SLT 235. Since the entry into force of s 335(1) of the Gambling Act 2005 (in 2007) the fact that a contract relates to gambling does not prevent its enforcement.

25 *Jones v Randall* (1774) 1 Cowp 37.

tory requirement is of limited relevance. Bell[26] refers to the common law principle in the following terms: 'It is essential to the contract of insurance that there shall be a subject in which the insured has an interest, a premium given or engaged for, and a risk run.' The scope of insurable interest is formulated in broad terms by Sheriff Guthrie, who in his edition of Bell's *Principles* states that: 'Interest is not limited to property but extends to every real and actual advantage and benefit arising out of or depending on the thing to which it refers. But one cannot insure a mere expectancy.'[27] As discussed below, the English common law and statutory formulations of insurable interest in non-life insurance have adopted a narrower approach.

Marine insurance

7.16 Legislation requiring insurable interest was first introduced in the field of marine insurance. The Marine Insurance Act 1745 made marine policies lacking interest, or with no further proof of interest than the policy itself, void. This Act was repealed by the Marine Insurance Act 1906, section 4 of which makes policies lacking insurable interest void. Insurable interest is defined as 'any legal or equitable relation to the adventure or any insurable property at risk therein'.[28] The effect of that definition is to limit insurable interest to legal or equitable relations and to exclude loss suffered by a person who does not have a legal relationship with the property (e.g. a beneficiary under a will). It is not necessary that the insured has an insurable interest at the time of entering into the contract provided he has such an interest at the time of the loss.[29]

Life assurance

7.17 The Life Assurance Act 1774[30] made insurable interest a statutory requirement for life assurance policies. Where there is no insurable interest the contract is void. The statute is silent on the issue of when insurable interest must exist. However, it was held in *Dalby v India and London Life Assurance Co*[31] that insurable interest is required only at the time of insuring and not at the time of death.

7.18 The Life Assurance Act 1774 does not define the circumstances in which there is an insurable interest in a person's life. However, the common law recognises that a person has an unlimited insurable interest in his own life.[32] An unlimited insurable interest in the life of a spouse

26 *Principles* (4th edn, 1839) § 457.
27 *Principles* (10th edn, 1899) § 461.
28 1906 Act, s 5(2).
29 1906 Act, s 6(1).
30 s 1.
31 (1854) 15 CB 365, 139 ER 465.
32 *Griffiths v Fleming* [1909] 1 KB 805 at 821.

is recognised both by common law[33] and by statute.[34] Provision is also made for policies effected by spouses on their own life for the benefit of their spouse and/or children to be deemed a trust for their benefit with the result that, following death, the policy proceeds do not form part of the deceased's estate but are instead paid directly to the beneficiary.[35]

7.19   In the case of all other relationships, whether within or outside a family, insurable interest can only exist where there is a financial interest in the life of the assured.[36] The financial interest can arise from a contractual relationship, common examples being agency, partnership and employment. In *Turnbull & Co v Scottish Provident Institution*,[37] for example, a firm of merchants insured the life of their agent in Iceland, through whom they carried on a lucrative business, and were held entitled to recover the proceeds after his death. In such cases the sum assured is limited to the financial interest. Insurable interest can also arise from a financial interest based on an obligation of aliment. Under section 1 of the Family Law (Scotland) Act 1985 parents owe an obligation of aliment to their children but children do not owe an obligation to their parents. It follows that parents do not have an insurable interest in the lives of their children *qua* parent[38] but may have such an interest *qua* creditor or employer.

7.20   The Law Commissions have suggested that the requirement for insurable interest in life assurance might be ended or alternatively that its scope should be widened.[39] In particular they have suggested that where there is a relationship of natural affection, a policyholder should be able to insure the life for an unlimited amount. In circumstances in which there is no relationship of natural affection, the consent of the person whose life is to be assured would be an alternative basis for insurable interest. The rationale for these proposals is that the law currently adopts an unnecessarily strict approach to insurable interest in life assurance and could in principle operate without it (as occurs, for example, in Australia). No legislative proposals have been brought forward as yet.

. 33 *Wight v Brown* (1845) 11 D 459.
34 See, for spouses, the Married Women's Policies of Assurance (Scotland) Act 1880, s 1; and for civil partners, the Civil Partnership Act 2004, s 253(1).
35 Married Women's Policies of Assurance (Scotland) Act 1880, s 2. Unlike the position in England under the Civil Partnership Act 2004, s 70, this provision has not been extended to civil partners in Scotland.
36 The general principle is stated in Bell, *Principles* § 457.
37 (1896) 34 SLR 146.
38 There is a statutory exception (limited to a sum assured of £800) in the case of policies issued by 'friendly societies' under the Friendly Societies Act 1992, s 99.
39 See generally The Law Commission and Scottish Law Commission, *Insurance Contract Law Issues Paper 4*, 'Insurable Interest' (2008).

Indemnity insurance

The requirement of insurable interest

7.21   In the case of non-marine indemnity insurance, the requirement of insurable interest is recognised both by common law[40] and statute. Despite its title, the Life Assurance Act 1774 applies to insurance on any event with the exception of 'ships, goods and merchandises'. The Gaming Act 1845, which does not apply to Scotland, made contracts of gaming or wagering void. However, the common law principle (in Scotland) requiring insurable interest resolved any uncertainty in the application of the statutory provisions. Moreover, modern legislation has relaxed the common law rule, with financial contracts for the mitigation of risk, such as derivatives, in mind.[41] The same approach can be taken in relation to the issue of whether the Life Assurance Act 1774 applies to heritable property. In England, that issue remained unresolved until recent case law confirmed that it did not.[42] In Scotland it has been assumed that the general principle of insurable interest applies equally to heritable property. Thus, in *Arif v Excess Insurance Group*,[43] it was held that one partner in a hotel business could not claim under a fire policy in which he was named as the insured because the hotel was partnership property and the policy made no reference to the insured acting other than as a principal.

The scope of insurable interest in non-marine indemnity insurance

7.22   Bell's definition of insurable interest[44] clearly extends its scope beyond the ownership of heritable or moveable property. It can exist in relation to property which one does not own, subject to the existence of a financial interest. In *Fehilly v General Accident*,[45] the issue arose as to whether a tenant of a ballroom had an insurable interest in the building. A clause in the lease obliged the tenant to keep the building in good repair but gave the tenant the option of terminating the lease if major work was required. When the building was destroyed by fire the tenant claimed the full value of the building from the insurer. The insurer argued that the tenant was entitled only to recover to the extent of his

40 Bell, *Principles* § 457. For this history, see L J Macgregor, 'Illegality' in K G C Reid and R Zimmermann (eds) *A History of Private Law in Scotland* (2000) II, 129.
41 Financial Services and Markets Act 2000, s 412 (the scope of application of which is, since 2007, now limited to Northern Ireland) and Gambling Act 2005, s 335.
42 The Court of Appeal held in *Mark Rowlands Ltd v Berni Inns Ltd* [1986] 1 QB 211, [1985] 3 All ER 473, [1985] 3 WLR 964 that the Life Assurance Act 1774 did not apply to fire insurance on buildings: this decision was followed in *Siu Yin Kwan v Eastern Insurance Co Ltd* [1994] 2 AC 199.
43 1986 SC 317. *Quaere* whether that approach contradicts the (limited) acceptance of the undisclosed principal doctrine to insurance contracts: see para **7.30** below.
44 *Principles* § 457.
45 *Fehilly v General Accident Fire and Life Insurance Corporation Ltd* 1982 SC 163, 1983 SLT 141.

loss, namely the market value of the lease. It was held that the tenant did not have an insurable interest in the full value of the building as the lease did not require the tenant to repair the fire damage. The tenant could only recover the market value of the lease. Similarly, a heritable creditor (such as a bank holding a standard security) has an insurable interest in property which is separate from that of the owner.[46]

7.23 In contracts for the sale of heritable property the purchaser has an insurable interest on conclusion of the contract (missives) and before the disposition has been recorded.[47] In contracts for the sale of goods a purchaser has an insurable interest from conclusion of the contract, irrespective of the time that risk or ownership passes:[48] the rationale being that loss of or damage to the property may diminish the value of the contractual rights of the purchaser. The general position is that it is not necessary to have a completed real right in property before there is an insurable interest; a sufficiently 'close relationship' with the property may suffice.[49] A seller of goods retains an insurable interest so long as he is in a legal position with regard to it such that any loss or damage to the property may result in loss to him. Trustees have an insurable interest in property held by them;[50] and, on one view, trustees may be *bound* to insure trust assets in order to discharge their duties as trustees.

7.24 Insurable interest can also exist in relation to potential legal liabilities in contract or delict. For example, if the tenant in *Fehilly* (above) had been contractually bound by the lease to reinstate the property following fire damage, he would have had an insurable interest in the full value of the building. Another example is the potential delictual liability which is insured under the third party section of a motor vehicle insurance policy. That form of insurance can cover both the insured and other drivers who may incur liability to third parties; and in that situation the other drivers are able to enforce the policy.[51]

FORMATION OF INSURANCE CONTRACTS

The proposal form

7.25 The normal contractual principles requiring an offer and an

---

46 *Bank of Scotland v Guardian Royal Exchange plc* 1995 SLT 763, OH.

47 *Sloans Dairies v Glasgow Corporation* 1977 SC 223.

48 As to the transfer of risk and ownership see Chapter 3, paras **3.76–3.78** and Chapter 6, paras **6.24–6.47**.

49 *Cowan v Jeffrey Associates* 1998 SC 496 at 502F per Lord Hamilton (Ordinary).

50 *Mitchell v Scottish Eagle Insurance Co Ltd* 1997 SLT 793 at 797E–F per Lord Prosser (Ordinary).

51 In England, it is presumed that the insured acts as agent for other drivers: see *Williams v Baltic Insurance Association of London Ltd* [1924] 2 KB 282. See para **7.28** below as regards the rights of the principal and agent. The Contracts (Rights of Third Parties) Act 1999 may also enable enforcement by third parties in England. In Scotland, the *ius quaesitum tertio* presumably provides a solution by recognising the rights of other persons covered by the policy.

acceptance apply to insurance contracts. In some cases the offer is made by the proposer for insurance on the insurer's standard proposal form.[52] This asks for information about the proposer and the risk which is to be insured. The insurer then has the option of accepting the offer, or of making a counter-offer to the proposer. A potential difficulty is that the proposer is unlikely to be aware of the precise contract terms at the time of completing the proposal form. It can therefore be argued that there is no consensus at the time when the insurer accepts the proposal. This outcome is avoided by the inclusion in proposal forms of a statement that the proposer is applying for insurance on the insurer's standard terms.[53] It follows that, even if the reality is that the insured is not familiar with the standard terms, an objective analysis of contract formation[54] will result in there being consensus when the insurer accepts the proposal.

Basis of contract clauses

7.26   In the past, it was possible for some or all of the information contained in a proposal form to be converted into terms of the contract. That outcome was achieved through a 'basis of contract' clause which stated that the relevant information formed the basis of the contract. The result was that the relevant information was treated as a warranty and in the event of misrepresentation the insurer was entitled to avoid the contract regardless of the materiality of the misrepresentation.[55] While reliance on that technique had diminished in the case of consumer insurance[56] as a result of self-regulation by insurers, it was ended by the Consumer Insurance (Disclosure and Representations) Act 2012.[57] But it remains possible for warranties to be expressly agreed and inserted into a consumer insurance policy.

The cover note

7.27   Cover notes are temporary contracts of insurance issued by insurers pending the issue of an insurance policy or certificate. Their use is most common in relation to those classes of insurance where there is a statutory obligation to insure, for example motor insurance. For such types of insurance it is important that the insured has proof of insurance (a certificate) right from the start of the period of cover. However, as

52 Completion of the proposal form can be in writing, orally or digitally. Proposal forms are not normally used for marine insurance or large commercial risks where the relevant information cannot be easily fitted into a standard format.
53 *General Accident Insurance Corporation v Cronk* (1901) 17 TLR 233. Even without this statement, it is submitted that there would be consensus if there were agreement on the following essential terms of the contract: subject matter, risk, premium, duration and sum insured.
54 Following the approach in *Muirhead & Turnbull v Dickson* (1905) 7 F 686, 13 SLT 151.
55 See the example in para **7.59** below (*Dawsons Ltd v Bonnin* 1922 SC (HL) 156).
56 See para **7.39** for the meaning of consumer insurance.
57 See s 6 of the Act.

technology has enabled insurers to speed up the process of issuing policies, cover notes are now much less common than they were in the past. Where they are issued, they normally incorporate, by reference, the insurer's standard policy terms. This avoids the problem which arose in *Re Coleman's Depositories Ltd.*[58] In that case a company applied for employers' liability insurance and was issued with a cover note. The policy, which was issued later, required immediate notification of claims. However, the insured delayed reporting an accident which occurred between the issue of the cover note and the policy. The insurer tried to avoid liability for the claim on the basis of the delay in notification but the court held that this term could not be implied into the cover note.

Agency and insurance contracts

7.28 The normal rules of agency law apply to insurance contracts. However, the application of these rules to the formation of insurance contracts is not always straightforward. The main difficulty is identifying the agent's principal. This problem arises from the manner in which insurance contracts are agreed. Most insurance agents who conclude insurance contracts are remunerated by the insurer. There is therefore a prima facie case for regarding them as agents of the insurer. However, an agent (particularly an independent broker) also advises the insured and can therefore be viewed as the agent of the insured. While it has been held that a Lloyd's broker[59] is always the agent of the insured,[60] there is no simple rule for other types of broker. In each case the position of the broker must be examined, particularly as regards the authority given by the insurer to the agent. An example of an agent being held to be the agent of the insurer is *Stockton v Mason*.[61] In that case, the insured advised his broker that he had changed his car from a Ford Anglia to an MG Midget. The broker confirmed that he would arrange for the change of car to be covered. The insured took this to mean that the existing cover for any authorised driver would apply to the MG. The plaintiff was injured as a passenger in the MG as a result of the negligent driving of the insured's son. The same day the insured received a letter from the insurers stating that only he himself was covered to drive the MG. The issue was therefore whether the insurers were bound by the broker's statement.[62] It was held by the Court of Appeal that the insurers were bound as the broker had implied authority to confirm temporary cover and had clearly led the insured to believe that the existing cover had been extended.

7.29 In the case of consumer insurance, the status of an agent has been

---

58 *Re Coleman's Depositories Ltd and Life and Health Assurance Association* [1907] 2 KB 798.
59 A broker entitled to do business at Lloyd's of London.
60 *Roberts v Plaisted* [1989] 2 Lloyd's Rep 341.
61 [1978] 2 Lloyd's Rep 430.
62 That issue was linked with the rule that a principal is deemed to know what his agent knows: see e.g. *Woolcott v Excess Insurance Co Ltd* [1979] 1 Lloyd's Rep 231.

clarified by the Consumer Insurance (Disclosure and Representations) Act 2012.[63] The Act defines circumstances in which the agent will be the agent of the insurer[64] and provides that in other cases it is to be presumed that the agent is the agent of the insured unless, in the light of the circumstances, it appears otherwise. Examples of factors which may tend to show that the agent is acting for the insured are where an agent agrees to provide impartial advice, or the customer pays a fee.

7.30   Also relevant in this context are issues related to an unnamed or undisclosed principal.[65] In the first case, the agent discloses that he is acting as an agent but not the name of the principal. In the second case, the agent appears to act as principal but is in reality acting as agent. In the context of insurance two approaches to these situations are possible: one is to hold that the identity of the insured is material to the contract and therefore that the insurer cannot be bound to an unnamed or undisclosed principal; the other is to focus more on the insured risk and to ask whether the identity of the insured matters for that purpose. In approaching this issue the courts have tended towards the latter view, with the result that an unnamed or undisclosed principal is entitled to enforce a contract entered into by their agent.[66] In those circumstances, and contrary to the normal rule in agency law, the agent is also entitled to sue in his own name on behalf of the principal.[67]

GOOD FAITH, THE DUTY OF DISCLOSURE AND MISREPRESENTATION

The principle of good faith

7.31   The general principles of contract law do not require the parties to a contract to act in good faith towards each other either during contractual negotiations or at the time of the performance of the contract. There is a duty to avoid making misrepresentations to the other party but no duty to volunteer information or to co-operate with the other party.

7.32   Insurance contracts are one of a category[68] of contracts in which

---

63 2012 Act, s 9 and Sch 2.
64 For example, where the agent acts in the capacity of an appointed representative (aka 'tied agent') of the insurer under FSMA 2000, s 39.
65 See Chapter 4, paras **4.52–4.72**.
66 *National Oilwell (UK) Ltd v Davy Offshore (UK) Ltd* [1993] 2 Lloyd's Rep 582; *Cochran & Son v Leckie's Tr* (1906) 8 F 975, (1906) 14 SLT 154.
67 *Vandepitte v Preferred Accident Insurance Corporation of New York* [1933] AC 70 (although in that case there was, on the facts, no agency).
68 The others are: cautionary obligations; sale of heritage; invitations to subscribe for shares in a company; partnership contracts (see generally W M Gloag *The Law of Contract* (2nd edn, 1929)).

there is an obligation of good faith imposed on the contracting parties. Lord President Inglis stated the common law in the following terms in *Life Association of Scotland v Foster*:[69] 'but contracts of insurance are in this, among other particulars, exceptional, in that they require on both sides uberrima fides [utmost good faith].'[70] The same principle is to be found in section 17 of the Marine Insurance Act 1906, which provides that if utmost good faith is not observed by either party, the contract can be avoided by the other.

7.33 The obligation to act in good faith applies to the contract of insurance at all times: during the negotiations; during the period of insurance; and at the time of making a claim.[71] Both the insurer and the insured must act in good faith. Although the reported cases have dealt mainly with breaches of good faith by the insured, it is clear from the decision of the Court of Appeal in *Banque Keyser Ullmann SA v Skandia (UK) Insurance Co Ltd*[72] that the insurer can also be in breach of the principle.

The duty of disclosure

Rationale for disclosure

7.34 The duty of disclosure is the element of the obligation of good faith which is relevant to contractual negotiations between the insurer and the proposer. The rationale for the duty was expressed by Lord Mansfield in the early case of *Carter v Boehm*[73] in the following terms:

> The specific facts upon which the contingent chance is to be computed lie most commonly in the knowledge of the insured only: the underwriter trusts to his representation and proceeds upon a confidence that he does not keep back any circumstance in his knowledge to mislead the underwriter into a belief that the circumstance does not exist, and to induce him to estimate the risk as if it did not exist.

Thus, the essential elements which underlie the duty of disclosure are the superior knowledge of the insured in relation to the risk and the reliance of the underwriter on the information given by the insured.

---

69 (1873) 11 M 351 at 359.
70 The '*uberrima*' aspect is arguably superfluous, for it is not possible to be more honest than honest. The South African Appellate Division, in a decision quoted with apparent approval by a Scottish Lord of Appeal in Ordinary, has said that the formulation '*uberrima fides*' 'is an alien, vague, useless expression without any particular meaning in law': *Mutual and Federal Insurance Co Ltd v Oudtshoorn Municipality* 1985 (1) SA 419 at 433C–F per Joubert JA, and quoted in *Manifest Shipping Co Ltd v Uni-Polaris Shipping Co Ltd* [2001] UKHL 1, [2003] 1 AC 469 paras [5]–[7] per Lord Clyde.
71 *Manifest Shipping Co Ltd v Uni-Polaris Insurance Co* [1997] 1 Lloyd's Rep 360 at 372 per Leggatt J.
72 [1990] 1 QB 665 (CA), affd on different grounds by the House of Lords, *sub nom Banque Financière de la Cité SA v Westgate Insurance Co Ltd* [1991] 2 AC 249.
73 (1766) 3 Burr 1905, 97 ER 1162.

What must be disclosed?

(a) Non-consumer insurance

7.35   The duty of disclosure requires the proposer to disclose every material circumstance which is known to him.[74] The insurer is required to disclose any facts known to him, but not to the proposer, which would reduce the risk.[75] A failure to observe the duty of disclosure allows the other party to avoid the contract.

7.36   The proposer clearly cannot be expected to disclose information he does not know,[76] but he is assumed to know information which is common knowledge in his business.[77] The proposer is also assumed to know information which he could discover by making enquiries. For example, in *Highlands Insurance Co v Continental Insurance Co*,[78] Continental insured the premises of a company in Tel Aviv which they re-insured with Highlands. The information provided to Highlands by Continental indicated that the premises were sprinklered. Following a fire, it was discovered that they were not and Highlands therefore refused to pay a claim. It was held that Continental had failed in its duty of disclosure by providing false information which could have been verified by making enquiries.

7.37   Where the proposer is asked for an opinion by the insurer, it is sufficient that the opinion is given to the best of the proposer's knowledge and belief.[79] There must, however, be a reasonable basis for the proposer's knowledge and belief. In *MacPhee v Royal Insurance Co Ltd*,[80] the owner of a cabin cruiser gave the wrong dimensions of his boat in a proposal for marine insurance. He had obtained these dimensions by telephoning the previous owner, not by taking them himself. The proposal form declared that it formed the basis of the contract and that the answers in it were true to the best knowledge and belief of the insured. The boat was destroyed by fire and the insurers refused to pay on the basis of the inaccuracy of the dimensions. It was held: (1) that it was not sufficient to show that the answers to the questions were untrue in fact – it had to be shown that they were untrue to the insured's best knowledge and belief; (2) that to provide answers to the best of a person's

---

74 1906 Act, s 18(1).
75 *Banque Keyser Ullmann SA v Skandia (UK) Insurance Co Ltd* [1990] 1 QB 665 (CA), affd on different grounds by the House of Lords, *sub nom Banque Financière de la Cité SA v Westgate Insurance Co Ltd* [1991] 2 AC 249.
76 *Joel v Law Union and Crown Insurance Co* [1908] 2 KB 863 at 884 per Fletcher-Moulton LJ: 'The duty is a duty to disclose and you cannot disclose what you do not know.'
77 1906 Act, s 18(1).
78 [1987] 1 Lloyd's Rep 109.
79 *Life Association of Scotland v Foster* (1873) 11 M 351.
80 1979 SC 304.

knowledge and belief requires a reasonable basis for the answer; and (3) that the insured did not exercise due care and as a result misled the insurer in a material manner.

7.38 The obligation to disclose includes factors which give rise to moral hazard, which is the likelihood that the character of the insured may exacerbate the risk faced by the insurer. Moral hazard encompasses the claims history of the insured, previous refusals of cover and criminal convictions. In principle, failure to disclose such material information entitles the insurer to avoid the contract.[81] However, criminal convictions which are 'spent' under the provisions of the Rehabilitation of Offenders Act 1974 need not be disclosed to insurers. Rehabilitation periods under the Act vary according to the severity of the sentence and sentences over thirty months cannot be rehabilitated.

(b) Consumer insurance

7.39 The Consumer Insurance (Disclosure and Representations) Act 2012 ('CIDRA 2012') responded to concerns that the general law relating to disclosure was overly harsh towards consumers, who faced the risk that their insurance claims could be avoided if they did not comply with the onerous duty of disclosure.[82] The insurance industry had taken steps to mitigate the harshness of the law through self-regulatory measures, which were later incorporated into the conduct of business rules of the FCA.[83]

> A 'consumer insurance contract' means a contract of insurance between—
>
> (a) an individual who enters into the contract wholly or mainly for purposes unrelated to the individual's trade, business or profession, and
> (b) a person who carries on the business of insurance and who becomes a party to the contract by way of that business (whether or not in accordance with permission for the purposes of the Financial Services and Markets Act 2000).[84]

7.40 The 2012 Act abolishes the duty of disclosure for the purposes of consumer insurance contracts and replaces it with a duty 'to take reasonable care not to make a misrepresentation'. The standard of care required is that of a reasonable consumer and the Act refers to examples of factors that may need to be taken into account in determining reasonableness:

---

81 See e.g. *Stewart v Commercial Union Assurance Co plc* 1993 SC 1 (failure to disclose an 'offence involving dishonesty').
82 The Act took effect generally from 6 April 2013.
83 See especially FCA Handbook, ICOBS 8.1.1 incorporating a modification of the duty of disclosure derived from the earlier (self-regulatory) Statements of Insurance Practice.
84 CIDRA 2012, s 1.

    (a)   the type of consumer insurance contract in question, and its target market,

    (b)   any relevant explanatory material or publicity produced or authorised by the insurer,

    (c)   how clear, and how specific, the insurer's questions were,

    (d)   in the case of a failure to respond to the insurer's questions in connection with the renewal or variation of a consumer insurance contract, how clearly the insurer communicated the importance of answering those questions (or the possible consequences of failing to do so),

    (e)   whether or not an agent was acting for the consumer.[85]

A misrepresentation made dishonestly is always to be taken as showing lack of reasonable care.

7.41   The Act also modifies the remedies available to an insurer following a qualifying misrepresentation. In the case of a deliberate or reckless misrepresentation the insurer is entitled to avoid the contract, to refuse to pay claims and to retain the premium (unless retention would be unfair to the insured). With regard to careless misrepresentation the position is more complex. If the insurer would not have entered the contract had the true position been stated, the contract can be avoided. If the insurer would have entered the contract on different terms, those terms are to apply. If the insurer would have entered the contract only at a higher premium the principle of proportionality is applied so as to adjust claims to correspond with the shortfall in the premium.[86]

Duration of the duty of disclosure

7.42   The duty of disclosure lasts until the contract is agreed between the insurer and the proposer. There is no obligation to disclose information during the period in which the insurance is in force.[87] However, if the contract is renewed, the duty of disclosure revives at each successive renewal since each renewal is treated as a new contract. In *Lambert v Co-operative Insurance Society*,[88] an 'all risks' policy covering jewellery was taken out by the insured in 1963. She failed to disclose at that time that her husband had been convicted for handling stolen goods. The policy was renewed each year until 1972. Prior to the last renewal in 1971, the insured's husband was convicted for two offences of dishonesty, but no disclosure was made to the insurer. When some jewellery was lost in 1972, the insurer denied liability on the basis of non-disclosure at the

---

85 CIDRA 2012, s 3.

86 Thus, if a premium of £200 were paid when it should have been £300, only two thirds of a claim will be paid.

87 *Banque Keyser Ullmann SA v Skandia (UK) Insurance Co Ltd* [1990] 1 QB 665(CA), affd on different grounds by the House of Lords *sub nom Banque Financière de la Cité SA v Westgate Insurance Co Ltd* [1991] 2 AC 249. A policy may, however, require the insured to report a material change of circumstances to the insurer and in some cases the cover may not extend to the new circumstances.

88 [1975] 2 Lloyd's Rep 485.

time the contract was agreed initially and at renewal in 1971. It was held that the duty of disclosure was the same at the outset and at renewal and that the insurer could avoid liability on the basis of either instance of non-disclosure.

Disclosure to intermediaries

7.43 Insurance contracts are often entered into through an intermediary such as an insurance broker. The normal rules of agency apply in this situation but there can be some difficulty in identifying for whom an agent is acting. Almost all agents are paid by the insurer in the form of a commission but, despite this, the courts have held that there are situations in which an agent is taken to be acting on behalf of the insured and not the insurer. The issue (sometimes referred to as 'transferred agency') is of considerable importance in the context of the duty of disclosure because a principal is deemed to know information known to his agent: it follows that, where an agent acts on behalf of an insurer, the insurer is deemed to know information known by the agent. Closely related to this issue is the question of whether a proposer is always bound by a signature on a proposal form.

7.44 The cases of *Bawden v London, Edinburgh and Glasgow Assurance*[89] and *Newsholme Bros v Road Transport & General Insurance Co*[90] illustrate the difficulties which can arise in agency situations. In *Bawden*, an illiterate proposer with one eye applied for accident insurance. The agent filled out the proposal form on his behalf. At the end of the proposal there was a declaration stating that the proposer had no physical infirmity. The proposer signed the proposal form and claimed under the insurance when he lost his good eye. The insurers tried to avoid liability on the basis of non-disclosure but the court held that the agent had acted for the insurer and therefore the insurer was aware of the insured's physical condition. In *Newsholme*, the agent entered incorrect information in the proposal despite being told the truth by the proposer. The proposer signed the proposal form in the knowledge that the information inserted by the agent was untrue. It was held[91] that the agent had acted for the insured and that the insured was bound by his signature. The result was that the insurer was able to avoid the policy on the basis of misrepresentation.

7.45 The approach adopted in *Bawden* was followed in *Stone v Reliance Mutual Insurance Society Ltd*,[92] but the *Newsholme* approach is supported by the cases of *Biggar v Rock Life Assurance Co*[93] and *McMillan v Accident Insurance Co Ltd*.[94] While these cases are not entirely irrelevant following the

---

89 [1892] 2 QB 534.
90 [1929] 2 KB 356.
91 *Bawden* was distinguished in this case.
92 [1972] 1 Lloyd's Rep 469.
93 [1902] 1 KB 516.
94 1907 SC 484.

introduction of the provisions of CIDRA 2012 dealing with the status of agents, they are of less direct relevance and subordinate to the statutory provisions. However, three principles derived from the cases would appear to remain good law: (1) a signature on a proposal form will normally bind the proposer whether the document has been read or not (*Newsholme*);[95] (2) an insurer's agent who acts fraudulently is acting outside his authority. Information fabricated by an agent cannot therefore be imputed to the insurer (*Biggar* and *Newsholme*); and (3) where the insurer's agent acts honestly but induces the proposer to sign a proposal form in the belief that it is complete and correct, the insurer cannot avoid liability on the basis of non-disclosure (*Bawden*).

Material information: non-life assurance

7.46   The duty of disclosure requires each party to the contract to disclose every material circumstance known to him.[96] Section 18(2) of the Marine Insurance Act 1906 provides that: 'Every circumstance is material which would influence the judgment of a prudent insurer in fixing the premium, or determining whether he will take the risk.' While the dictum of Lord President Inglis in *Life Association of Scotland v Foster*[97] suggested that materiality was to be judged in all forms of insurance[98] by reference to what a reasonable man would consider material, the decision of the Inner House in *Hooper v Royal London General Insurance Co Ltd*[99] makes clear that in the case of indemnity contracts, materiality is to be judged from the perspective of the prudent insurer. In that case, the pursuer, who had insured the contents of his home with the defender, failed to disclose a conviction for vandalism, despite there being a specific question relating to convictions in the proposal form. Shortly after the cover entered into force, the contents of the pursuer's home were destroyed by fire. The insurer refused to pay a claim on the basis of non-disclosure. The pursuer sued for payment on the basis that a non-disclosure could only be material if it would be considered as such by a reasonable person in the position of the insured. The court rejected that argument, holding that the test of the reasonable insurer was applicable to all insurance contracts with the sole exception of life cover.

7.47   Two issues have dominated recent judicial interpretation of the statutory definition of material information. The first is the meaning of 'influence'. Here, the focus has been on whether influence refers to a decisive influence or whether it simply refers to information which a prudent underwriter would wish to have but which would not necessarily

---

95 For a more recent application of this principle in the context of banking see *Grant Estates Ltd v The Royal Bank of Scotland plc* [2012] CSOH 133 at para [77] per Lord Hodge (Ordinary).

96 1906 Act, s 18(1).

97 (1873) 11 M 351 at 359.

98 It can be assumed that the statutory definition of materiality in the Marine Insurance Act 1906, s 18(2) would be excluded from this statement.

99 1993 SC 242.

change his mind on the decision to insure or the terms of insurance. The second major issue has been whether, in order to avoid a contract, an insurer simply has to prove non-disclosure or misrepresentation or whether it is necessary also to show that the non-disclosure or misrepresentation induced the insurer to enter into the contract.

7.48 In *Container Transport International Inc v Oceanus Mutual Underwriting Association (Bermuda) Ltd ('CTI v Oceanus')*,[100] the Court of Appeal held that a fact can be material even if its disclosure would not have changed the decision of the underwriter either as to the acceptance of the risk or the premium and the terms on which it would be accepted. In order to avoid the policy, an insurer simply had to show that there was non-disclosure of material information. This case formulated the law in a manner which clearly favoured insurers, in that they could avoid liability for non-disclosure of information which had no effect on their decision to insure. The matter subsequently came before the House of Lords in the case of *Pan Atlantic Insurance Co Ltd v Pine Top Insurance Co Ltd ('Pan Atlantic')*[101] in the form of two separate, but related, issues:

(a) Could a fact be material even if it would not have had any effect on a prudent insurer's decision to accept the insurance or the terms on which it was accepted (i.e. was *CTI v Oceanus* correctly decided on this point)?

(b) In order for an insurer to avoid liability under a policy was it enough simply to show that there had been non-disclosure of a material fact or was it also necessary for the insurer to prove that the non-disclosure had induced him to enter into the contract?

7.49 On the first point, the House of Lords (by a majority of 3:2) followed the decision in *CTI v Oceanus*. On the second point, the House of Lords unanimously overruled *CTI v Oceanus*, holding that it was necessary for an insurer to show that he had been induced into making the contract by the non-disclosure. Subsequent cases have established that inducement is a question of fact and must be established by the insurer as a causal factor, albeit not the only one, for entering the contract on the relevant terms.[102]

7.50 While *Pan Atlantic* may have settled the law in England, it was by no means inevitable that the same solution would be adopted in Scotland. While the general law of misrepresentation in Scotland requires inducement[103] for the avoidance of a contract, that in itself does not resolve the issue of the role of inducement in non-disclosure (as illus-

---

100 [1984] 1 Lloyd's Rep 476.
101 [1995] 1 AC 501.
102 *Assicurazioni Generali SpA v Arab Insurance Group* (BSC) [2003] 1 WLR 577 (CA); *Lewis v Norwich Union Healthcare Ltd* [2010] Lloyd's Rep IR 198.
103 *Menzies v Menzies* (1893) 20 R (HL) 108. Misrepresentation is considered in more detail below.

trated by the uncertainty in the law in England prior to *Pan Atlantic*). However, judicial consideration of *Pan Atlantic* in Scotland has proceeded on the basis that the same principles apply to Scotland.[104] Thus, avoidance of the contract was possible where a material non-disclosure led the insurer to set a premium 20 per cent lower than would otherwise have been the case because that was sufficient evidence of inducement.[105]

Material information – life assurance

7.51   In the case of life assurance, it was established in *Life Association of Scotland v Foster*[106] that the test of materiality in Scotland is that of the reasonable insured. In that case the insured replied in the negative to a question asking if she had a rupture. She later died from rupture and it was discovered that, at the time of making the proposal, she did have a small swelling on her groin. However, she did not appreciate that this was a symptom of rupture. Lord President Inglis, delivering the leading judgment, observed that the insured was obliged only to state such facts as a reasonable person would consider likely to influence the insurer's decision to enter into a contract.[107]

7.52   In England, the courts chose, in the context of life assurance, to follow the test of the reasonable insurer in determining materiality.[108] This resulted in the test being the same for both life and indemnity contracts. However, as far as Scotland is concerned, the decision of the Inner House in the case of *Hooper v Royal London General Insurance Co Ltd*[109] confirmed that there remains a distinction between life and indemnity contracts. Lord Justice-Clerk Ross justified the application of the reasonable insured test to life assurance on the basis that questions asked in a life assurance proposal form are 'subjective and not capable of assessment on any objective basis', whereas questions asked in indemnity proposal forms could be objectively ascertained.[110]

Misrepresentation

7.53   Misrepresentation is the giving of false information to the other contracting party. It is in essence an act of deception and therefore different from non-disclosure which involves the withholding of informa-

---

104 *Mitchell v Hiscox Underwriting Ltd* [2010] CSIH 18; *Gaelic Assignments Ltd v Sharpe* 2001 SLT 914 (OH); *Unipac (Scotland) Ltd v Aegon Insurance Co (UK) Ltd* 1996 SLT 1197 (IH).
105 *Mitchell v Hiscox Underwriting Ltd* (n 104).
106 (1873) 11 M 351.
107 At 359.
108 *Mutual Life Insurance Co of New York v Ontario Metal Products Co Ltd* [1925] AC 344.
109 1993 SC 242.
110 For a critique of this case, see Forte, 'The materiality test in insurance' 1994 LMCLQ 557. The issue was revisited in *Cuthbertson v Friends' Provident Life Office* [2006] CSOH 74, 2006 SLT 567, with Lord Eassie re-affirming the approach in *Life Association of Scotland v Foster*.

tion.[111] Misrepresentation can occur innocently, negligently or fraudulently. In all three instances, the general principles of contract law allow the contract to be avoided where one party has been induced by a misrepresentation into entering into the contract.[112] The Marine Insurance Act 1906 treats misrepresentation in the same manner as non-disclosure. Section 20(1) provides that there is a right to avoid the contract in the case of a material misrepresentation but there is no express reference to a requirement of inducement. The decision of the House of Lords in *Pan Atlantic* makes clear that, in England, inducement is required if the contract is to be avoided. Since the Scottish courts have followed *Pan Atlantic*, the position is the same in Scotland (and follows the general rule in Scots contract law).[113]

THE INSURANCE POLICY

Insured risks and exceptions

7.54 Most insurance policies contain some form of exception to the cover. They can be either general exceptions which apply to the whole policy (e.g. a motor policy which excludes the use of a car for business purposes) or specific exceptions which apply to a particular insured peril (e.g. a commercial vehicle policy which covers theft of goods from the vehicle, but not while the vehicle is left unattended overnight). The effect of the operation of an exception is that the insurer is off risk during the time that the exception operates but comes back on risk when the exception ceases to operate. For example, in *Roberts v Anglo-Saxon Insurance Association Ltd*,[114] the insurer of a van insured for business use only was held to be off risk when the van was used by the insured to drive to his golf club but was back on risk once the insured returned to his work.

Warranties: nature and definition

7.55 Warranties are fundamental terms of an insurance contract. Section 33(1) of the Marine Insurance Act 1906 makes clear the type of obligation which can be the subject of a warranty:

> A warranty, in the following sections relating to warranties, means a promissory warranty, that is to say, a warranty by which the assured undertakes that some particular thing shall or shall not be done, or that

---

111 Despite the clear difference in principle, the distinction may be more difficult to maintain in practice. For example, if a question in a motor insurance proposal relating to previous accidents involving the insured is left blank when the insured has been involved in several, is this a non-disclosure or a misrepresentation?

112 *Menzies v Menzies* (1893) 20 R (HL) 108.

113 See *Mitchell v Hiscox Underwriting Ltd* [2010] CSIH 18 for an example of avoidance of the contract as a result of misrepresentation.

114 (1927) 27 Ll L Rep 313.

some condition shall be fulfilled, or whereby he affirms or negatives the
existence of a particular state of facts.

Following this definition, warranties can be divided into two categories.

(1) Warranties relating to future facts: This is the most common form
of warranty. It requires the insured to conform to a certain pattern
of behaviour during the period of cover. Examples of such warranties are that the insured is obliged to set a burglar alarm when
premises are unoccupied (to deter burglars) or to maintain a sprink-
ler system in good working order at all times (to prevent the spread
of fire).

(2) Warranties relating to past or present facts: In this situation the
insured affirms or negatives the existence of a particular state of facts
at the time that the insurance contract is agreed. Where such a
warranty relates clearly to the past and present, it will not be taken
to apply to the future.

7.56   For example in *Kennedy v Smith & Ansvar Insurance Co Ltd*[115] a proposer for motor insurance completed a proposal form together with an
'Abstinence and Membership Declaration' in which he stated that he
was and had always been an abstainer from alcohol. However, the
euphoria of victory in a bowling match led him to consume his first ever
alcoholic beverage. Later, when driving home, he swerved off the road
and his two passengers were killed. The insurers denied liability under
the policy on the basis that, at the time of the accident, the abstinence
declaration was false as the insured was under the influence of alcohol.
The court held that the warranty could not be taken to cover the future
conduct of the insured (despite this being the intention of the insurer)
and therefore the insurer was liable to pay the claim. If the warranty is
based on the opinion of the insured, it can relate only to facts which
are known to the insured. In *Hutchison v National Loan Fund Life Assurance
Society*,[116] the insured warranted that she had no disease and enjoyed
good health. It was held that this did not form a warranty against
any latent disease which could only be discovered by post-mortem
examination.

Warranties: identification

7.57   No special form of words is needed to create a warranty. It will
often be the case that the word 'warranty' will be used, but this is not
necessary. What is required is a form of words which makes clear that
the relevant term is fundamental to the contract and that it requires
strict compliance. In this context a distinction has been drawn between
terms which are descriptive of the risk and those that are warranties: this
is a matter of construction of the policy and turns on the issue of whether
the term is intended to define the risk or to require strict compliance

---

115 1975 SC 266.
116 (1845) 7 D 467.

on the part of the insured.[117] It is possible, though no longer common, for commercial insurance policies to contain warranties created through the use of a 'basis of contract clause'. The effect of such a clause is to turn all the information given in the proposal form into a warranty relating to past or present facts.[118] Once this has occurred, any inaccuracy in the information given by the insured allows the insurer to avoid the contract, even if the information was not material to the insurer's assessment of the risk.[119]

The consequences of breach of warranty

7.58 The consequences of a breach of warranty are made clear by section 33(3) of the Marine Insurance Act 1906:

> A warranty, as above defined [in section 33(1)], is a condition which must be exactly complied with, whether it be material to the risk or not. If it be not so complied with, then, subject to any express provision in the policy, the insurer is discharged from liability as from the date of the breach of warranty, but without prejudice to any liability incurred by him before that date.   .

7.59 The case of *Dawsons Ltd v Bonnin*[120] illustrates the obligation of strict compliance with warranties. A proposer for motor insurance entered in the proposal form that a lorry was garaged in central Glasgow whereas in fact it was garaged on the outskirts of the city. The proposal form declared that it was to be the basis of the contract. The lorry was subsequently destroyed by fire. The fourth condition of the contract provided that any material misstatement or concealment on the part of the insured would render the policy void. The insurers disputed liability and the issue went to the House of Lords. It was held (1) that the misstatement in relation to the garage address was not material within the meaning of condition 4, but (2) that the 'basis of contract' clause had the effect of turning the garage address into a fundamental term of the contract and that, in this situation, it did not matter if the address was material within the meaning of condition 4 or not. It followed that the insurer could refuse to pay the claim.

7.60 *Dawsons Ltd v Bonnin* was later applied in the case of *Unipac (Scotland) Ltd v Aegon Insurance Co (UK) Ltd.*[121] In that case, the insured answered two questions in a proposal form incorrectly: one related to the

---

117 See e.g. *Farr v Motor Traders' Mutual Insurance Society Ltd* [1920] 3 KB 669, where the issue turned on the interpretation of a term (incorporated into the policy via a 'basis of contract clause') stating that taxis were driven in only one shift each day.

118 An example of such a clause is: 'I hereby confirm that the information contained in the proposal form is complete and accurate and will form the basis of the contract.'

119 *Unipac (Scotland) Ltd v Aegon Insurance Co (UK) Ltd* 1996 SLT 1197.

120 1922 SC (HL) 156, 1922 SLT 444.

121 1996 SLT 1197.

length of time for which the company had carried on business at the premises and the other to whether they were the sole occupiers. The proposal form contained a basis of contract clause which purported to make all the information in it the basis of the contract. The insured argued that the basis clause only made material facts the basis of the contract but the court held that this particular basis clause had the effect of turning all the information in the proposal form into a warranty. The court recognised that the effect of its decision was to allow the insurer to avoid the contract for non-disclosure or misrepresentation of information which was not material to the insurer's assessment of the risk, but took the view that this outcome was 'simply a consequence of what the parties have agreed to by contract and parties are free to agree what they like'.[122]

7.61 There is no need for the insurer to show a causal connection between the breach of warranty and a loss in order to avoid the contract. For example, in *Jones & James v Provincial Insurance Co Ltd*[123] the policy contained a warranty which provided that the insured was required to maintain his vehicle in an efficient condition. The warranty was not observed by the insured and when the vehicle was stolen the insurer was able to avoid liability for the theft despite there being no causal connection between the breach of warranty and the loss. This outcome was generally viewed as harsh for the insured and insurers responded by agreeing, through self-regulation, not to refuse to pay claims when breach of warranty has no connection with loss.[124] Section 6 of CIDRA 2012 now provides that representations made by the insured cannot be converted into a warranty by the terms of the contract, but there is no change to the general law of warranties in consumer insurance and so specific warranties may be inserted into the contract and must be observed by the insured.

7.62 Breach of warranty does not release the insurer from liability in relation to losses which have occurred before the breach. The breach operates to release the insurer only from any future liability under the policy. No specific action is required on the part of the insurer in order to be released[125] and the option is open to the insurer to waive the breach and allow the policy to remain in force.[126]

---

122 At 1202 per Lord Justice-Clerk Ross.
123 [1929] 35 Ll L Rep 135.
124 Self-regulation took the form of Statements of Practice agreed by the members of the Association of British Insurers ('ABI'). When FCA rules replaced the statements, this part of the statements was not carried forward but the statements continued to form the basis for decisions made by the Financial Ombudsman Service, which has the effect of binding insurers.
125 *Bank of Nova Scotia v Hellenic Mutual War Risks Association (Bermuda) Ltd ('The Good Luck')* [1992] 1 AC 233.
126 1906 Act, s 34(3).

Construction of insurance contracts

7.63 The normal rules for the construction of contracts apply to insurance.[127] Words and expressions used in the policy are given their ordinary, everyday meaning unless it is clear that a technical usage is intended.[128] Of particular importance is the *contra proferentem* principle which requires any ambiguity in a contract to be construed against the *proferens* (the person relying on the ambiguous term). This principle was applied in *Kennedy v Smith & Ansvar*,[129] discussed above, to determine whether a warranty covered the future conduct of the insured.

Assignation

7.64 The rights of the insured or the insurer under a contract of insurance can, in principle, be assigned to a third party.[130] There are, however, limitations on the extent to which assignation can take place. First, it is possible that the policy itself will contain a prohibition on assignation. An express contractual prohibition on assignation invalidates any assignation in breach of it.[131] Secondly, it is sometimes said that rights involving *delectus personae* cannot be assigned.[132] This is true in so far as it goes. But normally what is assigned is the right to payment under the policy and, as a general principle, there is no *delectus personae creditoris* in the payment of a sum of money.[133]

7.65 Where assignation is possible,[134] it will only be effective if it is intimated to the insurer. The Policies of Assurance Act 1867 is usually cited as requiring written intimation of 'the date and purport' of the assignation to be given to the insurer at a principal place of business. But the application of the 1867 Act to Scots law is doubtful;[135] and, in any event, policies of assurance are expressly covered by section 4 of the Transmission of Moveable Property (Scotland) Act 1862. It is therefore

---

127 *Smith v Accident Insurance Co* (1870) LR 5 Ex 302 at 307.

128 See, e.g., *Scragg v United Kingdom Temperance & General Provident Institution* [1976] 2 Lloyd's Rep 227, where the term 'motor racing' was held to have a technical meaning which excluded hill climbing in which each vehicle set off separately and raced against the clock.

129 At para **7.56**.

130 Bell, *Principles* (4th edn, 1839) § 520, referring to a life assurance policy, states 'and as it is assignable, it is useful as a fund of credit'.

131 *Apollo Engineering Ltd v James Scott Ltd* [2012] CSIH 88.

132 *Cole v C H Handasyde & Co* 1910 SC 68 at 73 per Lord President Dunedin. This decision, however, confuses the contractual relationship as a whole with individual rights arising out of it. Individual rights, particularly rights to payment, are normally freely assignable (unless there is an express prohibition).

133 See R G Anderson, *Assignation* (2008) para 2-34 ff.

134 Assignation occurs most commonly in life assurance. Although it results in a change in the person to whom the sum assured is payable, the life assured/creditor, and therefore the risk, remains the same. An assignation immediately following the conclusion of a life contract can effectively circumvent the requirement for insurable interest, but the courts have not limited assignation on this basis.

135 See Scottish Law Commission, *Discussion Paper on Moveable Transactions* (DP No 151, 2011) para 4.67.

possible that intimation of an assignation of rights under an insurance policy may be made in the normal way. The rights of the assignee are governed by the principle *assignatus utitur jure auctoris* (the assignee assumes the rights of the cedant) and priority among assignees is determined by the date of receipt of the notice. An example of this in the context of insurance is the case of *Scottish Widows' Fund and Life Assurance Society v Buist*.[136] The insured failed to disclose his addiction to alcohol at the time the contract was agreed. The policy was later assigned to a third party. When the insured died at the age of 30, the insurer sought to avoid the assignee's claim for payment. It was held that as the assignee stood in the same position as the cedant (the insured), the insurer could avoid the policy.

Third party rights

7.66   An insurance contract imposes obligations only on the insured and the insurer and therefore, in principle, third parties are not able to enforce the contract for their own benefit. This principle holds good even when a third party has a valid claim against the insured which is covered by an insurance policy. However, there are two important exceptions to this principle. First, a pursuer with a claim against an insured party may have direct rights of action against the insurer. One example is under the Third Parties (Rights against Insurers) Act 1930[137] which allows third parties with a valid claim[138] against an insured defender to obtain decree against the insurer where the insured is insolvent.[139] The effect of this provision is to create a statutory assignation of the insured's rights in respect of the particular claim to the third party.[140] Similarly, even outside of insolvency, it is possible for a pursuer to convene the primary wrongdoer's insurers as defenders to the action.[141]

7.67   Second, in the case of compulsory motor insurance, section 151 of the Road Traffic Act 1988 ('RTA 1988') requires insurers to pay directly to third parties any sums covered by a motor insurance policy.

---

136 (1876) 3 R 1078.
137 The 1930 Act will be repealed once the Third Parties (Rights against Insurers) Act 2010 is brought into effect. The 2010 Act implements recommendations made by the Law Commissions in *Third Parties (Rights Against Insurers) Act 1930* (Consultation Paper No 152, 1997).
138 The claim must be established in legal proceedings against the insured: *Bradley v Eagle Star Insurance Co Ltd* [1989] AC 957 at 960 per Lord Brandon. The 2010 Act permits the third party to proceed directly against the insurer but she cannot enforce rights under the insurance contract until the liability of the insured has been established (s 1(3)).
139 A dissolved company can be 'restored' to the register to permit a claim to proceed: see Companies Act 2006, s 1029.
140 *Cheltenham & Gloucester plc v Sun Alliance and London Insurance plc* 2001 SC 965 at para [10] per Lord President Rodger.
141 European Communities (Rights against Insurers) Regulations 2002 (SI 2002/3061).

The reference to compulsory (third party) insurance under the RTA 1988[142] has the effect of limiting the defences which would normally be available to the insurer. In particular, section 151 facilitates claims brought by third parties when a driver is not insured according to the terms of the policy. In those circumstances an insurer is liable to pay claims falling within compulsory insurance subject to a right of relief against any person who caused or permitted the use of the vehicle which gave rise to the liability.[143] To benefit from section 151, a third party must first obtain judgment against the insured and must give notice of the proceedings against the insured to the insurer, so as to allow the insurer the opportunity to defend the case.

7.68 Third, persons covered by an insurance policy (such as a driver under a motor policy) are able to enforce the policy despite not being a party to the contract.[144] In Scotland, the *ius quaesitum tertio* enables rights expressly granted to a third party in any contract to be enforced. In England, the Third Parties (Rights against Insurers) Act 1930 enables direct enforcement by a third party against the insurer following the insolvency of the insured. However, even when the insured is solvent, a third party who is expressly covered by the terms of the policy (e.g. as a driver in motor insurance) is able to enforce the policy.[145]

CLAIMS

Notice of loss

7.69 A policy will normally oblige an insured to notify the insurers of a loss within a specified time limit, or if none is stipulated, within a reasonable time. In principle, non-compliance with such a term defeats a claim under the policy, at least when the term is construed as a condition precedent to the liability of the insurer. However, there are two ways in which the insured may be protected from this outcome. One is that the courts will interpret such clauses *contra proferentem*, thereby extending the time period within which notification may be made.[146] The other is that such a clause may be struck down as unfair under the Unfair Terms in Consumer Contracts Regulations 1999.[147]

7.70 An additional obligation often contained in a policy is that 'full

142 RTA 1988, s 145.
143 It has been disputed whether this provision (RTA 1988, s 151(8)) correctly implements EU law: see *Churchill Insurance Co Ltd v Wilkinson* [2010] EWCA Civ 556, where the question of whether the insurer was entitled to relief from the insured, who was a passenger in a car and had consented to it being driven by an uninsured driver, was referred to the European Court of Justice.
144 See para **7.24** above.
145 See n 51 above.
146 See e.g. *Verelst's Administratrix v Motor Union Insurance Co Ltd* [1925] 2 KB 137, (1925) 21 Ll L Rep 227.
147 SI 1999/2083. See para **7.11** for general comment on the scope of the Regulations with regard to insurance.

particulars' of the loss must be given to the insurer and that the insured must co-operate with the insurer, such as by not admitting liability to or settling with a third party who has suffered loss. If such a clause is interpreted as a condition precedent to liability it may defeat a claim, but subject once again to interpretation *contra proferentem* and the possibility that the term may be invalid under the Unfair Terms in Consumer Contracts Regulations 1999. Conversely, if such a clause is interpreted as a standard contract term, any claim by the insurer for damages following breach must demonstrate loss resulting from the breach.[148]

Proximate cause

7.71 In order to claim under an indemnity policy,[149] the insured must show that loss or damage has been proximately caused by an insured peril. If loss or damage results from a cause other than an insured peril, the insurer is not liable.[150] The proximate cause of loss is the dominant or effective cause of that loss. It does not have to be the only cause of the loss, nor need it be the cause which operates closest in time to the loss. For example, in *Leyland Shipping Co Ltd v Norwich Union Fire Insurance Society Ltd*[151] there were two possible causes of loss. A marine policy covering a ship contained an exclusion relating to damage caused as a result of hostilities. The ship was torpedoed 25 miles from Le Havre by a German submarine during World War I. She was towed into port at Le Havre but subsequently ordered to anchor outside the harbour as it was feared that she would sink and block the harbour. At low tide the ship became grounded, took in water and sank. The insurers refused to pay the shipowner's claim on the basis that the proximate cause of the loss was the torpedoing, which was excluded. It was held that the torpedoing, not the grounding, was the proximate cause of loss.

7.72 Where two causes occur concurrently and it is not possible to say which is the proximate cause, there can be no claim if one of the causes is excluded. This situation occurred in *Wayne Tank & Pump Co Ltd v Employers Liability Assurance Corporation Ltd.*[152] Wayne Tank & Pump ('WTP') were engineers who installed machinery in a plasticine factory. They had a public liability policy with ELA which provided cover, inter alia, for damage caused by WTP at customers' premises. An exception to the cover was damage caused by the nature of goods sold or supplied on behalf of the insured. The machinery was switched on by a WTP employee before installation was complete, it caught fire and destroyed the factory. WTP were held liable to the factory owners in a separate

---

148 In *Porter v Zurich Insurance Co* [2009] EWHC 376 the insurer was unable to prove loss caused by the failure of the insured to comply with the claims co-operation clause (as opposed to loss caused by theft).
149 In the case of life assurance, it is necessary to show only that the event insured against (e.g. death) has occurred.
150 1906 Act, s 55(1).
151 [1918] AC 350.
152 [1974] QB 57.

action where it was established that there were two concurrent causes of the fire: (1) dangerous plastic material used by WTP (excluded); and (2) the premature switching-on of the machinery (covered). It was held by the Court of Appeal that the insurer was not liable as the exception should be allowed to operate to limit the insurer's liability. Conversely, where two causes occur concurrently and one is covered but no mention is made of the other, the insurers are liable.[153]

7.73   The potential uncertainty in the scope of cover illustrated by these cases can be addressed by the use of appropriate contract terms. For example, in *Jason v British Traders Insurance Co Ltd*[154] Jason was a market trader who was injured in a crash when a wheel came off his van. He claimed under an accident insurance policy from BTI. The policy provided cover for accidents which were, independently of other causes, the direct and immediate cause of injury. There was also an exclusion clause in respect of injuries caused by any physical defect or infirmity which existed prior to an accident. Following the accident, Jason suffered a coronary thrombosis and was disabled for about a year. The medical evidence showed that the stress of the accident had contributed to the condition but that Jason would have probably suffered this in any event within three years because of his existing medical condition. It was held that the insurers were not liable as the accident was not the independent cause of injury.

7.74   Loss caused by the deliberate act or criminal conduct of the insured is not covered by an insurance policy. The rationale lies in a correct construction of the contract[155] although there is also statutory authority for that approach.[156] In the case of compulsory third party motor insurance, however, statutory intervention has provided injured third parties with a right to claim under the policy even when the injury results from the criminal act of the insured.[157]

The indemnity principle

7.75   The objective of the principle of indemnity is to put the insured in the position he would be in had the loss not occurred. For example, in *Hercules Insurance Co v Hunter*,[158] the defender insured with the pursuers certain mill machinery and materials in Glasgow for a sum of £1,450. The property was destroyed by fire but the insurers refused to pay £1,450 on the basis that the goods destroyed were of lower value. It was established that the defender had deliberately overvalued the machinery.

---

153 *JJ Lloyd Instruments Ltd v Northern Star Insurance Co Ltd (The Miss Jay Jay)* [1987] 1 Lloyd's Rep 32.
154 [1969] 1 Lloyd's Rep 281.
155 *Beresford v Royal Insurance Co Ltd* [1938] AC 586 at 595 per Lord Atkin. In that case, the insurer avoided liability under a life policy as the insured had committed suicide, which at the time was a crime.
156 1906 Act, s 55(2)(a).
157 See para **7.67** above.
158 (1836) 14 S 1137.

It was decided that in a contract of indemnity it is the actual value of the property destroyed which the insured is entitled to recover and not the particular sum insured contained in the policy. The actual value of the goods was the value for which they could be sold.

7.76 There is no need for the principle of indemnity to be stated in the policy. If the nature of the policy is such that it is intended to compensate the insured to the extent of his loss, measured at the time it occurs, then the principle of indemnity applies. However, it is possible for the policy to provide that the principle of indemnity will not apply or that its application will be modified. This can occur in several ways:

(1) *Agreed value policy.* Agreed value policies are used for items which may be difficult to value when a loss occurs, such as works of art or antiques. The policy specifies the sum which is to be paid in the event of a total loss of the subject matter insured. Where there is a partial loss there is a pro-rata adjustment made.[159]

(2) *Replacement value or reinstatement policies.* A replacement value policy gives the insured the cost of replacing the item which has been destroyed and a reinstatement policy obliges the insurer to restore the property to its condition before the damage occurred. Some policies may give the insurer the option of either paying the value of the property destroyed or reinstating. Once agreement has been reached on the payment of money, the insurer no longer has the option to reinstate.

(3) *Excess clause.* An excess clause requires the insured to bear a certain amount of the loss but beyond this amount the insurer will be liable for the balance of the loss. It is common to find an excess clause in motor and home insurance policies because insurers regard such a clause as encouraging the insured to avoid a loss on the basis that it will not be possible to claim the entire loss from the insurer.

(4) *Franchise clause.* A franchise clause requires the insured to bear losses below a certain percentage of the sum insured; and where there is a loss above this percentage, it is borne in full by the insurer. For example a 5 per cent franchise on a policy covering goods valued at £1,000 would require the insured to bear any loss below £50, but any loss over £50 would be borne in full by the insurer.

(5) *Average clause.* An average clause is designed to deal with the problem of under-insurance. Where goods are insured for less than their true value, the insurer will not receive a premium which reflects the full value of the goods. For example, where goods worth £150,000 are insured for only £100,000, the insurer receives a premium based on £100,000 but is in reality exposed to the possibility of the loss

---

159 E.g. a policy states the value of goods to be £100, but the real value before loss is £60. The value after a loss is £30. The insured's claim against the insurer will be for £50 (three-sixths of £100).

of any £100,000 out of the total £150,000 of goods. An average clause prevents the insured from taking out a partial insurance and then recovering the full value of the goods which have been lost. It does this by adjusting the claim in relation to the proportion of the value of the goods which is insured.[160] The effect of this is that the insured is his own insurer for the portion of the value of the goods which is not insured.

7.77 Section 81 of the Marine Insurance Act 1906 provides that the principle of average applies to marine policies. In the case of other classes of insurance, it is necessary for there to be a specific clause providing for the application of the principle of average. If there is not, the insurer will not be able to reduce a claim on the basis that there has been under-insurance.[161]

Subrogation

7.78 The principle of subrogation follows logically from the principle of indemnity. It operates so as to prevent the insured from recovering more than a full indemnity under the policy. The possibility of the insured gaining more than a full indemnity arises in situations where the insured may be able to recover his loss from a third party as well as from the insurer. Subrogation has the effect of assigning to the insurer any rights which the insured may have against a third party who caused the loss.[162] For example, where motorist A negligently crashes into motorist B, A will be liable in delict to B. Assume that the cost of repairing B's car is £2,000. B then claims £2,000 from his insurer under his comprehensive motor policy. In this situation, B will have been fully indemnified for the loss by the insurer. The principle of subrogation would operate in this case to allow the insurer to exercise B's delictual rights against A in respect of loss caused to B.[163]

7.79 Subrogation is a common law principle and therefore applies without being referred to in the policy. It applies only to indemnity insurance and only when the insurer has paid a claim under the policy. In *Page v Scottish Insurance Corporation*,[164] the insurer tried to exercise subrogation against a person who had caused damage to the insured's car.

---

160 In the example cited, a loss of £30,000 would result in a claim for £20,000, i.e. (100/150 × £30,000).

161 *Sillem v Thornton* (1854) 3 E&B 868.

162 *Caledonia North Sea Ltd v London Bridge Engineering Ltd* 2000 SLT 1123 at 1139–1140 per Lord President Rodger (affd 2002 SC (HL) 117).

163 In the case of motor insurance, insurers have agreed among themselves (through so-called 'knock for knock' agreements) not to exercise subrogation rights against third parties (and their insurers) because the outcome would be that the number of claims within the system would increase. In other cases (where the numbers of claims are lower or there is an imbalance in claims between insurers) the exercise of subrogation rights is more common.

164 (1929) 33 Ll L Rep 134.

It was held that this could only be possible after the insurer had paid the insured's claim. Subrogation transfers from the insured to the insurer every right of the insured in contract or delict. This principle was applied in *Castellain v Preston*[165] where the insured was the vendor of a house which was burnt down between the conclusion of the contract for sale and the transfer of title. The contract provided for the risk to pass to the purchaser on conclusion of the contract. The vendor recovered the insurance money from the insurers and the purchaser then paid the price (as he was obliged to do under the contract). It was held that as the insurers had fully indemnified the vendor for his loss, the purchase price had to be passed to the insurers as they became subrogated to his rights once they had paid the claim.

7.80 In most cases the insured's rights in contract and delict will be passed to the insurer automatically when a claim is paid. However, there are circumstances in which this will not occur. One is where the policy contains a contractual exclusion of subrogation. Another is where the insured's right has been excluded by contract as in the case of *Mark Rowlands v Berni Inns Ltd*.[166] A lease provided that the landlord was obliged to insure the property and that the tenant was to pay an additional insurance rent. The property was damaged by fire, the insurer paid the landlord's claim under the policy and then tried to exercise a right of subrogation against the tenant. It was held that the effect of the lease was to prevent the landlord recovering damages from the tenant for any loss covered by insurance and as the landlord had no right of action against the tenant, the insurer could have no action.

7.81 A second situation where subrogation will not apply is where the loss has been caused by the insured himself or by a co-insured.[167] In the case of the insured causing the loss, the insurer can have no right of action because the insured has no right of action against himself and there is therefore nothing to transfer by way of subrogation. In the case of *Simpson & Co v Thomson*[168] a ship ran down and sank another belonging to the same owner, William Burrell. The underwriters of the sunken ship paid its value to Burrell and then made a claim against him on the basis that his other ship had caused the damage. It was held that this claim was not possible as Burrell could not have sued himself and the underwriters stood in his position once they had paid the claim. Of course, had the owner of the other ship been a third party such a claim would have been possible. In *Petrofina (UK) Ltd v Magnaload Ltd*,[169] Magnaload were sub-contractors involved in the construction of an extension to an oil refinery. The insurance policy provided cover for the work in progress and the construction equipment. Following the collapse

165 (1883) 11 QBD 380.
166 [1986] 1 QB 211.
167 The reference here is to loss caused carelessly or negligently: deliberate loss caused by the insured is not covered, see para **7.74** above.
168 (1877) 5 R (HL) 40, (1877) 3 App Cas 279.
169 [1984] QB 127, [1983] 2 Lloyd's Rep 91.

of a crane, the owner of the refinery claimed on the policy for damage caused to the contract works by the crane's collapse. The insurers then attempted to exercise subrogation rights against Magnaload, who were the sub-contractors responsible for the operation of the crane. It was held that as Magnaload were one of the parties insured by the policy, it was not possible for the insurers to exercise subrogation.

7.82 Finally, insurers have informally agreed that subrogation rights will not be exercised against the employees of an insured company or firm. This avoids the harsh outcome that resulted from the decision of the House of Lords in *Lister v Romford Ice and Cold Storage Co Ltd.*[170] In that case an employee of the insured was injured negligently by a co-employee and, following the payment of damages to the injured employee, the insurer sought to exercise the right of subrogation against the employee who caused the injury. It was held that the insurers were entitled to recover but the informal agreement not to exercise subrogation in this situation recognises the dissenting view of the minority in that case, which was that it was an implied term of the contract of employment that the insured would protect the employee from liability for injury caused to third parties, thereby precluding any claim by the employer or insurer.[171]

Contribution

7.83 Contribution relates to the rights of insurers among themselves. It applies in situations in which a loss is covered by more than one policy (e.g. where a bag stolen from a car is covered both by home contents insurance and by motor insurance).[172] In this situation, an insurer who pays the insured's claim in full is entitled to recover a proportion of the claim from the other insurer (i.e. half if two, one-third from each if three). In principle the insured is free to choose which insurer to claim against in cases of double/multiple insurance but cannot recover more than an indemnity.

7.84 In order to avoid paying a claim in full in cases of double insurance, insurers often use rateable proportion clauses which provide that they are only liable for their rateable proportion of the loss. However, as was held in *Legal and General Assurance Society Ltd v Drake Insurance Co Ltd,*[173] where there is double insurance and each policy has a rateable proportion clause, any payment made voluntarily by an insurer in excess of his rateable proportion cannot be recovered from the other insurer.

---

170 [1957] AC 555.
171 *Lister* was later distinguished in *Morris v Ford Motor Co Ltd* [1973] 1 QB 792, but Lord Denning's reference to *Lister* as an 'unfortunate decision' indicates that policy took priority over a strict application of the doctrine of precedent in *Morris*.
172 1906 Act, s 80(1).
173 [1992] 1 All ER 283.

Good faith and fraudulent claims

7.85   As noted earlier,[174] the duty of good faith applies at the time that the insured makes a claim under the policy. Claims made in breach of that duty have generally been characterised as 'fraudulent' and raise two key issues: first, what is the standard of conduct required from the insured during the claims process; and second, what are the consequences of breach?

7.86   A claim is fraudulent if it is based on substantial falsehood and is intended to secure a payment greater than the insured's entitlement. Some exaggeration in the value of a claim is part of the normal process of negotiation between insured and insurer, but a claim which is several times the real value of the loss is indicative of fraud. The effect of a fraudulent claim is that the insurer has the right to avoid all liability under the policy, not just liability for the claim to which the fraud relates. The reason for this is that a fraudulent claim is a breach of the duty of good faith. For example, in *The Litsion Pride*,[175] the insured attempted to claim for the loss of a ship during the Iran-Iraq war. The ship had sailed into a war zone, for which the policy required a large additional premium. When the ship was sunk by a helicopter attack the insured concocted false documents to give the impression that the failure to notify the insurers of entry into the war zone was due to an innocent oversight. It was held that the insurer could avoid the policy *ab initio*[176] or reject liability for the particular claim and allow the policy to continue in existence.

7.87   Subsequent cases have focused on the severity of this remedy for the insured, who may face the prospect of repaying prior claims following a fraudulent claim. As regards the standard of conduct required on the part of the insured during the claims process, it was established in the *The Star Sea*[177] that the insured owed no more than a duty of honesty and that the assumption made in *The Litsion Pride* that a duty of disclosure applied during the claims process was wrong. The rationale for this approach was that a more onerous duty of good faith was required in the context of negotiating the contract to enable the insurer to evaluate the risk, whereas in the post-contract situation an onerous duty of good faith provided a disproportionate benefit to the insurer in terms of avoiding liability. As regards the consequence of breach of the duty, the House of Lords in *The Star Sea* was inclined towards the view that it should only be prospective and should not enable avoidance of the contract *ab initio*. However, as the case did not turn on that issue (since a breach of good faith was not established on the facts), it was not conclu-

---

174 See above para **7.33**.
175 *Black King Shipping Corporation and Wayang v Mark Massie* [1985] 1 Lloyd's Rep 437.
176 Under the 1906 Act, s 17.
177 *Manifest Shipping Co Ltd v Uni-Polaris Shipping Co Ltd* [2001] UKHL 1, [2003] 1 AC 469 at 515 per Lord Scott.

sively resolved and remains subject to some uncertainty.[178] What is clear, however, is that breach of the duty permits the insurer to avoid liability for the fraudulent claim and any future claims under the policy (i.e. avoidance operates prospectively).

The Financial Ombudsman Scheme

7.88   An ombudsman scheme for the adjudication of consumer[179] insurance disputes has been available since the establishment in 1981 of the Insurance Ombudsman Bureau ('IOB'). The Financial Ombudsman Scheme ('FOS') replaced the IOB when FSMA 2000 took effect and has since then handled a large volume of insurance-related disputes. Complaints are determined according to what is fair and reasonable in all the circumstances of the case.[180] In considering what is fair and reasonable in all the circumstances of the case, the Ombudsman will take into account the relevant law, regulations, regulators' rules and guidance and standards, relevant codes of practice and, where appropriate, what he considers to have been good industry practice at the time. When a complaint has been determined[181] the Ombudsman must give both the complainant and the firm a written statement of the determination, stating reasons for it. The statement will invite the complainant to notify the Ombudsman in writing before the date specified in the statement whether he accepts or rejects the determination. If the complainant accepts the determination within the time limit set by the Ombudsman, it is final and binding on both the complainant and the firm. If not, the firm is not bound by the determination and both sides are free to pursue legal remedies in court. If a complaint is determined in favour of the complainant, the determination may include:

- a money award subject to a maximum of £150,000;[182] or
- a direction that the firm take such steps in relation to the complainant as the Ombudsman considers just and appropriate; or
- both of these.

In the case of a money award, the Ombudsman may decide to award compensation for the following kinds of loss or damage (in addition to or instead of compensation for financial loss):

---

178 At 515.
179 As to the meaning of 'consumer' for these purposes and the jurisdiction of the FOS see FCA Handbook DISP 2.
180 In the case of the compulsory jurisdiction, FSMA 2000, s 228(2) provides a statutory basis for this approach. In the case of the voluntary jurisdiction, FCA Handbook DISP 3.6.1R provides a contractual basis for the Ombudsman to determine a complaint in this manner.
181 A provisional decision, which gives both parties an opportunity to comment, is issued before the final decision.
182 With effect from 1 January 2012: for complaints notified before that date the limit is £100,000: see FCA Handbook DISP 3.7.4R.

- pain and suffering; or
- damage to reputation; or
- distress or inconvenience.

The limit on the maximum money award has no bearing on any direction that the Ombudsman may make as part of a determination. The result is that the complainant can receive benefits in excess of the monetary limit in circumstances in which a direction has a financial benefit for the complainant. Where the Ombudsman finds in a complainant's favour, he may also award an amount which covers some or all of the costs which were reasonably incurred by the complainant in respect of the complaint. A money award under the compulsory jurisdiction is enforceable through the courts in the same way as money awards made by the lower courts (the sheriff court in Scotland).[183]

7.89 No appeal to the courts is possible from a determination made by the Ombudsman. The rationale for excluding a right of appeal from FSMA 2000 was that it would be inconsistent with the objective of resolving disputes quickly and with minimum formality. In principle judicial review is available but this provides only a limited basis on which to mount a challenge. It is not normally possible to recover losses above the limit for FOS awards through subsequent court action following acceptance of a FOS award because the principle of *res judicata* applies so as to exclude the possibility of fresh proceedings based on the same cause of action.[184]

---

183 FSMA 2000, Sch 17 para 16.
184 *Clark v In Focus Asset Management & Tax Solutions Ltd* [2014] EWCA Civ 118.

Chapter 8

Money and Debt

PATRIMONIAL LAW

The general part

8.01   Private law is concerned with patrimonial rights: personal rights, real rights, intellectual property rights. Only rights, not physical things, are assets:[1] 'All rights, therefore, are incorporeal; and the distinction really is not between two kinds of right, but between things which are objects of right and the legal conception of right itself.' The paradigm focus in property law on real rights in land results in a tendency to identify patrimonial rights with their objects.[2] As the famous Roman and comparative lawyer, Barry Nicholas, elegantly observes:[3]

> The strictly comparable statement to 'I have bought a right of way over a plot of land' is not, 'I have bought a plot of land', but 'I have bought a right of ownership over a plot of land'. In each case I have acquired a right.

8.02   The relationship of a person to her rights is not her ownership (since ownership may be one of her rights), but her title.[4] Ownership is but one of the real rights and real rights are just one type of patrimonial right. Ownership is not necessary to describe the holding of personal rights. To speak of ownership of personal rights gives rise to a doubling of the rights involved and complicates unnecessarily the already difficult task of legal analysis.[5]

---

1   *Burghead Harbour Co v George* (1906) 8 F 982 at 996 per Lord Kinnear.
2   See paras **3.44–3.55** above. A statutory example is the Long Leases (Scotland) Act 2012, s 6 (where the right of ownership is identified with its object, the land).
3   B Nicholas, *An Introduction to Roman Law* (1962), p 107.
4   Cf. Bankton, *Institute*, I, 597, 1 'The terms Right and Title are promiscuously used in our law.' It is not clear whether Bankton is here referring to Scots law or English law.
5   In a curious *obiter dictum*, the Second Division in *Scottish Environmental Protection Agency v The Joint Liquidators of the Scottish Coal Company Limited* [2013] CSIH 108, 2014 SLT 259 at para [98] observed that 'strictly, it is not "ownership" that is transferred. It is the land which may be transferred and thereby result in the termination of one person's ownership and its creation in another.' But ownership is a transferable patrimonial right: Land Registration (Scotland) Act 1979, s 3;

8.03 In commercial law, the most important patrimonial rights are often not real rights in physical things, but personal rights to the performance of obligations.[6] Personal rights arising under the law of obligations have no physical object; their object is rather the counter-performance: to use a word of French origin, still often referred to in modern Scottish cases,[7] the object is the 'prestation'.

8.04 Obligations give rise to personal rights, whether those personal rights are born of contracts or promises or delicts or in order to prevent unjustified enrichment. Unlike real rights in land (some of which may endure forever) obligations (and thus their correlative personal rights), it has been said, are 'born to die'. This chapter will be concerned with the death of obligations, by performance or discharge; or with the maintenance of the obligation and the circulation of the creditor's position.

8.05 Since every contract creates rights and obligations, achieving performance is the core function of all commercial contracts. The basic principles, however, are little different in a commercial case than in any other case. The detailed rules on creation, variation, discharge and transfer of rights and obligations – the lifeblood of the corporate and financial world – are the core private law rules which comprise the general part of patrimonial law.[8]

Some vocabulary: rights and obligations

8.06 The English language has many attributes, but one major weakness is its legal vocabulary. Since this chapter is primarily concerned with 'obligations', a few words about the word 'obligation' may assist. The English word, 'obligation', focuses on the debtor, not the creditor:

> Obligation is that which is correspondent to a personal right, which hath no proper name as it is in the creditor, but hath the name of obligation

---

and, most clearly, Land Registration etc (Scotland) Act 2012, s 50. Land is the object of ownership; a disposition by an owner transfers ownership not the land; the land does not move: a point made, incidentally, by W N Hohfeld himself (1913) 23 Yale Law Journal 16 at 24 (whose mysterious analyses of equitable interests the Division cites at para [98]).

6 Or, indeed, intellectual property rights. See, further, Chapter 3: General Principles of Property Law.

7 *Johnston's Tr v Baird* [2012] CSOH 117 at paras [18]–[20] per Lord Uist; *Glasgow City Council v Morrison Developments Ltd* 2003 SLT 263 at paras [12] and [16] per Lord Eassie; and *Allied Dunbar Assurance plc v Superglass Sections Ltd* 2003 SLT 1420 at para [10] per Lord Eassie.

8 The institutional writers dealt with rules of the general part in some detail. But since then the general part of Scots private law has been neglected. Compare Book 1 of the German Civil Code; Part One of the Swiss *Code des Obligations*; Book 3 of the Dutch civil code; and Books I–III of the Draft Common Frame of Reference ('DCFR').

as it is in the debtor: and it is nothing else but a legal tie, whereby the debtor may be compelled to pay or perform something, to which he is bound by obedience to God, or by his own consent or engagement.[9]

8.07 Or, as the leading modern writer on the civil law of obligations explains:

> The substantive 'obligatio' can be traced back to Cicero. As to the literal meaning of the term, its root 'lig-' indicates that somebody or something is bound; just as we are all 'bound-back' (to God) by virtue of our 'religio'. . . . the English term 'obligation' is merely oriented toward the person bound, not towards the person entitled. With the words 'my obligations' I can refer only to my duties, not to my rights.[10]

8.08 The point is that words like 'obligation', 'debt' and 'duty' refer to the debtor's side of the legal relationship; the creditor's position, in contrast, the positive end of the relationship, is more difficult to describe. A creditor is said to hold a 'right' or a 'claim' against the debtor. As will be seen below, a claim, held by a creditor, is normally freely transferable; a liability owed by a debtor to a creditor, in contrast, cannot normally be transferred by the debtor without the creditor's consent. This fundamental principle forms the basis of much that occurs in the financial world.

Some corporate jargon

8.09 To identify rights and obligations in a corporate or financial context, however, may itself be a challenge. The term 'security' is particularly common. In this context, 'security' does not refer to a real right in security, like a standard security, which is a right additional to the creditor's principal right to payment; rather, in the corporate context, a 'security' is an instrument a company issues as an acknowledgement of investment in the company.[11] That investment may be by way of equity (shares) or debt (debentures, loan notes, bonds). In the corporate world, jargon abounds: words like 'convertible securities', 'bonds', 'stock',[12] 'debenture stock',[13] 'share warrants' etc all describe securities issued by a company. That security may or may not be certificated: that is to say,

---

9 Stair, *Institutions* 1.1.22. Of this passage, A H Campbell, *The Structure of Stair's Institutions* (1954) p 31, remarks: 'note how aptly Stair applies the metaphor of the *vinculum juris*. The chain does not, as the hasty beginner is apt to say, bind the debtor and the creditor; it binds the debtor, but the creditor's end lies freely in his hands to use or not as he pleases.'

10 R Zimmermann, *The Law of Obligations: Roman Foundations of the Civilian Tradition* (1990; pbk 1996) p 1.

11 Companies Act 2006, s 755(5): 'In this chapter "securities" means shares or debentures.'

12 See E Ferran, *Principles of Corporate Finance Law* (2008) pp 123–24.

13 Companies Act 2006, s 738: '"debenture" includes debenture stock, bonds and other securities of a company whether or not constituting a charge on the assets of the company.'

the security may be represented by a physical paper certificate; or the security may have been issued in dematerialised form. An 'issuer' of such security, the company, is normally the recipient of an investment, often, although not always, in money; the holder of the security is normally the investor, the creditor. A creditor who holds a corporate bond is someone who has lent money to the company and the company's obligation to repay is reified in the bond issued to the creditor. The term 'debenture' has no settled legal meaning,[14] other than an acknowledgement of indebtedness: an IOU. Determining the rights that a holder of such instruments may have, however, normally means trawling through the provisions of an overarching document (an offering circular, loan note instrument, debenture trust deed or articles of association). But the same general principles apply. And those principles essentially apply too where the issuer of the instrument is not a company, but Her Majesty's Government which must finance its activities on the capital markets as a company does, by issuing IOUs (government bonds) through the Debt Management Office.[15] Again, a similar barrage of jargon is encountered, such as 'gilts' and 'titans'.[16]

Money: the 'universal solvent'

8.10 Obligations may arise by consent (as with contracts or promises); or they may be imposed by law (under the law of delict or unjustified enrichment); or by statute. Sometimes an obligation will require something to be done: a service performed or goods delivered. Sometimes the obligation is simply to pay money. Even in cases where the initial obligation was for some performance, the law may convert this into an obligation to pay in the form of damages. For the purposes of the law of obligations, 'Money is the universal solvent; everything can be turned into money that is either a gain or a loss; money is asked and damages are due for reparation of every possible suffering and injury.'[17] That is a

---

14 See n 13 above. Companies which issue such bonds must keep a register of them: Companies Act 2006, s 743. In English law, 'debenture' sometimes also refers to a document that not only acknowledges indebtedness, but also grants fixed and floating charges to the creditor: see *Fons HF (in liquidation) v Corporal Ltd* [2014] EWCA Civ 304. In Scots law, a company wishing to acknowledge its indebtedness to a creditor and grant to the creditor a floating charge does so in a document called a 'Bond and Floating Charge'. The only difference between a 'Bond and Floating Charge' and a 'Floating Charge' is that the former contains an acknowledgement of the principal debt obligation in the same document as the grant of the security.

15 www.dmo.gov.uk

16 The financial markets play a central role in contemporary society. No more can be said about them here, but three useful introductory guides are W M Clarke, *How the City of London Works* (7th edn, 2008); R Vaitilingham, *Financial Times Guide to Using the Financial Pages* (6th edn, 2011); and N Ferguson, *The Ascent of Money* (2008).

17 *Auld v Shairp* (1874) 2 R 191 at 199 per Lord Neaves.

general principle of private law, whether the basis for the liability is contract or delict or unjustified enrichment.

DEBT AND DAMAGES

8.11 A fundamental distinction, of considerable practical importance, is made between debt and damages. A debt is a 'liquid' sum: that is, the amount owed is established. A contract or a document of debt[18] may provide for payment of a liquid sum. A claim for damages, in contrast, is the classic illiquid claim. Only on the court giving decree for the sum sued for is there a liquid sum payable. The major practical distinction between debt and damages is that there is an obligation on a creditor in a claim for damages to mitigate its loss; a creditor who claims payment of a debt has no such duty. The distinction is of particular importance in cases of anticipatory breach of contract where the innocent party has the option to accept the repudiation and claim damages (subject to the duty to mitigate), or to refuse to accept the repudiation, offer to perform its side of the contract, and then claim the moneys owed under the contract.[19]

MULTIPLE DEBTORS AND CREDITORS

General

8.12 Contract law is core to commercial law. Contractual matrices are often very deliberately constructed in order to take advantage of the basic principle of privity of contract: only the parties to a contract may sue on it.[20] A contract presupposes at least two parties, but contracts may have many more than two parties. In multipartite commercial contracts it is normal for each party to be a juristic rather than a natural person. In order to understand the implications for the respective parties to such a multipartite contract, there are a number of preliminary concepts to introduce.

Principal and accessory

8.13 Some patrimonial rights are dependent on the existence of another

---

18 For which, see n 111 below.
19 *White & Carter (Councils) Ltd v Macgregor* 1962 SC (HL) 1; *Société Générale, London Branch v Geys* [2012] UKSC 63, [2013] 1 AC 523.
20 For the difficulties relating to the law of *jus quaesitum tertio*, see Scottish Law Commission, *Review of Contract Law: Discussion Paper on Third Party Rights in Contract* (DP No 157, 2014). Cf. 'collateral warranties' provided to persons not otherwise party to the contract in terms of which the original warranties are given: *The Scottish Coal Company Ltd v Trustees of FIM Timber Growth Fund III* [2009] CSOH 30; *Scottish Widows Services Ltd v Harmon/CRM Facades Ltd (in liquidation)* 2012 SLT 68; *Royal Bank of Scotland plc v Carlyle* [2013] CSIH 75, 2014 SC 188.

right. Such dependent rights are known as 'accessory rights'. Both personal rights and real rights may be accessory. The classic example of an accessory right is a security right. That security right may be personal (such as that arising out of a cautionary obligation) or real (such as that arising out of a pledge). The principal obligation is normally a personal obligation to render some performance. The accessory principle has a number of aspects. The first is that it is not possible to constitute a properly accessory obligation, without the existence of a principal obligation. The second is that discharge of the principal leads to discharge of the accessory. And the third is that wherever the principal goes, so too does the accessory.

Primary and secondary liability

8.14   The distinction between primary and secondary liability may be used in a number of senses. Contractual liability may be said to have primary and secondary aspects: the primary liability is performance, the secondary liability is to pay damages for breach; and that secondary liability is contractual.[21] Another sense is this. Suppose Anne and Brian are partners of a Scottish general partnership. They enter into a contract with ACME plc for the supply of a payroll system. The contract is entered into by Anne and Brian 'for and on behalf of the partnership'. Because a Scottish partnership is a juristic person,[22] it is the partnership that is primarily liable under the contract. But the partners of a partnership are jointly and severally liable for the firm's debts. The result, therefore, is that Anne and Brian are secondarily liable under the contract with ACME plc.

All for one and one for all: the private law of solidarity

8.15   There are three introductory general principles:

(a) In Scots law, 'joint' liability means that each debtor is liable, *pro rata*, for his own share. 'Several' liability, in contrast, means that each debtor is liable for the whole amount.[23] So if Jack and Jill are 'jointly' liable to Christine for £100, Jack is liable for £50 and Jill is liable for £50. Where Jack and Jill are 'severally' liable for £100, Christine can sue either Jack or Jill for £100. To confuse matters, the words 'joint' and 'several' are used in precisely opposite senses in English law.

(b) The most common form of liability, however, is 'joint and several'

---

21 It is in this sense that the distinction was tirelessly championed by Lord Diplock: see e.g. *Moschi v Lep Air Services Ltd* [1973] AC 331 at 350; *Photo Production Ltd v Securicor Transport Ltd* [1980] AC 827 at 848–50. But as Bernard Rudden has pointed out ('Correspondence' (1990) 10 Oxford Journal of Legal Studies 288) the primary-secondary distinction can be traced to R J Pothier, *Traité des Obligations* (1761) § 183.

22 See Chapters 1 and 5 above.

23 See generally W W McBryde, *The Law of Contract in Scotland* (3rd edn, 2007) para 11-01.

liability, otherwise known as liability *in solidum*. In short, obligants who are jointly and severally liable in this way (co-obligants) are potentially liable to the creditor for the full amount and liable among themselves *pro rata* (i.e. for his own share). So, again, if Jack and Jill are jointly and severally liable to Christine for £100. Christine can sue either Jack or Jill for the full £100. If she recovers £100 from, say, Jill, it is for Jill to seek relief from Jack for his share.

(c) Joint and several liability may arise either in contract or in delict, or where one debtor is liable in delict and the other in contract, providing the events contributed to producing the same legal wrong and loss.[24]

Solidarity among creditors

8.16 The law of joint and several creditors in Scots law is underdeveloped and it is not easy to find a concise statement of the law.[25] The statements in the international instruments provide a useful systematic benchmark of what the law ought to be in the absence of authority.[26] There are two relationships to be distinguished. The first is the relationship between the co-creditors and the debtor (the external relationship). The second is the relationship between the creditors *inter se* (the internal relationship). The law of solidarity is primarily concerned with the external relationship.

8.17 The general principles are best illustrated by examples. Suppose Primus, Secundus and Tertius own land in common. They sell the land to David for £90,000. The contract may provide that David shall pay each of them £30,000. Alternatively, the contract may provide that David's debt is owed to Primus, Secundus and Tertius *in solidum* (or, more commonly, 'jointly and severally'). In that case, David can choose which of the creditors to pay. Payment of the whole amount to any of the entitled creditors discharges David. A pure case of solidarity among creditors is found where creditors are trustees. Each trustee is empowered, in dealings with third parties, to discharge the debtor or assign the claim against the debtor without first obtaining the consent of the other trustees.[27] Another case is the joint bank account. Subject to the express terms on which the account is to be operated, the bank is discharged if it complies with an instruction from either of the account holders without reference to the other account holder's consent. In each of these

---

24 See the discussion in *Grunwald v Hughes* 1965 SLT 209 and *Ruddy v Chief Constable of Strathclyde Police* [2012] UKSC 57, 2013 SC (UKSC) 126 at para [33]. Cf. *Fleming v McGillivray* 1946 SC 1.

25 See e.g. Gloag, *Contract* (2nd edn, 1929) pp 202–04; McBryde, *Contract* (3rd edn, 2007) para 11-24. Cf. the curious entry for *Correi credendi* in *Trayner's Latin Maxims* (4th edn, 1894).

26 DCFR III.-4:201 to III.-4:207 and UNIDROIT Principles of International Commercial Contracts 2010 ('PICC') Art 11.2.1.

27 Trusts (Scotland) Act 1961, s 2.

cases, a single co-creditor who receives payment of the whole amount may be obliged to account for that money to his fellow creditors.

THE LAW OF TRIANGLES: RIGHTS OF RELIEF

General

8.18 Commercial contracts, we have seen, are often multilateral. But it is also common in commercial situations for complex contractual matrices to be formed by chains of multiple bilateral contracts. The interaction of these contracts, in determining which party bears the ultimate risk for a loss incurred, may be a matter of some complexity. A party who is primarily liable may have various bases for a right of relief against another party, which, in turn, may have a right of relief against another party still. And so on. For more than two thousand years, Lord Rodger of Earlsferry memorably pointed out, lawyers have been wrestling with questions of 'legal eternal triangles'.[28]

Legal bases for rights of relief

8.19 Commercial contracts are often about allocating risks. Where risks materialise and liability is incurred, there is a question of working out which party is ultimately liable. So the driver of a car who culpably injures another road user is primarily liable in delict to pay damages to the injured party. But in most cases the driver will have a right of relief against his insurers: although the driver is primarily liable *in delict* to the injured party, the insurer is primarily liable to the driver *in contract*.[29]

8.20 A right of relief may be based on an express contractual provision; on an implied contractual provision; in unjustified enrichment; in *negotiorum gestio*; in subrogation; or in express or implied assignation. Subrogation and assignation are dealt with in detail below.[30] Rights of relief based on contractual provisions are self-explanatory; difficulties arise not with express rights of relief, but with the express exclusion of a liability that would otherwise have formed the basis of an action for relief in the context of contribution.[31]

8.21 Both unjustified enrichment and *negotiorum gestio* may be taken together. Rights of relief arise in a three-party situation. So suppose Paula pays David's debt to Claire. David's debt having been discharged, Paula

---

28 *Heaton v Axa Equity Law Life Assurance Society plc* [2002] UKHL 15, [2002] 2 AC 329 at para [85].

29 There is a statutory right for someone injured by the insured driver of a motor vehicle to sue the insurer directly: European Communities (Rights against Insurers) Regulations 2002 (SI 2002/3061), reg 3.

30 See para **8.71** below.

31 See para **8.22** below.

has a claim against him in order to prevent David being unjustifiably enriched.[32]

Contribution

8.22 This doctrine is best illustrated by example. Suppose Nicola, while cycling to work along the Broomielaw, is hit by a car driven by Andrew. She is injured and sues Andrew for damages. Andrew's position, however, is that the accident was wholly or partially caused by the fault and negligence of Richard, whose careless driving required Andrew to take evasive action, as a result of which, says Andrew, he hit Nicola. Andrew can convene Richard as an additional defender to the civil action by way of a 'third party notice'.[33] Suppose, however, that, when Nicola's personal injuries action comes to court, Andrew has not (yet) been able to identify Richard. If Andrew has to pay the full amount to Nicola he (or his insurers) may subsequently seek contribution from Richard,[34] even in the event that the decree obtained by Nicola against Andrew was essentially of consent.[35]

8.23 So much for the simple example. In the commercial context, difficult questions can arise where the contracts regulating the parties' relationships contain indemnity, exclusion or limitation clauses.[36] Suppose a ship owner, Farstad Supply SA, sues Enviroco Ltd for damages incurred when Enviroco was engaged to clean Farstad's ship, with Farstad's negligence causing a fire. Enviroco argues that a third party, ASCO UK Ltd, was also at least partially responsible for the fire. ASCO chartered the ship from Farstad. In terms of the charterparty between Farstad and ASCO, Farstad indemnified ASCO for any losses or liabilities that ASCO might incur in relation to loss or damage caused to the vessel even as a result of ASCO's negligence. The question arises whether, despite the contractual provision in the charterparty, Enviroco can seek contribution from ASCO, leaving ASCO to obtain its relief from Farstad. Lord Hodge, in a judgment upheld by the Supreme Court, answers the question in the negative: a contractual arrangement entered into in good faith (prior to the loss or damage incurred), which

---

32 See generally H L MacQueen, 'Payment of another's debt' in D E L Johnston and R Zimmermann (eds) *Unjustified Enrichment: Key Issues in Comparative Perspective* (2002).

33 Rules of the Court of Session ('RCS') r 26.1; Ordinary Cause Rules ('OCR') r 20.1.

34 Law Reform (Miscellaneous Provisions) (Scotland) Act 1985, s 3.

35 *Comex Houlder Diving Ltd v Colne Fishing Co Ltd* 1987 SC (HL) 85. On the facts of that case, however, contribution was disallowed because the pursuer had paid pursuant to a foreign action which, the House of Lords held, was not covered by the 1985 Act.

36 The facts of this example are taken from *Farstad Supply A/S v Enviroco Ltd* [2008] CSOH 63, 2008 SLT 703, revd [2009] CSIH 35, 2009 SC 489, revd [2010] UKSC 18, 2010 SC (UKSC) 87. The commendably concise opinion of the Lord Ordinary, Lord Hodge, ultimately upheld in the Supreme Court, is the most lucid treatment of this difficult area.

excludes the liability of a party who has caused the loss (here ASCO) to the party who has suffered the loss (here Farstad), means that ASCO could not have been sued by Farstad. And, because ASCO could not have been sued by Farstad, Enviroco may not seek contribution from ASCO.[37]

PERFORMANCE BY PAYMENT[38]

Performance

8.24 Discharge of a contractual obligation normally involves a type of performance. What amounts to performance depends on the terms of the contract. A contract to build a tram system, for instance, is discharged by construction of the system. A contract for the sale of heritable property is discharged by delivery of a disposition which confers vacant possession.[39] In return for such a service or disposition, however, the builder or the seller, as the case may be, is entitled to payment. Payment obligations, at the risk of stating the obvious, are discharged by payment.[40]

Payment

8.25 Payment is normally conceived, by lawyers as well as laymen, to be in 'money'. But what is 'money'? Most cash is money but not all money is cash. Cash is of significance for day-to-day transactions between citizens and small businesses. But these transactions represent only a tiny fraction of what, in both law and economics, is considered to be 'money'. In 2010, notes and coins in circulation represented only 2.1 per cent of the total UK money supply.[41] Most money, in the commercial world, is invisible. For lawyers – especially in times of financial crisis – the law of money is a subject of considerable difficulty.[42] Today, the Bank of England refers to 'broad money' when speaking of the 'money supply'. In that context, the Bank of England's concept of money includes all sorts of important categories of money with which even the *Financial Times* subscriber may have rather limited familiarity.

8.26 For legal purposes, however, 'money' has a rather narrower meaning. A salary, a mortgage repayment, a dividend: each is rarely, if ever, paid in cash. Payments are effected rather by entries in bank accounts. Suppose a university employee is paid net of tax £2,000 in salary per month by her employer (the University). The employee, on

---

37 2008 SLT 703 at para [19] per Lord Hodge (Ordinary), approved 2010 SC (UKSC) 87 at paras [40] and [43] per Lord Hope of Craighead.

38 See further Chapter 9: Payment Obligations.

39 *Morris v Rae* [2012] UKSC 50, 2013 SC (UKSC) 106 at para [35] per Lord Reed.

40 See generally C Proctor (ed) *Goode on Payment Obligations in Commercial and Financial Transactions* (2nd edn, 2009).

41 R G Lipsey and K A Chrystal, *Economics* (12th edn, 2011) p 458.

42 See generally C Proctor (ed) *Mann on the Legal Aspect of Money* (7th edn, 2012).

working for a month, has a claim against the University for £2,000. In principle, the employee could ask to be paid in legal tender. But the usual practice is for the salary to be paid, net of tax, into a bank account. The employee's claim against the University is substituted for a claim against the employee's own bank (assuming the employee's bank account is in credit). Let us suppose too that the University's bank is RBS. The employee's bank is the Clydesdale Bank plc. The University would have effected the payment to the employee by instructing RBS to make a payment to the employee's bank, so there would have been a change in the debt relationship between the University and RBS. Then there would have been a change in the debt relationship between RBS and the Clydesdale; and then between the Clydesdale and the employee. No cash changes hands and, as a proportion of the funds that are transferred each day, cash payments comprise a very small proportion of daily payment operations.

8.27 As can be seen, in the modern world, the banking system plays a central role; so central, indeed, that the European Commission has proposed a Directive to confer on consumers a right to basic banking services.[43] The proposal is limited to consumers; juristic persons will have no such right.

In God we trust:[44] legal tender

8.28 A debtor is required to pay debts not in any old money, but in 'legal tender'.

> No creditor is bound to receive payment of a debt due to him by cheque or otherwise than in the current coin of the realm. A creditor may even refuse to accept Scottish bank-notes, and insist on his debtor bringing him current coin of the realm to the amount of his debt. Nevertheless, if he choose [sic] to accept these bank-notes in payment, I do not think it is capable of being disputed that he would be held, according to our law and practice, to have been paid in cash. In the same way, if he receives, although not bound to do so, a cheque from his debtor and gives him a receipt for the sum contained in the cheque, that is regarded as a payment in cash if the cheque is duly honoured, and the payment in cash is not at the date of the honouring of the cheque, but at the date of its receipt by the creditor.[45]

8.29 Not all 'cash' is legal tender. As Lord Young points out, only 'current coin of the realm' is legal tender. Banknotes, in Scotland, are not legal tender. Three Scottish banks have retained the note-issuing

---

43 EU Legislative Proposal COM/2013/0266 final – 2013/0139 (COD).
44 'In God we Trust', the unofficial motto of the United States of America, has adorned US coins since the 1860s and all federal reserve dollar bills since the 1960s. 'Legal tender' is defined in 31 US Code § 5103: 'United States coins and currency (including Federal reserve notes and circulating notes of Federal reserve banks and national banks) are legal tender for all debts, public charges, taxes, and dues.'
45 *Glasgow Pavilion Ltd v Motherwell* (1903) 6 F 116 at 119 per Lord Young.

function first conferred upon them in 1848. The present law relating to the issue of banknotes is found in the Banking Act 2009 and associated regulations.[46] Scottish banknotes are not legal tender in either Scotland or England. They are promissory notes.[47] English banknotes with a value of less than £5 are legal tender in Scotland.[48] But the only notes under £5 were £1 notes, and Bank of England £1 notes ceased to be legal tender in March 1988.[49] Silver and copper coins – i.e. those for denominations of under £1 – are legal tender, but only for a debt up to a maximum value of £18.20.[50]

8.30 Coins of £1 and £2 are legal tender for the payment of debts of any amount and, indeed, are the only currency units that are legal tender in Scots law for the payment of a commercial debt. Can a creditor in a commercial debt of millions of pounds require the debtor to pay in £1 and £2 coins? Or can a debtor require a creditor to accept a truck-load of coins? The short answer is that Lord Young's principle that a creditor is bound to accept only legal tender applies only where the parties have not otherwise agreed, expressly or impliedly, how 'payment' is to be effected. For debts which run into tens of thousands, never mind hundreds of millions, of pounds, the parties will always agree, expressly or impliedly, to payment in bank moneys, not in legal tender.[51]

Cheques

8.31 As Lord Young pointed out in *Glasgow Pavilion Ltd v Motherwell*,[52] the parties are free to agree that something other than legal tender will amount to 'payment'. It would be quite competent, for example, to provide that the 'current coin of the realm' is *not* acceptable as payment. And for commercial payments the only practical solution is a 'payment' by way of replacement of the principal debtor's obligation with another obligation, normally from a bank. The key point, however, is that, in the absence of agreement, the creditor is not bound to accept something other than legal tender.[53] Traditionally, one type of payment subject to a special rule was payment by cheque. The Scottish authorities were

---

46 Banking Act 2009, Part 6; and the Scottish and Northern Ireland Banknote Regulations 2009 (SI 2009/3056). These make important changes to the definitions of words like 'asset', 'property', 'sum' or 'fund' in Scottish insolvency legislation in the case of a bank insolvency.

47 Subject to special rules. So it is a criminal offence to deface a banknote: Currency and Bank Notes Act 1928, s 12.

48 Currency and Bank Notes Act 1954, s 1(2).

49 They remain redeemable as promissory notes at the Bank of England.

50 Coinage Act 1971, s 2(1A).

51 For full treatment of this difficult subject from an English and international perspective see Proctor *Legal Aspect of Money* (n 42).

52 (1903) 6 F 116 at 119.

53 *Child Maintenance and Enforcement Commission v Wilson* [2013] CSIH 95, 2014 SLT 46.

summarised – without acknowledgement – by Lord Reid in an English criminal appeal in this way:[54]

> Normally everyone who accepts a cheque in payment takes it in discharge of the debt. But in law, unless anything is said to the contrary, the discharge is presumed to be subject to a resolutive condition that if the cheque is dishonoured the discharge is void *ab initio*; the condition operates retrospectively so that the debt revives in its original form. I can illustrate the meaning of that by supposing that the debt carried interest. When the cheque for the principal sum and accrued interest is accepted, discharge of the obligation causes the interest to cease to accrue. But when the cheque is dishonoured and the debt for the principal sum revives, interest becomes payable for the period between the acceptance of the cheque and its dishonour so there is no question of the debt being deferred or suspended during the period between acceptance of the cheque and its presentation for payment.

8.32 It is worth mentioning too that domestic contracts may be denominated in foreign currencies – US dollars, Euros, Swiss francs etc – and it is possible to sue, before the Scottish courts, for the payment of a debt – or, indeed, for damages[55] – in a foreign currency.[56]

The basics of bank accounts

8.33 Most debts are paid not in cash, but through the banking system. The details of bank payments are considered below. This paragraph contains some introductory general principles relating to bank accounts. A bank account represents a debtor-creditor relationship.[57] So if John pays money into his bank, and John's account is in credit, the bank is John's debtor. Similarly, if John has an overdraft with his bank and his account is overdrawn, John is his bank's debtor. An instruction to a bank to pay a sum that exceeds either the amount standing to the account holder's credit or agreed borrowing facilities, may be treated at the banker's option as a request for an overdraft. An overdraft is a loan repayable on demand.

8.34 Working out whether the bank is a creditor or debtor, and whether the account holder is debtor or creditor, is important for matters such as the law of arrestment. For, under the law of arrestment, 'it may be

54 *DPP v Turner* [1974] AC 357 at 367–68. This reflects the position of Gloag, *Contract* (2nd edn, 1929) pp 272–73 and *Leggat Brothers v Gray* 1908 SC 67.

55 In *Fullemann v McInnes's Exrs* 1993 SLT 259, the Lord Ordinary (Cullen) calculated the damages due for personal injuries suffered by a Swiss tourist in Scotland, and awarded decree, in Swiss francs (the sum awarded was a record at the time). See further *The Despina R* [1979] AC 685.

56 See A F Rodger (later Lord Rodger of Earlsferry), 'The strange demise of *Hyslops v Gordon*' in A J Gamble (ed) *Obligations in Context: Essays in Honour of Professor D M Walker* (1990) p 1 and authority there cited; and P Beaumont and P McEleavy (eds) *Anton's Private International Law* (3rd edn, 2011) para 12.12.

57 Bank moneys, wrote an eighteenth-century Lord Advocate, 'in plain Scots, are Debts': Sir James Stuart, *Dirleton's doubts and questions in the law of Scotland, resolved and answered* (1715) p 68.

stated as a rule without exception, that the arrestment will be laid in the hands of the parties who would have been defenders in an action for payment of the sum arrested'.[58] In other words, an arrestment is served in the hands of the arrester's debtor's debtor.

8.35 The main characteristic of the current account is that sums are credited and debited. The private law principles of a current account relationship are not limited to bank accounts.[59] Suppose it becomes necessary to know, at a particular moment in time, what the state of the account is where there have been payments to account by the debtor and further advances by the creditor. The question can be particularly important where, for example, an insolvency event has occurred. According to the rule in *Clayton's Case*,[60] the presumption is that the earliest credit extinguishes the earliest debit.

8.36 The principle is illustrated by example. Suppose John carries on business as a farmer. In that business he has a running account with a supplier. John dies. At the date of his death, John was indebted to the supplier in the sum of £9,000. The supplier agrees to allow John's executor to carry on the business. Further supplies are required for the business after John's death, for which the supplier extends a further £3,000 of credit to the executor. After four years, the executor has paid some £10,000 to account. Had the debt owed by John's estate been discharged? If the principle in *Clayton's Case* applies, the answer would be yes. The additional £3,000 would remain to be paid by the executor. But it may be that the principle does not apply. The principle is merely a presumption. A debtor may indicate, when making payment, that the payment is to be attributed to a particular debt. The parties may expressly agree that a particular payment should be attributed to a particular debt. Or the creditor may appropriate the payment to a particular debt. Only where there is no such appropriation does the principle apply.[61] In a case on similar facts to the example given in this paragraph of John's executor, the court held that the presumption had been displaced.[62]

8.37 The decision of the Court of Appeal in *Re Yeovil Glove Co Ltd*[63] provides an example of the importance of the principle in modern commercial circumstances. But this decision is best discussed in the context of corporate insolvency.[64]

58 J Graham Stewart, *Diligence* (1898) p 38.
59 *McKinlay v Wilson* (1885) 13 R 210.
60 The actual case name is *Devaynes v Noble* (1816) 35 ER 781. For illuminating discussion and criticism of the rule in English law, see D Fox, *Property Rights in Money* (2008) paras 7.62–7.64 and 8.43–8.47.
61 *Hay & Co v Torbet* 1908 SC 781.
62 *Macdonald, Fraser & Co v Cairn's Exrx* 1932 SC 699.
63 [1965] Ch 148.
64 See para **14.92** below.

Payments through the banking system

8.38 Reference has already been made to the law of bank payments. The law relating to bank payments is mainly the law of interlinked mandates and payment orders. The law of bank payments is, therefore, to a large extent but a modern application of the basic principles of payment orders that have been around for millennia.[65] Much often turns on the particular wording of the contractual relationships under which cards are issued and payments processed.[66]

8.39 In addition, the common law in this area is now subject to the Payment Services Regulations 2009.[67] 'Payment services' include (a) direct debits, including one-off direct debits; (b) payment transactions executed through a payment card or a similar device; and (c) credit transfers, including standing orders.[68] It is not possible here to summarise these provisions. In practical terms, perhaps the most important provisions relate to 'unauthorised payment transactions'. Customers who become aware of unauthorised payment transactions are required to notify their bank without undue delay, and in any event no later than thirteen months after the debit date.[69] Failure to do so may mean they lose their rights to 'redress'.[70] But the customer remains entitled to redress, though he has not notified the bank, where the bank has failed to provide the customer with information about the transaction.[71] Importantly, where a customer alleges that a particular payment transaction was unauthorised, the onus is on the bank to demonstrate that the transaction was authorised.[72]

8.40 Where an executed payment transaction was not properly authorised,[73] the bank must immediately (a) refund the amount of the unauthorised payment transaction to the payer; and (b) where applicable, restore the debited payment account to the state it would have been in if the unauthorised payment transaction had not taken place.[74]

---

65 B Geva, *The Payment Order of Antiquity and the Middle Ages: a Legal History* (2011); R G Anderson, *Assignation* (2008) chapters 4 and 5; J S Rogers, *A History of the Law of Bills and Notes* (1995).

66 *Re Charge Card Services Ltd* [1987] Ch 150, affd [1989] Ch 497; *Mercedes-Benz Finance Ltd v Clydesdale Bank plc* 1997 SLT 905; *Duncan v American Express Services Europe Ltd* [2009] CSIH 1, 2009 SLT 112.

67 SI 2009/209 ('2009 Regs'), implementing EU Payment Services Directive 2007/64/EC. See generally H Beale (ed) *Chitty on Contracts* (31st edn, 2012) vol II, ch 34.

68 2009 Regs, Sch 1, para 1(c). The most obvious transaction excluded from the scope of the 2009 Regulations is where there is no bank involved: the payment for goods or services in physical cash: Sch 1, para 2(a).

69 2009 Regs, reg 59(1).

70 2009 Regs, regs 61, 75, 76 and 77.

71 2009 Regs, reg 59(2).

72 2009 Regs, reg 60. Cf. *Tidal Energy Ltd v Bank of Scotland plc* [2014] EWCA Civ 1107; a payer who inserts the wrong details on a CHAPS transfer form bears the risk of the funds arriving in the wrong account; there is no claim against the bank in negligence.

73 2009 Regs, reg 55.

74 2009 Regs, reg 61.

There are also specific provisions for payment transactions authorised by the payee.[75] The time limits for action where the payer alleges that the amount debited was not authorised is eight weeks.[76] There are various regulatory requirements for banks and other entities which issue 'electronic money'[77] to comply with, including capital adequacy requirements.[78]

DISCHARGE OF DEBTS

Express discharges

8.41 Most contractual obligations are discharged by performance. Take the example of the home owner, Jess. Jess obtains a loan for £100,000 payable over 20 years from Banca d'Italia. She grants the bank a standard security in 'all sums' terms. After 20 years she has repaid both capital and interest. On first principles, therefore, the security is now empty of all content: there is no principal debt for the security to secure. But because the security is in 'all sums' terms, Jess will wish an express discharge from the Bank of both her indebtedness and the security. In the case of all sums securities, discharge of a debt does not discharge the security; while discharge of the security alone only discharges the debt if the only basis for the debt was the undertaking contained in the security (as in a bond and floating charge[79] or a Form A standard security).[80] Discharge of a Form B standard security,[81] in contrast, discharges only the security: in principle, any outstanding personal obligation would remain undisturbed. In the case of standard securities, the 1970 Act provides a form of discharge for registration.[82] Discharges are also of relevance in the law of insolvency since the giving up of a valuable claim by a creditor, for no consideration, may amount to a gratuitous alienation.

---

75 2009 Regs, reg 58.

76 2009 Regs, reg 64.

77 Electronic Money Regulations 2011 (SI 2011/99) (implementing EU Electronic Money Directive (2009/110/EC) reg 2 defines 'electronic money' as meaning 'electronically (including magnetically) stored monetary value as represented by a claim on the electronic money issuer which—(a) is issued on receipt of funds for the purpose of making payment transactions; (b) is accepted by a person other than the electronic money issuer'. There are various exclusions in reg 3. Recital (7) of the Directive says: 'It is appropriate to introduce a clear definition of electronic money in order to make it technically neutral. That definition should cover all situations where the payment service provider issues a pre-paid stored value in exchange for funds, which can be used for payment purposes because it is accepted by third persons as a payment.' 'Funds' are defined in the 2009 Regulations to cover: 'banknotes and coins, scriptural money', and electronic money [defined in terms of the Electronic Money Directive, Art 2]'.

78 See 2011 Regs (n 77).

79 See n 14 above.

80 Conveyancing and Feudal Reform (Scotland) Act 1970, Sch 2. A Form A security contains both the security and the obligation to pay.

81 Which contains only the security; the obligation to pay is found elsewhere, normally in a separate document.

82 1970 Act, Sch 4.

Good faith payment

8.42 It sometimes happens that a debtor pays the wrong person. Suppose an individual takes out a life insurance policy. The proceeds are to be held by his testamentary trustees for the benefit of a dependent child. The insured dies. The trustees are all dead. Someone appears and claims the money from the insurance company. As the insurance company is checking the claimant's identity another person appears also claiming to be the person entitled to payment. The insurance company's obvious remedy is to raise a multiplepoinding:[83] a debtor in double distress or holding in a representative capacity with doubt about who is properly entitled to be paid, may raise an action and offer to consign the money into court – allowing the claimants to the fund (the fund *in medio*) to fight it out – and seek exoneration and discharge from the court.[84] But it is also a general principle that where a debtor makes payment,

> *bona fide* to him who had not the true right, but where there was another with a preferable right, which the defender neither did, nor was obliged to know: and therefore the law secures the payer, without prejudice to the pursuer to insist against the obtainer of the payment.[85]

8.43 Without a judicial process such as a multiplepoinding, however, a fund holder may have a practical difficulty in demonstrating that payment to the wrong creditor was made in good faith.

Prescription

8.44 A classic method by which obligations are discharged is as a result of the creditor doing nothing. Once the prescriptive period has elapsed the debtor's obligation is extinguished. There are two relevant periods: the short negative prescription (five years)[86] and the long negative prescription (20 years).[87] Most of the obligations referred to in this chapter are subject to the five-year prescription; only a few fall into the long negative prescription (such as the obligations arising from the issue of a bank note).[88]

Waiver

8.45 At common law, it may be possible to establish that a creditor, by its actions, must be taken to have waived its right to performance. Waiver may arise in two ways. The first is by facts from which the inference can be drawn that the creditor has abandoned his right. The debtor need not demonstrate that he has acted to his detriment in reliance upon

---

83 As in *Carmichael v Carmichael's Executrix* 1920 SC (HL) 195.
84 See Bell, *Commentaries* (7th edn, 1870) II, 277.
85 Stair, *Institutions*, IV.40.33; for further references, see R G Anderson, *Assignation* (2008) para 7-01.
86 Prescription and Limitation (Scotland) Act 1973, s 6 and Sch 1. The five-year period is sometimes known as the *quinquennium*.
87 1973 Act, s 7 and Sch 3.
88 1973 Act, Sch 1, para 2(b). For all this, see D E L Johnston, *Prescription and Limitation* (2nd edn, 2012).

the acts or omissions indicating abandonment.[89] The second is a type
of personal bar:[90] where the creditor has acted, or omitted to act, in such
a way as to allow it properly to 'be inferred . . . that the defenders were
abandoning their right, and whether the pursuers had acted in reliance
upon a belief induced by the conduct of the defenders'.[91]

NOVATION AND DELEGATION

8.46 Obligations, as has been seen, have a positive end (the creditor's
claim) and a negative end (the debtor's obligation). The circulation of
creditors' claims is considered below. The debtor's position under an
obligation cannot be transferred without the consent of the creditor.
Where the content of the obligation, between the original debtor and
creditor, is altered by consent, this is known as novation. An agreement
between A and B, that B's obligations will be performed by C, resulting
in B's discharge, is known as delegation. Case law has not yet admitted
the proper transfer of debts: that is to say that a debt undertaken by David
on day 1 to Caroline may be transferred – with Caroline's consent –
in order that Tony becomes the debtor in place of David under the obligation constituted on day one.[92] At present, if the transfer occurs on day
50, the law allows only David to undertake, on day 50, a new obligation.
Similarly, the law has not yet evolved to allow the transfer of whole contractual positions. Lawyers often speak of the assignation of 'contracts'.
But that expression is a shorthand for the assignation of the creditor's
claims and the discharge of the debtor's obligations in return for a transferee undertaking a new obligation. Sometimes certain 'transfers' of
positions under financial contracts are said to take place by way of
novation. These are discussed below.[93]

8.47 These principles can be important in business transfer cases.
Suppose Camus SA has a contract with Kafka GmbH to supply office
equipment on a monthly basis. Kafka GmbH's trading name in Scotland
is 'Metamorphosis'. Kafka GmbH sells its assets, including its business
name and contractual rights, to Stevenson Ltd. Stevenson Ltd carries on
the business as before. No notice of the transfer is given to Camus SA
which continues to supply the goods, as before, to the Metamorphosis
business premises in terms of the contract it has with Kafka GmbH.

89 *Presslie v Cochrane McGregor Group Ltd* 1996 SC 289 at 291 per Lord Morison.
90 See E C Reid and J Blackie, *Personal Bar* (2006).
91 *Lousada & Co Ltd v J E Lesser (Properties) Ltd* 1990 SC 178 at 189 per Lord
    Justice-Clerk Ross. Lord Hodge summarises the law in the context of a share
    purchase agreement in *McMullen Group Holdings Ltd v Harwood* [2011] CSOH 132,
    paras [69]–[76].
92 Rights and obligations are often transferred by statute, such as the Acts of
    Parliament used to restructure banks. There is legislation too for the restructuring
    of insurance businesses. And employment contracts may transfer in their entirety
    on the transfer of an undertaking: Transfer of Undertakings (Protection of
    Employment) Regulations 2006 (SI 2006/246).
93 See para **8.76** below.

Stevenson Ltd accepts the goods and pays for them. Stevenson Ltd then becomes insolvent. The question arises: who is Camus SA's debtor or debtors? There are at least two possibilities. One is that Kafka GmbH has been replaced by Stevenson Ltd, Stevenson Ltd in that case being known as an *exprommisor*. For that situation to arise, however, it would have been necessary for Camus SA to have consented to Kafka GmbH's discharge. An alternative analysis, and one favoured in recent case law, is that Stevenson Ltd is an *adprommisor*, an additional debtor. Camus SA can therefore sue either Kafka GmbH or Stevenson Ltd or both.[94]

CONFUSION

8.48 Confusion (sometimes also known in English as 'merger')[95] is a doctrine that operates on two levels. The first, and most common, effect relates to the creditor succeeding to the debtor's position in an obligation or the debtor succeeding to the creditor's position. This may happen by succession, as where a child is indebted to a parent; the parent dies; and the child inherits the parent's claim against the child. There are also many corporate examples, as where a company buys back its own shares[96] or bonds. The general principle of confusion of debtor and creditor, from which there are exceptions, is that confusion leads to discharge.

8.49 Finding clear statements of the law is not, however, easy. The DCFR position may thus be gratefully adopted: 'An obligation is extinguished if the same person becomes debtor and creditor in the same capacity.' The caveat about capacity relates to a case where, for instance, a sole trustee expends money from his private patrimony on trust affairs. The trustee is entitled to be reimbursed for his expenses from the trust estate. But there is only one legal person, the trustee. The claim is held by the trustee (in his private capacity) against himself (in his capacity as trustee).

8.50 The second level on which confusion may operate is that of creation of an obligation. Andrea cannot enter into a contract with herself. Again, there is an exception where Andrea is acting in different capacities. And it is quite common in the corporate sphere for single persons to act in all sorts of different capacities. Trusts have already been mentioned. Another example is the case of the one-(wo)man company: Andrea may be shareholder, director and creditor of the company. She may pass resolutions as shareholder; as director; or enter into a service contract, *qua* director, with the company, which requires her own express approval *qua* shareholder; or grant the company loans for which the company will grant her security.[97] In such circumstances it is impor-

---

94 *MRS Distribution Ltd v D S Smith (UK) Ltd* 2004 SLT 631.
95 As in DCFR III.-6:201.
96 See Companies Act 2006, s 690 ff.
97 See the facts of *Salomon v A Salomon & Co Ltd* [1897] AC 22, HL.

tant that good records are kept, essentially recording Andrea's own thought processes.[98]

SET-OFF

General

8.51 'Set-off' is not a term of art in Scots law, but it is a useful general expression covering various institutions each of which implement the same general principle. The principle is simple and, indeed, common sense. Suppose Alan owes Stéphanie £10,000. Stéphanie owes Alan £8,000. The various rules of set-off allow Alan, if required by Stéphanie to pay £10,000, to pay that debt in part by setting off Stéphanie's liability to Alan of £8,000. Alan is, in principle, bound to pay only £2,000.

Compensation

8.52 *Compensatio* is regulated by the Compensation Act 1592, which remains in force.[99] The Act provides (in its entirety):

> Oure soverane lord and estaitis of parliament statutis and ordanis that ony debt de liquido ad liquidum instantlie verifiet be wreit or aith of the partie befoir the geving of decreit be admittit be all jugis within this realme be way of exceptioun, bot not eftir the geving thairof in the suspensioun or in reductioun of the same decreit.

> [Our sovereign lord and estates of parliament statutes and ordains that any debt *de liquido ad liquidum* instantly verified by writing or oath of the party before decree be admitted by all judges within this realm by way of exception, but not after the giving thereof in the suspension or in reduction of the same decree].[100]

8.53 Most contract debts for a fixed amount are 'liquid' claims; a claim for damages, in contrast, is the classic illiquid claim. The 1592 Act applies only to liquid claims. There must be an element of mutuality of obligation between the parties in order for compensation to apply (there must be, to use the Latin, a *concursus debiti et crediti*). In the above example, for instance, there is mutuality of obligation between Alan and Stéphanie. But it would not be possible for Alan to seek to plead compensation because Stéphanie's sister happened to owe him money. If Alan assigns his claim against Stéphanie to Jack, Stéphanie can plead such defences she had against Alan (including compensation) up to the moment when she receives intimation of the assignation in favour of Jack.

---

98 See, for instance, *Neptune (Vehicle Washing Equipment) Ltd v Fitzgerald* [1996] Ch 274.

99 RPS 1592/4/83; APS III, 573, c 61.

100 In *Donaldson v Donaldson* (1852) 14 D 849 at 855, Lord Cunninghame described the Compensation Act as 'a just and positive statute, most creditable to the wisdom and sound views of the ancient Scottish legislature'.

8.54 A creditor must assert a plea of compensation and specify the debt to be compensated. Compensation does not occur automatically. Example:

> Suppose a Bank is indebted to A on account 1, but holds claims against A on accounts 2 and 3. The Bank holds security in respect of A's indebtedness on account 2. The indebtedness on account 3 is unsecured. In Scots law, the Bank can compensate its liability on account 1 against account 3, leaving only a secured balance. This is so even if there are competing creditors; in other words, the doctrine of catholic and secondary creditors[101] does not apply to compensation.

8.55 In some circumstances, the court retains an equitable discretion to allow an illiquid claim for damages to be pled in defence of an admitted debt, where the illiquid claim can be rapidly quantified.[102] A defence of compensation need not arise from the same or related contractual relationship out of which the pursuer seeks payment.[103] So claims on unrelated contracts may found compensation.

8.56 A defender cannot refuse a claim by compensating a claim the pursuer owes to the defender in a different capacity. So if Peter sues Paul for €100 but Peter is indebted to Paul for €100 in the latter's capacity as trustee for the Third Lanark Supporters' Trust, Paul cannot refuse payment. There is *concursus* of legal personalities, but no *concursus* of patrimonies.[104] This principle must not, however, be taken too far.

8.57 Take the truster-as-trustee trust. Suppose Hamburg Bank loans €10m to Alba Heritable Investments Limited. Alba has other current accounts in credit with the Bank to the tune of €5m. And suppose the Bank sues for payment of the €10m. All other things being equal, Alba could compensate that claim with its liquid counterclaim of €5m. The Bank cannot cut out that claim by declaring a trust of the claim to the €10m, at least where the declaration has not been intimated to Alba and Alba's counter-claims arose before intimation.[105] The interposition of a trust does, however, prevent compensation being pled in respect of claims which arise in Alba's favour against the Bank subsequent to notice of the declaration of trust.[106]

8.58 Similarly, compensation cannot be pled against a claim for repayment of a fund which has been specifically appropriated to a particular purpose; so, where a firm of accountants had collected debts owed to a company and held them in an account which the client company was

---

101 For which, see W M Gloag and J W Irvine, *The Law of Rights in Security, Heritable and Moveable including Cautionary Obligations* (1897) p 58 ff and para **8.83** below.

102 *Inveresk plc v Tullis Russell Papermakers Ltd* [2010] UKSC 19, 2010 SC (UKSC) 106 at paras [58], [71], [81], [89] and [107] per Lord Rodger.

103 *Turner v Inland Revenue Commissioners* 1994 SLT 811.

104 See para **1.11** above.

105 Cf. *Royal Insurance (UK) Ltd v Amec Construction (Scotland) Ltd* [2008] CSOH 107, 2008 SC 201.

106 Cf. *Johnston v Johnston* (1875) 2 R 986 at 997 per Lord President Inglis.

free to utilise, the firm could not seek to compensate against those funds its claim for payment of fees.[107] And where money on deposit with a bank is held in the name of A and B, the Bank cannot refuse to pay A on the basis of B's outstanding indebtedness.[108] Where, however, Alpha Ltd is in administration and the administrator sues a debtor, Bravo Ltd, Bravo Ltd may still plead compensation.[109]

8.59 Compensation is not automatic; it has to be pled and sustained in court: compensation, it has been said, is 'the operation of the judge rather than the law'.[110] Compensation cannot therefore be pled against a claim for payment that arises out of a document registered in the Books of Council and Session for execution: the effect of registration is the equivalent of a court decree.[111]

Contractual set-off

8.60 The careful draftsperson of a corporate or financial contract, however, does not wish to leave matters of mutual debit and credit to the vagaries of subsequent litigation. Contracts thus make bespoke provision for set-off. The principle of contractual set-off is so self-evident that it is not mentioned in any legal textbook.[112] The whole point of contractual set-off provisions is to entitle the parties to the contract to achieve the effects of compensation by declaration or notice or some other contractually specified procedure.

Insolvency set-off: 'balancing of accounts in bankruptcy'

8.61 The general principles of compensation are the subject of an equitable extension on insolvency:[113] this is the law of 'balancing of accounts in bankruptcy'.[114] On insolvency a debtor to the insolvent estate may withhold payment of its debt on the basis of a claim against the insolvent

---

107 *Mycroft, Petr* 1983 SLT 342; *Melville Dundas Ltd v Hotel Corporation of Edinburgh Ltd* [2006] CSOH 136, 2007 SC 12 at para [24]. See further G L Gretton, 'Scotland' in W Swaddling (ed) *The Quistclose Trust: Critical Essays* (2004) p 169 at p 172.

108 *Anderson v North of Scotland Bank* (1901) 4 F 49 at 55 per Lord McLaren.

109 This is important because, in terms of Insolvency Act 1986, Sch B1, para 4(6), the consent of the court or the administrator is required to institute legal proceedings against a company in administration. But there is nothing to stop a defender pleading compensation, or, indeed, balancing of accounts in bankruptcy, in defence to a claim brought by a company in administration.

110 Erskine, *Institute*, III.4.12. For the background, see R G Anderson, *Assignation* (2008) para 8-43 ff.

111 *McLaughlin, Petr* [2010] CSIH 24 at para [7]. This decision also deals with the important question of quantification of a claim due under a document of debt.

112 See R G Anderson, 'Security over bank accounts in Scots law' (2010) 4 Law and Financial Markets Review 593.

113 *Atlantic Engine Co (1920) Ltd (in liquidation) v Lord* Advocate 1955 SLT 17 at 20 per Lord President Cooper (Ordinary); *Secretary of State for Trade and Industry v Frid* [2004] UKHL 24, [2004] 2 AC 506 at para [32] per Lord Hope of Craighead.

114 The classic discussion is in Bell, *Commentaries* (7th edn) II, 118–20.

115 *Scott's Tr v Scott* (1887) 14 R 1043 at 1051 per Lord President Inglis.

estate that is neither liquid nor even presently due;[115] as long as the claim existed prior to insolvency (assuming the debt that the insolvency administrator seeks to recover is also a pre-insolvency debt). A claim that the proponer would otherwise be able to rank on the insolvent's estate is certainly covered.[116] But so too are defences that the defender would have had to any claim for payment made by the insolvent. Contingent claims are covered.[117] A balancing of accounts under Scots law, like compensation, must be asserted; it does not occur automatically.[118] The general principles of balancing of accounts apply also on corporate insolvency whether liquidation, receivership or administration.[119] The right can be invoked by an insolvent debtor as well as by a creditor against an insolvent debtor.[120] The general principles apply too on the insolvency of credit institutions, although within a special framework of provisions applicable to those institutions.[121]

Netting

8.62 'Netting' is the name for contractual set-off on a grand scale – millions of banking transactions that occur every day as a result of consumer purchases, mortgage payments, bank withdrawals and so on. In so far as these are carried out with bank money, cash rarely, if ever, moves. The payments are effected by multiple account entries between the respective banks of the parties. This is the process of 'netting'. The process is of fundamental importance to finance transactions on regulated market exchanges. Under the regulations, netting is defined thus:[122]

'netting' means the conversion into one net claim or obligation of different claims or obligations between participants resulting from the issue and receipt of transfer orders between them, whether on a bilateral or

116 *Secretary of State for Trade and Industry v Frid* [2004] 2 AC 506 at paras [32] and [34] per Lord Hope of Craighead.

117 W A Wilson, *The Scottish Law of Debt* (2nd edn, 1991) para 13.10 and authorities there cited.

118 *National Westminster Bank Ltd v Halesowen Presswork & Assemblies Ltd* [1972] AC 785 at 822D–G per Lord Kilbrandon.

119 *Integrated Building Services Engineering Consultants Ltd v Pihl UK Ltd* [2010] CSOH 80 at paras [21] and [34] per Lord Hodge (Ordinary), pointing out that Lord Hope of Craighead's *dicta* in *Melville Dundas Ltd v George Wimpey UK Ltd* [2007] UKHL 18, 2007 SC (HL) 116 at para [33], that a balancing of accounts is available only on bankruptcy or liquidation, were not intended to be definitive. See too *Joint Administrators of Connaught Partnerships Ltd (in administration) v Perth & Kinross Council* [2013] CSOH 149.

120 *Borthwick v Scottish Widows' Fund and Life Assurance Society* (1864) 2 M 595 at 599 per Lord Mackenzie (Ordinary).

121 *Joint Administrators of Heritable Bank plc (in administration) v Winding Up Board of Landsbanki Islands HF* [2011] CSIH 61, 2012 SC 209, affd [2013] UKSC 13, 2013 SC (UKSC) 201.

122 Financial Markets and Insolvency (Settlement Finality) Regulations 1999 (SI 1999/2979) reg 2(1), reflecting Settlement Finality Directive (1998/26/EC), Art 2(k).

multilateral basis and whether through the interposition of a clearing house, central counterparty or settlement agent or otherwise.

8.63 Netting may be by novation or by contract consolidation; by settlement, or by payment; or by 'close-out' netting:[123] the conversion of non-monetary obligations into money claims through the exercise of a right to cancel or close out transactions. Settlement or payment netting is not subject to the usual mandatory insolvency rules such as, for example, those that would normally prevent the holder of a collateral security from enforcing it where the security giver is in administration;[124] nor the rule that pre-insolvency debts cannot be set off against post-insolvency debts and vice versa.[125]

CIRCULATING CREDIT (AND ACCESSORY RIGHTS)

Assignation

8.64 Contracts are at least bilateral and many are multilateral. The creditor in any claim arising out of the contract (like most other creditors) is entitled to transfer his claim to performance without the consent of the debtor. The transferor is called the cedent or assignor; the transferee is the assignee. Transfer to the assignee occurs, however, only on intimation of the assignation to the debtor. Intimation must be in writing and, if it is to comply with the terms of the legislation,[126] should include a copy of at least the operative terms of the assignation and the cedent's signature.[127] It is likely that intimation will be abolished as a constitutive requirement for assignations.[128] But intimation is presently necessary, and intimation will remain important for practical purposes, such as to provide a cut-off date for the debtor's defences;[129] and to prevent the debtor paying the assignor in good faith, and thus destroying by performance the asset for which the assignee has paid good money.[130]

8.65 The general principle is that the debtor cannot be prejudiced by the assignation. A doctrinal reason for that general principle is that the assignee merely exercises the cedent's rights. This is the rule known as

---

123 See the Financial Collateral Arrangements (No 2) Regulations 2003 (SI 2003/3226), reg 3.
124 Settlement Finality Directive (1998/26/EC, as amended by 2009/44/EC), implemented in the UK by SI 1999/2979 (n 122), reg 13.
125 Settlement Finality Directive, Art 3(1) (as amended by 2009/44/EC).
126 Transmission of Moveable Property (Scotland) Act 1862, s 2.
127 Cf. R G Anderson, 'A strange notice' (2009) 13 Edin LR 484 (discussing *Christie Owen and Davies plc v Campbell* [2009] CSIH 26, 2009 SLT 518).
128 Scottish Law Commission, *Discussion Paper on Moveable Transactions* (2011).
129 See para **8.53** above.
130 Consumer Credit Act 1974, s 82A (implementing Consumer Credit Directive 2008/48/EC, Art 17), which required debtor notification of assignments of claims arising out of regulated agreements was repealed by the Financial Services and Markets Act 2000 (Regulated Activities) (Amendment) (No 2) Order 2013 (SI 2013/1881).

assignatus utitur iure auctoris. It is but a positive formulation of the well-known negative formulation much referred to in property law: *nemo dat quod non habet.*[131] As a result, the debtor can raise all defences against a claim by the assignee that he could have raised, prior to intimation, against the cedent. One important defence is that of compensation.[132] Generally speaking, contractual prohibitions on assignation render any assignation in breach of that prohibition ineffective.[133] As a general principle, and in the absence of any express provision to the contrary, the cedent warrants that the debt is due and owing at the date he grants the assignation, but not the debtor's solvency.[134] That principle does not apply where the assignation is gratuitous, or where the cedent is acting in a representative capacity, such as *qua* executor or *qua* trustee.

8.66 In commercial relationships there can also be the important question of accessory security rights such as standard securities and floating charges.[135] Assignation of securities is a specialised subject, of considerable practical importance. In short, the assignation of a standard security is effective only on registration in the Land Register;[136] an assignation of a floating charge is effective on intimation of the assignation to the debtor.[137] In the standard security case, however, intimation to the debtor remains a practical requirement.

8.67 Two examples demonstrate some of the issues that arise. Suppose Jim grants an all sums standard security to Maria but primarily in respect of a twenty-year term loan for £150,000. In year five, Maria decides she wishes to have the capital now, so she 'sells' her claim against Jim to Nina, who pays Maria £130,000 in consideration of an assignation of the claim and the security. The assignation is registered in the Land Register and intimated to Jim. Jim, however, needs additional finance. Nina is willing to make further advances to Jim of £50,000. One difficulty is that, in year three, Jim granted another all sums security to Fenster Finance LLP when he bought new double glazing for his flat in respect of a debt to Fenster of £25,000. Nina will make the further advance of £50,000 only if the further advance is covered by the first-ranking security.

8.68 There are two points to make. First, it is sometimes said that the assignation must specify the sum for which the standard security is

---

131 See para **3.92** ff above.
132 See para **8.53** above.
133 *Linden Gardens Trust Ltd v Lenesta Sludge Disposals Ltd* [1994] 1 AC 85, followed in *James Scott Ltd v Apollo Engineering Ltd* 2000 SC 228. This rule is amended for commercial contracts by the Small Business, Enterprise and Employment Bill 2014, cl 1.
134 This is known as 'warrandice *debitum subesse*': see *Reid v Barclay* (1879) 6 R 1007.
135 For a general outline, see paras **11.21** and **11.22** below.
136 Conveyancing and Feudal Reform (Scotland) Act 1970, s 14. For detailed discussion, see A J M Steven, 'Accessoriness and security over land' (2009) 13 Edin LR 387 and R G Anderson, *Assignation* (2008) ch 2.
137 *Libertas-Kommerz GmbH v Johnson* 1977 SC 191; see too *Joint Liquidators of Simclar (Ayrshire) Ltd v Simclar Group Ltd* [2011] CSOH 54, 2011 SLT 1131.

assigned with the consequence that the effect of assignation of an all
sums standard security is to crystallise the amount due under the security.[138] But the need to specify arises because it is possible, in principle,
(although rarely encountered in practice) for Maria to retain her all
sums security but assign part of a claim against Jim, say £50,000 with
part of the security, i.e. to the extent of £50,000.[139] But it is sufficient
specification, where an all sums security is to be assigned, to indicate
that the amount for which an all sums security is being assigned is for 'all
sums'.[140]

8.69   The second issue is whether the debtor's consent is required to the
assignation of a standard security. As a matter of general principle, the
whole point of assignation is that it is effective without the debtor's consent. And that general principle applies where there is a standard security granted in respect of the claim. It should be remembered too that
the granter of a standard security is not always the debtor in the obligation. So if Beth takes a loan for £100,000, it may be that her husband,
Peter, will grant a standard security limited to £100,000 over a property
he owns, but with no personal obligation on his part. Beth need not
consent; neither need Peter.

8.70   Suppose Mercedia Holdings Ltd has a *bond and floating charge*, for
all sums, from a subsidiary, Tochter Ltd. Tochter Ltd is to be acquired
by Acheteur Ltd: Acheteur Ltd will acquire all of the shares in Tochter
Ltd which are presently held by Mercedia Holdings Ltd. Tochter Ltd
already has considerable outstanding indebtedness to other creditors.
Acheteur Ltd thus proposes to take an assignation of Mercedia Holdings
Ltd's bond and floating charge. The bond and floating charge is in 'all
sums' terms. At the date of the proposed assignation, Tochter Ltd's
indebtedness to Mercedia Holdings Ltd is £10,000. Following the assignation, Acheteur Ltd proposes to invest some £500,000 by way of debt
in Tochter Ltd. The question arises whether that additional investment
is covered by the floating charge. The short answer appears to be that,
in principle, there being no rule of statute or common law to the contrary, the post-assignation investment is covered.

8.71   There are difficulties with the assignation of an *all sums standard
security* where the assignee wishes to make further advances.[141] But what-

---

138 The pioneering analysis of this difficult subject is G L Gretton, 'Assignation of all
        sums standard securities' 1994 SLT (News) 207.
139 These issues tend to arise when the transfer is implied as a result of the doctrine
        of catholic and secondary creditors (for which see para **8.74** below), or to effect a
        cautioner's relief (for which see para **8.18**): see R G Anderson and S Eden,
        'Transfer of preferences on payment' (2003) 7 Edin LR 398.
140 1970 Act, s 14(1) provides that the effect of registration of an assignation of a
        security is 'to vest the security in the assignee as effectually as if the security . . .
        had been granted in the assignee's favour'. Had an all sums security originally
        been granted in favour of an assignee for all sums, it would be effective to cover
        sums acquired by the original grantee by assignation.
141 The potential difficulties are set out by Gretton (n 138).

ever those difficulties may be, an all sums security – at the risk of stating the obvious – is an all sums security: there is thus nothing to prevent the secured creditor taking assignations of the unsecured claims held by other creditors, with the result that a claim originally unsecured becomes secured.

Cessio legis: subrogation

(a) Rights of relief and accessory securities

8.72 Where a cautioner pays the principal debtor's debt, the cautioner has a right of relief against the principal debtor.[142] The basis for the right of relief may be mandate, *negotiorum gestio*, unjustified enrichment, express assignation or *cessio legis*. In a number of European legal systems, *cessio legis* is a form of implied assignation: the cautioner who pays the principal debtor's creditor, for example, obtains, by virtue of the payment, an implied assignation of the creditor's claim. No document is required. The implied assignation is known as subrogation. In France, subrogation is much more common than assignation *(cession de créance)*, because subrogation is effective without intimation. In England, subrogation is today seen as a remedy for unjust enrichment. Traditionally the Scottish sources referred to the *beneficium cedendarum actionum*: this is sometimes seen as a right to demand an express assignation, sometimes as an implied assignation.[143] The English view, however, appears to be gaining some traction in Scotland.[144]

8.73 The difficulty with the English view based on enrichment of the cautioner, is that the enrichment arises only because the cautioner's debt has been discharged. But if the debt has been discharged, there is nothing to assign and, importantly, any accessory securities must have been discharged. Even if the security is non-accessory – as with the 'all sums' security – an assignation of it is pointless since, *ex hypothesi*, the claim it secured has been discharged. The underlying rationale for a true *cessio legis*, therefore, is to provide a doctrinal basis for explaining why the payer's right of relief extends to securities.[145] On the *cessio legis* analysis, therefore, on payment of another's debt, the payer is considered to have bought the creditor's rights against the principal debtor; the claim, with accessory securities, is transferred, not discharged.[146]

---

142 See para **8.18** ff above.

143 The implied assignation cases are found, in particular, in relation to the doctrine of 'catholic and secondary creditors': para **8.81** below.

144 *Joint Liquidators of Simclar (Ayrshire) Ltd v Simclar Group Ltd* [2011] CSOH 54, 2011 SLT 1131, especially at para [34].

145 See Anderson and Eden (n 139) and authority there cited.

146 *Caledonia North Sea Ltd v London Bridge Engineering Ltd* 2000 SLT 1123 at 1140 per Lord President Rodger (affd 2002 SC (HL) 117).

(b) Insurance

8.74   But otherwise, in the most important practical case – insurance –
the English law of subrogation in the case of payments by an insurer has
been adopted into Scots law,[147] and the First Division has expressly, if
improbably, held that subrogation is not a species of assignation.[148] This
development has been unfortunate since the English law had developed
in its own peculiar way as a result of curious historical features, the most
important of which is that the idea of assignment was not properly
recognised at law until 1875; and, to this day, English law still does not
recognise, at law, the assignment of part of a claim.

8.75   The idea of subrogation in modern insurance law can be illustrated by an example. Suppose Alan takes out a policy of home and
contents insurance with ACME Insurance SA. On Friday, he has a
plumber visit to fix his radiators. On Sunday, Alan goes on holiday for a
week. When he returns his whole house has been flooded. Alan claims
on his insurance policy with ACME. ACME indemnify Alan for his
losses which, it turns out, were caused by the fault and negligence of the
plumber. Having paid Alan, ACME has a right to sue the plumber for
negligence. Importantly, the insurer *must* bring the claim in Alan's
name.[149] The consequence of obtaining a decree in Alan's name where,
in the interim, Alan has become insolvent is unclear.

Obligations: novation and delegation

8.76   Only rights or claims, and not liabilities, may be assigned. Assignation is effective without the debtor's consent. Where a *debtor* wishes to
effect a transfer of a *liability*, however, this can occur only with the creditor's consent. There are two functional ways in which this can be done.
The first is by novation or delegation (their effects are similar). The
second is by 'transfer of a contractual position'.

8.77   First, novation. In financial practice, novations are just as
common as assignations. The whole law of syndicated lending, for instance, presupposes that the banks participating in the nominal lender's
position, after the funds have been advanced, will change. The market
standard documentation (written under English law) refers to transfers
by novation. Novation is used because it is often the case that even the

---

147   This development may be traced to the decision in *Simpson & Co v Thomson*
        (1877) 5 R (HL) 40. In 1840, however, the Whole Court, in *Sligo v Menzies* (1840)
        2 D 1478 at 1490–91 had held that the rights of a cautioner in Scots law, including
        the right to be subrogated to the creditor's position, were accurately expressed
        by the terms of the French *Code civil* (opinion of Lord Mackenzie, with which the
        Lord President, Lord Fullerton, Lord Jeffrey and Lord Murray concurred).

148   *Esso Petroleum Co Ltd v Hall Russell & Co Ltd* 1988 SLT 33 at 43D–E per Lord
        President Emslie (affd 1988 SLT 874 (HL)).

149   *Esso Petroleum Co Ltd v Hall Russell & Co Ltd* 1988 SLT 874 (HL) at 878H per Lord
        Goff, followed in *Caledonia North Sea Ltd v London Bridge Engineering Ltd* (n 146).
        Lord Bingham's speech in *Caledonia North Sea* must be read subject to the
        correction at 2003 SLT (News) 295.

lenders have obligations under the contract which they would wish to transfer. For a valid novation, it will be recalled, the consent of the debtor – in the case of a loan, the borrower – is required. In most syndicated loan contracts, however, the borrower will consent in advance to 'transfers by novation' of the positions of other parties to the loan or other structured finance agreement, even if that involves those parties effectively 'transferring' their obligations.[150] 'Transfer by novation' is sometimes also encountered in relation to the transfer of company shares. In private companies, shares are transferable only with the consent of the directors of the company in which the shares are held. Where the shares are certificated, transfer of the share involves cancellation of the transferor's certificate and the re-issue of a new share certificate to the transferee. This procedure is described in standard English works as 'transfer by novation'.[151]

8.78 As has been seen,[152] subject to the terms of the parties' agreement, the effect of a novation is to discharge the original obligation and replace it with a new obligation. There is no reason in principle, however, why the law should not admit the transfer of full contractual positions, without the need for the formality of discharge and constitution, providing the original parties to the contract, together with the proposed transferee, all consent.[153]

Selling debt

8.79 In the same way that there may be a contract to acquire the real right of ownership of land, parties to a commercial transaction can contract to acquire personal claims, such as receivables. Receivables are what, in a corporate balance sheet, is recorded under the heading 'debtors'. The moneys owed to the company by those debtors represent assets. Suppose, then, Utopia SA seeks to raise finance by 'selling' its receivables to Caledonia Bank Ltd. The parties enter into a contract of sale. Caledonia Bank Ltd agrees to purchase and Utopia SA agrees to sell, a specified portfolio of receivables. The effect of the sale agreement is to give Caledonia Bank Ltd a personal right under the purchase agreement to transfer of Utopia SA's personal rights against its debtors: Caledonia Bank Ltd has a personal right to personal rights. Whether Caledonia Bank Ltd, in fact, ever seeks transfer of the receivables by inti-

---

150 See e.g. *The Argo Fund Ltd v Essar Steel Ltd* [2006] EWHC 600 (Comm), [2006] 1 All ER (Comm) 56; *Habibsons Bank Ltd v Standard Chartered Bank (Hong Kong) Ltd* [2010] EWCA Civ 1335, [2011] QB 943; *McKillen v Maybourne Finance Ltd* [2012] EWCA Civ 864.

151 L Gullifer, *Goode's Law of Credit and Security* (4th edn, 2008) para 3-03 also admits the 'mortgage by novation'.

152 See para **8.46** above.

153 The idea is recognised in both Art 9.3 ff PICC (n 26 above) and DCFR III.-5:302. These provisions apply *mutatis mutandis* the principles of transfer of obligations whereby the transferee becomes an additional rather than a substitute debtor unless the original debtor is discharged.

mated assignation is a matter for Caledonia Bank Ltd. Until Caledonia Bank Ltd intimates an assignation it is at risk of Utopia SA's insolvency. There are a number of markets for receivables financing depending on which party bears the risk of non-payment.[154]

Securitisation

8.80 Securitisation is often complex[155] but the basic underlying legal concepts are not. Securitisation involves the sale of a portfolio of receivables to a corporate vehicle specially incorporated for the purpose ('SPV'). The SPV pays for the portfolio by issuing financial instruments on the capital markets, using the proceeds of the issue to fund the purchase and/or ring-fencing the asset pool.[156] The originator (the Bank) gets a large capital sum today on a portfolio of loans that may have a term of 25 years. The SPV obtains the rights to payment under the original loan contracts and uses those repayments to service its own obligations to the holders of the financial instruments it has issued. And the holders of the instruments are, in theory, able to secure an investment in a particular asset which they consider desirable.

8.81 Nonetheless, despite the simplicity of the basic legal structure, the elaborate corporate structures and documentation involved can give rise to all sorts of intricate legal questions, which go well beyond the scope of this chapter.[157] The sale of the receivables under Scots law is problematic because intimation remains a constitutive requirement for a completed assignation. If a portfolio of receivables comprises tens of thousands of loans, it is not practicable to intimate the sale to the debtors under each individual loan, not least because the income streams are to continue to be paid to the originator. In practice, therefore, the standard Scots law structure is for the originator to declare a trust over the portfolio in question in favour of the SPV.[158]

Financial collateral

8.82 National law on concepts such as assignation must, however, yield to principles applicable to transnational financial markets where finan-

---

154 See H Beale et al (eds) *The Law of Security and Title-Based Financing* (2nd edn, 2012) paras 7.100–7.129.

155 *Re Sigma Finance Corporation (in administration)* [2009] UKSC 2, [2010] 1 All ER 571 did not concern a securitisation, but provides for the student a useful insight into the voluminous nature of structured finance documentation.

156 See the Regulated Covered Bonds Regulations 2008 (SI 2008/346) as amended for a regulated securitisation structure sometimes employed by banks. There are other securitisation structures that are not encompassed by this regulatory regime.

157 A flavour of the documentation can be found in *Citibank NA, MBIA Assurance SA v QVT Financial LP* [2007] EWCA Civ 11. For a helpful overview, see Beale (n 154) paras 7.130–7.139.

158 See discussion at para **11.90** below.

cial assets are involved. The Financial Collateral Regulations[159] apply to such arrangements where the parties choose to invoke the regime. The Regulations implement for the UK the EU Financial Collateral Directive.[160] Neither the Directive nor the Regulations are easy to understand.[161] Financial collateral means 'financial instruments', 'cash' or 'credit claims'. The key concepts are 'control' and 'appropriation'. The idea of the Directive is to allow financial collateral arrangements – such as re-purchase agreements – to have effect according to the terms without disruption from local EU laws of insolvency or set-off.

CATHOLIC AND SECONDARY CREDITORS[162]

8.83 Gloag and Irvine's classic description of this curiously named doctrine is this:[163]

> Where a party has granted to one creditor a right in security over two or more objects, and to another creditor a postponed right over one of such objects, these rights are known as catholic and secondary securities, and the holders thereof as catholic and secondary creditors. The rules which regulate the rights of parties holding this relation are the same, whether the objects of security are all heritable, or partly heritable and partly moveable.

8.84 Suppose Delta Ltd is indebted to each of the Caledonian Bank and the Bank d'Ecosse. The Caledonian Bank has a first-ranking standard security over Delta Ltd's retail premises. The Bank d'Ecosse has a second-ranking standard security over the same property. The Caledonian Bank also has a first-ranking standard security over the company's warehouse. Generally speaking a secured creditor can exercise his rights in any manner he chooses to facilitate the recovery of his debt. But where the effect of his course of action would be to prejudice the secondary creditor's rights, e.g. by first exhausting the estate over which there is a secondary security so as to render the secondary creditor's rights worthless, then the *beneficium cedendarum* operates in favour of the secondary creditor.

8.85 In our example, therefore, the Caledonian Bank must first seek to recover its debt out of a sale of the warehouse. Only once the warehouse has been sold and indebtedness of Delta remains outstanding, can

159 Financial Collateral Arrangements (No 2) Regulations 2003.
160 Financial Collateral Directive 2002/47/EC (as amended).
161 See generally G L Gretton, 'Financial collateral and the fundamentals of secured transactions' (2006) 10 Edin LR 209. The main appellate consideration of the Regulations has been in two appeals from the British Virgin Islands to the Privy Council: *Cukurova Finance International Ltd v Alfa Telecom Turkey Ltd* [2009] UKPC 19, [2009] 3 All ER 840 and [2013] UKPC 2 and discussion in Beale (n 154), ch 3.
162 See generally Bell, *Commentaries* (7th edn, 1870), II, 417; Gloag and Irvine, *Rights in Security* p 61.
163 Gloag and Irvine, p 58. Where Gloag wrote 'subjects' I have replaced it with 'objects'.

the Caledonian Bank seek to enforce the standard security against the retail premises. In the event that the Caledonian Bank attempts to enforce against the retail premises, the secondary creditor, the Bank d'Ecosse, has the *beneficium cedendarum actionum* with respect to the 'catholic' security, (here the standard security over the warehouse), in so far as the catholic creditor (here Caledonian Bank) has not exhausted the proceeds in discharge of Delta's outstanding indebtedness to the Caledonian Bank. The right arises in favour of the secondary creditor from the date that the catholic security is constituted:

> [the right] did not come first into existence when the catholic creditor proceeded to sell. It existed from the date of completion of the security, although its operation was suspended till there could be occasion to act on it. It was a right all along vested in the secondary creditor, that, whenever the catholic creditor should proceed to sell, the secondary creditor might require him to respect his interests, so far as not injurious to himself.[164]

8.86 Importantly, the right in favour of the secondary creditor is not merely to demand an assignation of the security from the catholic creditor, it operates *ex lege* as an assignation of both the debt and the security:

> Nor is actual assignation by the catholic creditor indispensable for the protection of the secondary creditor, for the law implies it, and would give effect to it in any process of distribution. That is clear, and is the simple doctrine as between the catholic and secondary creditors themselves.[165]

8.87 The doctrine of catholic and secondary creditors applies to all rights in security,[166] except floating charges.[167]

---

164 *Littlejohn v Black* (1855) 18 D 207 at 227 per Lord Deas. *Littlejohn* was cited with approval in *Szepietowski v National Crime Agency* [2013] UKSC 65, [2014] AC 338 at paras [81]–[84] per Lord Reed.
165 *Littlejohn v Black* at 218 per Lord Ivory. This passage is cited by Gloag and Irvine, p 61 for the proposition that: 'Such an assignation will be assumed in any process for the distribution of the balance remaining after the catholic debt is paid.'
166 See Chapter 11: Non-Judicial Real Security.
167 *Forth & Clyde Construction Co Ltd v Trinity Timber Plywood Co Ltd* 1984 SC 1. For application of the doctrine to the landlord's hypothec, see *Butter v Sir James Riddel* (1790–92) Bell's Octavo Cases 154.

Chapter 9

Payment Obligations

9.01 This chapter deals with the concept of payment and introduces the fundamental distinction between payment made in discharge of money obligations and different forms of payment promise. The focus is on negotiable instruments and, in particular, on bills of exchange where the (intangible) right to payment is embodied in a tangible instrument. Students often find the law of negotiable instruments to be a set of dry, arcane and technical rules and question its relevance in commercial practice. It is the aim of this chapter to contribute to the understanding of its intricate contents and to clarify its (historical and) current commercial significance.

INTRODUCTION

9.02 Payment is essentially an act accepted in performance of money obligations. It is the outcome of a claim for debt, for a definite sum of money established in an agreement between the parties in return for the performance of an obligation by one party to the other. All issues relating to payment depend on the terms of the obligations originally undertaken as amended/discharged according to subsequent mutual agreement by the parties.[1]

9.03 There are different ways in which a payment can be made and in the United Kingdom the Payment Council has identified the following: cash, cheque, direct debit, direct credit, mobile payment, cards, and wholesale interbank transfer.[2] With the exception of cash, various highly technical (statutory, contractual and market) rules govern the creation, processing, clearing and settlement of the payment instructions. An introductory discussion of payment methodologies or even a detour on the structure of clearing and settlement of payment is a complex exercise that exceeds the scope of this chapter.

9.04 This chapter will rather highlight the distinction between payment and the acceptance of a payment promise and, in particular, the acceptance of a payment promise represented by a negotiable instru-

---

1 See Chapter 2: General Principles of Contract.
2 National Payments Plan (2011): www.paymentscouncil.org.uk/files/ payments_council/pc_npp_report_2011_final-pdf.pdf

ment. While it is the layman's view to characterise the transaction where the debtor gives his creditor a negotiable instrument as a 'payment' of the debt, a distinction has to be drawn from payment made in discharge of money obligations. This is because, in the case of a negotiable instrument, there is technically only a payment promise and the creditor is not allowed to sue the debtor until the maturity of the instrument:[3] as will be clarified in the sections below, even if the creditor has taken the negotiable instrument the original debt still exists and his right on the underlying obligation is preserved.

9.05 This chapter is structured as follows. First, it considers the legal nature and peculiar elements of negotiable instruments, explaining the relevance of the historical and comparative perspective in understanding the current legal framework, commercial advantages and future use. Second, it addresses the legal nature, modes of circulation, liabilities and ways of enforcement of some of the most relevant types of negotiable instruments. Particular attention is focused on the bill of exchange, as its regulation provides a set of default rules that apply to most negotiable instruments. Reference is also made to other widely used types of negotiable instruments and in particular to cheques, promissory notes, bankers' drafts and travellers' cheques.

NEGOTIABLE INSTRUMENTS

Nature and essential characteristics

9.06 A negotiable instrument is a document that embodies a monetary obligation capable of being transferred by endorsement and delivery, free from defects in the title of prior parties. In essence, with a negotiable instrument an undertaking to pay a sum of money[4] or an order to pay a sum of money to the person giving the order or to a third person[5] are locked up in a document,[6] which remains distinct from the obligation that determined the issuance of the instrument. This is different from other documents commonly employed for commerce where physical possession does not confer ownership rights on the embodied obligation, nor does it involve any entitlement to claim money.[7]

9.07 In the absence of an *ad hoc* statutory definition of negotiable instruments, three fundamental features can be singled out from the common law, as shaped by the evolution of medieval mercantile custom and usage:

---

3 I.e. the payment is therefore 'conditional' until the instrument is due.
4 E.g. promissory note. See para **9.48** below.
5 E.g. bill of exchange. See para **9.24** below.
6 A mere receipt for money is not a negotiable instrument: see *Akbar Khan v Attar Singh* [1936] 2 All ER 545 (PC).
7 E.g. bill of lading, which is a document of title to goods carried as cargo: see *Simmons v London Joint Stock Bank* [1891] 1 Ch 270.

(a) The possession of the document confers on the holder[8] the right of action, the 'right to sue in his own name on the contract':[9] there is no need for the holder to join the original parties of the embodied monetary obligation to any proceedings.

(b) As the contractual right itself does not exist independently of the document, the modes of circulation are different (and surely less cumbersome) from the contractual rules on assignation.[10] When the instrument is payable to the bearer, it can be transferred by mere delivery. When it is payable to order, transfer is effected by its holder's indorsement, followed by delivery.

(c) In contrast to the rights acquired by an assignee under a contract, the delivery of the instrument (when complete and regular on its face) to a purchaser in good faith and for value confers on the transferee 'a right of action better than the right of him under whom he derives title'.[11] More accurately, the *bona fide* holder for value transferee acquires good title to the document and to the embodied rights, notwithstanding any defect in title of the party[12] from whom he took it.[13]

9.08 It follows from the above that a negotiable instrument enjoys a dual nature: it is a specific item of property capable of being possessed, transferred and destroyed like any other moveable, but it also resembles an obligation, as it embodies an autonomous contractual right to pay a certain sum of money enforceable by the holder of the document in his own name. The explanation for this is rooted in the evolution of commercial law as shaped by merchant practice in England. Negotiable instruments are not in fact a peculiar feature of Scottish law and the driver for their original reception is largely ascribable to the need to circumvent the prohibition on assignment of *choses* in action[14] at

---

8 I.e. the payee, the indorsee or the bearer of the instrument, as defined in the Bills of Exchange Act 1882 ('BoEA'), s 2.

9 *Crouch v Credit Foncier of England* (1873) 8 QB 374 (CA) at 382 per Blackburn J.

10 I.e there is no need for intimation to the debtor for the assignee to acquire a preferential right of payment: see *Connal & Co v Loder* (1868) 6 M 1095 at 1102 per Lord Neaves; *Grigor Allan v Urquhart* (1887) 15 R 56.

11 *Dixon v Bovill* (1856) 3 Macq 1 at 16 per Lord Cranworth.

12 This is different from the contractual rule *assignatus utitur jure auctoris* according to which the transferee does not acquire better rights than his transferor: see *Buist v Scottish Equitable Life Assurance Society* (1878) 5 R (HL) 64.

13 *Whistler v Forster* (1863) 14 CBNS 248 at 257 per Willes J. In general, see D V Cowen, *The Law of Negotiable Instruments in South Africa* (5th edn, Juta, 1985) p 52.

14 Under English law, a *chose* in action (a *chose* being a French word meaning 'thing') 'describes all personal rights of property which can only be claimed or enforced by action, and not by taking physical possession': *Torkington v Magee* [1902] 2 KB 427 at 439 per Channell J.

common law.[15] In *Picker v London & County Banking Co Ltd*, Bowen LJ clearly stated that 'at common law in general a *chose* in action is not transferable. Therefore, the right of action can only pass by delivery of the instrument where the instrument is negotiable or clothed by statute with the attributes of a negotiable instrument.'[16] This has never been the case in Scotland where in principle all personal rights have always been capable of transfer,[17] unless assignation was expressly prohibited.[18]

9.09   To sum up with a definition approved by the authorities, where an instrument is:

> 'by the custom of the trade transferable like cash, by delivery, and is also capable of being sued upon by the person holding it *pro tempore*, it is entitled to the name of a *negotiable instrument*, and the property in it passes to a *bona fide* transferee for value, though the transfer may not have taken place in the market overt.[19] But that if either of the above requisites be wanting i.e., if it be either not accustomably transferable, or, though it be accustomably transferable, yet if its nature be such as to render it incapable of being put in suit by party holding it *pro tempore*, it is not a *negotiable instrument*, nor will delivery of it pass the property of it to a vendee, however *bona fide*, if the transferor himself have not a good title to it, and the transfer be made out of market overt.'[20]

9.10   The law on negotiable instruments is today primarily regulated under the Bills of Exchange Act 1882 ('BoEA') and, to a limited extent, by the Cheques Act 1957 and associated case law. Quite interestingly, even if the very title of the BoEA refers to a negotiable instrument rarely used in inland trade, cheques, share warrants and debentures – probably among the most common negotiable instruments in commer-

---

15 Historically, at common law the general rule was that a *chose* in action could not be assigned or otherwise transferred as the right to bring a personal action enforcing a right was founded on the personal relationship between obligor and obligee and in order to prevent the maintenance of actions (i.e. the possible oppression of the obligor by an assignee more powerful than the obligee). See M Smith and N Leslie, *The Law of Assignment* (2nd edn, 2013) pp 208–16.

16 (1887) 18 QBD 515 (CA) at 519. See also *Master v Miller* (1791) 4 TR 320 at 340 per Buller J.

17 Erskine, *Institute* III, 5, 2: 'The general rule is, that whoever is in the right of any subject, though it should not bear to assignees, may at pleasure convey it to another, except where he is barred either by the nature of the subject or by immemorial custom.'

18 E.g. rights strictly personal into which an element of *delectus personae* enters as in the case of rights which are alimentary by nature. See R G Anderson, *Assignation* (2008) p 238.

19 I.e. on an open market. The doctrine of market overt provided that sale of goods made on an open market was binding not only on the parties involved, but also on third parties. According to the Sale of Goods Act 1979, s 22(1) (repealed in 1994), the purchaser in good faith of stolen goods in market overt acquired a valid title against the true owner.

20 J W Smith, *A Selection of Leading Cases on Various Branches of the Law* (Maxwell, 1837) p 259, cited with approval by Blackburn J in *Crouch v Credit Foncier of England* (1873) LR 8 QB 374 (CA) at 381.

cial practice – can only be understood with some knowledge of the provisions on bills of exchange. This explains why the law of negotiable instruments is still largely dominated by the study of bills of exchange and it explains the space in this chapter dedicated to the analysis of this particular instrument.

Historical evolution

9.11 It is generally agreed among historians that negotiable instruments originated and developed in the thirteenth century from a variation of certain Italian notarial exchange contracts and the contract of *cambium*, as effected under the machinery of the bill of exchange (the *tratta*).[21] In essence, the *tratta* consisted of an instrument specifically devised by the 'sedentary merchants' for long distance trade in order to obviate the risk of the physical transport of money from one fair to another or from one country to another.[22] According to medieval commercial practice, in its infancy the *tratta* involved four parties, as it was easier for creditors who wished to collect, and debtors who wished to pay, to appoint exchangers to do it for them.[23] The letter was 'addressed by B [the drawer – often an exchanger[24]] to C [the drawee/acceptor – often an exchanger], asking C to pay to a third person D [the payee] a sum of money, which A [the payer] has entrusted to B for this purpose. This letter is handed by B to A, who sends it on to D; and D presents it for payment to C'.[25] Briefly, the instrument provided that the drawee (C) who had accepted the bill was bound to the instruction of the drawer (B) and the payee (D) could sue the drawee to recover his property.

9.12 From the picture above, it should be clear that some of the peculiar characteristics of the current forms of negotiable instruments were not yet present in the earlier schemes. Namely:

(a) the payee (D) could not assign his rights under the bill to a third party;

(b) the drawee (C), even if he had accepted the bill, could successfully plead the fact that he had not received funds from the drawer (B) as a defence against the payee (D); and, above all,

(c) the drawee (C) could exploit any other defence against the payee which could have been adopted by the drawer.

---

21 See R De Roover, *L'Evolution de la Lettre de Change XIV–XVIII siècles* (Librairie Armand Colin Paris, 1953).

22 See N S Gras, *Business and Capitalism, an Introduction to Economic History* (FS Crofts, New York, 1939) pp 37–44.

23 In general, see E Jenks, 'The early history of negotiable instruments' (1893) LQR 70 at 74.

24 I.e. a merchant engaged in the business of paying out one currency in exchange for an equivalent amount of another, charging a commission for the service.

25 W S Holdsworth, *A History of English Law* (Methuen & Co, 1925) vol VIII p 131.

The *tratta*, in its infancy, was therefore a letter of payment, a mandate by a written command to pay.[26] That the *tratta* at that stage possessed full negotiability is largely a myth. It was freely transferable, but not negotiable, as it did not protect a *bona fide* acquirer for value of the instrument (the 'holder in due course'[27]) in the absence of title in his author.

9.13 The *tratta* was occasionally received in British mercantile practice as early as the fourteenth century, but it was not until about the middle of the fifteenth century that instruments similar to the bills of exchange were used by English merchants.[28] The need in Britain for an instrument suited to the settlement of foreign accounts, such as the bill of exchange, was primarily determined in the fifteenth century by the unprecedented growth of foreign trade. When English merchants became the principal dealers in commodities (wool and cloth exports), they found a very efficient and reliable model already existing in international market practice. Hence, when they became the principal dealers in exchanges, they imported the scheme of the bill of exchange adopted by the Italian banking houses.[29]

9.14 Negotiability developed in Britain only at the end of the eighteenth century, probably in response to the business practice of employing negotiable instruments in the credit system to raise finance and to accommodate the needs of those who were unable to secure credit directly from banks.[30] Bills of exchange were often discounted by their holders: 'the trader who needed cash could indorse his bill to a bank or discount house, which would charge the seller a sum representing interest on the time remaining before the bill was to be paid, as well as a commission'.[31] An alternative explanation is that negotiability developed in Britain from the growth in the market for investment securities. This view is supported by the case law where the most frequent examples involving the concept of negotiability[32] are about government bonds rather than bills of exchange.[33]

---

26 M M Postan 'Private financial instruments in medieval England' in Postan (ed), *Medieval Trade and Finance* (1973) p 57.
27 For the meaning of holder in due course, see BoEA, s 29.
28 J M Holden, *The History of Negotiable Instruments in English Law* (Athlone Press, 1955) p 22.
29 Postan, 'Private financial instruments in medieval England' (n 26) p 63.
30 J S Rogers, *The Early History of the Bills and Notes* (1995) p 121.
31 M Lobban, 'Commercial Law' in Cornish, Anderson, Cock, Lobban, Polden and Smith (eds), *The Oxford History of the Laws of England Volume XII 1820–1914 – Private Law* (2010) p 729.
32 See *Goodwin v Robarts* (1876) 1 App Cas 476 and *Crouch v Credit Foncier of England* (1873) 8 QB 374.
33 The leading case (the same rule was later applied to other instruments including government bonds) is *Miller v Race* (1758) 1 Burr 452 at 457 per Lord Mansfield where it was established that although bank notes were not goods, nor securities, nor documents for debts, they were 'treated as money, as cash, in the ordinary course and transaction of business, by the general consent of mankind; which gives them the credit and currency of money, to all intents and purposes'.

9.15   The history of negotiable instruments and their origin in mercantile custom in Scotland is not distant from the English evolution up to the drafting of the BoEA in 1882. The proposal to apply the law only in England and Ireland because of the possible differences with Scots law was rejected, as it was found that these were insignificant.[34] More accurately, as will be clarified below, there are only two points on which Scots and English law differ materially under the BoEA: the application of the English doctrine of consideration[35] and the fact that in Scotland the bill operates as an assignment of the sum for which it is drawn in favour of the holder, provided that the drawee of a bill (other than a cheque)[36] has in his hands funds available for the payment.[37]

Legal recognition and types

9.16   Documents can be recognised as negotiable either by statute or by mercantile usage.[38] Agreement between the parties alone is not *per se* sufficient to make an instrument negotiable.[39] Whether an instrument is negotiable in accordance with merchant law depends on the custom and must be proved,[40] with the exception of the obvious circumstances where the court will simply take judicial notice of it,[41] and unless the instrument expressly states that it should not be negotiable.[42]

9.17   Instruments negotiable by virtue of a statutory provision often confirm judicial acceptance of a mercantile use of the instrument as negotiable. This has been, for example, the case of bills of exchange and cheques that qualified as negotiable instruments even before the statutory consolidation under the BoEA.[43] However, it is worth noting that the law merchant rarely ceases to operate altogether after a statutory

---

34 Following the evidence taken from Sheriff Dove-Wilson of Aberdeen, who pointed out the similarities with Scotland and the advantages of a code for the mercantile community. See R Ferguson, 'Legal ideology and commercial interest: the social origin of commercial law codes' (1977) 4 British Journal of Law and Society 18.

35 BoEA, s 27.

36 The principle has been abolished in relation to cheques in Scotland by s 254(2) of the Banking Act 2009.

37 BoEA, s 53(2).

38 *Dixon v Bovill* (1856) 3 Macq HL 1 at 16 per Lord Cranworth and *Edelstein v Schuler & Co* [1902] 2 KB 144 at 154 per Bigham J.

39 *Crouch v Credit Foncier of England* (1873) 8 QB 374 at 386 per Blackburn J.

40 *Bechuanaland Exploration Co v London Trading Bank Ltd* [1898] 2 QB 658 at 666 per Kennedy J.

41 *Edelstein v Schuler & Co* at 155 per Bigham J.

42 *London & County Banking Co Ltd v London and River Plate Bank Ltd* (1888) 20 QBD 232 at 239 per Manisty J.

43 M D Chalmers, 'An experiment in codification' (1886) 3 LQR 125. For an historical enquiry on the subject, see Holden, *The History of Negotiable Instruments*, p 199.

consolidation, but that it continues to apply save in so far as it is inconsistent with the rules set out in the statute.[44]

9.18 There is not a final comprehensive list of the various types of negotiable instruments. The list is not closed, as:

> 'the law merchant is not a closed book, nor is it fixed or stereotyped. . . . Practices of men change, and courts of law in giving effect to the dealings of the parties will assume that they have dealt with one another on the footing of any relevant custom or usage prevailing at the time in the particular trade or class transaction.'[45]

The indirect corollary is that a relatively short period of usage is not generally a bar to negotiability, even if it is also true that the custom must have prevailed for some time in order to achieve certainty and notoriety.[46]

9.19 Finally, there are circumstances where the law expressly restricts the sphere of application of negotiable instruments, i.e. the extent to which negotiable instruments can be used for making payment or for giving security. This is, for example, the case of inland transactions between individuals regulated under section 123 of the Consumer Credit Act 1974 where, outside non-commercial agreements,[47] negotiable instruments (other than a bank note or a cheque) taken in regulated consumer credit agreements[48] and consumer hire agreements[49] in discharge of a sum payable by the debtor or hirer cannot be enforced.[50]

Advantages and foreseeable decline in use

9.20 Up until the enactment of section 25(6) of the Supreme Court of Judicature Act 1873,[51] negotiable instruments had a crucial importance in commercial practice in England: an assignee had to join the assignor as a party when seeking to enforce his rights against the debtor[52] and, therefore, the only way to assign a promise to pay money at common law was by the use of negotiable instruments. The scenario was in part different in Scotland where obligations, by their nature, were regarded as capable of being transferred to other people without the consent of the

---

44 E.g. BoEA, s 97(2) and the interpretation offered in *Bank of England v Vagliano Bros* [1891] AC 107.

45 *Bank of Baroda Ltd v Punjab National Bank Ltd* [1944] 1 AC 176 (PC) at 183 per Lord Wright.

46 *Edelstein v Schuler & Co* at 154 per Bigham J and, generally, see Holden, *The History of Negotiable Instruments*, pp 251–56.

47 I.e. an agreement not made by the creditor or owner in the course of a business carried on by him. See Consumer Credit Act 1974, s 123(5) and s 189(1).

48 Consumer Credit Act 1974, s 8.

49 Consumer Credit Act 1974, s 15.

50 Consumer Credit Act 1974, s 125(1).

51 The provision was repealed, but substantially re-enacted by s 136 of the Law of Property Act 1925.

52 The relevance of the change is addressed in *Re Westerton* [1919] 2 Ch 104 at 133 per Sargant J and *Marchant v Morton, Down & Co* [1901] 2 KB 829 at 832 per Channell J.

debtor or without the debt being reified into moveable bonds.[53] In other words, assignation of rights was settled in Scotland before and independently of the advent of the doctrine on procuration *in rem suam* as accepted by the decisions of the Court of Session in the nineteenth century.[54] It follows that the growth of negotiable instruments in Scotland has to be primarily explained by the possibility of avoiding the formalities of intimation and the *assignatus* rule[55] in commercial transactions.[56]

9.21 Notwithstanding the above-mentioned statutory interventions in England and the case law development in Scotland, together with the constant decline in commercial practice for bills in inland trade,[57] negotiable instruments are still widely popular in Britain. In particular, today bills are mainly used in the context of credit lines granted by banks to their customers and as a method of making payment in international sales and in domestic trade, as transferability facilitates discount. With forfaiting,[58] for example, a seller-exporter will be able to raise medium term finance, allowing a period of credit to the buyer-importer (who could use or resell the goods before having to pay for them) and avoiding the risk of the buyer-importer's default. The transaction works as follows: the seller draws on the buyer (no recourse)[59] bills on its own order and the buyer accepts it. If the bills bear an unconditional guarantee from the buyer bank,[60] the seller is then able to discount them without recourse through his own bank[61] and does not have to wait for the

---

53 This is the conventional doctrinal position: see K Luig, 'Assignation' in K Reid and R Zimmerman (eds), *A History of Private Law in Scotland* (2000) p 419 and R G Anderson, *Assignation*, p 92. A different view is suggested by D M Walker (ed), *Stair's Institutions of the Law of Scotland* (6th edn, 1981) III.i.3 and W Guthrie (ed), *Bell's Principles of the Law of Scotland* (10th edn, 1899) p 1459.

54 *Carter v McIntosh* (1862) 24 D 925 per Lord Justice-Clerk Inglis and *British Linen Co Bank v Carruthers and Fergusson* (1883) 10 R 926 per Lord President Inglis.

55 I.e. the rule according to which the transferee does not acquire better rights than his transferor.

56 See R G Anderson, *Assignation*, p 92.

57 As defined under BoEA, s 4(1). The decline was primarily due to the strengthening of the banking system with the granting of overdraft facilities for which the bankers could routinely consent to renewal rather than discounting bills (not to mention the costs associated with *ad valorem* stamp duty on bills). See Holden, *The History of Negotiable Instruments*, pp 294–303 and P Mathias, 'Capital, credit and enterprise in the Industrial Revolution' (1973) 2 Journal of European Economic History 121 at 136.

58 This is a type of non-recourse finance, which assists the export seller's cash flow (i.e. the seller receives an immediate payment of the cash value of the bill without recourse in case the buyer defaults on payment) whilst giving the buyer a period of credit: see A Ripley, *Forfaiting for Exporters* (1996).

59 I.e. the bill excludes recourse on the seller if the buyer does not pay.

60 Or an *aval* (in substance a guarantee for the payment of the debt) available in the legal systems that have adopted the Geneva Uniform Law on Bills of Exchange and Promissory Notes 1930 and that may take effect as an anomalous indorsement under BoEA, s 56 in the UK: see *G & H Montage GmbH v Irvani* [1990] 1 WLR 667.

61 I.e. to negotiate the bills in return for a payment slightly lower than the face value.

buyer's payment. When the instrument at maturity is presented to the buyer and if it is dishonoured, it is for the buyer bank that issued an unconditional guarantee to pay.[62]

9.22 It has recently been argued that the simple forms of circulation of negotiable instruments together with the strong protection of the innocent purchaser for value are largely anachronistic: the focus on transfer is not helpful as today most negotiable instruments (e.g. cheques and promissory notes) do not pass from person to person outside the banking system.[63]

9.23 The autonomy of the payment obligation from any contract, which caused negotiable instruments to be regarded as equivalent to cash, is also generally considered as out of date under the current electronic payment system. The explanation for that is simply that the law of negotiable instruments developed before the formation of the modern currency and banking systems, and a system of transfer of claims was essential for the creation of an efficient payment system. The same idea of (indispensable) reification of claims into paper documents has been questioned under modern commercial practice of money transfer, as has been the case for the circulation of securities held by intermediaries.[64] As remarked with an extreme formulation, the law of negotiable instruments 'is a museum of antiquities – a treasure house crammed full of ancient artefacts whose use and function have long since been forgotten'.[65]

BILLS OF EXCHANGE

Definition

9.24 As suggested earlier, the fundamental source of the law on bills of exchange (and on negotiable instruments in general) is the BoEA. According to the BoEA, section 3(1), a bill of exchange is and can only consist of[66] 'an unconditional order in writing, addressed by one person to another, signed by the person giving it, requiring the person to whom it is addressed to pay on demand or at a fixed or determinable future time a sum in money to or to the order of a specified person, or to the bearer'. Before examining the elements of the definition and the modes

---

62 Or an *aval*: see n 57. On this issue, in general, see A G Guest, *Chalmers and Guest on Bills of Exchange and Cheques* (17th edn, 2009) para 2-109.

63 J S Rogers, *The End of Negotiable Instruments – Bringing Payment Systems Law Out of the Past* (2012).

64 J S Rogers, 'Policy perspectives on revised UCC Article 8' (1996) 43 UCLA L Rev 1431.

65 G Gilmore, 'Formalism and the law of negotiable instruments' (1979) 13 Creighton L Rev 441.

66 An instrument which does not comply with the conditions set up under BoEA, s 3(1) or which requires an additional act to be done is not a bill of exchange: see BoEA, s 3(2).

of circulation, an illustration of the way in which a bill of exchange is drawn and an outline of some basic terms are offered. In particular, below is an example of a bill of exchange drawn in Glasgow on 14 December 2013 that contains an unconditional order ('pay') in writing addressed by A Ltd (the 'drawer'), to Bank B Ltd (the 'drawee'), signed on behalf of A Ltd by a director, requiring the drawee to pay at a fixed or determinable future time ('sixty days after sight') a sum in money (£ 50,000) to the order of a specified person (C), the 'payee' of the bill. It could also be possible that the order requires Bank B Ltd to pay the sum specified in the bill not to the order of C (a named payee – 'order bill'), but to whoever is in possession of the bill ('bearer bill').

Glasgow, December 14, 2013

£50,000
at sixty days after sight pay to the order of C the sum of fifty thousand pounds drawn under Bank B Ltd.

To Bank B Ltd   *for and on behalf of A Ltd*
                                   (signed) a director of A Ltd

Hence,

(a) The person who draws the bill[67] is known as the 'drawer'. He is primarily liable on the bill before the bill is accepted;

(b) The person on whom the bill is drawn[68] is termed the 'drawee' and – it will be clarified below – if he has funds available to pay it, the bill operates as an assignment to the holder of the sum for which it was drawn without need of acceptance (an 'intimated assignation').[69] The position is different in England and Wales where a drawee is not strictly a party to the bill and does not incur any liability on the bill until he agrees to comply with the instructions and honour the bill on maturity to the payee or to the holder (becoming, therefore, the 'acceptor');[70]

(c) The person in whose favour the bill is payable is known as the 'payee';

(d) A payee[71] who warrants to a transferee that the bill will be honoured by signing his name in the back of the instrument qualifies as 'indorser' and the person to whom it is indorsed is the 'indorsee'. The indorser's position is very similar to that of the drawer and several cases have suggested that the indorser is in

---

67 I.e. the one who gives the unconditional order.
68 I.e. the one who is the subject of the drawer's order.
69 BoEA, s 53(2).
70 BoEA, s 17(2)(a). As suggested below, it follows that in England and Wales, if the drawee does not accept the bill (or in Scotland if the drawee does not have funds available to pay it), the bill becomes dishonoured 'by non acceptance' and the payee has an immediate right of action against the drawer under BoEA, s 43(2).
71 And, similarly, the following transferees.

effect a new drawer who gives a new order as to the payment of the bill to the drawee;[72]

(e) The payee who physically retains the bill, or the transferee who obtains possession of it by indorsement completed by delivery or by mere delivery, is known as the 'holder'.

9.25 As stated in the definition above, the order to the drawee[73] does not have to be in a specified form, but it must be imperative,[74] it must be in writing,[75] signed by the drawer[76] and not be subject to any qualifications or limitations (i.e. it must be 'unconditional').[77] Moreover, the obligation must be exclusively[78] for a certain sum of money[79] with no ambiguity as regards its date of payment:[80] a bill is valid only if payable on demand (at sight, on presentation or if no time for payment is mentioned in it)[81] or at fixed date or, in any case, at an ascertainable future date.[82] Finally, it must be payable either to a specified person (the payee)[83] or to the bearer.[84]

9.26 Apart from the case of an unsigned document,[85] an instrument which fails to comply with all the requirements of BoEA, s 3(1)(i.e. an 'inchoate instrument') may still be converted to a bill of exchange by the

---

72 *Penny v Innes* (1834) 1 CM & R 439 and *Steele v McKinlay* (1880) 5 App Cas 754.

73 The drawee must be named or otherwise indicated with reasonable certainty: see *Gray v Milner* (1819) 8 Tauton 739.

74 I.e. it cannot be a precative request or a mere invitation to pay. An instrument reading 'Bank B Ltd, please let the bearer have £50,000, and place it to my account and you will oblige. A director of A Ltd (signed)' is not a bill of exchange, as it does not contain an order made by one party having a right to call on the other to pay: see *Hamilton v Spottiswoode* (1849) 154 ER 1182 and *Little v Slackford* (1828) 1 M&M 171.

75 Not necessarily written in English: see *Arab Bank Ltd v Ross* [1952] 2 QB 216.

76 In the absence of the drawer's signature, the acceptor is not liable on the bill: see *McCall v Taylor* (1865) 19 CB (NS) 301.

77 BoEA, s 11(2) provides that if the instrument is conditional, such defect cannot be cured by the happening of the event in question.

78 The order should not require the drawee to do any other act: see *Dickie v Singh* 1974 SLT (Notes) 3.

79 A sum is certain within the meaning of BoEA, even if the amount is not designated in English currency or if it has to be paid with interest or in instalments: see BoEA, s 9. If A Ltd writes and sends to Bank B Ltd the following order: 'Bank B Ltd, please pay to C the proceeds of a sale value about £50,000', the order is not a bill of exchange, the sum not being certain: see *Jones v Simpson* (1823) 2 B&C 318.

80 See *Korea Exchange Bank v Debenhams (Central Buying) Ltd* [1979] 1 Lloyd's Rep 100.

81 BoEA, s 10(1).

82 BoEA, s 11(2). If the bill is undated, it is still valid and the holder may insert the date: see BoEA, s 3(4)(a) and s 20, respectively.

83 Or, possibly, several payees either as joint or alternative payees: see BoEA, s 7(2).

84 A bill is payable to the bearer when it is explicitly written in the document or when the 'only or last indorsement is an indorsement in blank': see BoEA, s 8(3). Moreover, according to BoEA, s 7(3) a bill is payable to bearer 'where the payee is a fictitious or not existing person'.

85 Which cannot be cured by the holder.

transferee who has *prima facie* authority to fill it up as a complete bill and rectify any omission of any material particular,[86] provided that this is done within a reasonable time, and strictly in accordance with the authority given.[87]

Transfer

9.27 This section deals with the rules governing the transfer of bills between holders. Subject to the contrary explicit wish of a drawer who creates a bill of exchange without allowing for its transfer,[88] the method by which a bill is transferred is termed 'negotiation'. It involves the circulation 'from one person to another in such a manner as to constitute the transferee the holder of the bill'.[89] When the bill is negotiable, it continues to be so until it is restrictively indorsed[90] or 'discharged by payment or otherwise'.[91] The law distinguishes between the actual mode of transfer depending on whether the bill is a bearer bill or is payable to order.

Bearer bills

9.28 Bearer bills are transferred by (actual or constructive[92]) delivery of the instrument from one person to another, and the rights under them will vest in the holder.[93] A signature is not required to negotiate a bearer bill.[94] Once the bill passes to the hands of a holder in due course, 'a valid delivery of the bill by all parties prior to him so as to make them liable to him is conclusively presumed'.[95] This simply means that there will be no flaw in the title of the holder in due course even if the delivery was unauthorised. Bearer bills are payable when it is expressly so established,[96] when the last indorsement is in blank[97] or when the payee is a fictitious or non-existing person.[98] That said, these instruments are rarely used in practice because of the potential risks involved for the holder in losing the possession of the document vis-à-vis the right of the acceptor in

---

86 BoEA, s 20(1).
87 BoEA, s 20(2). See *Mckeekin v Russell* (1881) 8 R 587.
88 I.e. the bill can only be enforced by the original payee: see BoEA, s 8(3).
89 BoEA, s 31(1).
90 I.e. when the drawer instructs the drawee that payment should only made to a specified payee and further negotiation is prohibited: BoEA, s 35(1), (2).
91 BoEA, s 36. I.e. cancellation, renunciation or when the acceptor has become himself a holder: see BoEA, ss 61–63.
92 E.g. when a person holding a bill as owner agrees to transfer ownership to a third party, but continues to hold the bill as agent of that other person.
93 BoEA, s 31(2).
94 BoEA, s 58(2).
95 BoEA, s 21(2).
96 BoEA, s 8(3).
97 BoEA, s 8(3).
98 BoEA, s 7(3). See *Bank of England v Vagliano Bros* [1891] AC 107 and *Clutton & Co v Attenborough* [1897] AC 90.

good faith and without notice of a defect in title always to achieve a
good discharge by payment of the bill.[99]

Order bills

9.29   When the bill is payable to order, it is transferable by indorsement
and delivery of it.[100] To qualify as a valid indorsement, the indorsement
must be written on the instrument, signed by the indorser[101] and must
be for 'the entire bill'.[102] Delivery without indorsement still allows the
transferee to sue on the bill in his own name, but not to become a holder
in due course.[103] A transferee of an unindorsed bill will therefore acquire
the bill in the same position as an assignee.[104] Order bills are payable
when it is so expressly established in the document (and there are no
words suggesting that it should not be transferable)[105] or when the only
or last indorsement is in blank[106] and the holder converts the blank
indorsement into a special indorsement 'by writing above the indorser's
signature a direction to pay the bill to or to the order of himself or some
other person'.[107]

Entitlement to benefit from the obligation on the bill

9.30   When a bill is issued and negotiated, it circulates through the
hands of 'holders'. It follows that the right to enforce payment of a bill
belongs to the holder who, as mentioned above, is 'the payee or indorsee
of a bill or note who is in possession of it, or the bearer thereof'.[108]
According to the combination of sections 27 and 38 of the BoEA, three
types of holder can be identified: the mere holder, the holder for value
and the holder in due course.

Mere holder

9.31   The mere holder has not given value for the bill, but he still
enjoys a number of important rights. He can sue on the bill in his own
name,[109] convert a blank indorsement on an order bill into a special
one,[110] negotiate an order bill[111] and provide good discharge to an

---

 99 BoEA, s 59.
100 BoEA, s 31(3).
101 BoEA, s 32(1).
102 BoEA, s 32(2).
103 *Hood v Stewart* (1890) 17 R 749.
104 I.e. subject to any defects in the right of the transferor to obtain payment: see
    Whistler v Forster (1863) 14 CBNS 248 per Willes J.
105 BoEA, s 8(4).
106 I.e. it consists of the simple signature of the indorser, but no indorsee is identified:
    see BoEA, s 34(1).
107 BoEA, s 34(4).
108 BoEA, s 2.
109 BoEA, s 59(1).
110 BoEA, s 34(4).
111 BoEA, s 31(3).

acceptor in good faith and without notice of the defect in title. However, the drawee can raise a number of defences against an action brought by a mere holder based on defect in title of prior parties,[112] with the exception, possibly, of the absence of consideration under section 27 BoEA for the enforcement of an obligation, as this doctrine does not form part of Scots law,[113] and the presumption is that 'onerosity of a bill is to be assumed'.[114] That said, non-onerosity may possibly be pleaded in evidence when the bill is regarded to be invalid on other grounds such as fraud, error, undue influence or illegality.

Holder for value

9.32 A holder for value is a holder who has provided valuable consideration for the bill consisting of any consideration sufficient to support a simple contract or an antecedent debt or liability.[115] A holder for value may also be someone who did not give value himself, so long as value was given by some other party in the chain between the holder and the acceptor.[116] As suggested above, because the defence of absence or failure of consideration is irrelevant in Scotland, the position of the holder for value is similar to that of a mere holder,[117] as he does not acquire better title than his transferor.

Holder in due course

9.33 The holder in due course enjoys advantages not available to other holders. He holds the bill free from any defects of title of prior parties, as well as from mere personal defences available to prior parties among themselves.[118] Every holder of a bill is *prima facie* deemed to be a holder in due course, unless it is proven that the requirements set out in the definition under BoEA, s 29(1) are not met. In particular, a holder in

---

112 BoEA, s 38(2).
113 In England, old authorities have clearly established that a mere holder who does not give consideration for the bill (i.e. a mere holder who is not a holder for value) cannot succeed in his claim against an immediate or a remote party. The absence of consideration therefore has been held to be a valid defence against the holder in *Forman v Wright* (1851) 11 CB 451 at 492 and *Milnes v Dawson* (1850) 5 Exch 948 at 950.
114 *Law v Humphrey* (1876) 3 R 1192 at 1193 per Lord President Inglis and reference to BoEA, s 30(1).
115 BoEA, s 27(1).
116 BoEA, s 27(2).
117 *Nova (Jersey) Knit Ltd v Kammgarn Spinnerei GmbH* [1977] 1 WLR 713.
118 BoEA, s 38(2).

due course must be a holder of the bill other than the payee[119] who has taken it without notice of defect in title,[120] in good faith and for value.[121] Moreover, the bill must not be overdue[122] at the time of transfer[123] and must be complete and regular on its face.[124] Finally, contrary to the case of the holder for value,[125] in order to be a holder in due course it is necessary to give value personally.[126]

Liabilities of the parties on the bill

9.34 Having considered what amounts to a bill complete with all the necessary parties and the way it is negotiated, this section looks at how far the parties involved may incur liability on the bill. A drawer, acceptor or indorser who has no capacity to contract is not liable on the bill[127] and will be liable only if he has signed it in such a capacity[128] (or if the bill has been signed by an agent in a representative capacity on his behalf).[129] Where a signature on a bill is forged or placed on it without the authority of the person whose signature it purports to be,[130] such signature is inoperative and no title to the bill can be derived from it, unless the party against whom it is sought to retain it or enforce payment of the bill is personally barred from raising the question of forgery or want of authority.[131] This applies also to a company, which will make itself liable as a drawer, acceptor or indorser of a bill only if it is competent to

---

119 I.e. he can only be a subsequent possessor of a bearer bill or an indorsee in possession of an order bill: BoEA, s 29(1)(b). See the description of the exceptions to the *nemo dat* rule offered in *Whistler v Forster* (1863) 14 CB 196 per Willes J.

120 BoEA, s 29(2)(a) – i.e. actual notice of a fact that constitutes defect in title. See *Raphael v Bank of England* (1855) 17 CB 161.

121 BoEA, s 29(2)(b). BoEA, s 90 suggests that a thing is deemed to be done in good faith 'where it is in fact done honestly, whether it is done negligently or not'. On the interpretation of the provision, see *Jones v Gordon* (1877) 2 App Cas 616 at 628 per Lord Blackburn.

122 I.e. already matured.

123 BoEA, s 29(1).

124 BoEA, s 29(1). This is the case of an inchoate instrument or a bill, which contains on its face an irregular indorsement. See *Arab Bank Ltd v Ross* [1952] 2 QB 216 and *Lombard Banking Ltd v Central Garage & Engineering Ltd* [1963] 1 QB 220.

125 BoEA, s 27(2).

126 See Guest, *Chalmers and Guest on Bills of Exchange and Cheques* (n 62) para 4-057.

127 BoEA, s 22(1).

128 BoEA, s 23.

129 E.g. signature by procuration. In other words, an agent will not be personally liable on the bill if he signs it as drawer, indorser of an acceptor and adds words to his signature indicating that he signs for or on behalf of a principal: see BoEA, s 26(1).

130 Unless the unauthorised signature has been ratified: see BoEA, s 24(2).

131 In other words, the party barred must have led the other party to believe that the signature was in order and the other party must have acted as if the bill was fully valid: see BoEA, s 24 and s 54(2)(a).

do so under the law relating to corporations.[132] However, the lack of capacity to contract does not release other parties from liability on the bill.[133] For example, a transferor of a bearer bill by mere delivery may face liability outside the bill for breach of warranty on the fact that the bill is genuine to a transferee (provided that the transferee is a holder for value).[134] Liability of specific parties on the bill is as follows:

Liability of the drawer

9.35 The drawer promises that the bill will be accepted and paid according to the terms of his promise written on the instrument (its tenor) when presented to the drawee. If the drawee dishonours the bill by not accepting or not paying it, and provided that the holder has given notice of dishonour, then the drawer is in a position similar to the one of a joint guarantor and he will be obliged to compensate the holder or an indorser who was compelled to pay it.[135]

Liability of the drawee (and of the acceptor)

9.36 While in England and Wales the drawing of a bill creates no obligations upon the drawee to accept or pay the bill,[136] in Scotland, as mentioned above, a bill does constitute an assignation of funds, which the drawer has in the hands of the drawee.[137] However, once the bill is accepted, the acceptor is liable to pay in accordance with the terms of his acceptance[138] and, among other things, he cannot deny to a holder in due course 'the existence of the drawer, the genuineness of his signature, and his capacity and authority to draw the bill'.[139]

Liability of an indorser

9.37 The liability of the indorser is similar to that of the drawer of a bill. He promises that the bill will be accepted and paid according to its tenor and that should the bill be dishonoured (and provided that the holder has given notice of dishonour), he will have to compensate the holder or a subsequent indorser.[140] No dispute on the 'genuineness and

---

132 BoEA, s 22(2). Note that the strict rule according to which the capacity of the company depended on the powers conferred in the articles has been relaxed with the abolition of the *ultra vires* rules in relation to third parties under the Companies Act 2006, s 39.

133 E.g. *Wauthier v Wilson* (1912) 28 TLR 239 where a father was found liable on note made jointly by himself and his minor son.

134 BoEA, s 58(3).

135 BoEA, s 55(1).

136 See *Credit Lyonnais Bank Nederland NV v Export Credits Guarantee Department* [1998] 1 Lloyd's Rep 19 at 39 per Hobhouse J.

137 BoEA, s 53(2). See *Williams v Williams* 1980 SLT (Sh Ct) 25 and *British Linen Bank Co v Carruthers and Fergusson* (1883) 10 R 923 at 928 per Lord Shand.

138 BoEA, s 54(1).

139 BoEA, s 54(2)(a).

140 BoEA, s 55(2)(a).

regularity in all respects of the drawer's signature and all the previous indorsements'[141] is allowed when the other party satisfies the criteria for a holder in due course. However, as suggested above, the indorser called to make a payment on a bill, which has been dishonoured, is in a position similar to a joint guarantor and he will have the right to be repaid by the drawer.[142]

Exemptions

9.38 It is possible for the drawer or for an indorser to exclude or limit the liability that would ordinarily fall on him to guarantee the drawee by express stipulation after the signature in the bill of the words *sans recourse* (or its English equivalent 'without recourse').[143] However, this device is not available to an acceptor who may only mitigate his liability by qualified acceptance under BoEA, s 19(2).

Enforcement

9.39 A demand bill matures immediately and the payee (or other holder) simply presents for payment to the drawee. Unless the terms of the bill so require[144] or it is necessary to fix the maturity date of the instrument,[145] the presentation of the bill for acceptance is not essential,[146] as the holder of an unaccepted bill may still act against the drawer (or any prior indorser).[147] The failure to pay a demand bill duly presented for payment amounts to dishonour by non-payment[148] with slightly different procedures following the refusal depending on whether it is a foreign or inland bill.[149] This is different from the term bill where the bill must first be presented and accepted by the drawee.[150] If the bill is dishonoured by non-acceptance, the holder can enforce his rights against the drawer (and any prior indorser) without waiting for the maturity of the bill.[151] Where the bill is accepted, presentation for

---

141 BoEA, s 55(2)(b).
142 BoEA, s 55(1)(a).
143 BoEA, s 16(1).
144 BoEA, s 39(2).
145 BoEA, s 39(1).
146 BoEA, s 39(3).
147 BoEA, s 42 and s 43(2).
148 BoEA, s 47(1).
149 In the case of a foreign bill (i.e. a bill which is not drawn and payable within the British Islands or it is drawn within the British Islands by a non-resident person), notice is not sufficient to preserve the holder's right of recourse. The bill must be also noted and protested: see BoEA, s 51(2). While noting is an act preliminary to protest consisting in the making of a note or minute on the face of the bill, protest is a solemn declaration made by a public notary that a bill has been dishonoured. Protest in Scotland is required also in the case of inland bills for the purpose of summary diligence (i.e. the procedure for obtaining warrant for diligence might be done on a bill of exchange without first resorting to a court action): see BoEA, s 98.
150 BoEA, s 45(1).
151 BoEA, s 43(2).

payment on its maturity is necessary to establish dishonour of non-payment[152] and drawer/indorser liability.[153]

9.40 Drawers' (and prior indorsers') liability on the bill is based not only on the fact that the bill has been dishonoured for non-acceptance or non-payment, but also on the fact that the holder has given them notice of dishonour within a reasonable time.[154] Similar rules to notice of dishonour by non-acceptance apply to dishonour by non-payment.[155] This is subject to the important Scottish qualification mentioned above under section 53(2) of the BoEA whereby presenting a bill for acceptance or for payment has the effect of assigning the drawer's funds (held by the drawee) to the holder.[156]

Discharge

9.41 There are various ways according to which a bill may be discharged so that no party can sue or be sued on the instrument. The obvious one is the payment at or after maturity of the bill by or on behalf of the drawee (or acceptor) to the holder in good faith and without notice that his title to the bill is defective ('payment in due course').[157] A bill may also be discharged where the acceptor of a bill becomes the holder at or after its date of maturity;[158] when the holder, after maturity, waives his rights against the acceptor either in writing or by delivering the bill to him;[159] where the bill is intentionally and clearly cancelled[160] by the holder or his agent;[161] where materially altered, it is avoided against any party who did not assent to the alteration;[162] and, where applicable, via a five-year prescription starting from the date on which the obligation under the instrument becomes enforceable.[163]

CHEQUES

Definition and distinguishing elements

9.42 Cheques are probably one of the most common forms of negotiable instruments: they operate as an order from the drawer directed to a

152 BoEA, s 45.
153 BoEA, s 47(1).
154 BoEA, s 48.
155 BoEA, s 49.
156 See *British Linen Co Bank v Carruthers and Fergusson* (1883) 10 R 923 at 926 per Lord President Inglis; *Kirkwood & Sons v Clydesdale Bank* 1908 SC 20; *Sutherland v Royal Bank of Scotland plc* 1997 SLT 329.
157 BoEA, s 59 (1). And the bill ceases to be negotiable: BoEA, s 36(1).
158 BoEA, s 61.
159 BoEA, s 62(2).
160 BoEA, s 63 (1); *Bank of Scotland v Dominion Bank* [1891] AC 592.
161 BoEA, s 63(1).
162 BoEA, s 64(1). See *Hong Kong and Shanghai Banking Corporation v Lo Lee Shi* [1928] AC 182 (PC); *Smith v Lloyd's TSB Group* [2001] QB 541 at 556 per Pill LJ.
163 Prescription and Limitation (Scotland) Act 1973, s 6(3) and Sch 1(1)(e).

drawee bank (the paying bank) to make a payment to the holder of the cheque. The law relating to cheques is to be found in the BoEA Part III (sections 73–81) and in the Cheques Acts 1957 and 1992, together with the associated case law. In essence, a cheque is 'a bill of exchange drawn on a banker and payable on demand'[164] and the rules set out for bills of exchange apply to cheques as default rules, unless otherwise provided under the BoEA.[165] However, apart from the necessary involvement of a banker, there are certain substantial operational differences between the two,[166] including the fact that by nature a cheque is not intended to be a credit instrument (it is payable on demand) and the fact that in commercial practice it is not usually discounted or sold by the payee.

Crossed cheques

9.43 A crossing is essentially an instruction given to a banker to pay the proceeds of a cheque not in cash to the person who presents the cheque, but to the holder's own account. This is a common arrangement in many cheque forms today and it is aimed at reducing the risk of loss, particularly when the cheque is sent through the post: if the cheque is crossed, it will be difficult for a finder who does not have a bank account to collect, and the proceeds will be easier to monitor/trace. More accurately, when two parallel transverse lines are drawn across its face to which may be added the words 'and the company' or 'not negotiable'[167] or both, the cheque is 'crossed' and must be presented for payment through a bank account (general crossing),[168] unless the crossing bears the name of the bank to whom the payment is to be made and in that case the cheque must be presented for payment through the designated bank (special crossing).[169] Apart from the drawer,[170] a holder may also cross an uncrossed cheque or make the instrument more restrictive, but not less.[171] Finally, when a cheque bears either a general or special crossing and it has not been altered,[172] the drawee bank will be liable to the 'true owner' of the cheque for any loss incurred.[173]

9.44 A crossed cheque that bears across its face the words 'account payee' or 'a/c payee', either with or without the word 'only' cannot be

164 BoEA, s 73.
165 BoEA, s 73.
166 See *Ramchurn Mullick v Luchmeechund Radakissen* (1954) 9 Moo PCC 46 at 69 per Parke B.
167 In the words of Lindley LJ, 'everyone who takes a cheque which is marked "non negotiable" takes it at his own risk, and his title to the money is as defective as his title to the cheque itself': *Great Western Railway Co v London and County Banking Co* [1901] AC 414 at 424.
168 BoEA, s 76(1).
169 BoEA, s 76(2).
170 BoEA, s 77(1).
171 BoEA, s 77(2), (3) and (4).
172 BoEA, ss 64 and 78.
173 BoEA, s 79(2). See *Phillip v The Italian Bank* 1934 SLT 78.

passed by negotiation and is only valid as between the drawer and the drawee.[174] In essence, this type of crossing amounts to a direction to the collecting bank that the proceeds of the cheque should not be collected for a person other than the nominated payee.[175] As matters stand, it is questionable whether following the changes for the transferability of crossed cheques brought about by the Cheques Act 1992,[176] cheques should be regarded as negotiable instruments.

The clearing system

9.45 The cheque must be physically presented for payment to the branch of the paying bank on which it is drawn.[177] Given the huge volume of cheques that circulate every day through the banking system, this operation is simplified by the use of a centralised clearing system that favours the process of presentation for payment of cheques in bulk between banks, with the aim of achieving only a single balance among participating banks. Today, cheques are not therefore individually paid, but only a balance is transferred between the two banks at the end of each trading day. The current clearing process and the procedures involved usually operate within a 48-hour period over three days and are subject to variations. Under one of the most common scenarios, when the drawer and the payee have their accounts with different banks and the cheque is paid in the branch where the payee has his account, it is encoded in magnetic ink and a computerised credit entry is made on the payee's account before being sent together with the other cheques drawn on the drawer's bank to the central clearing department of the payee's bank. Once all the cheques have been verified with the encoded details, they are delivered to the central clearing department of the drawer's bank where a balance in the drawer's account is taken and a provisional settlement between the total amount of cheques presented between the two banks each day is performed. The cheque is finally forwarded to the drawer's bank branch and, unless the account's funds are not adequate (and the bank resolves to dishonour the cheque), it is paid.

Protection of the collecting bank

9.46 Among the functions of the banker is to collect the proceeds of cheques paid in by the customer and to credit them to his account. In this capacity a bank acts as the agent of the customer, whereas a bank that discounts a cheque (rare now that most cheques are crossed) acts as principal on its own behalf. If the customer does not have good right to the cheques, the law protects the banker from liability for the value

---

174 BoEA, s 81A(1).
175 *National Bank v Silke* [1891] 1 QB 435.
176 BoEA, s 81A.
177 BoEA, s 45(3) and *Barclays Bank plc v Bank of England* [1985] 1 All ER 385 at 392.

of the cheque to the true owner by means of the 'holder in due course' doctrine and by section 4 of the Cheques Act 1957. In particular, if the instrument is complete and regular on its face and it is taken by the banker in good faith, for value and without notice that it has been dishonoured,[178] then the banker can claim to be the true owner of the instrument as against any former true owner.[179] Other than in the cases where the banker cannot claim the holder in due course status,[180] a banker who has acted in good faith[181] and without negligence[182] in receiving payment for a customer[183] or, having credited the customer's account, receives payment for himself, does not incur any liability to the true owner of the instrument by reason only of having received payment thereof, even if the customer has no title or a defective title to the cheque.[184]

Protection of the paying bank

9.47 A paying banker shall not be responsible or incur any liability, nor shall the payment be questioned if, in the ordinary course of business, he pays a crossed cheque (even if crossing has not been altered)[185] or analogous instrument in good faith and without negligence in accordance with the appearance of the instrument.[186] Apart from the case of cheques crossed 'account payee', which are not transferable,[187] a banker who pays a (crossed or uncrossed) cheque payable to order to the wrong person because an indorsement has been forged is also protected from liability.[188] Lastly, and specifically aimed at reducing time spent in checking indorsement, when a banker 'in good faith and in the ordinary course of business pays a cheque drawn on him which is not indorsed or is irregularly indorsed' he does not, in doing so, incur any liability by reason only of the absence of, or irregularity in the indorsement, and the bank is deemed to have paid the cheque in due course.[189]

---

178 BoEA, s 29.
179 Cheques Act 1957, s 2.
180 This occurs frequently since most cheques nowadays are crossed 'a/c payee' and not discounted, with the result that a bank rarely becomes a holder in due course. The additional protection for the collecting bank under s 4 of the Cheques Act 1957 is therefore necessary.
181 Cheques Act 1957, s 4.
182 In accordance with normal and proper banking practice: see *Marfani & Co Ltd v Midland Bank Ltd* [1968] 1 WLR 956. While the collecting bank will not be liable under the tort of conversion, it has a 'duty of care to ensure that cheques are collected only for those entitled to receive payment': *Nimmo v Bank of Scotland* 2005 SLT (Sh Ct) 133 at 137G per Sheriff Evans.
183 *Great Western Railway Co Ltd v London and County Banking Co Ltd* [1901] AC 414.
184 Cheques Act 1957, s 4.
185 BoEA, s 79(2).
186 BoEA, s 80.
187 BoEA, s 81A(1).
188 BoEA, s 60.
189 Cheques Act 1957, s 1.

OTHER NEGOTIABLE INSTRUMENTS

Promissory notes

9.48 While a bill of exchange is essentially an unconditional order addressed by one person to another requiring the person to whom it is addressed to pay on demand or at a fixed or determinable future time a sum certain in money to the order of a specified person, or to the bearer, a promissory note is simply a promise made by one person, known as 'the maker' to another.[190] Once this difference is taken into account, the law governing promissory notes under Part IV of the BoEA (sections 83–89) is very similar to the law of bills of exchange and, unless otherwise expressly provided,[191] the rules on bills of exchange apply with few necessary adjustments to promissory notes.[192] In particular, in applying these rules, the maker of the note[193] is deemed to correspond with the acceptor of the bill, and the first indorser with the drawer of an accepted bill payable to his own order.[194]

9.49 The definition of a promissory note under BoEA follows that of a bill of exchange and, quite interestingly, many of the cases that are used to describe and explain the sections of the bills of exchange are promissory note cases:[195] according to the BoEA section 83(1):

> a promissory note is an unconditional promise in writing made by one person to another, signed by the maker, engaging to pay, on demand or at a fixed or determinable future time, a sum certain in money, to, or to the order of, a specified person or to bearer.

9.50 A promissory note is not mere evidence of indebtedness (such as an IOU), but it involves an explicit promise on the face of the document to be negotiable.[196] Moreover, in order to establish the liability of the maker of a formally complete document it must be delivered to the payee or bearer.[197] The liability of the maker is similar to that of an acceptor of a bill of exchange: the maker promises that he will pay the note according to its tenor[198] and he is precluded from denying to a holder in due course the existence of the payee and his capacity to indorse.[199]

---

190 In English law simple promises are not enforceable whereas in Scotland they are. See Chapter 1: General Principles of Contract.
191 E.g. the provisions relating to presentment for acceptance and to acceptance. See BoEA, s 89(3).
192 BoEA, s 89(1).
193 I.e. the party primarily liable.
194 BoEA, s 89(2).
195 E.g. *Williamson v Rider* [1963] 1 QB 89.
196 I.e. not subject to the rules on assignation, but transferable by delivery or delivery and indorsement.
197 BoEA, s 84.
198 BoEA, s 88(1).
199 BoEA, s 88(2). An interesting comparison can be made with the preclusions concerning the acceptor of the bill under BoEA, s 54.

9.51 Presentation for payment of notes contained in the BoEA is regulated differently from the corresponding provisions relating to bills of exchange. In the case of notes payable on demand, once the note has been indorsed, it must be presented for payment within a reasonable time of the indorsement and, if this is not done, the indorser is discharged.[200] This is different from the case of a bill of exchange where the delay in presenting the bill for payment also releases the drawer:[201] in that case both the drawer and the indorser are under a joint guarantee. In all other circumstances, and similarly to the case of bills of exchange, presentation for payment to the maker is a necessary precondition to establish the indorser's liability.[202]

Bankers' drafts

9.52 A banker's draft is generally used (especially where large sums of money are involved) to overcome the risks inherent in the possibility that an ordinary cheque is dishonoured by a drawer with insufficient funds in the account. In essence, it is the result of an action taken by the customer of the bank who transfers to the bank funds equivalent to the amount of the draft and instructs the bank to issue the draft as an undertaking to pay in a way which is *de facto* the same as cash.[203] More accurately, a banker's draft is a document drawn by a branch of a bank on its head office or on another branch and as such it cannot be qualified as a bill of exchange (or a cheque) under section 3(1) of the BoEA. However, it can be used by the holder as a bill of exchange or as a promissory note within the definition of section 5(2) of the BoEA:[204] in the first case the bank is protected under section 4 of the Cheques Act 1957 and in the case of a crossed draft by the provisions of BoEA[205] relating to crossed cheques.

Travellers' cheques

9.53 Travellers' cheques are means by which a person travelling can acquire cash from overseas banks in the course of a journey abroad. Even if they take a variety of forms (and not all of them will closely resemble negotiable instruments), travellers' cheques are usually purchased by a customer of the bank and signed before an official of the bank either as an order from the issuing bank to other banks to pay the cheques, or as an order from the customer to the bank to pay himself

---

200 BoEA, s 86.
201 BoEA, s 45.
202 BoEA, s 87(1). This means that the person under the primary liability must have been unsuccessfully approached.
203 Cheques Act 1957, s 5.
204 See *Abbey National plc v JSF Finance & Currency Exchange Ltd* [2006] EWCA Civ 328.
205 BoEA, ss 79 and 80.

as payee or another payee whose name is left in blank (not dissimilar in these two cases to the structure of a bill of exchange) or, possibly, as a promise by the issuing bank to repay the paying bank that cashes the cheque for the payee (not dissimilar to the structure of a promissory note). Given that the cheques need to be signed before the issuing bank and countersigned by the same customer before the paying bank, it has been suggested that the payment order or promise is conditional and, therefore, the instrument, even if treated as a negotiable instrument by modern mercantile custom, cannot technically be regarded as negotiable within the meaning of sections 3(1), 73 and 83 of the BoEA.

Chapter 10

Conventional Security: Cautionary Obligations

GENERAL

Concept of a cautionary obligation

10.01 The concept of a cautionary obligation is quite simple. It arises where one party (the cautioner) enters into an agreement with another party (the creditor) whereby the cautioner undertakes that, should a third party (the debtor) fail to complete his obligations to the creditor, the cautioner will perform instead. Or to put it another way, cautionary obligations are guarantees in respect of the obligations of another legal person. It follows that cautionary obligations require three parties: a cautioner, a creditor and a debtor.

10.02 Cautionary obligations frequently relate to monetary debt obligations owed by a debtor, such as bank loans, credit transactions or the business of commercial agents. However, the terms 'debt' and 'debtor' do not carry that specific meaning and can refer to any obligation. Cautionary obligations can also secure the performance of non-monetary obligations, such as the proper conduct of an employee.

Dependent and independent obligations

10.03 There is generally no distinction between the terms 'guarantee' and 'caution'.[1] However, not all agreements that carry the label 'guarantee' are cautionary obligations in the technical sense. Cautionary obligations are said to be accessory to, or dependent on, a principal debt obligation. It may be the case that a so-called guarantee is entered into independently of the existence or extent of a principal debt obligation. In this case, it is better to think of the guarantor as having granted a separate principal obligation in favour of the creditor to indemnify the creditor on the occurrence or non-occurrence of a risk: in other words a contract of insurance or indemnity.

10.04 In theory, the distinction between a cautionary obligation and a separate principal obligation is a simple one: it depends on whether the parties intend the second obligation to be conditional on the debtor's breach of the first obligation. If they do, the second obligation is caution-

---

1 *Aitken's Trs v Bank of Scotland* 1944 SC 270 at 281 per Lord Mackay.

ary; if they do not, it is a separate principal obligation. In practice, the classification of an obligation as a cautionary obligation or as a separate principal obligation will often depend on the particular facts of the case, making an abstract test quite difficult. If the obligation mentions the principal debt generally but is otherwise 'totally unconnected'[2] with the existence[3] or extent[4] of that principal debt then the obligation may be considered independent rather than cautionary.

10.05 Between these two poles of connected and totally unconnected, the parties are free to set out the terms of their agreement as they see fit. There is generally no particular form in which a cautionary obligation must be set out; an obligation may designate itself as a guarantee, yet its contents may suggest an independent obligation.[5] Despite apparent connection with the existence and extent of the principal debt, it is possible to vary, exclude or embellish the rights of the parties to such a degree that the obligation should properly be considered as an independent obligation. This may be the case, for example, because of the exclusion of the so-called cautioner's common law rights of recourse, or by specifically derogating from the rule that the cautioner's liability can be no greater than that of the principal obligation. In an attempt to avoid such confusion, the Draft Common Frame of Reference ('DCFR') proposes that if the obligation is to be independent rather than cautionary it must expressly or impliedly say so – the presumption being that the obligation is cautionary.[6]

Proper and improper caution

10.06 Within the category of cautionary (as opposed to independent) obligations, a further distinction may be made between proper caution and improper caution.

10.07 Proper caution arises where the cautioner is bound explicitly as a cautioner, for the debts of a named debtor.[7]

10.08 Improper caution arises where a cautioner appears on the face of the document establishing the obligation to be bound as a co-debtor in the principal obligation, but the parties' intention is that the apparent co-debtor should be a cautioner. In such cases, the creditor who knows of the true nature of the transaction is bound to treat the apparent co-debtor as cautioner, with the normal rights of a proper cautioner.[8] The

---

2 *Sutton & Co v Grey* [1894] 1 QB 285 at 288 per Lord Esher MR.
3 *Yeoman Credit Ltd v Latter* [1961] 1 WLR 828.
4 *Goulston Discount Co Ltd v Clark* [1967] 2 QB 493.
5 *Wilson v Tait* (1840) 1 Rob App 137.
6 C von Bar and E Clive (eds), *Principles, Definitions and Model Rules of European Private Law: Draft Common Frame of Reference (Full Edition)* (2010) IV.G.-1:101(b) and IV.G.-2:101.
7 G J Bell, *Principles of the Law of Scotland* (4th edn, 1839) § 247; J Erskine, *An Institute of the Laws of Scotland* (Nicolson ed, 1871) III.iii.61.
8 *Paterson v Bonar* (1844) 6 D 987; cf. Bell, *Principles* § 246.

only exceptions to this rule are the benefit of discussion (in so far as it continues to apply)[9] and the benefit of division. Both are taken to have been impliedly waived by consenting to be bound as a co-debtor.[10]

10.09 Where the creditor is aware of the true relationship of the parties to each other, but this fact is not disclosed by the document establishing the cautionary obligation, the position is somewhat difficult. On the one hand, the justification for affording special rights to an improper cautioner is the creditor's awareness of the true nature of the relationship between the parties. As a result of such knowledge, it would be inequitable to allow the creditor to ignore that information and treat the cautioner simply as a co-debtor. On the other hand, where the true relationship is not disclosed by the document itself, treating the supposed cautioner differently from the other co-debtors potentially amounts to a modification of the agreement between the parties by the court. It is suggested that the solution lies in interpreting the cautionary agreement or promise in light of the 'underlying factual matrix' known to the parties at the time it was constituted.[11] If the facts known to the creditor at that point mean that the creditor should have been aware that one party's obligations were merely cautionary, then that party should be afforded the protections afforded to cautioners (other than the benefit of division, which can be regarded as having been waived by the express terms binding the cautioner as 'co-debtor').

CONSTITUTION AND VALIDITY

Promise or contract

10.10 Cautionary obligations may be constituted as contracts or promises, and are subject to the same rules of formality as any other voluntary obligation. It is sometimes unclear from the dealings between the parties whether the cautioner offers to enter into a contract of guarantee, requiring acceptance, or whether the cautioner simply promises to pay if the debtor fails, requiring only communication to the promisee. This should be decided according to the normal rules of interpretation.[12]

Formal validity

10.11 With two exceptions, cautionary obligations – like most other

---

9 The benefit of discussion no longer applies to caution for payment obligations: Mercantile Law Amendment Act Scotland 1856, s 8.

10 G J Bell, *Commentaries on the Law of Scotland* (7th edn, 1870) I.365.

11 *Multi-Link Leisure Developments Ltd v North Lanarkshire Council* [2010] UKSC 47, 2011 SC (UKSC) 53.

12 Cf. S Eden, 'Cautionary obligations and representations as to credit', *Stair Memorial Encyclopaedia* (1994) ('SME') vol 3, paras 882–884.

voluntary obligations – do not need to be in writing.[13] With one exception, there is no particular form of words that must be used.

10.12 If a cautionary obligation is constituted as a unilateral obligation, otherwise than in the course of business, then it must be in writing and signed by the granter.[14] In addition, if a cautionary obligation relates to a regulated credit agreement, it must be constituted in the prescribed written form, or it is ineffective.[15] If neither of these cases apply, the cautionary obligation need not be in writing in order to meet the rules on formal validity. Most commercial guarantees are constituted by formal writing, for obvious reasons.

10.13 If an agreement is constituted in writing, the written terms are presumed to represent the entire agreement on that matter, subject to extrinsic evidence of additional terms.[16] Parties may not lead extrinsic evidence which would otherwise vary the written terms, unless the document fails to accurately express the common intention of the parties.[17] However, the subsequent words or conduct of the parties entitled to the benefit of obligations under the agreement may personally bar that person from insisting on the rights contained in the written document, if those words or conduct are inconsistent with the existence of the right.[18] Of course it should be remembered that, while the parties may not bring evidence to contradict a court's construction of a particular term, once that construction has been established it remains open to the parties to argue that the words used should be interpreted by the court in a particular way according to the factual matrix.[19]

10.14 The DCFR proposes that cautionary obligations must be written in a prescribed form in order to be valid.[20]

Substantive validity

Generally

10.15 Cautionary obligations are subject to the normal rules of capacity, error, misrepresentation, fraud, force and fear, undue influ-

13 Requirements of Writing (Scotland) Act 1995, s 1(1). Previously, the Mercantile Law Amendment Act Scotland 1856, s 6, required that cautionary obligations be constituted in writing, but the section was notoriously difficult to apply and has since been repealed for cautionary obligations coming into existence after 1 August 1995 (see Requirements of Writing (Scotland) Act 1995, s 14 and Sch 5).
14 Requirements of Writing (Scotland) Act 1995, s 1(2)(a)(ii).
15 Consumer Credit Act 1974, ss 105, 106 and the Consumer Credit (Guarantees and Indemnities) Regulations 1983 (SI 1983/1556).
16 Contract (Scotland) Act 1997, s 1.
17 Law Reform (Miscellaneous Provisions) (Scotland) Act 1985, s 8.
18 *Gatty v Maclaine* 1921 SC (HL) 1.
19 *Multi-Link v North Lanarkshire Council* (n 11).
20 DCFR IV.G.-4.104.

ence, facility and circumvention, and illegality, as any other voluntary obligation.

Wrongs by the debtor against the cautioner

10.16 Misrepresentation, undue influence, facility and circumvention, or fraud by the principal debtor on the cautioner will not generally have any effect on the validity of a cautionary obligation. This is because caution is constituted by a contract between cautioner and creditor, or by a promise by the cautioner to the creditor: the creditor is not normally responsible for the conduct of the principal debtor unless the debtor can be said to be acting as agent for the creditor.[21]

10.17 However, a cautionary obligation may be indirectly vulnerable to a wrong committed by the principal debtor against the cautioner. Where the cautioner's relationship with the principal debtor is such that there may be a risk of undue influence or particular reason to suspect a misrepresentation, and the caution is given gratuitously, the creditor has an obligation (a) to ensure that the cautioner has sufficient information about the nature of the obligation being entered into, and (b) to promote taking independent legal advice.

10.18 This rule, based on a limited requirement of good faith, was set out in *Smith v Bank of Scotland*.[22] The wife of a bank's debtor entered into a standard security with her husband in favour of the bank over their matrimonial home, securing sums due by the husband's partnership to the bank. The wife was therefore a cautioner to the partnership's debt. She averred that her husband had misrepresented the indebtedness to her. The House of Lords held that the standard security should be set aside. This was not because, as in England, the bank was to be clothed with constructive knowledge of the misrepresentation, but because it had failed in its duty of good faith to the wife by not warning her of the consequences of entering into the security and advising her to take separate legal advice.

10.19 More recent cases have affirmed the effect of the decision, although not always its basis in the principles of Scots contract law. In particular, *Smith* did not clarify whether a failure of good faith alone was sufficient to allow a cautioner to escape liability, or whether lack of good faith needed to be coupled with an actionable wrong by the debtor. An actionable wrong was required in *Royal Bank of Scotland plc v Wilson*,[23] which also added that the rule in *Smith* is relevant only where the obligation is gratuitous. The term 'gratuitous', however, was given a fairly wide meaning. A joint security which covers all sums due to the creditor by either party would not be 'gratuitous' for present purposes, as both

21 See *Young v Clydesdale Bank* (1889) 17 R 231.
22 (1997) SC (HL) 111.
23 2003 SLT 910.

parties would have the benefit of the other's potential liability for their debt.

10.20 There is no closed group of relationships to which the rule in *Smith* applies. The requirement is simply that there is some objective risk of wrongdoing by virtue of the nature of the relationship between debtor and cautioner. This risk exists in practically all non-commercial cases,[24] and would therefore include relationships between a parent and child, husband and wife, and cohabitees.

10.21 On the basis of the above, it is suggested that a cautioner may seek reduction of a cautionary obligation where (a) there was an objective risk of wrongdoing by the debtor against the cautioner by virtue of their non-commercial relationship; (b) the caution is granted gratuitously; (c) the creditor failed to take steps to mitigate that risk; and (d) the debtor did in fact commit an actionable wrong against the cautioner.

10.22 One exception to the general rule that a debtor cannot directly affect the validity of a cautionary obligation is force and fear. If a debtor induces a cautioner to enter into a cautionary obligation by force and fear, the resulting cautionary obligation is void by lack of consent, despite the good faith of the creditor.[25]

Wrongs by the creditor against the cautioner

10.23 Cautionary obligations are not contracts *uberrimae fidei* (utmost good faith), and therefore do not require full disclosure of material facts from the creditor to the cautioner. Nonetheless, the creditor must disclose all material risks within its knowledge if the cautioner is 'excusably ignorant'.[26] Further, as discussed above, the creditor must not act in bad faith. Thus, if the creditor is aware that the cautioner misunderstands the facts or the nature of the transaction, the creditor cannot remain silent.

10.24 Where the creditor makes a positive representation, the cautioner may seek reduction of the obligation should the representation prove to be materially false, provided the cautioner would not have entered the contract on the basis of the true circumstances.[27] Positive representations may include false statements, partial truths, or concealment when a duty to speak exists.[28] Damages may also follow if the misrepresentation was fraudulent or negligent.[29]

---

24 *Royal Bank of Scotland plc v Etridge (No 2)* [2001] UKHL 44 at para [89] per Lord Nicholls.
25 *Hislop v Dickson Motors (Forres) Ltd* 1978 SLT (Notes) 73.
26 *Smith* at 117–18 per Lord Clyde.
27 See *Ritchie v Glass* 1936 SLT 591; *Lees v Todd* (1882) 9 R 807.
28 E.g. *Railton v Mathews and Leonard* (1844) 6 D 536.
29 *Bryson & Co Ltd v Bryson* 1916 1 SLT 361; Law Reform (Miscellaneous Provisions) (Scotland) Act 1985, s 10.

Error

10.25   An error as to the essentials of the contract will render the cautionary obligation void, regardless of the actions or inactions of the debtor or cautioner.[30] Thus where the cautioner erroneously grants a guarantee under essential error as to identity of the debtor, or believing the guarantee to be a different kind of obligation altogether,[31] the cautionary obligation may be void. In such cases, it is thought that despite apparent agreement, there is latent *dissensus* which cannot be resolved through normal contractual interpretation. However, as a general rule, the cautioner will not be released because of a misunderstanding of the terms of the guarantee or the extent of the indebtedness of the debtor, unless that error was induced by the creditor.[32] In these latter cases – depending on the terms of the caution – there is still consent, albeit the outcome of giving that consent has turned out to be different from what the cautioner expected.

10.26   Where the cautionary obligation is a unilateral gratuitous obligation (whether or not given in the course of business), it may be susceptible to reduction on the ground of unilateral essential error, without needing to show that the error was induced.[33]

Gratuitous alienations

10.27   Upon the insolvency of the cautioner, his or her creditors, trustees in bankruptcy, administrators, or liquidators (as appropriate) may apply to the court to reverse a gratuitous alienation made by the insolvent party. Gratuitous alienations may be reversed only if they were made in the previous two years. However, if the transaction was for the benefit of an 'associate' of the insolvent party, the time limit is extended to five years.[34] Cautionary obligations can be particularly susceptible to challenge on this ground, as by their nature there will frequently be no consideration given for them by the creditor.

10.28   If a caution is challenged, the creditor may object on the grounds that (a) the cautioner's assets were greater than his liabilities immediately after or at any time following the grant of the guarantee, or (b) that the guarantee was granted for adequate consideration.[35]

---

30 Stair, *Institutions of the Law of Scotland* (1981) I.x.13.
31 E.g. *Ellis v Lochgelly Iron and Coal Co Ltd* 1909 SC 1278.
32 *Stewart v Kennedy* (1890) 17 R (HL) 25; see also para **10.24** above.
33 *Hunter v Bradford Property Trust Ltd* 1970 SLT 173.
34 Insolvency Act 1986, s 242(2); Bankruptcy (Scotland) Act 1985, s 34(3).
35 Insolvency Act 1986, s 242(3); Bankruptcy (Scotland) Act 1985, s 34(4).

Consumer protection

Pre-contractual duties

10.29 Pre-contractual duties in relation to cautionary obligations are currently regulated by common law, as discussed above at paragraph **10.17**, where it was seen that creditors must take steps to inform the cautioner in practically all non-commercial transactions.[36] It may be that 'non-commercial' is a somewhat narrower definition than 'consumer', as it can conceivably exclude commercial consumers. In practice, corporate lenders are likely to supply the same information to commercial consumers granting cautionary obligations as they are to non-commercial guarantors.[37]

10.30 The DCFR proposes that where the cautioner is a consumer, the duty incumbent on the creditor would not simply be to mitigate the risk by promoting independent legal advice. In cases where there is a risk of undue influence, the creditor ought to actually ensure that the cautioner has taken it. Where no information is provided or independent advice is not taken at least five days prior to entry into the cautionary obligation, the cautioner would be free upon receiving such information or advice to entirely revoke the agreement.[38]

Unfair terms

10.31 The Unfair Terms in Consumer Contracts Regulations 1999 are applicable to cautionary obligations where (a) both the debtor and the cautioner enter into their respective obligations as consumers, and (b) the cautioner has been unable to influence the substance of the agreement.[39]

10.32 It was at one time thought that cautioners could not be considered as consumers for the purposes of the regulations, because the creditor could not be considered as a supplier to the cautioner.[40] The argument went that it was impossible to be categorised as a supplier where the only supply was by the cautioner to the creditor – in other words, that the creditor was the recipient of services, not the supplier of them. However, discussing the Distance Selling Directive,[41] the ECJ decided that there was no need for the consumer to be the person to whom such services were supplied in order for the protections to apply.[42]

---

36 See *Etridge (No 2)* (n 24).
37 See also *Bankers Trust International plc v PT Dharmala Sakti Sejahtera (No 2)* [1996] CLC 518.
38 DCFR IV.G.-4.103.
39 *Barclays Bank plc v Kufner* [2008] EWHC 2319 (Comm).
40 *Bank of Scotland v Singh* 17 June 2005, Queens Bench Division (unreported, referred to in *Williamson v Governor of the Bank of Scotland* [2006] EWHC 1289 (Ch)).
41 Directive 85/577/EEC.
42 *Bayerische Hypothetken-und Wechselbank AG v Dietzinger* (Case C-45/96) [1998] ECR I-1199.

This decision was based on the nature of cautionary obligations as subsidiary to a relevant supply of services (i.e. the credit extended to the debtor), and therefore the regulations may not apply to independent obligations. No case has yet settled the matter in Scots law, although it is expected that a Scottish court would follow the English decision in *Barclay's Bank*.[43]

10.33 The Unfair Contract Terms Act 1977 also applies to cautionary obligations. In particular, the Act restricts specific types of unreasonable contract terms where either (a) the cautioner is a consumer and the creditor is not, or (b) the cautionary obligation is in standard form. Note that, as the 1977 Act does not require a link with a 'supply', there is no need for the debtor to be a consumer, in contrast with the 1999 Regulations.

LIABILITY OF CAUTIONER

Amount and limits

10.34 Cautionary obligations are accessory to liability for a principal debt. It follows that, unless expressly provided for, a cautioner is liable only to the extent of the principal debt, plus interest and expenses.[44] Unless otherwise specified, the cautioner will be liable for the full extent of the loss sustained by the creditor resulting from the debtor's default. This is also called the principle of co-extensiveness. Any express liability over this amount might indicate that the obligation is not a cautionary obligation but an independent obligation, as discussed above. If a specific limit is provided for then naturally the creditor cannot recover more than that agreed amount from the cautioner.

10.35 It follows from the principle of co-extensiveness that any repayment of debt will reduce the cautioner's liability accordingly. Where the caution is for a fixed debt, liability will not be affected by further advances. However, where the guarantee is a continuing guarantee, further advances may increase the cautioner's liability.[45]

10.36 Where a limit is placed on the cautioner's liability, it is a matter of construction as to the effect of that limit. Either the cautioner guarantees part of the debt, or guarantees the whole debt up to a particular limit on liability.[46] In the former case, in the event of the debtor's bankruptcy, the cautioner is entitled to share in any dividends or securities, thus reducing liability proportionately.[47] So if the debt is £1,000, and the cautioner guarantees £100, a dividend of £500 from the debtor's

---

43 [2008] EWHC 2319 (Comm).
44 *Struthers v Dykes* (1847) 9 D 1437.
45 See paras **10.38–10.40** below.
46 See *Veitch v National Bank of Scotland* 1907 SC 554.
47 *F W Harmer & Co v Gibb* 1911 SC 1341.

bankruptcy will reduce the cautioner's liability to £50. If liability is for the whole amount, subject to a limit, then the creditor can seek recovery up to that limit ignoring any dividends paid from the bankrupt estate.

10.37 Repayment of the principal obligation can be made either by the debtor, or by the cautioner. If the latter repays the debt, the cautioner may then seek recovery of that expenditure from the debtor, as discussed below.[48]

Further advances

10.38 A cautioner may guarantee specific obligations, past debts or future debts. Where additional debts have been incurred after the creation of the cautionary obligation, it is a matter of construction of the agreement whether these further advances are to be included in the guarantee. If so, the guarantee is sometimes referred to as a continuing guarantee. If not, and the cautioner has agreed to be held liable only for debt which existed or was in the contemplation of the cautioner at the time the cautionary obligation was created,[49] any credit extended subsequently will not be secured by the prior cautionary obligation.

10.39 Where further advances are made and the debtor later makes a payment to the creditor, it is necessary to determine whether this payment goes towards reducing the secured or the unsecured portion of the debt. In the first instance, it is open to the debtor to specify which portion should be reduced – this is called appropriation. Failing an appropriation by the debtor, it is open to the creditor to make the decision.[50]

10.40 If neither the debtor nor creditor makes the appropriation, the presumption is that the payment will be set against the earliest outstanding indebtedness. In effect, the cautioner's liability will be reduced first before the (unsecured) further advances. Thus, if a debtor borrows £100 in respect of which a cautionary obligation is granted, then later borrows a further £50, any repayment will be notionally attributed to the debt of £100 first, until that debt is extinguished and only £50 remains. This is sometimes referred to as the rule in Clayton's case.[51]

ENFORCEMENT

Default of the principal

10.41 Cautionary obligations are guarantees that, should the principal debtor fail to perform obligations owed to the creditor, the cautioner will perform instead. It follows that the debtor must have breached the principal obligation before the creditor may seek to enforce the caution.

48 At para **10.51**.
49 *Scott v Mitchell* (1866) 4 M 551.
50 *Jackson v Nicoll* (1870) 8 M 408.
51 *Devaynes v Noble* (1816) 35 ER 781.

Non-payment of a debt is often called 'default', although this is not a term of art. Typically, commercial facilities will expand the definition of default to include, for example, the commencement of formal insolvency proceedings against the debtor, or the debtor's breach of any financial covenants. Furthermore, in practice, many guarantees state that the guarantor will perform the principal obligations 'on demand', regardless of whether the debtor is in default, which might indicate that such guarantees are separate principal obligations rather than cautionary obligations.

Debt must be proved

10.42 A creditor cannot sue a cautioner unless the debt has been proved. A debt may be proved by obtaining a decree for payment, by probative deed, or by the debtor's admission. It is no longer possible to prove a debt by oath.[52] The debt may be proved against the principal debtor, or the creditor, or both. In practice, it may be better to prove the debt against both the principal debtor and the creditor to avoid certain complications that may arise from one of the parties' non-involvement.[53]

RIGHTS OF A CAUTIONER

Generally

10.43 Unless expressly agreed, cautionary obligations include certain implied terms that reflect the special position the law affords a cautioner. These equitable rights are: the benefit of discussion, division, relief, and assignation of debt. It is open to the parties to modify or exclude these rights, and so they should not be regarded as a package of rights afforded in all circumstances but as context-sensitive specialties of cautionary obligations.

Right to benefit of discussion

10.44 At common law, a proper cautioner is entitled to expect that the creditor will exhaust all potential legal methods of recovering from the debtor before seeking to enforce the caution – sometimes called the benefit of discussion. By Act of Parliament, the benefit of discussion no longer applies to caution for monetary debts.[54] This means that a creditor may now proceed against the cautioner of a monetary obligation immediately upon the default of the debtor.

---

52 Requirements of Writing (Scotland) Act 1995, s 11; see *Royal Bank of Scotland plc v Malcolm* 1999 SCLR 854.
53 See W M Gloag and J M Irvine, *Law of Rights in Security Heritable and Moveable including Cautionary Obligations* (1897) pp 790–91.
54 Mercantile Law Amendment Act Scotland 1856, s 8; Gloag and Irvine, *Rights in Security*, p 788. It remains possible for the benefit of discussion to be included as an express term of the contract of cautionary.

Right to division

10.45 Where a number of proper cautioners are bound jointly (but not severally) as co-cautioners, each co-cautioner is liable for only a pro-rata share of the debt – provided that the debt is capable of division. Therefore, a co-cautioner can refuse to pay until the other co-cautioners are called to pay.[55]

10.46 The right of division is subject to an exception if one of the joint cautioners is insolvent. In this case, the solvent cautioners can be required to increase their pro-rata share as if the insolvent cautioner did not exist, subject to any agreed limit on liability.[56] So, for example, if only one cautioner out of five remains solvent, then that single cautioner can be held liable for the whole debt. That cautioner may then attempt to exercise his right of relief. This is discussed in more detail below.[57]

Right of relief

10.47 The right of relief has two elements. First, the cautioner has a right to be relieved, based on the implied mandate between the debtor and the cautioner. The idea is that the debtor has impliedly commissioned the cautioner to pay on his or her behalf.[58] Like any other agent, a cautioner is entitled to be relieved of obligations incurred as a result of being agent.

10.48 The right to relief based on implied mandate arises when the cautioner is put in distress – that is, where the creditor takes legal steps against the cautioner to enforce the caution[59] – or where the debtor is on the brink of becoming insolvent. Once this right arises, the cautioner does not need to actually perform the obligations under the cautionary obligation before demanding that the debtor either obtain the cautioner's discharge or repay the debt. In appropriate circumstances the cautioner may be able to protect his position by exercising the right of retention or compensation over money due to the principal debtor.[60]

10.49 There are also certain occasions where the cautioner does not need to be put in distress before pressing the debtor for relief. Most importantly, where the caution is for an indefinite period of time, the cautioner may at any time give the debtor a reasonable time to obtain a discharge before demanding repayment of the debt, 'it being unreasonable that a man should always have a cloud hanging over him'.[61]

10.50 On the basis of this implied mandate, the cautioner is entitled

55 Bell, *Principles* § 62; SME vol 3, para 927.
56 Erskine, *Institute* III.iii.63.
57 At paras **10.77–10.82**.
58 *Smithy's Place Ltd v Blackadder & McMonagle* 1991 SLT 790 at 795 per Lord Cameron of Lochbroom.
59 Erskine, *Institute* III.iii.65.
60 See Chapter 2: General Principles of Contract.
61 *Ranelagh v Hayes* (1683) 23 ER 405 at 406 per Sir Francis North.

to a lien over any assets belonging to the debtor that may be in the cautioner's possession.[62]

10.51 Secondly, the cautioner has a right to relief arising from payment of the debt in full. This will trigger a deemed assignation of the debt and any securities from the creditor to the cautioner.[63]

Right to assignation of debt

10.52 In addition to the automatic transfer of the creditor's right, a cautioner who has intervened and paid the debt fully on behalf of the debtor is entitled to an assignation of the right and any securities the creditor may hold over the debtor's assets, as well as an assignation of any diligence that has been executed by the creditor.[64] In effect, the cautioner who has paid fully should be put in the shoes of the creditor. Whether the security was held without the cautioner's knowledge, or was obtained after creation of the cautionary obligation, is irrelevant.[65]

10.53 It is not clear what such an assignation would add to the automatic assignation discussed above, but, in practice, having a deed of assignation may make the cautioner's position clearer to the other parties involved.

TERMINATION

Extinction of principal obligation

10.54 The existence of a proper caution entirely depends on the existence of a principal debt. Should the agreement from which the principal debt flows be found to be void as a result of operation of the principles of contract law, for example as a result of essential error or illegality, the cautioner will be released from any obligation: there is nothing for the caution to support.[66] This is called the accessory principle. Similarly, if the principal obligation is voidable, and is subsequently reduced, the cautionary obligation will come to an end.

10.55 As a caveat to this rule, it may be the case that a cautionary obligation will be unaffected by voidness resulting from a lack of capacity[67] or a defect in form.[68] In such cases, the cautioner must have been aware of the debtor's lack of capacity if the cautioner is to remain bound

---

62 *McPherson v Wright* (1885) 12 R 942.
63 *Smithy's Place Ltd* (n 58 above) at 795 per Lord Cameron of Lochbroom; Bell, *Principles* § 558.
64 Bell, *Principles* § 255; see also *Sligo v Menzies* (1840) 2 D 1478.
65 *Duncan, Fox & Co v New South Wales Bank* (1880) 6 AC 1; *Forbes v Jackson* (1882) 19 Ch D 615.
66 *Garrard v James* [1925] Ch 616.
67 *Stevenson v Adair* (1872) 10 M 919.
68 Erskine *Institute* III.iii.64.

when the debtor is not. The reason for this is variously ascribed to the operation of personal bar or to the nature of the risk underwritten by the cautioner.[69] The DCFR only holds the cautioner bound where 'relevant facts were known to the security provider at the time when the security became effective',[70] but in Scots law there may be a presumption that the cautioner is aware of the debtor's condition.[71]

10.56 Since full repayment of a debt extinguishes that debt, full repayment of the principal debt will release the cautioner from liability.

Material alterations

10.57 Just as total extinction of the principal debt releases the cautioner, so too will material alteration to the principal debt without the consent of the cautioner. A material alteration to the obligation which is being guaranteed means that it is no longer the same thing as the original debt upon which the cautionary obligation was entirely dependent.[72]

10.58 The impact that variation of the principal debt can have on a cautionary obligation can be explained in a number of ways, which largely depend on how the guaranteed liability is defined in the particular cautionary obligation in question. If the guarantee secures a particular and definite obligation (e.g., '*this* debt'), the novation of that obligation effectively amounts to frustration of the guarantee because the debt that has been guaranteed no longer exists.[73] Where the terms of the guarantee are more general (e.g., '*the* debt'), an alteration of the principal debt may be prejudicial to the cautioner, thus permitting relief.[74] Of course, the terms of the guarantee may even permit alteration to the debtor's liability, but in such cases the accessory principle must be at least partially ignored – which may suggest an independent rather than cautionary obligation.

10.59 It is thought that giving time, as discussed below, may also constitute a material alteration depending on the terms of the particular cautionary obligation.

Prejudicial conduct

No general duty to act reasonably

10.60 From time to time it is suggested that a creditor owes a cautioner a duty to act reasonably in exercising rights under the cautionary obligation. While case law does not necessarily support this proposition as a

---

69 SME vol 3, para 838.
70 DCFR IV.G.-2.103(3).
71 Erskine, *Institute* III.iii.64.
72 Cf. J J Gow, *The Mercantile and Industrial Laws of Scotland* (1964) p 323.
73 *Calder & Co v Cruikshank's Tr* (1889) 17 R 74.
74 *N G Napier Ltd v Crosbie* 1964 SLT 185.

general principle, there are certainly instances where the unreasonable actions of a creditor can release the cautioner from the cautionary obligation. Rather than asserting that a creditor owes the cautioner a duty to act reasonably, it is perhaps more accurate to state that the creditor cannot act in a manner that is prejudicial to the cautioner and later insist upon the caution.[75] The meaning of prejudicial conduct has been elaborated upon by the courts, and while the list is never closed, it is possible to identify particular types of conduct which are likely to be classed as prejudicial.

Giving time

10.61   Giving time consists in the creditor legally binding him or herself (for example, by agreement) not to demand immediate payment of the principal debt when it falls due.[76] It is thought to be prejudicial to the rights of the cautioner,[77] because it may temporarily restrict or remove some of the cautioner's rights of relief – for example, the right to call on the debtor to repay the debt. However, it may be that the existence of prejudice is merely ancillary to the fact that, by giving time, the creditor has materially altered the principal debt.[78] As we have seen above, a material alteration to the principal debt will release the cautioner without consideration of prejudice.

10.62   A distinction must be made between situations in which the creditor becomes legally disabled from demanding payment, and situations in which the creditor simply fails to press for immediate payment. An example of the former may be agreeing to accept repayment in instalments rather than a lump sum; an example of the latter may be neglecting to immediately demand payment when it falls due. The latter does not affect the existence of the original obligation, nor does it alter the nature of the obligation.

Discharging securities

10.63   The release of real security rights (for example, standard securities, pledges, liens) can have a significant impact on the risk and extent to which the cautioner will be called upon to perform. Furthermore, the release of a security would be prejudicial to the cautioner's right to assignation of securities. For these reasons, a cautioner is entitled to assume that the creditor will not voluntarily release securities securing the debt. Discharge of a security interest will release the cautioner, but only to the extent of the security released.

10.64   The same effect will result where a security interest is lost due

---

75 *Lord Advocate v Maritime Fruit Carriers Co Ltd* 1983 SLT 357.
76 See e.g. *Rouse v Bradford Banking Co* [1894] AC 586.
77 E.g. *C and A Johnstone v Duthie* (1892) 19 R 624 at 627 per Lord McLaren.
78 *Richardson v Harvey* (1853) 15 D 628.

to the negligence or omission of the creditor. *Fleming v Thomson*[79] illustrates the potentially severe consequences for a legal practitioner involved in secured lending. In that case, the solicitors for the creditor failed to properly register a bond and disposition in security (a form of heritable security since replaced by the standard security[80]) in the General Register of Sasines. Not only was the security ineffective for want of registration, but the cautioner was released too.

Discharging a co-cautioner

10.65 Where caution has been granted by multiple co-cautioners, releasing one cautioner from his or her cautionary obligations will automatically release the others.[81] It does not matter whether the co-cautioners are liable severally (in other words, separately) rather than jointly or jointly and severally. It is thought that the reason behind this is that each co-cautioner is entitled to assume that the others will remain bound: their release has substantially the same effect as the discharge of a real security.

10.66 There is one potential exception or limit to this rule. Where each of the cautioners is bound severally for less than the whole debt, discharge of one will have no effect on the others.[82]

10.67 In practice, the procedural aspects of releasing co-cautioners will be set out in the agreement. The consent of the other cautioners to the discharge of one of their number will prevent such problems arising.

Discharge of the cautioner

By agreement

10.68 It is open to the parties to a cautionary obligation, as with any other contract, to simply agree that their respective obligations shall be at an end.

10.69 Where the cautionary obligation is reduced to writing, it is good practice to obtain the discharge in writing too – although it is no longer the case that it must be.[83] Even if writing is required for some reason, the creditor may, by words or conduct, become personally barred from insisting on the caution.[84]

---

79 (1826) 2 W & S 277.
80 Conveyancing and Feudal Reform (Scotland) Act 1970, s 9(3).
81 Mercantile Law Amendment Act Scotland 1856, s 9.
82 *Morgan v Smart* (1872) 10 M 610.
83 Requirements of Writing (Scotland) Act 1995, s 1; Cf. *Charles and James McPherson v John and James Reid Haggart* (1881) 9 R 306.
84 *Gatty v Maclaine* 1921 SC(HL) 1.

Revocation by the cautioner

10.70   Provided that doing so will not breach the terms of the cautionary obligation, a cautioner may give notice to the creditor that further advances will not be guaranteed – in effect withdrawing from future liability. In such cases the cautioner will continue to be held liable for advances made prior to the notice. The cautioner is then, as at any other time, free to call upon the principal debtor to repay the debt and obtain a discharge of the caution from the creditor.

10.71   It is implied that a cautioner may revoke liability for further advances where liability is on a continuing basis, whether or not there is a cap on the amount the cautioner can be held liable for.[85] The terms of the cautionary obligation may, and frequently do, expressly override this implied term. No such implied term exists where the cautionary obligation is for a definite period of time, or for the finance of a particular transaction.

10.72   The DCFR proposes additional protection for consumer cautioners by permitting revocation after three years, even where an agreed time limit exists. This exception would not apply, again, if the caution related to a specific transaction or contractual obligation. It would require that the cautioner must give at least three months' notice.[86]

Operation of law

Prescription

10.73   Prescription of liability under the cautionary obligation will release the cautioner. The relevant period is five years from the time at which the cautionary obligation becomes enforceable.[87] In the absence of contrary agreement, a cautionary obligation becomes enforceable upon default of the principal obligation, meaning that the cautionary obligation and principal debt both prescribe together.

10.74   In practice, it is common to state that the guarantee will become enforceable 'on demand'. If this is the case, then the date of demand is the relevant date for the purposes of prescription, regardless of the date of default.[88]

Death

10.75   The death of the cautioner will, upon notice being given to the creditor, have the same effect as revocation – that is, determination of any future liability. As noted above, revocation is not possible where it would contradict the terms of the guarantee, in which case the

---

85 Bell, *Principles* § 266.
86 DCFR IV.G.-04.107.
87 Prescription and Limitation (Scotland) Act 1973, s 6.
88 See e.g. *Royal Bank of Scotland v Brown* 1983 SLT 122.

cautioner's estate remains bound in relation to any further advances. Notice of the death must be given to the creditor. In the absence of notice, it does not appear to be relevant whether the creditor was in fact aware of the cautioner's death. However, it is possible that knowledge of the death coupled with failure by the creditor to notify the cautioner's estate of the cautionary obligation will bar claims as to further advances.

10.76 Death of the creditor or debtor will generally determine the obligation, thereby preventing future liabilities, but not liability for previously incurred debts.[89]

Insolvency

Generally

10.77 Insolvency of any of the parties has certain effects on cautionary obligations established between them, but does not generally terminate or otherwise alter their obligations. Instead, it is better to think of insolvency as having an effect on the way in which the creditor and cautioner may enforce their respective rights under the cautionary obligation.

Of the debtor

10.78 Upon the insolvency of the debtor, the creditor may elect to rank in the insolvency for the debt. Typically the creditor will be paid at a discount for every pound of the debt in full satisfaction of the whole debt, if there is any payment at all. This payment is called a dividend. Once the dividend is paid, the creditor is then free to seek recovery of the balance of the debt from the cautioner. However, because the debt has been settled in full as far as the insolvent estate is concerned, the cautioner cannot seek to rank in the insolvency after assignation,[90] and is therefore left without a remedy.

10.79 On the other hand, the creditor may seek to enforce against the cautioner directly and bypass the debtor's insolvency. If the debt is settled in full, the cautioner, exercising the rights of relief discussed below, is then entitled to rank in the insolvency.

10.80 Complications can arise where the caution is limited by amount. As a matter of construction, it must be established whether the guarantee was (a) for the whole debt, subject to a limit, or (b) for part of the debt only. In the first case, should the creditor choose to rank in insolvency, the cautioner will be precluded from doing so as discussed above. This is because the cautioner would effectively be ranking on the insolvent estate for the same debt, thus counting it twice – so called 'double ranking'. Of course, the agreed limit will still apply. In the second case, should the cautioner repay the guaranteed part of the debt in full, both

---

89 *Woodfield Finance Trust (Glasgow) Ltd v Morgan* 1958 SLT (Sh Ct) 14.
90 See *Mackinnon v Monkhouse* (1881) 9 R 608; See also para **10.52**.

the creditor and the cautioner may rank in insolvency: the cautioner for the part of the debt guaranteed, and assigned by virtue of the rights of relief discussed below; the creditor for the parts of the debt not covered by the guarantee.[91]

Of the cautioner

10.81 Should the cautioner become bankrupt before the cautionary obligation becomes enforceable, the creditor is entitled to rank in the cautioner's insolvency on a contingent basis. After the obligation is enforceable, the creditor may simply rank on the cautioner's insolvent estate for the debt. If there are co-cautioners, the creditor may only rank for the cautioner's pro-rata liability of the debt, leaving the creditor to recover the balance from the other co-cautioners.

Of the principal debtor and co-cautioners

10.82 If the principal debtor and some, but not all, of the co-cautioners become insolvent, the creditor is again entitled to choose between two options. First, the creditor may rank on the insolvent estates for the full debt, thereafter seeking the balance from the solvent cautioners.[92] This would have the effect of preventing the solvent cautioners from ranking on the insolvent estates for the same debt.[93] Alternatively, the creditor may recover the full amount from the solvent cautioners, leaving them to rights of relief against the insolvent estates. In this case, the solvent cautioners are entitled to rank on the debtor's estate for the full amount they have paid, but may rank on the insolvent co-cautioners' estates only for the extent to which they have paid more than their pro-rata share.[94]

---

91 *Veitch v National Bank of Scotland* 1907 SC 554.
92 See *Morton's Trs v Robertson's Judicial Factor* (1892) 20 R 72.
93 See para **10.78** above.
94 Bell, *Commentaries*, I.354.

Chapter 11

Non-Judicial Real Security

INTRODUCTION

Why grant or seek rights in security?

11.01 Personal rights are only as valuable as the person who owes the correlative obligation. If that person is unwilling or unable to pay or perform, the value of the right will be seriously diminished. The expense and hassle of enforcing a small debt may mean that it is not worth pursuing if the debtor resists. Even if a creditor successfully obtains a decree for payment and does diligence, expenses may not cover the full cost of recovery. Further, the debtor may not have sufficient assets to pay the creditor. A right to payment of £500 against a solvent debtor will be worth more than one for £5,000 against an insolvent one, if the so-called dividend which the insolvency official pays out to the insolvent debtor's creditors is less than 10p for every pound owed.[1]

11.02 Creditors have a strong interest in protecting themselves against these risks before giving credit to debtors. The mechanisms which allow them to do so are known as rights in security. Rights in security take two forms: personal security (known in Scots law as caution) and real or proprietary security. Personal security gives the creditor a secondary personal right: the basic idea is that, if the debtor does not pay the creditor another person will (thus the term personal security). In real security, the creditor's secondary right is not against a different person but against a thing, a *res* (thus the term real security). The thing over which the right is granted is sometimes referred to as the object of the right in security or the security subjects.

11.03 As discussed in Chapters 3 and 12, certain forms of diligence enable a creditor to acquire a real right in the debtor's property which allows the value of the asset to be realised and applied to payment of the debt. For that reason, diligence is sometimes referred to as judicial security. This Chapter is concerned with non-judicial real security. Judicial security is discussed in chapter 12. Rights in security may be granted in respect of obligations other than debts but debts are the most common form of secured obligation and, for the sake of simplicity, the rest of this

1 See generally Chapters 13 and 14.

chapter will proceed on the assumption that the secured obligation is a debt.

11.04   The reasons why a creditor might want a right in security are obvious, but why would the debtor be willing to grant one? Without a right in security a creditor might not be willing to lend at all or might only advance credit at a much higher rate of interest. Given the possibility of diligence and insolvency processes where debts are not paid, granting a right of security does not really put the debtor at greater risk of losing the asset. The assets will be sold off one way or another anyway. Those who are really prejudiced by rights in security are the other creditors of the person who gives security because the security holder's real right will entitle him or her to preferential access to the asset in question but the other creditors have no say in the granting of the right.

Timing and parties

11.05   While the grant of the right in security is usually contemporaneous with the creation of the debt, this need not be the case. It is perfectly permissible to grant a right in security to secure the payment of a pre-existing debt.

11.06   Also, while the right in security will usually be granted by the debtor, this need not be the case. A third party may well be willing to grant a right in security for another's debt. David may want to borrow money from Carol but she is unwilling to lend it to him without security. David has no suitable assets, so he asks Oliver to put up security for him. Oliver agrees and pledges his antique clock in security for David's debt. In that situation, if David does not pay the debt, Carol could sue David for the price. She could also sell the clock (although she might have to apply to the court for authority to do so) so the proceeds could be applied to satisfaction of the debt. She could not, however, sue Oliver for the price. Oliver's clock is, in a manner of speaking, liable for the debt but Oliver has no personal liability.

11.07   In order to keep things simple, the rest of this chapter has been written on the assumption that the right in security has been granted by the debtor but it should be borne in mind that the rules discussed are equally applicable where the right in security is granted by a third party. Unless a specific case is being discussed, the debtors and owners will be referred to using the masculine pronoun and creditors will be referred to using the feminine pronoun.

11.08   Granting a right of security for someone else's debt is one reason why someone might own an asset burdened by a right in security without being liable to pay the relevant debt. The other reason is transfer of the burdened asset. Since rights in security are real rights, they affect the asset even after transfer.

Types of real security

11.09 Scots law recognises a wide range of real rights in security. They may be subdivided into conventional rights and tacit or automatic rights. Those in the former category are created as a result of a juridical act by the debtor and creditor; those in the latter are created by operation of law, without the need for any juridical act on the part of either owner or security holder. Real rights in security may also be subdivided into possessory and non-possessory security rights. For the former, the creditor must take possession of the object of the right, while this is not necessary for the latter.

Voluntary rights in security

- Pledge: a possessory right in security over corporeal moveables.
- Standard security: a non-possessory security over heritable property constituted by registration.
- Floating charge: a non-possessory right in security which can be granted only by companies and a small number of other types of juristic person.
- Aircraft mortgage: a non-possessory security over aircraft.
- Ship mortgage: a non-possessory security over ships.

Tacit rights in security

- Lien: a possessory right in security which arises in favour of creditors who obtain possession of their debtor's property in the course of carrying out their obligations to the debtor.
- Landlord's hypothec: a non-possessory right securing the right to rent over corporeal moveables belonging to the debtor which are on the property which has been let out.
- Solicitor's lien: a solicitor's right in security over papers owned by the client in security of outstanding fees.
- Maritime lien or hypothec: a right in security over the ship for seamen's wages, for the price of foreign repairs and for damage done by the ship.

In English law, the term 'charge' is sometimes used to mean a right in security. Sometimes English lawyers use the term 'charge' in contradistinction to a mortgage to refer to a particular type of right in security. English influence on Scots law means that the term 'charge' is sometimes used in Scotland too. In Scotland, a charge is a right in security.

GENERAL PRINCIPLES APPLICABLE TO RIGHTS IN SECURITY

11.10 Scots law recognises a number of different kinds of right in security. The appropriate right in security will vary depending on the nature of the thing which is being used as security, the granter of the security and the circumstances in which it arises. However, there are certain principles which are applicable to most of all kinds of right in security.

Nemo plus juris ad alium transferre potest quam ipse haberet

11.11 The general rule that no-one can grant a greater right than he has himself applies to the grant of rights in security as much as it does to the creation of other real rights. This means that, while the debtor and the owner of the object of the security right need not be the same person, the granter of the security right requires to be the owner of the object of the security right. There are some exceptions to this, however.

11.12 The protection which sections 24 and 25 of the Sale of Goods Act 1979 gives to those who buy goods from non-owning sellers or buyers who are nonetheless in possession of the goods was discussed in Chapter 3.[2] This protection also extends to pledges: Sam sells some machinery to Bertha and remains in possession. By virtue of section 17 of the Sale of Goods Act 1979, ownership has passed to Bertha. Sam needs to borrow some money and pledges Bertha's machinery in security for the loan. Section 24 of the 1979 Act means that, provided the pledgee is in good faith, the pledge will be validly constituted and thus effective even against Bertha.

Prior tempore potior jure

11.13 Multiple rights in security may be granted in the same object. If the object is of sufficient value to pay all of the security holders then this is unproblematic. Where the asset is not sufficiently valuable to satisfy all the security holders, it becomes necessary to rank the rights in security to determine who has first call on the proceeds of the object of the right in security and who has to wait until others have been paid.

11.14 As might be expected, given that they are real rights, rights in security rank according to their date of creation. Colin lends £100,000 to Doreen which is initially unsecured. Later she borrows £50,000 from Carol and grants to her a standard security over her flat. Colin becomes concerned about the debt which Doreen owes him. To calm him down, Doreen grants him a right in security over the flat. Doreen defaults so the standard securities are enforced and the flat is sold. The sale raises £100,000 after the expenses have been paid. Who gets what? Colin was the first lender but that is not what matters. What matters is who has the prior real right. Carol has the prior real right, so she will be paid first, leaving only £50,000 for Colin.

11.15 It is open to the holders of rights in security to vary the *prior tempore* rule by a ranking agreement.

2 Paras **3.108–3.118**.

Publicity principle

11.16 Because rights in security are real rights, third parties need to be aware of dealings with them. For this reason, as with other real rights, the creation, modification or transfer of a right in security requires some means of publicity. Broadly speaking, this publicity is achieved by transfer of possession where the right in security is possessory, and by registration when it is not. In most cases the relevant publicity is a constitutive requirement, so the right in security will not be created until the publicity step has been taken.

11.17 Additional publicity is required for rights in security over property owned by companies.[3] When a right in security other than a pledge is granted by a company, 'particulars' giving the basic details of the right in security must be submitted for registration in the charges section of the entry for the relevant company in the Companies Register, within 21 days.[4] Failure to do so will prevent the security holder from relying on it in a dispute with an insolvency official or other creditor.[5] This means that, if a company grants a standard security or a ship mortgage, it must be registered twice: once in the Land Register or the Merchant Shipping Register in order to constitute the right in security and once in the charges section of the Companies Register. It is open to the secretary of state to make an order under section 893 of the Companies Act 2006 which would avoid the need for double registration by requiring the keeper of the 'special register' (such as the Land or Merchant Shipping Register) to communicate relevant registrations to the Registrar of Companies. Thus far, no section 893 order has been made.

Accessoriness principle

11.18 Rights in security exist to ensure the payment of debts or the fulfilment of other obligations. For this reason, the right in security is said to be accessory to the relevant debt or other obligation. The idea behind the principle of accessoriness is that the right in security depends for its existence on the existence of the debt. The most important implications of the principle of accessoriness are that the right in security cannot be enforced if the debt is not enforceable,[6] and that rights in security are extinguished by payment of the debt in question.[7]

11.19 The accessoriness principle is not enforced with the full rigour which might be used: it is possible to grant a security for sums which are

---

3 There are some cases where registration is not required so as to facilitate financial market transactions: rights in security held by central banks such as the Bank of England (Banking Act 2009, s 252) and rights in security granted as part of financial collateral arrangements (Financial Collateral Arrangements (No 2) Regulations 2003 (SI 2003/3226), reg 4(4)).

4 Companies Act 2006, s 859A.

5 Companies Act 2006, s 859H.

6 *Nisbet's Creditors v Robertson* (1791) Mor 9554.

7 Bell, *Commentaries* I, 711.

yet to be lent or for all sums due or to become due. In the former case, the right in security exists but only becomes enforceable when the money is advanced. In the latter, payment of everything which is owed to the creditor at a particular moment suspends, but does not extinguish, the security because it remains in force to secure any further debts which become due to the security holder.

Obligations on the party in possession

11.20 Rights in security are subordinate real rights. The existence of a subordinate real right means that there are at least two persons with an interest in the object of the right: the owner and the holder of the security right. Only one of the two parties with an interest can be in possession of the object. For this reason, certain obligations are imposed on the party in possession to prevent the other party's interest in the object from being harmed. The detail varies depending on the particular right in security.

Transfer of rights in security

11.21 In principle, rights in security are assets which may be transferred by the rightholder. However, a right in security is worth nothing without the right whose performance it secures. It might be thought that, because rights in security are accessory, they should follow the right which they secure automatically. So, if Adam has a right to payment secured by a right in security and he assigns the right to payment to Eve, both the personal right to payment and the right in security would pass to Eve when the assignation of the right to payment was intimated to the debtor. This idea is sometimes expressed by the maxim *accessorium sequitur principale*.

11.22 However, there is a potential conflict between the publicity principle and the principle of accessoriness in such a case. The latter might suggest that the right in security should follow the right to which it is accessory. On the other hand, the publicity principle suggests that any change to a right in security should be accompanied by some form of publicity. In the case of the standard security, the publicity principle prevails, so the right in security can only be transferred by registration of the relevant deed in the Land Register.[8] Thus it may lag behind the right to payment, which may be transferred by intimation of the assignation. The position regarding the transfer of other rights in security is mixed. A floating charge may be assigned[9] but there is doubt as to when and whether the right of pledge may be assigned. If assignation of the

---

8 Conveyancing and Feudal Reform (Scotland) Act 1970, s 14(1).
9 There is no statutory provision for assignation of floating charges but it is possible as a matter of general principle and has been recognised by the court: *Libertas-Kommerz v Johnson* 1977 SC 191.

right of pledge is possible, it appears to require transfer of possession from the assignor to the assignee.[10]

11.23 The requirement of publicity for transfer of a right in security raises the possibility of a security being held by the assignor when the right to payment has already passed to the assignee. Can the right in security survive such a separation, given that it is accessory to the right to payment? The drafters of the legislation governing the standard security appear to have assumed that it could. Were this not the case, we might expect to see some provision which holds back the transfer of the right to payment until the assignation of the right in security has been registered.

Sale by the security holder

11.24 In most cases the right in security is enforced by sale of its object. This sale is effected by or on behalf of the first-ranking security holder, who has a duty to get as high a price as can reasonably be obtained.[11] Although the security holder is not the owner, she has the power to make the buyer owner. The transfer also has the effect of discharging any security rights (including those arising from diligence) which rank alongside or below that of the selling security holder.[12] The proceeds are used to pay the expenses of the sale and the debt due to the security holder. Any surplus proceeds must be remitted to security holders with lower rankings (if there are any) and then (if anything is left) to the owner of the object of the security right.[13]

11.25 Imagine that Derek owns a factory. He borrows money from Ellie and grants a standard security over the factory to her. She registers it promptly. A few months later, he grants a second standard security to Felicity (who also registers). Unfortunately, Derek does not pay either of them and Ellie takes the relevant steps to enforce the security.[14] Ellie sells the factory to Betty for a price which is greater than the total amount due to her and to Felicity. The grant by Ellie is effective to make Betty the owner and to discharge both standard securities. Ellie has a duty to pay Felicity with the money left over after her expenses and the debt due to her have been paid. The surplus left over after Felicity has been paid must be given to Derek.

Extinction

11.26 The two main reasons for extinction of a security right have already been discussed: payment of the secured debt and enforcement of the security or of a prior ranking security. A right in security will also

---

10 A J M Steven, *Pledge and Lien* (2008) paras 4-18–4-27.
11 E.g. Conveyancing and Feudal Reform (Scotland) Act 1970, s 25.
12 E.g. CFR(S)A 1970, s 26.
13 E.g. CFR(S)A 1970, s 27.
14 Discussed below, in paras **11.39–11.44**.

be extinguished if the security holder discharges the right or if the object of the security ceases to exist. So, if flour which has been pledged is used to make bread, the security right in the flour will cease to exist because the flour has been destroyed by specification.

Some attention will now be given to the detailed rules governing the most important rights in security.

VOLUNTARY RIGHTS IN SECURITY

Pledge

11.27 Giving a pledge is the most basic way of granting real security: giving something to the creditor which she is entitled to hold on to until the obligation is fulfilled. Only corporeal moveables may be pledged: the requirement for delivery means that pledge of incorporeals is impossible and the only right in security which can be granted over heritable property is the standard security.[15] So a car or antique painting can be pledged.

Creation

11.28 Pledge is effected by delivery to the creditor together with an agreement that the object is to secure the debts.[16] Delivery is necessary to satisfy the requirement of publicity and the pledge only subsists while possession is maintained.[17] The agreement is considered as a real contract (real because it does not come into effect until the thing (*res*) is delivered). The agreement usually does not need to be in writing.[18]

11.29 The exception to this rule is a pledge under an agreement regulated by the Consumer Credit Act 1974.[19] The only creditors permitted to take pledges which are covered by the 1974 Act are those authorised by the Financial Conduct Authority: pawnbrokers.[20] Therefore, while the pledge agreement need not normally be in writing, it does need to be in writing if the creditor is a pawnbroker.

Obligations

11.30 The security holder has possession of the pledged object but is not entitled to use it or take its fruits unless this is necessary for the care of the object or the parties have agreed otherwise.[21] The security holder is obliged to take ordinary care of the pledged object but is entitled to

15 Conveyancing and Feudal Reform (Scotland) Act 1970, s 9(3).

16 Bell, *Principles* § 1363.

17 Bell, *Principles* § 1364; *Wolifson v Harrison* 1977 SC 384.

18 Requirements of Writing (Scotland) Act 1995, s 1(1).

19 Consumer Credit Act 1974, s 8(3) with Financial Services and Markets Act 2000, s 19 and Financial Services and Markets Act 2000 (Regulated Activities) Order 2001 (SI 2001/544) art 60B(3).

20 CCA 1974, ss 61A and 114.

21 Bell, *Principles* § 206; *Moore v Gledden* (1869) 7 M 1016.

payment of reasonable expenses for costs incurred as a result.[22] The owner is entitled to return of the property on payment of the debt.

Enforcement

11.31 Where the 1974 Act does not apply, the common law continues to govern the security holder's right to enforce a pledge. The default rule at common law is that authority to sell must be obtained from a sheriff before the sale can be effected.[23] However, it is open to the parties to agree that the security holder should have the power to sell without needing to go to court.[24]

11.32 Where an object has been pawned, i.e. pledged under a regulated consumer credit agreement, and the debtor defaults, the security holder is entitled to enforce without recourse to the courts. There are two possible enforcement mechanisms: one for small, short-term debts and the other for other debts.

11.33 The small debt rule applies where the period for repayment is six months (the statutory minimum for consumer loans secured by pledge),[25] the debt secured is £75 or less and the pledged object was not already in the possession of the security holder by virtue of a prior pledge. If the small debt rule applies, ownership of the pledged object passes to the security holder on the debtor's default.[26] Where the small debt rule does not apply, the pawnbroker has the power to sell the pledged object.[27]

11.34 The small debt rule is less favourable to debtors because, where there is no sale, there is no chance of obtaining a price greater than the debt and generating a surplus which is payable to the debtor.[28] The rule is poorly drafted: it depends on the value of the debt secured rather than on the value of the item pledged. If David pledged a watch worth £1,000 for a debt of £50 repayable within six months, the watch will be forfeited if he fails to pay within the allotted time. If, however, the loan had been for £100 rather than £50, the creditor would have had a simple power of sale and so David would have received around £900. (The precise amount would depend on the expenses of the sale.) A fairer rule would depend on the value of the item which has been pledged rather than on the debt which is secured.

Standard security

11.35 If pledge is the most basic right in security, the standard security

22 Bell, *Principles* § 206; Erskine, *Institute* III.i.33.
23 Bell, *Principles* § 207.
24 *North-Western Bank Ltd v Poynter, Son & Macdonalds* (1894) 22 R (HL) 1.
25 Consumer Credit Act 1974, s 116.
26 CCA 1974, s 120(1)(a).
27 CCA 1974, s 120(1)(b).
28 CCA 1974, s 121(3).

is arguably the most important. It is the only right in security which can be granted over heritable property.[29] In many cases, the most valuable asset which can be used as a security is land. This restriction is subject to a slight caveat because a floating charge can also cover heritable property but only certain kinds of person can grant a floating charge.[30]

11.36 Standard securities are usually granted over land but they can also be granted over any real right in land.[31] In practice, the most important application of this rule is that standard securities can be granted over registered leases.

Creation

11.37 Since a standard security is a real right in land, it requires to be granted by formal writing.[32] It also requires to be registered in the Land Register (if the property burdened by the standard security is on the Land Register) or recorded in the General Register of Sasines (if the property has yet to be registered in the Land Register).[33] Section 48(2) of the Land Registration etc (Scotland) Act 2012 gives Scottish Ministers power to set a date after which the Sasine Register will be closed to standard securities. After this date, all grants of standard securities will require to be registered in the Land Register.

Obligations

11.38 In contrast to pledge, the object of the standard security is not in the creditor's possession. Therefore, the most important obligations which apply while the security subsists protect the creditor's interest by controlling what the owner can do with the property. These obligations are set out in the 'conditions' of the standard security. Schedule 3 to the Conveyancing and Feudal Reform (Scotland) Act 1970 sets out standard conditions which, by default, apply to every standard security. It is open to the parties to vary these conditions. The default rules contain the obligations which might be expected for the protection of the value of the object of the security, for example: to keep the property in good repair;[34] a prohibition on alterations without the consent of the creditor;[35] to insure the property[36] and not to let the property without the creditor's consent.[37]

---

29 Conveyancing and Feudal Reform (Scotland) Act 1970, s 9(3).
30 See para **11.56**.
31 Conveyancing and Feudal Reform (Scotland) Act 1970, s 9(2).
32 Requirements of Writing (Scotland) Act 1995, s 1(2)(b).
33 Conveyancing and Feudal Reform (Scotland) Act 1970, s 9(2).
34 CFR(S)A 1970, Sch 3, para 1.
35 CFR(S)A 1970, Sch 3, para 2.
36 CFR(S)A 1970, Sch 3, para 5.
37 CFR(S)A 1970, Sch 3, para 6.

Enforcement

11.39 As well as containing rules on what can be done to the security subjects, the standard conditions contain rules about the enforcement of the standard security. Where the debtor fails to pay the debt, the creditor must serve a calling-up notice on the debtor.[38] The calling-up notice gives the debtor two months to pay the debt.[39] Failure to do so puts the debtor in default in terms of standard condition 9(1)(a). That, in turn, enables the creditor to sell the security subjects.[40]

11.40 If the property is used for residential purposes, significant further procedural requirements apply. Notification of the calling-up notice must be given to the relevant local authority.[41] This notification allows the local authority to make provision for housing anyone evicted from the property. Further, before the property can be sold the creditor requires either a court order or written consent to the sale and certification that the subjects are unoccupied from the debtor, the owner (if that is a different person) and anyone with family law occupancy rights.[42] The requirement of consent means that any of the people on the list can force the creditor to obtain a court order.

11.41 A court will not grant warrant to sell a residential property unless the 'pre-action requirements' have been complied with.[43] The pre-action requirements are set out in section 24A of the 1970 Act. Essentially, the requirements are threefold. First, there are information duties: the creditor must provide the debtor with information about the obligations which are unfulfilled and the consequences of not fulfilling them.[44] Further information must be given about sources of advice and assistance for debt management.[45] Secondly, there is a duty to encourage the debtor to make contact with the relevant local authority (so that emergency housing can be arranged).[46] Thirdly, there are duties aimed at a consensual outcome: the creditor must make reasonable efforts to agree a plan of action with the debtor which will remedy the defaults[47] and the creditor is barred from making an application for warrant to sell if the debtor is taking reasonable steps towards dealing with the defaults.[48] Further detail on the content of these pre-action requirements

---

38 CFR(S)A 1970 s 19; *Royal Bank of Scotland plc v Wilson* [2010] UKSC 50, 2011 SC (UKSC) 66.
39 CFR(S)A 1970, Sch 6 Form A.
40 CFR(S)A 1970, s 20(2); Sch 3, para 10(2).
41 CFR(S)A 1970, s 19A.
42 CFR(S)A 1970, ss 20(2A) and 23A.
43 CFR(S)A 1970, ss 24(1A)–(1D).
44 CFR(S)A 1970, s 24A(2).
45 CFR(S)A 1970, s 24A(5).
46 CFR(S)A 1970, s 24A(6).
47 CFR(S)A 1970, s 24A(3).
48 CFR(S)A 1970, s 24A(4).

can be found in the Application by Creditors (Pre-Action Requirements) (Scotland) Order 2010.[49]

11.42 Once the pre-action requirements have been complied with, the creditor can go to court for her warrant, but she must give notification of her application to the debtor, the owner and the occupier of the security subjects (often these will all be the same person) and give notification to the local authority.[50] Section 24 also contains guidance on when warrant to sell should be granted. The court must consider not only whether the debtor is in default and whether the pre-action requirements have been complied with but also whether warrant to sell is reasonable in all the circumstances.[51]

11.43 In determining whether the warrant is reasonable, subsections (6) and (7) of section 24 direct that the court must have regard to the nature and reasons for the default, the debtor's ability to address the problem within a reasonable time, what the creditor has done to help, participation by the debtor in a statutory debt payment programme and the ability of the debtor or other occupants of the security subjects to find alternative accommodation. Sections 24B and 24C give 'entitled residents' the right to make an application to the court about the warrant to sell. Essentially, this gives the owner, spouses, civil partners, cohabitants and the parents of children who live in the property the right to a say about whether the warrant to sell should be granted.

11.44 If it proves impossible to find a buyer willing to pay a price which would cover the debt secured by the standard security, and any other securities ranking alongside or below it, in the two months after the property was first advertised for sale, the creditor can apply for a decree of foreclosure.[52] When such an application is made, the court may either grant the decree or order that the property should be re-exposed for sale at a price fixed by the court.[53] If the decree of fore-closure is granted, it must then be registered. On registration of the decree, the creditor becomes the owner and her security along with all rights in security which rank alongside or below hers are extinguished.[54]

All sums due securities

11.45 As discussed above, sale may be by private bargain or public auction and the price is applied to pay secured creditors according to their ranking. Ordinarily, standard securities rank according to the rule *prior tempore potior jure*. However, some special rules are necessary to deal with standard securities which secure 'all sums due or to become due' to the creditor from the debtor. This means that every debt owed by the

---

49 SSI 2010/317.
50 CFR(S)A 1970, s 24(3).
51 CFR(S)A 1970, s 24(5)(b).
52 CFR(S)A 1970, s 28(1).
53 CFR(S)A 1970, s 28(4).
54 CFR(S)A 1970, s 28(6).

debtor to the creditor is secured by the standard security, even if the debt is created after the right in security has been granted. Such securities present a challenge to potential second-ranking security holders.

11.46 Imagine that David has borrowed £75,000 from Bank of Shetland Ltd and granted a standard security for all sums due or to become due. Later he needs another loan and he approaches Bank of Orkney Ltd. Bank of Orkney is not keen to lend because of the prior-ranking security but David produces documents proving that only £25,000 of the debt to Bank of Shetland is still outstanding and that his house is worth £250,000. This should reassure Bank of Orkney but it is worried because Bank of Shetland's security is for all sums due and ranks first. What if Bank of Shetland later lent David £250,000? Would Bank of Orkney then find itself ranking behind a security which would use up the whole value of the property?

11.47 Bank of Orkney's concern is addressed by section 13 of the 1970 Act. It allows a lower-ranking security holder to freeze the amount which can be covered by a prior-ranking all-sums-due standard security by notifying the prior-ranking holder of the creation of the lower-ranking security. So if Bank of Orkney obtains a standard security from David, it can notify Bank of Shetland of that fact. After that notification, Bank of Shetland's prior ranking will be limited to the amount which is outstanding at the time of notification and interest on that sum together with any further sum which they are obliged to advance to David under their contract with him.[55] In that way, Bank of Orkney can be reasonably confident there will be enough value in the house to secure its loan as well.

11.48 The same procedure can be used if the security subjects are sold. Usually the seller will obtain a discharge of any standard security burdening the property but this is not necessarily the case. Instead of borrowing from Bank of Orkney, David may sell the property to Betty. Even if some of the price Betty pays to David is used to clear the last £25,000 of the loan, the security will not be extinguished because it is for all sums due and to become due. However, Betty can prevent David from borrowing on the security of her house by notifying Bank of Shetland that the house now belongs to her. Since there is no debt outstanding, Betty will only be at risk if Bank of Shetland is obliged to advance further sums to David.

Floating charges

11.49 Pledge is not a very convenient mechanism for granting security over corporeal moveable property. It requires that the pledged items be in the possession of the security holder. That means that the debtor cannot use them. It also means that the creditor has to find somewhere to put them. Further, businesses whose major assets are corporeal move-

55 CFR(S)A 1970, s 13(1).

ables often want to be able to sell them and buy others frequently: their stock in trade is continually turning over. Even if the problems surrounding possession could be overcome, this would present another challenge to pledge as a security mechanism. Those who buy from the debtor would want to get an unburdened right but it would not be convenient to get a release of the security right from the creditor in every case. Furthermore, creditors do not want the administrative burden of accepting the grant of a security right for each new item of stock.

11.50 These concerns led to pressure for the introduction of a security right which could cover corporeal moveables, was non-possessory and could handle rotating stock. English law appeared to have developed just such a security: the floating charge. Although the floating charge was the product of case law development in England, it was introduced by statute in Scotland.

11.51 The floating charge is part of equity in English law. Broadly speaking, equity recognises the transfer or creation of property rights more readily than either common law rules in England or Scots property law. English law has a set of rules which deal with what happens when there is a conflict between the common law rules and those in equity. Scots law does not have a division between law and equity and therefore does not have rules which deal with the relationship between law and equity. Indeed, such a division makes little sense in the context of a civilian system of property law. For this reason, certain aspects of the floating charge have made it a rather poor fit in Scots law, causing some anomalous results and conceptual difficulties.

The basic idea

11.52 Two key concepts distinguish the floating charge from other kinds of security in Scots law: it is a global security and there is a gap between creation of the charge and its attachment.

11.53 As a global security, the floating charge can be granted 'over all or any part of the property which may from time to time be comprised in its property and undertaking'.[56] So the floating charge is not limited to corporeal moveables: heritable property and incorporeals can also be subject to a floating charge. Further, while a floating charge over a particular asset or particular class of assets might be granted, the most common floating charge is the global security which covers the company's whole property and undertaking. Traditional voluntary rights in security cover particular assets; the floating charge can cover everything in the company's 'property and undertaking'.

11.54 The key concept in the floating charge is the gap between

---

56 Companies Act 1985, s 462(1). Cf. Bankruptcy and Diligence etc (Scotland) Act 2007, s 38(1), which is not yet in force.

creation of the charge and its attachment. While other rights in security give the creditor a real right as soon as they are created, this is not the case with the floating charge.

11.55 As the name suggests the charge 'floats' over the company's assets. While the charge is floating, the creditor has no real right in them. This means that, when an asset which is under the shadow of the charge is transferred, the acquirer takes it free of any right in security. When a new asset is acquired, it falls under the shadow of the charge and thus becomes liable to be affected by the charge if it attaches. When the charge attaches, it has effect 'as if the charge were a fixed security'.[57] Therefore, the floating charge holder acquires a real right at the moment of attachment rather than at the moment of creation.

Creation

11.56 Floating charges can only be granted by companies and a small number of other juristic persons (notably limited liability partnerships).[58] There is no specific legislative requirement that the charge be in writing. In practice, charges are always made in writing as this greatly facilitates registration of the 'particulars' of the charge in the Companies Register. Since the floating charge can only be granted by companies or other entities subject to their publicity regime, all floating charges require to be registered in accordance with the special regime for publicity of rights in security granted by companies.[59]

11.57 As discussed above,[60] the companies registration regime is different from registration in the Land Register: registration is retrospective rather than constitutive. It is not something which needs to be done in order to create the right in security. Rather, it is something which requires to be done once a right in security has been created. In contrast to other rights in security, the floating charge is created by a private act between the parties: delivery of the signed deed granting the charge to the creditor.[61] This is dangerous because it means that there is a 21-day 'blind period' during which the floating charge exists but third parties have no notice of it.

11.58 If Part 2 of the Bankruptcy and Diligence etc (Scotland) Act 2007 is ever brought into force, this will change. It requires registration of a subscribed document granting the floating charge in a new Register of Floating Charges. Only once that step has been completed would the

---

57 Companies Act 1985, s 463(2); Insolvency Act 1986, s 53(7), Sch B1, para 115(3).
58 Companies Act 1985, s 462(1); Limited Liability Partnership (Scotland) Regulations 2001 (SSI 2001/128) reg 3.
59 There are some cases where registration is not required: see above n 3.
60 Para **11.17**.
61 *AIB Finance Ltd v Bank of Scotland* 1993 SC 588; Companies Act 2006, s 859E(1).

charge come into existence.[62] There is no immediate prospect of Part 2 of the 2007 Act being brought into force.

Attachment and enforcement

11.59 Only once a floating charge has attached does the chargeholder have a real right in security and thus the right to the value of the items affected by the charge. When does attachment occur? For a long time, the principal mechanism for enforcing a floating charge was the appointment of a receiver. If the debtor defaulted on his obligations, the chargeholder was entitled to appoint a receiver.[63] The appointment of the receiver triggered the attachment of the charge and the receiver took control of the assets covered by the charge and sold them to pay off the debt.[64] Since the charge usually covered all of the company's 'property and undertaking', the receiver had effective control of the company. These receivers were known as administrative receivers. However, the power to appoint receivers has been significantly restricted by statute. The basic rule is that, if the floating charge was granted after 15 September 2003, the holder of the floating charge cannot appoint an administrative receiver.[65] It remains competent to appoint receivers to enforce charges whose scope is limited to particular assets.

11.60 Does this mean that the chargeholder is now left without a mechanism for enforcement? No. Instead of being entitled to appoint a receiver, the chargeholder can appoint an administrator.[66] There are two important differences between the appointment of a receiver and of an administrator: first, the administrator must act for the benefit of the company's creditors as a whole rather than just for the benefit of the chargeholder;[67] secondly, appointment of the administrator does not automatically trigger the attachment of the floating charge.

11.61 If a company goes into administration, the charge only attaches when the administrator delivers a paragraph 115 notice to the Registrar of Companies.[68] This is a notice which says that the only way the administrator will be able to pay out to unsecured creditors is by invoking the 'carve-out' provision in section 176A(2)(a) of the Insolvency Act 1986.[69] The 'carve-out' rule is discussed at paras **11.72–11.74** below but the basic import of such a notice is that the company's secured debts are greater in value than its assets.

---

62 Bankruptcy and Diligence etc (Scotland) Act 2007, s 38(3). Again, there are some exceptions for central banks and financial collateral arrangements: 2007 Act, s 38(3A)–(3B).

63 Insolvency Act 1986, ss 51–52.

64 IA 1986, ss 53(7), 55 and Sch 2.

65 IA 1986, s 72A. A number of exceptions are set out in ss 72B–72GA, preserving the right to appoint administrative receivers for certain classes of debtor. These are limited to public sector activity and financial and capital markets.

66 IA 1986, Sch B1, para 14(1).

67 IA 1986, Sch B1, para 3(2).

68 IA 1986, Sch B1, para 115(3).

69 IA 1986, Sch B1, para 115(2).

11.62 The third trigger which can cause a floating charge to attach is the company going into liquidation.[70] In making such a notice, the administrator is saying that the company's secured debts are greater in value than its assets.[71]

Ranking: other rights in security

11.63 Once a charge has attached, it becomes necessary to determine how the floating charge ranks. The basic principles discussed above would suggest that the floating charge should rank ahead of unsecured creditors who have a merely personal right, and that it should rank with other rights in security according to whether they were created before or after attachment, when the chargeholder gets her real right. Unfortunately, the picture is not quite that simple.

11.64 The rules just stated are the starting point[72] but there are some important variations. The first of these is the so-called negative pledge clause. The document creating the floating charge may contain a clause which forbids or restricts the grant of other rights in security which would rank prior to or equally with the floating charge.[73] If such a pledge is included, the floating charge will rank ahead of any right in security created after the floating charge comes into existence.[74] This applies despite the fact that these rights in security have been granted before the floating charge has attached and thus before the chargeholder has a real right.

11.65 Imagine that Bust Co Ltd grants a floating charge over its whole property and undertaking to Bank of Shetland on 14 June, which is duly registered. On 31 August, it grants a standard security to Bank of Orkney which is registered the same day. On 2 September, the charge attaches. The respective ranking depends on whether a negative pledge clause has been included in the floating charge or not. If there is such a clause, then Bank of Shetland's floating charge will rank ahead of Bank of Orkney's standard security. If there is no such clause, Bank of Orkney's standard security will rank ahead of Bank of Shetland's floating charge.

11.66 As might be expected, nearly all floating charges include a negative pledge clause. If Part 2 of the Bankruptcy and Diligence etc (Scotland) Act 2007 comes into force, the default rule will be changed so that no security granted after the floating charge was created will rank ahead of it.[75] This will render negative pledge clauses unnecessary.

11.67 The negative pledge clause is effective to prevent the debtor

70 Companies Act 1985, s 463(1).
71 See further in Chapter 14: Corporate Insolvency.
72 CA 1985, s 464(4); IA 1986, s 60, Sch B1, para 116.
73 CA 1985, s 464(1)(a).
74 CA 1985, s 464(1A).
75 Bankruptcy and Diligence etc (Scotland) Act 2007, s 40(2).

from making grants of rights in security which will rank ahead of the floating charge, but it has no effect against involuntary securities. Thus the charge will rank behind 'effectually executed diligence' and tacit securities such as lien and the landlord's hypothec.[76]

11.68 Floating charges rank among themselves according to their date of registration in the Companies Register.[77] If a floating charge has been granted to cover future advances, the amount secured by the charge may be frozen by giving notification of a subsequent floating charge in a manner very similar to that which applies to standard securities which secure future advances.[78] If Part 2 of the 2007 Act comes into force, the power to freeze the debt secured will also be available to subsequent grantees of other rights in security.[79]

Ranking: unsecured creditors

11.69 The second major variation on the normal rules of ranking is that the floating charge is subject to rights of certain unsecured creditors. First, the floating charge ranks behind 'preferential debts'.[80] These cover certain obligations owed to employees, contributions to occupational pension schemes and levies on coal and steel production.[81] Secondly, the chargeholder's right is subject to the prescribed part under section 176A of the Insolvency Act 1986.

11.70 The prescribed part carves out a portion of what would otherwise be payable to the chargeholder for the benefit of unsecured creditors. The prescribed part was introduced because of concerns that the global nature of the floating charge meant that the chargeholder would 'scoop the pool' and leave nothing for unsecured creditors.

11.71 Whether a carve-out is made and the size of the carve-out depends on the size of the company's 'net property', which is the property left for the satisfaction of the chargeholder once prior-ranking security holders and preferential debts have been paid.[82] If the net property is less than £10,000, then the carve-out is only made if the liquidator, administrator or receiver thinks that the benefit of making it would outweigh the cost.[83] Even if the net property is £10,000 or more, the liquidator, administrator or receiver can apply to the court for an

---

76 CA 1985, s 463(1); IA 1986, s 60(1)(b). The interpretation of the phrase 'effectually executed diligence' has been the subject of some controversy: S Wortley, 'Squaring the circle: revisiting the receiver and "effectually executed diligence"' 2000 JR 325.
77 CA 1985, s 464(4)(b).
78 CA 1985, s 464(5).
79 Bankruptcy and Diligence etc (Scotland) Act 2007, s 40(5)(b).
80 Companies Act 1985, s 464(4); Insolvency Act 1986, ss 59, 175, and Sch B1, para 116.
81 IA 1986, s 386.
82 IA 1986, s 176A(6).
83 IA 1986, s 176A(3), Insolvency Act 1986 (Prescribed Part) Order 2003 (SI 2003/2097) reg 2.

order that the carve-out should not be made on the basis that the cost would outweigh the benefit.[84]

11.72 Assuming that a carve-out is to be made, the next step is to determine how big it should be. If the net property is £10,000 or less, the prescribed part is 50 per cent of that net property. If the net property is more than £10,000, the prescribed part is £5,000 plus 20 per cent of the surplus above £10,000.[85] The prescribed part is subject to an upper limit of £600,000.[86] So, if the net property is £7,000, the prescribed part would be £3,500 because that is half of the net property. If the net property is £15,000, the prescribed part would be £6,000: £5,000 plus 20 per cent of £5,000, which is the amount by which the net property exceeds £10,000. No matter how big the net property is, the prescribed part will never be more than £600,000.

Floating charges and purchasers

11.73 As noted above, the floating charge was the product of equity in English law. For the purposes of equity, a buyer who has paid for property and taken possession is considered to be the owner, although some of the necessary formalities have still to be completed. That means that, even if the charge granted by the seller attaches before the disposition has been registered, the buyer who has paid and taken possession is safe.

11.74 In *Sharp v Thomson*,[87] this set of circumstances arose under a Scottish floating charge. The purchasers had paid the price, obtained possession of the property and received delivery of the disposition, but they had not registered the disposition when the charge attached. An orthodox Scots property law analysis suggested that the chargeholder should prevail over the purchaser in these circumstances: the seller was the owner of the property when the charge attached. However, the House of Lords found in favour of the purchasers. The best explanation of the result is that the term 'property and undertaking' as it is used in the floating charge legislation does not quite cover everything which the granter of the charge owns.[88] The *Sharp* exception has not been applied in any other case and appears to be restricted to cases where payment has been made for an asset but the transfer has not been complete when the charge attaches.

TACIT RIGHTS IN SECURITY

11.75 The rights in security considered hitherto occur as a result of a grant by the debtor. However, some rights in security occur automati-

---

84 IA 1986, s 176A(5).
85 Insolvency Act 1986 (Prescribed Part) Order 2003, reg 3(1).
86 Reg 3(2).
87 1997 SC (HL) 66.
88 *Sharp v Thomson* read with *Burnett's Tr v Grainger* 2004 SC (HL) 19.

cally, without the need for any grant. They are known as tacit rights
in security.

Lien

11.76 The simplest tacit right in security is lien. It can be thought of
as the tacit security equivalent of pledge. Like pledge, lien is a possessory
right in security. In contrast to pledge, it may be possible to have a lien
of land as well as of corporeal moveable property.[89]

Special and general liens

11.77 Liens are either special or general. Special liens arise on the basis
of mutuality of obligations. The creditor has an obligation to deliver the
debtor's property but that obligation is conditional on the debtor fulfilling his obligation to her.[90] It can arise in any case where a creditor finds
herself in possession of the debtor's property as a result of the same transaction which gave rise to the debtor's obligation to the creditor. This
personal right to retain the property is fortified by the real right of lien,
so it is effective even in insolvency. Thus, where ownership passes to the
buyer before delivery, the seller has a lien for the price.[91] Similarly, a
repairer has a lien entitling her to retain possession of the repaired item
until the owner pays for the repair.[92]

11.78 General liens are broader in scope than the special lien: it is not
necessary for the creditor to show that her position and the debtor's obligation to her arise from the same transaction. They arise by reason of
usage in relation to particular professions. The most important instances
are the general lien of the solicitor,[93] the factor (a commercial agent in
possession of the principal's goods),[94] the broker (a commercial agent
who does not have possession of the principal's goods),[95] and the
banker.[96] In these cases, the creditor is entitled to maintain possession of
items acquired in the course of acting in the relevant capacity for rights
to payment accrued in that capacity. Thus a solicitor who holds title
documents which relate to the debtor's house may exercise a lien over
the documents because the debtor has yet to pay the solicitor for acting
on his behalf in litigation. In the case of a solicitor, banker or broker, the
items will often be documents rather than items of inherent value.

---

89 A J M Steven, 'Property issues in lien' (2010) 14 Edin LR 455. Cf. *McGraddie v
   McGraddie* [2010] CSOH 60.
90 Bell, *Principles* § 1419.
91 Sale of Goods Act 1979, s 41.
92 *Lamonby v Foulds Ltd* 1928 SC 89.
93 E.g. *Liquidator of Grand Empire Theatres v Snodgrass* 1932 SC (HL) 73.
94 E.g. *Mackenzie v Cormack* 1950 SC 183.
95 E.g. *Glendinning v Hope & Co* 1911 SC (HL) 73.
96 E.g. *Clydesdale Bank Ltd v Liquidators of James Allan Senior & Son Ltd* 1926 SC 235.

Enforcement and extinction

11.79 Like pledge, the right in security is lost if possession is lost (unless the creditor is deprived of possession by undue means).[97] Also like pledge, the general rule is that court sanction is required for sale.[98] In contrast with pledge, however, there is little scope for a power of sale to be agreed by the parties. Lien is subject to equitable control by the courts. If its exercise is inappropriate, the court may order the property to be handed over, sometimes on condition that the debt in question be consigned to the court.[99]

Landlord's hypothec

11.80 The other important tacit right in security in Scots law is the landlord's hypothec. It gives the landlord a right in security over corporeal moveables belonging to the tenant which are to be found on the leased premises,[100] for rent which is due and unpaid.[101] Certain moveables are excluded: notably cash, documents of debt or clothes.[102] The hypothec does not apply to residential or agricultural leases.[103] In effect, that means that it only applies to commercial leases.

11.81 Someone who acquires property subject to the hypothec from the debtor takes it free from the hypothec if the acquirer is in good faith.[104] If there is reason to fear that the tenant will attempt to defeat the hypothec by removing or disposing of property, the landlord can obtain an interdict prohibiting such actions. If the tenant disposes of property in breach of such an interdict then the acquirer must not only be in good faith but must also have given value in order to be safe from the hypothec.[105]

11.82 The landlord's hypothec has no specific mechanism for enforcement.[106] It is open to the landlord to do diligence or to rely on the hypothec in insolvency proceedings.

FUNCTIONAL SECURITIES

11.83 The security devices discussed so far are proper rights in security: that is to say they are legal institutions whose specific function is to secure performance of obligations. However, certain other institutions can be used in a way which closely mirrors the effect of a right in secur-

---

97 Bell, *Principles* § 1415.
98 Bell, *Principles* § 1417.
99 *Onyvax Ltd v Endpoint Research (UK) Ltd* [2007] CSOH 211.
100 Bankruptcy and Diligence etc (Scotland) Act 2007, s 208(2)(a).
101 BD(S)A 2007, s 208(8).
102 Bell, *Principles* § 1276.
103 BD(S)A, 2007,s 208(3).
104 BD(S)A 2007, s 208(5)(a).
105 BD(S)A 2007, s 208(5)(b).
106 BD(S)A 2007, s 208(1).

ity. Often these are resorted to because of perceived deficiencies in the proper rights in security.

Assignation in security

11.84   It does not appear to be possible to grant a right in security over incorporeal property in Scots law. It is likely (although the point is disputed) that the diligence of arrestment gives the arresting creditor a judicial right in security in a right which is arrested,[107] and the attachment of a floating charge which covers incorporeal property seems to create a right in security in that incorporeal property. But there is no equivalent to pledge or the standard security for incorporeals.

11.85   Instead, a debtor who wants to use incorporeal property as collateral for a loan must use an assignation in security. As the name suggests, this is a transfer of the relevant property to the creditor. As such, it must comply with the usual formalities for such a transfer (intimation in case of personal rights, registration in case of registered intellectual property rights). The difference between assignation in security and normal assignation is that the creditor has an obligation to retransfer the assigned property when the debt is paid off. Of course, this transfer must also be done in the usual way.

11.86   Thus assignation in security differs from a proper right in security in two important ways: the security taker becomes the owner of the claim assigned, and payment of the debt does not bring the security arrangement to an end automatically. Since the security giver has a mere personal right to the return of the property, there is also the risk that it will be transferred to a third party by the creditor.

Retention of title

11.87   Buyers of goods often require to be able to use them before they can pay for them. One way of allowing this to happen, which protects the seller, is to use a retention of title clause. Section 17 of the Sale of Goods Act 1979 provides that, where there is a contract for the sale of goods, ownership passes when the parties intend that it should. That leaves it open to the parties to agree that, although the goods have been delivered, the seller will remain the owner until the price is paid. Indeed, there is nothing to stop the parties from agreeing that ownership does not pass until the buyer has paid all sums due by it to the seller (even if some of the debts arise from completely separate contracts).

11.88   There were some suggestions that arrangements of this kind circumvented the rules on publicity for rights in security, because the seller has a real right while the buyer has possession and there is no public register. This argument was correctly rejected by the House of

---

107 For arrestment, see paras **12.27–12.34**.

Lords in *Armour v Thyssen Edelstahlwerke AG*.[108] A true right in security over property involves someone giving the creditor a real right in his property so that she can have recourse to it if the debt is not paid. In retention of title, the creditor merely keeps something which already belongs to her (ownership of the goods); she acquires no new real right.

Trusts

11.89   As discussed in Chapter 3, assets held in trust are protected from the trustee's insolvency and from diligence by the trustee's personal creditors. Trusts can also be created with minimal formalities and no publicity, and it is possible to have a 'truster-as-trustee' trust: whereby the owner of property declares that he holds property for the benefit of a third party rather than for his own benefit. Furthermore, any kind of asset can be held in trust: be it heritable or moveable, corporeal or incorporeal. There is no restriction on who can create a truster-as-trustee trust. It is open to sole traders and partnerships as well as to companies and limited liability partnerships.

11.90   All of these factors combine to make the trust very tempting as a functional security device. The basic idea is straightforward: Alf declares that he holds certain assets in trust and that his creditor, Betty, is the beneficiary. Alf retains possession and can carry on using the assets. If Alf becomes insolvent, his other creditors will have no access to the assets because they are held in trust. This is not a problem for Betty, however, because she is a beneficiary of the trust as well as being Alf's creditor. As beneficiary of the trust, she is entitled to satisfaction from the trust assets.

11.91   There is some authority for the validity of using trusts in this way.[109] However, it remains rather controversial.[110] Commercial trusts often appear to have little in the way of trust purposes. Trust purposes are essential to the constitution of a trust because the point of a trust is to allow certain assets to be dedicated to a particular use. The insolvency protection might be regarded as ancillary to this function: the main point is that the trustee administers the assets in accordance with the trust purposes and the insolvency protection is just there to deal with the unfortunate and hopefully unusual case of a trustee who gets into financial difficulties.

11.92   In a commercial trust, this order of priorities is reversed. The main reason for using the trust is to take advantage of the insolvency protection. Connected to that is the concern that there is little in the way of a 'divesture' by the truster. The parties will rarely envisage that the debtor will use the trust assets for the benefit of the creditor or that

---

108 1990 SLT 891.
109 *Tay Valley Joinery Ltd v CF Financial Services Ltd* 1987 SLT 207.
110 See *Clark Taylor & Co Ltd v Quality Site Development (Edinburgh) Ltd* 1981 SC 111.

she will have any particular right in respect of the trust assets prior to the debtor's insolvency. He will simply continue to do his usual business with them (although this may generate profits which can be used to pay the creditor). The truster/trustee continues to use the assets as before and the only purpose of the trust is to avoid sharing the asset with other creditors in insolvency.

11.93 Another objection to the use of trusts as security devices relates to one of their main attractions: they are private. Since a trust can be created without the publicity of registration, delivery or intimation which normally attends the creation of a right in security or an assignation in security, it might be argued that the use of trusts in this way subverts the publicity principle.

REFORM

11.94 Certain aspects of the Scots law of rights in security have been subject to sustained criticism. There has been particular dissatisfaction with the absence of a non-possessory right in security over corporeal moveables or a proper right in security over incorporeals. The floating charge addresses these concerns to some degree but it can only be granted by certain kinds of debtor and there are concerns about how well it fits with the rest of Scots property law.

11.95 In light of these pressures, the Scottish Law Commission is undertaking a project for the reform of rights in security over moveable property.[111] The core concept is a non-possessory right in security created by registration. The right would cover all types of moveable property and could be granted by natural persons and partnerships as well as companies and limited liability partnerships.

11.96 Some dissatisfaction has also been expressed regarding the law of heritable security. Reform of heritable security is part of the Scottish Law Commission's eighth programme of law reform. As yet, no discussion paper has been published so the details of the proposed reform are not known.[112]

---

111 Scottish Law Commission, *Discussion Paper on Moveable Transactions* (SLC DP 151, 2011).
112 Scottish Law Commission, *Eighth Programme of Law Reform* (SLC 220, 2010) paras 2.27–2.33.

Chapter 12

Judicial Security: Diligence

INTRODUCTION

What is diligence?

12.01 Diligence is the term used in Scots law to describe debt enforcement processes. A creditor will 'do diligence' in order to obtain repayment of an obligation by exercising particular rights against the debtor's property. Imagine that Anna owes Brian £5,000. Despite his polite requests, she has refused to pay it back. If Anna consented to grant Brian a right in security when they agreed the loan contract, known as a conventional or voluntary security, Brian could now recover his money by enforcing that right against Anna's property.[1] If Anna did not grant Brian security at the time, he can ask the court to do so now without Anna's consent, known as a judicial or involuntary security. Brian will again recover his money by enforcing that right against Anna's property. The process by which Brian asks the court for a judicial security, and the range of rights it is possible for the court to grant him, are known as diligence.

Which diligence?

12.02 There are a number of different types of diligence. Which diligence a creditor chooses will depend on the nature of the assets the debtor has in his patrimony. For example, where a debtor owns corporeal heritable property such as land or buildings, the creditor may use the diligence of inhibition or alternatively the diligence of adjudication. Where the debtor owns corporeal moveable property, the creditor may use attachment. The application of each type of diligence is explained below. The creditor must know or make an educated guess as to what property is within the debtor's patrimony in order to work out which diligence is likely to be effective. There is no point inhibiting a debtor who does not own heritable property, for example.

12.03 Diligences can also be divided into two categories – seize diligences and freeze diligences – based on their effect on the debtor's property. A seize diligence enables the creditor to transfer property out

1 Chapters 10 and 11.

of the debtor's patrimony without the debtor's consent. The creditor may transfer the property into his own patrimony in satisfaction of the debt. Alternatively, the creditor may transfer the property by sale to a third party, using the proceeds of the sale to satisfy the debt. In either case, the purpose of the transfer is repayment of the debt. Attachment is an example of a seize diligence. A freeze diligence, on the other hand, prevents the debtor transferring property out of his patrimony or granting subordinate real rights in respect of it without the creditor's consent. The creditor will normally consent only if the debtor agrees to repay the debt with the proceeds of the transfer or grant. Inhibition is the main example of a freeze diligence.

12.04   A creditor may use more than one type of diligence in respect of the same debt. If Anna owned a car worth £2,500 and had savings in a bank account of £2,500, Brian might seek both to attach the car and to arrest the savings in the bank account. Together, these two processes might enable him to recover the full £5,000 which Anna owes him. Alternatively, a creditor may use more than one type of diligence in respect of the same item of property. The most common example of this is in relation to heritable property, where a creditor might first use the freeze diligence of inhibition to prevent the debtor selling the property, and then use the seize diligence of adjudication to transfer rent money paid for the property from the debtor's tenants to the creditor in repayment of the debt.

General principles

12.05   Some general principles of property law are particularly relevant to the law of diligence. In the first place, diligence can only be effected against assets in the debtor's personal patrimony. If Anna is a trustee, Brian cannot do diligence against assets in the trust patrimony. Only assets in Anna's personal patrimony are available for diligence processes. (It is possible for a trustee to have run up debts in the name of the trust. In this situation, the creditor could do diligence against the assets in the trust patrimony, but not against assets in the trustee's personal patrimony. The difference between a trust patrimony and a personal patrimony is discussed in Chapter 3: General Principles of Property Law.)

12.06   Any right the creditor receives from the debtor as a result of diligence can be no better than the right held by the debtor in the first place. This is an application of the principle *nemo plus juris ad alium transferre potest, quam ipse haberet*, discussed above.[2] Where the creditor acquires a personal right held by the debtor, he acquires it on the same terms as the debtor.[3] For example, imagine Anna has £5,000 in a bank account. Anna deposited the money some months ago subject to an agreement that she would not withdraw it for two years, in return for which she

---

2 At para **3.96** above.
3 In this context, the *nemo plus* principle is expressed by the equivalent maxim *assignatus utitur jure auctoris*.

would obtain a higher than normal rate of interest. Brian can acquire a right in Anna's bank account by way of arrestment. However, he cannot oblige the bank to pay the funds over to him any earlier than they would have paid the funds over to Anna. His right is subject to the same restrictions as Anna's right. Similarly, if Brian acquires a real right in Anna's property, it will be acquired subject to any existing subordinate real rights.[4]

12.07 Diligence works on a 'first come, first served' basis. Where a debtor has several creditors, the first to effect diligence on a particular asset is able to recoup his debt in full before the second creditor has any claim. Imagine that, in addition to owing Brian £5,000, Anna also owes Dorothy £5,000. Anna has savings in a bank account of £7,500. Brian arrests these savings on 1 May. Dorothy arrests them two days later. Since Brian obtained his arrestment first, he is entitled to recover his £5,000 in full. Dorothy will only be able to obtain the remaining £2,500 of savings towards repayment of her debt. In this situation, it does not matter which creditor loaned money to Anna first, or which creditor has been waiting the longest for repayment. All that matters is which creditor was first to obtain a right via diligence. This is an application of the principle *prior tempore potior jure* discussed above.[5]

Procedure

12.08 The effect of diligence procedures can be to remove the debtor's property without his consent, which is a significant interference with the debtor's property rights. For that reason, the procedural rules governing how diligence is carried out must be adhered to strictly in order to ensure that the debtor is fairly treated.[6] Where even a small mistake is made, the whole procedure is likely to be invalidated, meaning the creditor must begin again from the start.

12.09 The first step in any diligence procedure is to establish that the debt exists. In most cases, this requires the creditor to raise a court action seeking repayment of the debt. The creditor will have to produce evidence which proves the existence of the debt, the amount, and the date by which it should have been repaid. This would normally be done by production of the written contract between the debtor and creditor. If the evidence proves the existence of the debt on a balance of probabilities, the court will grant a decree setting out the details of the obligation owed by the debtor.

---

4 It is sometimes said that a creditor doing diligence takes *tantum et tale*, but it is not clear that this maxim correctly applied is anything other than a restatement of the *nemo plus* principle. For discussion, see Lord Rodger's speech in *Burnett's Tr v Grainger* 2004 SC (HL) 19 and R G Anderson, 'Fraud on transfer and on insolvency: ta...ta...tantum et tale?' (2007) 11(2) Edin LR 187.

5 At para **3.34** above.

6 See the comments of Lord President Rodger in *Atlas Appointments Ltd (No 2) v Tinsley* 1997 SC 200 at 210.

12.10   Parties have the option to avoid the expense and inconvenience of court action by agreeing in the contract to an expedited enforcement procedure known as summary diligence.[7] Where a contract contains a clause stating that the parties 'consent to registration for execution' or 'consent to registration for summary diligence', they are effectively consenting to a court decree coming into existence without the need to go to court. The consent takes effect when the document is registered in the Books of Council and Session. In this situation, the registered document is proof of existence of the debt equivalent to a court decree. A form of summary diligence is also available where the right to payment is embodied in a negotiable instrument.[8] The creditor in this instance can instruct a notary public to present the bill to the debtor,[9] and if payment is refused, the notary can issue a formal certificate protesting the bill for non-payment.[10] A negotiable instrument noted and protested for non-payment is also proof of the existence of a debt equivalent to a court decree.

12.11   Once decree[11] is obtained, the creditor must arrange for it to be served on the debtor[12] accompanied by a 'charge for payment', a formal notice demanding payment of the debt within a 14-day period known as the 'days of charge'.[13] If the days of charge expire without payment of the debt, the creditor is entitled to proceed with an appropriate type of diligence. Diligence must follow within two years of the date of service of the charge.[14]

12.12   Where the debtor is a natural person, it will also usually be necessary to provide him with a debt advice and information package ('DAIP') before diligence can be enforced. The DAIP is a booklet prepared by the Accountant in Bankruptcy on behalf of the Scottish Government[15] which sets out the debtor's rights in relation to legal proceedings, gives advice on how the debt might be managed and suggests where further support and guidance might be sought within the

---

7 Summary diligence is not competent for debts arising under a regulated consumer credit agreement: Consumer Credit Act 1974, s 93A.

8 For an explanation of negotiable instruments, see paras **9.06–9.09**.

9 A debtor is usually referred to as a 'drawee' in this context: see para **9.24**.

10 Bills of Exchange Act 1882, s 51.

11 Decree is defined in the Bankruptcy and Diligence etc (Scotland) Act 2007, s 221.

12 Service will be carried out by officers of court, namely sheriff officers in the case of a sheriff court decree, or messengers-at-arms in the case of a Court of Session decree. Officers of court are regulated by their professional body, the Society of Messengers-at-Arms and Sheriff Officers (SMASO), in line with the Officers of Court's Professional Association (Scotland) Regulations 2011 (SSI 2011/90).

13 The period of payment will be 14 days if the debtor is within the UK. It is increased to 28 days if the debtor is outside the UK or his whereabouts are unknown: Debtors (Scotland) Act 1987, s 90(3).

14 Debtors (Scotland) Act 1987, s 90(5).

15 Debt Arrangement and Attachment (Scotland) Act 2002, s 10(5).

debtor's local area.[16] For most forms of diligence, a set period of time must elapse after provision of the DAIP before the diligence can proceed. The details will be discussed with reference to each of the specific forms of diligence below.

Protection from diligence

12.13 The Scottish Government operates a voluntary Debt Arrangement Scheme ('DAS') which provides guidance and support to natural persons resident in Scotland.[17] Where an individual with debt problems contacts DAS, it has authority to act as an intermediary between the debtor and his creditors in order to set up a debt payment programme ('DPP').[18] A DPP usually enables the debtor to make repayments over a longer period of time than initially agreed without incurring additional interest, and may even allow for some discount on the amount to be repaid. A creditor is not obliged to consent to a DPP, but a DAS administrator has the authority to overrule the creditor's refusal if the proposal is, in his view, 'fair and reasonable'. Where a DPP is in operation, it is not competent for creditors to take other steps to enforce the debt, such as diligence.[19]

12.14 A debtor is also protected from diligence where a 'time to pay' direction is in effect. When a debtor receives intimation of a court action seeking to establish the existence of a debt, he may ask the court for a period of time to repay it in manageable instalments with reference to his financial situation.[20] An application for a time to pay direction can be made at any point between when the action is raised and expiry of the days of charge. Where a time to pay direction is in effect, the right of any creditor to serve a charge for payment or do diligence is suspended.[21]

ATTACHMENT

12.15 The diligence of attachment gives the creditor the right to seize and sell the debtor's corporeal moveable property at auction in order to recoup the debt. Prior to the 2002 Act, this type of diligence was known

16 A copy of the DAIP can be found on the AIB website at www.aib.gov.uk/guidance/publications/debtbankruptcy/DAIP (accessed May 2014).
17 Authority for the scheme is set out in part 1 of the Debt Arrangement and Attachment (Scotland) Act 2002, with detailed provision in the Debt Arrangement Scheme (Scotland) Regulations 2011 (SSI 2011/141).
18 Further information can be found on the DAS website at www.dasscotland.gov.uk (accessed May 2014).
19 Debt Arrangement and Attachment (Scotland) Act 2002, s 4. The Bankruptcy and Debt Advice (Scotland) Bill, s 8, proposes that a moratorium on diligence should be imposed for six weeks from the date on which the debtor first gives written notice of his intention to apply for a DPP, with potential to extend the time limit if the application takes longer to process.
20 Debtors (Scotland) Act 1987, s 1.
21 1987 Act, s 9.

as poinding (pronounced 'pinding') and warrant sale. Poinding was considered a harsh and humiliating experience for a debtor, and a sustained political campaign for its abolition was led by then-MSP Tommy Sheridan. Attachment, an attenuated form of the diligence, was introduced by sections 10–57 of the Debt Arrangement and Attachment (Scotland) Act 2002.

Procedure

12.16 A creditor seeking to use the diligence of attachment must first serve a charge. Where the debtor is a natural person, the creditor must also provide the debtor with a DAIP. When the days of charge have expired,[22] or in the case of a natural debtor no earlier than 12 weeks after the DAIP was provided,[23] the creditor can execute the attachment by instructing officers of court to attend any premises where the debtor has goods. The officers will make up a schedule identifying every asset owned by the debtor and estimating the value of that item.[24] A copy of the schedule must be served on the debtor.[25] The officer of court must give a signed report to the sheriff within 14 days of executing the attachment including the schedule and specifying whether anyone other than the debtor asserted ownership of any of the listed goods.[26] Once the report is received, the officer has six months in which to arrange for the goods to be removed from the debtor's premises[27] and sold at public auction.[28] The proceeds of goods sold are acquired by the creditor in satisfaction of the debt.[29] If the auction raises funds in excess of the debt, the surplus must be returned to the debtor.[30] Ownership of any goods not sold is transferred to the creditor, who again must pay the debtor the value of any surplus in excess of the debt.[31] The officer then makes a report of the auction to the sheriff, which brings the attachment to an end.[32]

12.17 Any person interfering with an attached article, for example by giving it away or destroying it, between execution of the attachment and the auction may be found in contempt of court and will incur personal liability to the creditor for the value of the item.[33]

22 Debt Arrangement and Attachment (Scotland) Act 2002, s 10(3).
23 2002 Act, s 10(3)(c).
24 2002 Act, s 13A.
25 2002 Act, s 13A(3).
26 2002 Act, s 17.
27 2002 Act, s 19.
28 2002 Act, ss 27–30. The traditional Scots law term is 'roup'.
29 2002 Act, s 31(1)(b).
30 2002 Act, s 31(1)(c).
31 2002 Act, s 31(2).
32 2002 Act, s 32.
33 2002 Act, s 21.

Exempt articles

12.18 A significant number of goods are exempt from attachment. Most importantly, the creditor has no right to attach articles inside the debtor's dwellinghouse without obtaining an exceptional attachment order, discussed below. Further exemptions are listed in section 11 of the 2002 Act. These include: tools of the trade or other equipment used in the debtor's profession, trade or business; any vehicle reasonably required by the debtor not exceeding £1,000 in value; a mobile home which is the debtor's only or principal residence; and money, which must be dealt with by the separate diligence of money attachment.[34]

12.19 Only assets owned by the debtor may be attached, although the fact the debtor is in possession of the goods gives rise to a presumption of ownership.[35] Third-party owners may overturn this presumption by making representations to the officers of court or, later, to the sheriff.[36] Goods owned in common by the debtor and a third party may be attached, with the third party entitled to receive his share of the proceeds from the sale of the item.[37]

Exceptional attachment

12.20 Where a creditor wishes to attach goods inside the debtor's dwellinghouse, he must seek an exceptional attachment order from the court.[38] The exceptional circumstances in which such an order will be granted are detailed in section 47 of the 2002 Act – essentially, there must be no other way for the creditor to recoup his debt, and it must be reasonably clear that there are sufficient assets in the debtor's dwellinghouse to make the order worthwhile. Even where the order is granted, the creditor may only attach 'non-essential' assets as defined in Schedule 2 to the Act, which excludes clothing, most household goods and furnishings, articles required for the care or upbringing of a child, educational articles such as books, and medical aids or equipment.[39] Exceptional attachment is therefore effectively limited to luxury goods inside the debtor's home.

MONEY ATTACHMENT

12.21 A specific attachment procedure applies where the property the creditor wishes to obtain is money. The precise legal definition of 'money' is complex,[40] but for the purposes of this diligence, it is inter-

---

34 See paras **12.21–12.26** below.
35 Debt Arrangement and Attachment (Scotland) Act 2002, s 13, restating the position at common law.
36 2002 Act, s 34.
37 2002 Act, ss 35–36.
38 2002 Act, s 46.
39 2002 Act, s 47.
40 See Chapter 8: Money and Debt.

preted as cash (in other words, coins and banknotes) and banking instruments (such as cheques, money orders, promissory notes and postal orders) in any currency.[41] Money attachment is regulated by sections 174–198 of and Schedule 3 to the Bankruptcy and Diligence etc (Scotland) Act 2007.

Procedure

12.22   The procedure follows a similar pattern to that of attachment of goods. A creditor must serve a charge, and provide a DAIP where the debtor is a natural person. When the days of charge expire,[42] and no earlier than 12 weeks after the DAIP was provided,[43] the creditor can instruct officers of court to attend the debtor's premises,[44] attach any money belonging to the debtor up to the value of the debt and remove it from the premises.[45] A schedule of money removed must be prepared by the officers of court and served on the debtor.[46] Any foreign currency removed must be converted into sterling[47] and all cash must be deposited in a bank account.[48] Banking instruments should be valued by the officer at their open market value and stored in a secure place.[49] The officer must give a signed report to the sheriff within 14 days of executing the attachment.[50] Once the report is received, the creditor has 14 days in which to apply to court for a payment order, authorising transfer of the attached money to the creditor up to the value of the debt.[51] If no application is made for a payment order within the time limit, the attachment is terminated and the money restored to the debtor.[52] If a payment order is applied for and granted, the officers of court will realise any banking instruments and pay over the money to the creditor.[53] The officer then makes a final statement to the sheriff, which brings the money attachment to an end.[54]

12.23   Any attempt by the debtor to frustrate money attachment, for example by inducing someone to cancel an attached cheque made out to the debtor and issue a new cheque in its place, is unlawful and may be dealt with as a contempt of court.[55]

41 Bankruptcy and Diligence etc (Scotland) Act 2007, s 175.
42 2007 Act, s 174(2)(a)–(c).
43 2007 Act, s 174(2)(d).
44 Excluding his dwellinghouse: 2007 Act, s 174(3). See para **9.24** below.
45 2007 Act, s 177.
46 2007 Act, s 179.
47 2007 Act, s 177(3).
48 2007 Act, s 177(5).
49 2007 Act, s 177(7)–(8).
50 2007 Act, s 182.
51 2007 Act, s 183.
52 2007 Act, s 187.
53 2007 Act, s 184.
54 2007 Act, s 189.
55 2007 Act, s 193.

Limitations on money attachment

12.24 The attachment process can only be carried out from Monday to Saturday between the hours of 8am and 8pm, avoiding public holidays, unless the creditor has a court order authorising officers of court to enter the debtor's premises outside these times.[56] The creditor has no right to attach money kept in a dwellinghouse.[57] Cash or instruments which have 'an intrinsic value greater than any value it may have as a medium of exchange' – for example, a gold coin which is valuable because it is made of gold, as opposed to a £50 note which is valuable for what it represents rather than the paper it is printed on – are also exempt from attachment.[58]

12.25 Only money owned by the debtor may be attached although, as with attachment of goods, possession gives rise to a presumption of ownership.[59] Third-party owners may overturn this presumption by making representations to the officer of court or, later, the sheriff.[60] Money owned in common by the debtor and a third party may be attached, although the third party may apply for relief where the attachment is unduly harsh.[61] The third party is entitled to receive his share of the proceeds, for example where a banking instrument owned in common is realised.[62]

12.26 It is open to the debtor to apply for release of the money attachment prior to a payment order being made on the grounds that it is unduly harsh.[63]

ARRESTMENT

12.27 The diligence of arrestment enables the creditor to seize incorporeal property and corporeal moveables owned by the debtor, but in the possession of a third party. For example, the creditor may arrest furniture belonging to the debtor which is being kept in a storage facility, or arrest funds belonging to the debtor held in a savings account controlled by the bank. The rules of arrestment are based in the common law, but extensively modified by sections 73A–73T of the Debtors (Scotland) Act 1987.

Procedure

12.28 The creditor must first serve a charge on the debtor. At present,

56 2007 Act, s 176.
57 2007 Act, s 174(3).
58 2007 Act, s 175(1).
59 2007 Act, s 178, restating the position at common law.
60 2007 Act, s 183.
61 2007 Act, s 191.
62 2007 Act, s 192.
63 2007 Act, s 185.

there is no requirement to provide a DAIP where the debtor is a natural person – provision is made for this requirement in section 73D of the 1987 Act, but the section is not yet in force. On expiry of the days of charge,[64] the creditor instructs officers of court to serve a 'schedule of arrestment' on the arrestee – the third party who has possession of the debtor's property.[65] The schedule is a formal notice advising the arrestee that (i) funds held by him on behalf of the debtor up to the value of the debt and/or (ii) all moveable property held by him on behalf of the debtor have been arrested, meaning the arrestee is prohibited from releasing the property from his possession.[66] The arrestee is then obliged to send a form of disclosure to the creditor, the debtor and anyone else who claims ownership of the arrested property.[67] The form sets out the nature and value of any items arrested. It must be sent out within three weeks of service of the schedule of arrestment, or else the arrestee may be subject to a financial penalty.[68] The arrestee must release funds to the arrestor 14 weeks after service of the schedule if the debt has not been repaid, or earlier on receipt of a mandate by the debtor authorising release.[69] Where goods have been arrested, the creditor must raise an action of furthcoming, by which the arrestee will be ordered to sell the goods and transfer the sale proceeds to the arrestor. Once the arrested property has been released to the creditor, the arrestment is at an end.[70]

Arrestable property

12.29   Corporeal moveable property owned by the debtor but in the possession of a third party can be arrested.[71] It is also competent to arrest ships. In addition, incorporeal property – in other words, personal rights – owed to the debtor by a third party can be arrested.[72] Money in a bank account falls into this category, since strictly speaking this is an obligation owed by the bank to the debtor. Imagine that, before Brian loaned Anna £5,000, Anna had loaned £500 to Felix. Brian can arrest the obligation to repay owed by Felix to Anna, with the effect that Felix will repay his £500 not to his creditor Anna, but to his creditor's creditor Brian.

12.30   Two important exceptions exist to these general principles. One

---

64 Debtors (Scotland) Act 1987, s 73A.
65 1987 Act, s 73B.
66 The form of the schedule is prescribed by the Diligence (Scotland) Regulations 2009 (SSI 2009/68), Sch 7.
67 Debtors (Scotland) Act 1987, s 73G. The form of disclosure is prescribed by the Diligence (Scotland) Regulations 2009, Sch 8.
68 1987 Act, s 73G.
69 1987 Act, s 73J. The sum to be released is specified in s 73K. The court may make an order preventing automatic release of funds in certain circumstances: see ss 73L–73N.
70 An arrestee who releases funds to the wrong person in good faith is protected per Debtors (Scotland) Act 1987, s 73P.
71 *Moore and Weinberg v Ernsthausen Ltd* 1917 SC (HL) 25.
72 *Boland v White Cross Insurance Association* 1926 SC 1066.

is that benefit payments cannot be arrested, whether in the hands of the relevant government authority,[73] or after payment into the debtor's bank account.[74] The other is that funds held by a bank or other financial institution are subject to a minimum amount protected from arrestment, known as the protected minimum balance, currently £415.[75] The PMB does not apply where the account is held in the name of a company, LLP, partnership or unincorporated association.[76]

Earnings arrestment

12.31 A person's employer becomes his debtor at the point in the week or month where wages fall due. It is therefore open to the employee's creditor to arrest earnings in the hands of the employer.[77] As with the example of Anna and Felix above, the employer in this case will pay the wages over not to the employee, but to the employee's creditor. In practice, earnings arrestment is often likely to be the most useful form of diligence available to the creditor of a natural person.

12.32 Specific rules for arrestment of earnings are set out in sections 46–50 of the Debtors (Scotland) Act 1987, although the procedure is broadly the same as for any other arrestment. The creditor first serves a charge on the debtor. Where the debtor is a natural person, a DAIP must also be provided. On expiry of the days of charge,[78] or no earlier than 12 weeks after provision of the DAIP,[79] the creditor serves an earnings arrestment schedule[80] on the employer specifying the amount of the debt. The employer must provide the creditor with details of how, when and how much the debtor is paid in wages.[81] The employer must then make deductions from the debtor's net earnings on every payday and transfer the funds to the creditor until the debt is paid off. Regulations set out the amount to be deducted, dependent on the debtor's earnings and whether he is paid weekly or monthly.[82] Where an employer fails to comply with an earnings arrestment, he may be held personally liable for the sums due to the creditor.[83]

73 See for example the Social Security Administration Act 1992, s 187(1) and the Tax Credits Act 2002, s 45(1).
74 *North Lanarkshire Council v Crossan* 2007 SLT (Sh Ct) 169, reversed on appeal by Temporary Sheriff Principal Kearney on 2nd May 2009. The appeal decision is unfortunately unreported, although a copy of the opinion can be found at www.govanlc.com/nlc-crossan-judgment.pdf (accessed May 2014).
75 Debtors (Scotland) Act 1987, s 73F and Sch 2.
76 1987 Act, s 73F(2)(a).
77 1987 Act, s 47.
78 1987 Act, s 90.
79 1987 Act, s 47(3).
80 The form of the earnings arrestment schedule is prescribed in the Act of Sederunt (Proceedings in the Sheriff Court under the Debtors (Scotland) Act 1987) 1988 (SI 1988/2013), art 38 and schedule (Form 30).
81 Debtors (Scotland) Act 1987, s 70A.
82 1987 Act, s 49 and Sch 2.
83 1987 Act, s 57.

12.33   The legislation also provides for two other forms of diligence against earnings. Where two or more creditors seek to arrest their common debtor's earnings in the hands of his employer at the same time, the provisions on a *conjoined arrestment order* will apply.[84] Where the diligence is used to enforce a court award of maintenance, because the debtor has defaulted on an order to make periodical payments of aliment in respect of his child, for example, the provisions on a *current maintenance assessment* will apply.[85] Both schemes operate in much the same way as an earnings arrestment.

Admiralty arrestment

12.34   It is possible to arrest a ship and the cargo on board where the debtor has a real right in the ship. The effect is usually to prevent the ship sailing to its next destination until the debt is repaid. This form of diligence is unlikely to be used often in practice, although the situations where it does have application will normally involve substantial amounts of debt. Admiralty arrestment is regulated by section 213 and Schedule 4 of the Bankruptcy and Diligence etc (Scotland) Act 2007.[86]

INHIBITION

12.35   Inhibition is a diligence against real rights in land.[87] It is a 'freeze' diligence, which prevents the debtor from, for example, selling a piece of land, or granting a lease over it, without the creditor's consent. Normally the creditor will consent only if the proceeds of the debtor's transaction with the property will be used to repay the debt. Inhibition might therefore be viewed as a bargaining tool employed by the creditor to persuade the debtor to repay his debt 'voluntarily', as opposed to a 'grab' diligence like attachment described above, where the creditor simply takes property from the debtor in satisfaction of the debt. Inhibition is now largely regulated by sections 146–168 of the Bankruptcy and Diligence etc (Scotland) Act 2007.

Procedure

12.36   A creditor may begin the process of inhibition by instructing officers of court to serve a 'schedule of inhibition' on the debtor. The schedule is a formal notice advising the debtor that he is being inhibited,

---

84   1987 Act, ss 60–66.
85   1987 Act, ss 51–59.
86   For a fuller account, see *Stair Memorial Encyclopaedia*, vol 8, paras 322–327.
87   Strictly speaking, the form of inhibition discussed in this section is known as inhibition in execution. Two other forms of inhibition are competent: inhibition on the dependence, discussed at paras **12.58–12.62** below, and the rare process of inhibition on a document of debt, for which see *Stair Memorial Encyclopaedia*, vol 8, paras 134 and 138A. The procedure and effect of inhibition on a document of debt are largely the same as those described here.

accompanied by extract of the court decree in respect of the debt.[88] Where the debtor is a natural person, the schedule must be accompanied by a DAIP.[89] The schedule of inhibition, along with a certificate of execution (certifying that the schedule was served on the debtor), must then be registered in the Register of Inhibitions and Adjudications, also known as the Personal Register.[90] Unlike other forms of diligence, there is no need for the creditor to wait for expiry of the days of charge before registering the inhibition. The inhibition takes effect from the beginning of the day on which it is registered.[91]

12.37 A variation on this procedure is available to creditors who worry that the debtor, once alerted to the fact an inhibition is shortly to be registered, will attempt to dispose of his property quickly before the inhibition can take effect. A creditor with this concern may begin the process of inhibition by registering a 'priority notice'[92] in the Register of Inhibitions. The priority notice is effectively a statement that the creditor intends to register a schedule of inhibition in the near future. Officers of court would then serve the schedule on the debtor as outlined above. The schedule and certificate of execution must then be registered within 21 days of the priority notice being registered. If this time limit is adhered to, the effect of the inhibition will be backdated to the beginning of the day on which the schedule was served.[93] Accordingly, any attempted disposal of the property by the debtor after the schedule was served would be caught by the inhibition nevertheless.

12.38 Once registered, the inhibition remains in effect for five years, at which time it prescribes.[94] Alternatively, the inhibition may be discharged by the creditor, in full or in relation to a specific property only. The inhibition will also be brought to an end where the debtor satisfies his obligation to the creditor, normally by repaying the debt in full.[95]

Effect of inhibition

12.39 Inhibition affects all heritable property in Scotland within the debtor's patrimony.[96] The creditor need not specify what property the debtor has in his patrimony – the creditor may not even know what

---

88 The form of the schedule is prescribed by the Diligence (Scotland) Regulations 2009, regs 3(1)(a) and (2) and Sch 1.
89 Bankruptcy and Diligence etc (Scotland) Act 2007, s 147.
90 This will be renamed the Register of Inhibitions if and when the abolition of adjudication provided for in the 2007 Act is brought into force: see para **12.46** below.
91 Titles to Land Consolidation (Scotland) Act 1868, s 155.
92 Referred to somewhat confusingly in the statute as a 'Notice of Inhibition': 1868 Act, s 155(2)(a).
93 1868 Act, s 155(2)–(3).
94 Conveyancing (Scotland) Act 1924, s 44(3).
95 Bankruptcy and Diligence etc (Scotland) Act 2007, ss 157–58.
96 2007 Act, s 150.

heritage the debtor owns. In other words, the inhibition affects a specific person, rather than specific property.

12.40 Inhibition does not give the creditor any real rights in respect of the debtor's heritage. Instead, it has a 'freeze' effect on the debtor's capacity to interact with his property. It prohibits the debtor from voluntarily conveying his heritage to a third party, and from voluntarily granting subordinate real rights in his heritage.[97] If the debtor proceeds to convey property or grant a subordinate real right despite the inhibition, the creditor can reduce that transaction. In practice, this means the debtor will be unable to transact with his heritage without the creditor's consent.

12.41 Inhibition only strikes at voluntary actions by the debtor. If, for example, heritage is transferred out of the debtor's patrimony by a bank exercising its power of sale under a standard security, that is not a voluntary action on the debtor's part. Similarly, if the debtor is under a personal obligation, which predates the inhibition, to transfer property to a third party, the debtor's actions in fulfilment of that obligation will not be considered voluntary.[98] Imagine that Anna owns a house. On 3 May, she concludes missives to sell the house to Evan. On 4 May, she is inhibited by Brian. On 5 May, Anna delivers the disposition in respect of the house to Evan, who registers it in the Land Register, resulting in ownership of the house transferring to Evan. Although the property is transferred out of Anna's patrimony after the inhibition takes effect, Anna's actions are not voluntary: she could not have refused to deliver the disposition to Evan without breaching her personal obligation to him.[99]

12.42 Inhibition does not affect heritage acquired by the debtor after the date of inhibition.[100] However, a person is said to acquire property for the purposes of this rule at the beginning of the day on which the deed conveying or otherwise granting a real right in the property is delivered.[101] Imagine Anna has concluded missives for the purchase of a cottage from Zoe. On 5 May, Zoe delivers the disposition in respect of the cottage to Anna. On 6 May, Brian registers his inhibition against Anna in the Personal Register. On 7 May, Anna registers her title to the cottage in the Land Register. Ownership of the house does not transfer to Anna until the moment the title is registered. However, the cottage will nevertheless be caught by the inhibition because the disposition –

97 2007 Act, s 160.
98 This is thought to be a correct statement of the law, although the 2007 Act introduced some scope for doubt: see the discussion of *Playfair Investments Ltd v McElvogue* (n 99 below) in G L Gretton and K G C Reid, *Conveyancing 2012* (2013).
99 *Halifax Building Society v Smith* 1985 SLT (Sh Ct) 25; *Playfair Investments Ltd v McElvogue* [2012] CSOH 148, 2013 SLT 225.
100 Titles to Land Consolidation (Scotland) Act 1868, s 157. Property acquired after the date of the inhibition is referred to as 'acquirenda'.
101 Bankruptcy and Diligence etc (Scotland) Act 2007, s 150(3).

the deed transferring the real right to Anna – had been delivered prior to the inhibition taking effect. Anna now owns the house, but cannot transfer it or grant any subordinate real rights in it without breaching the inhibition.

ADJUDICATION

12.43 Like inhibition, adjudication is a form of diligence against heritable property.[102] Unlike inhibition, adjudication allows the creditor to obtain a real right in security over the property. The rules of adjudication are based largely on the common law.

Procedure

12.44 Unlike other diligences, a creditor cannot simply proceed to adjudication once he has obtained decree in respect of the debt.[103] Instead, he must raise a second action of adjudication, competent only in the Court of Session. In practice, he will usually have inhibited the debtor first, although this is not required. The summons in the action for adjudication must specify the particular property the creditor wishes to adjudge, including the title sheet number if the property is in the Land Register.[104] Unless the debtor has a relevant defence (which is unlikely, since any defence which could be made out would have been used in response to the earlier action for repayment), the court will pronounce a decree of adjudication including details of the property in question. The creditor must then register the extract decree against the title to the property in the Land Register or Register of Sasines.

Effect of adjudication

12.45 Once the creditor has registered extract decree of adjudication against title to the property concerned, he has a right in security over that property. Unlike a standard security, adjudication does not confer on the creditor a power to sell the heritage. Instead, the adjudger has the power to eject the debtor from the property if necessary,[105] grant leases

---

102 Strictly speaking the form of diligence discussed in this section is known as 'adjudication for debt'. Other forms of adjudication are discussed below: see paras **12.48–12.51**.

103 See para **12.09** above.

104 Land Registration (Scotland) Act 1979, s 4(2)(d). This section will be repealed by the Land Registration etc (Scotland) Act 2012, s 119 and Sch 5, para 19(2) when it is brought into force, and authority for the requirement that the summons in an action for adjudication narrate the title sheet number will be found in the 2012 Act, ss 26(1) and 113(1).

105 Heritable Securities (Scotland) Act 1895, s 5. It appears that where the property concerned is the debtor's principal residence, the adjudger will have to comply with the requirements of the Conveyancing and Feudal Reform (Scotland) Act 1970 as amended by the Mortgage Rights (Scotland) Act 2001 and the Home Owner and Debtor Protection (Scotland) Act 2010 before an order for ejection can be obtained.

over the property and keep the rent paid by the tenants in satisfaction of the debt.[106] If the debt has not been repaid at the end of ten years – known as 'expiry of the legal' – the adjudger may raise another court action seeking declarator of expiry of the legal. This decree, if granted, can be registered in the Register of Sasines or the Land Register with the effect that ownership of the property is transferred to the adjudger. If the value of the property exceeds the amount of the debt remaining, any surplus must be paid to the debtor.[107]

Abolition of adjudication and replacement with land attachment

12.46 The Bankruptcy and Diligence etc (Scotland) Act 2007 contains provisions abolishing adjudication[108] and introducing in its place a new diligence of land attachment.[109] The new diligence will work in a similar way to attachment of moveables, discussed above,[110] but focused on a specific piece of heritable property. The creditor will first serve a charge on the debtor. When the days of charge have expired, the creditor will register a notice of land attachment against the title to the property in the Land Register or Register of Sasines, and against the name of the debtor in the Register of Inhibitions.[111] Once registered, the creditor obtains a right in security over the property.[112] After six months have elapsed, if at least £3,000 of debt remains outstanding, the creditor can apply to the court for a warrant to sell the property.[113] The debt outstanding can be recouped from the sale proceeds and any surplus returned to the debtor.[114]

12.47 It is unclear at present when, if ever, these provisions will be brought into force.

Other forms of adjudication

12.48 Lawyers tend to use the broad term 'adjudication' to refer to what is in fact only one form of adjudication process, namely adjudication for debt. This is the process outlined above. Other forms of adjudication do exist, although they are virtually unknown in practice nowadays. For the sake of completeness, three of these will be mentioned here.

---

106 Heritable Securities (Scotland) Act 1895, ss 6–7.
107 *Hull v Campbell* [2011] CSOH 24, 2011 SLT 881.
108 2007 Act, s 79.
109 2007 Act, ss 81–128.
110 At paras **12.15–12.20**.
111 Bankruptcy and Diligence etc (Scotland) Act 2007, ss 81(3) and 83.
112 2007 Act, s 81(5).
113 2007 Act, s 92.
114 2007 Act, s 116.

Adjudication in security

12.49 Adjudication in security is akin to diligence on the dependence, discussed below.[115] An action of adjudication in security can be brought by a creditor before the debt is due to be repaid in circumstances where the creditor has reasonable grounds to suspect that the debtor is on the verge of insolvency. If granted, decree has the same effect as in adjudication for debt. This form of adjudication will be abolished by section 172 of the 2007 Act, if ever brought into force.

Adjudication in implement

12.50 Adjudication in implement is not a form of diligence, despite sharing the same name. This is the mechanism by which a buyer of heritable property can obtain judicial title if the seller refuses to deliver a valid disposition in implement of the missives.[116] The effect is to give the adjudger a right of ownership over the property, rather than a right in security. In modern practice, a buyer in this situation is more likely to rescind the contract and seek damages.

Declaratory adjudication

12.51 Declaratory adjudication is also not a form of diligence. This is a mechanism by which the court can confer title to land on the adjudger when the identity of the previous owner is not known and cannot be discovered. This remedy is unheard of in modern practice.

OTHER DILIGENCES

12.52 For the sake of completeness, brief mention is made here of some other forms of diligence. These diligences are little used, obsolete or have been abolished.

12.53 Where a debtor has died, the diligence of *confirmation as executor-creditor* is available to his creditor(s). The creditor will take charge of the deceased's estate and recoup his debt from any assets. This diligence remains competent although it is seldom used in practice.[117]

12.54 At common law, it was possible to imprison debtors for wilful or neglectful refusal to pay, considered a diligence directed against the person rather than his property. *Civil imprisonment for debt* is no longer possible,[118] except in enforcement of a limited class of alimentary debts, including child support.[119]

---

115 At paras **12.58–12.62**.
116 *Mackay v Campbell* 1966 SC 237; *Boag, Ptr* 1967 SLT 275; *Hoey v Butler* 1975 SC 87. Authority for the sheriff court equivalent is found in the Sheriff Courts (Scotland) Act 1907, s 5A.
117 For a fuller account, see *Stair Memorial Encyclopaedia*, vol 8, paras 350–358.
118 Debtors (Scotland) Act 1880, s 4.
119 For a fuller account, see *Stair Memorial Encyclopaedia*, vol 8, paras 347–349.

12.55   The diligence of *mails and duties* is available to heritable creditors where the security subjects have been let. Where the diligence is used, the tenant will make rent payments directly to the creditor rather than the landlord-debtor. The diligence is not available to standard security holders, rendering it effectively obsolete in modern practice. It will be abolished by section 207 of the Bankruptcy and Diligence etc (Scotland) Act 2007, if brought into force. A related diligence, known as *poinding of the ground* or *real poinding*, allowed a heritable creditor to recoup his debt by poinding (attaching) corporeal moveables on the security subjects belonging to the debtor or the debtor's tenant. This diligence was abolished alongside all other forms of poinding.[120]

12.56   The diligence of *sequestration for rent*, formerly a mechanism for enforcement of the landlord's hypothec, has also been abolished.[121] A landlord seeking to enforce the hypothec must now use one of the other diligences described above.

DILIGENCE ON THE DEPENDENCE

12.57   Diligence on the dependence is not a specific form of diligence, but rather a way in which many of the diligences explained above can be used. When a pursuer raises a court action, often the ultimate goal will be to obtain money from the defender, perhaps in implement of a contract (as with an action for repayment of debt), perhaps in damages for a delictual loss and so on. A devious defender who suspects that he is likely to lose the case may seek to frustrate the pursuer by ridding himself of his assets. If the defender does so successfully, the pursuer's eventual court decree will be worthless, since a decree cannot be enforced against a person with no property. As the adage says, you can't get blood from a stone.[122]

12.58   The law seeks to prevent this evasion of the judicial process by allowing a pursuer in an action with a financial conclusion to carry out certain forms of diligence 'on the dependence of the action'. The diligence process takes effect when the court action is first raised, or at some point during the life of the case, and prevents the defender disposing of his assets whilst the action is ongoing. If the pursuer wins the case, the diligence can then be fully enforced if necessary to obtain payment in terms of the court decree. If the pursuer loses the case, the diligence is discharged and the defender's assets remain with him.

12.59   The forms of diligence which can be used in this way are

---

120   Debt Arrangement and Attachment (Scotland) Act 2002, s 58.
121   Bankruptcy and Diligence etc (Scotland) Act 2007, s 208.
122   A defender in this situation is sometimes referred to as 'judgment proof'. See L M LoPucki, 'The death of liability' (1996) 106 Yale Law Journal 1.

inhibition,[123] arrestment[124] and attachment[125] (referred to in this context as 'interim attachment'). A pursuer seeking to use diligence on the dependence must include a crave or conclusion for the specific diligence sought in the writ or summons raising the action.

12.60 It used to be the case that diligence on the dependence would be granted automatically by the court if requested by a pursuer seeking a sum of money. However, the effect on the defender can be quite severe – a large part of the defender's assets can effectively be frozen for years if the case is complicated or there are delays in the court process – so that an automatic grant of diligence on the dependence was eventually found to be in violation of the defender's right to peaceful enjoyment of his possessions under article 1 of the First Protocol to the European Convention on Human Rights.[126] The automatic nature of diligence on the dependence was considered the heart of the violation. An order granted after the court had been addressed on why the diligence was necessary in a particular case, where the defender had an opportunity to make arguments against the grant of diligence, would not contravene the defender's Convention rights.[127]

12.61 The Convention-compliant approach to diligence on the dependence was put on a statutory footing in 2008 by virtue of amendments to the Debtors (Scotland) Act 1987.[128] The court will grant warrant for diligence on the dependence if satisfied (i) that the pursuer has a prima facie case on the merits of the action; (ii) that there is a 'real and substantial' risk that any decree obtained by the pursuer will be unenforceable because the defender is on the verge of insolvency or is likely to dispose of his assets, and (iii) it is reasonable in all the circumstances of the case.[129] On paper, the process is now in line with Convention standards, although doubts have been expressed over whether the reforms have led to any real change in the court's attitude towards granting diligence on the dependence.[130]

123 Debtors (Scotland) Act 1987, s 15A(1)(b).
124 1987 Act, s 15A(1)(a).
125 Debt Arrangement and Attachment (Scotland) Act 2002, s 9A.
126 *Karl Construction Ltd v Palisade Properties plc* 2002 SC 270; *Fab Tek Engineering Ltd v Carillion Construction Ltd* 2002 SLT (Sh Ct) 113.
127 *Karl Construction v Palisade Properties* and *Fab-Tek Engineering Ltd v Carillion Construction* (n 126 above); *Gillespie v Toondale Ltd* [2005] CSIH 92, 2006 SC 304.
128 1987 Act, ss 15A–15N.
129 1987 Act, s 15F.
130 J Fordyce, 'Diligence on the dependence – a return to the old regime?' 2009 SLT (News) 71.

Chapter 13

Insolvency: Bankruptcy

INTRODUCTION

13.01 Insolvency describes a situation in which a legal person is unable to meet their obligations to creditors. In certain circumstances, the law allows the creditors of a debtor in this position to seize the debtor's assets and sell them off in satisfaction of the debts. The creditors will receive a certain percentage of what is owed. The remainder of the debts are written off, and the debtor is able to start afresh. Where the debtor is a company or limited liability partnership, the relevant insolvency process may be receivership, administration or liquidation. These processes are discussed in Chapter 11. Where the debtor is a natural person, trust, partnership, body corporate or unincorporated association, the relevant insolvency process is sequestration, colloquially referred to as bankruptcy. This chapter sets out the rules of sequestration: when it can happen, the legal effect and the results for both debtor and creditors.

13.02 Although personal insolvency processes have existed in Scotland for centuries, the law is now largely codified in the Bankruptcy (Scotland) Act 1985. At the time of writing, the Bankruptcy and Debt Advice (Scotland) Act 2014 ('BDA Act'), which makes several significant reforms to the 1985 legislation, has just received Royal Assent.[1] It is not yet clear when the 2014 Act will come into force. The changes to the law it proposes will be considered where relevant. Further reform to the drafting of the 1985 Act may follow. The 1985 Act has been substantially amended over the years, with the result that many of its sections are long and unwieldy with complex numbering. In May 2013, the Scottish Law Commission published its Report on the Consolidation of Bankruptcy Legislation in Scotland,[2] which essentially reviewed the current drafting of the 1985 Act and made detailed suggestions to streamline and improve it. These recommendations will, it seems, be implemented in codifying legislation in due course.[3]

---

1 The Act, supporting documentation and a history of its passage through Parliament may be found at www.scottish.parliament.uk/parliamentarybusiness/Bills/64534.aspx (accessed May 2014).
2 Scot Law Com No 232, available at www.scotlawcom.gov.uk/publications/reports/2010-present/ (accessed May 2014).
3 Policy Memorandum to the BDA Bill, paras 305 and 306.

Why have insolvency law?

13.03 Imagine that Gordon owes money to four different creditors. The debts amount to £100,000, with interest added each month. When the loans were taken out, Gordon's business was doing well, and he was confident he could repay on the agreed terms. Since then, the recession has struck, and Gordon's business is failing. Despite using all of his meagre turnover towards his debt repayments, there is not enough to make his minimum payments. Each month, he incurs penalty costs which put him further into debt. It is hard to see how Gordon will ever recover.

13.04 The law allows sequestration to happen in this context for two reasons. In the first place, the law aims to ensure creditors are treated equally. It is not possible for Gordon to repay them all. Each creditor could individually attempt diligence in respect of their debts,[4] but there are not sufficient assets for them all to be repaid – it would be a case of 'first come, first served' which is considered unfair on the creditors who were slower to act, especially those who delayed taking action in a spirit of compassion towards Gordon. Four creditors doing diligence also means four times the amount of time and money spent, and court time used, which is inefficient. Insolvency gives creditors the option to cut their losses in an efficient and equitable manner. The law also seeks to protect Gordon in this situation. His debts have arisen through a combination of bad judgement and bad luck. Gordon took a risk when starting his business – if no one was prepared to take that risk, a country's economy would never grow. Enabling Gordon to escape from his debts is therefore both a humane recognition that people make mistakes and an economic second chance that may allow Gordon to become a financially contributing member of society once again.

Different types of insolvency

13.05 The word insolvency can be used to describe a range of situations which have different legal consequences. Where a debtor is unable to pay his debts as they fall due, this is referred to as simple or practical insolvency, and does not necessarily indicate that a debtor is in real financial trouble. If Gordon owns shop premises worth £500,000, and his only debt is a credit card bill of £500, his financial situation is very healthy. However, if his credit card bill must be paid today, and there is no cash in his bank account to pay it, he will be practically insolvent. This is a short-term problem: he will be able to obtain the money he needs, perhaps by asking the bank for an overdraft secured against his house. In business, this kind of liquidity problem often arises because clients are late in paying their bills, which in turn leaves the business

---

4 For a discussion of diligence, see Chapter 12.

owner unable to pay his own creditors. Sequestration would not usually be necessary or sensible here.

13.06   Absolute insolvency describes the situation where a debtor's total liabilities exceed his total assets, alternatively referred to as 'balance sheet insolvency'. A debtor in this situation will not inevitably be sequestrated. Some absolutely insolvent debtors continue to operate for long periods, by borrowing money to pay off the most immediate debts in the hope or expectation that their overall financial health will improve. This type of solution cannot continue indefinitely, however, and eventually the creditors may wish to take action.

13.07   Apparent insolvency is the critical test for sequestration. This is a term created by the Bankruptcy (Scotland) Act 1985 ('1985 Act') to describe a number of situations in which the debtor's financial situation is deemed sufficiently precarious to give creditors grounds for sequestration. Section 7 provides that a debtor's apparent insolvency shall be constituted where:

- The debtor gives written notice to his creditors that he has ceased to pay his debts in the ordinary course of business.[5] In other words, the debtor gives notice that he is practically insolvent.
- The debtor grants a trust deed (a kind of negotiated sequestration, discussed below);[6] or is served with a charge and the days of charge expire without payment;[7] or a decree of adjudication is granted against any part of his estate;[8] or a debt payment programme is revoked.[9] Apparent insolvency will not be constituted by any of these events if the debtor can demonstrate that he was practically solvent at the time the event occurred.[10]
- A creditor in respect of a liquid debt of £750 or more has served on the debtor a formal notice[11] requiring payment, and three weeks have passed without payment being made, security being provided, or the debtor formally denying the existence of the debt.[12]

---

5 Bankruptcy (Scotland) Act 1985, s 7(1)(b).
6 1985 Act, s 7(1)(c)(i). A trust deed is a mechanism by which a debtor voluntarily transfers all his assets to a third-party trustee to distribute to his creditors in satisfaction of his debts: see paras **13.73–13.76**.
7 1985 Act, s 7(1)(c)(ii). Service of a charge is the first formal step in enforcing a court decree for repayment of debt: see the discussion at paras **12.09–12.12**.
8 1985 Act, s 7(1)(c)(iv). Adjudication is a form of diligence directed against a debtor's heritable property which enables the creditor to take rents paid in respect of any lease over the property. See the discussion at paras **12.43–12.47**.
9 1985 Act, s 7(1)(c)(vii). A Debt Payment Programme is an agreement between debtor and creditor negotiated through the government Debt Arrangement Scheme, usually on favourable terms to the debtor. See para **12.13**.
10 1985 Act, s 7(1)(c).
11 The form is prescribed by the Bankruptcy (Scotland) Regulations 2008 (SSI 2008/82) reg 3 and Sch 1 (Form 1).
12 1985 Act, s 7(1)(d).

- The debtor's estate has been sequestrated in Scotland or subjected to an equivalent bankruptcy process elsewhere in the EU.[13] In this situation, rather than insolvency triggering sequestration, it is the sequestration which constitutes apparent insolvency. This might happen where the sequestration is initiated by the debtor, discussed below.[14]

13.08 Where the debtor is a partnership, in addition to the situations outlined above, apparent insolvency will be constituted where any of the partners is apparently insolvent for a debt of the partnership.[15] Where the debtor is an unincorporated body, apparent insolvency will be constituted where any person who represents the body or holds property on behalf of the body in a fiduciary capacity is apparently insolvent for a debt of the body.[16]

THE SEQUESTRATION PROCESS

13.09 The process of sequestration generally goes through the following stages:

(a) an application is made for sequestration by the debtor, a creditor or another person qualified to petition the court;

(b) an award of sequestration is made, including the appointment of a trustee in sequestration to deal with the debtor's estate;

(c) the trustee investigates the debtor's estate, establishing his assets and liabilities and challenging any recent transactions designed to defeat the sequestration process;

(d) the trustee realises the debtor's assets, distributing property or funds amongst the creditors of the estate. Creditors will generally receive a percentage of what they are owed, referred to as their 'dividend' from the estate; and

(e) the sequestration is terminated and the debtor is discharged, free of debt.

This chapter will look at each of these stages in detail.

The role of the Accountant in Bankruptcy

13.10 The Accountant in Bankruptcy ('AiB') is a government agency set up under the Bankruptcy (Scotland) Act 1985[17] to oversee the operation of personal insolvency law in Scotland. The AiB operates from an office in Kilwinning staffed by civil servants with legal qualifications,

---

13 1985 Act, s 7(1)(a) and (ba).
14 At paras **13.14–13.16**.
15 1985 Act, s 7(3)(a).
16 1985 Act, s 7(3).
17 1985 Act, ss 1–1C.

accountancy qualifications or various other skills. One of its main functions is to supervise the performance of those administering the insolvency process, including insolvency lawyers. This means providing guidance to practitioners on law and procedure, in addition to investigating complaints from debtors or creditors about the administration of a sequestration in which they were involved. The AiB also has a record-keeping role, with responsibility for maintaining the Register of Insolvencies.[18] In a limited range of situations, the AiB can step in to act as an insolvency practitioner itself. More information on the AiB's role and functions can be found on its website.[19]

13.11   The chief executive of the agency holds the statutory post of Accountant in Bankruptcy, an officer of the court. At the time of writing, the post is held by Rosemary Winter-Scott.

APPLYING FOR SEQUESTRATION

Who can be sequestrated?

13.12   Provision as to which legal persons are liable to sequestration is made in sections 5 and 6 of the 1985 Act. In the first place, the estate of a natural person can be sequestrated, whether that person is alive or dead.[20] In addition, it is competent to sequestrate the legal estate belonging to or held by or for: a trust in respect of debts incurred by the trust;[21] a partnership or limited partnership, including a dissolved partnership or dissolved limited partnership;[22] a body corporate other than a company or LLP;[23] and an unincorporated body.[24]

Obtaining a sequestration

13.13   A debtor who is a natural person can apply to the AiB to sequestrate his own estate. An 'entity debtor' (trust, partnership, body corporate or unincorporated body) can apply to the AiB to sequestrate its estate with the concurrence of a creditor. Alternatively, creditors and other qualified persons can petition the court to make an award of sequestration in respect of the estate of a debtor.

---

18 A public register containing details of all sequestrations awarded by the Scottish courts, in addition to information on protected trust deeds for creditors and details of limited companies in receivership or liquidation. It can be consulted at www.roi.aib.gov.uk/roi (accessed May 2014).
19 www.aib.gov.uk (accessed May 2014).
20 1985 Act, s 5.
21 1985 Act, s 6(1)(a).
22 1985 Act, s 6(1)(b) and (d). A limited partnership is not the same legal entity as a limited liability partnership, as discussed at para **1.24** ff. A limited partnership can be sequestrated; an LLP cannot.
23 1985 Act, s 6(1)(c) and (2).
24 1985 Act, s 6(1)(c).

Application by debtor

13.14 A natural person is permitted to apply for sequestration of his own estate,[25] provided the total amount of his debts is £3,000 or more,[26] and there has been no award of sequestration made against him within the five years prior to the application.[27] The debtor's application will be competent only where he meets one of the conditions set out in section 5(2B)(c) of the 1985 Act,[28] namely that he is apparently insolvent,[29] has granted a trust deed which cannot be converted into a protected trust deed,[30] or has been granted a 'certificate of sequestration'.[31] This certificate can be granted by certain authorised persons who have reviewed the debtor's financial statements and confirmed that the debtor is unable to pay his debts as they fall due.[32] Alternatively, he can qualify as a 'low income, low asset' debtor[33] if his weekly income does not exceed the national minimum wage, he does not own any land, the total value of his assets (excluding liabilities) on the date of the application does not exceed £10,000 and he has no single asset worth over £1,000.[34] The BDA Act proposes the introduction of compulsory state-funded financial education for living debtors, requiring that advice be sought from a money advisor prior to any application for sequestration.[35] Additionally, the debtor's financial position will be assessed, and if he is deemed able to make an ongoing contribution to his debts from his income, his application for sequestration will include consent to make this ongoing contribution throughout the sequestration process.[36]

13.15 An 'entity debtor' (a trust, partnership, body corporate or unin-

25 1985 Act, s 5(2)(a). The estate of a deceased person can currently be sequestrated only by way of the petition procedure outlined below: see paras **13.17–13.19**. However, the BDA Act, s 11 proposes that the executor of an insolvent estate should be able to apply to the AiB for sequestration.
26 1985 Act, s 5(2B)(a).
27 1985 Act, s 5(2B)(b).
28 1985 Act, s 5(2B)(b).
29 1985 Act, s 5(2B)(c)(i). See para **13.07**.
30 1985 Act, s 5(2B)(c)(ii). See para **13.75**.
31 1985 Act, s 5(2B)(c)(ib).
32 1985 Act, s 5B.
33 1985 Act, s 5(2B)(c)(ia).
34 1985 Act, s 5B and Bankruptcy (Scotland) Act 1985 (Low Income, Low Asset Debtors etc) Regulations 2008 (SSI 2008/81) regs 2 and 3. The BDA Act proposes to replace this scheme with a new 'minimal asset process'. This will be available firstly to debtors who have been in receipt of welfare benefits for at least six months. Alternatively, a debtor will be able to apply using this process where he owes between £1,500 and £10,000, the total value of his assets (excluding liabilities) does not exceed £2,000, he has no single asset over £1,000 and does not own land. Household items will not be included in the calculation of his assets. A vehicle worth up to £3,000 will also be excluded where its use is 'reasonably required' by the debtor. See BDA Act, ss 5–7 and Sch 1.
35 BDA Act, s 1 inserting new sections 5(4BA), 5(2B)(ba) and 5C into the 1985 Act. Further financial education may be a compulsory requirement of discharge of bankruptcy: BDA Act, s 2.
36 BDA Act, ss 3 and 4.

corporated body) may apply for sequestration only with the concurrence of a qualified creditor.[37] Where the debtor is a trust, the majority of trustees must make the application.[38] For a partnership, consensus of all the partners is required.[39] For bodies corporate and unincorporated, a person authorised to act on behalf of the body must make the application.[40]

13.16 A debtor makes his or its application to the AiB by completing a prescribed form[41] available from the AiB website,[42] and paying a fixed fee, currently £200. If the AiB is satisfied that the debtor meets the conditions set out in the statute, it will award sequestration forthwith.[43] The AiB must also record the sequestration in the Register of Inhibitions and Adjudications.[44]

Petition to the sheriff

13.17 A qualified creditor can petition the sheriff to award sequestration in respect of the estate of a debtor who is apparently insolvent.[45] A qualified creditor is one who, at the date of the petition, is owed at least £3,000 by the debtor in question, or more than one creditor whose debts add up to at least £3,000.[46] Where the debtor is a natural person, the creditor must provide him with a Debt Advice and Information Pack at least two weeks and not more than 12 weeks before the petition is made.[47] Where the debtor is deceased, the creditor must wait until six months after the death unless the debtor was apparently insolvent at some point in the four months preceding his demise.[48]

13.18 The sheriff can also be petitioned by the executor of a deceased debtor's estate,[49] a trustee acting under a trust deed[50] or by an official in an alternative insolvency process (although this is rare).[51]

13.19 The petition must be presented to the court in the sheriffdom in which the debtor was habitually resident or had a place of business

---

37 1985 Act, s 6(3)(a), (4)(a) and (6)(a). For the meaning of 'qualified creditor', see para **13.17**.
38 1985 Act, s 6(3)(a).
39 1985 Act, s 6(4)(a).
40 1985 Act, s 6(6)(a).
41 1985 Act, s 5(4B).
42 www.aib.gov.uk/guidance/publications/forms/debtorsapplforms (accessed May 2014).
43 1985 Act, s 12(1).
44 1985 Act, s 14(1A).
45 1985 Act, s 5(2)(b).
46 1985 Act, s 2(4). For information on the DAIP, see para **12.12**.
47 1985 Act, s 5(2D).
48 1985 Act, s 8(3)(b).
49 1985 Act, s 5(3). The BDA Act, s 11 proposes that the executor of an insolvent estate should be able to apply to the AiB for sequestration.
50 1985 Act, s 5(2)(b)(iv).
51 1985 Act, s 5(2)(b)(ii)–(iv) and s 5(3)(ba)–(c).

during the previous 12 months.[52] A copy of the petition must be sent to the AiB.[53] The sheriff will cite the debtor to a hearing between six and 14 days after the petition was presented.[54] The purpose of the hearing is to ascertain whether the defender can show cause why the petition should not be granted. He may argue that the procedural formalities in respect of the petition have not been carried out correctly, or that the applicant was not entitled to petition the court because the debts were not due or the debtor was not apparently insolvent. If good cause is shown, or if the debtor pays or secures the debt, the petition will be dismissed.[55] The court may continue the petition in certain circumstances if it appears matters can be resolved without the need for sequestration.[56] Otherwise, sequestration will be awarded.[57] The sheriff clerk must record the sequestration in the Register of Inhibitions and Adjudications and notify the AiB.[58]

CONSEQUENCES OF THE AWARD OF SEQUESTRATION

13.20 In the case of debtor application, the date of sequestration is the date on which the award was made by the AiB.[59] Where sequestration has been awarded by the court following on a petition, the date of sequestration is backdated to the date on which warrant to cite the debtor in respect of the petition was first granted by the sheriff.[60] An award of sequestration has several immediate consequences. In the first place, a trustee in sequestration is appointed to deal with the debtor's estate. Secondly, the debtor's estate immediately vests in the trustee. Thirdly, diligence is equalised. Finally, a sequestrated debtor is subject to certain legal restrictions.

The trustee in sequestration

13.21 On making an award of sequestration, the AiB or the sheriff must appoint a person to act as the trustee in sequestration. This person must be a qualified insolvency practitioner (almost invariably a lawyer) and consent to taking on the role.[61] It is normally the case that the application or petition will nominate someone to act as trustee,[62] failing which the AiB will take on the role.[63] In the unusual situation where an interim trustee has been appointed to safeguard the debtor's assets

---

52 1985 Act, s 9.
53 1985 Act, s 5(6).
54 1985 Act, s 12(2).
55 1985 Act, s 12(3A).
56 1985 Act, s 12(3B) and (3C).
57 1985 Act, s 12(3).
58 1985 Act, s 14(1).
59 1985 Act, s 12(4)(a).
60 1985 Act, s 12(4)(b).
61 1985 Act, s 2(3).
62 1985 Act, s 2(1) and (1A).
63 1985 Act, s 2(1B) and (2).

whilst the application for sequestration is ongoing, the same person will usually continue into the role of trustee in sequestration.[64] Where the debtor has applied through the 'low income, low asset' route, the AiB must act as the trustee.[65]

13.22 The trustee's functions are set out in section 3 of the 1985 Act. In summary, these are:

- to recover, manage and realise the debtor's estate, wherever situated;
- to distribute the estate amongst the creditors according to their respective entitlements;
- to ascertain the reasons for the debtor's insolvency and the circumstances surrounding it; and
- to ascertain the state of the debtor's liabilities and assets.

These duties should be performed only in so far as, in the trustee's view, it would be of financial benefit to the estate of the debtor and in the interests of creditors to do so.[66] The trustee also has a responsibility to ensure accurate records of the sequestration are maintained and supplied to the AiB, and to keep all interested parties up to date on progress.[67]

13.23 In practice, the trustee's first duties on being appointed will be to secure the debtor's estate as necessary[68] (by requiring the debtor to physically hand over assets, for example) and to prepare a statement of the debtor's financial affairs.[69] The debtor is required to provide the trustee with a list of assets and liabilities to assist the trustee in preparation of his statement.[70]

13.24 The trustee also has the option to call a 'statutory meeting' of creditors,[71] at which the creditors vote to approve the appointment of a trustee (or replace him) and submit claims on the estate.[72] This used to be a compulsory but ill-attended aspect of the sequestration process, which is little used since the 1985 Act was amended to make the meeting optional. If the trustee wishes to call a meeting, he must do so within 60 days of being appointed.[73]

64 1985 Act, s 2(5)–(6B). Prior to the reforms introduced by the Bankruptcy and Diligence etc (Scotland) Act 2007, an interim trustee would be appointed in every case, followed by a 'permanent trustee' at a later stage after sequestration was awarded. The interim trustee under the old regime had more extensive powers than he does now. The distinction between interim and permanent trustees was considered to be unnecessarily cumbersome, hence its abolition and the introduction of the current system.
65 1985 Act, s 2(1C).
66 1985 Act, s 3(8).
67 1985 Act, s 3(1)(e)–(g).
68 1985 Act, s 18.
69 1985 Act, s 20.
70 1985 Act, s 19.
71 1985 Act, ss 20A and 21A.
72 1985 Act, ss 21A–24.
73 1985 Act, s 21A(2).

13.25 At the statutory meeting, or any other meeting, it is open to creditors to elect up to five of their number as 'commissioners' whose task it is to oversee the trustee's dealings with the estate.[74] In practice, this tends not to happen except in particularly large or complex sequestrations. Commissioners have a responsibility to supervise and provide guidance to the trustee on his management of the estate,[75] although he is not obliged to follow their advice.[76] Commissioners will also audit a trustee's accounts, and determine what payment in respect of fees and outlays he is entitled to in any accounting period.[77] Commissioners must act gratuitously, and owe fiduciary duties to the debtor and other creditors.

Vesting of the estate

13.26 On appointment, the trustee is issued with an 'act and warrant' by the sheriff or AiB. The effect of the act and warrant is to divest the debtor of all property in his patrimony at that moment and transfer it to the trustee's patrimony.[78] The estate is said to vest in the trustee *tantum et tale*, meaning the trustee acquires no better right to the property than the debtor had.[79] If the debtor owned property subject to a right in security, the trustee's ownership will also be subject to that right in security.

13.27 In respect of moveable property, the trustee acquires any personal rights held by the debtor, such as a right to repayment of debt from a third party. However, the trustee does not automatically acquire any onerous obligations owed by the debtor, such as the obligations he may owe as a tenant under a lease. The trustee will not be liable for such obligations unless he specifically adopts the relevant contract. Where delivery, possession or intimation would normally be required to complete title to a piece of moveable property, this will be deemed to have occurred by virtue of the trustee's appointment.[80]

13.28 In respect of heritable property, as a matter of general property law principle, the trustee must register the act and warrant against the title to the property in the Land Register or Register of Sasines in order to acquire a real right in that property. This cannot be done until at least 28 days after the sequestration has been recorded in the Register of

---

74 1985 Act, s 30.
75 1985 Act, s 4.
76 1985 Act, s 3(2).
77 1985 Act, s 53(5).
78 1985 Act, s 31(1).
79 It is not clear that the maxim *tantum et tale* correctly applied is anything other than a restatement of the *nemo plus* principle. For discussion, see Lord Rodger's speech in *Burnett's Tr v Grainger* 2004 SC (HL) 19 and R G Anderson, 'Fraud on transfer and on insolvency: ta...ta...tantum et tale?' (2007) 11(2) Edin LR 187. The *nemo plus* principle is explained in detail at para **3.96** ff.
80 1985 Act, s 31(4).

Inhibitions and Adjudications.[81] The 28-day window was introduced to avoid the situation where the disposition in respect of the sale of a house by the debtor was delivered prior to the award of sequestration, but not registered until afterwards, leaving the prospective house buyer without the sale price, the house or any effective remedy against the debtor or the trustee.[82]

13.29 Certain property is exempt from vesting. Property which the debtor holds in trust is specifically excluded.[83] Property exempt from attachment, such as household goods and tools of the debtor's trade,[84] do not vest in the trustee.[85] Property subject to confiscation orders or related restraints under the Proceeds of Crime Act 2002 will not vest.[86] Protected tenancies, including assured or Scottish secure tenancies, are excluded.[87]

13.30 More broadly, the rules on vesting apply to assets and not to income, so any income received by the debtor will not vest unless it has been derived from his assets.[88] Dividends paid on shares owned by the debtor will therefore vest in the trustee. Wages or periodical payments from a pension fund will not. It is open to the trustee to seek a voluntary contribution of income from the debtor by way of an Income Payment Arrangement,[89] or to apply to court for an Income Payment Order transferring to the trustee income which is surplus to that reasonably required by the debtor.[90]

13.31 Property acquired by the debtor after the date of sequestration but prior to him being discharged,[91] known as *acquirenda*, will vest in the trustee.[92] A debtor must immediately inform the trustee of any acquirenda or he commits a criminal offence.[93]

Equalisation of diligence

13.32 Once an award of sequestration has been made, it is no longer

---

81 1985 Act, s 31(1A), (1B) and (3).
82 See *Burnett's Tr v Grainger* 2004 SC (HL) 19.
83 For a full discussion, see paras **12.18–12.19**.
84 Bankruptcy (Scotland) Act 1985, s 33(1)(b).
85 1985 Act, s 33(1)(a)–(aa).
86 1985 Act, ss 31A–31C.
87 1985 Act, s 31(9) and (10).
88 1985 Act, s 32(1).
89 1985 Act, s 32(4B).
90 1985 Act, s 32(2). IPOs are likely to become rare if the proposals for a debtor contribution outlined in the BDA Act, ss 3 and 4 are implemented: see para **13.14**.
91 For an explanation of the procedure for discharge of the debtor from the sequestration, see paras **13.66–13.70**.
92 1985 Act, s 32. The BDA Act, s 16 proposes changing the period of acquirenda to cover all property acquired by the debtor from the date of sequestration until four years later, rather than from the date of sequestration to the date of discharge, as it is at present.
93 1985 Act, s 32(7).

competent for creditors to enforce their right to repayment of debt through diligence.[94] The sequestration has the same effect as if the trustee had carried out all relevant forms of diligence against the debtor's estate for the benefit of all creditors.[95] The law also does not wish to reward creditors who aggressively pursued debts at a time when the debtor was close to bankruptcy, since this is considered unfair both on the debtor and other creditors. To this end, any diligence process started in the period of 60 days prior to the award of sequestration will not create a preferential right in favour of the creditor who performed the diligence.[96] Any right or asset obtained by a creditor through a diligence process started during this period must be handed over to the trustee to be shared amongst creditors with the rest of the estate.[97] Any right of inhibition obtained by a creditor during this period must be assigned to the trustee to exercise for the benefit of all creditors.[98] This is known as equalisation of diligence, since the creditor's rights are equalised with those of the trustee and other creditors.

Personal effects on the debtor

13.33 In addition to being divested of his assets, the debtor is also subject to certain legal restrictions as a result of the sequestration. He is not permitted to leave Scotland.[99] He is not permitted to obtain credit over a value of £500[100] without advising the creditor about the sequestration.[101] He is not permitted to act as a director of a company or to be involved in the promotion, formation or management of a company without the leave of the court.[102] Breach of any of these restrictions is a criminal offence. In addition, an undischarged bankrupt is not entitled to practise as a solicitor[103] or in various other professions, and may not become an MP or take up various other public offices.[104] Section 9 of the BDA Act proposes a new requirement on the debtor to sign a 'statement of undertakings' at the time the sequestration is applied for, confirming his understanding of the obligations placed on him by the 1985 Act.

---

94 For more detail on the process and effect of diligence, see Chapter 12. The BDA Act, s 8 proposes that a moratorium on diligence should be imposed for six weeks from the date on which the debtor first gives written notice to the AiB of his intention to apply for sequestration, with potential to extend the time limit if the application takes longer to process.
95 1985 Act, ss 14(2) and 37(1).
96 1985 Act, s 37(2)–(7).
97 1985 Act, s 37(2)–(7).
98 1985 Act, s 37(2)–(3).
99 1985 Act, s 67(3).
100 The BDA Act, s 51 proposes to increase this figure to £2,000.
101 1985 Act, s 67(9).
102 Company Directors Disqualification Act 1986, s 11(1).
103 Solicitors (Scotland) Act 1980, s 18(1).
104 Insolvency Act 1986, s 427.

INVESTIGATING THE ESTATE

13.34   Although the estate automatically vests in the trustee at the date
of sequestration, he must take practical steps to ingather it. The trustee
is given power to take possession of the estate and any document in the
debtor's possession related to his assets or business and financial
affairs.[105] The trustee is also entitled to access such documents in the
hands of a third party, and to require delivery of title deeds or documents belonging to the debtor which are in the hands of a third party.[106]
In order to obtain information necessary for his investigation of the
estate, the trustee may request the debtor or any other person to appear
before him for questioning in respect of the debtor's assets, and may
apply for a court order compelling attendance if a person will not
comply.[107] A person who fails to attend or produce documents commits
a criminal offence.[108] The trustee's examination is performed under
oath, so a charge of perjury is possible where a person fails to tell the
truth.[109]

13.35   The trustee is also given powers to manage the debtor's estate
as necessary for the discharge of his functions. Specifically, he is empowered to: carry on the debtor's business; bring, defend or continue any
legal proceedings related to the debtor's estate; create a right in security
over any part of the estate; make payments or incur liabilities in order
to acquire property which is the subject of a right or option; borrow
money; and effect or maintain insurance policies.[110] Additionally, the
trustee may adopt or decline to adopt any contract entered into by the
debtor prior to sequestration, or enter into new contracts, if he considers
it would be beneficial for the administration of the debtor's estate.[111]

CHALLENGEABLE TRANSACTIONS

13.36   Another aspect of the trustee's role in investigating the estate is
to counteract any steps the debtor may have taken during the run-up to
the sequestration in an attempt to defeat his creditors. Return to the
example of our businessman, Gordon. As the only person with full
knowledge of his financial situation, he is aware that he is insolvent some
time before any of his creditors come to realise that fact. Gordon suspects
bankruptcy is on the horizon. He does not want his shop to be taken
from him and sold to pay off his creditors, so he agrees to 'sell' it to his
brother Graeme for a small amount of money. The brothers agree

---

105 1985 Act, s 38(1)–(2).
106 1985 Act, s 38(2) and (4).
107 1985 Act, ss 44–47.
108 1985 Act, ss 44(3) and 45(4).
109 1985 Act, s 47(1).
110 1985 Act, s 39(2)(a)–(f).
111 1985 Act, s 42.

privately that, once the sequestration is over and Gordon has been discharged, Graeme will 'sell' the shop back to Gordon for the same nominal sum. This would allow Gordon to write off his debts and yet still hold on to one of his biggest assets. The law does not consider this to be fair. Accordingly, the trustee has the power to investigate transactions entered into by the debtor in the period prior to the sequestration, and to undo steps taken to defeat the interests of creditors.

13.37 The two most significant types of challengeable transaction are gratuitous alienations and unfair preferences. The trustee is also empowered to challenge financial orders on divorce, excessive pension contributions and extortionate credit transactions. Each of these will be discussed below.

Gratuitous alienations

13.38 The essence of a gratuitous alienation is that the debtor has simply given away part of his estate. Section 34 of the 1985 Act sets out what is required for a transaction of this type to be challenged. In the first place, there must have been an alienation, meaning the debtor must have transferred property out of his estate.[112] This would include the debtor making a cash payment, or renouncing a right or preference. The transfer must have been made within the two years prior to the date of sequestration,[113] unless it was made to an associate of the debtor, in which case any transfer within five years prior to the sequestration is potentially challengeable.[114] 'Associate' is defined to include spouses, relatives and in-laws, business partners, the debtor's employee or employer and a company controlled by the debtor alone or with associates.[115] It does not include a friend of the debtor. The transfer will be considered to have taken place on the date on which it became effectual:[116] so, on the date of registration for transfer of heritable property, for example. If all these requirements are met, the alienation can be challenged by the trustee or any creditor.[117]

13.39 Three defences are available to a debtor where a transaction has been challenged on this basis. First, if the debtor can show that at any time after the alienation his assets exceeded his liabilities, the transaction will stand.[118] Secondly, if the debtor can prove that the transaction was

112 1985 Act, s 34(2)(a).
113 1985 Act, s 34(2) and (3)(b). Where the debtor is deceased, the alienation must have been made within two years prior to his death, and his estate sequestrated within 12 months after his death: s 34(2)(b)(iii), (2)(c) and (3)(b).
114 1985 Act, s 34(2) and (3)(a). Where the debtor is deceased, the alienation must have been made within five years prior to his death, and his estate sequestrated within 12 months after his death: s 34(2)(b)(iii), (2)(c) and (3)(a).
115 1985 Act, s 74.
116 1985 Act, s 34(3).
117 1985 Act, s 34(1). A trustee under a trust deed is also entitled to make a challenge under this section.
118 1985 Act, s 34(4)(a).

for adequate consideration (in other words, was not 'gratuitous'), this will be a defence to a challenge.[119] What will be considered adequate consideration is a question of fact, although the court has indicated that it need not mean 'the best possible price which could have been achieved' so long as the price actually paid was reasonable.[120] Attempts to argue that consideration was given by the transferee in separate transactions are unlikely to find favour with the court, as with the husband who claimed that the transfer of his house to his wife had been paid for by a number of gifts given to him in the past.[121] Thirdly, if the debtor can demonstrate that the alienation was a permitted gift such as a Christmas present or a charitable donation (made to someone other than an associate of the debtor), the transaction will stand.[122] The debtor must show that a gift of this type was reasonable at the time it was made, which may be difficult to do if the debtor was in financial difficulties at that point.

13.40   If the debtor is unable to defend the transaction, the court has three options: to order reduction of the deed effecting the transfer, which would be the normal remedy for heritable property; to order restoration of the property to the estate, which would be the normal remedy for moveables; or to grant 'such other redress as may be appropriate'.[123] The court has tended to interpret these remedies quite strictly. In *Short's Trustee v Chung*,[124] the debtor had sold two flats to a third party at significant undervalue, and the third party had in turn gifted them to his wife, Mrs Chung. Both transactions were gratuitous and therefore liable to reduction, but Mrs Chung argued this would be inequitable, since the flats had increased significantly in value whilst in her ownership. She suggested the appropriate remedy would be for her to retain ownership, instead paying back the value of the flats at the time they were alienated. The court disagreed, reading the statute to mean that property should be restored to the estate wherever possible. Since it was possible in this situation, restoration was the appropriate remedy. In *Cay's Trustee v Cay*,[125] the debtor had gifted £35,000 to his wife. She argued that it would not be equitable for the court to order restoration of the full amount to the estate, since she had already used £20,000 of the money to pay off debts of her husband. The court found no statutory basis for determining an equitable remedy where restoration to the estate was possible, as it was in this case, and so ordered the full amount to be restored.[126]

---

119 1985 Act, s 34(4)(b).
120 *Lafferty Construction v McCombe* 1994 SLT 858.
121 *Matheson's Tr v Matheson* 1992 SLT 685. See also *MacFadyen's Tr v MacFadyen* 1994 SLT 1245.
122 1985 Act, s 34(4)(c).
123 1985 Act, s 34(4).
124 1991 SLT 472.
125 1998 SC 780, 1998 SCLR 456.
126 See also *Nottay's Tr v Nottay* 2001 SLT 769.

13.41 The statute does make clear, however, that a third party who has acquired the property in good faith and for value should not be prejudiced.[127] So, where a debtor has gifted property to his wife, and his wife has sold that property on to a good faith third party for value, the court cannot order the property to be restored to the estate. The appropriate remedy in this situation would be for the wife to return the proceeds of the sale to the estate.

13.42 In addition to the statutory regime, it remains possible for a challenge to be made to a gratuitous alienation at common law.[128] This right, originally available only to creditors, has been extended to the trustee by the 1985 Act.[129] In order to make a successful common law challenge, the challenger faces a somewhat heavier burden of proof than in the statutory regime, having to demonstrate all three of the following components. First, the alienation must have been gratuitous in the sense described above. Secondly, it must have had a prejudicial effect on creditors. Thirdly, the debtor must have been absolutely insolvent at the time the alienation was made, or else have been rendered absolutely insolvent by the alienation, and remained so until the challenge to the transaction was made. This should be contrasted with a statutory challenge, in which the onus of proof would be on the debtor to show that he was *not* insolvent in order to defend the transaction. If a common law challenge can be successfully made out, the advantage to the challenger is that any alienation can be challenged without limit of time. The common law route also enables a creditor to bring a challenge outwith the context of the sequestration process, although a creditor may be unwilling to take on this difficulty and expense when a successful challenge would only lead to the property being restored to the debtor for diligence at the hands of any creditor.

Unfair preferences

13.43 A challenge to a gratuitous alienation protects all creditors from dishonest behaviour on the part of the debtor. A challenge to an unfair preference protects the majority of creditors from dishonest behaviour on the part of the debtor in collusion with a creditor. A preference is unfair if the debtor has given it to one creditor at the expense of the others. Imagine that Gordon, on the verge of bankruptcy, decides he wishes to maintain a good relationship with his creditor Heather so that she will lend him money once again after the sequestration has been dealt with. He grants her a standard security over his shop, which is his principal asset. In the sequestration proceedings which follow Heather, as a secured creditor, will obtain repayment of her debt in full first. The

---

127 1985 Act, s 34(4).
128 J McLaren (ed), *Bell's Commentaries on the Law of Scotland* (7th edn, 1870, rep 1990), II, 170.
129 1985 Act, s 34(8). A trustee under a trust deed is also entitled to make a challenge under this section.

remaining creditors will be left to share any surplus sale proceeds from the shop once Heather's debt has been paid. Gordon and Heather are happy, but the other creditors are out of pocket. The law considers this to be inequitable, so such preferences are challengeable.

13.44 Grant of a security to a creditor is one example of a preference which could be unfair. Paying off a debt before it falls due, particularly when other debt payments are overdue, is another example. Any action by the debtor which favours one creditor over the others may fall within this category.

13.45 The statute allows a challenge to be made to any unfair preference granted to a creditor within the six months prior to the date of sequestration.[130] A challenge can be brought by the trustee or any creditor.[131]

13.46 The statute also sets out four categories of transactions which cannot be challenged as creating an unfair preference:

(a) a transaction in the ordinary course of trade or business.[132] This would include paying a debt as it fell due, or performing any other obligation under a contract at the required time;

(b) a payment in cash for a debt which had fallen due, unless the transaction was collusive with the purpose of prejudicing the general body of creditors;[133]

(c) a transaction where the debtor and creditor undertake reciprocal obligations.[134] Again, this exception does not apply where there was collusion to defeat the interests of other creditors; or

(d) the grant of a mandate by the debtor to pay over arrested funds.[135]

13.47 As with gratuitous alienations, if the debtor is unable to defend the transaction, the court has three options: to order reduction of the deed effecting the preference, as with the grant of a standard security; to order restoration of the property to the estate, as with early payment of a debt; or to grant 'such other redress as may be appropriate'.[136] Where a creditor transfers property acquired via an unfair preference to a third party, the third party's title will be protected so long as the transfer was in good faith and for value.[137]

---

130 1985 Act, s 36(1). Where the debtor is deceased, the preference must have been granted within the six months prior to his death, and his estate sequestrated within twelve months after his death: s 36(1)(c).

131 1985 Act, s 36(4). A trustee under a trust deed is also entitled to make a challenge under this section.

132 1985 Act, s 36(2)(a).

133 1985 Act, s 36(2)(b).

134 1985 Act, s 36(2)(c).

135 1985 Act, s 36(2)(d). For the rules of arrestment, see paras **9.27–9.30**.

136 1985 Act, s 36(5).

137 1985 Act, s 36(5).

13.48 Fraudulent preferences can also be challenged at common law.[138] This right, originally available only to creditors, has been extended to the trustee by the 1985 Act.[139] Despite the use of the word 'fraudulent', it is not necessary for a challenger to demonstrate a fraudulent intention on the part of the debtor or the creditor in receipt of the preference.[140] What the challenger must prove is that the debtor carried out a voluntary act[141] which preferred one creditor to the prejudice of others, at a time when he was absolutely insolvent and knew himself to be so. An inference of fraud can be drawn in the circumstances.[142] It is irrelevant whether the creditor was aware of the debtor's state of solvency.

13.49 It has been said that the first three statutory defences outlined above will also operate as a defence against a common law fraudulent preference claim. McBryde argues[143] that these are only examples of situations in which a defence might be made out: the real question is whether the defender can show his act was not voluntary, he was not insolvent, or he did not know himself to be insolvent. If that is the case, a wider range of potential defences is available to the debtor at common law. The advantage of a successful common law challenge here, as with gratuitous alienations, is that preferences granted at any time can be challenged, not just those granted within the six-month statutory time limit. Additionally, an interested creditor need not wait until sequestration proceedings are underway in order to bring his challenge.

Recall of financial orders on divorce

13.50 On divorce or dissolution of civil partnership, the court can make a number of financial orders to ensure that both parties leave the relationship with a fair share of the property. A party can be ordered to pay a capital sum to his former spouse or partner,[144] to transfer specific property,[145] or to share rights in a pension fund.[146] The trustee may ask the court to retrospectively reconsider an order of this kind[147] in the following circumstances:

- on the date the order was made, the party subject to the order

---

138 J McLaren (ed), *Bell's Commentaries on the Law of Scotland* (7th edn) II 170.
139 1985 Act, s 36(6). A trustee under a trust deed is also entitled to make a challenge under this section.
140 The term fraudulent in this context has carried over from the old law of fraud, on which see Stair, *Institutions* 1.9.16.
141 *Nordic Travel Ltd v Scotprint Ltd* 1980 SC 1.
142 *Liquidator of Letham Grange Development Co Ltd v Foxworth Investments Ltd* [2013] CSIH 13, 2013 SLT 445.
143 *Bankruptcy* (2nd edn, 1995), p 317.
144 Family Law (Scotland) Act 1985, s 8(1)(a).
145 FL(S)A 1985, s 8(1)(aa).
146 FL(S)A 1985, s 8(1)(baa).
147 1985 Act, s 35. A trustee under a trust deed is also entitled to make a challenge under this section.

was absolutely insolvent, or was rendered absolutely insolvent as a result of the order;[148] or

- within five years of the order being made, the party subject to the order was sequestrated.[149]

The court has the power to order the debtor's former spouse or partner to return any or all property or capital transferred. However, it can only do so after having regard to all the circumstances of the case, including the financial circumstances in which the debtor's former spouse or partner now finds himself.[150]

Recovery of excessive pension contributions

13.51 As previously discussed, any share the debtor may have in a pension fund is not considered an asset capable of vesting in the trustee. Payments received from a pension fund are classed as income, and remain with the debtor. For this reason, a debtor who fears bankruptcy may choose to make substantial contributions to his pension fund in order to keep the funds out of reach of his creditors. If the trustee considers that the debtor's pension contributions have unfairly prejudiced his creditors, he may make an application to court for an order restoring the position to what it would have been had the contributions not been made.[151] The court, having satisfied itself that the contributions were excessive in the circumstances and designed to put assets beyond the reach of creditors,[152] may make such order as it thinks fit. This is likely to include ordering the pension fund administrators to restore some or all of the pension contributions to the debtor's estate, and to adjust the benefits the debtor or any dependant is entitled to receive from the pension fund.[153]

Extortionate credit transactions

13.52 A debtor in a difficult financial position may find himself borrowing money on extremely uncompetitive terms. If a debtor has entered into a credit transaction within three years prior to the sequestration on terms which the trustee considers extortionate,[154] he can apply to court to have the transaction varied or set aside, and for funds or property paid over in respect of the transaction to be restored to the

---

148 1985 Act, s 35(1)(b).
149 1985 Act, s 35(1)(c). Where the debtor is deceased, he must have died within five years of the order being made and the estate must have been sequestrated within 12 months after his death: s 35(1)(c)(iii).
150 1985 Act, s 35(2).
151 1985 Act, s 36A. A trustee under a trust deed is also entitled to make a challenge under this section.
152 1985 Act, s 36A(6).
153 1985 Act, ss 36B–36C.
154 1985 Act, s 61(2). A trustee under a trust deed is also entitled to make a challenge under this section.

estate.[155] The statute defines an extortionate transaction as one which required 'grossly exorbitant' payments to be made or otherwise 'grossly contravened' the principles of fair dealing.[156] Where the trustee makes an application under this section of the statute, it will be presumed that the transaction was extortionate, with the onus of proof resting on the credit provider to demonstrate the terms were fair and reasonable.[157]

REALISING THE ESTATE

13.53 Once the trustee has ascertained the contents of the estate and restored any property to which the creditors are entitled in terms of the challengeable transactions outlined above, his next task will be to realise the property in order that it can be paid over to creditors.[158] In addition to the management powers outlined above[159] which enable the trustee to take possession of the estate, the trustee is empowered to sell off any part of it by public sale or private bargain.[160] Estate property cannot, however, be bought by the trustee, any associate of his or any commissioner.[161]

13.54 Where the estate contains heritable property subject to a security, both the secured creditor and the trustee have power to sell.[162] The trustee cannot exercise his power here without the agreement of the secured creditor, unless it is clear that the sale proceeds will pay off the debt to that creditor in full.[163] Once either party indicates an intention to sell, the other party cannot take steps to do so.[164] Where one party has commenced sale proceedings, the other is entitled to seek a remedy from the court if the sale is unduly delayed.[165]

13.55 As an exception to the general rule on heritable property, the trustee does not have an automatic right to sell the debtor's family home, defined to mean a place in which the debtor and/or his current or former spouse or civil partner and/or any child of the family was resident on the day immediately preceding the sequestration.[166] The trustee must seek consent to the sale from the spouse or civil partner. If there is no spouse or civil partner, but the debtor lives in the home with a child of

---

155 1985 Act, s 61(4).
156 1985 Act, s 61(3).
157 1985 Act, s 61(3).
158 1985 Act, s 3(1)(a).
159 1985 Act, s 39(2). See paras **13.34–13.35**.
160 1985 Act, s 39(3).
161 1985 Act, s 39(8). For an explanation of the role of commissioner, see para **13.25**.
162 1985 Act, s 39(4).
163 1985 Act, s 39(4)(a).
164 1985 Act, s 39(4)(b).
165 1985 Act, s 39(4)(c).
166 1985 Act, s 40(4).

the family, the trustee must seek the consent of the debtor.[167] If consent is not given, the trustee can apply to court for authority to make the sale.[168] The court can give or refuse authority subject to any appropriate conditions after having regard to the needs and financial resources of any resident of the house, and the interests of the creditors.[169] If the trustee does not exercise the power of sale within three years of the date of sequestration, the family home will reinvest in the debtor.[170] It should be noted that where a secured creditor seeks to sell the family home, he is not subject to the conditions outlined above, although he will have to comply with the usual protections available to a debtor where a home is sold under a standard security.[171]

PAYMENT OF CREDITORS

13.56 Having realised the estate, the trustee must then arrange to pay the creditors and eventually bring the sequestration to an end.

Submission of claims

13.57 Any creditor who believes he has a right in the sequestration must submit a claim to the trustee.[172] Where a statutory meeting has been held, claims will normally have been submitted in advance since, without a claim, a creditor has no right to vote at the meeting.[173] Otherwise, a claim must be submitted at least eight weeks before the end of any accounting period, or the creditor will not be entitled to share in payments made by the trustee at the end of that period.[174] So long as a claim has been submitted once, it will be included in every subsequent dividend paid out by the trustee.[175] The form of the claim is prescribed by statute, which requires the creditor to provide details of each debt owed to him and any security held in respect of that debt, as well as an account or voucher as evidence that the debt exists.[176] A creditor who submits a false claim or evidence in support of it commits an offence.[177]

13.58 A creditor is entitled to claim the amount owed plus interest due

---

167 1985 Act, s 40(1)(a) and (4)(c).
168 1985 Act, s 40(1)(b).
169 1985 Act, s 40(2).
170 1985 Act, s 39A.
171 See the discussion at paras **11.35–11.48**.
172 1985 Act, ss 22 and 48.
173 1985 Act, ss 22(1) and 48(2).
174 1985 Act, s 48(1). The BDA Act, s 14 proposes an additional requirement that all claims must be submitted within 120 days of the trustee inviting creditors to submit unless there is a reasonable explanation why the creditor has taken longer to come forward.
175 1985 Act, s 48(2). In other words, it is not necessary to resubmit the claim in every accounting period.
176 1985 Act, ss 22(2)(a) and 48(2) and (3). The form is prescribed by the Bankruptcy (Scotland) Regulations 2008 (SSI 2008/82), reg 3 and Sch 1 (Form 4).
177 1985 Act, ss 22(5) and 48(7).

at the date of sequestration.[178] Where the debt is secured, unless the creditor wishes to surrender the security for the benefit of the estate, the value of the security must be deducted from his claim.[179] If a creditor has not exercised his rights under a security within twelve weeks of the date of sequestration, he can be compelled to transfer the security to the trustee in exchange for payment of the secured debt.[180] Where the debtor has previously been ordered by the court to pay aliment or a periodical allowance to a spouse, civil partner or child, or where he undertook to make such payments in a formal written agreement, a claim can be made in respect of any arrears.[181] A claim can also be made in respect of a contingent debt: that is, a debt which may come into existence at some future point.[182] For example, if the debtor is defending a court action at the date of sequestration, and may be ordered to make a damages payment at the conclusion of the proceedings, the pursuer may wish to submit a claim in respect of that potential future payment. A creditor in this situation has the option to submit a claim at the time of sequestration, the value of which will be estimated by the trustee, or alternatively to wait until the debt comes into existence and make the claim at that stage (the risk being that the whole estate may already have been paid out by then).[183]

Adjudication of claims

13.59   When the trustee has funds available to make payment, he will accept or reject every claim submitted in respect of the estate,[184] and determine where a claim should rank in the order of priority.[185] He is entitled to ask the creditor or any relevant person for further evidence in support of the validity or value of a claim if he considers it necessary.[186] Where a claim is rejected, the trustee must give the claimant written reasons for the rejection,[187] and the claimant is entitled to appeal the decision to the sheriff.[188] The debtor may also appeal any acceptance or rejection of claims against his estate.[189]

Distribution of estate

13.60   The trustee will pay the claims he has accepted in the order of priority set out by the statute.[190] It should be recalled that secured debts

178 1985 Act, Sch 1, para 1(1).
179 1985 Act, Sch 1, para 5(1).
180 1985 Act, Sch 1, para 5(2).
181 1985 Act, Sch 1, para 2.
182 1985 Act, Sch 1, para 3. See also *Crighton v Crighton's Tr* 1999 SCLR 16.
183 1985 Act, Sch 1, para 3(3).
184 1985 Act, s 49(2).
185 1985 Act, s 51(1). See the discussion on ranking at para **13.60**.
186 1985 Act, s 48(5) and (6).
187 1985 Act, s 48(4).
188 1985 Act, s 48(6).
189 1985 Act, s 48(6).
190 1985 Act, s 51.

do not form part of this list, since the security will have been exercised separately from the sequestration, or surrendered to creditors in exchange for full repayment of the secured debt.[191] Broadly speaking, priority is given to the expenses of the sequestration itself, which is why a creditor is unwise to apply for sequestration if the debtor's estate is limited. After the expenses are paid, certain debts are seen as more deserving than others. The order of payment is as follows:

(a) outlays and remuneration of the interim trustee, if appointed;
(b) outlays and remuneration of the trustee;
(c) deathbed and funeral expenses of the debtor if appropriate, and expenses reasonably incurred in administering the deceased's estate;
(d) expenses incurred by a creditor who petitioned for sequestration;
(e) preferred debts (primarily debts owed to employees including arrears of pension contributions, holiday pay and wages up to four months prior to the date of sequestration, subject to a limit of £800 per employee);[192]
(f) ordinary debts;
(g) interest on preferred debts and ordinary debts accrued after the date of sequestration; and
(h) postponed debts (including repayment of a loan made to a debtor by his spouse or civil partner, and any payment owed to the transferee in respect of a gratuitous alienation successfully challenged by the trustee).[193]

13.61 Each category of debts will be paid in full before the next category is entitled to any payment at all. For example, if the whole value of the estate is required to cover the expenses of the sequestration (categories (a) to (h) above), preferred creditors and everyone below them on the list will receive nothing.

13.62 Where there are insufficient funds to pay every creditor within a particular category in full, each creditor in that category will be paid a rateable portion of what he is owed.[194] So, imagine that Gordon has £1,500 of ordinary debt, of which Ian is owed £500 and Isabel is owed £1,000. Once all prior ranking creditors in the sequestration have been paid, only £750 remains in the estate – half of what is needed to pay all the ordinary debts. Accordingly, each ordinary creditor receives half of what he is owed, meaning Ian is paid £250 and Isabel is paid £500. Any creditor ranked lower than an ordinary creditor will receive nothing at all.

13.63 In the highly unlikely event that surplus funds remain in the

191 See para **13.58**.
192 1985 Act, s 51(2) and Sch 3.
193 1985 Act, s 51(3).
194 1985 Act, s 51(4).

estate once all debts are paid in full, those funds will be paid over to the debtor.[195]

13.64 An alternative mechanism for dealing with the claims of creditors in a sequestration is for the parties to agree a composition contract, which is a form of negotiated settlement.[196] It is open to the debtor to make an offer of composition, setting out what percentage of each creditor's claim he is prepared to pay, at any point after sequestration has been awarded. The debtor must offer to pay at least 25p of every £1 owed.[197] The offer should be made in writing to the trustee, who will discuss it with the commissioners if any have been elected, or the AiB, before deciding whether to place it before the creditors.[198] If he does so, a majority of creditors in number, or creditors owed more than a third of the total debt in value, must reject the offer in writing within five weeks of it being placed before them. If no rejection is received, the composition will be approved by the trustee.[199] The BDA Act proposes to remove this option from the legislation, so that composition will no longer be possible.[200]

TERMINATING THE SEQUESTRATION

13.65 Once the estate has been paid out to creditors, or a composition contract has been agreed, the sequestration can be brought to an end. This requires both the debtor and the trustee to be discharged.

Discharge of debtor

13.66 The debtor is automatically discharged one year after the date of sequestration.[201]

13.67 It is open to the trustee or any creditor to apply to the sheriff for deferment of the discharge, which would usually occur if the 12-month period has been insufficient time in which to investigate the estate.[202] If

---

195 1985 Act, s 51(5).
196 1985 Act, s 56 and Sch 4.
197 1985 Act, Sch 4, para 3.
198 1985 Act, Sch 4, para 2.
199 1985 Act, Sch 4, para 6.
200 BDA Bill, s 17.
201 1985 Act, s 54(1). The BDA Act, ss 17 and 18 propose to amend the 1985 Act so that the debtor will no longer be automatically discharged. A new process will be introduced whereby the trustee must apply to the AiB for the debtor to be discharged only when the trustee is satisfied that the debtor has fully co-operated and that all statutory issues and investigations have been completed. If the debtor cannot be traced, his discharge should be deferred indefinitely. Discharge of living debtors may be conditional on undertaking financial education: BDA Act, s 2. Debtors dealt with through the 'minimum asset process' (see para **13.14** above) will be discharged automatically subject to certain restrictions continuing for 12 months post-discharge, and again may be required to participate in financial education: BDA Act, ss 2 and 7.
202 1985 Act, s 54(3).

the debtor wishes to contest the application for deferment, he will lodge a declaration that he has made full and fair surrender of his estate and disclosure of his assets,[203] following which the sheriff will fix a hearing at which the debtor, the trustee and any interested creditor are entitled to make representations.[204] The sheriff will then either dismiss the application, or if good cause is shown, grant a deferment for a period not greater than two years.[205] The debtor can appeal this decision, and may also apply to have the sequestration discharged at any point prior to the expiry of the deferment period.[206] It is open to the trustee or any creditor to apply for further periods of deferment if good cause can be shown.[207]

13.68   Alternatively, in a case where composition has been approved, the AiB will discharge the debtor, bringing the sequestration process to an end.[208] The debtor is reinvested in the estate, which can be used to pay off his debts as agreed in the composition contract.

13.69   Discharge of the debtor has three main effects. First, the various restrictions to which the debtor was subject as a result of the sequestration are lifted.[209] Secondly, the debtor is discharged from all debts due at the date of the sequestration with a few limited exceptions.[210] Thirdly, any new estate acquired by the debtor after the discharge vests in him, not in the trustee.[211] Unless the discharge has come about as the result of composition, discharge of the debtor does not bring the sequestration itself to an end, so the debtor remains under an obligation to co-operate with the trustee.

13.70   It is open to the AiB to apply to the sheriff for qualifications to the discharge where the debtor is a natural person.[212] This would occur where the debtor has not co-operated with the trustee during the investigations or has otherwise failed to conduct himself appropriately during the sequestration process. The sheriff can grant a bankruptcy restrictions order, with the effect that the debtor remains subject to some or all of the legal restrictions which affected him during the sequestration for a further period of time. Alternatively, the AiB can deal with the matter non-judicially by asking the debtor to give a bankruptcy restrictions

---

203 1985 Act, s 54(4).
204 1985 Act, s 54(5).
205 1985 Act, s 54(6).
206 1985 Act, s 54(8).
207 1985 Act, s 54(9).
208 1985 Act, Sch 4, paras 11–13.
209 See para **13.33**.
210 1985 Act, s 55(1) and (2).
211 Although see the proposed change to the rules on *acquirenda* outlined in para **13.31**.
212 1985 Act, ss 56A–56K. The BDA Act, s 33 proposes that applications for and administration of bankruptcy restrictions orders should in future be dealt with by the AiB.

Undertaking, promising that he will not participate in any of the restricted activities for a set period of time after the discharge.[213]

Discharge of the trustee

13.71 It is not mandatory for the trustee to seek a discharge from the sequestration, but in most cases he will wish to do so, as discharge signals an end to his liability to debtors and creditors in respect of his dealings with the estate.[214] The trustee can apply to the AiB for discharge once he has made a final division of the debtor's estate amongst the creditors.[215] He must supply the AiB with accounts detailing his intromissions with the estate. If no objections to his discharge are made by the debtor or any creditor, and the AiB is satisfied that the accounts are in order, discharge will be granted.[216] A separate procedure is set out for situations where the AiB acted as trustee.[217] Alternatively, in a case where composition has been approved, the AiB will discharge the trustee at the same time as discharging the debtor.[218]

13.72 If, following the discharge of the trustee, it is discovered that the debtor had further assets in his estate at the time of the sequestration, it is possible for a new trustee to be appointed to deal with the new assets. In this sense, a sequestration that is not terminated by composition is never really terminated at all. In the overwhelming majority of cases, however, discharge of the trustee marks a practical end to the sequestration process.

TRUST DEED FOR CREDITORS

13.73 A debtor and his creditors may seek to avoid the expense and administrative burden of sequestration by agreeing amongst themselves that the debtor will transfer some or all of his estate to a trustee to administer on the creditors' behalf. In addition to being less expensive, a voluntary arrangement of this sort allows for greater flexibility than formal sequestration, meaning the debtor may negotiate to retain particular assets, perhaps in exchange for a contribution from his income for a set period of time, for example. If the voluntary arrangement ceased to function effectively, it would remain open to parties to instigate formal sequestration proceedings.

13.74 A simple trust deed is essentially a private arrangement, regulated under the general law of trusts. In this situation, the trustee would not be able to make use of the statutory powers enabling a formal trustee

---

213 1985 Act, s 56G. The BDA Act, s 52 proposes to repeal provision for bankruptcy restrictions undertakings.
214 1985 Act, s 57(5).
215 1985 Act, s 57(1).
216 1985 Act, s 57(2) and (3).
217 1985 Act, s 58A.
218 1985 Act, Sch 4, paras 11–13.

in sequestration to investigate the estate or challenge transactions unless these were explicitly provided for in the trust deed. The major drawback to an ordinary trust deed, however, is that it can only bind creditors who expressly agree to its terms, meaning other creditors are not prevented from performing diligence or raising sequestration proceedings.

13.75 If a trust deed meets certain requirements, however, it will be deemed a protected trust deed which binds all creditors.[219] The requirements are that the debtor has not been sequestrated or agreed to a debt payment programme;[220] the trustee is a person capable of acting as a trustee in a formal sequestration process;[221] the deed provides for vesting in the trustee of all assets that would vest in a formal sequestration process;[222] the debtor has been provided with independent legal advice prior to signing the deed;[223] the trustee publicises the existence of the deed in the Edinburgh Gazette;[224] and the trustee sends a copy of the deed and other relevant information to every creditor known to him.[225] Unless a majority of creditors by number or a third of the creditors by value object to the trust deed in writing within five weeks, all creditors will be deemed to have agreed to its terms.[226] The trustee then sends copies of the relevant information to the AiB, who will record the details in the Register of Insolvencies.[227] Once registered, the trust deed will be protected.[228]

13.76 Where a trust deed is protected, it prevents a creditor from petitioning for sequestration or performing diligence, even where he was not aware of the deed or objected to it.[229] It allows the trustee or any creditor to challenge a gratuitous alienation[230] or unfair preference,[231] and enables the trustee to challenge a financial order on divorce.[232]

---

219 See the Protected Trust Deeds (Scotland) Regulations 2008 (SSI 2008/143).
220 2008 Regulations, reg 4. For an explanation of a DPP, see para **9.13**.
221 2008 Regulations, reg 5.
222 2008 Regulations, reg 6.
223 2008 Regulations, reg 6.
224 2008 Regulations, reg 7.
225 2008 Regulations reg 8.
226 2008 Regulations, reg 9.
227 2008 Regulations, regs 11 and 12.
228 2008 Regulations, reg 3.
229 2008 Regulations, reg 11.
230 1985 Act, s 34(2) and (8).
231 1985 Act, s 36(4) and (6).
232 1985 Act, s 35(2).

Chapter 14

Corporate Insolvency and Dissolution*

INTRODUCTION: FINDING THE LAW

14.01 This chapter deals with the dissolution of juristic persons. A major reason for dissolution is insolvency and the greater part of this chapter is concerned with the corporate insolvency procedures and associated rules. But insolvency does not necessarily mean dissolution; and dissolution, like the death of natural persons, may occur for reasons other than insolvency. The Scots·law of corporate insolvency is not always easy to access. All insolvency law in Scotland, whether individual or corporate, flows from the law of sequestration. To identify the corporate rules, therefore, it is often necessary to jump between the Insolvency Act 1986 and the Bankruptcy (Scotland) Act 1985; to read the already heavily amended provisions of the 1985 Act subject to provisions of the Insolvency (Scotland) Rules 1986; to consider this domestic mass of legislation in the context of the EU Insolvency Regulation;[1] and all against a background of case law interpreting those provisions as well as various common law rules. Recent amendments of the 1986 Rules have largely removed cross-references to the 1985 Act,[2] but for isolated instances.[3] The Scottish Law Commission has proposed a long-overdue consolidation of the Bankruptcy (Scotland) Act 1985,[4] but because corporate insolvency, in broad terms, is a matter reserved to Westminster, there appears to be no prospect of Scots corporate insolvency law being set down in consolidated form.

---

* The author, Ross G Anderson, is indebted to Elisabeth Roxburgh, Advocate, for many insightful comments and criticisms, but any errors are his alone.
1 See para **14.15** ff below.
2 Insolvency (Scotland) Rules 1986 (SI 1986/1915) ('the 1986 Rules') as amended by the Insolvency (Scotland) Amendment Rules 2014 (SSI 2014/114).
3 1986 Rules, r 4.76.
4 Scottish Law Commission, *Report on the Consolidation of Bankruptcy Legislation in Scotland* (SLC Report No 232, 2013). The draft Bill contained in that report, however, must now be revised to take into account the additional amendments to the Bankruptcy (Scotland) Act 1985 introduced by the Bankruptcy and Debt Advice (Scotland) Act 2014.

GENERAL PRINCIPLES OF INSOLVENCY

Paritas creditorum principle

14.02 Insolvency is, by definition, unfair: where liabilities exceed assets, creditors must lose out.[5] In those circumstances, Scots law, like most legal systems, favours egalitarian over individual equity.[6] The principle is known in the 1986 Act as the '*pari passu* principle'.[7] Each unsecured creditor receives the same pro-rata dividend from the insolvent estate: a general creditor, A, with a claim of £1m will receive the same dividend as B, a general creditor for £100: if the dividend is 5p in the pound (5 per cent) A receives £50,000 and B £5. Scots law is particularly reluctant to listen to individual creditors who argue for special treatment.[8]

Ranking

14.03 In general terms, whereas the unsecured or general creditors rank *pari passu*, secured creditors are entitled to look to the particular asset over which they hold a security. A bank, holding a standard security over an insolvent company's ownership of land, is entitled to sell the land and pay itself from the proceeds. In the example of the standard security, for the purposes of corporate insolvency law, the standard security is a 'fixed charge'. Fixed charges are essentially proper rights in security.[9] Fixed securities may be contrasted with 'floating' charges. Floating charges have been dealt with in the context of rights in security; it is important to emphasise, however, that floating charges play a central role in corporate insolvency law: their function is as much a tool for taking control of a restructuring or insolvency procedure, since a qualifying floating charge confers on the holder the power to appoint an administrator.

14.04 The differences between fixed and floating charges are important in relation to ranking. It will be recalled that, in principle, a fixed charge ranks ahead of a floating charge. That principle is often inverted in practice because almost all floating charges contain a negative pledge clause.[10] But whereas the holders of fixed charges can enforce their security outwith a corporate insolvency process, a floating charge holder, in

---

5 G L Gretton, 'Ownership and insolvency' (2004) 8 Edin LR 389–395.

6 In the litigation arising out of the fraudulent scheme concocted by one Carlo Pietro Giovanni Guglielmo Tebaldo Ponzi (the original 'Ponzi Scheme'), *Cunningham v Brown* (1923) 263 US 1 (68 L Ed 873) at 13 (877), Taft CJ observed that '[this] is a case the circumstances of which call strongly for the principle that equality is equity, and this is the spirit of the bankrupt law'.

7 Insolvency Act 1986, s 107; *Re Nortel GmbH (in administration)* [2013] UKSC 52, [2014] AC 209, para [35] per Lord Neuberger.

8 *Mansfield v Walker's Tr* (1833) 11 S 813 at 828 per Lord Craigie: 'It is a rule established, beyond all memory, that there are no [individual] equities in competitions among creditors' (affd (1835) 1 Sh & McL 203, 3 Ross LC 139).

9 See Chapter 11: Non-Judicial Real Security.

10 See para **14.53** below.

Scots law, can enforce the floating charge only through a corporate insolvency procedure such as administration or liquidation (or, in more limited circumstances, through receivership or administrative receivership). Such procedures are not cheap. Insolvency practitioners – normally chartered accountants or solicitors – charge significant professional fees. And the expenses of the administrator or liquidator, as the case may be, rank before the floating charge holder.[11] The remuneration of insolvency practitioners and their advisers is a subject of importance. Suffice it to say for present purposes that the insolvency practitioner's fees may be authorised either by the company's creditors or by the court, with the result that many of the reported insolvency cases deal with questions of remuneration.[12]

14.05 At this juncture it is useful to put the insolvency practitioner's expenses into context and to list the priority rules. Taking liquidation as the paradigm insolvency procedure, the order in which the company's assets are to be distributed, under the 1986 Rules, is:[13]

(a) the expenses of the liquidation;[14]
(b) the expenses properly incurred of a CVA which was in force when a winding-up order was made in relation to a company;
(c) any preferential debts,[15] such as the company's obligations to pay wages and salaries to the company's employees or to make contributions to occupational pension schemes;
(d) ordinary debts (that is to say a debt which is neither a secured debt nor a debt mentioned in this rule);
(e) interest at the official rate on–
  (i) the preferential debts, and
  (ii) the ordinary debts,

---

11 For voluntary liquidation, see 1986 Act, s 115, for which see *Re Toshoku Finance UK plc* [2002] 1 WLR 671; for winding up by the court, see n 14 below. The court retains a residual discretion, under s 156, to alter the priorities.

12 The conduct of professional advisers – whether of accountants or solicitors or both – was criticised in *Joint Administrators of Martin Groundland & Co Ltd, Petrs* [2011] CSOH 14; *Liquidator of St Margaret's School Edinburgh Ltd, Noter* [2013] CSOH 4, 2013 SLT 241 and *Quantum Distribution (UK) Ltd (in liquidation)* [2012] CSOH 191, 2013 SLT 211. A summary of the normal procedure – which, for the uninitiated, is not apparent from the face of the legislation – is contained in Lord Glennie's opinion in *Joint Liquidators of Park Gardens Investments Ltd, Petrs* 2011 SC 243.

13 1986 Rules, r 4.66.

14 1986 Rules, r 4.67 contains detailed provision for liquidation expenses, the important practical element of which is the liquidator's remuneration. Administration expenses are also regulated by r 4.67 when read subject to the modifications in r 2.39B.

15 Insolvency Act 1986, s 386 defines 'preferential debts' with reference to the list in Schedule 6, which includes remuneration of the company's employees and the company's contributions to occupational pension schemes.

between the said date of commencement of the winding-up and the date of payment of the debt; and

(f) any postponed debt, namely a creditor's right to any gratuitous alienation[16] which has been reduced or restored to the company's assets or to the proceeds of sale of such an alienation.

14.06 Creditors holding fixed securities (such as a standard security or an assignation in security) are able to realise their securities without being subject to this order of priority. Another example – this time of a creditor who holds a fixed security – is the landlord for its hypothec. This order of priority affects only those who cannot enforce security other than through the insolvency process, the most important example of which is the floating charge holder. Preferential debts are paid in priority to the floating charge holder in the event that the assets of the company are insufficient to meet the preferential debts in full.[17]

Prescribed part

14.07 Since being amended by the Enterprise Act 2002, the Insolvency Act 1986 also makes provision for a fund – the 'prescribed part' – for unsecured creditors.[18] The prescribed part applies to liquidation (including where there is a provisional liquidator), administration, and receivership. The rules relating to the prescribed part are dealt with more fully below.[19]

Contracting-out and ranking agreements

14.08 On insolvency, by definition, a company cannot comply with its obligations. It is not therefore possible for a company to contract out of the operation of insolvency law. So suppose A Ltd has a contract with B Ltd. The contract provides that, on A Ltd suffering an 'insolvency event', B Ltd shall have no obligation to pay anything to A Ltd and that A Ltd may not enforce any rights that A Ltd may have against B Ltd. Such a provision is invalid because it is an attempt to contract out of the operation of insolvency law on A's assets. Similarly, any contractual provision designed to transfer A Ltd's assets to another company, which transfer is intended to take effect after the commencement of a winding-up, is void.[20] The rule against contracting out is also the rationale for what is known in English law as the 'anti-deprivation' principle:[21] Alexandra cannot agree with Brian that, on the event of Alexandra's bankruptcy, certain of Alexandra's assets will become Brian's property. The 'anti-deprivation' principle has always been of more limited importance

---

16 See para **14.85** below.
17 Companies Act 1985, s 464(6) read with Insolvency Act 1986, s 175.
18 Insolvency Act 1986, s 176A.
19 See paras **11.70** above and **14.60** below.
20 Insolvency Act 1986, s 127(1).
21 See *British Eagle International Airlines Ltd v Compagnie Nationale Air France* [1975] 1 WLR 758 and R M Goode, 'Perpetual trustee and flip clauses in swap transactions' (2011) 127 LQR 1.

in Scotland since, at common law, it has never been possible to transfer patrimonial rights *solo consensu*. But however that may be, the important point is that the various rules described seek to implement a general public policy: to prevent a fraud on the insolvency statutes.[22] Fraud, in this sense, means insolvency fraud.[23] Commercial agreements, such as intellectual property licences, entered into in good faith with no intention to deprive the insolvent estate, but which contain resolutive conditions bringing the contract to an end on insolvency, do not therefore normally offend the principle.

14.09　A ranking agreement does not amount to contracting out of insolvency law. Suppose Alpha Ltd is a first ranking creditor by virtue of an all sums floating charge containing a negative pledge. Bravo sarl is a second ranking creditor but it holds a fixed security over particular heritable assets in Scotland. It is possible for Alpha and Bravo to agree as between themselves as to how they exercise their rights *qua* secured creditors.

Pre-insolvency and post-insolvency debts

14.10　It has been seen that the general principle that unsecured creditors of an insolvent company rank *pari passu*. That principle is rudimentary. But the principle assumes that it is possible to identify who is actually a creditor of the company. Identifying who is a creditor may be more difficult than might be imagined, especially in relation to contingent liabilities:[24]

> A fundamental principle that underlies insolvency law is that all creditors as at the date of bankruptcy or winding up are entitled to share equally in the debtor's funds. If a person is a creditor at that date, even if he is merely a contingent creditor, he is entitled to share equally with the other creditors. If, however, he is not a creditor in any sense at that date, he cannot participate in the division of the assets among the creditors. Thus a person who has a mere *spes obligationis* would have no locus to participate in such a division.

Future liabilities and contingent liabilities

14.11　On insolvency – including, for these purposes, working out whether a company is insolvent at all[25] – it is often necessary to consider future or contingent liabilities. As Bell put it, 'debts are either presently

---

22　*Belmont Park Investments Pty Ltd v BNY Corporate Trustee Services Ltd* [2011] UKSC 38, [2012] 1 AC 383 at paras [102]–[106] per Lord Collins; para [121] per Lord Walker (founding on *R v J* [2005] 1 AC 562, para [64] per Lord Rodger of Earlsferry); and paras [159]–[165] per Lord Mance. Cf. the dictum of Lord Coalston quoted in para **14.84** below.

23　*Belmont Park* (n 22) para [151] per Lord Mance. For the Scottish authorities on fraud on insolvency, see para **14.65** below.

24　*Liquidator of Ben Line Steamers Ltd, Noter* [2010] CSOH 174, 2011 SLT 535, para [30] per Lord Drummond Young.

25　1986 Act, s 123(1)(e), for which, see para **14.24** below.

due; or due at a future day certain; or due provisionally, in a certain event. The first are called pure; the second, future; the last, contingent debts.'[26] Future obligations are presently owed, but are payable only in the future *(debitum in praesenti, solvendum in futuro)*. A sum due on someone's death will become due sometime (under the law of mortality). Contingent obligations, in contrast, may never become due. A sum due only on a person marrying may never become due because not everyone marries. The law on contingent debts is of general importance: debts presently due, though payable in the future, may be arrested; a contingent obligation, where the contingency has not yet been purified, may not be.[27] For insolvency purposes, contingent liabilities may be very relevant where a court has to consider whether a company is balance sheet insolvent.

CORPORATE INSOLVENCY PROCEDURES

14.12 The principles applicable to companies apply, *mutatis mutandis*, to limited liability partnerships (LLPs). At the end of the chapter something will be said of limited partnerships (LPs) and partnerships, neither of which are bodies corporate, but both of which, as has been seen in Chapter 5, are juristic persons.

14.13 In this chapter, the following insolvency procedures are considered:

- Liquidation
- Receivership and Administrative Receivership
- Administration
- Company Voluntary Arrangements (CVAs)
- Schemes of Arrangement
- Section 110 Reorganisation

14.14 A few words, by way of summary, about each procedure. Winding-up, otherwise known as liquidation, kills a company. Solvent as well as insolvent companies may be wound up. Administration is a temporary insolvency procedure designed to keep the company alive as a going concern. A company may exit administration by way of a CVA or a scheme of arrangement or, indeed, by liquidation. But while a CVA is an insolvency procedure, schemes of arrangement may be used in solvent as well as insolvent reconstructions. Receivership is a method for enforcing a floating charge and is thus not always recognised by the courts of other jurisdictions as an *insolvency* procedure.[28] Confusingly, where a receiver is appointed under a floating charge over the whole or substantially the

---

26 Bell, *Commentaries* (7th edn, 1870) I, 332. See too Erskine, *Institute*, III.1.6 approved by the House of Lords in *Re Sutherland* [1963] AC 235 at 248 per Lord Reid.

27 *Costain Building and Civil Engineering Ltd v Scottish Rugby Union plc* 1993 SC 650 at 661 per Lord President Hope (a decision of five judges).

28 It is not referred to in the Annexes to the EUIR: para **14.15** below.

whole of a company's property, the receiver is known as an 'administrative receiver'. But receivership and administration are quite distinct procedures and, since 2003, administrative receivership is, for private companies, rare.

EUROPEAN INSOLVENCY REGULATION[29]

14.15 All insolvency proceedings opened in the UK, whether they have an EU element or not, must state whether, for the purposes of the European Insolvency Regulation ('EUIR'), they are 'main' or 'secondary' proceedings.[30] The idea behind the EUIR is to avoid conflicts between courts in different member states. In general terms, the EUIR provides that the courts of the member state where the insolvent person (the 'debtor') has its 'centre of main interests' ('COMI') has jurisdiction to open main insolvency proceedings.[31] In the case of juristic persons, the presumption is that the debtor's COMI is in the member state where it has its registered office.[32] There is a considerable body of case law, domestic and with the Court of Justice of the European Union, on how a company's COMI is to be determined.[33] But providing a debtor's COMI is in Scotland, any main proceedings opened in Scotland – and the insolvency practitioners appointed pursuant to those proceedings – are entitled to automatic recognition by all courts in the EU.[34] Those UK insolvency proceedings, which are recognised throughout the EU, are listed in Annex A to the EUIR:

- Winding up by or with the supervision of the court
- Creditors' voluntary winding-up (with confirmation by the court)[35]
- Administration (including appointments made by filing prescribed particulars with the court)[36]
- Voluntary arrangements under insolvency legislation (for Scottish purposes, company voluntary arrangements (CVAs))
- Bankruptcy or sequestration

14.16 The officers appointed pursuant to these proceedings – liquidators (including provisional liquidators), CVA supervisors, administrators, trustees in sequestration and – for Scottish purposes – a judicial

29 Council Regulation (EC) No 1346/2000 on insolvency proceedings: [2000] OJ L160/1.
30 EUIR, Arts 3 and 17. For a useful summary of the issues to be considered when drafting pleadings, see W W McBryde, 'Insolvency jurisdiction' 2004 SLT (News) 185.
31 EUIR, Art 3(1).
32 EUIR, Art 3(2).
33 Case C-341/04 *Eurofood IFSC Ltd* [2006] ECR I-3813, [2006] Ch 508 (ECJ).
34 EUIR, Art 16(1).
35 A members' voluntary winding-up is not included because it can occur only where a company is solvent.
36 So-called 'out of court' appointments.

factor[37] – are all recognised, for the purposes of the EUIR, throughout the EU.[38] Importantly, it should be emphasised that receivership is not recognised under the EUIR as an insolvency procedure.[39]

14.17 Generally speaking, the Scottish courts are reluctant to subject foreign companies to Scottish insolvency proceedings,[40] especially if those companies have no assets in Scotland. But where the principal assets of a company, incorporated outside the EU, are in Scotland, the court may exercise its discretion to place the company into liquidation in Scotland under the provisions in the Insolvency Act 1986 dealing with unregistered companies.[41] There are also provisions for the mutual recognition of certain insolvency proceedings outside the EU,[42] and the Insolvency Act contains an important provision which gives the UK courts power to assist foreign insolvency practitioners and courts.[43]

INTRA-UK INSOLVENCY

14.18 If, for the purposes of the EUIR, the company's centre of main interests is the 'UK', the Insolvency Act confers jurisdiction on the courts of the country where a company is incorporated: Scottish courts for Scottish companies and English courts for English companies.[44] But averments (or, in the case of out-of-court appointments, statements) in EUIR-compliant terms are still required. In the event of a Scottish registered company, with its centre of main interests in, say, London, the Insolvency Act nonetheless confers jurisdiction on the Court of Session. The converse also holds true: an English-registered company with its centre of main interests in Edinburgh, is nonetheless to be wound up by the English courts. Under the Insolvency Act 1986, although not under the EUIR, a reference to a company's 'insolvency' covers administrative receivership.[45]

---

37 See further para **14.95** below.
38 EUIR, Annex C.
39 Cf. the domestic UK position referred to in para **14.18** below.
40 *Banco Nacional de Cuba v Cosmos Trading Corporation* [2000] 1 BCLC 813 at 819 quoted with approval by Lord Hodge in *HSBC Bank plc, Petr* [2009] CSOH 147, 2010 SLT 281.
41 1986 Act, s 220: 'For the purposes of this Part "unregistered company" includes any association and any company, with the exception of a company registered under the Companies Act 2006 in any part of the United Kingdom'. See too s 51(1)(b) discussed at n 178 below in the context of receivership.
42 Cross-Border Insolvency Regulations 2006 (SI 2006/1030), implementing the UNCITRAL Model Law, for which see L Chan Ho, *Cross-Border Insolvency: A Commentary on the UNCITRAL Model Law* (3rd edn, 2012); and the Foreign Judgments (Reciprocal Enforcement) Act 1933 (for certain Commonwealth countries), discussed in *Rubin v Eurofinance SA* [2012] UKSC 46, [2013] 1 AC 236.
43 1986 Act, s 426, for which see *Re HIH Casualty & General Insurance Ltd* [2008] UKHL 21, [2008] 1 WLR 852 and *Rubin v Eurofinance*.
44 1986 Act, s 120. Cf. Civil Jurisdiction and Judgments Act 1982, s 43(5).
45 1986 Act, s 247(1).

LIQUIDATION

14.19 'Liquidation' is used in the Companies and Insolvency Acts in the same sense as it might be used by a totalitarian state security service: to liquidate is to kill. A synonym for liquidation is 'winding up' and this latter term better describes the process, which may be swift but may, in some cases, be tortuous. Death of a company comes only with the expiry of the three-month period following publication of a notice of dissolution in the register of companies at the end of the winding-up process.[46] The date of liquidation, however, is either on the date of the resolution to wind up (in a members' or creditors' voluntary liquidation)[47] or on the date of a petition (in the case of a creditors' winding-up), as the case may be.[48] But, for companies, liquidation may not be the end: companies, unlike mortal men and women, are potential revenants and, by the process of 'restoration to the register', may be brought back from the dead.[49]

Liquidation types

14.20 The first distinction in the types of liquidation is between voluntary and compulsory liquidation. A voluntary liquidation is one instigated by the company itself, normally by a special resolution of the members;[50] a compulsory liquidation, in contrast, is instigated by court procedure. The result is that there are three types of winding-up:

- Members' voluntary winding-up
- Creditors' voluntary winding-up
- Compulsory winding-up

Voluntary winding-up

14.21 A members' voluntary liquidation can occur only where the company is solvent.[51] A creditors' voluntary liquidation may involve insolvency. Otherwise, the distinction between a members' and a creditors' voluntary winding-up depends upon whether the directors have delivered a statement of solvency: such a statement is a pre-requisite for

---

46 1986 Act, s 201(2) (MVL and CVL), s 204(4) (early dissolution) and s 205(2) (all other cases).
47 1986 Act, s 86.
48 1986 Act, s 129(2). It is possible for an administration to be converted into a creditors' voluntary liquidation by the administrators filing a conversion notice with the Registrar: 1986 Act, Sch B1, para 83. In such a case, the liquidation is deemed to have commenced from the date that the company went into administration: Sch B1, para 83(8)(b).
49 See para **14.95** below.
50 1986 Act, s 84(2). The other basis is the example of a joint venture company, which is formed for a specific purpose and that purpose has been fulfilled: s 84(1)(a).
51 1986 Act, s 89: the directors must deliver to the Registrar of Companies a statutory declaration of solvency within 15 days.

a members' voluntary winding-up.[52] In a creditors' voluntary winding-up ('CVL') the creditors, in practice, will appoint the liquidator.[53] As with dissolution of a partnership, on a resolution to wind up the company voluntarily, the company must cease to carry on its business, except in so far as may be required for its beneficial winding-up.[54] An important difference between a CVL and a compulsory winding-up is that, in the case of a CVL, the liquidator is able to exercise many of his powers without court sanction,[55] and such a liquidator has the power to sell heritable property free of an inhibition.[56] In both voluntary and compulsory liquidation, because the company continues in existence as a juristic person, the difficulties encountered winding up a partnership are largely avoided.[57]

Compulsory winding-up

14.22   Insolvency is perhaps the most common ground for a compulsory winding-up.[58] But insolvency is not the only ground on which a company may be wound up by the court. The other reasons that tend to arise in practice are: (a) that there has been a special resolution of members that the company be wound up by the court; (b) the company has not commenced business within a year of incorporation; (c) the limited CVA moratorium has come to an end without a CVA being put in place;[59] or (d) because it is 'just and equitable' to do so. Of these four examples, in all except (c), the company will be solvent.[60]

14.23   It remains competent for a floating charge holder to enforce its floating charge by petitioning to have the company wound up.[61] The basis for doing so is that the floating charge holder's security will otherwise be placed in 'jeopardy'; and the court is satisfied that events have occurred – or are about to occur – which render it unreasonable for the company to retain the power to dispose of the property subject to the floating charge.[62]

Insolvency: timings and duties

14.24   In practice, the most common reason that a company is wound up at the instance of a creditor is because that company is unable to pay

---

52 1986 Act, s 90.
53 1986 Act, s 100(2).
54 1986 Act, s 87(1).
55 1986 Act, s 166(2) and (3).
56 1986 Act, s 166(1A).
57 Compare Partnership Act 1890, s 36 and 1986 Act, s 87(2).
58 1986 Act, s 122(1)(f).
59 1986 Act, s 122(1)(fa).
60 1986 Act, s 122.
61 1986 Act, s 122(2).
62 1986 Act, s 122(2).

its debts.[63] There are four distinct bases on which a creditor can demonstrate the company's inability to pay its debts:

(a) a statutory demand to pay a sum exceeding £750 has been served on the company at its registered office and the company has neglected to pay that sum for three weeks thereafter or to secure or compound for it to the reasonable satisfaction of the creditor ('apparent insolvency');[64]

(b) the *induciae*[65] of a charge for payment on an extract decree, or an extract registered bond, or an extract registered protest, have expired without payment being made ('apparent insolvency');[66]

(c) if it is proved to the satisfaction of the court that the company is not paying its debts as they fall due ('practical insolvency');[67] and

(d) a company is also deemed to be unable to pay its debts if it is proved to the satisfaction of the court that the value of the company's assets is less than the amount of its liabilities, taking account of prospective and contingent liabilities ('balance sheet insolvency').[68]

14.25 The expiry, without payment, of a statutory demand, or charge for payment, provides the clearest basis for a creditor to petition for a winding-up. Often, however, matters are more complicated because the basis of the creditor's claim relates to the viability of the company. Both practical insolvency and balance sheet insolvency have been elaborated upon in the case law. So, where practical insolvency is the basis for presentation of a petition, difficulties may arise where the company disputes that the creditor's claim is due at all.[69] A claim in respect of which there is a genuine and good faith defence to liability is not a claim which will found a winding-up petition. Conversely, however, if the claim on which the petition is based is one which the company does not or cannot substantially dispute, and which has not been settled, the petitioner has standing to present the winding-up petition on the ground of practical insolvency. The shortcomings of the practical insolvency test (otherwise

---

63 1986 Act, s 122(1)(f).

64 1986 Act, s 123(1)(a).

65 G Watson (ed) *Bell's Dictionary and Digest of the Law of Scotland* (7th edn, 1890; repr 2012) s.v. *induciae legales*: 'the days which intervene between the citation of a defender and the day of appearance in the action or process; or the days which are allowed to a debtor to obey a charge or decree'. The standard period of notice in a Court of Session summons is 21 days: RCS r 13.4(1)(a); for petitions, see n 159 below. But the standard period of notice for a charge for payment is 14 days: Debtors (Scotland) Act 1987, s 90(3).

66 1986 Act, s 123(1)(c).

67 1986 Act, s 123(1)(e).

68 1986 Act, s 123(2).

69 *MacPlant Services Ltd v Contract Lifting Services (Scotland) Ltd* 2009 SC 125.

known as the 'cash-flow' test), particularly in relation to future liabilities, have been explained by the Supreme Court thus:[70]

> [T]he 'cash-flow' test is concerned, not simply with the petitioner's own presently-due debt, nor only with other presently-due debt owed by the company, but also with debts falling due from time to time in the reasonably near future. What is the reasonably near future, for this purpose, will depend on all the circumstances, but especially on the nature of the company's business. . . . The express reference to assets and liabilities is in my view a practical recognition that once the court has to move beyond the reasonably near future (the length of which depends, again, on all the circumstances) any attempt to apply a cash-flow test will become completely speculative, and a comparison of present assets with present and future liabilities (discounted for contingencies and deferment) becomes the only sensible test. But it is still very far from an exact test.

14.26 In relation to balance sheet insolvency, meanwhile, the Supreme Court has emphasised that s 123(2) should not be paraphrased to mean that the company had reached the 'point of no return'. The correct test is whether, on the balance of probabilities, the petitioner has satisfied the court that a company has insufficient assets to be able to meet all its liabilities, including prospective and contingent liabilities.[71] In order to qualify as a contingent creditor, the creditor need show only that the obligation has a basis at common law or under statute at the date of the winding-up petition, though it may be subject to a contingency which will be purified only at some later stage.[72] But a company, which is managing to pay its debts as they fall due, may nonetheless be insolvent, as where a company is able to pay debts which fall due only by borrowing.[73] Lord Hodge has said of the balance sheet test that:[74]

> It is clear that when the court looks at balance sheet insolvency under section 123(2) it is not simply taking a snap shot of the balance between a company's assets and it liabilities then and there. It is not concerned with temporary imbalances. Rather in considering that balance the court looks to the future and asks whether it is clear in practical terms that because of an incurable deficiency in its assets it will not be able to meet its future or contingent liabilities. In other words, the section allows the court to have regard to the interests of contingent or prospective creditors (the latter being creditors with existing debts which are not yet due for payment) and form a judgment whether it has been established that the company cannot reasonably be expected to meet those liabilities. . .

The various tests which provide a basis for petitioning for a company's

---

70 *BNY Corporate Trustee Services Ltd v Eurosail-UK 2007-3BL plc* [2013] UKSC 28, [2013] 1 WLR 1408 at paras [37]– [38] per Lord Walker.

71 *BNY Corporate Trustee Services* at para [48].

72 *Liquidator of Ben Line Steamers Ltd, Noter* [2010] CSOH 174.

73 *Bucci v Carman, Re Casa Estates (UK) Ltd (in liquidation)* [2014] EWCA Civ 383.

74 *Joint Building Society Special Administrators of Dunfermline Building Society v FM Front Door Ltd* [2011] CSOH 175 at para [25].

winding-up may be relevant in other contexts. A debtor of a company in financial difficulties, as has been seen, may refuse to pay on the basis of the defence of 'balancing of accounts in bankruptcy'.[75] For such a case to be made out, however, in cases where the company is not yet in formal insolvency proceedings, very clear averments of insolvency are required.[76]

Publicity

14.27 As was observed above, although a company remains in existence during the winding-up process, the date of liquidation is backdated to the date of the special resolution to wind up,[77] or the presentation of the petition,[78] as the case may be. In the case of a resolution to wind up, as soon as a resolution is passed, there is a duty on the officers of the company to publicise it in the Edinburgh Gazette within 14 days,[79] and to lodge it with the Registrar of Companies,[80] and the Accountant in Bankruptcy, within 15 days.[81] In the case of a compulsory winding-up, a copy of the court order must be forwarded to the Registrar of Companies and Accountant in Bankruptcy 'forthwith'.[82] As a result, they are entered on the Register of Insolvencies held by the Accountant in Bankruptcy. But neither winding-up resolutions nor court orders – unlike sequestration orders[83] – are registered in the Personal Register.[84] In the case where an administration is converted into a members' voluntary liquidation by notice, however, the conversion takes place only on registration of the notice with the Registrar of Companies,[85] but the liquidation is then backdated to the date of the administration.[86]

Effect of winding up

14.28 On the court making a winding-up order, the person appointed is known as the 'interim' liquidator. Within 28 days of his appointment there must be summoned a meeting of the creditors to appoint a liquidator (who may be, and often is, the interim liquidator).[87] The most

---

75 See para **8.61** above.
76 See e.g. *J & A Construction (Scotland) Ltd v Windex Ltd* [2013] CSOH 170.
77 1986 Act, s 86.
78 1986 Act, s 129(2).
79 1986 Act, s 85.
80 1986 Act, s 84(3) and Companies Act 2006, ss 29 and 30.
81 1986 Act, s 84(3) and 2006 Act, ss 29 and 30 read with Scotland Act 1998, Sch 8, para 23.
82 1986 Act, s 130(1). Where liquidation is to follow from administration on the basis of a conversion notice under 1986 Act, Sch B1, para 83(2), the administrator must send a notice to the Registrar and, 'as soon as is reasonably pacticable', file a copy of the notice with the court and send copies to creditors.
83 Bankruptcy (Scotland) Act 1985, ss 1A and 14.
84 That is to say, the Register of Inhibitions and Adjudications, indexed under the names of individual natural and juristic persons.
85 *Cartwright v Register of Companies, Re Globespan Airways Ltd (in liquidation)* [2012] EWCA Civ 1159, [2013] 1 WLR 1122 at paras [41]–[50] per Arden LJ.
86 1986 Act, Sch B1, para 83(3) and (8)(b).
87 1986 Act, s 138(2) and (3).

important practical consequence of liquidation is that legal proceedings may be commenced against a company in liquidation (including provisional liquidation) only with the consent of the court.[88]

14.29 Liquidation, unlike sequestration, does not result in the vesting of the company's assets in the liquidator. Corporate insolvency uses the law of legal personality rather than the law of property to effect a collective procedure for realisation of the company's assets: the liquidator replaces the company's directors as the person able to bind the company.[89] Care is needed with the word 'vesting', because, although there is no automatic 'vesting' of the company's assets in the liquidator, the respective positions of a trustee in sequestration and a liquidator are similar.[90] Neither the trustee nor the liquidator is owner of immoveable property unless he or she is registered as such. Both can do so, although the power of a trustee in sequestration is now limited.[91] The liquidator can do so by deducting title in favour of himself,[92] or by virtue of an order of the court,[93] although such orders are, in practice, unknown. Such an order takes effect only when an extract has been recorded or registered as the case may be.[94]

14.30 A company must publicise the fact that it is in liquidation in all business correspondence.[95] But where a third party, for instance, enters into an oral contract with someone purporting to represent the company in liquidation, other than the liquidator, it is likely that the transaction – at least in so far as it purports to dispone any of the company's

---

88 1986 Act, s 130(2). In *Pillar Denton Ltd v Jervis, Re Games Station Ltd* [2014] EWCA Civ 180 at para [31], Lewison LJ said that 'the precise scope of [these sections] is still to some extent uncertain'. But the prohibition on proceedings without the consent of the court extends to proceedings brought against the company elsewhere in the EU: *Re ARM Asset Backed Securities SA* [2014] EWHC 1097. For CVLs, the court, on the application of the liquidator, may direct that proceedings can be brought against the company only with the leave of the court: 1986 Act, s 113.

89 1986 Act, s 91(2) (members' voluntary), s 103 (CVL) and s 169(2) (compulsory). The same is true on administration: Sch B1, para 64(1). But the board retains a residual power to challenge the appointment of a provisional liquidator, receiver or administrator, as the case may be: *Stephen, Petr* [2011] CSOH 119.

90 G L Gretton, 'The title of a liquidator' (1984) 29 JLSS 357 summarised in G L Gretton and A J M Steven, *Property, Trusts and Succession* (2nd edn, 2013) paras 22.68–22.70. Gretton's approach is largely adopted by the Inner House in *Liquidators of the Scottish Coal Co Ltd, Noters* [2013] CSIH 108, 2014 SLT 259, paras [111]–[113].

91 Bankruptcy (Scotland) Act 1985, s 31(1A) and (1B).

92 Titles to Land Consolidation (Scotland) Act 1868, s 25. The Scottish Law Commission has proposed that this provision be repealed: *Report on Sharp v Thomson* (SLC Report No 208, 2007) paras 4.3 to 4.6.

93 1986 Act, s 145.

94 Conveyancing (Scotland) Act 1924, s 4; Land Registration (Scotland) Act 1979, s 3(6).

95 1986 Act, s 188.

property – is void.[96] Importantly, where the company has granted a floating charge, liquidation causes the floating charge to attach.[97]

ADMINISTRATION

Outline

14.31   It was as a result of the Enterprise Act 2002 that administration was given the primacy that it now enjoys in corporate insolvency practice. The amendments introduced by the 2002 Act are now mainly found in Schedule B1 to the Insolvency Act 1986. There were also consequential amendments to the Insolvency (Scotland) Rules 1986 where the relevant provisions on administration are found in Part 2.

14.32   An administration must have a statutory objective, selected by the administrator according to a threefold statutory hierarchy:

(a)   to rescue the company as a going concern; or

(b)   to achieve a better result for the company's creditors as a whole than would be likely if the company were wound up (without first being in administration); or

(c)   to realise property in order to make a distribution to one or more secured or preferred creditors.[98]

The procedure is intended to be quick and efficient.[99] The general rule is that administrators are under a duty to have regard to the interests of the company's creditors as a whole.[100] On occasion, that duty may involve the subordination of one creditor's interests to the greater good.[101] It is under (b) that there may be a transfer of the company's undertaking. 'One of the main advantages of administration over liquidation', the Court of Appeal has remarked,

> is precisely that administrators have power to continue the insolvent company's business, protected (unlike the company's directors) by the moratorium on the pursuit of claims by creditors, so that it can be prepared and marketed for sale as a going concern, and the proceeds of sale distributed to the company's creditors, either by the administrators themselves, or (less commonly now) in a subsequent liquidation. . . continuation of the company's business is commonly a prerequisite of a beneficial sale. Once a business is closed down, its value rapidly declines

---

96 1986 Act, s 127.

97 Companies Act 1985, s 463(1).

98 1986 Act, Sch B1, para 3. These provisions were introduced by the Enterprise Act 2002. Prior to that Act, administrators were not able to make distributions to creditors.

99 1986 Act, Sch B1, para 4. Cf. Sch B1, para 52(1).

100 1986 Act, Sch B1, para 3(2).

101 *Joint Administrators of Rangers Football Club plc, Noters* 2012 SLT 599 at paras [57] [59] and [62] discussed by G L Gretton, 'The laws of the game' (2012) 16 Edin LR 414.

to an amount no greater than the aggregate of the forced sale value of its constituent assets.[102]

14.33   Purpose (c), however, is available only when (a) and (b) are not viable options. Administrators may therefore seek to realise property for the purposes of making a distribution to a secured creditor only if rescuing the company as a going concern or achieving a better result for the creditors as a whole is not reasonably practicable and realising the property for the purposes of making a distribution to a secured creditor does not unnecessarily harm the interests of the general creditors.[103]

14.34   An administrator may be appointed by (a) the court; (b) the company (i.e. a resolution of the members) or the directors (i.e. the managers); or (c) the holder of a qualifying floating charge ('QFC').[104] A little more will be said about each in turn.

Appointment by QFC holder

14.35   Appointment may be made either by petitioning the court or 'out of court' by filing a notice of appointment with the court. A floating charge 'qualifies' where it is created by an instrument which states that paragraph 14 of Schedule B1 to the Insolvency Act 1986 applies to it, or purports to confer on the holder of the charge a power to appoint an administrator, or purports to confer on the holder the power to appoint a receiver or administrative receiver.[105] In addition, the charge must relate to the whole or substantially the whole of the company's property.[106] The power of a QFC holder to appoint is likely to be limited only if there is a prior QFC in favour of another creditor in place. Where such a prior QFC does exist, at least two business days' notice must be given to the prior QFC holder, by way of a filing of a 'Notice of Intention to Appoint'.[107] Importantly, a QFC holder has a power to appoint an administrator only when the floating charge is enforceable:[108] in other words, there has been a demonstrable event of default under the charge. In practical terms, one of the great attractions of the out-of-court procedure is that it can be done quickly and cheaply. If necessary, it can be done in the middle of the night, by faxing the appropriate forms to the Petitions Department of the Court of Session.[109]

---

102   *Kavanagh v Crystal Palace FC 2000 Ltd* [2013] EWCA Civ 1410, [2014] ICR 251, paras [19]–[20] per Briggs LJ.
103   1986 Act, Sch B1, para 3(4).
104   1986 Act, Sch B1, para 2.
105   1986 Act, Sch B1, para 14(2). The conditions in para 14(2) are alternatives, so a floating charge need satisfy only one of the conditions to be characterised as a QFC: *Stephen, Petr* [2011] CSOH 119.
106   1986 Act, Sch B1, para 14(3)(a).
107   1986 Act, Sch B1, para 15.
108   1986 Act, Sch B1, para 16.
109   1986 Rules, r 2.12.The date of the appointment is then dated to the timing of the fax transmission: r 2.12(3).

Moratorium

14.36 The most important practical consequence of administration is the moratorium. A company in administration is protected from attempts by creditors to enforce any contractual rights or rights in security against the company, whether by litigation, diligence or other enforcement.[110] A company must publicise on all business documents, including websites, that it is in administration.[111]

Power to deal with company's property

14.37 On administration, subject to limited exceptions, the floating charge does not attach. The administrator is empowered to deal freely with the company's property, which would otherwise fall within the charge, without the charge holder's consent. The power extends to disposing of the property, as by sale,[112] so, if an administrator sells the company's stock, the buyer takes free from the charge and the price becomes an asset of the company. Property which is subject to a fixed security is in a different position. The administrator cannot dispose of that property without the consent of either the charge holder or the court.[113] A court will supply consent only on the condition that the proceeds are used to pay the secured creditor[114] and that the sale leaves the secured creditor, *qua* secured creditor, no worse off than if the secured creditor itself had sold the secured assets.[115] These powers allow an administrator to continue the company's business. But, as Briggs LJ has explained, the economic realities will often make any trading difficult and, in practice, it is often necessary for the administrators to make employees redundant:[116]

> An administrator's ability to continue the business pending sale is inevitably constrained by acute economic considerations. The company will not be in administration unless it is insolvent and, indeed, hopelessly insolvent, in the sense that the directors had reached the view that, without protection from its creditors, the company could not realistically expect to trade out of its difficulties. In most cases, that insolvency will have arisen because of the manner in which the company had been conducting its business. Thus, leaving aside pre-packs, administrators will typically need urgently to reform and economise upon the manner in which the business is being conducted immediately prior to their appointment, both to maximise the period before a lack of resources compels closure, and to make the business more attractive to purchasers. Dismissal of employees is, unfortunately for them, a principal method

110 1986 Act, Sch B1, para 43, explained in *Re Globespan Airways Ltd* [2013] 1 WLR 1122 at para [6] per Arden LJ.

111 1986 Act, Sch B1, para 45.

112 1986 Act, Sch B1, para 70.

113 1986 Act, Sch B1, para 71.

114 1986 Act, Sch B1, para 71(3).

115 Cf. *O'Connell v Rollings* [2014] EWCA Civ 639 at para [70] per Kitchin LJ.

116 *Kavanagh v Crystal Palace FC 2000 Ltd* [2013] EWCA Civ 1410, [2014] ICR 251, para [22].

by which the administrators can achieve the economies necessary for those two purposes. Those who are kept on have to be paid their wages and salaries in full, as a prior claim on the limited funds available to the administrators.

Pre-pack administrations

14.38 Insolvency carries considerable stigma and, at all events, even the suspicion that a company may be on the verge of insolvency can lead to a crisis of confidence among the company's creditors. Credit may be withdrawn. The company's goodwill may be irretrievably damaged. The most efficient way for an administrator to realise a company's assets in order to achieve the purposes of administration˘ is often, therefore, as Briggs LJ indicated in the passage quoted in the previous paragraph, to sell the assets before creditors know about the insolvency event. This is the practice of the 'pre-pack' sale of the company's business. The details of the sale are negotiated with the buyer prior to appointment of the administrator. Normally, the accountant advising on the sale is also the administrator. When the sale is due to complete, the administrator is appointed out of court and the sale is completed on the same day. The driver behind the sale will be the QFC holder. Other creditors are not consulted prior to the sale. Pre-packs are particularly important for small businesses where the only prospective buyers are likely to be the management of the OldCo.

14.39 The legal basis for the whole scheme is the power of an administrator, as agent of the company,[117] to do anything necessary or expedient for the management of the affairs, business and property of the company.[118] Unless the administrator proposes to dispose of property subject to a fixed security without the consent of the fixed security holder,[119] the court's consent is not required.[120] The practice has proved controversial because of the lack of scrutiny of the administrators' role, the fees charged,[121] and the general result that unsecured creditors receive nothing. There are special statements of insolvency practice to regulate how administrators must act in these circumstances, and to which a recent independent review has recommended changes.[122]

117 1986 Act, Sch B1, para 69.
118 1986 Act, Sch B1, para 59(1).
119 See text and notes 113 and 114 above.
120 See *Re Transbus International Ltd (in liquidation)* [2004] 1 WLR 2654; *Re Kayley Vending Ltd* [2009] EWHC 904 (Ch), [2009] BCC 578; *Clydesdale Financial Services Ltd v Smailes* [2009] EWHC 1745 (Ch), [2009] BCC 810.
121 For the need for disclosure and approval of pre-administration costs incurred by the creditors, see 1986 Rules, r 2.25(1)(ka) and r 2.39C.
122 See e.g. Statement of Insolvency Practice 16 (Scotland): Pre-Packaged Sales in Administrations, dated 1 November 2013, and available from www.icas.org.uk. The recommended improvements are found in the review by Louise Graham, *Graham Review into Pre-Pack Administration* (June 2014), Annex 1. The main recommended change is the creation of a pool of independent experts from which one would be instructed to examine the terms of a proposed pre-pack.

Business names and phoenixing

14.40 A company subject to an insolvency proceeding undergoes a mandatory change of name to include, in its corporate name, an indication that it is 'in administration' or 'in liquidation' as the case may be. These facts must be disclosed on all of the company's business correspondence and websites.[123] One of the primary rationales for a pre-pack sale, as has been seen, is to preserve the goodwill of the business by effecting a sale before the insolvency is publicised. Goodwill is accessory to a business name.[124] The purchasers under a pre-pack sale, therefore, will often wish to carry on the new business under the same trading name as before. The purchaser may want the new entity to take the corporate name of the seller or be able to exercise registered trade marks or unregistered business names of the seller.

14.41 But there is a major legal catch to giving effect to such an arrangement: the rules against phoenixing.[125] 'Phoenixing' is the phenomenon whereby an insolvent OldCo sells its business and assets to a NewCo, perhaps for an undervalue;[126] the NewCo trades on debt free under the same name as the OldCo previously traded, while the OldCo is placed into insolvent liquidation. Section 216 of the Insolvency Act was introduced to deal with this phenomenon. Section 216(3) prohibits someone who has been a director of a company in the 12 months prior to its insolvent liquidation, from being concerned in any way with the carrying on of a business using the same or similar name as was used by the insolvent company. The prohibition lasts for a period of five years following the liquidation. The name under which OldCo carried on its business is the 'prohibited name'.[127] The sanctions for breach are severe: criminal penalties plus personal liability for the debts and other liabilities of NewCo as are incurred at a time when the former director of OldCo was involved with management of NewCo.[128] It is important to recognise that s 216 does not, in terms, expressly apply to administration. But s 216 has important practical implications for the sale of a business by an administrator, particularly in a pre-pack situation, for two reasons.

---

123 1986 Act, s 188 (liquidation); Sch B1, para 45 (administration).

124 *Commissioners of Inland Revenue v Muller & Co's Margarine Ltd* [1901] AC 217 at 224 per Lord Macnaghton.

125 See C Wilson, 'Prohibited names and phoenix companies' 2005 SLT (News) 207.

126 For which see para **14.85** below. Careful consideration should be given to the value paid for the goodwill and intellectual property transferred: *Western Intelligence Ltd v KDO Label Printing Machines Ltd* [1998] BCC 472.

127 1986 Act, s 216(2)(a) refers to the name 'by which the liquidating company was known'. That may be its corporate name or its trading name; s 216(2)(b) covers a name which is so similar as to suggest an association with the insolvent company. In *Advocate General v Reilly* [2011] CSOH 141, Lord Bannatyne held that 'Aquaseal UK Ltd' was sufficiently similar to the liquidating company's name of 'Aqua Seal IT Ltd' to be a prohibited name.

128 1986 Act, s 217(1)(a). See *ESS Production Ltd (in administration) v Sully* [2005] EWCA Civ 554. The right of action is personal to individual creditors. The liquidator of OldCo has no right of action: *Re Prestige Grinding Ltd* [2006] BCC 421.

First, it is thought that around 60 per cent of pre-packs are to connected parties, such as to former directors;[129] and, secondly, following such a sale, the OldCo will normally be placed into insolvent liquidation. The OldCo directors, if concerned with the management or with the carrying on of the NewCo business, may thereby incur liability under s 217 for NewCo's debts.

14.42 The prohibition in s 216 is, however, subject to three exceptions. First, s 216(3) is expressed to be subject to the leave of the court.[130] An application for leave of the court may be sought prior to the OldCo's insolvent liquidation or within seven days. Where such an application is made, the director in question may carry on a business under the prohibited name until the court decides to grant leave or for six weeks, whichever is the earlier.[131] Second, there is no breach of s 216(3) where the company which goes into insolvent liquidation had been known by that name for the whole of the 12-month period ending with the company's liquidation and which, during that time, had not been dormant.[132] Finally, there is an exception for a director who has acted in terms of s 216(3) where 'the whole or substantially the whole' of the business of the OldCo has been acquired from an insolvency office holder such as an administrator or liquidator. In order to invoke this exception, notice must be given in a prescribed form to the creditors of the company and published in the Edinburgh Gazette within 28 days of the completion of the sale.[133] The purpose of this provision is to support the rescue of a business but to ensure that the 'phoenix' company is disclosed as such.[134] But nice questions may arise where only part of the business is acquired (as where the underperforming part of the business is left behind) and there is uncertainty as to whether 'the whole or substantially the whole' of the business has been acquired. Careful thought is thus needed in advance in order to decide which exception may be invoked. But providing such matters are addressed at the outset, in most pre-pack cases it should be possible for the directors to avoid personal liability. Finally, it should be mentioned that there is a relatively old statement of insolvency practice for administrators dealing with such sales to connected parties.[135]

14.43 Where liability is incurred, under ss 216 and 217, it tends to be

---

129 *Graham Review* (n 122) para 7.50. The words 'connected with' are defined in 1986 Act, s 249. 'Associate', for these purposes, is defined in s 435.
130 1986 Act, s 216(3) and 1986 Rules, r 4.79.
131 1986 Rules, r 4.81 (the 'second excepted case').
132 1986 Rules, r 4.82 (the 'third excepted case').
133 1986 Rules, r 4.80(3) (the 'first excepted case').
134 *Penrose v Secretary of State for Trade and Industry* [1996] 1 WLR 482 at 489 per Chadwick J, approved by the Court of Appeal in *ESS Production Ltd v Sully* [2005] EWCA Civ 554.
135 Statement of Insolvency Practice 13 (Scotland): Acquisition of assets by directors (dated 1 August 1998) which pre-dates the Enterprise Act 2002, the Companies Act 2006 and the amendments to the 1986 Rules.

in cases that arise outside administration and where, perhaps, the transferees have not had the benefit of specialist legal advice. One example is *Glasgow City Council v Craig*.[136] The defenders operated two businesses from adjacent units. One business, operated by a company called Arigo Ltd, was an Italian restaurant. The other, a wine bar, was operated by a company called Degreefresh Ltd. Degreefresh also operated other businesses from other addresses. At the end of 2004, Degreefresh took an assignation of Arigo Ltd's lease. Degreefresh Ltd then operated the Italian restaurant business, named Arigo, as before. In January 2005, Arigo Ltd was placed into insolvent liquidation. Degreefresh Ltd, in January 2005, wrote to the local authority acknowledging that it was now liable for payment of the domestic rates for both shop units. Degreefresh Ltd paid the rates for both properties until it itself was placed in insolvent liquidation in September 2007. The local authority therefore sought to recover all the unpaid rates, for both units, from the directors personally on the basis of s 217.

14.44 The defenders accepted that none of the exceptions in the 1986 Rules applied.[137] The Lord Ordinary accepted that Arigo was a prohibited name for the purposes of s 216(2). The question arose for decision whether the directors were liable for the rates in respect of both Arigo and Degreefresh or just for the debts of Degreefresh which arose in respect of the latter's use of the Arigo name. Lord Glennie held, as a general principle, that liability under s 217 may be incurred even where only part of NewCo's business is carried on under OldCo's name. But Parliament did not intend to extend liability beyond the liabilities incurred by Degreefresh while carrying on business under the prohibited name, for there is no warrant for imposing personal liability on directors who have carried on a business under a name that is not prohibited. The 'relevant debts' under s 217 are thus limited to those 'incurred by the company while carrying on business under a prohibited name'.[138]

Exiting administration

14.45 All other things being equal, administration automatically comes to an end after 12 months.[139] The company's creditors may agree to extend the administration for six months; or the administrator may petition the court to extend the administration.[140] Prior to the Enterprise Act 2002, where an administration failed to rescue a company, it was expected that the company would be wound up. It is now the case that an administrator may make the distributions to the company's secured

---

136 [2008] CSOH 171, 2009 SC 185.
137 See n 130 to n 133 above.
138 *Glasgow City Council v Craig* at para [21].
139 1986 Act, Sch B1, para 76(1).
140 1986 Act, Sch B1, para 76(2). The court may extend the period of administration for longer than six months.

creditors avoiding the need for a winding-up.[141] That objective having occurred, where the administrator 'thinks' that the purpose[142] of the administration has been achieved, the administrator can bring the administration to an end without winding-up.[143] This decision is effective only on notice to both the Registrar and the court, but the court's consent is not required.[144]

14.46   It remains competent for a company to exit administration by being wound up. This can be done seamlessly by the administrators filing a notice to that effect. The notice takes effect on registration.[145] In the liquidation that follows, creditors, whose debts existed prior to the administration, and who remain undischarged, may rank in the liquidation, with their claims being calculated from the date of the administration.[146] Otherwise, it is possible for a company, following administration, to be dissolved without going to into liquidation.

COMPANY VOLUNTARY ARRANGEMENTS

14.47   The law on CVAs is found in Part 1 of, and Schedule A1 to, the Insolvency Act 1986 and in Part 1 of the 1986 Rules.[147] The procedure is designed to allow a company to come to an arrangement with its creditors which will allow it to continue trading. The company need not be insolvent.[148] A CVA is often combined with other procedures such as administration. It is a hybrid procedure: a cross between a scheme of arrangement and a private contract. Subject to the CVA terms, the directors may remain in control. A CVA looks like a contractual document and, according to the terms of the Act, binds all those who voted for or against it, as well as those that would have been entitled to vote on it had they known about it.[149] It is a standard term of a CVA that no legal proceedings may be brought against the company. In the absence of such a term, however, unlike administration, the only statutory moratorium available on a CVA is the limited statutory moratorium available for small companies between the lodging of an application for it with the court and the holding of meetings to approve the CVA. The moratorium lasts only until the meetings have taken

---

141 1986 Act, Sch B1, para 3(1)(c). Distributions to unsecured creditors may be made only with the permission of the court: Sch B1, para 65(3).

142 1986 Act, Sch B1, para 80.

143 *Re Kaupthing Singer & Friedlander Ltd (in administration)* [2010] EWCA Civ 518 at paras [7]–[8] per Etherton LJ; *Re Nortel GmbH (in administration)* [2013] UKSC 52 at para [34] per Lord Neuberger.

144 *Joint Administrators of Station Properties Ltd* [2013] CSOH 120.

145 *Re Globespan Airways Ltd (in liquidation)* [2013] 1 WLR 1122.

146 1986 Act, Sch B1, para 83(6)(b) and *Re Kaupthing Singer & Friedlander Ltd (in administration)* at paras [7]–[8] per Etherton LJ.

147 For more detailed treatment, see R M Goode, *Principles of Corporate Insolvency Law: Student Edition* (4th edn, 2011) para 12.26.

148 1986 Act, s 1(1).

149 1986 Act, s 5(2)(b).

place or for 28 days.[150] If such a moratorium is in force, this must be publicised in all of the company's business documents and websites.[151]

INTERACTIONS

Provisional liquidation and administration

14.48 A creditor petitioning for a winding-up may seek the appointment of a provisional liquidator.[152] The court may appoint a provisional liquidator before the petition to wind up has been heard. A provisional liquidator's purpose is to take control of the company's business and assets, normally with a view to their preservation and prevention of their dissipation. Since the appointment of a provisional liquidator, however, has much the same practical effect as a liquidator being appointed, the court will do so only if it is satisfied that it is likely that a liquidator will, indeed, be appointed when the petition is heard.[153]

14.49 A hearing is bound to be required.[154] The general rule is that presentation of a liquidation petition prevents the company or the directors seeking to appoint an administrator.[155] But it may be impossible to obtain the appointment of a provisional liquidator in the face of a qualifying floating charge holder who has caveats in place:[156] on being alerted that there is to be a hearing on the appointment of a provisional liquidator, the QFC holder may proceed to file a notice of appointment, which suspends the liquidation petition.[157] Once a provisional liquidator has been appointed, however, it is not possible for the qualifying floating charge holder to appoint an administrator.[158]

Administration and liquidation

14.50 On the presentation of a winding-up petition, the standard period of notice is eight days.[159] Since an administrator may be appointed by the holder of a qualifying floating charge 'out of court', that is to say by filing forms with the Petition Department of the Court

150 1986 Act, Sch A1, para 8.
151 1986 Act, Sch A1, para 16.
152 1986 Act, s 135.
153 Cf. *Revenue and Customs Commissioners v Rochdale Drinks Distributors Ltd* [2011] EWCA Civ 1116.
154 Cf. *Teague, Petr* 1985 SLT 469 and, in England *Practice Direction (Ch D: Companies Court: Appointment of Provisional Liquidator)* [1997] 1 WLR 3.
155 1986 Act, Sch B1, para 25.
156 'Caveat' in this context relates to notices filed with the Court of Session that prevent interim orders being granted against a party who has lodged such a caveat without a hearing: *Bell's Dictionary* (7th edn) 'caveat'.
157 1986 Act, Sch B1, para 40(1)(b).
158 1986 Act, Sch B1, para 17(a). Appointment by the company or the directors is prevented by the general rule in the 1986 Act, Sch B1, para 25.
159 RCS 74.22(2). That rule, however, is subject to RCS r 14.6(2) which allows for the period of notice to be shortened.

of Session, there is thus a potential for conflict. So where, during the period allowed by the court for intimation of the winding-up petition, a notice of appointment of an administrator is filed with the court, the winding-up petition is immediately suspended on the filing of the notice.[160]

ENFORCING FLOATING CHARGES: RECEIVERSHIP

Fixed and floating charges

14.51 Under the Companies Acts, where a company grants a right in security, such as a standard security in respect of Scottish land, the charge must be registered at Companies House within 21 days of its creation.[161] In the English law jargon of the Companies Acts, a right in security granted by a company is a 'charge'. In Scots law, the provisions on registration of company charges have long been problematic, not least because, in Scotland, they were generally unnecessary: it was already a general principle of Scots law that rights in security could be created only with some form of publicity.[162] The registration of company charges regime thus leads, with one exception, to a system of dual publicity for all rights in security granted by companies and LLPs. The exception is the floating charge, which is registered only at Companies House.[163] A standard security granted by a company and registered in the Land Register may therefore be 'invalid against a liquidator' if the charge is not registered at Companies House within 21 days of its registration in the Land Register. In transactional practice, the 21-day rule is of central importance.

14.52 Floating charges, in Scots law, are creatures of statute. As in the United States prior to the introduction of the Uniform Commercial Code,[164] floating charges are not recognised at common law.[165] They were introduced to Scots law by legislation[166] in terms of which certain bodies corporate – which today means companies, LLPs and industrial

---

160 1986 Act, Sch B1, para 40(1)(b).

161 Companies Act 2006, Part 25, as amended by the Companies Act 2006 (Amendment of Part 25) Regulations 2013 (SI 2013/600).

162 For all this, see G L Gretton, 'The registration of company charges' (2002) 6 Edin LR 146.

163 All charges created by a company must also be registered in the granter company's own statutory registers: that is to say, the file of prescribed information that must be kept at the company's registered office and available for inspection: 2006 Act, s 859P.

164 *Benedict v Ratner* 268 US 353 (1925).

165 *Carse v Coppen* 1951 SC 233 at 239 per Lord President Cooper: 'a floating charge is utterly repugnant to the principles of Scots law and is not recognised by us as creating a security at all'.

166 Companies (Floating Charges) (Scotland) Act 1961.

and provident societies – are permitted to grant floating charges.[167] Prior to attachment, the status of a floating charge is difficult to explain conceptually. But despite the constant conceptual problems floating charges have caused, the importance of the floating charge in daily financial practice cannot be overstated. Just two aspects of its importance can be mentioned here.

14.53 The first relates to its ranking with other 'fixed' rights in security. In principle, a floating charge ranks behind prior fixed securities.[168] But a floating charge is also allowed to contain a so-called 'negative pledge clause': that is to say, a clause prohibiting the company from creating any subsequent security ranking prior to, or *pari passu* with, the floating charge.[169] In other words, a floating charge containing such a clause (and all do) ranks ahead of any fixed rights in security which are created after the floating charge has been executed but before the floating charge has attached. And since the clause takes effect as soon as the floating charge has been executed but remains latent for up to 21 days, it may prejudice a subsequent bona fide third party creditor who takes a standard security in good faith.[170]

> **Example:** suppose, on day 1, Alpha Limited executes a floating charge, containing a negative pledge, in favour of Bank of Bermuda SA. On day 4, Alpha Limited grants a standard security in favour ABC Banking Corporation Inc. On day 7 the standard security is registered in the Land Register. On day 10 both the floating charge and the standard security are registered at Companies House. On first principles, because the standard security has been created as a subordinate real right prior to enforcement of the floating charge, the standard security ought to prevail over the floating charge. Because the floating charge contained a negative pledge, however, the effect is to invert the ordinary ranking.

14.54 The second important aspect of floating charges is their role in corporate insolvency. Indeed, under the modern law, one of the main rationales for taking an all-encompassing floating charge may have less to do with its effect as a security instrument, and more to do with the control it provides to a creditor and, in particular, the right it confers on the holder to appoint an administrator.

Receivership and administrative receivership

14.55 Prior to 1972, the only way to enforce a floating charge in Scotland was to kill the company by liquidation. Receivership was thus

---

167 Companies Act 1985, s 462 (applied, implicitly, to LLPs by the Limited Liability Partnerships (Amendment) Regulations 2009 (SI 2009/1833)); Co-operative and Community Benefit Services Act 2014, s 62.
168 Companies Act 1985, s 463(1)(b).
169 Companies Act 1985, s 464, for which see para **11.65** above.
170 *AIB Finance Ltd v Bank of Scotland* 1993 SC 588.

introduced as a method for enforcing floating charges in 1972.[171] That Act allowed enforcement by way of an appointment by the floating charge holder of an insolvency practitioner on an event of default under the instrument creating the floating charge.[172] A receiver whose appointment covered the 'whole or substantially the whole of the company's property and undertaking' was known as an 'administrative receiver'.[173] Other receivers – such as those appointed in respect of specific assets – are plain 'receivers'. The distinction is crucial because, for floating charges executed after September 2003,[174] it is no longer possible to appoint an 'administrative receiver'. But it remains possible to appoint a receiver who is not an administrative receiver, such as where a receiver is appointed in respect of a particular asset.

14.56 In either case, however, a receiver's primary duties were owed to the floating charge holder rather than to the general creditors. The result was that, where companies encountered difficulties, the most sophisticated creditor, the bank, which invariably held the floating charge, was able to place the company in receivership, instigate a fire sale of the assets, and take whatever could be realised. The unsecured creditors, in contrast, often unsophisticated, usually unrepresented and always ignored, received nothing. It was dissatisfaction with the operation of administrative receivership that led to its abolition for most companies.[175] The abolition of administrative receivership means that, in practice, by far the most important insolvency proceedings are administration (where the business might be saved) and liquidation (where there is little or nothing left to save).

Abolition of administrative receivership

14.57 The Enterprise Act 2002 was introduced in order to promote a rescue culture. A prescribed part for unsecured creditors was introduced. And the general position is that a floating charge holder's only practical option is to place the company into administration: a procedure that, generally speaking,[176] prevents all creditors, the floating charge holder included, from enforcing rights in security. From September 2003 it has not been possible to appoint an administrative receiver – at least in respect of most private companies.[177]

---

171 Floating Charges and Receivers (Scotland) Act 1972.
172 1986 Act, s 52. The receiver is subject to the Receivers (Scotland) Rules 1986 (SI 1986/1917), as amended.
173 1986 Act, s 259(b).
174 When 1986 Act, s 72A came into force.
175 1986 Act, s 72A. For the exceptions, see n 177 below.
176 See para **14.36** above.
177 But there are a host of exceptions where floating charges have been granted in respect of major financial transactions: see 1986 Act, s 72B–72GA. For a reported example where an administrative receiver was appointed under s 72E, see *Cabvision Ltd v Feetum* [2006] Ch 585.

Remnants of receivership

14.58 It is still possible to have a receivership that is not an administrative receivership, as where the receiver is not to be appointed over the 'whole or substantially the whole' of the company's property and undertaking. It is also now competent to appoint a receiver in respect of Scottish-based assets pursuant to a Scottish floating charge created by a company that is not registered in Scotland and which the Court of Session would not have jurisdiction to wind up.[178] The Act allows a receiver to be appointed to a company 'in respect of which a court of a member state other than the United Kingdom has under the EU Regulation jurisdiction to open insolvency proceedings'.[179] The receiver so appointed is empowered to act only with respect to charged assets located in Scotland.[180] This provision is important in finance transactions concerning assets located in Scotland but which are held by corporate vehicles incorporated elsewhere.[181]

14.59 When a receiver is appointed, all business documents, including websites, must publicise the fact that the company is in receivership.[182] A receiver is deemed to be the agent of the company in respect of such property of the company as is attached by the floating charge under which he has been appointed.[183] But the receiver may be personally liable on such contracts as he does conclude while holding office, unless he expressly qualifies his liability.[184]

The prescribed part

14.60 One of the many criticisms of administrative receivership was that the receiver acted solely in the interests of the creditor in the strongest position, namely the floating charge holder. When administrative receivership was abolished, one of the amendments that was introduced was the introduction of the prescribed part: that is to say, a proportion of the assets that would otherwise be paid to the floating charge holder would be carved out to form a fund for the payment of something to the unsecured creditors. The prescribed part applies, however, only where the company's net property, that would otherwise be

---

178 1986 Act, s 51(1)(b) and (2), as a result of amendments introduced in 2011. For the background to the amendments, see H Patrick, 'Receivership of foreign based companies' 2010 SLT (News) 177.
179 1986 Act, s 51(1)(b).
180 1986 Act, s 51(2ZA).
181 See further para **5.77** above.
182 1986 Act, s 64.
183 1986 Act, s 57(1). The receiver's powers, over and above those contained in the charge, are set out in 1986 Act, Sch 2.
184 1986 Act, s 57(2). But even if he is personally liable, he is entitled to an indemnity from the funds subject to the charge: s 57(3). There are special provisions dealing with employment contracts: s 57(2A)–(2D).

available to the floating charge holder, exceeds £10,000.[185] In so far as the company's net property exceeds £10,000, the prescribed part represents £5,000 of the first £10,000; and 20 per cent of the company's net property thereafter.[186]

14.61   Where the company has net property that would be available to a floating charge holder that is less than the prescribed minimum (currently £10,000); and the liquidator, administrator or receiver 'thinks that the cost of making a distribution to the unsecured creditors would be disproportionate to the benefits',[187] then the prescribed part does not apply. Separately, and in any event, it is possible for the administrator or liquidator to ask the court to disapply the prescribed part.[188] One common reason in practice for seeking to disapply is that the prescribed part will be small relative to the expense that would be involved in adjudicating on the unsecured creditors' claims. But the court has a discretion. And the mere fact that the dividend to individual unsecured creditors will be small is not, of itself, enough to justify the disapplication of the prescribed part.[189] The prescribed part may be disapplied only in general terms: it is not possible to seek its disapplication in relation only to specific creditors.[190]

CONSEQUENCES OF INSOLVENCY: REMEDIES AGAINST DIRECTORS AND TRANSFEREES

Personal liability for corporate insolvency and directors' disqualification

14.62   Directors of companies in financial difficulties may be subject to personal liability. Under s 212 of the Insolvency Act 1986, an officer[191] of a company who has 'misapplied or retained, or become accountable for, any money or other property of the company, or been guilty of any misfeasance or breach of any fiduciary or other duty in relation to the company' may be examined and, on the application of a liquidator or a creditor, be required (a) to repay, restore or account for the money or property or any part of it, with interest at such rate as the court thinks just, or (b) to contribute such sum to the company's assets by way of compensation in respect of the misfeasance or breach of fiduciary or

---

185 Insolvency Act 1986, s 176A(3)(a) read with Insolvency Act (Prescribed Part) Order 2003 (SI 2003/2097), art 2.
186 2003 Order, art 3. See further paras **11.71–11.72** above.
187 1986 Act, s 176A(3)(b).
188 1986 Act, s 176A(5).
189 See e.g. *Joint Administrators of QMD Hotels Ltd (in administration), Noters* [2010] CSOH 168.
190 *Re Courts plc (in liquidation)* [2008] EWHC 2339 (Ch).
191 Officer, in this context, includes, in principle, de facto or shadow directors: *Holland v Revenue and Customs Commissioners* [2010] UKSC 51, [2010] 1 WLR 2793 at para [51] per Lord Hope of Craighead.

other duty as the court thinks just.[192] Section 212 does not add anything to existing common law remedies, but s 212(3) confers discretion on the court concerning the remedy to be awarded once liability is established.[193]

14.63 Sections 213 (fraudulent trading) and 214 (wrongful trading) of the Insolvency Act, in contrast, provide statutory rights of action. The two sections are materially different. Section 213 deals with fraudulent trading, which is also a criminal offence.[194] It may lead to liability being imposed on 'any person' who has 'carried on the business of the company with intent to defraud creditors of the company or creditors of any other person, or for any fraudulent purpose'. Section 214, in contrast, applies to persons who are, or who have been, directors of the company. In terms of s 214(4), the court will take into account both (a) the general knowledge, skill and experience that may reasonably be expected of a person carrying out the same functions as are carried out by that director in relation to the company; and also (b) the general knowledge, skill and experience that that director has. Part (b) of this test refers to actual knowledge which the director has over and above the minimum to be expected of an ordinarily competent director. Part (b) is of particular importance to qualified professionals – such as lawyers and accountants – who act as company directors. For whereas part (b) of the test may increase the standard of care incumbent on the director, it will never lower the standard below that set out in part (a). Sections 213 and 214 are of real concern in practice, although reported case law involving applications under those sections is limited.

14.64 Finally, it should be mentioned that an insolvency practitioner is required to investigate, and report to the Secretary of State, the conduct of all persons who were directors of the company in the three years prior to insolvency.[195] The Secretary of State will consider these reports and decide whether a particular director is someone against whom disqualification proceedings under the Company Directors Disqualification Act 1986 should be instigated. The test is whether the director's conduct had fallen below the standards of probity and competence appropriate for persons fit to be directors of companies.[196]

192　See e.g. *Trustees of the Dyglen Engineering Ltd Pension Scheme No 2 v Russell* 2014 GWD 1-6 (Sh Ct).

193　*Stone & Rolls Ltd (in liquidation) v Moore Stephens (a firm)* [2009] 1 AC 1391 at paras [110]–[111] per Lord Scott.

194　Companies Act 2006, s 993(1): 'If any business of a company is carried on with intent to defraud creditors of the company or creditors of any other person, or for any fraudulent purpose, every person who is knowingly a party to the carrying on of the business in that manner commits an offence'.

195　Company Directors Disqualification Act 1986, s 7(3); Insolvent Companies (Reports on Conduct of Directors) (Scotland) Rules 1996 (SI 1996/1910) (as amended) containing reports D1 and D2.

196　See e.g. *Secretary of State for Business Innovation and Skills v Khan* [2012] CSOH 85, 2012 SLT 1090.

Fraudulent breach of trust and embezzlement

14.65 Bell used the term 'embezzlement' to describe the acts of an insolvent debtor which prefer particular creditors.[197] The term has proved evocative and its effect enduring. Under the law of prescription, for example, the prescriptive period is interrupted where the creditor is induced to refrain from making a relevant claim in relation to the obligation by the debtor's fraud;[198] while claims to make reparation or restitution for 'fraudulent breach of trust' are imprescriptible.[199] It is necessary to say something of these two elements: what must be demonstrated in order to satisfy the 'fraudulent' aspect; and, secondly, what is meant by 'trust' in this context.

Fraudulent breach of trust

14.66 It is often said in civil proceedings that any allegations of fraud must be specific.[200] But the specification indicated – identity of alleged perpetrator and specification of the allegedly fraudulent acts – is little different from the specification that ought to be required for any action. In Scots law, insolvency fraud has never required proof of the transferee's dishonesty.[201] In *Ross v Davey*, however, Lord Penrose said that, in Scots law, 'dishonesty is in general fundamental to the Scottish notion of fraudulent conduct'; at its lowest common denominator, he held, 'dishonest conduct or conduct from which dishonesty can be inferred', is the very essence of 'fraud'.[202]

14.67 *Ross v Davey* is, however, inconsistent with the traditional concept of fraud on insolvency: that is to say, in Bankton's strikingly modern phrase, 'statutory presumptive fraud'.[203] Indeed, it was early established in the nineteenth century that, in attacking an unfair preference under

---

197 Bell, *Commentaries* (7th edn, 1870) II, 170 (quoted in para **14.84** below).
198 Prescription and Limitation (Scotland) Act 1973, s 6(4).
199 Prescription and Limitation (Scotland) Act 1973, Sch 3, para (e)(ii).
200 *Royal Bank of Scotland plc v Holmes* 1999 SLT 563 at 569 per Lord Macfadyen: 'It is in my view essential for the party alleging fraud clearly and specifically to identify the act or representation founded upon, the occasion on which the act was committed or the representation made, and the circumstances relied on as yielding the inference that that act or representation was fraudulent. It is also, in my view, essential that the person who committed the fraudulent act or made the fraudulent misrepresentation be identified.'
201 *M'Gowan v Wright* (1853) 15 D 494 approved in *Dryburgh v Scotts Media Tax Ltd (in liquidation)* [2014] CSIH 45 at para [30] per Lord Drummond Young. More generally, see D Reid, 'The doctrine of presumptive fraud in Scots law' (2013) 34 Journal of Legal History 307.
202 *Ross v Davey* 1996 SCLR 369 at 388C–E. Lord Penrose allowed a proof before answer on the question.
203 Bankton, *Institute* I, 264, 85.

the 1696 Act, it was not necessary to prove fraud.[204] *Ross v Davey* is also inconsistent with binding modern authority on the proper test for the crime of embezzlement. The Appeal Court considered these requirements in *Moore v HM Advocate*.[205] In that case the accused was prosecuted in respect of various acts that, in broad terms, concerned insolvency fraud on a company in order to defeat his former wife's claims for financial provision on divorce. It was accepted that a conviction for embezzlement in Scots criminal law requires a 'dishonest purpose'. The Appeal Court candidly acknowledged, however, that there is a 'degree of vagueness' in the mental element required for the crime of embezzlement. A dishonest purpose may, therefore, be proved by 'bad faith' inferred from suspicious circumstances for which there was no *bona fide* explanation. In so doing, their Lordships drew heavily on the decision relating to the relevancy of the indictment in the trial of the City of Glasgow Bank directors in 1879.[206]

14.68 As a result, if a criminal conviction for fraud requires only that the Crown prove circumstances from which a jury could infer bad faith, then the test for determining a fraudulent breach of fiduciary duty,[207] fraud on creditors,[208] or, for that matter, fraudulent trading[209] may not be as high as is sometimes suggested. If that is so, the present position would appear to be similar to that in other European legal systems.[210]

14.69 As has been seen, claims for 'fraudulent breach of trust' are imprescriptible.[211] 'Trust' language is, for this reason, often bandied around in corporate insolvencies. Sometimes it is said, based on an imaginative reading of the legislation,[212] that the company is a trustee for its creditors; sometimes that the directors of the insolvent company are trustees for the company's creditors. But it is only the company that can reasonably be described as a trustee for its creditors, and, even then, as Lord President Emslie has pointed out, only in a general and non-

---

204 *Speir v Dunlop* (1827) 5 S 729 at 731 per Lord Justice-Clerk Boyle, followed in *Mitchell v Rodger* (1834) 12 S 802 at 810 per Lord President Hope: 'After the case of *Speir*, it is in vain to contend that fraud is an essential element in a reduction under the [Bankruptcy Act 1696].' Interestingly, the Lord President added: 'there is no inconsistency in holding a transaction to be good as to one of several parties, and yet not to the others'.

205 [2010] HCJAC 26, 2010 SCCR 451.

206 *HM Advocate v City of Glasgow Bank Directors* (1879) 4 Coup 161.

207 *Commonwealth Oil & Gas Co Ltd v Baxter* 2010 SC 156.

208 See para **14.85** below.

209 1986 Act, s 214.

210 Cf. e.g. Swiss *StGB/Code Pénal* Art 158 (*Ungetreue Geschäftsbesorgung/Gestion déloyale*) (lit: 'disloyal management').

211 Prescription and Limitation (Scotland) Act 1973, Sch 3, para (e)(ii).

212 1986 Act, s 130(4).

technical sense.[213] Not all breaches of fiduciary duty by a company director, however, amount to a breach of trust.[214] The remedy for breach of trust is normally damages or restitution. Clear averments are required for any case based on constructive trust.[215] But in England it has been held that claims based on constructive trust are subject to the ordinary law of limitation and do not fall within a similar exception for claims based on a fraudulent breach of trust.[216]

EFFECT OF INSOLVENCY ON PATRIMONIAL RIGHTS

14.70 Insolvency, in the general sense, means that the insolvent company cannot meet its liabilities, but there are a number of legal principles which regulate how the insolvency administrator can deal with the company's property and existing contractual relationships. It is often difficult to find a modern statement of these principles in the case law so it makes sense to explain some of the vocabulary sometimes encountered: adoption and judicial rescission, abandonment, and disclaimer.

General principle

14.71 On insolvency, a company remains the holder of its patrimonial rights: it remains creditor of its receivables, owner of its immoveable and corporeal moveable properties and holder of its intellectual property rights. Conversely the company remains the debtor in respect of its liabilities and remains liable for the performance of its obligations even after a liquidator, or other insolvency practitioner, has been appointed.[217] The effect of appointment of an insolvency practitioner is rather to invest the insolvency practitioner with the power to manage the company and the authority to enter into contracts on behalf of the company. Unless otherwise expressed, however, an insolvency practitioner is con-

---

213 *Nordic Travel Ltd v Scotprint Ltd* 1980 SC 1 at 10: 'There are no doubt certain acts which, in the interests of all his creditors . . . an insolvent person is obliged not to do, but to say that he is, literally, a trustee for his creditors is unwarranted in authority and wholly misleading.' The idea, in English law, of an insolvent company holding its assets in trust for creditors is set out in *Ayerst v C & K (Construction) Ltd* [1976] AC 167. But as Lord Hoffmann has pointed out, 'it is a special kind of trust . . . The creditors have only a right to have the assets administered by the liquidator in accordance with the provisions of the Insolvency Act 1986': *Buchler v Talbot* [2004] 2 AC 298 at para [28].
214 Cf. *Dryburgh v Scotts Media Tax Ltd* [2011] CSOH 147, revd [2014] CSIH 45.
215 *Ross v Morley and Williamson* [2013] CSOH 175; *Ted Jacob Engineering Group Inc v Robert Matthew, Johnson-Marshall & Partners* [2014] CSIH 18, especially at paras [98]–[101] per Lord Drummond Young. For penetrating criticism, see N Whitty, 'The "no profit from another's fraud" rule and the knowing receipt muddle' (2013) 17 Edin LR 37.
216 *Williams v Central Bank of Nigeria* [2014] UKSC 10, [2014] 2 WLR 355.
217 *Smith v Lord Advocate (No 1)* 1978 SC 259 at 270–271 per Lord President Emslie.

sidered as acting independently after appointment: creditors, with whom the insolvency practitioner contracts, in the absence of express limitations on the insolvency practitioner's liability, are entitled to look at the personal credit of the insolvency practitioner (and, on ordinary principles of agency, the professional firm which the insolvency practitioner represents).[218]

Adoption

14.72 An insolvency practitioner, such as a liquidator, is not liable to perform the insolvent company's obligations. But the liquidator is entitled, where he considers it in the interests of the creditors to do so, to 'adopt' certain contracts, procure the performance of the company's outstanding obligations, and then claim the benefits of that performance for the company's creditors. This is the general process known as 'adoption'.[219]

14.73 On insolvency, a liquidator has the same powers as a trustee in sequestration.[220] A trustee in sequestration is appointed to manage the assets of a bankrupt to ensure the orderly payment of a dividend to creditors. A trustee in sequestration does not, by virtue of his appointment alone, assume any personal liability to the creditors. The rationale for adoption is that the bankrupt's contracts may be profitable for the bankrupt's estate and thus benefit the general creditors.[221] But a distinction has to be made between the contract's constituent elements. Adoption applies only to the bankrupt's *liabilities* under the contract. By adoption, the trustee assumes (personal) liability for the bankrupt's liabilities under the contract. In a personal bankruptcy, the trustee is already vested in the bankrupt's *claims* under the contract.

14.74 On a corporate insolvency, the company remains creditor in respect of its own debtors, and it remains liable for its debts. Like the trustee in sequestration, therefore, a liquidator or administrator has the power to adopt any outstanding liabilities the company has under the contract, in order to obtain the counter-performance owed to the insolvent company. The effect of the administrator or liquidator as the case may be adopting, is that the company's liability under the contract ranks as an insolvency expense.

14.75 A contract is not adopted by the mere fact of the insolvency administrator claiming an accrued debt.[222] But the administrator cannot 'cherry-pick' the obligations adopted: adoption of a particular contract

---

218 *Smith* at 270 and 272 per Lord President Emslie.
219 Cf. *Edinburgh Heritable Security Co Ltd v Stevenson's Tr* (1886) 13 R 427 at 428 per Lord McLaren (Ordinary).
220 1986 Act, s 130(2).
221 For adoption by a trustee in sequestration, see Bankruptcy (Scotland) Act 1985, s 42.
222 *Sturrock v Robertson's Tr* 1913 SC 582; *Craig's Tr v Lord Malcolm* (1900) 2 F 541.

is all or nothing.[223] Special provisions apply to employment contracts and there are strict time limits in which an insolvency practitioner must decide whether the employees are to be retained and the contracts adopted.[224]

14.76 An insolvency practitioner may be deemed to have adopted contracts where he has taken post-insolvency benefits, such as where an administrator has retained 'beneficial occupation' by the company of leased premises. The rent under such leases becomes an insolvency expense. This is sometimes known as the '*Lundy Granite* principle'.[225] So where administrators had continued to possess under a lease and had, as part of a restructuring, purported to grant a sub-lease (in breach of the terms of the lease), the landlords were held entitled to require the administrators to treat the rent as an expense of the administration.[226] In England, there is continuing controversy about whether rent payable in advance – as where the quarter day on which the rent is payable falls before the date of administration – falls within the principle. The latest decision of the Court of Appeal imposes a 'pay-as-you-go' principle: such rent too is to be treated as an expense of the administration in so far as the administrator remains in beneficial occupation.[227] In Scotland, an insolvency practitioner, who has not caused the company to remain in beneficial occupation of the leased premises, is not liable for the rent. It should be remembered that the landlord retains a fixed security for unpaid rent by virtue of the landlord's hypothec, but in practice there may be limited corporeal moveables of value belonging to the company.

Rescission

14.77 All other things being equal, insolvency has no effect on existing contracts. But most professionally drafted contracts contain 'events of default' provisions, the result of which normally confers various rights on the solvent counterparty, such as accelerating the date for performance of the insolvent party's liabilities under the contract. Such provisions may be the subject of judicial scrutiny.[228] The solvent party normally has an option to rescind, but basic contractual principle means that there is no obligation on the solvent party to rescind the contract. It is open to the solvent party to claim the amounts due under the contract as a debt. But where the solvent party wants to rescind but has no con-

---

223 *Powdrill v Watson* [1995] 2 AC 394 at 449 per Lord Browne-Wilkinson.
224 1986 Act, s 57(5) (receivers), Sch B1, para 11 (power of administrator to employ agents or employees and to dismiss employees), for which see *Kavanagh v Crystal Palace FC 2000 Ltd* [2013] EWCA Civ 1410; 1986 Act, Sch 4, paras 12 and 13 (liquidator's powers in any winding-up exercisable without court sanction).
225 *Re Lundy Granite Co, ex parte Heavan* (1871) LR 6 Ch App 462 at 466 per James LJ, explained in *Re Toshoku Finance UK plc* [2002] 1 WLR 671 at paras [27] and [29] per Lord Hoffmann.
226 *Cheshire West and Chester Borough Council, Petr* [2010] CSOH 115.
227 *Re Games Station Ltd* [2014] EWCA Civ 180.
228 See *Belmont Park Investments Pty Ltd v BNY Corporate Trustee Services Ltd* [2011] UKSC 38, [2012] 1 AC 383.

tractual right to terminate the contract with the insolvent company, the solvent party may ask the court to terminate the contract judicially.[229]

Abandonment

14.78 In principle, any solvent person, natural or juristic, may abandon ownership of corporeal moveables.[230] At common law, the Crown acquires ownership of such abandoned objects.[231] But there is now a statutory procedure which must be followed by the finder of lost or abandoned corporeal moveable property.[232] Solvent creditors too may 'abandon' personal rights held against debtors by discharging the debtors or by doing nothing and allowing the period for negative prescription to expire.

14.79 Ownership of land is more difficult. When all land was feudal, the relationship of the owner was, in many respects, contractual. The very basis of the 'owner's' holding, indeed, was often under a 'feu contract'. For this reason, a trustee in sequestration had the power to adopt a feu contract or to refuse to adopt the feu as the case may be. A solvent vassal, meanwhile, could abandon his feu by a procuratory of resignation in favour of the feudal superior.[233] In the modern law, there appears to be no recognised procedure for the registration of a unilateral abandonment of ownership,[234] although that may change. In any case, such abandonment can be effective only from the date of registration.[235]

Disclaimer of onerous property

14.80 The 1986 Act contains an express provision allowing the liquidators of English companies to 'disclaim onerous property'.[236] That provision applies to the company's property wherever situated, so, in principle, the liquidator of an English company, which owns Scottish land, may attempt to disclaim ownership of the land by an informal notice. There is no equivalent express provision in the 1986 Act for liquidators of Scottish companies. But the 1986 Act applies to Scottish companies the general principles of bankruptcy and insolvency law and

---

229 1986 Act, s 186.
230 See K G C Reid, *The Law of Property in Scotland* (1996) paras 540 and 547–552.
231 Reid, *Property*, para 540 and 547.
232 Civic Government (Scotland) Act 1982, ss 67–79.
233 W Ross, *Lectures on the History and Practice of the Law of Scotland, relative to Conveyancing and Legal Diligence* (2nd edn, 1822) II, 222–223. Matters were simplified by the Conveyancing and Land Transfer (Scotland) Act 1874 (c 95), s 6 and Schedule O. All was washed away with the Abolition of Feudal Tenure etc (Scotland) Act 2000.
234 Abandonment could be covered by the general wording of the Abolition of Feudal Tenure etc (Scotland) Act 2000, s 4(1), (2) and (3)(a). An application to abandon could also be registrable in terms of the Land Registration (Scotland) Act 1979, s 2(4)(c).
235 Land Registration etc (Scotland) Act 2012, ss 22 and 31.
236 1986 Act, s 178.

a liquidator is given the same powers as the trustee of a bankrupt estate.[237] Adoption, as has been seen, is a power conferred on a trustee in sequestration, administrator or liquidator. The power to adopt is also a power to refuse to adopt. But whereas the power to adopt relates to the company's *liabilities*, disclaimer is a power which relates to the company's *assets*.[238] It is useful to make this distinction at the outset as it is not one that is otherwise made in those Scottish cases which do mention a power to disclaim.[239]

14.81 The question of whether Scottish liquidators have a power to disclaim similar to that set out in s 178 was thrown into sharp focus in *Joint Liquidators of the Scottish Coal Co Ltd, Noters*.[240] The liquidators applied to the court for directions on whether they were entitled to abandon on behalf of the company the ownership of various coalmines to which significant environmental liabilities attached. Although recognising that the case was unprecedented, the Lord Ordinary, Lord Hodge held that a trustee in sequestration does have the power to disclaim onerous property.[241] The liquidators too, the Lord Ordinary held, thus had the power to disclaim ownership of land either by declining to use the funds in the creditors' patrimony to deal with it, or by taking steps to terminate the company's ownership of land.[242] The effect of such a disclaimer was described thus:[243]

> Just as a trustee in sequestration can decline to deal with an asset and avoid the accompanying responsibility, so also, it seems to me, can a liquidator by refusing to manage the asset and meet its related liabilities. Such a refusal would not terminate the company's ownership of the asset. The asset would remain the property of the company until the company was dissolved. But it would not form part of the liquidator's patrimony in the winding up. Instead it would remain in a mummified patrimony of the company as, in contrast to the bankrupt in sequestration, there would be no one with power to take control of the asset during the winding up.

14.82 Disclaimer, the Lord Ordinary held, is available only to insol-

---

237 1986 Act, s 169(2).
238 This discussion is offered as an analysis of Scots law. The rather different evolution of English law in this area is charted in *Hindcastle Ltd v Barbara Attenborough Associates Ltd* [1997] AC 70 at 89H–96D per Lord Nicholls of Birkenhead. But Lord Nicholls too, in the context of the effect of disclaimer on a lease, at the outset of his speech carefully distinguishes the respective rights and obligations of the parties to a lease: p 85B–D. In England, a liquidator's power to disclaim is today statutory (1986 Act, s 178), but there is no equivalent power for an administrator: *Re Nortel GmbH (in administration)* [2013] UKSC 52 at para [104] per Lord Neuberger.
239 E.g. *Crown Estate Commissioners v Liquidators of Highland Engineering Ltd* 1975 SLT 58 at 59 per Lord Keith.
240 [2013] CSOH 124.
241 At para [28].
242 At para [34].
243 At para [28]. Further machinery may be required at the Land Register: see para [76].

vency practitioners; it can occur informally, and is effective as soon as the decision to disclaim is made.[244] As the Lord Ordinary put it, it may be effective from the date of 'declining to deal with' or 'declining to manage' the asset in question. In this respect, disclaimer would be different from abandonment of ownership, which any solvent person can do and which is effective only from the date of registration. Scots law, on the Lord Ordinary's analysis, would be similar to German law[245] and relative in effect: third party rights would be otherwise unaffected.[246]

14.83 Lord Hodge's decision, however, was overturned by the Second Division.[247] The Second Division held that, although it is possible for a Scottish insolvency administrator to refuse to adopt liabilities under contracts or leases, or to abandon assets in the form of ownership of corporeal moveables, Scots law does not recognise any power in an insolvency administrator to refuse to deal with ownership of immoveable property situated in Scotland. It was argued that preventing an insolvency administrator from disclaiming assets such as ownership of land would lead to a deemed adoption of environmental liabilities, creating a *de facto* insolvency preference for environmental liabilities. Such a preference, it was argued, had no statutory basis and would amount to a grave breach of the *pari passu* principle. The Second Division rejected that argument. As it stands, therefore, Scots insolvency law allows an insolvency administrator, in a functional sense, to deal with all the bankrupt's liabilities (by adoption), but only some of the company's assets (by refusal to adopt): namely personal rights and rights of ownership held in corporeal moveables. The exclusion of ownership of land from an insolvency administrator's powers is unexplained and, perhaps, unexplainable. There are, of course, strong policy arguments to be had. But in the absence of legislation the courts, over and again, have returned to the central principle of *paritas creditorum*.[248]

---

244 Compare, in England, 1986 Act, s 178(4)(a).
245 The Lord Ordinary in *Scottish Coal* at paras [28] and [76] referred to the provisions on *Dereliktion* under §928 *BGB* (*Aufgabe*). But that provision deals with the German equivalent of abandonment. The German equivalent to disclaimer is rather an insolvency administrator's power to disclaim (*Freigabe*) under §32(3) *Insolvenzordnung*. Whereas abandonment (*Aufgabe*) of ownership of land by a solvent owner under the BGB takes effect only on registration, disclaimer (*Freigabe*) under the *InsO* by an insolvency administrator is immediately effective: subsequent registration is declaratory of what has already happened.
246 1986 Act, s 178(4)(b). The principle has been recognised in Scottish cases on *confusio*: *Murray's Trs v Trs of St Margaret's Convent* (1906) 8 F 1109 at 1117 per Lord Kinnear; *Brookfield Developments Ltd v Keeper of the Registers of Scotland* 1989 SLT (Lands Tr) 105 at 110. See too *Mitchell v Rodger* (1834) 12 S 802.
247 [2013] CSIH 108, 2014 SLT 259.
248 *Re Nortel GmbH (in administration)* [2013] UKSC 52 at paras [100]–[114] per Lord Neuberger. The Supreme Court of Canada, in a Quebec case in many respects similar to *Scottish Coal*, lucidly focuses the policy issues. The SCC held in favour of the *pari passu* principle: *R v AbitibiBowater Inc* [2012] 3 SCR 443 at para [40] per Dechamps J: '[the Crown's] position would result not only in a super-priority, but in the acceptance of a "third-party-pay" principle in place of the polluter-pay principle'. Dechamps J's opinion repays reading.

CHALLENGABLE TRANSACTIONS: THE ACTIO PAULIANA[249]

14.84 'Wherever there is commerce, there must be bankrupts', the eighteenth-century judge, Lord Coalston, once observed; adding that, 'wherever there are bankrupts, there will be attempts to disappoint the law'.[250] Transactions entered into by an insolvent verging on insolvency (*vergens ad inopiam*) to the detriment of his creditors are challengeable at common law, as well as under statute. As Bell observed:

> From the moment of insolvency a debtor is bound to act as the mere trustee, or rather as the *negotiorum gestor*, of his creditors, who thenceforward have the exclusive interest in his funds. He may, as long as he is permitted, continue his trade, with the intention of making gain for his creditors and for himself; but his funds are no longer his own, which he can be entitled secretly to set apart for his own use, or to give away as caprice or affection may dictate. This is the great principle on which the creditors of an insolvent debtor are, by the law of Scotland, entitled to proceed in detecting embezzlement.[251]

Two classic examples of fraudulent transactions voidable at the instance of a creditor or the liquidator or administrator,[252] as the case may be, are gratuitous alienations and unfair preferences. It is worth emphasising, however, that such transactions remain capable of challenge at common law.[253] And, unlike under the statutory provisions, there are no time limits for challenging transactions at common law: this is consistent with the rule that obligations arising out of fraudulent breach of trust are imprescriptible[254] and to which a discharge from bankruptcy does not extend.[255]

Gratuitous alienations

14.85 A gratuitous alienation is the classic 'attempt to disappoint the law'. A company, seeing the writing on the wall, seeks to transfer assets, often to connected persons, without adequate consideration. Any preinsolvency creditor or a liquidator or an administrator is therefore entitled to reduce such transactions as being prejudicial to the general

---

249 The creditors' right to challenge can be traced to the *actio Pauliana* of Roman law and the term is often used internationally to describe equivalent actions in other legal systems: e.g. *l'action paulienne* or *Paulianische Anfechtung*. For the history, see the opinion of Advocate General Ruiz-Jabaro Colomer in Case C-339/07 *Seagon v Deko Marty Belgium NV* [2009] ECR I-767, [2009] 1 WLR 2168.

250 *Mansfield, Hunter & Co v Macilmun* (1770) Mor 'Bill of Exchange' App 1, No 1; Hailes 350 at 351. Cf. n 22 above per Lord Walker.

251 Bell, *Commentaries* (7th edn 1870) II, 170, approved in *Nordic Travel Ltd v Scotprint Ltd* 1980 SC 1 and in *Johnstone v Peter H Irvine Ltd* 1984 SLT 209.

252 1986 Act, s 242(1) and (7) (gratuitous alienations); and s 243(4) and (6) (unfair preferences).

253 See ss 242(7) and 243(6) and *Bank of Scotland, Petrs* 1987 SC 234 affd 1988 SC 245.

254 See para **14.66**.

255 Bankruptcy (Scotland) Act 1985, s 55(2)(c).

body of creditors for whose benefit these assets, or their proceeds, ought to have been retained. There are two periods during which gratuitous alienations may be challenged. The standard period is two years. But where the transferee is an 'associate',[256] the relevant suspect period in respect of which the liquidator or administrator may examine alienations is five years. If the alienation becomes 'completely effectual' within one of those periods, it was made on a 'relevant day'. In terms of the Act, all 'alienations' (which term includes a transfer, discharge or renunciation of a patrimonial right belonging to the company) on a relevant day are challengeable. A court will grant reduction or an order for restoration unless the defender can demonstrate that one of the defences has been fulfilled. The defences are that (a) the company assets were greater than its liabilities; or (b) the alienation was made for adequate consideration; or (c) the alienation was a conventional or charitable gift which, in all the circumstances, it was reasonable for the company to make.[257]

14.86 The relevant date is calculated from the date on which the suspect transaction became 'completely effectual'.[258] For example, suppose a company disponed heritable property on 20 January 2007 to an associate company for no consideration. That disposition was registered on 10 January 2009. The transferor company is wound up on 5 January 2014. The liquidator would be able to seek reduction of the disposition because the disposition became 'completely effectual' only on registration and registration was within the five-year period.[259] An action of reduction is brought at the instance of the liquidator or administrator as the case may be, and by action not petition.[260] Where the legal basis of a payment is reduced, the liquidator or administrator will be able to seek either repayment from the transferee on the basis of unjustified enrichment[261] or an order under the Act for restoration of the property.[262] An alienation is normally a transfer of an asset. But the dis-

---

256 Defined in Bankruptcy (Scotland) Act 1985, s 74(2) for natural persons to mean 'relative' which is further defined in subsection (4); s 74(5A)–(5C) provides, in broad terms, that a company is an associate of another company if it is controlled by the same person. Cf. 1986 Act, s 435(6).

257 1986 Act, s 242(4).

258 1986 Act, s 242(3). See e.g. *Craiglaw Developments Ltd v Gordon Wilson & Co* 1997 SC 356; *Jackson v Royal Bank of Scotland plc* 2002 SLT 1123; *Accountant in Bankruptcy v Orr* 2005 SLT 1019.

259 See n 262 below.

260 *Joint Administrators of Prestonpans (Trading) Ltd, Petrs* [2012] CSOH 184, 2013 SLT 138.

261 *Stak Realty Group Co Ltd (in administration) v McKenna* [2010] CSOH 29; *Joint Administrators of Questway Ltd v Simpson* [2012] CSOH 107.

262 An order for restoration under s 242(4) may be particularly useful where the asset alienated was ownership of land in order to avoid the difficulties of giving effect in the Land Register to a reduction. The liquidator or administrator will seek retransfer of the property to the company, failing which a warrant authorising the Deputy Principal Clerk of Session to execute and deliver the necessary dispositions: see e.g. *Joint Administrators of Oceancrown Ltd v Stonegale Ltd* [2013] CSOH 189, para [48].

charge, without consideration of patrimonial value,[263] of a good security or personal right to payment held by the company may also amount to an alienation. The relevant date for considering whether there was a shortfall in patrimonial value is the date on which the attacked transaction was entered into;[264] where consideration is represented by the transferee undertaking an obligation, it can constitute consideration only if it is undertaken as the counterpart of the alienation.[265] Agreements to pay 'as soon as I have money'[266] or 'when funds are available' or 'with the consent of the debtor' are not normally considered to amount to an enforceable obligation to pay on which a defence to an action of reduction may be founded.

Unfair preferences

14.87   The law on unfair preferences is said to be based on the notional distinction between formal insolvency (such as commencement of winding-up or administration) and constructive insolvency which is deemed, by statute, to have occurred at any earlier date.[267] This is often referred to as the 'suspect period'. Under s 243(1), the suspect period is the six months before the commencement of the winding-up. An unfair preference often involves the payment of a genuine debt to a genuine creditor. The transaction is attacked rather because, in the suspect period, that creditor has received payment of his debt before it was actually due. So in a case where a director of a company transferred £9,000 to himself in his capacity as a creditor of the company and, on the same day, resolved to wind up the company, it is likely that, in the absence of documentary evidence demonstrating that this was indeed a cash payment in respect of a presently due debt, it would amount to an unfair preference.[268] Similarly, where a director has acted as cautioner for a company and been called upon to pay the company's debts, payments made during the suspect period to the director in relief of his cautionary obligation are likely to amount to a preference.[269] There may be an overlap between s 242 and s 243. Suppose that a petition for Alpha Ltd's liquidation was presented on 1 June. On 14 February Alpha Ltd con-

263 *MacFadyen's Tr v MacFadyen* 1994 SC 416 at 421–422 per Lord McCluskey; *Matheson's Tr v Matheson* 1992 SLT 685 at 686G–H per Lord Marnoch (Ordinary): 'the giving of "consideration" involve[s] either the discharge of an existing obligation or an exchange of new obligations'.

264 *Liquidator of Letham Grange Development Co Ltd v Foxworth Investments Ltd* [2013] CSIH 13, 2013 SLT 445 at para [75] per Lady Paton (revd; see n 265 below).

265 *Henderson (Liquidator of Letham Grange Development Co Ltd) v Foxworth Investments Ltd* [2014] UKSC 41 at para [25] per Lord Reed.

266 *Rose v Falconer* (1868) 6 Macph 960.

267 Cf. Bell, *Commentaries* II, 193.

268 *Liquidator of 3G Design Engineering Ltd v White* [2012] CSOH 124, revd [2013] CSIH 20.

269 *Mitchell v Rodger* (1834) 12 S 802 followed in *Anderson v Dickens* [2008] CSOH 134, 2009 SCLR 609 at paras [73] and [93] per Temporary Judge Sir David Edward QC. See too *Baillie Marshall Ltd (in liquidation) v Avian Communications Ltd* 2002 SLT 189.

tracted to sell land to Bravo Ltd. Bravo was to pay £10,000 for the land. The market value of the land is £1 million. The transaction settled on 1 March and the disposition was registered on 14 March. The transaction is considered to have been a gratuitous alienation to the extent of £990,000.[270]

Payments in cash, ordinary course of trade and *nova debita*

14.88 The general rule in s 243 is that, in the suspect period, a company may not confer preferential treatment in favour of a creditor to the prejudice of the general body of creditors. Section 243(2) contains a number of exceptions: (a) transactions in the ordinary course of trade; (b) a payment in cash for a debt which, when it was paid, had become payable, unless the transaction was collusive; and (c) a transaction whereby the parties to it undertake reciprocal obligations (sometimes known as the *nova debita* principle).[271]

14.89 The onus is on any defender seeking to demonstrate that any of the above exceptions apply. A pursuer may not even need to lead any evidence if little in the way of evidence is offered by the defender, since the defender will thus fail to discharge the evidential burden.[272] A major difficulty is that in many, perhaps most, cases where the defences are pled, they cannot be made out because neither the insolvent company nor the transferees kept any records documenting the transactions which, later, those self-same parties, when called as defenders, seek to set up. It is often on insolvency that failures by former directors of a company to comply with their statutory obligation to keep proper records is thrown into sharp focus. The courts are generally unsympathetic to after-the-event attempts by such directors to place a commercially justifiable construction on the attacked transactions.[273]

Floating charges as preferences

14.90 The Insolvency Act also contains provisions on the enforceability of floating charges granted within the relevant suspect period.[274] The relevant suspect period is two years prior to the onset of insolvency where the floating charge is created in favour of connected persons; and 12 months from the onset of insolvency where the person in whose favour the charge is created is not a connected person. Where the person in whose favour the charge is granted is not a connected person the charge may be avoided only where, at the time the charge was created, the

---

270　1986 Act, s 242(6).

271　In *Nicoll v Steelpress (Supplies) Ltd* 1992 SC 119, the Inner House held that nothing less than full patrimonial value would found a relevant *novum debitum* defence.

272　As in *Short's Tr v Chung* 1991 SLT 472; *McLuckie Bros Ltd v Newhouse Contracts Ltd* 1993 SLT 641; and *Stak Realty Group Co Ltd (in administration) v McKenna* [2010] CSOH 29.

273　See e.g. authorities cited in n 261 above.

274　1986 Act, s 245. This provision applies to Scots and English law alike.

company was unable to pay its debts in terms of s 123, or became unable to pay its debts within the meaning of s 123 as a result of the creation of the charge.[275] There is no statutory definition of 'floating charge' and it thus 'bears the meaning attributed to it by judicial decision'.[276] Avoidance under s 245 is partial rather than catholic in effect. The charge is 'invalid except to the extent of the aggregate of':[277] (a) the value of so much of the consideration for the creation of the charge as consists of money paid, or goods or services supplied, to the company at the same time as, or after, the creation of the charge; (b) the value of so much of that consideration as consists of the discharge or reduction, at the same time as, or after, the creation of the charge, of any debt of the company; plus (c) interest.

14.91   In order to understand what the words 'at the time of or subsequently to the creation of . . . the charge' mean, a practical example is required. In *Re Shoe Lace Ltd*,[278] a Jersey company, Shoe Lace, had sought financial support from its parent company. The parent provided payments of £300,000 in April, £50,000 in May, £75,000 in June and £11,500 in July 1990. A debenture (including a floating charge) was created in July and with particulars registered at Companies House, within 21 days, in August 1990. Shoe Lace Ltd resolved that it was unable to pay its debts in September, sold its entire business and undertaking to a new company, Shoe Hut, and used the proceeds to pay, among others, all the debts due to its parent as floating charge holder. Shoe Lace went into liquidation in November 1990. The liquidator sought repayment of the sums paid to the parent company on the basis that the floating charge was invalid to the extent of the payments made in April, May, June and July. The directors of the company argued that the sums advanced to Shoe Lace and the indebtedness it incurred, representing the consideration for the charge, occurred 'at the same time as' the charge was created. Hoffmann J said this:[279]

> The degree of contemporaneity which such words connote must depend upon the context. It might not be unreasonable to say that two species of dinosaur became extinct 'at the same time' when millions of years separates their last known representatives. On the other hand, one would not say that the winner of a 100 metres race crossed the tape at the same time as the runner who came second, even though they were separated by less than a tenth of a second. The question, I think, is whether a businessman having knowledge of the kind of time limits imposed by the Insolvency and Companies Acts and using ordinary language would say that the payments had been made at the same time as the execution of the debenture. In my judgment no businessman would use such language of the payments made in this case.

275 1986 Act, s 245(3) and (4). For s 123, see para **14.24** above.
276 *Re Spectrum Plus Ltd (in liquidation)* [2005] 2 AC 680 at para [98] per Lord Scott.
277 1986 Act, s 245(2).
278 *Power v Sharp Investments, Re Shoe Lace Ltd* [1992] BCC 367.
279 At 369–370.

14.92 That view was affirmed by the Court of Appeal which held that Parliament included the words 'at the same time as, or after,' in the legislation 'for the purpose of excluding from the exemption moneys paid to the company before the creation of the charge, even though they were paid in consideration for the charge'.[280]

Clayton's Case and insolvency

14.93 Suppose, at January 2014, a company has a bank overdraft of £100,000. The overdraft is unsecured. The bank is concerned about the position and, in June 2014, the company creates a floating charge in favour of the bank. In July, the company pays £40,000 into the account, but a few days later instructs a payment out of £40,000. In November the company goes into insolvent liquidation. In an application of the rule in *Clayton's Case*,[281] it has been held that the payment, after the floating charge was created, of £40,000 must be taken to have extinguished the earliest debit; moreover, the post-floating charge advance by the bank of £40,000 is permitted post-floating charge consideration. In the result, therefore, the floating charge may be considered to be invalid under s 245 only in respect of the remaining £60,000.[282] It has been suggested that the new value provided by the bank post-floating charge has benefitted the business and the bank should be entitled to enjoy, to that extent, the benefit of the floating charge.[283] Nonetheless there is force in the view that the rule in *Clayton's Case* is based on an outdated understanding of a current account;[284] a floating charge for pre-creation indebtedness of £100,000, having been struck at by s 245, cannot be saved retrospectively by an application of *Clayton's Case* to post-creation payments; while the very grant of the floating charge, on the facts given in the example, may be considered to be an unfair preference, with the result that a court would reduce the floating charge.[285]

MAINTENANCE OF CAPITAL AND UNLAWFUL DISTRIBUTIONS

14.94 In corporate insolvency there is an overlap between the rules of insolvency law with the substantive rules of company law designed to protect creditors. As a general rule, company law imposes conditions on the circumstances in which a company may deal with its capital (the

---

280 [1993] BCC 609 at 619 per Sir Christopher Slade.
281 *Devaynes v Noble* (1816) 35 ER 781, for which see paras **8.36** and **8.37** above.
282 *Re Yeovil Glove Co Ltd* [1965] Ch 148.
283 Goode, *Corporate Insolvency Law* (n 147) para 13.122.
284 D Fox, *Property Rights in Money* (2008) para 7.64: '[if] it is accepted that a current account with a bank does not consist in a sequence of individuated debts, the foundation for applying the rule in *Clayton's Case* . . . can no longer stand'.
285 1986 Act, s 243(5).

'maintenance of capital' principle).[286] Companies may make distributions, by way of dividends, only out of profits available for distribution. The Companies Acts expressly prohibit, for instance, distributions of capital that have not been properly declared as a dividend (the 'unlawful distributions rule');[287] and at common law disguised returns of capital to shareholders are prohibited, even where the recipients are not shareholders, but corporate vehicles controlled, directly or indirectly, by the same person who controls the company making the distribution.[288]

JUDICIAL FACTORS AND PARTNERSHIPS

14.95 The Insolvency Act provisions which cover unregistered companies apply also to associations.[289] But those provisions cannot be invoked to confer on a Scottish court jurisdiction to wind up a partnership or limited partnership under the Insolvency Act: a conscious decision has been taken to subject Scottish partnerships and limited partnerships to the bankruptcy regime.[290] One exception to that general rule is found in respect of partnerships or limited partnerships which are regulated by the Financial Conduct Authority: in that case, the FCA can petition to have partnerships and limited partnerships wound up under the Insolvency Act regime.[291] Judicial factors have already been encountered in the context of partnerships. And it is, in principle, possible to have a judicial factor appointed in respect of a company's estate.[292] But judicial factors appointed to companies for reasons other than insolvency are not 'liquidators' for the purposes of the EUIR. Judicial factors are most commonly appointed, for insolvency reasons, to the bankrupt estates of a partnership or limited partnership or trust. A judicial factor appointed to such an estate because of bankruptcy enjoys the powers of a 'liquidator' for the purposes of the EUIR.[293]

---

286 The *locus classicus* is *Trevor v Whitworth* (1887) 12 App Cas 409 at 423–424 per Lord Watson.

287 Companies Act 2006, s 847.

288 *Aveling Barford Ltd v Perion Ltd* (1989) 5 BCC 677; *Progress Property Co Ltd v Moore* [2010] UKSC 55, [2011] 1 WLR 1.

289 1986 Act, s 220: 'For the purposes of this Part "unregistered company" includes any association and any company, with the exception of a company registered under the Companies Act 2006 in any part of the United Kingdom'.

290 *Smith, Petr* 1999 SLT (Sh Ct) 5. As the sheriff pointed out, the Scottish courts have, in the past, had jurisdiction to subject partnerships and limited partnerships to the corporate insolvency regime.

291 See, for instance, Financial Services and Markets Act 2000, s 367.

292 Either at common law or under the Companies Act 2006, s 996. See e.g. *Fraser, Petr* 1971 SLT 146 approved in *Weir v Rees* 1991 SLT 345 (which involved a public company). See too *McGuinness v Black (No 2)* 1990 SC 21.

293 EUIR Art 2(b) and Art 18.

RESTORATION TO THE REGISTER

14.96 Companies and LLPs are subject to various filing obligations. Failure to comply may result in the Registrar of Companies assuming that the company or LLP is not carrying on business and striking it from the register.[294] It is possible for the Registrar to fulfil his information obligations but the company or LLP or its officers are somehow not informed of the dissolution. In such a case, an application may be made to restore the company or LLP to the register. In other cases, an application for restoration may need to be made because, some time after the company or LLP has been wound up, a creditor – often a personal injuries claimant, such as a former employee of a company who, many years later, develops an industrial disease – wishes to sue the company or its insurers; or a company in a group has been wound up, but it has subsequently been established that the company continued to hold assets at the date of dissolution which had not been dealt with in the liquidation.

14.97 There are two procedures available for restoring the company to the register: (a) the administrative procedure; and (b) the court procedure. The administrative procedure is available only on the application of (former) members or directors of the company. There are three conditions: (i) immediately prior to dissolution the company was carrying on business; (ii) Crown consent is obtained where property has vested in the Crown as *bona vacantia*; and (iii) delivery of all necessary documentation and records.[295] Under both the administrative and the judicial procedure, the application should be made within six years of the company having been dissolved.[296]

14.98 The judicial procedure is more flexible. The general ground for seeking restoration is that it is just to do so.[297] The application may be brought by anyone appearing to the court to have an interest.[298] As a general rule, the six-year time limit also applies.[299] But there is an important exception to that rule where the purpose of the restoration is in order to bring an action for damages for personal injuries: in that case there is no time limit for bringing a restoration application.[300]

14.99 'The general effect of an order by the court for restoration to the

---

294 2006 Act, s 1000.
295 2006 Act, s 1025.
296 2006 Act, s 1024(4).
297 2006 Act, s 1031(1)(c).
298 2006 Act, s 1029(2). Express mention is made, for example, of those with a 'potential legal claim against the company'; of the trustees of any employee pension fund; and of the holders of an interest in land which is burdened by a right held by the company or which benefited from an obligation owed by the company: s 1029(2)(d). A party who would be liable to indemnify a restored defender, has an interest to oppose restoration: *City of Edinburgh Council, Petr* [2010] CSOH 20.
299 2006 Act, s 1030(4).
300 2006 Act, s 1030(1) and (4).

register is that the company is deemed to have continued in existence as if it had not been dissolved or struck off the register'.[301] In other words, the order has retrospective effect. Providing an order has been made restoring the company to the register, therefore, any acts purportedly done by the company will be deemed to have been done by the company;[302] similarly any actions raised against the company before the order for restoration will be deemed to have been raised against the company.[303]

RESTRUCTURING: SCHEMES OF ARRANGEMENT

14.100 A Scheme of Arrangement ('**SoA**') is a useful restructuring tool.[304] It is not limited to insolvent restructuring and is often used in cases of solvent restructuring too.[305] The law is now found in Part 26 of Companies Act 2006,[306] which applies too, with modifications, to LLPs[307] and to industrial and provident societies.[308] The legislation is skeletal: there is nothing in the legislation which prescribes the content of a scheme. It is for the company's lawyers to draft the scheme which will be presented to the court to approve. Interested parties must receive notice of the proposed scheme and they must consent to it. But consent is not required from those whose interests the SoA does not affect: thus, for example, a SoA which gives effect to a takeover offer to the shareholders and which has no effect on the creditors does not require the consent of the creditors.

14.101 The crucial point about a SoA, which explains why a company may wish to go to the expense of presenting one, is that the consent of only 75 per cent of each class of members or creditors is required.[309] Once 75 per cent is obtained and the court approves the scheme, the

301 2006 Act, s 1032(1).
302 Such as presentation of particulars for registration of a charge: *Hounslow Badminton Association v Registrar of Companies* [2013] EWHC 2961 (Ch).
303 *Peaktone Ltd v Joddrell* [2012] EWCA Civ 1035, [2013] 1 WLR 784.
304 Only an outline may be given here. For fuller treatment, see e.g. P L Davies and S Worthington (eds), *Gower and Davies Principles of Modern Company Law* (9th edn, 2012) ch 29; Goode, *Corporate Insolvency Law* (n 147), para 12.12.
305 As in *Scottish Lion Insurance Co Ltd, Petr* 2010 SC 349.
306 2006 Act, s 895. The provisions can be traced to the Joint Stock Companies Arrangement Act 1870 (33 & 34 Vict, c 104), s 2 (which applied only to arrangements with creditors).
307 Limited Liability Partnerships (Application of Companies Act 2006) Regulations 2009, reg 45.
308 Industrial and Provident Societies and Credit Unions (Arrangements, Reconstruction and Administration) Order 2014 (SI 2014/229) art 2(2) and Sch 2.
309 The classic definition of a 'class' is found in *Sovereign Life Assurance Co Ltd (in liquidation) v Dodd* [1892] 2 QB 573 at 583 per Bowen LJ: 'those persons whose rights are not so dissimilar as to make it impossible for them to consult together with a view to their common interest'. For an application of that definition to modern documentation, see *Redwood Master Fund Ltd v TD Bank Europe Ltd* [2006] 1 BCLC 149.

minority is bound. Importantly, however, there must be a 'meeting' of the class. A 'meeting' at which only one member of the class purports to attend and vote is not, however, a meeting at all.[310] A SoA becomes effective not on the court sanctioning the scheme, but only on the delivery of the court order to the Registrar of Companies.[311]

14.102 A SoA has three distinct stages. The first is an application to the court to call the requisite meetings of members or creditors or both as the case may be. The second is to hold the meetings to allow the members or creditors to vote on the proposed scheme. The third is for the petitioning company to apply to the court to sanction the scheme.[312]

14.103 The CA 2006 contains no detailed procedural provisions about notice of, and procedure to be adopted at, meetings and the like, so the requisite notice periods will depend on the content of the scheme.[313] Depending on the resolutions required, the notice periods set out in the articles of association must be complied with,[314] as must other notice periods set out in the CA 2006, if these provisions are invoked. So if the SoA proposes, as part of the scheme, that the company's share capital is to be reduced, the notice periods set out in the CA 2006 for securing a reduction of capital must be complied with.[315] But any notice of a meeting to consider the terms of a proposed SoA must be accompanied by an explanatory statement setting out the proposed scheme and its effects. And if the information in that explanatory statement becomes inaccurate and that information might affect the way shareholders vote, corrected information must be communicated to the members or creditors as the case may be.

14.104 A SoA can be between:

- a company and its members;
- a company and its creditors; or
- a company and its members and its creditors.

14.105 The SoA must, however, be in the nature of a 'compromise or arrangement' with creditors or members. Neither term is defined in the Act, although it is accepted that the two terms are not synonyms.[316] An arrangement which does not involve members giving up any rights may still be an 'arrangement' for SoA purposes between the members and the

---

310 *Re Altitude Scaffolding Ltd* [2006] BCC 904.
311 2006 Act, s 899(4).
312 *Re The British Aviation Insurance Co Ltd* [2006] BCC 14 at para [54] per Lewison J.
313 But see *Practice Statement: Schemes of Arrangements with Creditors* [2002] 1 WLR 1345 which has been referred to with approval in Scotland: *Scottish Lion Insurance Co Ltd, Petr* 2011 SC 534 at para [5].
314 So if the SoA proposes a change to the articles, the notice periods for proposing a resolution to change the articles – set out in s 307 and s 307A – must be complied with.
315 2006 Act, s 641 ff.
316 *Re Guardian Assurance Co* [1917] Ch 341.

company because, for instance, it is proposed that the membership, on the SoA being approved, will change.[317] But if members or creditors are to give up their rights, they cannot do so for no consideration: there must be 'some element of accommodation' or 'give and take' on each side.[318] The scheme may extend to releasing a third party guarantor, not otherwise party to the scheme, from its obligations.[319]

Court consideration of SoA

14.106 There are at least two stages involved in the court's consideration of sanctioning a scheme of arrangement. The first is a question of jurisdiction: have the statutory formalities been complied with in such a way as to confer a jurisdiction on the court to consider the scheme? If the formalities have not been complied with, it may not be competent for the court even to consider sanctioning the scheme. The second stage for consideration assumes that the court does have jurisdiction. At this stage the court addresses the question of whether, in broad terms, the scheme is fair and does not oppress those who did not vote for it.[320] In deciding whether to approve the Scheme, the court will consider whether:[321]

● the scheme is reasonable;
● those voting were representative of each class; and
● each class voted in good faith.

14.107 Difficulties can arise with the valuation of the claim of contingent creditors. This may be a matter of considerable practical importance given that the value of a creditor's claims is likely to determine its voting rights.[322]

SECTION 110 REORGANISATION

14.108 The 1986 Act, s 110 allows a company, on liquidation, to transfer all or part of its business and undertaking to another company, or LLP,[323] in consideration of shares in the transferee company or membership of the transferee LLP. Sometimes this is used as a form of 'de-merger' restructuring. As the specialist texts point out, however, 'it rarely has anything to do with insolvency, because the creditors have to be paid in full and almost invariably the winding up is a members' voluntary winding up'.[324]

---

317 *Re Savoy Hotel Ltd* [1981] Ch 351.
318 *Re NFU Development Trusts Ltd* [1972] 1 WLR 1548 at 1555C per Brightman J.
319 *Re La Seda de Barcelona SA* [2010] EWHC 1364, [2011] 1 BCLC 555.
320 *Re British Aviation Insurance Co Ltd* [2006] BCC 14.
321 *Re Anglo-Continental Supply Co Ltd* [1922] 2 Ch 723.
322 *Scottish Lion Insurance Co Ltd, Petr* 2011 SC 534.
323 1986 Act, s 110(1)(b).
324 Goode, *Corporate Insolvency Law*, para 1.50; see too *Gower and Davies Principles of Modern Company Law*, para 29.18.

Chapter 15

Alternative Dispute Resolution

INTRODUCTION

15.01 This chapter deals with the different forms of alternative dispute resolution ('ADR'). There is no single definition of ADR. At its widest it can encompass all types of dispute resolution which are not litigation. ADR can be a contractual form of dispute resolution where parties have contracted, either at the outset of their legal relations or when a dispute arises, to have their dispute dealt with in a particular way. It can be consensual or statutory. It includes the submission to and determination of disputes by third parties. It also includes non-adjudicative processes where the third party may be used as a facilitator rather than a dispute resolver. The types of ADR which are covered in this chapter are arbitration, expert determination, adjudication, and mediation.

ARBITRATION

What is arbitration?

15.02 Arbitration is a method by which parties may have their disputes determined conclusively by a third party. The third party is known as the arbitrator. In Scotland this third party was known as an arbiter until 2010 when the Arbitration (Scotland) Act 2010 ('2010 Act') introduced what was previously the English term 'arbitrator'. The arbitrator exercises a judicial function. Most arbitrations are based on an agreement between the parties to submit their disputes to that chosen method of dispute resolution. That agreement has the effect of excluding determination of that dispute by a court of law.

15.03 The arbitration agreement[1] is an agreement to submit present or future disputes to arbitration. It can be as simple as:

> If any dispute or difference of any kind whatsoever shall arise between the parties to the contract in relation to any matter or thing arising out

---

1 Arbitration (Scotland) Act 2010, s 4.

of or in connection with the contract the same shall be referred to and settled by arbitration.[2]

It often forms part of the contract which governs parties' relations generally. Arbitration agreements are to be found in many types of commercial contract although an arbitration agreement may also be entered into when a dispute arises. Arbitration agreements are regularly to be found in partnership agreements, leases, other contracts related to heritable property, and building and engineering contracts. An advantage of arbitration over litigation is that a technical person skilled in the area of the dispute can be the arbitrator. An arbitration is private: it enables parties to keep their quarrels out of the public eye.

15.04 An arbitration agreement need not be in writing although it may be hard to evidence otherwise. There are no formalities around the form such a written arbitration agreement should take.

Some arbitration agreements only cover certain types of disputes leaving the remainder to be determined by the courts or some other specified means. Where the arbitration agreement forms part of another agreement, the arbitration provisions themselves will be treated as if they were a separate agreement: i.e. the arbitration provisions survive termination of the underlying contract.[3] An arbitrator may rule on whether there is a valid arbitration agreement[4] and the extent of his jurisdiction including whether a claim that has been referred to him has prescribed.[5]

The legal framework for arbitration

15.05 Arbitrations in Scotland are regulated by the 2010 Act which applies to arbitrations which commenced on or after 7 June 2010.[6] The 2010 Act applies to domestic arbitration, arbitration between parties residing in different parts of the United Kingdom, and to international arbitration.

15.06 Prior to the 2010 Act, Scots arbitration law derived primarily from case law with very limited statutory provision. This gave rise to uncertainty as to what was the law of arbitration and certain gaps in its application. The UNCITRAL Model Law on International Commercial Arbitration was adopted into Scots law for international commercial

---

2 An arbitration agreement may be much longer than this. It can stipulate the body which will nominate an arbitrator. This may be as a fall-back in the event that parties cannot agree upon the identity of an arbitrator. It may also set out the desired qualifications of the arbitrator and any applicable institutional rules, that is the rules published from time to time by various arbitration appointing bodies.

3 2010 Act, s 5(1)–(2).

4 See Scottish Arbitration Rules (2010 Act, Sch 1), r 19.

5 See *Orkney Islands Council v Charles Brand Ltd* 2002 SLT 100.

6 Arbitration (Scotland) Act 2010 (Commencement No 1 and Transitional Provisions) Order 2010 (SSI 2010/195).

arbitrations in 1990.[7] An arbitration was international if parties had at the time of entering into the arbitration agreement (i) their places of business in separate states; or (ii) one party's habitual residence was in a different state; or (iii) the place of arbitration or place of closest connection to the subject matter of the dispute was in a different state from that of the parties' places of business.[8] However, there continued to be a demand for a modern arbitration law for domestic arbitration. It took until 2010 for such legislation to come into effect and this is the Arbitration (Scotland) Act 2010.

15.07 The general principles of the 2010 Act include fairness, party autonomy, and limited court intervention.[9] Anyone construing the 2010 Act is to have regard to these founding principles when doing so.

15.08 There must be a law of the arbitration agreement 'whose job it is to administer, control or decide what control there is to be over the arbitration'.[10]

The law of the arbitration agreement is not automatically the same law as the proper law of the contract which contains the arbitration agreement. Where the parties to the contract in which the arbitration agreement is contained are all based in Scotland it is likely the law of the arbitration agreement will be the same as the proper law. However, the parties may have chosen another system of law for the arbitration. They may do so by the use of provisions such as 'the place of the arbitration shall be Scotland' or 'the seat of the arbitration is Glasgow, Scotland'. Where an arbitration is seated in Scotland, section 6 of the 2010 Act provides that, unless the parties agree otherwise, the arbitration agreement is governed by Scots law. The reference to place or 'seat' will therefore usually determine the law of the arbitration agreement.[11]

An arbitration is seated in Scotland where the arbitration agreement states that it is; or the arbitration agreement provides for a third party to determine the seat and that third party has determined Scotland; or the court or arbitrator determines Scotland is the seat.[12] Where an arbitration is 'seated' in Scotland the Scottish Arbitration Rules apply.[13]

---

7 Law Reform (Miscellaneous Provisions) (Scotland) Act 1990, s 66 and Sch 7.

8 Model Law, art 1(3)(b)(ii).

9 2010 Act, s 1.

10 *Braes of Doune Wind Farm (Scotland) Ltd v Alfred McAlpine Business Services Ltd* [2008] EWHC 426 (TCC) per Mr Justice Akenhead at para 15.

11 See however *Braes of Doune Wind Farm (Scotland) Ltd v Alfred McAlpine Business Services Ltd* (n 10) where, unusually, an expression that the seat of an arbitration would be Glasgow did not prevent the court from determining that the *lex fori* was England because of other terms within the contract which could be said to be inconsistent with the seat being in Glasgow.

12 2010 Act, s 3.

13 2010 Act, s 7.

15.09 The Scottish Arbitration Rules ('SARs') are a set of procedural rules contained within Schedule 1 to the 2010 Act which set out the powers of the arbitrator as well as the circumstances in which the courts may intervene in the process or hear an appeal. Some of these rules may, by express agreement, be modified or disapplied. They are called the 'default rules' and are marked as such within Schedule 1 with a 'D'. All other rules are mandatory and are marked with an 'M'.[14]

Certain statutes provide for arbitration.[15] They may have their own arbitration rules and the SARs only apply to such arbitrations to the extent that they do not conflict.

15.10 Where legal proceedings have been raised in respect of a matter which is the subject of an arbitration agreement, either party to the arbitration agreement may apply to the court to sist the proceedings. The court is obliged to do so unless the applicant has submitted a defence to the substantive nature of the claim or acted in such a way as to indicate that that party wished to have the dispute resolved in legal proceedings (a form of personal bar).[16] This is regardless of whether the arbitration is seated in Scotland.

Appointing the arbitrator

15.11 Only an individual may be appointed as an arbitrator. An arbitrator must be aged over 16 and not an incapable adult under the Adults with Incapacity (Scotland) Act 2000. The arbitration agreement may identify an individual or individuals as arbitrators. More commonly it may identify a body which will appoint an arbitrator. It may also describe the qualifications or experience required of an arbitrator.

15.12 A number of bodies are authorised as arbitral appointments referees by the Scottish Ministers for the purposes of the SARs. The Arbitral Appointment Referee (Scotland) Order 2010 (SSI 2010/196) lists the bodies which include:

- Agricultural Industries Confederation Limited
- Chartered Institute of Arbitrators
- Dean of the Faculty of Advocates
- Institution of Civil Engineers
- Law Society of Scotland
- Royal Incorporation of Architects in Scotland
- Royal Institution of Chartered Surveyors
- Scottish Agricultural Arbiters and Valuers Association

15.13 Such bodies may nominate arbitrators either where they are stipulated in the arbitration agreement as the appointing body or where the appointment process within the arbitration agreement has broken down. An arbitrator, in accepting an appointment either through agree-

14 2010 Act, ss 8 and 9.
15 See for example the Bankruptcy (Scotland) Act 1985, s 65.
16 2010 Act, s 10.

ment with the parties or nomination by a body, is entering into a contract with the two parties to the arbitration. This contract shall contain his terms and conditions including daily or hourly rates and cancellation fees.

Commencing the arbitration

15.14   Arbitration will normally be commenced by one party serving a notice of arbitration on the other. This is often known as a preliminary notice. There is no set form for such a notice but it should include details of the parties, a description of the underlying contract and the arbitration agreement, and a brief description of the dispute and the claims being made. Its terms are important as it may be the relevant claim for the purposes of interrupting the prescriptive and limitation periods applicable to the rights and obligations in the underlying contract which are in dispute. An arbitration, in respect of which an arbitrator has been appointed, is 'appropriate proceedings' for the purposes of negative and positive prescription.[17]

15.15   The date of judicial interruption for an arbitration in Scotland is the date when the arbitration begins. This is either when parties have agreed it begins under the arbitration agreement or when one party gives the other party notice submitting the claim to arbitration in terms of the arbitration agreement. The notice of arbitration must identify the dispute and claims adequately. For there to be judicial interruption of a claim in an arbitration seated in Scotland, an arbitrator must have been appointed.[18] The interruption continues for the time that the arbitration is ongoing and has the effect of suspending the period of prescription or limitation for the duration of the arbitration.

Duties and obligations of the arbitrator

15.16   An arbitrator must act within the powers afforded to him both by the terms of the arbitration agreement and the applicable SARs as well as those implied by the law of the arbitration. The SARs set out certain of the duties which would otherwise be implied on the basis that the arbitrator is discharging a judicial function, such as the obligation to treat the parties fairly including giving each party a reasonable opportunity to put its case and respond to the other party's case.[19] As arbitration is of a judicial character an arbitrator must not have any interest in the dispute. He must not be biased towards one of the parties. He must be impartial and independent.[20]

15.17   The arbitrator may wish to seek his own expert opinion on any

17 Prescription and Limitation (Scotland) Act 1973, ss 4 and 9 as amended by s 23 of the 2010 Act.
18 2010 Act, s 23.
19 SAR 24(M).
20 SAR 24(1)(a)(M).

matter arising in the arbitration. He has an implied power to obtain the assistance of another person provided that his award is his own opinion and judgement, not that of another.[21] SAR 34(D) allows an arbitrator to obtain such an expert opinion provided that parties are given a reasonable opportunity to make representations on any written opinion and to hear any oral opinion and ask questions of the expert. It would be usual for the arbitrator first to consult with the parties before appointing such an expert.

The arbitration procedure

15.18   The arbitrator is afforded substantial discretion as to the procedure to be followed in the arbitration. Unless the arbitration agreement provides otherwise the arbitrator will determine the admissibility, weight and relevance of any evidence including whether to apply rules of evidence used in legal proceedings or any other rules of evidence.[22] Unless the agreement provides otherwise the arbitrator will be expected to determine the dispute in accordance with the applicable law.[23]

15.19   It will be in the arbitrator's discretion as to whether and to what extent he requires written submissions in the form of pleadings or other types of document or to hold hearings. This is subject to one of the founding principles to conduct the arbitration fairly and impartially.[24] Arbitrations may be conducted as 'documents only' arbitrations if the arbitration agreement so provides or both parties so agree with the arbitrator.

15.20   The arbitrator, if he is subject to SAR 26(D), is obliged to keep information as to the dispute, the proceedings, any award, or civil proceedings relating to the arbitration, confidential. Such an obligation regarding confidentiality may be separately implied at common law, but this rule puts it beyond doubt.

15.21   Another of the founding principles of the 2010 Act is that the object of arbitration is to resolve disputes without unnecessary delay and expense. SAR 25(M) provides that the parties must ensure that the arbitration is conducted without unnecessary delay and without incurring unnecessary expense.

15.22   Section 1 of the 2010 Act provides that the court shall not intervene in an arbitration except as provided for by that Act. These rights to intervene include supporting the arbitration process as it proceeds. For example, an arbitrator as a private judge does not have a power to force a witness to attend any hearing. He has no power to force parties to produce documents or other property relevant to the dispute. The right of the court to make the orders necessary in these circumstances

21 *Caledonian Railway Co v Lockhart* (1860) 22 D (HL) 8.
22 SAR 28(D).
23 SAR 47(D).
24 2010 Act, s 1(a).

was recognised by the common law prior to the 2010 Act but the SARs provide expressly for this through SAR 45(M).

15.23 Unless the arbitration agreement provides otherwise, the court will expect the party seeking any orders for disclosure of documents first to have obtained from the arbitrator a determination of what documents or other evidence should be disclosed under SAR 28(M). In those circumstances an application to the court to make an order to this effect does not need first to have been intimated to the other party.[25]

Resignation of the arbitrator/termination of the arbitration agreement

15.24 An arbitrator's tenure will continue until he has exhausted the reference, i.e. decided all that has been referred to him for determination unless both parties agree that he should be removed or he is removed by the court for a breach of the arbitration agreement or a ground set out in the arbitration agreement.

15.25 The SARs contain certain mandatory rules regarding the circumstances in which an arbitrator may resign or be removed. His tenure may come to an end if he becomes incapable under the Adults with Incapacity (Scotland) Act 2000. On an application to the Outer House of the Court of Session he may be removed where he has not been impartial and independent, has failed to treat the parties fairly, does not have the qualifications it has been agreed by the parties that he should have, or that substantial injustice will be caused by his breaches of the arbitration agreement.[26] A party may lose the right to object to the arbitrator's eligibility to act as arbitrator if it fails to raise the objection timeously and continues to participate in the arbitration.[27]

SAR 15 also provides that a challenge by one of the parties to his appointment under SAR 10 or 12 will entitle him to resign. He may also resign with the agreement of the parties or in those circumstances where the Outer House has authorised his resignation. When an arbitrator's tenure ends prematurely it may have implications for the arbitrator's liability in respect of his conduct and on his entitlement to recovery of his fees and expenses.[28]

Making the award

15.26 The arbitrator's determination is known as the award. The arbitrator may make a part award or, where the arbitration agreement so provides, a provisional award. The extent and nature of the type of determinations the arbitrator may make are dependent on what has

25 *SGL Carbon Fibres Ltd for a petition for an order to disclose documents* [2013] CSOH 21.
26 SARs 12(M), 13(M) and 14(M).
27 SAR 76(M).
28 SAR 16(M).

Alternative dispute resolution

actually been claimed by one or both of the parties. It may be an award of payment or damages. It may be a declarator, for example of a party's legal entitlement.[29] If parties have given the arbitrator the power it may include an order that a deed or other document be rectified or reduced to the extent permitted by the law applicable to the document in question.[30] The arbitrator has the power to award interest on the whole or any part of the sums which have been referred to arbitration even if some of them were paid prior to the award being made.[31]

15.27 The arbitration agreement may stipulate what form any arbitral award should take. For example a common form of award is one which is signed and dated by the arbitrator, and states the seat of the arbitration, when the award is to take effect, and the reasons for the award. SAR 51(1) and (2)(D), if not disapplied, provides what must be included in the award. An arbitrator may refuse to deliver his award until his fees and expenses have been paid in full.[32] However, the court may, on application, regulate that power.

15.28 Once the arbitrator has issued his final award, including dealing with fees and expenses, he is *functus*. He has no power to do anything further in the arbitration except where he has the power conferred by SAR 58(D), when he can correct a typographical or other error in the award which was an accident or omission or is required to clarify an ambiguity in the award.[33] This can only be done within 28 days of the award or later with leave of the court.

Arbitration fees and expenses

15.29 Parties are severally liable to pay the arbitrator's fees and expenses and the fees of any arbitral appointments referee, subject to the arbitrator allocating liability between the parties for these, if given the power to do so by the parties after the dispute has arisen. SAR 62(D) provides for such a power and that the arbitrator have regard, in doing so, to the principle that expenses follow success. The amount of these, if not agreed by the parties, shall be fixed by the Auditor of the Court of Session.[34]

15.30 The Outer House of the Court of Session has power, on the application of a party when the arbitrator's tenure has ended, to make orders regarding the arbitrator's fees which include the amount, whether any should be repaid or, where the arbitrator has resigned, about his liability in respect of 'acting as arbitrator' (SAR 16(M)).

29 SAR 49(D).
30 SAR 49(D).
31 SAR 50(M).
32 SAR 56(M).
33 This mirrors section 57 of the Arbitration Act 1996 in England where is it called the 'slip rule'. SAR 58 has also been described as 'the slip rule'. See *Arbitration Application 1 of 2013* [2014] CSOH 83 at para [15].
34 SAR 60(3) and (4)(M).

15.31 Parties will normally seek to recover their own legal expenses if they are successful in whole or in part. These may form part of an award where they have been included as part of the claim and the arbitrator has determined that they are recoverable. The level of recoverability will depend on the arbitration agreement. For example SAR 61(D) provides that what is recoverable is 'a reasonable amount . . . of all reasonably incurred expenses'.

Liability of an arbitrator

15.32 On the grounds of public policy an arbitrator is immune from liability for negligence on the basis that he acts in a judicial capacity. However, to attract such immunity, it must be shown that the arbitrator exercises a judicial function.[35] SAR 73(M) provides for an arbitrator's immunity from anything done or omitted in the performance or purported performance of his duties. The exception to this is where the act or omission is shown to have been in bad faith. The same immunity is also extended to any body appointing an arbitrator.

The effect of the award

15.33 An arbitration award is final and binding on the parties[36] subject to the right of any person to challenge the award under Part 8 of the SARs or by any available arbitral process of appeal or review. An award cannot be challenged simply because the arbitrator is wrong in law or in his findings of the facts. The purpose of arbitration is to exclude determination of such matters from the court. The rights to have any such award reviewed by the court are therefore extremely limited. An appeal under the 2010 Act is only competent where the appellant has exhausted any available arbitral process of appeal or review including that available under SAR 58(D) (correcting an award).[37]

Enforcement

15.34 Section 12 of the 2010 Act provides for the means of enforcement of an award. The court, either the Court of Session or sheriff court,[38] may order that an award be enforced as if it were an extract registered decree bearing a warrant for execution. The exceptions to this are where the time periods for those types of appeal available to the parties have not expired, or a period of correction is ongoing under SAR 58(D).

Challenging the arbitral award

15.35 There are three potential grounds for challenge of an award in Part 8 of the SARs: a jurisdictional appeal, a serious irregularity appeal,

---

35 *Arenson v Casson Beckman Rutley & Co* [1977] AC 405.
36 2010 Act, s 11.
37 SAR 71(M).
38 2010 Act, s 31(10).

and a legal error appeal. A legal error appeal is a restricted right to appeal on a point of law. It can be excluded. A right to a jurisdictional appeal or a serious irregularity appeal cannot be excluded, although under SAR 76(M) a party loses its right to object if timeous objection is not made on certain of the grounds (see para **15.37** below). The court which hears such appeals is the Outer House of the Court of Session. There is a right of appeal, with leave, to the Inner House whose decision on the appeal is final. An arbitration judge is nominated to hear the appeals in the Outer House.

15.36   As privacy can be one of the governing considerations for parties opting for arbitration, section 15 of the 2010 Act, as supported by Court of Session Rule 100.9, entitles a party to civil proceedings relating to the arbitration (other than enforcement) to apply to the court prohibiting disclosure of the identity of a party to the arbitration in any report of the proceedings.

A jurisdictional appeal

15.37   Under SAR 67(M), a party may appeal to the Outer House against an award on the ground that the arbitrator did not have jurisdiction to make the award. This is known as a 'jurisdictional appeal' and is available where the arbitrator did not have the jurisdiction to make the award that he did. The award is then in whole or in part *ultra vires*. An example would be where the arbitrator included in the award a finding on a matter not referred to him for a decision.[39] Another situation might be where he has done something he had no power to do, for example, found parties liable jointly and severally for payment when he had no power to do so.[40] If the appeal is successful the Outer House may vary the award or part of it, or set it aside in whole or in part. A party which participated in an arbitration where it was clear that the arbitrator intended to exercise a jurisdiction he did not have, and which did not record an objection, may have lost its right to object under SAR 76(1).[41]

A serious irregularity appeal

15.38   Under SAR 68(M), a party may appeal to the Outer House on the ground of serious irregularity. A serious irregularity is defined in SAR 68(2) as an irregularity of any of the following kinds which has caused or will cause substantial injustice to the appellant:

(a) the tribunal failing to conduct the arbitration in accordance with—
    (i) the arbitration agreement,
    (ii) these rules (in so far as they apply), or

---

39 *McIntyre v Forbes* 1939 SLT 62, OH.
40 *Carruthers v Hall* (1830) 9 S 66.
41 SAR 76(1) refers to timeous objection as defined under SAR 76(2)(M).

(iii) any other agreement by the parties relating to conduct of the arbitration,

(b) the tribunal acting outwith its powers (other than by exceeding its jurisdiction),

(c) the tribunal failing to deal with all the issues that were put to it,

(d) any arbitral appointments referee or other third party to whom the parties give powers in relation to the arbitration acting outwith powers,

(e) uncertainty or ambiguity as to the award's effect,

(f) the award being—

    (i) contrary to public policy, or

    (ii) obtained by fraud or in a way which is contrary to public policy,

(g) an arbitrator having not been impartial and independent,

(h) an arbitrator having not treated the parties fairly,

(i) an arbitrator having been incapable of acting as an arbitrator in the arbitration (or there being justifiable doubts about an arbitrator's ability to so act),

(j) an arbitrator not having a qualification which the parties agreed (before the arbitrator's appointment) that the arbitrator must have, or

(k) any other irregularity in the conduct of the arbitration or in the award which is admitted by—

    (i) the tribunal, or

    (ii) any arbitral appointments referee or other third party to whom the parties give powers in relation to the arbitration.

15.39 Assistance as to what is meant by substantial injustice can be found in some of the commentary to the English Arbitration Act 1996 from which the concept is drawn. 'It is designed as a long stop only available in extreme cases where the tribunal has gone so wrong in its conduct of the arbitration that justice calls out for it to be corrected.'[42] To the extent that a party has been aware of such an irregularity during the arbitration and has not made timeous objection, that party may not raise that objection in such an appeal.[43]

If the Outer House allows such an appeal the court may require the arbitrator to reconsider the award or any part of it. If that is inappropriate the court may set aside the award or part of it. The court may also, where the irregularity goes to the arbitrator's conduct, make such orders as it thinks fit regarding the arbitrator's entitlement to fees and expenses including making an order for repayment if appropriate.

Legal error appeal

15.40 SAR 69(D) provides that parties may appeal to the Outer House

---

42 The Departmental Advisory Committee on Arbitration (DAC) Report 1996, para 280 and *Arbitration Application 1 of 2013* (n 33 above).

43 SAR 76(M).

on the ground that the arbitrator erred on a point of Scots law, provided that parties have not excluded this ground from the arbitration agreement (a legal error appeal). An agreement between the parties that the arbitrator did not require to give reasons for his decision will be taken to be an agreement to exclude the court's jurisdiction to consider a legal error appeal.

Before such a legal error appeal will be entertained by the court, leave will be required unless the parties agree otherwise. Leave will be granted where the court is satisfied that:

(a) deciding the point will substantially affect a party's rights;
(b) the arbitrator was asked to decide the point; and
(c) the arbitrator's decision was obviously wrong or where the court considers the point of general importance, the arbitrator's decision is open to serious doubt.

15.41 In *Arbitration Application no 3 of 2011* for leave to appeal on grounds of legal error[44] Lord Glennie granted leave to appeal. The issue was where the burden of proof lay in a claim by an employer under a building contract alleging that he had overpaid. Lord Glennie found that the point would substantially affect the parties' rights; that the arbitrator had been asked to decide the point; that it was of general importance as it arose under a standard form of contract; and that it was open to serious doubt.

15.42 The court will determine whether leave is to be granted without a hearing, as provided for under SAR 70(5), unless satisfied a hearing is required. Lord Glennie in *Arbitration Application no 3 of 2011* set out the procedure to be followed when leave is required. This will be on the basis of a brief reading of the award against which an appeal is sought and the arguments put in writing by the parties. The court's decision as to whether to grant leave is final. If leave to appeal is granted the court will consider whether, on the points of law raised in the appeal, the arbitrator has made a legal error and, if so, what consequences flow from that. This will include ordering the arbitrator to reconsider the award or setting aside all or part of it.[45]

EXPERT DETERMINATION

What is expert determination?

15.43 Expert determination is a means whereby parties to a contract jointly agree that a third party (which may be a company or partnership) is to determine certain issues that might arise between them. Expert determination is often chosen as the means of resolving such issues as valuations in corporate acquisitions, rent reviews, valuations of

---

44 [2011] CSOH 164.
45 *Arbitration Application no 2 of 2011* [2011] CSOH 186 and *Manchester Associated Mills Ltd v Mitchells and Butler Retail Ltd* [2013] CSOH 2.

commercial assets or property, or breaches of warranties. It is often used to determine whether a condition precedent in some transaction relating to land has been purified e.g. whether satisfactory planning permission has been obtained or completion of certain works has been achieved.

15.44 Historically the role was often described as that of a valuer but the expert may determine issues well beyond those of valuation.

> Expert determination, understood as an alternative to arbitration, has taken root in Scottish legal practice, as a consequence of its attractiveness to the commercial community as a relatively quick and informal means of resolving matters of disagreement or potential disagreement. It is now a well-recognised means of resolving disputes in almost any area of commercial life, and owes its success to the fact that it generally works well and is found to be commercially useful. The difference between an expert and that of an arbiter has become well understood in general terms although the boundary between them can sometimes . . . be difficult to draw.[46]

15.45 An expert plays an entirely different role to an expert witness appointed by a party to a dispute or an expert appointed by a court or arbitration tribunal to assist it in matters of a technical nature. In terms of procedure, the different roles of arbiter/arbitrator and expert have been described as follows:

> A person who sits in a judicial or quasi-judicial capacity, as an arbiter ordinarily does, decides matters on the basis of submissions and evidence put before him, whereas an expert, subject to the provisions of his remit, is entitled to carry out his own investigations and come to his own conclusion regardless of any submissions or evidence adduced by the parties themselves.[47]

15.46 There is no statutory regulation of expert determination in the way that there is with arbitration. The only source of law relating to expert determination is case law. Much of the authority on expert determination is English. It has been acknowledged[48] that expert determination may have originated in England but it has taken root in Scottish legal practice. As an expert is a creature of contract the general principles of contract law apply in determining what the expert is required to do.

The expert determination agreement

15.47 The expert determination provision (the expert clause) is contained within the contract between the parties. It may specially state that the party agreed upon or to be appointed 'shall act as expert not arbitrator'. An expert clause may be limited to certain types of disputes arising under a commercial agreement on the basis that there will likely be another forum for resolution of disputes, whether it is arbitration or litigation.

46 *MacDonald Estates plc v National Car Parks Ltd* [2009] CSIH 79A at para [22] per Lord Reed.
47 *MacDonald Estates v NCP* at para [21] per Lord Reed.
48 *MacDonald Estates v NCP*.

15.48   An example of an expert clause is:

> In the event of a dispute or disagreement arising as to whether or not a
> Planning Decision is a Satisfactory Planning Permission the issue shall be
> referred to the Independent Expert to be determined in accordance with
> condition 24.

An expert clause will very often be drafted simply to require all documents and arguments to be handed over to the expert who then makes
his own investigations and reaches a determination. The provision will
normally stipulate the period of time within which the expert is expected
to make his determination and whether it is to be final and binding.
Most expert clauses will provide that the determination is final and
binding. Where the clause does not do so, the court may imply a term to
that effect if the wording of the contract points to this being the agreement of the parties.[49] The expert clause may state that the determination
is final and binding 'in the absence of manifest error.' In determining
what is 'manifest error' it has been said that: 'such clauses are intended
to be confined to oversights and blunders so obvious and so obviously
capable of affecting the determination as to admit of no difference of
opinion'.[50]

Appointing an expert

15.49   Where the expert clause identifies the expert, the issue can be
put directly to that individual. Most expert clauses provide that parties
should attempt to agree an individual, often of a specified discipline,
first. The expert clause may, as well as specifying the desired discipline,
describe other expected attributes of an expert, for example, with ten
years' experience of the field within which the expert is to make a determination. Alternatively the expert clause will provide for an appointing
body, often the professional body for the discipline expected of such an
expert, to nominate one. The court does not have power to make an
appointment should the clause be silent on who is to make the appointment. In these circumstances the expert clause will not be enforceable.
An expert is not immune from liability for negligence unless parties have
conferred on the expert a quasi-judicial role to allow him to claim
immunity from action.

Commencing the expert determination

15.50   An expert clause will often provide that parties jointly submit
the issue or dispute to the expert for determination. An expert determination does not interrupt the running of prescription in the same way
that commencing arbitration does. This is on the basis that an expert
determination does not regulate parties' rights and obligations vis-à-vis

---

49 *Homepace Ltd v Sita South East Ltd* [2008] EWCA Civ 1.
50 *Veba Oil Supply & Trading GmbH v Petrotrade Inc* [2001] EWCA Civ 1832 at para
    [33] per Simon Brown LJ.

one another. It determines a state of facts or provides opinion as to value.

The process

15.51 The procedure for the determination may be set out in the expert clause. There is no procedure prescribed by law. If the procedure is not set out in the expert clause, a procedure will need to be laid down by and agreed with the expert. An expert does not require the parties to submit competing submissions although an expert will require sight of relevant documents. An expert can make a determination without such submissions. This is a feature which distinguishes expert determination from the arbitration process. This procedure will provide that both parties will submit their positions at the same time, or that there is one joint submission of the dispute, or that each party makes its own separate representations. Expert clauses will provide the time within which the expert has to reach a determination. There will often be very tight timescales specified for the issue of the determination, for example, within a matter of days.

The question which often arises is whether one party can proceed if the other refuses to co-operate? This may require the party wishing the referral to make an application to the court for an order for specific implement forcing the unwilling party to comply with the agreement.[51] This can be contrasted with the situation where the contractual machinery is unworkable, in which case the expert clause is unenforceable.

15.52 An expert is likely to be asked to determine a value or the substance of a particular legal obligation or right. An expert may be asked to determine issues of fact and law. He may find that a party is due to be paid a certain sum as this is a determination as to a party's rights but any order for payment would need to be made by the courts (on enforcement see para **15.55** below). The expert clause will state whether the expert is to give reasons for his or her decision.

Grounds for challenging an expert determination

15.53 Experts are not subject to the same control by the courts as arbitrators on the basis that they do not, in the main, exercise a judicial or quasi-judicial function although they must act independently and impartially. The fact that the expert may be patently wrong is not a ground for challenge. It does not mean that the expert has not done what he was appointed to do or that he has asked himself the wrong question. It is only where he has departed from those instructions that his determination is open to challenge.[52]

---

51 *Sudbrook Trading Estate Ltd v Eggleton* [1983] 1 AC 444.
52 *Jones v Sherwood Computer Services plc* [1992] 1 WLR 277. Note also that a decision will not be binding in the case of fraud or collusion between the expert and one of the parties.

15.54   Such conduct by an expert must be so fundamental as to amount to a departure from instructions in a material respect. In *Jones v Sherwood Computer Services plc* an accountant had been appointed as expert to determine the amount of sales for the purposes of calculating the consideration under a share sale agreement. Payment of a deferred consideration depended upon the amount by which the purchased company's sales exceeded a certain level. Competing methods of calculating sales had been proposed by each party's accountant. The expert followed one party's method of making the calculations. The unsuccessful party challenged this determination on the basis that the expert had made mistakes of mixed fact and law. The approach to determining whether the expert's determination could be set aside was as follows:

(a) examine what had been remitted to the expert as a matter of contract;

(b) examine the nature of the alleged mistake; and

(c) establish if the expert departed from his instructions in a material respect e.g. valued the wrong number of shares or shares in the wrong company. If so, the determination was not binding.

This approach was followed in *Nikko Hotels (UK) Ltd v MEPC plc*[53] where it was held that an expert who answered the question in the wrong way could not be challenged. If, however, he answered the wrong question his decision was a nullity as being outside the scope of his remit.

Enforcement

15.55   There are no statutory provisions underpinning enforcement of an expert determination. It cannot be enforced in the same way as an arbitrator's award. It may not of itself be enforceable where it is limited to valuation or technical issues without monetary findings. Sometimes such a determination sets in train a number of entitlements and contractual obligations that can in themselves be enforced. If direct enforcement of the determination is sought this would require to be done by seeking various findings in a court action, including findings of whatever financial consequences flow from such a determination.

ADJUDICATION

What is adjudication?

15.56   Adjudication is a form of interim determination of disputes commonly used in the construction industry. It is a fast process which produces a binding decision until litigation or arbitration determines the dispute or the parties reach agreement. It is based in statute. Since the

---

53 [1991] 2 EGLR 103.

coming into force of Part II of the Housing Grants, Construction and Regeneration Act 1996 ('the Housing Grants Act')[54] either party to a construction contract has a right to refer a dispute or difference to adjudication at any time. Since 2011 it applies to oral as well as written contracts. The Housing Grants Act does this by providing that all construction contracts, as therein defined, should contain provisions that:

- a party has a right at any time to refer a dispute or difference to adjudication;
- require the decision of an adjudicator within 28 days of the referral of a dispute; extended by 14 days if agreed to by the party referring or further extended by agreement of both parties;
- the adjudicator must act impartially;
- enable the adjudicator to take the initiative in ascertaining the facts and the law;
- the decision will be temporarily binding unless or until ultimately resolved by court or other legal proceedings or by agreement;
- the adjudicator may correct any clerical or typographical errors in his decision; and
- the adjudicator has immunity from acts or omissions unless the act or omission is in bad faith.[55]

15.57 If the construction contract does not contain the requirements set out above, section 114(4) of the Housing Grants Act provides that the adjudication provisions of the Scheme for Construction Contracts[56] have effect as implied terms of the contract. The Scheme will, in those circumstances, supplant the deficient or missing adjudication provisions in their entirety except for the choice of adjudicator or named nominating body within the contract.[57] Most of the standard forms of contract used in the construction industry contain their own adjudication provisions, thereby avoiding the need to revert to the Scheme. Other contracts expressly incorporate the Scheme.

15.58 Adjudication is considered to be a type of arbitration[58] and therefore the non-statutory rules that govern judicial control of arbitrators apply to adjudicators. An extensive body of case law has built up on the process and its enforcement, more or less consistently in Scotland and England and Wales. The authorities for expert determination and

---

54 This Act came into force for contracts entered into from 1 May 1998 onwards. It has been amended by Part 8 of the Local Economic Development and Construction Act 2009 which came into force for Scotland on 1 November 2011.
55 Housing Grants Act, s 108.
56 The Scheme for Construction Contracts (Scotland) Regulations 1998 (SSI 1998/687) as amended by the Scheme for Construction Contracts (Scotland) Amendment Regulations 2011 (SSI 2011/371). There are separate schemes for England and Wales, and Northern Ireland. There is no practical difference between the English and Scottish schemes.
57 *John Mowlem & Co plc v Hydra Tight Ltd* [2002] 17 Const LJ 358.
58 *Costain Ltd v Strathclyde Builders Ltd* [2003] ScotCS 352 at paras [7] and [8].

the extent of court intervention have also been relied upon in determining when and in what circumstances an adjudicator's decision can be challenged.

What can be referred to adjudication?

15.59 Any disputes or differences arising under a construction contract can be referred at the option of one of the parties. Although it is not compulsory,[59] if a party exercises that right the other party cannot prevent it. A construction contract is widely defined. It excludes certain agreements defined by the Construction Contracts Exclusion Orders,[60] namely the head agreement in a private finance initiative contract or equivalent contract, finance agreements and certain development agreements. It does not include contracts for manufacture or delivery except and to the extent that the contract also provides for installation. It does not apply to contracts with residential occupiers. Also excluded from the application of the Act are construction contracts where the operation is drilling for or extracting oil and natural gas; extracting minerals; tunnelling; or boring or constructing underground works for this purpose; assembly installation, demolition of plant or machinery or supporting steelwork where the primary activity on site is nuclear processing; power generation; water or effluent treatment; production and processing of chemicals, pharmaceuticals, oil, gas, steel, food or drink.[61]

15.60 Although these contracts and operations fall outside the Housing Grants Act and therefore adjudication is not implied as a right, this does not prevent parties in such contracts agreeing that adjudication will apply, whether it is in the Scheme or a contractual version. To constitute a dispute there will typically require to have been a claim made by one of the parties which has been rejected or ignored by the recipient.[62]

Appointing the adjudicator

15.61 The adjudicator may be appointed at any time after a dispute has arisen and must be a natural person. The adjudication agreement will provide for either the identity of the adjudicator or the name of a body (the adjudicator nominating body) which will appoint such an individual. If it does not, the Scheme for Construction Contracts applies and a party may apply to any adjudicator nominating body for appointment of an adjudicator. An adjudicator nominating body is defined as 'a body, not a natural person which holds itself out publicly as a body

---

59 Unless the contract provides that it is a mandatory first step in the dispute resolution process.
60 Construction Contracts (Scotland) Exclusion Order 1998 (SI 1998/686), Construction Contracts (Scotland) Exclusion Amendment Order 2006 (SSI 2006/513), and Construction Contracts (Scotland) Exclusion Order 2011 (SSI 2011/370).
61 See the Housing Grants Act, s 105(2) for its full terms.
62 *Cantillon Ltd v Urvasco Ltd* [2008] EWHC 282 (TCC).

which will select an adjudicator when requested to do so by a referring party'. Such bodies have been established by many of the professional bodies in the field and include the Royal Institution of Chartered Surveyors (Scotland), Royal Incorporation of Architects in Scotland and the Law Society of Scotland.

The adjudication process

15.62 The party seeking to refer the dispute (the referring party) will commence the process with a notice of intention to refer to adjudication. At that point an adjudicator will be agreed or nominated.

There is no statutory provision which counts commencement of adjudication as judicial interruption for the purposes of the Prescription and Limitation (Scotland) Act 1973. Court proceedings can be raised contemporaneously and, if both parties agree, sisted, particularly if there is a potential limitation issue.

The referring party must, if it is an adjudication under the Scheme, refer the dispute to the adjudicator within seven days of having first given notice of adjudication. The procedure, once an adjudicator has been nominated may be set down in the adjudication agreement. If not, the adjudicator has discretion as to how to conduct the enquiry subject to the 28-day period for his decision from the date of referral which may be extended as set out at para **15.56** above. Typically there will be a referral document with supporting information which the adjudicator will require the parties to answer by a written response, usually within seven to ten days. The procedure that then follows may depend on the size and nature of the dispute and whether the adjudicator wishes to hold a hearing or to deal with it on a 'documents only' basis and whether the period of 28 days has been extended.

The adjudication decision

15.63 The adjudicator must issue his decision within the statutory or longer period agreed upon by the parties. If he fails to do so he will be *functus* and any purported decision issued later will be of no effect.[63] The exception to the adjudicator no longer having any power beyond the agreed period of the adjudication is where the adjudicator is simply asked to correct an arithmetical error.[64]

15.64 The adjudicator is not obliged to give reasons for his decision unless parties have agreed that he do so under the adjudication agreement or he has been requested to do so by one of the parties after the adjudication has commenced but before he has issued his decision.

63 *Ritchie Brothers (PWC) Ltd v David Philp (Commercials) Ltd* [2005] CSIH 32, 2005 1 SC 384.
64 This was considered to be an implied power until the Housing Grants Act was amended. Section 108(3A) now provides that the contract shall include a provision in writing permitting the adjudicator to correct his decision so as to remove a clerical or typographical error arising by accident or omission.

Parties must comply with a decision even although it is an interim one. It has a temporarily binding effect. Parties may not retain the sums due under an adjudication to set off against other claims except in very limited circumstances where the adjudication decision allows for this either expressly or implicitly, or where the rules of insolvency regarding balancing of accounts apply. Parties may not refer the same dispute to adjudication more than once.

Enforcement

15.65 To enforce an adjudication decision an application must be made to the court. The summons or writ will seek decrees for the orders granted by the adjudicator. This can be met with a counterclaim or petition seeking that the adjudicator's decision be reduced. The general approach of the courts is to be supportive of adjudication and its temporary binding nature. As with expert determination or arbitration the fact that the adjudicator appears to have got it wrong is not sufficient to prevent enforcement of a decision.

15.66 The main grounds for a successful challenge to enforcement of an adjudicator's decision can be summarised as:

- where the adjudicator has exceeded his jurisdiction or failed to exhaust it; or
- where there has been a material breach of the rules of natural justice.

Although an adjudicator may and often has first to make a decision as to whether he has jurisdiction before he can proceed to deal with the substantive dispute, the adjudicator's decision on his own jurisdiction will not be determinative and a challenging party, provided it has reserved its position during the adjudication, may later challenge this in any enforcement proceedings.[65]

Parties may revisit any matters referred to and determined by adjudication in any subsequent dispute resolution process such as litigation or arbitration. The ultimate tribunal will look at the dispute as if no adjudication had taken place. However the implementation of an adjudicator's decision may change the orders or remedies sought e.g. a party may seek repayment of sums which were paid over following an adjudicator's decision.

NON-ADJUDICATIVE FORMS OF DISPUTE RESOLUTION

15.67 Parties may choose to settle their disputes through non-adjudicative procedures where a third party plays an independent role but does not issue any decision or recommendation. There are a number of

---

65 *Ballast plc v Burrell Company (Construction Management) Ltd* 2001 ScotCS 159.

forms of non-adjudicative dispute resolution. They are commonly described together as 'ADR' although the term 'ADR' is also used to cover all adjudicative forms of dispute resolution except litigation. The most commonly used one is mediation.

What is mediation?

15.68 Mediation is a process whereby a third party acts as an intermediary in negotiations between the parties. The advantages of a successful mediation are that it avoids the costs of court or arbitration proceedings. It may also preserve relationships between the parties to the dispute where formal proceedings might not. Mediation is a consensual process. There is no legislation which regulates the process apart from the Cross-Border Mediation (Scotland) Regulations 2011[66] which brought into effect parts of an EU Directive relating to cross-border disputes in civil and commercial matters.[67] This applies to disputes in which at least one of the parties is domiciled or habitually resident in a member state other than that of any one of the other parties to the dispute. The key provisions of the Directive cover enforceability of mediation settlement agreements, confidentiality, postponement of limitation periods and measures to ensure the quality of mediation. Set out below is the extent to which these provisions have been brought into effect by the Scottish regulations.

15.69 Mediation may be provided for in the contract between the parties as one of the stages of a dispute resolution process. This is usually where disputes 'escalate' through the stages starting with negotiation among senior executives of the parties, then mediation, with the ultimate forum being an adjudicative process such as litigation or arbitration. Such a dispute resolution clause can be called an 'escalation' clause or a 'multi tiered' dispute resolution clause.

15.70 Mediation can take place at any time. It may be before parties have begun an adjudicative form of dispute resolution and so avoid this. It may be during court or arbitration proceedings. Parties will agree at the outset of a mediation that it is to be confidential and privileged so that what goes on in mediation cannot be used or relied upon in any court or other proceedings.[68] Mediation is considered to be a form of 'without prejudice' negotiation.[69] Standard mediation agreements which cover these issues are usually signed up by parties and the mediator at the outset of a mediation. The role of a mediator may be facilitative (enabling the parties to reach a solution) or evaluative (analysing the

---

66 SSI 2011/234 in force on 6 April 2011.
67 EU Mediation Directive 2008/52/EC.
68 For confidentiality in cross-border mediations see the Cross-Border Mediation (Scotland) Regulations 2011, reg 3.
69 *Brown v Rice* [2007] EWHC 625 (Ch), [2007] All ER (D) 252, which would likely be followed in Scotland.

dispute and proposing solutions). A mediator must be independent. He must be, and be seen to be, impartial.

Initiation of mediation?

15.71   There may be a provision in the underlying contract between the parties which provides for mediation. Alternatively parties can agree outside their contract to go to mediation. There is an issue as to the enforcement of a mediation clause in a contract because it is an agreement to negotiate. Such clauses are not normally binding because they lack the certainty required for contractual obligations.[70] However, in *Cable & Wireless plc v IBM United Kingdom Ltd*[71] the dispute resolution clause contained the following provision:

> The Parties shall attempt in good faith to resolve any dispute or claim arising out of or relating to this Agreement or any Local Services Agreement promptly through negotiations between the respective senior executives of the Parties who have authority to settle the same pursuant to Clause 40.
>
> If the matter is not resolved through negotiation, the Parties shall attempt in good faith to resolve the dispute or claim through an Alternative Dispute Resolution (ADR) procedure as recommended to the Parties by the Centre for Dispute Resolution. However, an ADR procedure which is being followed shall not prevent any Party or Local Party from issuing proceedings.

15.72   One of the parties sought to enforce this and put court proceedings on hold until the dispute was referred to ADR. Mr Justice Colman found that the ADR provisions were sufficiently certain to be enforceable:

> Accordingly, in the present case I conclude that clause 41.2 includes a sufficiently defined mutual obligation upon the parties both to go through the process of initiating a mediation, selecting a mediator and at least presenting that mediator with its case and its documents and attending upon him. There can be no serious difficulty in determining whether a party has complied with such requirements.[72]

Mediation does not interrupt the running of the limitation period except in the case of cross-border disputes where the Scottish Regulations amend the law on prescription and limitation by basically extending the time-bar period where it would otherwise expire during or within eight weeks of a cross-border mediation ending.[73]

---

70 See *Walford v Miles* [1992] 2 AC 128.
71 [2002] EWHC 2059 Comm.
72 *Cable & Wireless v IBM United Kingdom* (n 71 above).
73 See the Cross-Border Regulations, regs 5 and 6. The 'end' of a mediation is defined as including when all parties agree to end it, when an agreement to mediate determines that the mediation has ended, when parties reach agreement in resolution of the dispute, where one party withdraws or 14 days after a mediator's tenure ends and no replacement is appointed.

Appointing a mediator

15.73 The mediation clause may provide the name of an appointing body. It is unlikely to name a mediator. Mediation services are offered by a number of organisations and parties seeking to appoint a mediator may approach one of these if they are unable to agree an individual between themselves. Most mediators operate under the code of conduct of their professional body or the mediation organisation of which they are a member.

The mediation process

15.74 A mediator will set the agenda for a mediation in consultation with the parties. It will usually involve exchanging some form of 'position' paper before a day, or occasionally more, is set aside when all parties come together for the mediation itself. The format of this day will depend on the mediator but it is likely to involve the mediator shuttling among the various parties holding private discussions with each of them. Typically in private discussion a mediator will undertake that nothing disclosed to him by one party will be disclosed to another without its permission.

There is no limit on the number of parties who may be involved in the mediation. For example it is common in actions involving multiple defenders, third parties and/or insurers that they all be represented at a mediation to enable a settlement binding on all parties to be achieved.

An agreement to mediate is usually signed by all parties and their representatives and the mediator before the mediation starts. This will contain provisions on confidentiality, that the parties present have authority to settle the dispute, and an ability to terminate the process at any time.

Settling the mediation

15.75 If a mediation is successful parties will normally agree and sign a settlement agreement recording the terms of the agreement at the end of the day of the mediation. Parties require to have authority to enter into such an agreement and its terms require to be certain enough to be enforceable, as with any other contract. In *Frost v Wake Smith and Tofields Solicitors*[74] the English Court of Appeal found, in dealing with allegations of negligence against a solicitor, that a solicitor had a duty to advise his client on the nature of the mediation process and the status of any agreement reached as a result of that process.

The role of the court in mediation

15.76 It is increasingly recognised by the courts that ADR can play an important part in resolution of disputes. At present the sheriff court rules relating to commercial actions provide that, at the case manage-

---

74 [2013] EWCA Civ 772.

ment conference, the sheriff has the power to make any order which he thinks 'will result in the speedy resolution of the action (including the use of alternative dispute resolution)'.[75]

15.77 In commercial actions in the Court of Session the Rules provide that at the preliminary hearing the commercial judge may make such order as he thinks fit for the speedy determination of the action.[76] The Court of Session Practice Note on Commercial Actions (No 6 of 2004)[77] states 'Both parties may wish to consider whether all or some of the dispute may be amenable to some form of alternative dispute resolution.' These provisions can be contrasted with the position in the courts in England where various practice directions and pre-action protocols require parties to consider ADR and face sanctions in the extent of recovery of legal fees if they fail to properly consider it. The Report of the Scottish Civil Courts Review of 30 September 2009 has a chapter on 'Mediation and Other Forms of Dispute Resolution'. It recommends that the court should not have power to compel parties to enter into ADR. It did not consider it necessary to make any specific provision in court rules for sanctions in expenses where a party has refused to engage in ADR. However, its proposals as to pre-action protocols and active case management provide an opportunity for the court to encourage parties to consider alternatives to litigation.

Other non-adjudicative dispute resolution forms

15.78 There are other forms of ADR. These include variations on mediation such as 'med arb' and 'neutral evaluation'. Med arb is where the third party combines the role of mediator and arbitrator. An individual acts first as mediator and then, if this does not resolve the issues, will proceed to act as arbitrator of the dispute. Neutral evaluation is where a neutral expert, usually in a complex technical or legal dispute, is employed to analyse the facts or law so that the real issues emerge, thereby enabling the parties to resolve a dispute.

75 Ordinary Cause Rules ('OCR'), r 223.
76 Rules of the Court of Session ('RCS') r 47.11(1)(e).
77 See s 11.

Index